Automata Theory and Logic

Martin Hofmann · Martin Lange

Automata Theory and Logic

Springer Vieweg

Martin Hofmann
Institut für Informatik
Lehr- und Forschungseinheit Theoretische
Informatik
Ludwig-Maximilians-Universität München
München, Germany

Martin Lange
Fachbereich Elektrotechnik und Informatik
Fachgebiet Theoretische Informatik /
Formale Methoden
Universität Kassel
Kassel, Germany

ISBN 978-3-662-72153-7   ISBN 978-3-662-72154-4   (eBook)
https://doi.org/10.1007/978-3-662-72154-4

This is a revised, extended and translated version of the German "Automatentheorie und Logik", by Martin Hofmann and Martin Lange, published by Springer in 2011 – ISBN: 978-3-642-18089-7, e-ISBN: 978-3-642-18090-3

This Springer Vieweg imprint is published by the registered company Springer-Verlag GmbH, DE, part of Springer Nature.
The registered company address is: Heidelberger Platz 3, 14197 Berlin, Germany

If disposing of this product, please recycle the paper.

To Annette, Johanna, Matthias and Elisabeth.
To Becky, Annika and Sophie.

Preface

The roots of this book date back to the year 2004 when Martin Hofmann and myself gave a course on *"Automatentheorie"* in the computer science programme at the Ludwig-Maximilians University of Munich. The course was inspired – at least for my part – by lectures on automata theory given by Franz Baader and Wolfgang Thomas that I had attended during my studies at RWTH Aachen in the mid '90s.

The course was well received by students and consequently was repeated in the summer terms 2006 and 2008 at LMU Munich, still shared, and then also beyond that point separately as I had left LMU Munich in 2010. In order to integrate the parts that we lectured on separately, Martin had at some point, in his very own way, *"just quickly typed the course notes in ASCII."* That was quickly turned into LaTeX sources and then given some structure and content details to make it proper hand-out lecture notes.

We then realised that the result was close to being publishable as a textbook on automata theory and logic. So we approached Springer, a publication agreement was made and some final touches were implemented.

This could well be the end of this foreword, at least the part outlining this book's history, but the acute reader may have already wondered about a 15 year gap in the story. During the talks about the publication of a book we asked the handling editor at Springer whether they would prefer to publish the book in English or in German, and fatally they left it up to us to decide. We managed to convince ourselves of the existence of good reasons beyond pure laziness for which we decided to stick with the German version.

In 2011, the book *"Automatentheorie und Logik"*, just under 250 pages long, appeared in Springer's eXamen.press series.

Over the next years, we received positive feedback from various colleagues who seemed to like the book a bit more than they liked buying it, at least when comparing such feedback to the royalty statements. From most of the feedback we could also deduce that an English version may have been appreciated a bit better.

In 2017 we had pretty much decided that it is time to produce an English version. Initial work quickly revealed some differences in our vision of the final result. Martin favoured a straightforward and quick translation including fixes of reported and obvious mistakes, while I grew increasingly discontent with the sparsity of the lecture-note style and favoured a more thorough reworking with the aim of better self-containment.

We never got to work out a common vision for how much "the English version" should deviate from the original book in German in terms of content and style. In January 2018, Martin sadly died in a snow storm on a day's hike in the mountains north of Tokyo which, needless to say, put the project to a halt.

In early 2022, I was approached by Springer asking if I was interested in producing a second edition of the book. I told them about our thoughts and efforts on an English version which had ground to halt, effectively before they had started properly. Springer was quite positive about the idea of an English version and so I convinced myself that I could do it on my own, and also do it in a way that Martin and I would have agreed to. I do not know about the second part. It could have been that Martin would have agreed to a more elaborate version, or perhaps we would still be discussing pros and cons. In any case, I decided to try to emulate as much of Martin's more minimalistic approach as possible, and failed. In the end, this book is not just a translation of the German version from 2011. It has seen some major overhauling in terms of chapter restructuring, addition of proofs and examples, bug fixes of course, unification in terminologies and, most importantly, the attempt to make it a self-contained reading material that can be used for self-study, not just as back-up course notes. Consequently, it grew by about 150 pages.

A line was drawn regarding genuinely new content: while research in automata theory and logic is still active and ongoing with new developments seen regularly, I decided to not include any additional concepts (apart from examples, proof details, references, etc.) compared to the German version. This was also done in order to retain the spirit of it being an actual collaboration between Martin and myself. While the amount of material in this English version that Martin has actually written is limited to the skeleton of one chapter, it was decided very early on that he would have to retain co-authorship of the book. Without him, the German version would have never been possible, and without that, there would also not be this English version. There has never been an equal distribution of the work and task load for this project. There has always been an unspoken understanding of both of us contributing in each one's way. Martin's strength has always been crunching the heavy and difficult things into digestible chunks, and I had often felt that I could contribute best by trying to make them presentable to those who are not blessed with Martin's intellectual abilities. So, even under more fortunate circumstances, I would have probably done quite a lot of the polishing work that has gone into the English version anyway. In any case, this does not diminish Martin's major role in the entire project, so his co-authorship remains to be genuine even though this book will only appear more than 7 years after his tragic and early death.

This book is directed at graduate students at the Master's level who have knowledge and competencies in standard topics of theoretical computer science, as is given in introductory courses on automata, formal languages, formal logic and computational complexity, or can be found in standard textbooks like the well-known ones by Hopcroft et al. for instance [HU80, HMU01]. This book then delves deeper into the world of automata by presenting deeply rooted connections between automata and logic along the lines of work started by Büchi and Rabin.

Also needless to say, such a project is hardly possible without the help of many people who deserve to be acknowledged and thanked. Florian Bruse, Lars-Eric Marquardt, Sören Möller proof-read a final draft version and found many mistakes. Peter Pashkin, Jannik Nordmeyer, Florian Redinger, Jamie Chen and Jiayu Ma reported typos as well. Étienne Lozes, Ulrich Schöpp, Steffen Jost, Krystian Kensy, Thomas Schwentick, Mirco Franzek and Michael Falk had reported bugs in the original German version. Étienne Lozes, Florian Bruse, Daniel Kernberger and Norbert Hundeshagen gave lectures or tutorials for a course on automata, logic and games at the University of Kassel that is based on the content of this book and thus have provided suggestions, exercises and fixes. Marco Sälzer and Eric Alsmann gave tutorials for a course on database theory, part of which is based on the material in Chapter 11 on automata on finite trees, and have similarly provided suggestions and exercises. Michael Möller redrew some of the original figures using TikZ. I would also like to thank the people at Springer for their support and also their patience regarding a few requests for deadline extensions.

Kassel, Germany,   *Martin Lange*
March 2025

Contents

Acronyms

ABA	alternating Büchi automaton
AcoBA	alternating co-Büchi automaton
AFA	alternating finite automaton
APA	alternating parity automaton
APA	alternating parity tree automaton
BFS	breadth-first search
CTL*	full branching-time computation tree logic
DAG	directed acyclic graph
DBA	deterministic Büchi automaton
DbuTA	deterministic bottom-up tree automaton
DcoBA	deterministic co-Büchi automaton
DFA	deterministic finite automaton
DFS	depth-first search
DMA	deterministic Muller automaton
DNF	disjunctive normal form
DPA	deterministic parity automaton
DPA$_e$	deterministic edge-based parity automaton
DPTA	deterministic parity tree automaton
DRA	deterministic Rabin automaton
DRA$_e$	deterministic edge-based Rabin automaton
DSA	deterministic Streett automaton
DSO	dyadic second-order logic
DtdTA	deterministic top-down tree automaton
FO	first-order logic
GNBA	generalised nondeterministic Büchi automaton
$\mathcal{L}_\mu$	modal μ-calculus
LAR	latest appearance record
LTL	linear-time temporal logic
LTS	labelled transition system
ML	modal logic
MSO	monadic second-order logic

NBA	nondeterministic Büchi automaton
NBA_e	nondeterministic edge-based Büchi automaton
NbuTA	nondeterministic bottom-up tree automaton
NBTA	nondeterministic Büchi tree automaton
NcoBA	nondeterministic co-Büchi automaton
$NcoBA_e$	nondeterministic edge-based co-Büchi automaton
NFA	nondeterministic finite automaton
NMA	nondeterministic Muller automaton
NMA_e	nondeterministic edge-based Muller automaton
NNF	negation normal form
NPA	nondeterministic parity automaton
NPA_e	nondeterministic edge-based parity automaton
NPTA	nondeterministic parity tree automaton
NRA	nondeterministic Rabin automaton
NRA_e	nondeterministic Rabin automaton
NSA	nondeterministic Streett automaton
NTA	nondeterministic (finite) tree automaton
NSA_e	nondeterministic Streett automaton
NtdTA	nondeterministic top-down tree automaton
PA	Presburger arithmetic
PSL	property specification language
REG_Σ	class of regular languages over alphabet Σ
S1S	second-order logic of one successor (function)
SCC	strongly connected component
SF_Σ	class of star-free languages over alphabet Σ
sNMA	symbolic nondeterministic Muller automaton
SnS	second-order logic of n successor (functions)
UBA	universal Büchi automaton
UcoBA	universal co-Büchi automaton
VWABA	very weak alternating Büchi automaton
WABA	weak alternating Büchi automaton
WAcoBA	weak alternating co-Büchi automaton
WAPA	weak alternating parity automaton
WNBA	weak nondeterministic Büchi automaton
WS1S	weak second-order logic of one successor (function)

Part I
Finite Words

Chapter 1
Regular Languages

We start by repeating some fundamental concepts from the theory of formal languages, in particular regular languages. Throughout this book we use the convention that $\mathbb{N}$ denotes the set of natural numbers beginning with 0. For $k \in \mathbb{N}$, $[k]$ denotes the interval $\{0, \ldots, k-1\}$.

1.1 Regular Expressions

Let $\Sigma = \{a, b, \ldots\}$ be a finite *alphabet*. A *finite word* over Σ is a sequence $w = a_0 \ldots a_{n-1}$ with $a_i \in \Sigma$ for $i \in [n]$. We write $|w|$ for the *length* of w, i.e. n in this case, and $w(i)$ for its i-th symbol a_i. The *empty word*, i.e. the sequence of length 0, is written as ε. Σ^* denotes the set of all (finite) words over Σ, and Σ^+ denotes the set of all non-empty finite words over Σ. The *concatenation* of two words w and v is simply written as wv, it denotes the sequence that is obtained by first iterating through w and then through v, i.e. $(wv)(i) = w(i)$ if $0 \le i < |w|$ and $(wv)(i) = v(i - |w|)$ if $|w| \le i < |w| + |v|$.

A *language* L is a set of words, i.e. a subset of Σ^*. This introduces all the usual set-theoretic operations like union, intersection, complement, difference, etc. into the world of formal languages. The *complement* of a language L is typically written as $\overline{L}$, and it is defined as $\Sigma^* \setminus L$.

Other important operations on languages are concatenation (lifted from words) and the Kleene closure, also known as Kleene iteration or the Kleene star. If L_1 and L_2 are languages over Σ then so is their *concatenation* $L_1 L_2 := \{w_1 w_2 \mid w_1 \in L_1, w_2 \in L_2\}$ that results from concatenating arbitrary words from L_1 with arbitrary words from L_2.

For a language L its *Kleene closure* is the language $L^* := \{w_1 \ldots w_n \mid n \in \mathbb{N}, w_i \in L \text{ for all } i = 1, \ldots, n\}$. It results from concatenating L with itself an arbitrary but finite number of times. Note that $n = 0$ is possible in this construction, hence, $\varepsilon \in L^*$ for any $L \subseteq \Sigma^*$. Another, yet equivalent, way of defining the Kleene closure makes its constituent parts more explicit:

© The Author(s), under exclusive
license to Springer-Verlag GmbH, DE, part of Springer Nature 2025
M. Hofmann and M. Lange, *Automata Theory and Logic*,
https://doi.org/10.1007/978-3-662-72154-4_1

$$L^0 := \{\varepsilon\} \, , \quad L^{i+1} := LL^i \, , \quad L^* := \bigcup_{i \in \mathbb{N}} L^i$$

We are particularly interested in one class of formal languages, namely the *regular* ones over some alphabet Σ, denoted REG_Σ. If Σ is clear from context, we also simply write REG. Note that $\mathrm{REG}_\Sigma \subseteq 2^{\Sigma^*}$ as it is a set of sets of finite words.

Definition 1.1 The class REG_Σ is the smallest set $\mathcal{C} \subseteq 2^{\Sigma^*}$ that satisfies the following two conditions.

a) $\varnothing \in \mathrm{REG}_\Sigma$ and $\{a\} \in \mathrm{REG}_\Sigma$ for any $a \in \Sigma$.
b) Whenever $L_1, L_2 \in \mathrm{REG}_\Sigma$ then $L_1 \cup L_2 \in \mathrm{REG}_\Sigma$, $L_1 L_2 \in \mathrm{REG}_\Sigma$ and $L_1^* \in \mathrm{REG}_\Sigma$.

Here, *smallest class* means that no language which is not covered by either of the two cases belongs to REG_Σ. Hence, a language L belongs to REG_Σ only if it is of either of the forms listed under (a), or it is built according to either of the constructions listed under (b). The latter means that there need to be languages L_1 (and L_2) for which it is already known that they belong to REG_Σ. Put differently, every regular language can be constructed in a finite number of steps from the languages listed in (a) using the operations in (b). Moreover, any language that cannot be constructed in this way is not regular.

Example 1.2 The set L of all words over the alphabet $\{a, b\}$ in which every a is eventually succeeded by some b is regular. To see this, it is helpful to characterise this differently: no word in L can end on the letter a. Since the alphabet only contains two letters, L consists of all words that either end on b or are empty. Hence, we have

$$L = \{\varepsilon\} \cup ((\{a\} \cup \{b\})^* \{b\}) \, .$$

It remains to be seen that $\{\varepsilon\}$ is a regular language. This is the case since $\{\varepsilon\} = \varnothing^*$ according to the comment made above.

When giving a formal description of a (regular) language we try to omit parentheses for better readability. We introduce the convention that the unary operation of Kleene closure takes precedence over the binary operations, and that concatenation takes precedence over union. We also omit curly braces around singleton sets. Then the language L of the previous example is also simply written as $\varepsilon \cup (a \cup b)^* b$. An even cleaner way of obtaining a neat description of regular languages is to introduce regular expressions.

Definition 1.3 Let Σ be an alphabet. *Regular expressions* over Σ are given by the following grammar.

$$\alpha := \varnothing \mid a \mid \alpha + \alpha \mid \alpha\alpha \mid \alpha^*$$

The language $L(\alpha)$ of a regular expression α is defined straightforwardly as

$$
\begin{aligned}
L(\varnothing) &:= \varnothing & \qquad L(\alpha + \beta) &:= L(\alpha) \cup L(\beta) \\
L(a) &:= \{a\} & \qquad L(\alpha\beta) &:= L(\alpha)L(\beta) \\
& & L(\alpha^*) &:= (L(\alpha))^*
\end{aligned}
$$

Thus, every regular expression defines a regular language in a natural way. The minimality condition in Def. 1.1 guarantees that every regular language can also be described by a regular expression.

The literature contains both the use of '+' and '∪' in regular expressions to denote unions. We will use either of them, whatever is more convenient in that moment. We will also often drop the strict distinction between an expression and the language defined by it writing, for example $L = (a + b)^* b$ instead of $L = L((a + b)^* b)$.

It is easy to see that every finite set of words is a regular language; it can be written in the form $w_1 + \ldots + w_n$, using only unions of concatenations of singleton letters (and possibly the empty word).

Condition (b) in Def. 1.1 means that REG_Σ is *closed* under the operations of union, concatenation and Kleene star, i.e. applying these operations to members of the class can never yield non-members of this class. REG_Σ is furthermore closed under several other operations, in particular the usual set-theoretic ones. This is not easy to see, in particular closure under the complement operation does not exactly follow directly from Def. 1.1. Once this is shown, closure under other operations follows immediately. For instance, closure under intersections would then simply be a consequence of the deMorgan law $L_1 \cap L_2 = \overline{\overline{L_1} \cup \overline{L_2}}$.

Note that the class of regular languages is *not* closed under infinitary unions, for otherwise every language would be regular since any language can be written as a possibly infinite union of finite languages, for instance as $\{w_1\} \cup \{w_2\} \cup \ldots$ by simply enumerating all its words.

Another closure result is quite easily obtained through reasoning about regular expressions, though.

Definition 1.4 Let Σ, Δ be alphabets and $h : \Sigma \to \Delta^*$ a mapping called a *morphism*. It is extended homomorphically to a mapping $\hat{h} : \Sigma^* \to \Delta^*$ via

$$\hat{h}(\varepsilon) \ := \ \varepsilon \ , \qquad \hat{h}(av) \ := \ h(a)\hat{h}(v)$$

for any $a \in \Sigma$, $v \in \Sigma^*$. Consequently, $\hat{h}$ is called a *homomorphism* (induced by h).

It is extended even further homomorphically to a mapping $\hat{h} : 2^{\Sigma^*} \to 2^{\Delta^*}$ via

$$\hat{h}(L) \ := \ \{\hat{h}(w) \mid w \in L\} \ .$$

We do not distinguish notationally between a homomorphism on words and on languages. The type will always be clear from the context.

It is often said that the class of regular languages is closed under homomorphisms which is not correct, strictly speaking. Since homomorphisms may map languages over one alphabet into another, a more precise formulation is the following one.

Theorem 1.5 *Let Σ, Δ be alphabets, $h : \Sigma \to \Delta^*$ a morphism and $\hat{h}$ its induced homomorphism. For any $L \in REG_\Sigma$ we have $\hat{h}(L) \in REG_\Delta$.*

Proof Let $L \in REG_\Sigma$, i.e. there is a regular expression α over Σ such that $L = L(\alpha)$. By induction on the structure of regular expressions we create an expression $\hat{h}(\alpha)$

such that $L(\hat{h}(\alpha)) = \hat{h}(L(\alpha))$. In fact, $\hat{h}(\alpha)$ is simply obtained as the homomorphic extension of h to regular expressions, i.e.

$$\hat{h}(\varnothing) := \varnothing \qquad\qquad \hat{h}(\alpha + \beta) := \hat{h}(\alpha) + \hat{h}(\beta)$$
$$\hat{h}(a) := h(a) \qquad\qquad \hat{h}(\alpha\beta) := \hat{h}(\alpha)\hat{h}(\beta)$$
$$\hat{h}(\alpha^*) := (\hat{h}(\alpha))^*$$

for any $a \in \Sigma$.

A straightforward induction shows that $L(\hat{h}(\alpha)) = \hat{h}(L(\alpha))$ holds indeed for any α. In the first base case we have $\alpha = \varnothing$. Then $L(\hat{h}(\varnothing)) = L(\varnothing) = \varnothing = \hat{h}(\varnothing) = \hat{h}(L(\varnothing))$. Note that in the first term, $\hat{h}$ is the syntactical mapping on expressions while the last two occurrences of $\hat{h}$ denote the semantical function on languages. In the second base case we have $\alpha = a$ for some $a \in \Sigma$. Then $L(\hat{h}(a)) = L(h(a)) = \{h(a)\} = \{\hat{h}(a)\} = \hat{h}(\{a\}) = \hat{h}(L(a))$ by the homomorphic nature of both versions of $\hat{h}$.

Then there are three step cases. First, let $\alpha = \beta_1 + \beta_2$. Then

$$
\begin{aligned}
L(\hat{h}(\beta_1 + \beta_2)) \;&=\; L(\hat{h}(\beta_1) + \hat{h}(\beta_2)) \;=\; L(\hat{h}(\beta_1)) \cup L(\hat{h}(\beta_2)) \\
&=\; \hat{h}(L(\beta_1)) \cup \hat{h}(L(\beta_2)) \;=\; \hat{h}(L(\beta_1) \cup L(\beta_2)) \\
&=\; \hat{h}(L(\beta_1 + \beta_2))
\end{aligned}
$$

by the definition of the syntactical $\hat{h}$, the induction hypothesis (twice), and then basic properties of the semantical $\hat{h}$.

Next, let $\alpha = \beta_1\beta_2$. Then

$$
\begin{aligned}
L(\hat{h}(\beta_1\beta_2)) \;&=\; L(\hat{h}(\beta_1)\hat{h}(\beta_2)) \;=\; L(\hat{h}(\beta_1))L(\hat{h}(\beta_2)) \\
&=\; \hat{h}(L(\beta_1))\hat{h}(L(\beta_2)) \;=\; \hat{h}(L(\beta_1)L(\beta_2)) \;=\; \hat{h}(L(\beta_1\beta_2))
\end{aligned}
$$

in the same way.

Finally, let $\alpha = \beta^*$. Then

$$
\begin{aligned}
L(\hat{h}(\beta^*)) \;&=\; L((\hat{h}(\beta))^*) \;=\; (L(\hat{h}(\beta)))^* \\
&=\; (\hat{h}(L(\beta)))^* \;=\; \hat{h}((L(\beta))^*) \;=\; \hat{h}(L(\beta^*))
\end{aligned}
$$

again by basic properties of both the syntactical and the semantical $\hat{h}$ and the induction hypothesis. $\qquad\square$

So instead of saying that "the class of regular languages is closed under homomorphisms" it would be more precise to say that homomorphisms map languages from one class of regular ones to another. On the other hand, a morphism h of type $\Sigma \to \Delta^*$ for two different alphabets Σ, Δ can always be seen as a morphism h' of type $\Sigma \cup \Delta \to (\Sigma \cup \Delta)^*$ by a straightforward extension: $h'(a) = h(a)$ if $a \in \Sigma$, and $h'(a) = a$ if $a \in \Delta$. It should be clear that the homomorphisms induced by h and h' behave in the same way on languages over Σ. Hence, there is little need to be too thorough in distinguishing homomorphism closure of some class from mappings between two classes in this case.

In order to obtain closure under complements (and perhaps further interesting operations) we need a different characterisation of the class of regular languages that turns out to be equivalent to the algebraic one in Def. 1.1, and which we recall in the following two sections.

1.2 Nondeterministic Finite Automata

Finite automata can be used to – as the name suggests – finitely represent regular languages which are, in general, infinite objects.

Definition 1.6 A *nondeterministic finite automaton* (NFA) is an $\mathcal{A} = (Q, \Sigma, q_I, \delta, F)$ with

- a finite *state set Q*,
- an *input alphabet Σ*,
- an *initial state $q_I \in Q$*,
- a *transition function $\delta : Q \times \Sigma \to 2^Q$* and
- a *set of final* or *accepting states $F \subseteq Q$*.

A *run* of $\mathcal{A}$ on a word $w = a_0 \ldots a_{n-1}$ is a sequence $\rho = q_0 \ldots q_n$ s.t. $q_0 = q_I$ and for all $i \in [n]$ we have $q_{i+1} \in \delta(q_i, a_i)$. The run ρ is called *accepting* if $q_n \in F$. We call $L(\mathcal{A}) := \{w \in \Sigma^* \mid$ there is an accepting run of $\mathcal{A}$ on $w\}$ the *language accepted* by $\mathcal{A}$. A language L is called *NFA-recognisable* if $L = L(\mathcal{A})$ for some NFA $\mathcal{A}$.

The association of a language with an NFA immediately yields an equivalence relation on NFA: we call two NFA $\mathcal{A}_1$ and $\mathcal{A}_2$ *equivalent*, whenever $L(\mathcal{A}_1) = L(\mathcal{A}_2)$. We assume that they are defined over the same alphabet. The name *equivalence* is justified as two equivalent automata simply are two possibly different syntactical representations of the same language.

We need a measure of size of such a representation in order to measure the efficiency of algorithms that use automata as representations of languages. For an NFA $\mathcal{A}$ with state set Q we simply define its *size* as $|\mathcal{A}| := |Q|$. Note that this is not entirely accurate: the space needed to write down $\mathcal{A}$ is generally dominated by the size of its transition function $\delta : Q \times \Sigma \to 2^Q$. It can equally be represented as a *relation* $\delta' \subseteq Q \times \Sigma \times Q$: we have $(q, a, q') \in \delta'$ iff $q' \in \delta(q, a)$. We will make use of this correspondence and use both kinds of notation interchangeably. Seeing δ as a finite relation, i.e. a set of tuples, makes the term $|\delta|$ well-defined; it simply counts the number of transitions. Note that this is still not an accurate measure for the space needed to write down δ, for example as a table with three columns, as each element connects two states via an alphabet symbol, and the space needed to write down a state is at least $\mathcal{O}(\log |Q|)$. Moreover, we clearly have $|\delta| \in \mathcal{O}(|Q|^2)$ in general only. Hence, even though using $|Q|$ as the size of an NFA is not an accurate measure for

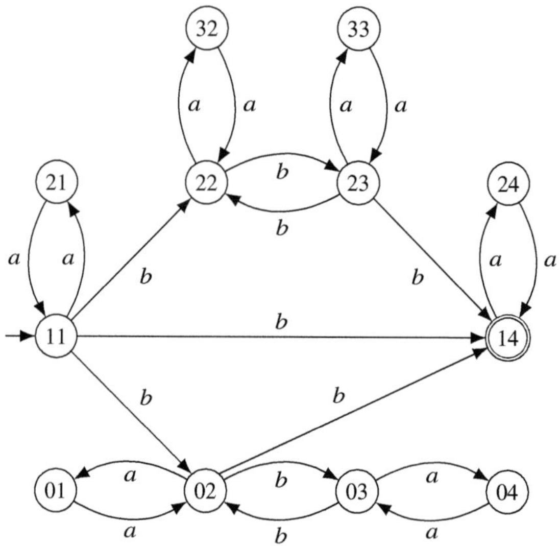

Fig. 1.1 Example NFA.

the real space needed to represent it, it is a measure that is easy to handle and is accurate up to a small polynomial.

NFAs can be drawn as node- and edge-labelled directed graphs. The states form the graph's nodes, and a transition (q, a, q') is drawn as an edge from q to q' that is labelled with a. The initial state is usually marked by an unlabelled incoming edge, emerging out of nowhere; final states are marked using double lines. An example of an NFA is shown in Fig. 1.1. We leave it as an exercise to determine its language and to find an equivalent NFA with four states only that recognises the same language.

The main theorem in the theory of regular languages states that a language is regular iff it can be recognised by an NFA. It is therefore sensible to ask whether the constructions under which regular languages are obviously closed, namely union, concatenation and Kleene star, can be executed directly on NFA. We will show how to do this exemplarily for the Kleene star; the other cases are left as exercises.

Theorem 1.7 *Let* $\mathcal{A}, \mathcal{A}_1, \mathcal{A}_2$ *be NFA over some alphabet* Σ.

a) There is an NFA $\mathcal{A}^\cup$ *s.t.* $L(\mathcal{A}^\cup) = L(\mathcal{A}_1) \cup L(\mathcal{A}_2)$ *and* $|\mathcal{A}^\cup| \le |\mathcal{A}_1| + |\mathcal{A}_2| + 1$.
b) There is an NFA $\mathcal{A}^;$ *s.t.* $L(\mathcal{A}^;) = L(\mathcal{A}_1)L(\mathcal{A}_2)$ *and* $|\mathcal{A}^;| \le |\mathcal{A}_1| + |\mathcal{A}_2| + 1$.
c) There is an NFA $\mathcal{A}^*$ *s.t.* $L(\mathcal{A}^*) = L(\mathcal{A})^*$ *and* $|\mathcal{A}^*| \le |\mathcal{A}| + 1$.

Proof We only show (c). The parts (a) and (b) are similar and left as exercises. Let $\mathcal{A} = (Q, \Sigma, q_I, \delta, F)$. Take a new state q_I' s.t. $q_I' \notin Q$. Let

$$\mathcal{A}^* := (Q \cup \{q_I'\}, \Sigma, q_I', \delta^*, F \cup \{q_I'\})$$

where for all $a \in \Sigma$ and all $q \in Q \cup \{q_I'\}$ we have

$$\delta^*(q,a) \ := \ \begin{cases} \delta(q_I,a) & \text{, if } q = q_I' \, , \\ \delta(q,a) \cup \delta(q_I,a) & \text{, if } q \in F \, , \\ \delta(q,a) & \text{, if } q \in Q \smallsetminus F \, . \end{cases}$$

Hence, states in $\mathcal{A}^*$ have the same outgoing transitions as their correspondents in $\mathcal{A}$ with the only exception that final states also inherit the outgoing transitions of the original initial state. The new initial state is a copy of the old one that is not reachable from any other state.

It remains to be seen that $L(\mathcal{A}^*) = L(\mathcal{A})^*$. For the "$\subseteq$"-part assume that $w \in L(\mathcal{A}^*)$ for some $w = a_1 \ldots a_n \in \Sigma^*$. Then we must have some accepting run $q_I', q_1, \ldots, q_n$ of $\mathcal{A}^*$ on w. From the observation above we immediately get that there are $i_0, i_1, \ldots, i_m$ s.t. $0 = i_0 < i_1 \ldots < i_m = n$ and for all $j = 1, \ldots, m$ we have that $q_{i_{j-1}}, \ldots, q_{i_j}$ is an accepting run of $\mathcal{A}$ on $a_{i_{j-1}+1} \ldots a_{i_j}$. Hence, this run partitions w into $v_1 \ldots v_m$ with $v_j = a_{i_{j-1}+1} \ldots a_{i_j}$ for each $j = 1, \ldots, m$. Then $v_j \in L(\mathcal{A})$ for each such j, thus, $w \in L(\mathcal{A})^*$.

For the "$\supseteq$"-part take some $w \in L(\mathcal{A})^*$. If $w = \varepsilon$ then clearly $w \in L(\mathcal{A}^*)$ since $\mathcal{A}^*$'s initial state is final, so $\mathcal{A}^*$ accepts ε. So suppose that $w \neq \varepsilon$. Hence, there is a partition $w = v_1 \ldots v_m$ s.t. $v_i \neq \varepsilon$ and $v_i \in L(\mathcal{A})$ for all $i = 1, \ldots, m$.

We now show by induction on m that $w \in L(\mathcal{A}^*)$. Note that the base case of $m = 0$ has already been proven since $w = \varepsilon$ if $m = 0$. So suppose that $m > 0$ and $v_1 \ldots v_{m-1} \in L(\mathcal{A}^*)$, i.e. there is an accepting run $\rho = q_I', q_1, \ldots, q_k$ of $\mathcal{A}^*$ on $v_1 \ldots v_{m-1}$. Since $v_m \in L(\mathcal{A})$ there is also an accepting run $\rho' = p_0, \ldots, p_\ell$ of $\mathcal{A}$ on v_m. We have, in particular, $p_0 = q_I$, $p_\ell \in F$ and $\ell \geq 1$, since $v_m \neq \varepsilon$. But then $q_I', q_1, \ldots, q_k, p_1, \ldots, p_\ell$, obtained by concatenating ρ with ρ' (but leaving out its first state), is an accepting run of $\mathcal{A}^*$ on $v_1 \ldots v_m$, as we have $p_1 \in \delta^*(q_k, v_m(0))$ because $p_1 \in \delta(q_I, v_m(0))$. $\qquad\square$

The proof above suggests that the size of the resulting NFA, for example for $L(\mathcal{A})^*$, is always *exactly* $|\mathcal{A}| + 1$ instead of just *at most* that. The formulation in the theorem however, using inequality, is based on the observation that during the course of constructing $\mathcal{A}^*$ one may discover that certain states of $\mathcal{A}$ are unreachable and therefore unnecessary or that some can be discarded using minimisation. $\mathcal{A}$ may also be structured in a way that makes it unnecessary to add a new initial state but instead re-use the old one.

Later we will need the fact that the class of NFA-recognisable languages is closed under further operations, in particular intersections.

Theorem 1.8 *Let $\mathcal{A}_1, \mathcal{A}_2$ be NFA over some alphabet Σ. There is an NFA $\mathcal{A}^\cap$ s.t. $L(\mathcal{A}^\cap) = L(\mathcal{A}_1) \cap L(\mathcal{A}_2)$ and $|\mathcal{A}^\cap| \leq |\mathcal{A}_1| \cdot |\mathcal{A}_2|$.*

Proof Let $\mathcal{A}_i = (Q_i, \Sigma, \delta_i, q_I^i, F_i)$ for $i \in \{1,2\}$. Define their *product NFA* as $\mathcal{A}^\cap := (Q_1 \times Q_2, \Sigma, \delta, (q_I^1, q_I^2), F_1 \times F_2)$ with

$$((q_1,q_2), a, (p_1,p_2)) \in \delta \quad \text{iff} \quad (q_1, a, p_1) \in \delta_1 \text{ and } (q_2, a, p_2) \in \delta_2$$

for all $q_1, p_1 \in Q_1$, $q_2, p_2 \in Q_2$ and $a \in \Sigma$. The claim about $\mathcal{A}^\cap$'s size should be clear. It remains to be seen that $L(\mathcal{A}^\cap) = L(\mathcal{A}_1) \cap L(\mathcal{A}_2)$.

"$\supseteq$" Suppose $w \in L(\mathcal{A}_1) \cap L(\mathcal{A}_2)$, i.e. $w \in L(\mathcal{A}_1)$ and $w \in L(\mathcal{A}_2)$. Then there are accepting runs $\rho_1 = q_0^1, \ldots, q_n^1$ of $\mathcal{A}_1$ and $\rho_2 = q_0^2, \ldots, q_n^2$ of $\mathcal{A}_2$ on w. Note that they are of equal length $n + 1$ if $n = |w|$. Moreover, $q_0^1 = q_I^1$, $q_0^2 = q_I^2$, $q_n^1 \in F_1$ and $q_n^2 \in F_2$. Consider the sequence $\rho = (q_0^1, q_0^2), \ldots, (q_n^1, q_n^2)$ obtained by *zipping* the pair of sequences of states ρ_1 and ρ_2 into a sequence of pairs of states. We observe that it starts in $\mathcal{A}^\cap$'s initial state (q_I^1, q_I^2), it ends in one of its final states since $(q_n^1, q_n^2) \in F_1 \times F_2$, and it follows $\mathcal{A}^\cap$'s transition function δ on the letters of w. Hence, ρ is an accepting run of $\mathcal{A}^\cap$ on w and therefore we have $w \in L(\mathcal{A}^\cap)$.

"$\subseteq$" This is shown analogously by unzipping an accepting run of $\mathcal{A}^\cap$ into accepting runs of $\mathcal{A}_1$ and $\mathcal{A}_2$. $\qquad\square$

Next we recall the fundamental result that the class of languages recognisable by NFA coincides exactly with the class of regular languages. I.e. for every NFA $\mathcal{A}$ we have that $L(\mathcal{A})$ is regular and, vice-versa, for every regular language L there is an NFA $\mathcal{A}$ s.t. $L = L(\mathcal{A})$. The second part is quite easy to see, in fact the main constructions have already been given in Thm. 1.7. We therefore leave a formal proof as an exercise.

Theorem 1.9 *For every regular language L there is an NFA $\mathcal{A}$ s.t. $L(\mathcal{A}) = L$.*

For the other direction we need some more machinery. There are various ways of showing regularity of an NFA-recognisable language. One of them uses the following result, known as *Arden's Lemma*.

Theorem 1.10 *Let $U, V, L \subseteq \Sigma^*$ s.t. $\varepsilon \notin U$ and $L = UL \cup V$. Then $L = U^*V$.*

Proof "$\subseteq$" Suppose $w \in L$. We show that $w \in U^*V$ by induction on $|w|$. In the base case, suppose that $|w| = 0$, i.e. $w = \varepsilon$. Note that if $\varepsilon \notin U$ then $\varepsilon \notin UL$ either. Since $L = UL \cup V$ and $w = \varepsilon$ we therefore must have $w \in V$. But since $\varepsilon \in U^*$ we have $V \subseteq U^*V$ and therefore $w \in U^*V$.

Now suppose that $|w| > 0$. Since $L = UL \cup V$ we can have that $w \in UL$ or $w \in V$. In the latter case we get $w \in U^*V$ just like in the base case above. Therefore we assume that $w \in UL$. Since $\varepsilon \notin U$, there must be $u, v \in \Sigma^*$ s.t. $w = uv$, $u \in U$ and $v \in L$. By assumption we have that $u \neq \varepsilon$, so therefore we have $|v| < |w|$ and we can apply the induction hypothesis to v and get that $v \in U^*V$. Now note that $U^+ = UU^* \subseteq U^*$ and therefore $UU^*V \subseteq U^*V$. Moreover, since $w = uv$ and $u \in U$, $v \in U^*V$ we have $w \in UU^*V$ and therefore $w \in U^*V$.

"$\supseteq$" Remember that $U^* = \bigcup_{i=0}^{\infty} U^i$, hence $U^*V = \bigcup_{i=0}^{\infty} U^iV$. We show by induction on i that $U^iV \subseteq L$ for all $i \in \mathbb{N}$ which then yields $U^*V \subseteq L$.

First, we have $U^0 = \{\varepsilon\}$ and therefore $U^0V = V$. So we get $U^0V \subseteq L$ simply because $L \supseteq V$ which follows immediately from $L = UL \cup V$.

Now consider $U^{i+1}V$ for some $i \geq 0$. By associativity of concatenation we have $U^{i+1}V = U(U^iV)$, and the inductive hypothesis yields $U^iV \subseteq L$. Hence, whenever $w \in U^{i+1}V$ then w can be decomposed into $w = uv$ s.t. $u \in U$ and $v \in U^iV$ which yields $v \in L$. By $L = UL \cup V$ we also have $L \supseteq UL$, and now we have that $w = uv \in UL$, so $w \in L$. Hence, $L \supseteq U^{i+1}V$ as well. $\qquad\square$

This gives us a tool for successively constructing a regular expression for the language of a given NFA. The trick is to view an NFA with n states as a system of n recursive equations for formal languages, and then to use Arden's Lemma to solve this system of equations.

Theorem 1.11 *For every NFA $\mathcal{A}$ we have that $L(\mathcal{A})$ is regular.*

Proof Let $L = L(\mathcal{A})$ for some NFA $\mathcal{A} = (Q, \Sigma, q_I, \delta, F)$. W.l.o.g. we assume that $Q = \{0, \ldots, n-1\}$ and $q_I = 0$.

For every $i \in [n]$, let X_i be the language of all words accepted by the NFA $\mathcal{A}_i = (Q, \Sigma, i, \delta, F)$, i.e. the one resulting from $\mathcal{A}$ by making i the initial state. Clearly, $L = X_0$. These languages can be defined recursively via

$$X_i = \Big(\bigcup_{a \in \Sigma} \bigcup_{j \in \delta(i,a)} \{a\} X_j \Big) \cup \begin{cases} \{\varepsilon\} & , \text{ if } i \in F, \\ \varnothing & , \text{ otherwise.} \end{cases}$$

Using some obvious equivalences on languages like $U_1 V \cup U_2 V = (U_1 \cup U_2)V$ and successive applications of Arden's Lemma it is possible to eliminate recursion from these equations and eventually construct a regular expression for all X_i, in particular X_0, thus showing that L is regular. $\qquad\square$

Example 1.12 Consider the language L of the following NFA.

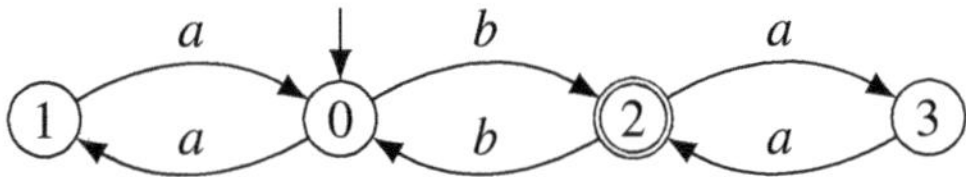

The corresponding system of equations is the following.

$$\begin{aligned} X_0 &= aX_1 \cup bX_2 & \text{(I)} \\ X_1 &= aX_0 & \text{(II)} \\ X_2 &= aX_3 \cup bX_0 \cup \{\varepsilon\} & \text{(III)} \\ X_3 &= aX_2 & \text{(IV)} \end{aligned}$$

We can replace X_3 in (III) by its right-hand side from (IV) which yields the following.

$$X_2 = aaX_2 \cup bX_0 \cup \varepsilon \qquad \text{(V)}$$

By Arden's Lemma we get a definition of X_2 that does not use recursion, at least not directly.

$$X_2 = (aa)^*(bX_0 \cup \varepsilon) \qquad \text{(VI)}$$

Using its right-hand side to replace X_2 in (I) and doing so likewise for X_1 with (II) yields

$$X_0 = aaX_0 \cup b(aa)^*(bX_0 \cup \varepsilon) = (aa \cup b(aa)^*b)X_0 \cup b(aa)^*$$

using some simplifications that allow us to apply Arden's Lemma again for X_0 to finally obtain

$$X_0 = (aa \cup b(aa)^*b)^*b(aa)^*$$

which gives us a regular expression for X_0 and, hence, for L.

1.3 Deterministic Finite Automata

Nondeterministic automata are not very suitable for showing that the class of regular languages is closed under complements. The problem lies with the existential quantification in the definition of acceptance by an NFA: $w \in L(\mathcal{A})$ iff *there is* an accepting run of $\mathcal{A}$ on w. Hence, $w \in \overline{L(\mathcal{A})}$ iff *every* run of $\mathcal{A}$ on w is *not* accepting. However, this universal quantification is not something that is built into the definition of NFA in general, unless it happens to coincide with existential quantification, i.e. whenever "there is" and "for all" expresses the same property. This is generally the case whenever the entities under consideration (here the runs) always exist uniquely. This takes us to the definition of a *deterministic* automaton.

Definition 1.13 An NFA $\mathcal{A} = (Q, \Sigma, q_0, \delta, F)$ is a *deterministic finite automaton* (DFA) if for all $q \in Q$ and $a \in \Sigma$ we have that $|\delta(q,a)| = 1$.

The following lemma formalises the key insight into the workings of a DFA as hinted at above: words in a DFA have unique runs. The proof is left as an exercise.

Lemma 1.14 *Let $\mathcal{A}$ be a DFA over Σ and $w \in \Sigma^*$. Then there is a unique run ρ of $\mathcal{A}$ on w.*

It is convenient to see the transition function of a DFA as being of type $Q \times \Sigma \to Q$. Moreover, it is also possible to relax the definition and to require $|\delta(q,a)| \leq 1$ only, i.e. states in a DFA may also be allowed not to have any successor under some alphabet symbol. It is always possible to transform such a DFA into one that satisfies the stronger requirement of Def. 1.13 by adding one more state.

DFA are easy to complement, as the next theorem shows.

Theorem 1.15 *For any DFA $\mathcal{A}$ there is a DFA $\overline{\mathcal{A}}$ s.t. $L(\overline{\mathcal{A}}) = \overline{L(\mathcal{A})}$ and $|\overline{\mathcal{A}}| = |\mathcal{A}|$.*

Proof Let $\mathcal{A} = (Q, \Sigma, q_I, \delta, F)$. Define $\overline{\mathcal{A}} := (Q, \Sigma, q_I, \delta, Q \setminus F)$. It should be clear that $\overline{\mathcal{A}}$ is also a DFA, and that it is of the same size as $\mathcal{A}$. It remains to be seen that $L(\overline{\mathcal{A}}) = \overline{L(\mathcal{A})}$.

"$\subseteq$" Suppose $w \in L(\overline{\mathcal{A}})$ for some $w \in \Sigma^*$. Take the unique run $\rho = q_0, \ldots, q_n$ of $\overline{\mathcal{A}}$ on w according to Lemma 1.14. By assumption, we must have $q_n \in Q \setminus F$ since w must end in an accepting state of $\overline{\mathcal{A}}$ which is any state in $Q \setminus F$.

Since $\mathcal{A}$ and $\overline{\mathcal{A}}$ have the same initial state and, most of all, same transition functions, ρ is also a run of $\mathcal{A}$ on w, and it does not end in an accepting state of $\mathcal{A}$. According to Lemma 1.14, there can be no other run of $\mathcal{A}$ on w and so we have $w \notin L(\mathcal{A})$, resp. $w \in \overline{L(\mathcal{A})}$.

"$\supseteq$" Suppose $w \in \overline{L(\mathcal{A})}$, i.e. $w \notin L(\mathcal{A})$. Likewise, the unique run of $\mathcal{A}$ on w must not end in F, so it ends in $Q \setminus F$, and it is therefore an accepting run of $\overline{\mathcal{A}}$ on w, witnessing the fact that $w \in L(\overline{\mathcal{A}})$. $\square$

The simplicity of the complementation construction is not the only reason for considering DFA separately from NFA. There are also applications, in particular games and tree automata as discussed in Part III, that require deterministic automata for some purpose. A natural and important question arising with Def. 1.13 is therefore: is the model of DFA genuinely weaker than that of NFA or can any regular language also be accepted by a DFA? The answer to this question lies in the famous *powerset construction* that transforms any NFA into an equivalent DFA thus showing that the class of regular languages are not only captured by NFA but also by DFA.

Theorem 1.16 *For any NFA $\mathcal{A}$ there is a DFA $\mathcal{D}$ s.t. $L(\mathcal{D}) = L(\mathcal{A})$ and $|\mathcal{D}| \leq 2^{|\mathcal{A}|}$.*

Proof Let $\mathcal{A} = (Q, \Sigma, q_I, \delta, F)$ be an NFA. Define $\mathcal{D} := (2^Q, \Sigma, \{q_I\}, \Delta, F')$ where, for each $S \subseteq Q$ and every $a \in \Sigma$ we have

$$\Delta(S, a) \ := \ \bigcup_{q \in S} \delta(q, a) \, ,$$

and $F' := \{ S \subseteq Q \mid F \cap S \neq \varnothing \}$.

It should be clear that $\mathcal{D}$ is indeed a DFA: when reading symbol a in state S, it takes a transition into a unique successor state, even though this is defined as the union of state sets in $\mathcal{A}$. Note that states in $\mathcal{D}$ are sets of states in $\mathcal{A}$. Moreover, the size estimation on $\mathcal{D}$ is also clear. It only remains to be seen that $L(\mathcal{D}) = L(\mathcal{A})$ holds.

"$\supseteq$" Suppose $w = a_0, \ldots, a_{n-1} \in L(\mathcal{A})$ and $\rho = q_0, \ldots, q_n$ is an accepting run of $\mathcal{A}$ on w. Since $\mathcal{D}$ is deterministic there is a unique run $\sigma = S_0, \ldots, S_n$ of $\mathcal{D}$ on w. We show that $q_i \in S_i$ for all $i = 0, \ldots, n$. This is rather obvious for $i = 0$ since $S_0 = \{q_0\}$ by construction.

Now suppose that $q_i \in S_i$ for some $i < n$. Note that $q_{i+1} \in \delta(q_i, a_i)$ because a run in $\mathcal{A}$ must follow $\mathcal{A}$'s transitions. But then we have $q_{i+1} \in S_{i+1} = \bigcup_{q \in S_i} \delta(q, a_i)$ since q_i is one of these states $q \in S_i$. Hence, eventually we get $q_n \in S_n$. But ρ is accepting, so $q_n \in F$ and therefore $S_n \cap F \neq \varnothing$, i.e. $S_n \in F'$. So σ is accepting as well and therefore $w \in L(\mathcal{D})$.

"$\subseteq$" Suppose $w = a_0, \ldots, a_{n-1} \in L(\mathcal{D})$, i.e. the unique run $\sigma = S_0, \ldots, S_n$ of $\mathcal{D}$ on w is accepting which entails that $S_n \in F'$, resp. $S_n \cap F \neq \varnothing$. I.e. there is some $q \in S_n$ s.t. $q \in F$. Our aim is to construct an accepting run $\rho = q_0, \ldots, q_n$ of $\mathcal{A}$ on w, and we will do this from back to front, i.e. starting with q_n. For this we choose the state q that we just identified to be an accepting state in $\mathcal{A}$. We also need to note that $q_n \in S_n$.

Now suppose that q_i for some $i > 0$ has already been picked from S_i. Remember that $S_i = \bigcup_{q \in S_{i-1}} \delta(q, a_{i-1})$. I.e. $q_i \in S_i$ does not hold for no reason, instead it can only be included in S_i if it is an a_{i-1}-successor of some state $q \in S_{i-1}$. So if $q_i \in S_i$ has already been selected, we can select some a_{i-1}-predecessor $q_i \in S_{i-1}$ and continue doing so until $q_0 \in S_0$ has been selected. But $S_0 = \{q_I\}$, so $q_0 = q_I$ showing that every back-to-front construction of such a run ρ must eventually end in $\mathcal{A}$'s initial state q_I. Since q_i is an a_{i-1}-successor of q_{i-1} iff q_{i-1} is an a_{i-1}-predecessor of q_i for all $i = 1, \ldots, n$, and $q_n \in F$, the run ρ constructed in this way is in fact accepting for $\mathcal{A}$ and we have $w \in L(\mathcal{A})$. $\qquad\square$

The converse direction – DFA-recognisable languages are NFA-recognisable – is of course trivial since every DFA is an NFA. Hence, we have that a language is regular iff it is NFA-recognisable iff it is DFA-recognisable. An important consequence of this is the aforementioned closure of the class of regular languages under complements, resulting from the combination of Thm. 1.16 and 1.15.

Corollary 1.17 *Let $L \subseteq \Sigma^*$ be regular. Then $\overline{L}$ is regular.*

Hence, for any regular language that is accepted by some NFA with n states we can construct an NFA for its complement by going through DFA. This comes with a blowup in size, though. The number of states of the complement automaton can only be bounded by 2^n, and it is possible to show that this is asymptotically optimal. Also note that 2^n is only an upper bound. The powerset construction can be carried out on-the-fly, starting with the initial state and then only adding reachable successor states, rather than constructing the transition table for the entire 2^Q. This leads to smaller DFA in general. For example, when the NFA to be determinised happens to be deterministic then the on-the-fly procedure simply returns its input and thus causes no blowup in this case.

1.4 Decidability and Complexity

Automata play a main role in decision procedures for logics which get reduced to questions about automata. To this end, we define or recall the most important decision problems on automata. These are not bound to the models of NFA and DFA that have occurred so far; these questions can equally be stated for any other automaton model to be introduced in the remainder of this book. In fact, it is helpful to regard these questions as effectively being about *languages*, and *automata* only serve as finite representations of these potentially infinite objects, so that algorithmic questions about such languages become well-defined.

The *word problem* or *membership problem* is the following.

> **given:** a language L (in the form of an automaton for example)
> over an alphabet Σ and a word $w \in \Sigma^*$
> **decide:** is $w \in L$?

The *emptiness problem* is the following.

> **given:** a language L
> **decide:** is $L = \varnothing$?

The *universality problem* is the following.

> **given:** a language L over some alphabet Σ
> **decide:** is $L = \Sigma^*$?

The *inclusion* or *subsumption problem* is the following.

> **given:** two languages L_1, L_2 over a common alphabet
> **decide:** is $L_1 \subseteq L_2$?

The *equivalence problem* is the following.

> **given:** two languages L_1, L_2 over a common alphabet
> **decide:** is $L_1 = L_2$?

It should be clear that the computational complexity of these problems may depend on the formalism used to represent languages. For example, the universality problem for NFA is PSpace-complete, i.e. it most likely requires exponential time to be decided. But the universality problem for DFA can be decided in polynomial time (in fact even in nondeterministic logarithmic space). So it would in fact be better to consider these problems as being parametrised by a class of automata. This is in fact what we will do in the following, for instance considering the emptiness problem for a specific automaton model. Here, however we focus on the interplay between these problems, and chosen representation formalisms are less relevant for such considerations.

We assume familiarity with standard time and space complexity classes like NLogSpace, P, NP, PSpace, ExpTime, ExpSpace, 2ExpTime, etc. and the role of complements in the form of co-$\mathcal{C}$ classes like co-NLogSpace. Another class that plays a certain role in the following chapters, especially when introducing Monadic Second-Order Logic, is Elementary, consisting of all problems that can be solved by an algorithm running in time

$$\left. 2^{2^{\cdot^{\cdot^{2^{n^{\mathcal{O}(1)}}}}}} \right\}_k$$

for some fixed k, on inputs of size n.

A third remark on the definition of these decision problems is concerned with the underlying language-theoretic objects, namely words as finite sequences of alphabet symbols. In Parts II and III we present a theory of automata and its applications for extensions thereof, namely infinite words, finite and infinite trees. The decision problems stated above still play the same roles; however, they clearly need to be rephrased slightly. For instance, the universality problem for automata operating on infinite words is then to decide whether $L = \Sigma^\omega$ instead of $L = \Sigma^*$, since that is the (notation used for the) set of all *infinite* words over the alphabet Σ.

The last remark concerns the exact formulation of these problems with regards to what counts as a positive or a negative answer. It would be more accurate to say that it is not the emptiness problem for automata which is used to solve the most fundamental problem for logics, the *satisfiability problem*, but in fact the *non-emptiness problem*, asking whether $L \neq \varnothing$ for some given L. The problems of *non-universality* and *non-inclusion* are obtained in an analogous way.

We will allow ourselves not to distinguish too rigorously between a problem and its complement problem. Especially when we are concerned with solutions in the form of deterministic algorithms there is no need for a separation, as any algorithm solving one of them can easily be modified to solve the corresponding other one by simply swapping yes/no answers. However, when allowing nondeterministic algorithms one needs to be a bit more careful in the distinction between such variants, as done in the formulation of the following result for instance: non-emptiness is in NLogSpace, and emptiness is therefore in co-NLogSpace.

Theorem 1.18 *The non-emptiness problem for NFA is in NLogSpace.*

Proof The key is to see that the language of an NFA $\mathcal{A} = (Q, \Sigma, q_0, \delta, F)$ is non-empty iff there is a path from q_0 to some $q_f \in F$ in the transition graph of $\mathcal{A}$ where edge labels are ignored. Such a path forms an accepting run on *some* word, and for the non-emptiness problem the exact word witnessing non-emptiness is irrelevant. Moreover, we need to see that such a path exists iff there is a path of length at most $|Q|$; any path longer than that would have to be of the form $q_0, \ldots, q, \ldots, q, \ldots, q_f$ for some $q \in Q$ and could be shortened by cutting out the loop from q to q.

Then a nondeterministic algorithm only needs to store a state q and a counter value c, initially $q = q_0$ and $c = 0$. It then accepts if $q \in F$, and rejects if $c = |Q|$. Otherwise it replaces q by some successor $q' \in \delta(q, a)$ for some $a \in \Sigma$ and increments c. It should be clear that this algorithm terminates and can nondeterministically find a path of length at most $|Q|$ if one exists. The space needed is indeed logarithmic only since a counter of value at most $|Q|$ needs at most $\lceil \log |Q| \rceil$ many bits, and a state can equally be stored as a number from $\{0, \ldots, |Q| - 1\}$. $\square$

This proof of course uses the standard argument for showing that the graph reachability problem is in NLogSpace. In fact, one could have argued directly that non-emptiness for NFA *is* just an instance of graph reachability. Moreover, it is then easy to see that non-emptiness (and therefore also emptiness) can be solved in deterministic linear time $\mathcal{O}(|\mathcal{A}|)$, using standard algorithms like depth- or breadth-first search.

The word problem for NFA can be solved in a similar style. The proof of the following theorem is left as an exercise.

Theorem 1.19 *The word problem for NFA is in NLogSpace.*

The other problems listed above are equally decidable for NFA.

Theorem 1.20 *Universality, inclusion and equivalence for NFA are in PSpace.*

Proof We consider the inclusion problem first. Suppose NFA $\mathcal{A}_1$ and $\mathcal{A}_2$ are given. Note that $L(\mathcal{A}_1) \subseteq L(\mathcal{A}_2)$ iff $L(\mathcal{A}_1) \cap \overline{L(\mathcal{A}_2)} = \varnothing$. According to Cor. 1.17, $L(\overline{\mathcal{A}_2})$ can be recognised by an NFA, for instance through the powerset construction on $\mathcal{A}_2$, switching accepting and non-accepting states. At last, Thm. 1.8 shows that it is possible to construct an NFA for $L(\mathcal{A}_1) \cap \overline{L(\mathcal{A}_2)}$ whose size is linear in the size of $\mathcal{A}_1$ and exponential in the size of $\mathcal{A}_2$.

Hence, inclusion can be solved by an exponential reduction to the emptiness problem for NFA which belongs to co-NLogSpace, according to Thm. 1.18. Moreover, this reduction can be carried out on-the-fly, i.e. there is no need to construct the entire NFA for $L(\mathcal{A}_1) \cap \overline{L(\mathcal{A}_2)}$ first and then to analyse its emptiness. Instead, the nondeterministic algorithm from Thm. 1.18 can be used so that it constructs successor states in the product automaton of $\mathcal{A}_1$ and the powerset automaton of $\mathcal{A}_2$ on-the-fly. The space needed for this is logarithmic in the size of this product automaton, which in turn is exponential in the size of the input, i.e. the space needed is polynomial only. According to *Savitch's Theorem* we have NPSpace = PSpace and therefore also co-NPSpace = PSpace which finishes the argument for the inclusion problem.

It is then easy to see that universality and equivalence are in PSpace as well. For equivalence this is the case because $L(\mathcal{A}_1) = L(\mathcal{A}_2)$ iff $L(\mathcal{A}_1) \subseteq L(\mathcal{A}_2)$ and $L(\mathcal{A}_2) \subseteq L(\mathcal{A}_1)$, i.e. equivalence can be checked by two successive inclusion checks which can still be done in polynomial space. For universality this is the case because $L(\mathcal{A}) = \Sigma^*$ iff $\Sigma^* \subseteq L(\mathcal{A})$ and it is easy to construct a (one-state) NFA recognising Σ^*. Hence, universality is a special case of inclusion.   □

Bibliographic Notes

The theory of finite-state machines, aka finite automata, as language acceptors in the sense of computability theory was started by Rabin and Scott [RS59] who invented the powerset construction for instance. Since then, regular languages and their theory, including logical and algebraic aspects, have been studied extensively and the main results are covered in many textbooks, for example by Hopcroft and Ullman [HU80], later with Motwani [HMU01], Harrison [Har78], Sipser [Sip13], and many others.

The equivalence between different representational formalisms for regular languages, in particular between finite automata and regular expressions, is known as *Kleene's Theorem* [Kle56]. *Arden's Lemma* is – not surprisingly – attributed to Arden [Ard60].

One aspect of the study of regular languages and finite automata that is seldomly covered in such textbooks but has some relevance for the automata-logic connection outlined here, is concerned with lower bounds. Meyer and Stockmeyer showed that the complexity of decision problems regarding regular languages is highly dependent on the representation, in particular, it becomes significantly more difficult from a computational point of view when such formalisms includes operators like complementation, intersection [MS73], squaring (in regular expressions) [MS72]. An investigation into the complexities of formal-language problems, depending on the representation formalism, is given in Stockmeyer's thesis [Sto74].

Exercises

Exercise 1 Determine the regular language that is recognised by the NFA in Fig. 1.1. Construct an equivalent DFA with 4 states only.

Exercise 2 Prove parts (a) and (b) of Thm. 1.7.

Exercise 3 Prove Thm. 1.9 by induction on the structure of a regular language, making use of the constructions in Thm. 1.7.

Exercise 4 Consider the NFA $\mathcal{A} = (\{0, 1, 2, 3\}, \{a, b\}, 0, \delta, \{3\})$ with the transition function δ given by $\delta(0, a) = \{1\}$, $\delta(0, b) = \{0, 3\}$, $\delta(1, a) = \{0\}$, $\delta(2, a) = \{3\}$, $\delta(3, a) = \{2\}$ and $\delta(q, b) = \varnothing$ for $q \in \{1, 2, 3\}$. Use the powerset construction from Thm. 1.16 to build a DFA $\mathcal{A}'$ s.t. $L(\mathcal{A}') = L(\mathcal{A})$.

Exercise 5 Prove Lemma 1.14. *Hint:* Note that this carries two obligations: first show that for every word there is at least some run. Then assume that there were two runs and show that they are equal componentwise.

Exercise 6 Consider, for $n \geq 1$, the languages $L_n = (a + b)^* a (a + b)^{n-1}$ of words whose n-th last letter is an a. Show that the following holds for any $n \geq 1$:

   a) L_n can be accepted by an NFA with at most $n + 1$ states.
   b) Every DFA recognising L_n must have at least 2^n states.

Exercise 7 Prove Thm. 1.5 using NFA instead of regular expressions as representation formalisms for regular languages.

Exercise 8 Show that the class REG is also closed under the following operations.

   a) *differences*: $L_1, L_2 \in \text{REG} \Rightarrow L_1 \setminus L_2 \in \text{REG}$
   b) *reversals*: $L \in \text{REG} \Rightarrow \{a_n \ldots a_1 \mid a_1 \ldots a_n \in L\} \in \text{REG}$
   c) *inverse homomorphisms*: let Σ, Δ be alphabets, $h : \Sigma \to \Delta^*$ be a morphism and $\hat{h}$ be the homomorphism induced by h. Show that for any such $h : \Sigma \to \Delta^*$ we have: $\hat{h}(L) \in \text{REG}_\Delta \Rightarrow L \in \text{REG}_\Sigma$.
   d) *shuffle product*: we define a mapping $\bowtie : \Sigma^* \times \Sigma^* \to 2^{\Sigma^*}$ via

$$\varepsilon \bowtie v := \{v\} \qquad aw \bowtie bv := \{a\}(w \bowtie bv) \cup \{b\}(aw \bowtie v)$$
$$w \bowtie \varepsilon := \{w\}$$

   for any $a, b \in \Sigma$, $w, v \in \Sigma^*$.
   This shuffling operation can be extended to languages in a natural way.

$$L_1 \bowtie L_2 := \bigcup_{w \in L_1} \bigcup_{v \in L_2} w \bowtie v$$

   Show that the following holds: $L_1, L_2 \in \text{REG} \Rightarrow L_1 \bowtie L_2 \in \text{REG}$.

Exercise 9 Prove Thm. 1.19.

Chapter 2
Monadic Second-Order Logic

This chapter introduces logic, in particular Monadic Second-Order Logic over finite words. Familiarity with mathematical logic, typically in the form of general First-Order Logic, is helpful but not strictly necessary for reading this chapter. For those who are familiar with logic in general it is worth noting that – throughout the entire book – the logics under consideration are interpreted over structures of particular shape, for instance over finite words only. This restriction has consequences in that generally invalid formulas may become valid, like $\forall x.a(x) \vee b(x)$ saying that every element of the domain of interpretation (here: position in a word) carries an a or a b. Moreover, it is common to adjust the syntax of logics interpreted over restricted domains to reflect parts of these structures. For example, with the position in a word we usually associate a total order, and in order to enable logics to formalise statements involving this ordering, we need to introduce syntactic symbols whose interpretation is tied to this order.

2.1 Syntax and Semantics

The syntax of Monadic Second-Order Logic is similar to that of First-Order Logic: it is built from atomic formulas formalising basic properties of the elements of an underlying structure, using Boolean connectives and quantification over such elements. Second-Order Logic generally also allows quantification over *relations* between the elements of the structure, but in the monadic fragment this is restricted to unary relations (i.e. subsets).

Definition 2.1 Let Σ be an alphabet. Fix two countable and disjoint sets $\mathcal{V}_1 = \{x, y, \ldots\}$ of *first-order variables* and $\mathcal{V}_2 = \{X, Y, \ldots\}$ of *second-order variables*. Formulas of *Monadic Second-Order Logic* (MSO) over Σ-words are given by the following grammar.

$$\varphi \ ::= \ x < y \mid X(x) \mid a(x) \mid \varphi_1 \vee \varphi_2 \mid \neg\varphi \mid \exists x\,\varphi \mid \exists X\,\varphi$$

© The Author(s), under exclusive
license to Springer-Verlag GmbH, DE, part of Springer Nature 2025
M. Hofmann and M. Lange, *Automata Theory and Logic*,
https://doi.org/10.1007/978-3-662-72154-4_2

where $a \in \Sigma$, $x, y \in \mathcal{V}_1$ and $X \in \mathcal{V}_2$.

Formulas of *First-Order Logic* (FO) over Σ-words are obtained by forbidding second-order variables and quantification over them in this grammar.

Note that, theoretically, this defines one logic MSO per alphabet and pair of variable sets. However, variables can be used interchangeably, and – as with the definition of regular languages in the previous chapter – we will assume that the underlying alphabet is fixed and clear from context. This is why we simply speak of MSO instead of MSO_Σ or something like that.

In general, we use lower case for first-order variables and upper case for second-order ones. Sometimes, other objects like e.g. identifiers can be used for the variables of either order. In this case the context must be used for disambiguation.

Intuitively, the first-order variables range over positions in a word providing the basis for an interpretation of MSO formulas to be either true or false, and the second-order variables range over sets of positions. Then $a(x)$ intuitively states that the position currently denoted by x carries the symbol a, and $X(x)$ means that it belongs to the set that is associated with the set variable X. The other symbols have the usual meaning.

We use the following standard abbreviations.

$$
\begin{aligned}
\forall x\, \varphi &:= \neg \exists x\, \neg \varphi & x \leq y &:= \neg(y < x) \\
\forall X\, \varphi &:= \neg \exists X\, \neg \varphi & x = y &:= \neg(x < y \vee y < x) \\
\varphi \wedge \psi &:= \neg(\neg \varphi \vee \neg \psi) & x > y &:= y < x \\
\varphi \rightarrow \psi &:= \neg \varphi \vee \psi & \mathbf{tt} &:= \exists x\, x = x \\
\varphi \leftrightarrow \psi &:= (\varphi \rightarrow \psi) \wedge (\psi \rightarrow \varphi) & \mathbf{ff} &:= \neg \mathbf{tt}
\end{aligned}
$$

In order to save parentheses we also introduce the convention that $\neg$ binds strongest, and that the binary operators take precedence in decreasing order of $\wedge, \vee, \rightarrow, \leftrightarrow$. We also introduce the notation $\exists x.\varphi$, resp. $\exists X.\varphi$ where the dot acts as a left parenthesis whose matching right counterpart is inserted as far right as possible, i.e. at the unique rightmost position that still allows the formula to be well-formed.

Example 2.2 Consider the formula

$$
\begin{aligned}
\varphi_{\mathrm{odd}} \;:=\; & \exists x_I\, \exists x_F.(\neg \exists y. y < x_I) \wedge (\neg \exists y. x_F < y) \wedge \\
& \exists X. X(x_I) \wedge X(x_F) \wedge \\
& \forall x. X(x) \leftrightarrow \forall y. x < y \wedge \neg \exists z\, (x < z \wedge z < y) \rightarrow \neg X(y)
\end{aligned}
$$

Intuitively, φ_{odd} states that there are two positions in a word – called x_I and x_F – s.t. there is none preceeding x_I and none following x_F. Hence, x_I and x_F need to be bound to the first and last position in a word. It then continues to state that there is a set X of positions that contains both the first and last position, and includes a position x iff it does not include its successor y. Note how we can make y denote the successor of x by stating that it comes after x and there is no position in between. Altogether, φ_{odd} therefore states that the underlying word has odd length.

Definition 2.3 An occurrence of a first- or second-order variable x or X in a formula φ is *bound* if it appears in the scope of a *quantifier* $\exists x$, resp. $\exists X$ in the syntax tree of φ. Otherwise, the occurrence is *free*. A variable with at least one free occurrence in a formula is called free. We also write $\varphi(X_1, \ldots, X_n, x_1, \ldots, x_m)$ to indicate that the free variables in φ belong to the set $\{X_1, \ldots, X_n, x_1, \ldots, x_m\}$. A formula without free variables is called a *sentence* or a *closed formula*.

Example 2.4 In the formula $\neg \exists y\, y < x$ the variable x is free and y is bound. In the formula $\forall x.(\neg \exists y\, y < x) \to X(x)$ the variable X is free and x, y are both bound.

As usual, the meaning of a formula depends on the values of the free variables it contains and it can be true or false depending on those values. A *sentence* thus is true or false on its own, provided an interpretation for formulas of the form $a(x)$ is given for $a \in \Sigma$. This will be done in the form of a word $w \in \Sigma^*$. Bound variables can be renamed without changing their meaning, e.g. $\exists x\, X(x)$ and $\exists y\, X(y)$ are equivalent formulas, but $\exists x\, X(x)$ and $\exists x\, Y(x)$ are not.

We introduce further short-hand notation in the form of some special terms which we can then be used just like first-order variables. This allows us to refer to the first and last position in a word in a more readable way:

$$first(x) \quad := \quad \neg \exists y\, y < x \qquad\qquad last(x) \quad := \quad \neg \exists y\, y > x$$

This is not restricted to terms containing a single free variable. Another useful abbreviation will allow us to refer to adjacent positions in a word more easily.

$$succ(x, y) \quad := \quad x < y \wedge \neg \exists z. x < z \wedge z < y \qquad pred(x, y) \quad := \quad succ(y, x)$$

We can even introduce terms that refer more directly to the first, last or some successor position. Suppose that $\varphi(x)$ is an arbitrary formula with a free first-order variable x. We use the following abbreviations.

$$\varphi(0) \quad := \quad \exists x. first(x) \wedge \varphi(x) \qquad \varphi(succ(y)) \quad := \quad \exists x. succ(y, x) \wedge \varphi(x)$$
$$\varphi(end) \quad := \quad \exists x. last(x) \wedge \varphi(x) \qquad \varphi(pred(y)) \quad := \quad \exists x. pred(y, x) \wedge \varphi(x)$$

We use the constant symbol 0 here for the first position in a word is natural. We can in fact refer to any position $k \in \mathbb{N}$ in a formula like $\varphi(k)$, essentially using unary representation:

$$k \quad := \quad \underbrace{succ(\ldots succ(0) \ldots)}_{k \text{ times}}$$

It should be clear that we cannot do the same for the constant symbol end whose interpretation then depends on an underlying word as words may have different lengths and therefore different last positions. The reader is invited to check the truth value of a formula $\varphi(k)$ on words of length less than k.

Bearing all these conventions and abbreviations in mind, φ_{odd} from above can be rewritten in a more readable form as follows.

$$\exists X. X(0) \wedge X(end) \wedge \forall x. X(x) \leftrightarrow \neg X(succ(x))$$

We define the formal semantics of MSO formulas over Σ as a relation $\vDash$ between interpretations and formulas. The former are pairs consisting of a Σ-word, providing information about which positions carry which letters in order to interpret formulas of the form $a(x)$, and *assignments* or *valuations* providing an interpretation of the free variables of the formula under consideration.

The overall goal is to show that MSO is yet another way of describing regular languages. We will introduce a slight deviation, though: when using words to interpret logical formulas we require the word to be non-empty. This avoids strange effects that may occur when interpreting logical formulas over empty domains: for example, tt should always be satisfied, and we expect $\exists y\, \varphi$ to be equivalent to φ if y is not a free variable of φ. But $\exists y\, \mathrm{tt}$ would be false in the empty word.

The restriction to words in Σ^+ instead of Σ^* is not a critical one. Note that $L \in \mathrm{REG}_\Sigma$ iff $L \smallsetminus \{\varepsilon\} \in \mathrm{REG}_\Sigma$. Note, though, that ε may of course occur as a subword of a non-empty word.

Definition 2.5 Let $w \in \Sigma^+$, $n = |w|$, and $I : (\mathcal{V}_1 \to [n]) + (\mathcal{V}_2 \to 2^{[n]})$ be an *assignment* of the first-order variables to positions in w and the second-order variables to sets of such positions.

We say that the *interpretation* of w and I *satisfies* the MSO formula φ, if $w, I \vDash \varphi$ holds according to the following rules.

$$
\begin{array}{lll}
w, I \vDash x < y & \text{iff} & I(x) < I(y) \\
w, I \vDash X(x) & \text{iff} & I(x) \in I(X) \\
w, I \vDash a(x) & \text{iff} & w(I(x)) = a \\
w, I \vDash \varphi \vee \psi & \text{iff} & w, I \vDash \varphi \text{ or } w, I \vDash \psi \\
w, I \vDash \neg\varphi & \text{iff} & w, I \nvDash \varphi \\
w, I \vDash \exists x\, \varphi & \text{iff} & \text{there is } i \in [n] \text{ such that } w, I[x \mapsto i] \vDash \varphi \\
w, I \vDash \exists X\, \varphi & \text{iff} & \text{there is } M \subseteq [n] \text{ such that } w, I[X \mapsto M] \vDash \varphi
\end{array}
$$

Here, $I[x \mapsto i]$ is the function that maps x to I and behaves like I on all other arguments; similarly for $I[X \mapsto M]$.

Two formulas are *equivalent*, written $\varphi \equiv \psi$, if $w, I \vDash \varphi$ iff $w, I \vDash \psi$ holds for any word w and any assignment I that fits w.

If φ is a sentence then $w, I \vDash \varphi$ iff $w, I' \vDash \varphi$ for all assignments I, I'. Thus, the meaning of a sentence does not depend on the variable assignment and we write $w \vDash \varphi$ instead of $w, I \vDash \varphi$ for some and, hence, for all I. More generally, $w, I \vDash \varphi$ iff $w, I' \vDash \varphi$ holds whenever I and I' agree on the free variables of φ – the meaning of a formula φ thus depends only on the restriction of the assignment to its free variables. Therefore, it suffices to define satisfaction $w, I \vDash \varphi$ for finite, partial assignments I, for long as $I(x)$, resp. $I(X)$ is not undefined for any free variable x, resp. X of φ. Also, we have $\varphi \equiv \psi$ iff they agree on all pairs of words and assignments of the smallest set of variables containing the free variables of both of them.

A sentence φ of MSO over Σ then defines a language of words over Σ via $L(\varphi) := \{w \mid w \vDash \varphi\}$. A language $L \subseteq \Sigma^+$ is *MSO-definable* if there is some MSO sentence φ s.t. $L(\varphi) = L$.

If $w, I \models \varphi$ holds for at least one interpretation (w, I) then φ is said to be *satisfiable*. An interpretation (w, I) with $w, I \models \varphi$ is called a *model* of φ. Its *size* is $|w|$. A formula that has no model is called *unsatisfiable*. A formula φ such that $w, I \models \varphi$ holds for all (w, I) is called *valid*. Notice that a formula φ is valid if $\neg\varphi$ is unsatisfiable.

A natural question that arises with this notion of (un-)satisfiability is: can we decide automatically whether a given MSO formula is satisfiable? We formulate this as a decision problem – called the *satisfiability problem* – similar to those defined in Sect. 1.4 for NFA.

> **given:** an MSO formula φ
> **decide:** is φ satisfiable?

A weaker equivalence relation between formulas when compared to semantical equivalence '$\equiv$' is only concerned with the existence of models: two formula φ, ψ are *equi-satisfiable*, if φ has a model iff ψ has a model. Note that satisfiability-preserving effective translations suffice to transfer the decidability of the satisfiability problem of one logic to another.

Likewise the notion of equivalence gives rise to the *equivalence problem*:

> **given:** MSO formulas φ and ψ
> **decide:** does $\varphi \equiv \psi$ hold?

We observe that from a computational point of view, there is no need to consider both problems separately.

Theorem 2.6 *The satisfiability problem for MSO is decidable iff the equivalence problem is decidable.*

Proof Note that $\varphi \equiv \psi$ iff $\varphi \leftrightarrow \psi$ is valid, i.e. $\neg(\varphi \leftrightarrow \psi)$ is unsatisfiable. This yields a polynomial-time (and even logarithmic space) reduction from the equivalence problem to the complement of the satisfiability problem. Hence, if the latter is decidable then so is the former.

For the converse direction note that φ is unsatisfiable iff $\varphi \equiv \mathrm{ff}$. $\qquad\square$

We remark that it is the *unsatisfiability* problem rather than the satisfiability problem that is computationally equivalent to the equivalence problem. For as long as we are only interested in decidability this makes no difference and we could say that equivalence is decidable if satisfiability is. When not just considering decidability but also computational complexity this could of course make a difference and needs to be taken into consideration. However, as we will see in Sect. 2.3, these two problems are of very high complexity, and the difference between satisfiability and unsatisfiability is not the real issue there.

In order to estimate the computational complexity of such problems for MSO (or in fact any logic) we need to measure the size of an input containing formulas, i.e. we need a size measure on formulas. An obvious definition is the length of a string representation of a formula. However, this can be unnatural for formulas which contain parts that are reused multiple times and then also lead to exponentially larger size measures. We therefore measure the size of a formula in terms of the number of different subformulas it contains.

Definition 2.7 The set $Sub(\varphi)$ of *subformulas* of an MSO formula φ is inductively defined as follows.

$$
\begin{aligned}
Sub(x < y) &:= \{x < y\} & Sub(\varphi \vee \psi) &:= \{\varphi \vee \psi\} \cup Sub(\varphi) \cup Sub(\psi) \\
Sub(X(x)) &:= \{X(x)\} & Sub(\neg \varphi \vee \psi) &:= \{\neg \varphi\} \cup Sub(\varphi) \\
Sub(a(x)) &:= \{a(x)\} & Sub(\exists x\, \varphi) &:= \{\exists x\, \varphi\} \cup Sub(\varphi) \\
& & Sub(\exists X\, \varphi) &:= \{\exists X\, \varphi\} \cup Sub(\varphi)
\end{aligned}
$$

Then let $|\varphi| := |Sub(\varphi)|$ denote the *size* of φ.

We give a few more examples of MSO formulas, in fact FO formulas, defining certain languages. The reader is also encouraged to check how φ_{odd} given above defines $\{w \in \{a, b\}^+ \mid |w| \text{ is odd }\}$.

Example 2.8 Let $\Sigma = \{a, b\}$. Let $\varphi := \forall x \, \neg(a(x) \wedge b(x))$. For every $w \in \Sigma^+$ we have $w \models \varphi$ since no position can hold both an a and a b.

The formula $\psi := \forall x \, \forall y.(a(x) \wedge b(y)) \to x < y$ does not hold for every word. We have $aaabbbb \models \psi$, but $aabab \not\models \psi$ because $aabab(2) = b$ and $aabab(3) = a$ but of course $3 \not< 2$. It defines the language $a^* b^*$ or, to be precise, $a^+ b^* \cup a^* b^+$.

$\Sigma^* ab \Sigma^*$ is FO-definable by the formula $\exists x \, \exists y. a(x) \wedge b(y) \wedge succ(x, y)$.

Now let $\Sigma = \{a, b, c\}$. The language comprising of all words w with the property that each a is eventually followed by a b and between such a and the first subsequent b there are only symbols a (and no symbol c) is FO-definable by the following formula.

$$\forall x.a(x) \to \exists y.b(y) \wedge x < y \wedge \forall z.x < z \wedge z < y \to a(z)$$

Remember the formula $succ(x, y)$ defined above using quantification and reference to '$<$' in order to assert that y is the successor of x. It is possible to introduce MSO with $succ(x, y)$ as a primitive binary predicate in place of $x < y$. This leads to two (syntactically) different logics MSO[$<$] (as introduced in Def. 2.1) and MSO[$succ$] with the corresponding modification. The reason for not distinguishing between these two in the first place is the following result.

Theorem 2.9 *A language L is MSO[$<$]-definable iff it is MSO[$succ$]-definable.*

Proof The right-to-left direction is trivial as any subformula $succ(x, y)$ of some φ defining L can be rewritten using '$<$' in the way shown to introduce $succ$ as an abbreviation. The other direction works in a similar way. It suffices to show that $x < y$ can be expressed in MSO[$succ$]. This can be done as follows.

$$x < y \; := \; \forall X.\big(\forall u.\forall v.X(u) \wedge succ(u, v) \to X(v)\big) \to \forall z.succ(x, z) \wedge X(z) \to X(y)$$

In other words, $x < y$ if and only if every set that is closed under successors and contains x's successor also contains y. $\qquad \square$

Thm. 2.9 does not hold for FO: the two logics FO[$<$] and FO[$succ$] do not have the same expressive power; the former is genuinely more expressive than the latter.

In other words, the translation of $x < y$ into a formula over *succ* does indeed require second-order quantification as used in the proof of Thm. 2.9. By convention, when we speak of FO we mean FO$[<]$.

2.2 MSO-Definability and Regularity

In this section we will show that the class of MSO-definable languages coincides exactly with the class of regular languages.

2.2.1 From Automata to Formulas

We show that every NFA can be translated into an MSO formula defining the same language.

Theorem 2.10 *For every regular language L over some alphabet Σ there is an MSO formula φ_L such that $L(\varphi_L) = L$.*

Proof Let $\mathcal{A} = (Q, \Sigma, q_I, \delta, F)$ be an NFA for L. We assume that $Q = \{1, \ldots, n\}$ and introduce second-order variables $X_1, \ldots, X_n$ representing these states in the sense that an assignment of X_q corresponds exactly to the sets of positions in which $\mathcal{A}$ can be in state q in an accepting run. Then φ_L can be constructed as $\exists X_1 \ldots \exists X_n \ldots$ so that the existential quantification over sets of positions corresponds to the existential quantification over runs in the definition of acceptance of a word by an NFA.

Note that there is a slight mismatch: a run on a word w of length n has length $n + 1$ itself. This can easily be remedied for example by not demanding that the first position in a word belongs to the assignment of the set corresponding to the initial state, but to one of its successors under the first symbol in the word. Thus, $X_q(i)$ should hold if $\mathcal{A}$ is in state q *after* processing $w(i)$. To that end we define the following auxiliary formulas with free variables as indicated. Let $\mathbf{X} = (X_1, \ldots, X_n)$.

$$uniq(\mathbf{X}) \;:=\; \forall x \bigvee_{q \in Q} X_q(x) \wedge \bigwedge_{q' \neq q} \neg X_{q'}(x)$$

$$init(\mathbf{X}) \;:=\; \bigvee_{a \in \Sigma} a(0) \wedge \bigvee_{q' \in \delta(q_I, a)} X_{q'}(0)$$

$$run(\mathbf{X}) \;:=\; \forall x \, \forall y.succ(x, y) \rightarrow \bigwedge_{q \in Q} \bigwedge_{a \in \Sigma} \left(X_q(x) \wedge a(y) \rightarrow \bigvee_{q' \in \delta(q, a)} X_{q'}(y) \right)$$

$$acc(\mathbf{X}) \;:=\; \bigvee_{q \in F} X_q(\mathrm{end})$$

Note that $\bigvee_{q \in \varnothing} \ldots := \mathrm{ff}$ by convention. These formulas state, successively, that (I) every position is "labelled" with a unique state, (II) the first position is labelled with a successor of $\mathcal{A}$'s initial state under the symbol at that position, (III) the labels at two successive positions agree with $\mathcal{A}$'s transition table, and (IV) the last position is labelled with an accepting state.

We now put

$$\varphi_L \quad := \quad \underbrace{\exists X_1 \ldots \exists X_n . \, \mathit{uniq}(\mathbf{X}) \wedge \mathit{init}(\mathbf{X}) \wedge \mathit{run}(\mathbf{X}) \wedge \mathit{acc}(\mathbf{X})}_{\psi(\mathbf{X})} \ .$$

Correctness of this formula follows from the following observation. Let $w \in L(\mathcal{A})$ and $\rho = q_0, \ldots, q_m$ be an accepting run of $\mathcal{A}$ on w. Hence, $q_0 = q_I$, $q_m \in F$, and $q_{i+1} \in \delta(q_i, w(i))$ for all $i \in [m]$. Consider the assignment I_ρ that assigns to each X_q to the positions at which ρ hits state q (shifted by 1 to account for the problem with the indices mentioned above): $I(X_q) := \{i - 1 \mid q_i = q\}$. It is then not hard to see that $w, I_\rho \models \psi(\mathbf{X})$ because ρ has all the properties formulated in the four conjuncts in $\psi(\mathbf{X})$ under this interpretation for $\mathbf{X}$. Hence, $w \models \varphi_L$. Likewise, given any assignment for $\mathbf{X}$ satisfying these four conjuncts, it is easily possible to extract a run (by adding q_I at the beginning) from it. $\square$

Note that the passage from an NFA for L to φ_L is constructive.

2.2.2 From Formulas to Automata

We are now interested in the converse of the result just proved to the effect that the language of an arbitrary MSO-sentence is regular. Note that the method of choice for proving statements about formulas – induction on the formula structure – cannot directly be employed. The reason is simply that a subformula of a sentence is in general not a sentence itself, so the inductive hypothesis would not be applicable. The problem here is that we only defined the notion of *language* for sentence, not for open formulas because the set of models of a formula is a set of pairs of words and assignments in general, and it was only the observation that assignments are irrelevant for sentences that allowed us to see this simply as a set of words.

There is, however, a simple trick that can be used to make the induction work: note that the language of a possibly open subformula of a sentence would not have to be a word over the same alphabet Σ as that of the sentence's language. In fact, there is a very natural way to regard an interpretation (w, I) consisting of a word $w \in \Sigma^+$ and an assignment of a finite number of second-order variables $X_1, \ldots, X_n$ by sets of positions in w, as a word w_I again, namely over the alphabet $\Sigma \times \{0, 1\}^n$. This way, the external assignment for the word gets internalised as follows.

$$w_I(i) \quad := \quad \begin{pmatrix} \chi_1(i) \\ \vdots \\ \chi_n(i) \\ w(i) \end{pmatrix}$$

where, for each $i = 0, \ldots, |w| - 1$ and each $j = 1, \ldots, n$ we have

$$\chi_j(i) \;=\; \begin{cases} 0 & \text{, if } i \notin I(X_j)\,, \\ 1 & \text{, if } i \in I(X_j)\,. \end{cases}$$

We can think of w_I as of a word with multiple tracks: one Σ-track containing the original word w, and one additional $\{0,1\}$-track for each second-order variable.

Example 2.11 Let $w = aabab$ and I be such that $I(X) = \{0,3,4\}$ and $I(Y) = \{1,3\}$ Then w_I could be written as follows.

$$\begin{array}{c} X: \\ Y: \\ w: \end{array} \quad \underbrace{\begin{pmatrix}1\\0\\a\end{pmatrix}\begin{pmatrix}0\\1\\a\end{pmatrix}\begin{pmatrix}0\\0\\b\end{pmatrix}\begin{pmatrix}1\\1\\a\end{pmatrix}\begin{pmatrix}1\\0\\b\end{pmatrix}}_{w_I}$$

We say that w_I *could be* this multi-track word and not that it *is*, simply because the representation using such vector symbols obviously requires us to fix an order on the variables. Ideally, the variables are ordered as in $X_1, \ldots, X_n$ for instance. However, later on, we will make use of the projection construction that eliminates single tracks from such words. It does not change the order but it causes us to deviate from the situation in which the tracks correspond to variables $X_1, \ldots, X_n$. In order to avoid technical overkill, we will simply assume that there is some correspondence between the second-order variables in a formula and the additional $\{0,1\}$-tracks. In fact, this will be a one-to-one correspondence between the *free* variables and these tracks.

We could extend this construction to the first-order variables, indicating the assignment of such a variable x by an additional track of the form 0^*10^*. Note that an assignment I assigns a single position to a first-order variable.

We can avoid the additional technicalities with the following trick, though.

Definition 2.12 An MSO formula φ over Σ is called *normalised* if it is derivable from the grammar

$$\varphi \;::=\; sing(X) \mid X < Y \mid X \subseteq Y \mid X \subseteq a \mid \varphi \vee \varphi \mid \neg\varphi \mid \exists X\,\varphi$$

where $a \in \Sigma$, $X, Y \in \mathcal{V}_2$.

The term "normalised" is slightly misleading. Clearly, such normalised formulas are not just of a special form in the original syntax. Instead we have extended the syntax by new atomic formulas $sing(X)$, $X < Y$, $X \subseteq Y$ and $X \subseteq a$ for $a \in \Sigma$ with one, resp. two free second-order variables X, Y. Intuitively they state that (i) X denotes a singleton set, (ii) for every position in X there is a later one in Y, (iii) the set denoted by X is a subset of that denoted by Y, and (iv) all the positions in the set for X carry the letter a. We therefore need to extend the semantics accordingly as well.

$$\begin{array}{llll} w, I \vDash sing(X) & \text{iff} & |I(X)| = 1 \\ w, I \vDash X < Y & \text{iff} & \text{for all } i \in I(X) \text{ there is } j > i \text{ with } j \in I(Y) \\ w, I \vDash X \subseteq Y & \text{iff} & I(X) \subseteq I(Y) \\ w, I \vDash X \subseteq a & \text{iff} & w(i) = a \text{ for all } i \in I(X) \end{array}$$

The justification for calling formulas of this new form normalised is given by the following lemma. It states that every formula in the original syntax can be translated into the new syntax in a way that is almost equivalence-preserving. Note that the result cannot be equivalent since normalised formulas have no first-order variables. However, first-order variables can be seen as special second-order variables. Suppose I is an assignment of first-order variables $\mathcal{V}_1 = \{x_1,\ldots,x_n\}$ and second-order variables $\mathcal{V}_2 = \{X_1,\ldots,X_m\}$. Take new second-order variables $Y_1,\ldots,Y_n$ and let $\hat{I}$ be the assignment of the second-order variables $\{Y_1,\ldots,Y_n,X_1,\ldots,X_m\}$, defined by

- $\hat{I}(X_j) := I(X_j)$ for every $j = 1,\ldots,m$,
- $\hat{I}(Y_j) := \{I(x_i)\}$ for every $j = 1,\ldots,n$.

This simple reinterpretation of first-order objects as singleton second-order objects is what allows us to almost preserve equivalence in a translation from original MSO formulas to normalised ones.

Lemma 2.13 *For every MSO formula $\varphi(x_1,\ldots,x_n,X_1,\ldots,X_n)$ there is a normalised MSO formula $\varphi'(Y_1,\ldots,Y_n,X_1,\ldots,X_m)$ such that $|\varphi'| = \mathcal{O}(|\varphi|)$ and for all $w \in \Sigma^+$ and I we have $w, I \vDash \varphi$ iff $w, \hat{I} \vDash \varphi'$.*

Proof The elimination of first-order variables and quantifiers is realised by the following translation. Let $Y_1,\ldots,Y_n$ be fresh second-order variables not occurring in φ.

$$
\begin{aligned}
tr(x_i < x_j) &:= Y_i < Y_j & \qquad tr(\psi_1 \vee \psi_2) &:= tr(\psi_1) \vee tr(\psi_2) \\
tr(a(x_i)) &:= Y_i \subseteq a & tr(\neg\psi) &:= \neg tr(\psi) \\
tr(X(x_i)) &:= Y_i \subseteq X & tr(\exists X_i\,\psi) &:= \exists X_i\, tr(\psi) \\
tr(\exists x_i\,\psi) &:= \exists Y_i.sing(Y_i) \wedge tr(\psi)
\end{aligned}
$$

Then simply let $\varphi' := tr(\varphi)$. The claim on the size of φ is obvious. Correctness is shown by a standard induction on the structure of φ. Details are left as an exercise. $\square$

Lemma 2.13 allows us to restrict our attention to normalised formulas φ over some alphabet Σ. In particular, they contain no first-order variables. Moreover, assume that the second-order variables occurring in φ are $X_1,\ldots,X_n$ and that all quantifiers in φ use different variables. Lemma 2.13 then also allows us to see the set of models of any subformula $\psi(X_1,\ldots,X_n)$ as a set of words over the extended alphabet $\Sigma \times \{0,1\}^n$. We will also denote this as $L(\psi(X_1,\ldots,X_n))$.

The goal is to construct, given such a normalised formula φ, an NFA $\mathcal{A}_\varphi$ such that $w, I \vDash \varphi$ iff $w_I \in L(\mathcal{A}_\varphi)$. Note that this is general enough to be proved by induction on the structure of φ. The next lemma provides the base case for this induction.

Lemma 2.14 *Let Σ and $n \in \mathbb{N}$ be given. There are NFA $\mathcal{A}_\psi$ for $\psi \in \{sing(X_i), X_i < X_j, X_i \subseteq X_j, X_i \subseteq a \mid a \in \Sigma, i,j \in \{1,\ldots,n\}\}$ such that for all $w \in \Sigma^+$ and all assignments $I : \{X_1,\ldots,X_n\} \to 2^{[m]}$ with $m = |w|$ we have*

$$
w, I \vDash \psi \quad \text{iff} \quad w_I \in L(\mathcal{A}_\psi).
$$

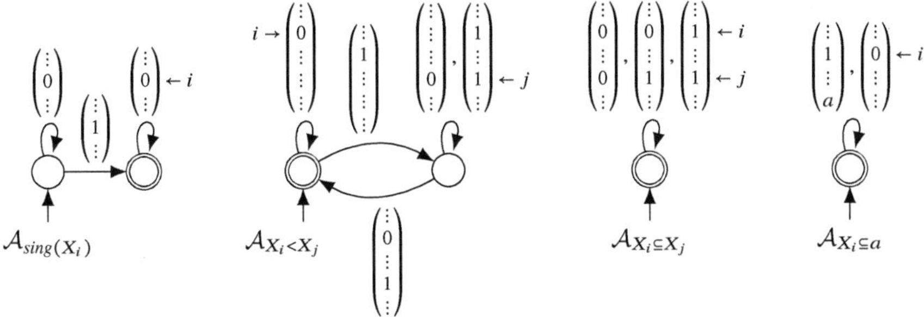

Fig. 2.1 NFA for the base cases in the proof of Lemma 2.14.

Proof The four NFA, depending on the type of atomic formula, are shown in Fig. 2.1. A close inspection shows that these correctly accept words encoding interpretations for formulas of these atomic kinds: take for instance $\mathcal{A}_{sing(X_i)}$ on the left. It accepts a word $v \in (\Sigma \times \{0,1\}^n)^*$ that represent some interpretation-extended word w_I, iff its i-th track is of the form $0^* 1 0^*$, i.e. if the interpretation encoded in w_I assigns a single position to X_i, resp. $I(X_i)$ is a singleton set. $\qquad\square$

The NFA for formulas of the form $\varphi \vee \psi$ is obtained from $\mathcal{A}_\varphi$ and $\mathcal{A}_\psi$ using the union construction for NFA, cf. Thm. 1.7. The automaton for $\neg\varphi$ is obtained from $\mathcal{A}_\varphi$ by complementation, cf. Cor. 1.17. What remains is to transfer the effect of existential second-order quantification to NFA. Interestingly, this seemingly most complex logical operation corresponds to almost the simplest operation on NFA: alphabet *projection*. For a word w_I over $\Sigma \times \{0,1\}^n$ and $j \in [n]$ we denote by $w_I\!\downarrow_j$ the word that results from w_I by simple removing the j-th additional track. Clearly, $w_I\!\downarrow_j$ is a word over $\Sigma \times \{0,1\}^{n-1}$, and it represents a pair of a Σ-word and an assignment of one less second-order variable than w_I does.

Lemma 2.15 *Let $\psi(X_1,\ldots,X_n)$ be a formula and $\mathcal{A}_\psi$ be an NFA recognising its language in the sense above. Let $j \in \{1,\ldots,n\}$. There is an NFA $\mathcal{A}_{\exists X_j \psi}$ such that $L(\mathcal{A}_{\exists X_j \psi}) = \{w_I\!\downarrow_j \mid w_I \in L(\mathcal{A}_\psi)\}$ and $|\mathcal{A}_{\exists X_j \psi}| = |\mathcal{A}_\psi|$.*

Proof Let $\mathcal{A}_{\exists X_j \psi}$ result from $\mathcal{A}_\psi$ by replacing every transition label $(a, \chi_1, \ldots, \chi_n)$ with $a \in \Sigma$, $\chi_j \in \{0,1\}$ for $j = 1, \ldots, n$, by $(a, \chi_1, \ldots, \chi_{j-1}, \chi_{j+1}, \ldots, \chi_n)$. Clearly, $\mathcal{A}_{\exists X_j \psi}$ is an NFA over the alphabet $\Sigma \times \{0,1\}^{n-1}$, if $\mathcal{A}_\psi$ is an NFA over the alphabet $\Sigma \times \{0,1\}^n$, and the size claim is obviously true. Correctness remains to be seen.

Suppose that ρ is an accepting run of $\mathcal{A}_{\exists X_j \psi}$ on some word $w_{I'}$ with $n-1$ additional tracks that interpret the variables $X_1, \ldots, X_{j-1}, X_{j+1}, \ldots, X_n$. Since $\mathcal{A}_{\exists X_j \psi}$ resulted from $\mathcal{A}_\psi$ by projection of the j-th track, it is possible to follow ρ through $\mathcal{A}_\psi$ by reconstructing the symbols from $\{0,1\}$ on the original j-th track. Let $S \subseteq [m]$ for $m = |w_{I'}|$ be the set of positions at which this track sees the symbol 1. Hence, there is a set S s.t. $\mathcal{A}_\psi$ accepts the word w_I where $I = I'[X_j \mapsto S]$. Assuming that $\mathcal{A}_\psi$ is correct, we therefore have that $w, I' \models \exists X_j \psi$. The converse direction is shown in the same way. $\qquad\square$

The automaton for $\exists X_j\,\psi$ thus works like $\mathcal{A}_\psi$ but guesses the contents of the X_j-track nondeterministically. This completes the construction of logical operations on automata needed to prove the main result.

Theorem 2.16 *Every MSO-definable language is regular.*

Proof Let $L = L(\varphi)$ for some MSO-sentence φ. We want to show that L is regular, namely NFA-recognisable. In order to do this by induction on the structure of φ, we need to extend the claim to arbitrary formulas: let $L \subseteq (\Sigma \times \{0,1\}^n)^+$ such that $L = L(\varphi(X_1,\ldots,X_n))$ for some MSO formula φ not containing any first-order variables. We can then use induction; the base cases are covered by Lemma 2.14. For the step cases, Lemma 2.15 shows how to construct NFA for existential quantifications, Thm. 1.7 for unions and Cor. 1.17 for complements. $\qquad\qquad\square$

2.2.3 Consequences of the Translations

The two constructions above, from NFA to MSO and back, have important consequences. By putting Thm. 2.10 and 2.16 together we obviously obtain that these two formalisms are equi-expressive.

Corollary 2.17 *A language $L \subseteq \Sigma^+$ is regular iff it is MSO-definable.*

The second consequence combines this with decidability of NFA non-emptiness.

Corollary 2.18 *Satisfiability and equivalence for MSO are decidable.*

Proof According to Thm. 2.6 it suffices to consider the satisfiability problem. Given some $\varphi \in \mathrm{MSO}$, according to Thm. 2.16 it is possible to construct an NFA $\mathcal{A}_\varphi$ s.t. $L(\mathcal{A}_\varphi) = L(\varphi)$. Then decidability of MSO satisfiability follows from decidability of NFA emptiness, cf. Thm. 1.18. $\qquad\qquad\square$

We also consider the existential fragment EMSO of MSO. It consists of all those formulas that – when brought into negation normal form – do not contain universal second-order quantifiers. For example $\exists X\,\forall y.P_a(y) \rightarrow \exists x.x < y \wedge X(x)$ is an EMSO formula but $\forall x.(\exists X\,\forall y.P_a(y) \rightarrow X(y)) \rightarrow P_b(x)$ is not because the quantification over X is on the left (negative) side of the implication and thus is effectively universal. Universal first-order quantification is, however, allowed in EMSO. Surprisingly, EMSO is as expressive as full MSO.

Theorem 2.19 *A language $L \subseteq \Sigma^+$ is MSO-definable iff it is EMSO-definable.*

Proof It suffices to note that the formulas constructed in the proof of Thm. 2.10 belong to EMSO. Hence, by translating an MSO formula into an NFA and then back into MSO, we effectively obtain an equivalent EMSO formula. $\qquad\qquad\square$

Some of these translations come with certain costs. While the construction of EMSO formulas from NFA is polynomial, the translation from MSO to NFA is not. The reason is that each negation operation requires a complementation construction on NFA which incurs an exponential blowup. One may be tempted to try to optimise the translation and eliminate negation first by putting formulas into negation normal form. This cheap trick does not work, though. This transformation would leave universal quantifiers, and it is impossible to translate universal quantification into an equally simple operation like projection on NFA. It would be helpful to work with DFA instead to handle universal quantifiers, but determinism is not an invariant of the translation: while it is possible to construct DFA for the union of two DFA-recognisable languages at a quadratic blowup only, it is then the existential quantification that causes problems because projection genuinely creates nondeterministic automata. Hence, all these ideas only shift the exponential blowups around, and the translations seem to involve a number of nested exponential constructions that is dependent on the formula. It is reasonable to ask whether this may be unavoidable, i.e. whether NFA equivalent to some MSO formulas may need to be non-elementarily larger. The following section shows that this is indeed the case.

2.3 The Complexity of MSO

We will show that the non-elementary blowup in translating MSO formulas into NFA is unavoidable. To this end, we first define two fast-growing families of functions in input parameter n:

$$2_0^n := n \qquad\qquad F_0^n := n$$

$$2_{k+1}^n := 2^{2_k^n} \qquad\qquad F_{k+1}^n := F_k^n \cdot 2^{F_k^n}$$

The functions $n \mapsto 2_k^n$ for any $k \geq 0$ are ultimately what we are interested in, namely to show that the blowup in translating MSO formulas of size n into NFA cannot be bounded by an elementary function. The functions $n \mapsto F_k^n$ will be helpful for technical reasons. Clearly, we have $F_k^n \geq 2_k^n$ for all $n, k \geq 0$, so it suffices to use the functions F_k^n for any lower bounds.

The goal is to construct satisfiable formulas φ_k^n s.t. the shortest word in $L(\varphi_k^n)$ has length F_k^n. Specifically, we will construct formulas $dist_k^n(x, y)$ with two free variables x, y s.t.

$$w, I \vDash dist_k^n(x, y) \quad \text{iff} \quad I(y) - I(x) = F_k^n$$

for all interpretations (w, I) and all $n, k \geq 0$. Then take the sentence $\varphi_k^n := \exists x\, \exists y\, dist_k^n(x, y)$ for instance. Clearly, it would be satisfiable, but any word fulfilling it would have to have length at least $F_k^n + 1$.

In order to construct $dist_k^n(x, y)$ we proceed by induction on k. For $k = 0$ this is simple: remember that $F_0^n := n$, hence, we can simply take

$$dist_0^n(x, y) := \exists x_0 \ldots \exists x_n . x_0 = x \wedge \Big(\bigwedge_{i=0}^{n-1} succ(x_i, x_{i+1}) \Big) \wedge x_n = y \, .$$

Now suppose that $dist_k^n(x, y)$ is already defined. In order to construct $dist_{k+1}^n(x, y)$ it is helpful to imagine a given word $w = a_0 a_1 \ldots a_m$ for some large m to be equipped with an additional track of symbols 0 and 1 that act as bit values of an F_k^n-bit counter s.t., when read in chunks of length F_k^n starting in position x, we see the binary representations of the numbers $0, 1, \ldots$ successively along this track. Note that there are $2^{F_k^n}$ many such values, and each takes up F_k^n positions. Hence, writing them all down consecutively takes up $F_k^n \cdot 2^{F_k^n} = F_{k+1}^n$ many positions in the underlying word. So if this enumeration starts at position x and ends just before position y then we have $y - x = F_{k+1}^n$. The following picture shows the evaluation of a monadic second-order variable B representing bits in such a counter with two positions x and y in a fictitious word (over an arbitrary alphabet). To ease the construction of the formulas in the following, we additionally require the first position of every block of F_n many bits to be marked, using another second-order variable M.

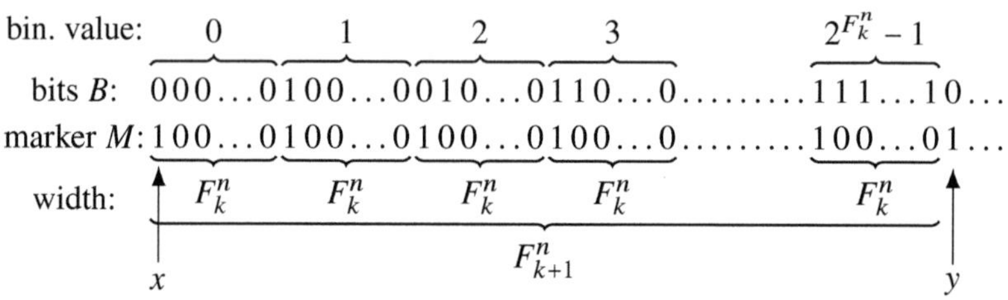

bin. value: 0   1   2   3 $2^{F_k^n} - 1$

bits B: $000\ldots01\,00\ldots00\,10\ldots01\,10\ldots0\ldots\ldots\ldots111\ldots10\ldots$

marker M: $100\ldots01\,00\ldots01\,00\ldots01\,00\ldots0\ldots\ldots\ldots100\ldots01\ldots$

width: F_k^n F_k^n F_k^n F_k^n F_k^n

F_{k+1}^n

x y

Note that bits in the binary values are given in increasing order of significance when reading from left to right.

We define

$$dist_{k+1}^n(x, y) \;\; := \;\; \exists M \, \exists B . mark_{k+1}^n(x, y) \wedge init_{k+1}^n(x) \wedge count_{k+1}^n(x, y) \wedge fin_{k+1}^n(y)$$

where $mark_{k+1}^n(x, y)$ expresses the correct marking of the first position in each block:

$$M(x) \wedge \forall z . x < z \rightarrow \big(((\exists y' . z < y' \wedge dist_k^n(x, y')) \wedge \neg M(z))$$
$$\vee \, \exists x' . x \leq x' \wedge dist_k^n(x', z) \wedge (M(z) \leftrightarrow M(x')) \big)$$

It says that position x is marked, and thereafter all positions in the same block (recognisable by being left of some y' that is at distance F_k^n from x) are not marked. All positions further away than that (recognisable by being equal to or right of some position at distance F_k^n from x) obtain their marker value from the position at distance F_k^n to the left of themselves.

Formula $init_{k+1}^n(x)$ expresses that the first F_k^n positions starting at x carry the symbol 0:

$$\exists y' . dist_k^n(x, y') \wedge \forall z . x \leq z \wedge z < y' \rightarrow \neg B(z)$$

Formula $fin_{k+1}^n(y)$ expresses that the F_k^n positions before y carry the symbol 1:

$$\exists x'.dist_k^n(x',y) \wedge \forall z.x' \le z \wedge z < y \to B(z)$$

Formula $count_{k+1}^n(x,y)$ expresses that each block of width F_k^n between x and y carries a binary value that is the successor of the value written down in the block to its left. This is easier to express than one may expect: a recipe for increasing a binary value by one is the following.

Flip the least significant bit. For the i-th bit, $i > 0$, assume that the new value of bit $i-1$ has already been determined. Then note that the old and new value b_{i-1} and b'_{i-1} of bit $i-1$ together with the old value b_i of bit i uniquely determine the new value b'_i of bit i. It is helpful to depict these four values as bits placed in positions $i-1$ and i in consecutive blocks.

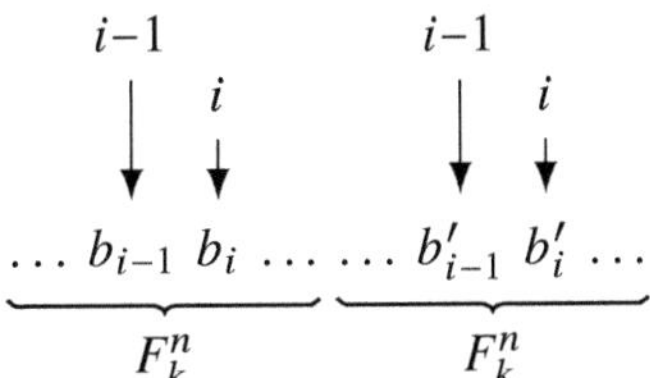

Then there are only eight different possibilities for combinations of these four values, determined by how a binary value gets incremented: all lowest set bits are unset, the first unset bit is set and all higher bits are preserved. Hence, by comparing b_{i-1} and b'_{i-1} we can easily determine which of these three phases the i-th bit falls into: if they are equal or b_{i-1} has already been increased to b'_{i-1}, then b_i and b'_i must be equal. If b_{i-1} has been decreased to b'_{i-1} then b_i must be decreased to b'_i as well if it is set, or must be increased if it is unset. The following table shows all these combinations.

b_{i-1}	b'_{i-1}	b_i	b'_i
0	0	0	0
0	0	1	1
1	1	0	0
1	1	1	1
0	1	0	0
0	1	1	1
1	0	0	1
1	0	1	0

It is not hard to see that the formula

$$next(b_{i-1},b_i,b'_{i-1},b'_i) \; := \; (b_{i-1} \to b'_{i-1}) \leftrightarrow (b_i \leftrightarrow b'_i)$$

expresses exactly this relationship between these four values. We can use this to construct $count_{k+1}^n(x,y)$ as

$$\forall x' \forall y'.x \le x' \wedge y' < y \wedge dist_k^n(x',y') \to$$

$$\Big((M(x) \to (B(x) \leftrightarrow \neg B(y))\Big) \wedge$$

$$\left(\neg M(x) \to \exists x'' \, \exists y'' . succ(x'', x') \wedge succ(y'', y') \wedge next(x'', x', y'', y') \right)\right)$$

This shows that satisfiable MSO formulas can have truly large models. Combining this with the fact that NFA cannot, we obtain the impossibility of an equivalence-preserving translation of MSO formulas into relatively small NFA.

Theorem 2.20 *There is no translation of MSO formulas of size n into equivalent NFA of size at most $2_k^{p(n)}$ for any polynomial function $p : \mathbb{N} \to \mathbb{N}$ and any $k \geq 0$.*

Proof Consider the family $(\varphi_n)_{n \geq 1}$ with $\varphi_n := \exists x \, \exists y \, dist_n^1(x, y)$. Clearly, each φ_n is satisfiable, and $L(\varphi_n) = \{ w \in \Sigma^* \mid |w| \geq F_n^1 \}$. It is a routine exercise to show that every NFA recognising $L(\varphi_n)$ needs to have at last F_n^1 many states. Note that the function $n \mapsto F_n^1$ grows non-elementarily, i.e. much faster than $2_k^{p(n)}$ for any fixed $k \geq 0$ and any polynomial p. Hence for any such k, p there is some n_0 s.t. $F_n^1 > 2_k^{p(n)}$ for all $n \geq n_0$, showing that any family $(\mathcal{A}_n)_{n \geq 1}$ of NFA growing in size at a rate of at most $2_k^{p(n)}$, must contain some NFA $\mathcal{A}_n$ s.t. $L(\mathcal{A}_n) \neq L(\varphi_n)$. $\qquad\qquad \square$

This already gives a non-elementary gap between the sizes of MSO and equivalent NFA. However, the construction is not optimal yet: the size of (φ_n) grows exponentially in n, since every $dist_{k+1}^n(x, y)$ contains several occurrences of $dist_k^n(x', y')$ for different variables x', y'. It is not hard, though, to rewrite φ_n so that it only contains polynomially many subformulas in n: simply replace $dist_k^n(x', y')$ by $\exists x' \, \exists y'. x' = x \wedge y' = y \wedge dist_k^n(x, y)$. Then $dist_k^n(x, y)$ still contains several occurrences of $dist_k^n(x, y)$ but they are all syntactically equal. Hence, the number of subformulas of φ_n then grows only linearly in n.

Thm. 2.20 only precludes the existence of an elementary and *equivalence-preserving* translation from MSO into NFA. But Cor. 2.18 reduces decision problems on MSO to satisfiability, resp. non-emptiness of NFA. The existence of a translation from MSO into equi-satisfiable NFA – i.e. a mapping $\varphi \mapsto \mathcal{A}_\varphi$ s.t. $L(\mathcal{A}_\varphi) \neq \varnothing$ iff φ_n is satisfiable – would not contradict Thm. 2.20. In fact, such a mapping trivially exists. Take two NFA $\mathcal{A}_0$ and $\mathcal{A}_1$ s.t. $L(\mathcal{A}_0) = \varnothing$ and $L(\mathcal{A}_1) \neq \varnothing$. Then the mapping

$$\varphi_n \mapsto \begin{cases} \mathcal{A}_1 & \text{, if } \varphi_n \text{ is satisfiable,} \\ \mathcal{A}_0 & \text{, otherwise.} \end{cases}$$

cleary has the desired property. However, it is not helpful in order to decide satisfiability of MSO since, in order to use it to know what φ_n gets mapped to, one needs to "know" whether it is satisfiable. Moreover, NFA are not really used in this translation – one could equally just take two Boolean values to signal the outcome of this function on any argument.

So the real question behind all this simply is: can the satisfiability problem for MSO be decided in a way that is asymptotically significantly better than translating formulas into NFA according to Thm. 2.16 and testing those for non-emptiness? That test can be done in nondeterministic logarithmic space in the size of the resulting NFA which are of non-elementary size compared to the original MSO formulas. Hence, the space (and also time) complexity of this procedure is still non-elementary.

The answer is negative, as the following theorem shows. Note that $(k - 1)$-ExpSpace $\subsetneq k$-ExpSpace for any $k > 1$. Hence, any k-ExpSpace-hard problem does not belong to $(k - 1)$-ExpSpace. Moreover, $\bigcup_{k \geq 0} k$-ExpSpace $= \bigcup_{k \geq 0} k$-ExpTime, and the following theorem could equally be stated about elementary time instead of space complexity. Moreover, k-ExpSpace $= k$-NExpSpace, i.e. it is irrelevant whether Turing Machines as a computational model for this complexity class are assumed to be deterministic or allowed to be nondeterministic.

Theorem 2.21 *The satisfiability problem for MSO is hard for k-ExpSpace for any* $k \geq 0$.

Proof (Sketch) Let $k \geq 0$. A standard problem that is k-ExpSpace hard is the following: given a Turing Machine $\mathcal{M}$ whose space is bounded by a function $2_k^{p(n)}$ for inputs of length n, and an input w, does $\mathcal{M}$ accept w? We show that this can be polynomially reduced to the satisfiability problem for MSO by constructing a formula $\varphi_{\mathcal{M},w}$ that is satisfiable iff $w \in L(\mathcal{M})$, and of polynomial size in $|\mathcal{M}|$ and $|w|$ only.

Let $\mathcal{M} = (Q, \Sigma, \Gamma, q_I, \Delta, q_{\mathrm{acc}})$ with state set Q, input and tape alphabets Σ, Γ, initial and accepting state q_I, q_{acc}, and transition function $\delta \subseteq Q \times \Gamma \times Q \times \Gamma \times \{-1, 0, 1\}$. Assume that there is a special blank-tape symbol $\square \in \Gamma \setminus \Sigma$. Let $w = a_0 \dots a_{n-1}$.

Note that a computation of $\mathcal{M}$ on w can be represented as a word $C_0 \# C_1 \# \dots \# C_m$ by concatenating successive configurations which can also be represented as words $C_0, C_1, \dots$ over the alphabet $Q \times \Gamma \cup \Gamma$. Then, $\varphi_{\mathcal{M},w}$ only has to express the conjunction of the following properties. Formalising these properties in MSO is left as an exercise.

- A model is of this specific form, i.e. it can be decomposed into blocks separated by the special symbol #, and each block is of length $2_k^{p(n)}$ and contains exactly one symbol from $Q \times \Gamma$ whereas all other symbols are from Γ.
- The first block is of the form $(q_I, a_0)a_1 \dots a_{n-1} \square \dots \square$.
- The last block is of the form $\dots (q_{\mathrm{acc}}, a) \dots$ for some $a \in \Gamma$.
- Each C_{i+1} is a legal successor of the preceding C_i, i.e. for every position x in C_i labelled with a symbol $(q, a) \in Q \times \Gamma$, there is a transition $(q, a, q', b, d) \in \delta$ s.t. the following hold.

    - If $d \in \{-1, 1\}$ then position x in C_{i+1} carries the symbol b, and position $x + d$ carries the symbol (q', c) where c is the symbol at position $x + d$ in C_i. I.e. $\mathcal{M}$ has written b at the tape head and moved the head accordingly.
    - If $d = 0$ then the symbol at position x is (q', b). I.e. $\mathcal{M}$ has written b and not moved the tape head.

    All other positions remain unchanged between C_i and C_{i+1}. $\qquad\square$

$$
\begin{array}{ll}
I(X_1) = 1\ 0\ 1\ 0\ 1 & \qquad I(X_1) = 1\ 0\ 1\ 0\ 1\ 0\ 0\ \ldots \\
I(X_2) = 0\ 1\ 1\ 0\ 0 & \qquad I(X_2) = 0\ 1\ 1\ 0\ 0\ 0\ 0\ \ldots \\
w = a\ a\ b\ a\ b & \qquad I(a) = 1\ 1\ 0\ 1\ 0\ 0\ 0\ \ldots \\
\text{positions: } 0\ 1\ 2\ 3\ 4 & \qquad I(b) = 0\ 0\ 1\ 0\ 1\ 0\ 0\ \ldots \\
& \qquad \text{domain}: 0\ 1\ 2\ 3\ 4\ 5\ 6\ \ldots
\end{array}
$$

Fig. 2.2 Word and MSO interpretation (left), corresponding WS1S interpretation (right).

2.4 Weak Second-Order Logic of One Successor

Historically, the automata-logic connection that is developed here started with the question of the decidability of a logic called *Second-Order Logic of One Successor* (S1S) which is syntactically very similar to MSO. S1S formulas are interpreted over the natural numbers, though, with a variable interpretation assigning members of $\mathbb{N}$ to first-order variables and subsets of $\mathbb{N}$ to second-order variables. If the interpretation of second-order variables is restricted to *finite* subsets than the logic is called *Weak Second-Order Logic of One Successor* (WS1S).

Note that this is not far away from the interpretation of MSO over (finite) words. The most notable difference is a purely technical one: in a WS1S-interpretation, every position, i.e. natural number, can belong to an arbitrary number of finite sets interpreting the second-order variables. In MSO, though, every position (of the underlying Σ-word) belongs to the interpretation of exactly one symbol from Σ, and arbitrarily many sets interpreting the second- order variables from $\mathcal{V}_2$. Fig. 2.2 depicts the difference. Note though, that belonging to exactly one of finitely many sets can be defined in MSO, for instance via

$$
\varphi_{\text{uni}}^{\Sigma} \;:=\; \forall x.\ \bigvee_{a \in \Sigma} a(x) \wedge \bigwedge_{\substack{b \in \Sigma \\ b \neq a}} \neg b(x) \ .
$$

Hence, we could equally have introduced MSO as a logic being interpreted over finite initial intervals of the natural numbers, i.e. the positions in a finite word, without distinguishing between alphabet symbols a and second-order variables X. Then, an MSO formula with n free second-order variables (and no free first-order variables) could be seen as being interpreted over a finite word over the alphabet $\{0,1\}^n$, so that a single alphabet letter provides the interpretation of all free second-order variables.

This may even be the more natural interpretation for these second-order formulas as it leads to a slightly simpler syntax without alphabet symbols. The reason for why MSO has been introduced in the slightly more cumbersome way is the use of automata theory in its traditional form where automata accept words over an arbitrary but fixed alphabet.

There is, however, another difference between MSO and WS1S that is not simply due to a choice of presentation. Consider the formula $\varphi := \forall x \exists y\, x < y$. As an MSO formula, φ is unsatisfiable, as no finite word can provide a position further to the right of any position. However, as a WS1S formula, φ is satisfiable. Note that it does not contain second-order variables, let alone free ones. Hence, satisfiability of φ

boils down to checking whether in the domain of natural numbers, for every element there is a greater one which is clearly true.

Thus, MSO over finite words and WS1S are not the same logic. They are, however, not only almost identical syntactically and very similar semantically, but they are also similar in terms of their computational complexity. It is easy to reduce satisfiability of one of them to the other.

Lemma 2.22 *For every MSO formula φ there is an equi-satisfiable $\psi \in$ WS1S s.t. $|\psi| = \mathcal{O}(|\varphi|)$.*

Proof The trick is to see that a model of an MSO formula over an alphabet Σ can fit into a finite prefix of the ordered natural numbers, and that quantifier relativisation can be used to restrict attention of all the logical operators to such a finite prefix. Let z be a fresh first-order variable not occurring in φ and let

$$\psi \; := \; \exists z. \varphi_{\mathrm{uni}}^{\Sigma} \!\restriction_z \wedge \varphi \!\restriction_z$$

where relativisation of quantification w.r.t. some first-order variable z is defined via

$$(\exists x.\varphi)\!\restriction_z \; := \; \exists x. x < z \wedge \varphi\!\restriction_z \; , \quad (\exists X.\varphi)\!\restriction_z \; := \; \exists X.(\forall x. X(x) \to x < z) \wedge \varphi\!\restriction_z \; ,$$

commutes with Boolean operators and does not change atomic formulas.

Now suppose that φ is an MSO formula over some alphabet Σ and first- and second-order variables from $\mathcal{V}_1, \mathcal{V}_2$, and that it has a model (w, I) for some $w \in \Sigma^+$ and corresponding assignment I. Let I' be the interpretation for the resulting WS1S formula ψ that agrees with I on all variables in $\mathcal{V}_1 \cup \mathcal{V}_2$, and additionally satisfies

$$I'(z) = |w| \quad \text{and} \quad I'(a) = \{i \mid w(i) = a\} \text{ for any } a \in \Sigma \; .$$

A straightforward induction on the structure of $\varphi\!\restriction_z$ shows that we have $I' \vDash \psi$. So, ψ is also satisfiable. Likewise, a finite word model for φ can be extracted from a satisfying assignment of ψ. $\qquad\square$

The converse direction, reducing WS1S satisfiability to MSO satisfiability over finite words, is not as easy as that. In particular, this would have to capture the satisfiability of the WS1S formula $\forall x \exists y\, x < y$ on a genuinely finite domain. We do not attempt to find some elaborate construction that realises this. Instead, we observe that the translation of MSO into NFA from Sect. 2.2.2 can be modified to capture WS1S using NFA.

Theorem 2.23 *The satisfiability problem of WS1S is decidable.*

Proof As in the case of MSO, we can assume WS1S formulas to be normalised so that first-order variables have been replaced by second-order ones. Let $2_{\mathrm{fin}}^{\mathbb{N}}$ denote the set of finite subsets of $\mathbb{N}$. We build, for each WS1S formula $\varphi(X_1, \dots, X_n)$, an NFA $\mathcal{A}_\varphi$ over the alphabet $\{0, 1\}^n$ s.t. for every variable interpretation $I : \{X_1, \dots, X_n\} \to 2_{\mathrm{fin}}^{\mathbb{N}}$ we have

$$I \vDash \varphi \quad \text{iff} \quad enc(I) \begin{pmatrix} 0 \\ \vdots \\ 0 \end{pmatrix}^* \subseteq L(\mathcal{A}_\varphi) \tag{2.1}$$

where $enc(I)$ is the shortest word representing I over the alphabet $\{0,1\}^n$ in the sense that $j \in I(X_i)$ iff the symbol in the i-th component of the j-th symbol in $enc(I)$ is 1. Note that being shortest means that $enc(I)$ does not end with leading zeros, resp. trailing zeros in a word representation with the least significant bit at the word's beginning. So $enc(I)$ must not end on $\mathbf{0} := (0, \ldots, 0)$. Thus, (2.1) demands that $\mathcal{A}_\varphi$ is built such that it accepts the encoding of I regardless of how many leading zeros its representation contains.

The inductive construction of $\mathcal{A}_\varphi$ is similar to the construction of NFA for MSO formulas. For atomic formulas they are in fact the same. Also, disjunctions can be handled using an ordinary union construction on NFA since this preserves (2.1). However, projection and complementation, used on the NFA side to handle existential quantification and negation on the formula side, do not generally preserve the invariant (2.1). When applied straightforwardly, they will result in NFA that only recognise a subset of $enc(I)\mathbf{0}^*$, namely $enc(I)\mathbf{0}^m$ for all $m \geq m_0$ for some $m_0 > 0$. It is then necessary to amend $\mathcal{A}_{\exists X_i . \varphi}$, resp. $\mathcal{A}_{\neg \varphi}$ after projection or complementation in order to maintain (2.1), by making those states final from which an ordinary final state can be reached under a sequence of $\mathbf{0}$-symbols.

At last, it remains to be seen that this modified construction can be used to decide WS1S. We claim that the construction guarantees that φ is satisfiable iff $L(\mathcal{A}_\varphi) \neq \varnothing$. So suppose that φ has a model I. According to (2.1), we have $enc(I)\mathbf{0}^* \subseteq L(\mathcal{A}_\varphi)$. Since the left side is clearly non-empty, we get that $L(\mathcal{A}_\varphi) \neq \varnothing$ as well.

Suppose, on the other hand, that $L(\mathcal{A}_\varphi) \neq \varnothing$. Let n be the number of free variables in φ. Then there must be a shortest word $w \in (\{0,1\}^n)^* \setminus (\{0\}^n)^*$ s.t. $w(\{0\}^n)^* \subseteq L(\mathcal{A}_\varphi)$. Then w uniquely induces an interpretation I (namely such that $enc(I) = w$) which yields $I \vDash \varphi$ according to (2.1). Hence, φ is satisfiable. $\square$

The following exemplifies the difference in the NFA constructions for MSO and for WS1S.

Example 2.24 Consider the formula $\varphi := \forall X_1 \exists X_2 \, X_1 < X_2$ where $X_1 < X_2$ expresses that the maximum of X_2 is strictly larger than the maximum of X_1, if the latter exists. Note that $X_1 < X_2$ is generally definable in MSO, resp. WS1S. Here we consider it as an atomic formula in order to keep the example reasonably small. Since φ does not contain any first-order formulas, we simply need to normalise it to $\neg \exists X_1 \neg \exists X_2 \, X_1 < X_2$ in order to translate it into an NFA. The first step consists of building an NFA $\mathcal{A}_{X_1 < X_2}$ for $X_1 < X_2$, for instance the following one.

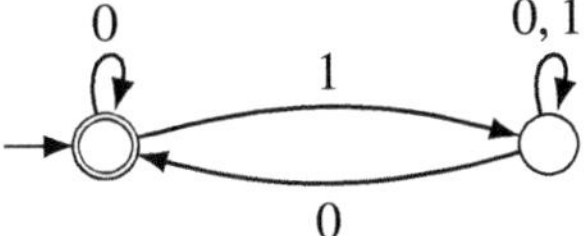

Next we project each alphabet symbol onto the first component, resulting in the following NFA $\mathcal{A}'$.

In a construction for MSO, this could be taken as $\mathcal{A}_{\exists X_2\, X_1 < X_2}$. However, for WS1S, this is not correct (yet). Note that it does not satisfy (2.1) from the proof of Thm. 2.23. Take, for instance, the WS1S interpretation $I : X_1 \mapsto \{2, 4, 5\}$ with $enc(I) = 001011$. Note that $enc(I)$ is not accepted by $\mathcal{A}'$, and therefore $enc(I)0^* \not\subseteq L(\mathcal{A}')$. However, if we donate leading zeros to the encoding of X_1, for instance as in 0010110, then we obtain an accepted word.

The key observation now is that for MSO, the matter of leading zeros is simply decided by the length of the underlying word that determines the length of representations of the encodings of the variable interpretations. For WS1S however, there is no such underlying word length: a variable interpretation can take any length that includes the largest indices in the sets associated with any second-order variable. Most of all, if the shortest of these encodings is captured by the construction, and (2.1) is maintained, then this guarantees that the NFA make no additional assumptions on the representation of such words $enc(I)$ other than the ability to write them down on a prefix of $\mathbb{N}$. Hence, we modify $\mathcal{A}'$ above to

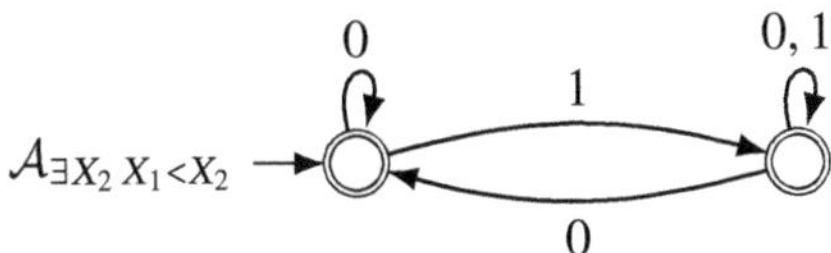

in order to ensure that it also accepts the shortest encodings of such interpretations. Note that the state on the right has become final because it can reach the final state on the left through a series of 0-symbols. Moreover, $L(\mathcal{A}_{\exists X_2\, X_1 < X_2}) = \{0, 1\}^*$. Hence, $L(\mathcal{A}_{\neg \exists X_2\, X_1 < X_2}) = \varnothing$, and this complementation obviously maintains (2.1). Next, we project it down to the alphabet $\{()\}$ of the empty tuple, yielding $L(\mathcal{A}_{\exists X_1\, \neg \exists X_2\, X_1 < X_2}) = \varnothing$ as well, and therefore $L(\mathcal{A}_\varphi) = \{()\}^*$, confirming that φ is satisfiable.

Note how the construction for MSO would deviate after building $\mathcal{A}_{\exists X_2\, X_1 < X_2}$ as the intermediately constructed $\mathcal{A}'$ above, accepting $\overline{(0 + 1)^* 1}$. Complementing it yields some $\mathcal{A}_{\neg \exists X_2\, X_1 < X_2}$ accepting $(0 + 1)^*$, and projecting it onto empty tuples yields $\mathcal{A}_{\exists X_1\, \neg \exists X_2\, X_1 < X_2}$ recognising $()^+$. Finally, complementing it yields $\mathcal{A}_\varphi$ accepting $\{\varepsilon\}$. Now, since its language is non-empty as well, one may be inclined to deduce that φ should be satisfiable as an MSO formula which it is not. However, note that in the MSO construction, $\mathcal{A}_\varphi$ accepts all words w, adorned by an encoding of the interpretation I of its free variables (here: none), such that $w, I \vDash \varphi$. Thus, the construction shows that ε is the only model for φ, and this can be taken in one of two ways.

First, we recall that, by convention, models of logical formulas should be non-empty, i.e. satisfiability of φ should correctly correspond to $\mathcal{A}_\varphi$'s ability to accept a *non-empty* word. Here, $\mathcal{A}_\varphi$ does not, so this does indeed confirm that φ is unsatisfiable as an MSO formula. Second, if we allowed the empty word as domain for the interpretation of MSO formulas we would find that $\varepsilon \vDash \forall X_1 \exists X_2\, X_1 < X_2$ indeed for trivial reasons, as the only available set for interpreting X_1 is $\varnothing$. We can then choose $\varnothing$ as well as the interpretation of X_2, and $X_1 < X_2$ is indeed satisfied, even though it looks like it should not, simply because $\varnothing$ has no maximal element.

2.5 Presburger Arithmetic

Presburger Arithmetic (PA) is the first-order theory of the natural numbers with addition. Its syntax is given by the grammar

$$\varphi ::= x + y = z \mid \varphi \vee \varphi \mid \neg \varphi \mid \exists x\, \varphi$$

where $x, y, z \in \mathcal{V}_1$. As with WS1S, the first-order variables are interpreted as unbounded natural numbers, and $+$ denotes the usual addition relation. Formally, let $I : \mathcal{V}_1 \to \mathbb{N}$ be a variable assignment. Satisfaction of a PA formula by an interpretation I is explained inductively as follows.

$$
\begin{array}{lll}
I \vDash x + y = z & \text{iff} & I(x) + I(y) = I(z) \\
I \vDash \varphi \vee \psi & \text{iff} & I \vDash \varphi \text{ or } I \vDash \psi \\
I \vDash \neg \varphi & \text{iff} & I \nvDash \varphi \\
I \vDash \exists x\, \varphi & \text{iff} & \text{there is } c \in \mathbb{N} \text{ with } I[x \mapsto c] \vDash \varphi
\end{array}
$$

Besides the usual Boolean operators, universal quantification etc., several additional constructs can be defined.

$$
\begin{array}{rcl \qquad rcl}
\varphi(0) & := & \exists n.n + n = n \wedge \varphi(n) \\
x \leq y & := & \exists z\, x + z = y \\
succ(x, y) & := & x < y \wedge \neg \exists z. x < z \wedge z < y
\end{array}
$$

$$
\begin{array}{rcl}
x = y & := & x + 0 = y \\
x \neq y & := & \neg(x = y) \\
x < y & := & x \leq y \wedge x \neq y
\end{array}
$$

Not only 0 but in fact every natural number can be used as a constant and this notation can be extended to variables as well.

$$\varphi(\mathrm{k}{+}1) \quad := \quad \exists y.succ(\mathrm{k}, y) \wedge \varphi(y)$$

$$\varphi(\text{succ}(x)) \ := \ \exists y.succ(x,y) \wedge \varphi(y)$$

We can define limited forms of multiplications, namely those between a variable and a constant.

$$\varphi(0 \cdot x) \ := \ \varphi(0) \ , \quad \varphi(1 \cdot x) \ := \ \varphi(x) \ , \quad \varphi((k+1) \cdot x) \ := \ \varphi(k \cdot x + x)$$

Also note that addition is not restricted to a binary operation only.

$$\sum_{i=1}^{n} x_i = z \ := \ \exists y_2 \ldots \exists y_{n-1}.x_1 + x_2 = y_2 \wedge \left(\bigwedge_{i=3}^{n-1} y_{i-1} + x_i = y_i \right) \wedge y_{n-1} + x_n = z$$

Example 2.25 Let $P = \{(m_0, r_0), \ldots, (m_{n-1}, r_{n-1})\}$ with $m_i \geq 1$, $r_i \geq 0$ for all $i \in [n]$. For every such fixed parameter list P, PA can define the set of all numbers that are congruent to r_i modulo m_i:

$$\varphi_P(x) \ := \ \bigwedge_{(m,r) \in P} \exists y.x = m \cdot y + r$$

Then the PA formula

$$\exists z \forall x.x > z \wedge \varphi_{\{(3,0)\}}(x) \rightarrow \exists u \exists v \, x = 15u + 27v$$

asserts that any large enough multiple of three can be written as a nonnegative linear combination of the numbers 15 and 27 whose greatest common divisor is 3.

WS1S can now be used to derive a fairly simple argument showing that Presburger Arithmetic – precisely: its satisfiability problem – is decidable. Note that the satisfiability problem asks, given a PA formula φ, for the existence of an interpretation $I : \mathcal{V}_1 \rightarrow \mathbb{N}$ s.t. $I \vDash \varphi$. As usual, it suffices to consider interpretations that map the free variables to natural numbers. Hence, a PA sentence is satisfiable iff it is satisfied by the empty interpretation iff it is valid.

The trick in the reduction to WS1S satisfiability is to regard a natural number by its binary encoding. We choose to write the least significant bit on the left; this is not a fundamental but a very natural choice as we will see.

Let I be a PA interpretation of the (first-order) variables $x_1, \ldots, x_n$. With this we associate a WS1S interpretation $\hat{I}$ of corresponding second-order variables $X_1, \ldots, X_n$ via

$$\hat{I}(X_j) = \{b \mid I(x_j) \div 2^b \equiv 1 \bmod 2\}$$

for any $j \in \{1, \ldots, n\}$, Here $\div$ denotes integer division as usual.

This turns the first-order PA interpretation I, mapping a variable x_j to a number $p \in \mathbb{N}$, into a second-order WS1S interpretation $\hat{I}$, mapping the variable X_j to the set of positions corresponding exactly to the set bits in the binary representation of $I(x_j)$. Note that this is necessarily a finite set. With this we can formulate the core of the reduction establishing decidability of PA.

Theorem 2.26 *For every PA formula φ there is a WS1S formula Φ s.t. $|\Phi| = \mathcal{O}(|\varphi|)$ and for any PA variable interpretation I we have $I \models \varphi$ iff $\hat{I} \models \Phi$.*

Proof We give an inductive construction of $\Phi := tr(\varphi)$. W.l.o.g. we assume that φ uses the variables $x_1, \ldots, x_n$ only. The translation simply replaces any first-order PA variable x_i with the second-order WS1S variable X_i. The only interesting case is that of atomic addition formulas. The other cases are handled via

$$tr(\varphi \vee \psi) \;:=\; tr(\varphi) \vee tr(\psi) \;, \quad tr(\neg\varphi) \;:=\; \neg tr(\varphi) \;, \quad tr(\exists x_i\, \varphi) \;:=\; \exists X_i\, tr(\varphi) \;.$$

Moreover,

$$tr(x_i + x_j = x_k) \;:=\; \exists C.\neg C(0) \wedge \forall y.\big(X_k(y) \leftrightarrow odd_y(X_i, X_j, C)\big) \wedge$$
$$\big(C(\mathrm{succ}(y)) \leftrightarrow two_y^+(X_i, X_j, C)\big)$$

where

$$odd_y(A, B, C) := \big(A(y) \wedge \neg B(y) \wedge \neg C(y)\big) \vee \big(\neg A(y) \wedge B(y) \wedge \neg C(y)\big) \vee$$
$$\big(\neg A(y) \wedge \neg B(y) \wedge C(y)\big) \vee \big(A(y) \wedge B(y) \wedge C(y)\big)$$
$$two_y^+(A, B, C) := \big(\neg A(y) \rightarrow B(y) \wedge C(y)\big) \wedge \big(\neg B(y) \rightarrow A(y) \wedge C(y)\big) \wedge$$
$$\big(\neg C(y) \rightarrow A(y) \wedge B(y)\big) \;.$$

Note that $tr(x_i + x_j = x_k)$ formalises addition of two binary numbers according to the standard textbook method: at every position we introduce a carry bit which is unset at the least significant position, and then in every next position it is set whenever at least two bits of the two summands and the carry bit at the previous position are set. Moreover, a bit in the resulting sum is set whenever an odd number of the two bits of the summands at this position and the carry bit are set.

It is then straightforward to show by induction that $I \models \varphi$ iff $\hat{I} \models \Phi$ holds. Likewise, $|\Phi|$ is clearly linear in $|\varphi|$. $\qquad\qquad\square$

Putting this reduction from PA to WS1S together with the statement of Thm. 2.23 we obtain decidability of PA.

Corollary 2.27 *The satisfiability problem for PA is decidable.*

The automata-theoretic procedure obtained in this way has non-elementary worst-case complexity, inherited from WS1S. In practice, however, one sees that the automata for WS1S formulas that stem from the translation of PA formulas remain relatively small and that, as a result, the automata-theoretic procedure is competitive. Indeed, there exists a theoretical justification for this phenomenon.

Proposition 2.28 *The minimal DFA for a WS1S formula resulting from the translation of a PA formula of size n has size $2^{2^{\mathcal{O}(n)}}$.*

Bibliographic Notes

The automata-logic connection presented here for Monadic Second-Order Logic on finite words was started by Büchi and Elgot [BE58, Büc60, Elg61] and independently by Trakhtenbrot [Tra61]. The main focus of attention was WS1S, the Weak Second-Order Logic of One Successor, which was found to be decidable using the theory of finite automata on finite words, even though the domain of interpretation in this logic is comprised of the natural numbers. Weakness, i.e. the fact that second-order predicates only ever range over finite subsets of the natural numbers, makes the theory of finite words applicable.

The exposition here considers Monadic Second-Order Logic over finite words. It is different in that the domain of interpretation of any formula is always finite a priori. Hence, MSO and WS1S do not share the same validities. The fact that decidability of both can be established in a very similar manner is the reason for them not always being distinguished very clearly. Some discussions on the semantic differences between MSO on finite words and WS1S can be followed in works of Klarlund [Kla99], or Ayari and Basin [AB00]. While the construction of finite automata for MSO formulas is slightly cleaner than that for WS1S and is often what is presented in the literature, Fiedor et al. [FHJ$^+$17] describe how to construct automata for WS1S formulas efficiently.

The automata-logic connection, in particular the automata-theoretic approach to the decidability of logics like MSO, is covered in a survey paper by Thomas [Tho97].

The original proof of decidability of PA is due to Presburger [Pre27] using quantifier elimination. The logic has received quite some attention since then, probably because of its decidability which is in contrast to the undecidability of Peano Arithmetic [Göd31, Kle43] that contains both addition and multiplication. It is worth noting that Skolem Arithmetic, the pendant of Presburger Arithmetic with only multiplication and no addition, is decidable, too [FR79, Chp. 5]. As with Presburger Arithmetic, Skolem Arithmetic can also be shown to be decidable using automata-theoretic constructions [BG00], in this case automata operating on trees rather than words. Trees are the topic of Part III.

Presburger Arithmetic has remained an object of study to date. A problem that had been open for a long time was the exact complexity of its satisfiability problem. Note that the translation into WS1S only yields a non-elementary upper bound on the time and space complexity, and this is known not to be optimal. Fischer and Rabin gave a doubly exponential lower bound [FR74] which is close to a triply exponential upper bound given by Oppen only shortly afterwards [Opp78]. Later, Berman showed that the complexity lies in between: it is complete for the class of problems that can be solved by an alternating Turing Machine in doubly exponential time with linearly many alternations only [Ber80]. Note that alternating doubly exponential time with arbitrarily many alternations is the same as deterministic doubly exponential space [CKS81] which is between nondeterministic doubly exponential time and deterministic triply exponential time.

The automata-theoretic approach to Presburger Arithmetic has also been investigated further. Prop. 2.28 about upper bounds on the size of minimal DFA for PA formulas is due to Klaedtke [Kla08]. The findings there agree with those about the computational complexity made above: the dependency is doubly exponential on the size resp. length of a formula but only linear on the number of its quantifier alternations. A considerable amount of work has been spent on extending the decidability result for Presburger Arithmetic, and the automata-theoretic approach has played a significant role in this, cf. an overview by Haase [Haa18].

Exercises

Exercise 10 Show that every regular language is MSO-definable by induction on the structure of regular expressions. *Hint:* Construct, for every regular expression α, an MSO formula $\varphi_\alpha(x, y)$ s.t. for any word $w \in \Sigma^+$ and any I with $0 \leq I(x) \leq I(y) < |w|$ the following holds:

$$w, I \vDash \varphi_\alpha(x, y) \quad \text{iff} \quad w(I(x)) \ldots w(I(y)) \in L(\alpha)$$

Exercise 11 Complete the proof of Lemma 2.13 by carrying out the induction on the structure of MSO formulas.

Exercise 12 Write down MSO formulas $\varphi(x, y)$ that express the following properties.

a) $x = y$ (without using the symbols '=' and '<'),
b) $y = x + k$, i.e. y is k positions behind x for any fixed $k \in \mathbb{N}$.

Construct MSO sentences φ that define languages which are informally described as follows.

c) Every k-th position contains the letter a (for some fixed $k \in \mathbb{N}$).
d) Let $\Sigma = \{a_0, \ldots, a_{n-1}\}$. A letter a_i (not at the word's end) is followed by $a_{(i+1) \bmod n}$.
e) Every a is succeeded somewhere by a b and vice-versa for as long as the word's end is not reached. In between there are only symbols c.
f) The (finite) language consisting of all words that are permutations of a fixed word $w \in \Sigma^+$.
g) The language of all words of the form $u\#v$ s.t. u, v do not contain the symbol $\#$ and all letters occurring somewhere in u also occur somewhere in v and vice-versa.

Which of these languages, resp. properties, are already FO-definable?

Exercise 13 Construct an MSO sentence that defines exactly the languages recognised by the following NFA.

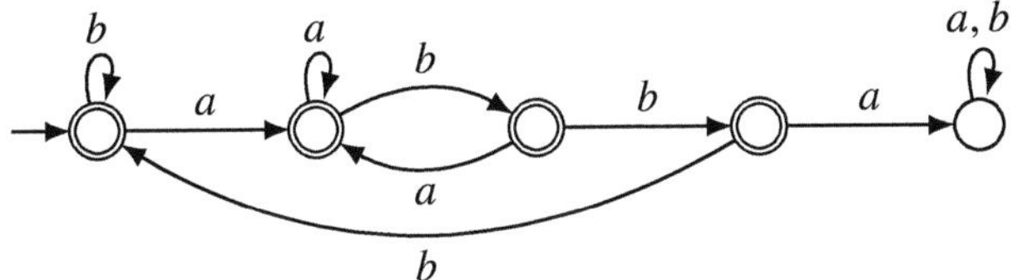

Exercise 14 Construct NFA that recognise exactly those languages that are defined by the following MSO-sentences.

a) $\forall x.a(x) \to \forall y.x < y \to b(y)$
b) $\exists x.b(x) \wedge \forall y.y < x \to a(y)$
c) $\forall X \exists y \forall x.X(x) \to x \le y \wedge a(y)$
d) $\exists X \exists Y.(\forall z.X(z) \vee Y(z)) \wedge \forall x \forall y.X(x) \wedge Y(y) \to x < y \wedge a(x) \wedge b(y)$
e) $\forall x.(\exists z\, x < z) \to \exists y.x < y \wedge (a(x) \leftrightarrow \neg a(y))$

Exercise 15 In accordance with EMSO let AMSO be the fragment of MSO that contains formulas of the form $\forall X_1 \dots \forall X_n \psi$ where ψ is a first-order formula. Show that a language is MSO-definable iff it is AMSO-definable.

Exercise 16 The *word problem* – also known as the *model checking problem* – for MSO is: given a word $w \in \Sigma^+$ and an MSO sentence φ, decide whether $w \in L(\varphi)$.

Construct an algorithm that solves the word problem for MSO. Its space usage should only be polynomial in the size of its input, i.e. $|w| + |\varphi|$.

Exercise 17 Four people are trying to cross a bridge. They only have one torch. At any time, at most two people can cross the bridge. They can wait in the darkness on either side, but they can only cross the bridge with the help of the torch's light. Person A needs 5 min to cross the bridge, person B needs 10 min, person C 20 min and person D 25 min. The torch's battery lasts for 60 min.

a) Explain why MSO is suitable to model this problem rather than WS1S.
b) Write a formula expressing the solvability of this problem. It should be satisfiable iff there is a way for all four people to cross the bridge under the constraints listed above.

Exercise 18 A farmer needs to take his dog, his cat and his mouse across a river in a boat. The boat can take at most him and one animal, and it needs him to sail from one side of the river to the other. Whenever the farmer is with his animals, they are generally kind and leave each other alone. However, whenever he is not with them, he needs to ensure that . . .

- the dog and the cat are not together on one side of the river, since the cat would talk the dog into closing the deal on a very disadvantageous financial investment;
- the cat and the mouse are not together on one side of the river, since the mouse would get the cat to start smoking.

Write an MSO formula whose models represent valid solutions to the problem of taking all four animals across the river. *Hint:* Use $\{F_\ell, D_\ell, C_\ell, M_\ell, F_r, D_r, C_r, M_r\}$ as the underlying alphabet where the letter F_ℓ indicates, for example, that the *F*armer is on the *l*eft side, etc. A solution can then be represented by a word composed of blocks of length 4 of the form $F_{s_F} D_{s_D} C_{s_C} M_{s_M}$ determining the location of all four protagonists.

Exercise 19 For $n \geq 1$ the n-queens problem is the following: place n queens – the chess piece – onto an $n \times n$ chess board without one queen being able to capture another in one move. In other words: each row, each column and each diagonal may contain at most one queen.

Construct MSO formulas φ_n that are satisfiable iff the n-queens problem is solvable. *Hint:* An $n \times n$ chess board with placed queens can be seen as a word of length n^2 over $\{0, 1\}$, for instance representing the square board row by row.

Exercise 20 Complete the proof of Thm. 2.21 by writing down MSO formulas that express the properties stated in this proof.

Exercise 21 We introduce *Dyadic Second-Order Logic* (DSO) similar to MSO over finite words. In DSO, second-order variables are interpreted as *binary* predicates. Hence, atomic formulas $X(y)$ from MSO get replaced by formulas of the form $X(y, z)$ with the straightforward interpretation that the pair of positions y and z belongs to the set of position pairs X:

$$w, I \vDash X(x, y) \quad \text{iff} \quad (I(x), I(y)) \in I(X)$$
$$w, I \vDash \exists X.\varphi \quad \text{iff} \quad \exists M \subseteq \{0, \ldots, |w| - 1\}^2 \text{ s.t. } w, I[X \mapsto M] \vDash \varphi$$

The aim of this exercise is to study the expressiveness and decidability of DSO, compared to MSO.

a) Show that $\{a^n b^n \mid n \geq 1\}$ is DSO-definable.
b) Show that every CFL is DSO-definable. *Hint:* Assume that a CFL is given as a normalised context-free grammar G with derivations of the form $A \to BC$ and $A \to a$ only. Each nonterminal A defines a set of position pairs (i, j) in a given word $w = a_0 \ldots a_{n-1}$ s.t. $A \Rightarrow^* a_i \ldots a_j$. I.e. we can use nonterminals as second-order variables. Write a DSO formula which states that

   - every pair of the form (i, i) belongs to A only if $A \to a$ and a is the letter at position i;
   - every pair of the form (i, j) with $i < j$ belongs to A only if $A \to BC$ and corresponding pairs for B and C can be found,
   - the subword from the first to the last position can be derived from G's starting symbol.

c) Show that $\{a^n b^n c^n \mid n \geq 1\}$ and $\{ww \mid w \in \Sigma^+\}$ are DSO-definable.
d) Show that the satisfiability problem for DSO is undecidable. *Hint:* It is undecidable to decide, given two context-free languages, whether their intersection is non-empty.

Chapter 3
Alternating Finite Automata

Nondeterminism is a concept that is not inherently self-dual in the following sense: a nondeterministic automaton may intuitively "guess" at some point to make a choice that turns out to be good for accepting a word. This is why it is typically easy to construct NFA for languages which are defined via existential quantification, for instance $\Sigma^* aba \Sigma^*$ – the set of all words for which *there is* a subword of the form *aba*. Consider, however, its complement – the set of all words that do *not* contain the subword *aba*. By complementation closure of REG, this is also a regular language, but constructing a regular expression or an NFA for it directly by hand is more difficult. What is missing is the ability to "guess" that taking some transition is good for showing that the input should be *rejected*. Such an automaton could equally go through the input from left to right and at some point make this guess, confirming that the input contains the subword *aba*, and thus reject it altogether.

We extend the model of NFA to so-called *alternating finite automata* (AFA) by adding the ability to make choices leading to rejection, in particular combining this with nondeterministic guesses leading to acceptance. We then study the expressive power of this model with respect to the class of regular languages. As it turns out, languages accepted by AFA are still regular, i.e. we have only increased the pragmatic power of finite automata, not the expressive power. Conversely, it confirms the robustness and importance of the class REG of regular languages.

Technically, we extend the model of NFA by *universal branching*, the dual concept of *nondeterministic branching*. The latter describes the ability to choose a successor state in a run towards an accepting end. Universal branching requires accepting ends to be reached through *all* possible successor states. This can also be seen as a model of parallel processing of the input word. At nondeterministic branching points, the automata select successors state to continue with; at universal branching points, the automata intuitively split into several copies, and each of them processes the remainder of the input word starting from a different successor state.

It is not hard to imagine that this power could be used to construct a simple automaton for recognising the language of all words that do not contain *aba*: upon reading a *b* simply continue to the next position. Upon reading an *a*, branch universally: one copy continues with the next position in the same manner, the other copy

© The Author(s), under exclusive
license to Springer-Verlag GmbH, DE, part of Springer Nature 2025
M. Hofmann and M. Lange, *Automata Theory and Logic*,
https://doi.org/10.1007/978-3-662-72154-4_3

checks that this a is not followed by ba. When all launched copies accept, the word does not contain aba anywhere.

This view of alternating automata running copies in parallel is merely useful for intuition. Acceptance of a word by an AFA is defined without referring to parallelism, just like acceptance by an NFA is not defined by referring to guesses. It is simply unnecessarily cumbersome to try to formalise the notions of parallelism and guessing at this point. Instead, the notion of a run can be extended accordingly to explain acceptance by an AFA.

3.1 Run Trees

The transition function of an NFA $\mathcal{A}$ maps a state q and an alphabet symbol a to a set $\{q_1, \ldots, q_k\}$ of successor states. The connection between the q_i is implicitly understood to be a *disjunction* – $\mathcal{A}$ can continue in q_1 *or* q_2 *or* ... in order to accept. Likewise, one could see the combination of these states to be conjunctive which yields the model of universal automata. Alternating automata should possess both modes of branching, hence we need to make the connection explicit. This is done by replacing sets with Boolean combinations, represented by propositional formulas.

Definition 3.1 Let Q be a set. The set $\mathbb{B}^+(Q)$ of *positive Boolean formulas* over Q is the smallest set satisfying

- $Q \subseteq \mathbb{B}^+(Q)$,
- whenever $f, g \in \mathbb{B}^+(Q)$ then $f \vee g \in \mathbb{B}^+(Q)$ and $f \wedge g \in \mathbb{B}^+(Q)$.

For example, $(q_2 \vee q_3) \wedge (q_1 \wedge q_2) \in \mathbb{B}^+(\{q_1, q_2, q_3\})$. We use the usual rules of associativity, commutativity, idempotence and the usual precedence of $\wedge$ over $\vee$ to minimise the use of parentheses and to write formulas in shortest ways possible.

Definition 3.2 An *alternating finite automaton* (AFA) is an $\mathcal{A} = (Q, \Sigma, q_I, \delta, F)$ just like an NFA but with $\delta : Q \times \Sigma \to \mathbb{B}^+(Q)$.

As with NFA, the size $|\mathcal{A}|$ of an AFA is the numbers of its states.

Hence, the transition function of an AFA maps a pair of a state and an input letter to a Boolean combination of states, representing a combination of nondeterministic and universal branchings leading to successor state. For instance, we can read $q_1 \wedge (q_2 \vee q_3)$ as universal branching between q_1 on one side, and the other side consisting of a follow-up nondeterministic branching between q_2 and q_3. However, it will be more convenient to compress these alternating choices into one step, associated with the processing of one input letter. To do so, we need a formal definition of satisfaction of a Boolean formula.

Definition 3.3 Let Q be a set, and $M \subseteq Q$. *Satisfaction* of a Boolean formula $f \in \mathbb{B}^+(Q)$ by M is defined inductively as follows.

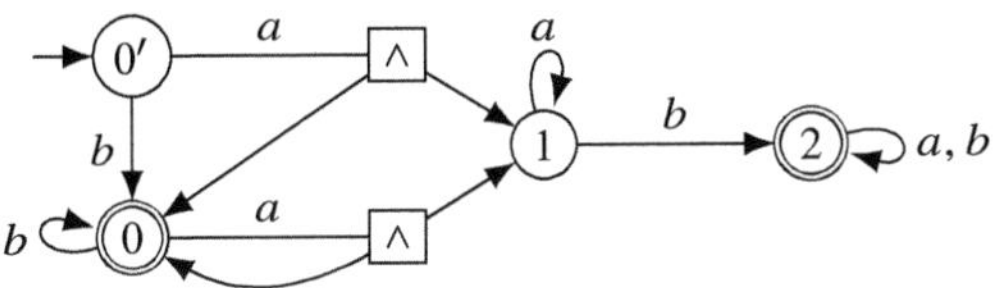

Fig. 3.1 Graphical representation of the AFA from Ex. 3.5.

$$
\begin{aligned}
M &\models q &&\text{iff} && q \in M \\
M &\models f \vee g &&\text{iff} && M \models f \text{ or } M \models g \\
M &\models f \wedge g &&\text{iff} && M \models f \text{ and } M \models g
\end{aligned}
$$

If $M \models f$ then we say that M is a *model* of f.

Intuitively, M is a model of f if f evaluates to *true* under the usual rules of Boolean formula evaluation when all states $q \in M$ are set to *true* and all states $q \notin M$ are set of *false*. For example, let $f := q_1 \wedge (q_2 \vee q_3)$. We have $\{q_1, q_2\} \models f$ and $\{q_1, q_3\} \models f$, but $\{q_2, q_3\} \not\models f$ and $\{q_1\} \not\models f$.

Runs of AFA will become trees rather than linear sequences of transitions, i.e. words. For the purposes of this chapter, we only need so-called *unordered trees* in which there is no particular order on the child nodes of any node. Part III of this book will deal with *ordered trees* instead (that arise as inputs to automata, not as structures used to explain the processing of such inputs). Here it suffices to regard a tree as a directed graph without cycles and which possesses a designated root node with no predecessors. Each node in a tree resides on a particular *level* which measures the distance of this node to the tree's root. Hence, the root itself is on level 0, its successors comprise level 1, etc.

We will speak of a Q-labelled tree for some set Q as a function which assigns values from Q to each node of the tree. We will not distinguish formally between the labelling function and the underlying tree structure.

Definition 3.4 A *run* of an AFA $\mathcal{A} = (Q, \Sigma, q_I, \delta, F)$ on a word $w = a_0 \ldots a_{n-1} \in \Sigma^*$ is a Q-labelled tree ρ with the following properties.

- The root node v_0 is labelled with $\mathcal{A}$'s initial state: $\rho(v_0) = q_I$.
- Let v be a node on level i for $i \in [n]$, and $v_1, \ldots, v_k$ be the successors of v on level $i + 1$. Then we have $\{\rho(v_1), \ldots, \rho(v_k)\} \models \delta(\rho(v), a_i)$.

The run is called *accepting* if all its leaves are on level n, and they are all labelled with accepting states.

As with NFA we define $L(\mathcal{A}) := \{w \in \Sigma^* \mid \text{there is an accepting run (tree) of } \mathcal{A}$ on $w\}$.

Note that – as with NFAs – (accepting) runs need not be unique.

Example 3.5 Let $L = \{w \in \{a, b\}^* \mid |w| \geq 1$ and for every position labelled with a there is some later position labelled with $b\}$. There is a simple AFA recognising L which conceptually follows the description of that language. Consider

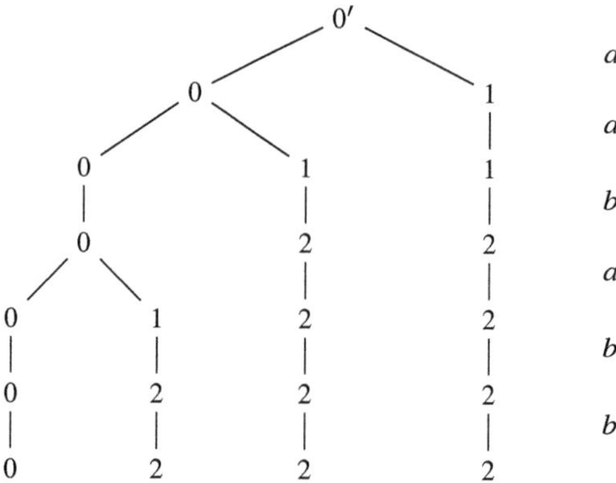

Fig. 3.2 Run of the AFA from Ex. 3.5 on the input word *aababb* aligned with the transitions between the run's levels.

$\mathcal{A} = (\{0, 0', 1, 2\}, \{a, b\}, 0', \delta, \{0, 2\})$ with the transitions defined as follows.

$$\delta(0', a) = \delta(0, a) := 0 \wedge 1 \qquad \delta(1, a) := 1 \qquad \delta(2, a) := 2$$
$$\delta(0', b) = \delta(0, b) := 0 \qquad\quad \delta(1, b) := 2 \qquad \delta(2, b) := 2$$

Fig. 3.1 introduces a way to represent such AFA graphically with nodes that do not represent states but Boolean operators in the transition function. Disjunctions underneath conjunctions can be represented in a similar way with nodes carrying a symbol '$\vee$'. They could also be shown just like nondeterminism usually is, i.e. using several edges with the same label.

Intuitively, $\mathcal{A}$ uses state 0 to search for occurrences of the letter *a*. When one is found, the transition to $0 \wedge 1$ makes $\mathcal{A}$ continue looking for further symbols *a* in the remainder of the input word *and* to search for an occurrence of the letter *b*. State 2 is used to signal that such a *b* has been seen. State $0'$ behaves in the same way as 0 and is only used to make sure that the empty word is not accepted.

An accepting run of $\mathcal{A}$ on the word *aababb* is shown in Fig. 3.2. Note that it is possible to construct an NFA (and therefore also an AFA) with only two states which recognises L.

Run trees can, as they grow deeper, become wider than the number of states of the underlying automaton. Hence, a level may contain nodes which are labelled with the same state. This occurs multiple times in the run shown in Fig. 3.2. However, one will not find two such nodes such that the two subtrees under these nodes differ. Runs with this property are of particular interest and are therefore given a special name.

Definition 3.6 A run ρ of an AFA on some word is called *memoryless* or *history-free* if for any two nodes v, v' on the same level such that $\rho(v) = \rho(v')$, the subtrees rooted at v and v' are isomorphic.

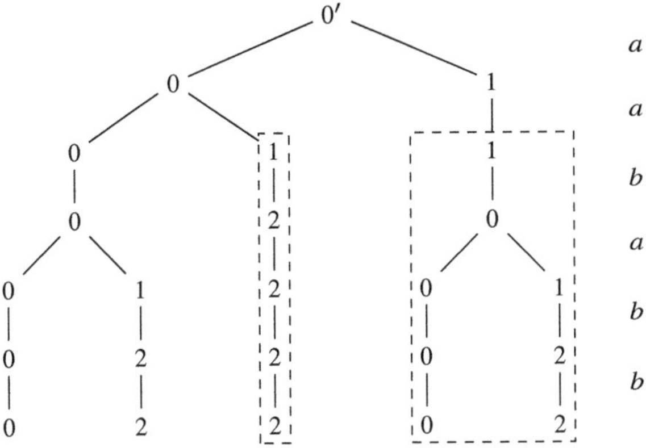

Fig. 3.3 Non-memoryless run of the AFA from Ex. 3.7.

The name suggests that the decision made by the AFA of how to branch in node v on level i in a history-free run only depends on the current state $\rho(v)$ and the suffix of the input word from position i, but not on any decision made earlier, i.e. the *history* of v in this run.

History-freedom is not a trivial property. The AFA of the previous Ex. 3.5 only has memoryless runs, but it is equally possible to construct AFA without this property.

Example 3.7 Consider the AFA $\mathcal{A}' := (\{0, 0', 1, 2\}, \{a, b\}, 0', \delta, \{0, 2\})$ which only differs from the AFA $\mathcal{A}$ of Ex. 3.5 in a single transition:

$$\begin{aligned}
\delta(0, a) &= \delta(0', a) &&:= 0 \wedge 1 & \delta(1, a) &:= 1 & \delta(2, a) &:= 2 \\
\delta(0, b) &= \delta(0', b) &&:= 0 & \delta(1, b) &:= 0 \vee 2 & \delta(2, b) &:= 2
\end{aligned}$$

In state 1, $\mathcal{A}'$ can move to state 2 as $\mathcal{A}$ does, in order to signal that a letter b has been found and the rest of the word is irrelevant for this branch of the run. Likewise, it can move (back) to state 0 to continue scanning for further symbols a.

The run in Fig. 3.2 is not only a run of $\mathcal{A}$ on $aababb$, it is also a run of $\mathcal{A}'$ on this word. As said before, it is memoryless. Fig. 3.3 shows a non-memoryless run of $\mathcal{A}'$ on the same word. The two subtrees violating history-freedom are marked in dashed boxes.

The next theorem shows that, while it is possible to construct AFA that only have memoryless runs, it is not possible to construct an AFA and a word on which there are no memoryless runs.

Theorem 3.8 *Let $\mathcal{A}$ be an AFA and $w \in \Sigma^*$. We have $w \in L(\mathcal{A})$ iff there is a memoryless and accepting run of $\mathcal{A}$ on w.*

Proof "$\Leftarrow$" This direction is trivial, since every memoryless accepting run is an accepting run.

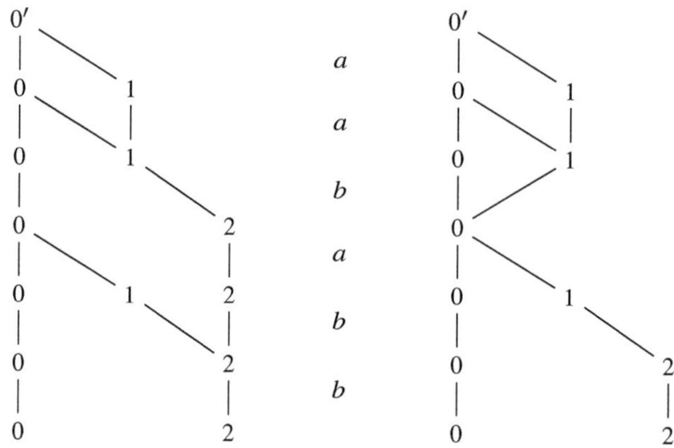

Fig. 3.4 DAG representations of the memoryless runs obtained from the one in Fig. 3.3 by means of the construction in the proof of Thm. 3.8.

"$\Rightarrow$" Let $\mathcal{A} = (Q, \Sigma, q_0, \delta, F)$ be an AFA and $w = a_0 \ldots a_{n-1} \in L(\mathcal{A})$. Then there is an accepting run ρ of $\mathcal{A}$ on w. We now construct a memoryless run by successively replacing subtrees, starting on level n.

Consider two nodes v, v' on level n, s.t. $\rho(v) = \rho(v')$. Then the subtrees rooted at v and v' are trivially isomorphic because v and v' are both leaves. Now suppose that the property of history-freedom is satisfied by all nodes on levels below i for some $i < n$, and take two nodes v, v' on level i such that $\rho(v) = \rho(v')$. Take the run ρ' which is obtained from ρ by replacing the subtree at node v' with the subtree at node v. Since the labels at their roots are the same, the result is still an accepting run of $\mathcal{A}$ on w. By successively eliminating violations of history-freedom in this way, one finally arrives at a memoryless run. $\square$

Memoryless runs can easily be represented as *directed acyclic graphs* (DAGs) by *sharing* equal subtrees. The result of this sharing, when applied to the run in Fig. 3.2 is shown in Fig. 3.4. Note that there are two possibilities to eliminate the violation of history-freedom in the run in Fig. 3.3 since there are only two subtrees in positions where there should be equal ones, and a memoryless run is obtained by replacing either of them with the other. One possibility – shown on the left – in fact leads to the memoryless run from Fig. 3.2. The other – shown on the right – leads to a different memoryless run.

The following statement will be useful when analysing the expressive power of AFA in the next section.

Corollary 3.9 *Let $\mathcal{A} = (Q, \Sigma, q_1, \delta, F)$ be an AFA over Σ, $w = a_0 \ldots a_{n-1} \in \Sigma^*$. We have $w \in L(\mathcal{A})$ iff there is a sequence $S_0, \ldots, S_n$ of subsets of Q such that*

- *$S_0 = \{q_1\}$,*
- *$S_{i+1} \models \bigwedge_{q \in S_i} \delta(q, a_i)$ for all $i \in [n]$, and*
- *$S_n \subseteq F$.*

This follows immediately from Thm. 3.8 with the observation that the levels of a DAG representation of a memoryless run of $\mathcal{A}$ on w form a sequence with the three stated properties.

3.2 Expressiveness and Succinctness

A question arising immediately with the introduction of a new automaton model is the one after its expressive power. In particular, how does the class of languages acceptable by AFA compare to the class of regular languages? It is not hard to see that AFA are at least as powerful as NFA, i.e. every regular language is AFA recognisable.

Theorem 3.10 *For every NFA $\mathcal{A}$ of size n there is an AFA $\mathcal{A}'$ of size at most $n + 1$ states such that $L(\mathcal{A}') = L(\mathcal{A})$.*

Proof Let $\mathcal{A} = (Q, \Sigma, q_I, \delta, F)$ be an NFA. W.l.o.g. we assume $\bot \notin Q$. Let $\mathcal{A}' := (Q \cup \{\bot\}, \Sigma, q_I, \delta', F)$ be the AFA uniquely given by

$$
\delta'(q,a) := \begin{cases} \bigvee_{p \in \delta(q,a)} p & \text{, if } q \in Q \text{ and } \delta(q,a) \neq \varnothing, \\ \bot & \text{, otherwise.} \end{cases}
$$

Clearly, $|\mathcal{A}'| \leq |\mathcal{A}| + 1$. Correctness of the construction uses the observation that any run tree of an AFA whose transitions are purely disjunctive can be pruned to a single branch, and that this branch is still an accepting run (tree) if the original one is. It now suffices to see that this branch is also a run of the NFA $\mathcal{A}$. Conversely, any accepting run of $\mathcal{A}$ is in fact an accepting run tree of $\mathcal{A}'$ on the same word. $\square$

The more interesting question concerns the opposite direction: we will show that AFA can only recognise regular languages by translating AFA into equivalent NFA, making use of Cor. 3.9. This is analogous to the powerset construction for transforming NFA into equivalent DFA.

Theorem 3.11 *For every AFA $\mathcal{A}$ of size n there is an NFA $\mathcal{A}'$ of size at most 2^n such that $L(\mathcal{A}') = L(\mathcal{A})$.*

Proof Let $\mathcal{A} = (Q, \Sigma, q_I, \delta, F)$ be an AFA. Define the NFA $\mathcal{A}' := (2^Q, \Sigma, \{q_I\}, \Delta, F')$ s.t. $F' := \{S \mid S \subseteq F\}$ and

$$
\Delta(S,a) := \{S' \mid S' \models \bigwedge_{q \in S} \delta(q,a)\}
$$

for any $S \in 2^Q$, $a \in \Sigma$. The bound on the size of $\mathcal{A}'$ is obvious. It remains to be seen that $L(\mathcal{A}') = L(\mathcal{A})$.

"$\supseteq$" Suppose $w = a_0 \ldots a_{m-1} \in L(\mathcal{A})$. According to Cor. 3.9 there is a sequence $\rho = S_0, \ldots, S_m$ of state sets such that $S_0 = \{q_I\}$, $S_m \subseteq F$ and $S_{i+1} \models \bigwedge_{q \in S_i} \delta(q, a_i)$

or, equivalently, $S_{i+1} \in \Delta(S_i, a_i)$ for $i \in [m]$. Hence, ρ is an accepting run of $\mathcal{A}'$ on w.

"⊆" Analogously. $\square$

So AFA are not more expressive than NFA but the translation given here incurs an exponential blowup. This is similar to the situation between NFA and DFA, so the question arises whether AFA are truly more succinct than NFA.

Example 3.12 Let $\Sigma = \{a\}$. We leave it as an exercise to prove that the language $L_{29393} := \{w \in \Sigma^* \mid |w| \equiv 0 \bmod 29393\}$ cannot be recognised by an NFA with less than 29393 states.

However, there is an AFA with only 57 states which recognises L_{29393}. This may seem random at first, but the construction principle becomes clearer when one is presented with a simple connection between the numbers 57 and 29393. We have

$$29393 = 7 \cdot 13 \cdot 17 \cdot 19 \qquad \text{and} \qquad 57 = 1 + 7 + 13 + 17 + 19 .$$

For $n \geq 1$ let $\mathcal{A}_n = (Q_n, \Sigma, (n, 0), \delta_n, F_n)$ with $Q_n := \{(n, 0), \ldots, (n, n-1)\}$, $F_n := \{(n, 0)\}$ be the standard DFA for the languages $L_n := \{w \in \Sigma^* \mid |w| \equiv 0 \bmod n\}$. Their transition relation forms a simple cycle: $\delta_n((n, i), a) := (n, i + 1 \bmod n)$. Usually it would suffice to name the states $0, \ldots, n-1$, but here they are tagged with the constant n as we will compose several such DFA, and this will avoid problems with different states of the same name.

Now consider $\mathcal{A} := (Q, \Sigma, 0, \delta, F)$ with

$$Q := \{0\} \cup Q_7 \cup Q_{13} \cup Q_{17} \cup Q_{19}$$
$$F := \{0\} \cup F_7 \cup F_{13} \cup F_{17} \cup F_{19}$$

and

$$\delta(0, a) := (7, 1) \wedge (13, 1) \wedge (17, 1) \wedge (19, 1)$$
$$\delta((n, i), a) := \delta_n((n, i), a)$$

for $n \in \{7, 13, 17, 19\}$ and $i < n$.

We have $L(\mathcal{A}) = L_{29393}$. Note that the only state in which there is universal branching is state 0. In all other states, $\mathcal{A}$ behaves deterministically. A run tree (on a word of length > 0) therefore consists of a root from which four paths branch off. These branches form runs of the DFA $\mathcal{A}_n$ for $n \in \{7, 13, 17, 19\}$.

The first one only contains accepting states on levels $0, 7, 14, 21, \ldots$, the second on levels $0, 13, 26, 39, \ldots$, and so on. Since 7, 13, 17 and 19 are pairwise co-prime, the only levels of this run tree on which all states are accepting are those which are multiples of $7 \cdot 13 \cdot 17 \cdot 19$, i.e. of 29393.

So we have seen that at least *some* regular languages can be recognised by small AFA – when compared to using NFA or even DFA as models of regular languages. However, here "small" is measured in absolute terms, for instance in the sense that 57 is clearly smaller than 29393. One could and in fact should argue, though, that they only differ by a constant factor, and most of the analyses regarding automata sizes do not consider constant factors as significant differences. So the question arises whether there is also an asymptotic size gap between AFA and NFA. The following theorem can be proved by suitably generalising the example above. This is left as an exercise.

Theorem 3.13 *There is a family of regular languages $(L_n)_{n\geq 1}$ which can be recognised by AFA of size polynomial in n such that any family of NFA recognising these are of size exponential in n.*

In other words, there can be no polynomial translation from AFA into equivalent NFA. Then the question arises after the succinctness gap between AFA and DFA. Clearly, AFA can be translated into DFA at a doubly exponential blowup by combining the two powerset constructions from AFA to NFA (Thm. 3.11) and then on to DFA (Thm. 1.16). Theoretically, it could be the case that this is not optimal, for instance if NFA resulting from the translated AFA were of such a shape that they could be translated into DFA more efficiently. Likewise, it could be the case that the two lower bounds do not combine in the sense that there is a family of AFA which can only be translated into exponentially larger NFA, but these are different from NFA which can only be translated into DFA at an exponential blowup. This, however, is not the case, as the next theorem states. The proof is deferred to the exercises.

Theorem 3.14 *There is a family of regular languages $(L_n)_{n\geq 1}$ which can be recognised by AFA of size polynomial in n such that the smallest family of DFA recognising these are of size doubly exponential in n.*

3.3 Closure Properties

We investigate the possibility to prove closure properties of regular languages via AFA directly. It turns out that for some operations, like complementation for instance, AFA provide easier constructions than NFA do. For other operations like concatenation for example, the additional expressive power of AFA is not helpful. We start with a complementation construction.

Definition 3.15 Let $\mathcal{A} = (Q, \Sigma, q_I, \delta, F)$ be an AFA. The *dual AFA* to $\mathcal{A}$ is the AFA $\overline{\mathcal{A}} := (Q, \Sigma, q_I, \overline{\delta}, Q \setminus F)$, where for each $q \in Q$, each $a \in \Sigma$ and each $f, g \in \mathbb{B}^+(Q)$ we have $\overline{\delta}(q, a) := \overline{\delta(q, a)}$ with $\overline{q} := q$, $\overline{f \vee g} := \overline{f} \wedge \overline{g}$ and $\overline{f \wedge g} := \overline{f} \vee \overline{g}$.

Note that the dual AFA has no more states than the original one. This is in contrast to the case of NFA where complementation incurs a blowup in general. Still, the dual AFA recognises the complement language. The key observation in the proof of this statement is the following lemma.

Lemma 3.16 *Let $\mathcal{A} = (Q, \Sigma, q_I, \delta, F)$ be an AFA and $\overline{\mathcal{A}}$ be its dual AFA. For any $q \in Q$ and any word $w \in \Sigma^*$ there is an accepting run tree of $\mathcal{A}$ for w with the root labelled q iff there is no accepting run tree of $\overline{\mathcal{A}}$ for w with the root labelled q.*

Proof By induction on the length of w. Suppose $|w| = 0$, i.e. $w = \varepsilon$. The only run tree for ε with root label q is the one consisting of the root only, i.e. the root is also the only leaf. Now q is an accepting state in $\mathcal{A}$ iff it is not an accepting state in $\overline{\mathcal{A}}$, so the statement holds in this case as accepting runs have all leaves labelled with accepting states.

Now suppose $|w| > 0$, i.e. $w = av$ for some $a \in \Sigma, v \in \Sigma^*$. Since $|v| < |w|$ we can assume that the induction hypothesis holds for v already. We will now assume that there is an accepting run tree of $\mathcal{A}$ on w and show that there cannot be one of $\overline{\mathcal{A}}$ on w. The converse direction is entirely analogous and therefore omitted here.

Let ρ be an accepting run tree for $\mathcal{A}$ on $w = av$ and root label q. Since $|w| > 0$, there is a layer of nodes directly underneath the root. Let $q_1, \ldots, q_k$ be the labels of these nodes. Considering the fact that subtrees of an accepting run tree form accepting run trees on suffixes we have

- $Q' := \{q_1, \ldots, q_k\} \models \delta(q, a)$, and
- there are accepting run trees of $\mathcal{A}$ on v with root labels q_i for all $i = 1, \ldots, k$.

By the induction hypothesis, no accepting run tree of $\overline{\mathcal{A}}$ on v can be formed with a root label from Q'.

We now show by a separate induction on the structure of the Boolean formula $\delta(q, a)$ that any model of $\overline{\delta(q, a)}$ must contain a state in Q', from which we can conclude the impossibility to build an accepting run tree of $\overline{\mathcal{A}}$ on w with root label q. Remember that a run tree of $\overline{\mathcal{A}}$ on $w = av$ is such that the labels of the successor nodes of the root form a model of $\overline{\delta(q, a)}$.

Suppose $\delta(q, a) = p$ for some $p \in Q$. Then $\overline{\delta(q, a)} = p$ and the only models of $\overline{\delta(q, a)}$ are sets containing p. Since $Q' \models \delta(q, a)$ we must have $p \in Q'$ which immediately proves the base case of this inner induction.

If $\delta(q, a) = \psi_1 \vee \psi_2$ then $\overline{\delta(q, a)} = \overline{\psi_1} \wedge \overline{\psi_2}$. By the induction hypothesis, any model of $\overline{\psi_i}$ must contain a state from Q' for $i \in \{1, 2\}$. Now note that the only models of $\overline{\psi_1} \wedge \overline{\psi_2}$ are those which contain – as subsets – models of $\overline{\psi_i}$ for $i \in \{1, 2\}$. Hence, they must also contain at least some state from Q'.

The last case of $\delta(q, a) = \psi_1 \wedge \psi_2$ is proved analogously. $\qquad\square$

As a specialisation of this lemma with q being the initial state we get the following complementation result.

Corollary 3.17 *For any language $L \subseteq \Sigma^*$ we have: if L is recognised by an AFA of size n, then $\Sigma^* \setminus L$ is also recognised by an AFA of size n.*

The fact that complementation on AFA is easy and every NFA is also an AFA according to Thm. 3.10 suggests a simpler decision procedure for MSO based on a modular translation of formulas into AFA instead of NFA. There is, however, a problem with the size of the resulting automata. If no operation incurs an exponential blowup then the translation from formulas to automata is polynomial contradicting Thm. 2.20.

Put differently, *some* construction on AFA which would be used in a modular translation from MSO formulas must incur an exponential blowup, but it is not the complementation construction. Clearly, it also cannot be either of the constructions for atomic formulas as they get translated into NFA of fixed size and therefore also into AFA of fixed size. There are only two candidates left: disjunctions and existential quantification which are handled by union and alphabet projection on the automata side.

It is easy to construct a (small) AFA which recognises the union of the languages given as AFA. In fact, the same holds for conjunctions and virtually any Boolean combination of languages. The proof of the following theorem is left as an exercise.

Theorem 3.18 *For any AFA $\mathcal{A}_1, \mathcal{A}_2$ over a common alphabet there are AFA $\mathcal{A}^{\cup}$ and $\mathcal{A}^{\cap}$ of size at most $|\mathcal{A}_1| + |\mathcal{A}_2| + 1$ such that $L(\mathcal{A}^{\cup}) = L(\mathcal{A}_1) \cup L(\mathcal{A}_2)$ and $L(\mathcal{A}^{\cap}) = L(\mathcal{A}_1) \cap L(\mathcal{A}_2)$.*

It may seem surprising that alphabet projection or, more generally, homomorphism closure on AFA should incur an exponential blowup. Still, an example witnessing its failure is quite easy to construct.

Example 3.19 Let $\Sigma = \{a, b\}$, $h : \Sigma \to \Sigma$ with $h(a) = h(b) = a$ and $\mathcal{A} = (\{1, 2\}, \Sigma, 1, \delta, \{1\})$ with

$$\delta(1, a) := 1 \ , \quad \delta(1, b) = \delta(2, a) = \delta(2, b) := 2 \ .$$

There is no immediate and well-defined way of obtaining an AFA $(\{1, 2\}, \{a\}, 1, \delta',$ $\{1\})$ by applying the morphism h to the transition function δ as there is in the case of NFA. We would obtain $\delta'(1, a) = \delta(1, a) = 1$ but also $\delta'(1, a) = \delta(1, b) = 2$. Maybe a natural way of fixing these diverging values of the transition function is to interpret it such that $\delta'(1, a) = 1 \wedge 2$. But then we would have $L(\mathcal{A}') = \varnothing \neq \{a\} = \hat{h}(L(\mathcal{A}))$.

One may possibly argue that the construction should form a disjunction rather than a conjunction out of cases in which two different alphabet letters get mapped to the same one by the morphism. But this is equally arbitrary, and likewise one can construct simple examples showing the failure of such an ad-hoc construction. Hence, the correct way of obtaining an AFA for $\hat{h}(L(\mathcal{A}))$ is to transform $\mathcal{A}$ into an NFA by means of Thm. 3.11, then applying the alphabet construction and then interpreting the resulting NFA as an AFA.

Hence, there is no gain in translating MSO formulas into AFA rather than NFA. When using NFA, alphabet projection is cheap and complementation is costly, and for AFA it is simply the other way round.

It is worth noting that alphabet projection is not the only construction which can be used rather simply on NFA but not on AFA. Another prominent example is concatenation.

Example 3.20 Consider the AFA $\mathcal{A}$ and $\mathcal{B}$ over the singleton alphabet $\{a\}$ shown in Fig. 3.5. We have $L(\mathcal{A}) = \varnothing$ and $L(\mathcal{B}) = a^*$. Hence, $L(\mathcal{A})L(\mathcal{B}) = \varnothing$. However, applying the concatenation construction known for NFA to these results in the AFA $\mathcal{C}$ shown in Fig. 3.5 as well. It is obtained by adding, to every accepting state of $\mathcal{A}$, the possibility to move to a successor of the initial state of $\mathcal{B}$. This extra possibility can be realised using disjunctions in the transition function.

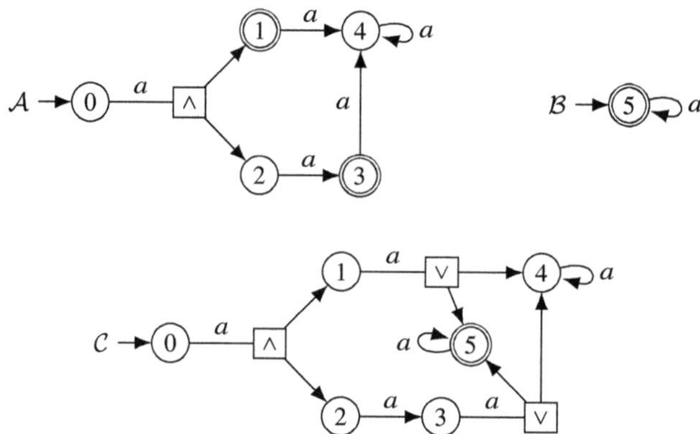

Fig. 3.5 Naïvely concatenating the two AFA above results in the AFA below.

Note that $L(\mathcal{C}) = aaaa^*$. An accepting run on a^n for $n \geq 3$ has two paths which split in the root node labelled 0: one traverses the states $2, 3$ followed by $n - 2$ visits of state 5; the other traverses state 1, followed by $n - 1$ visits of 5.

Recall, though, that $L(\mathcal{A})L(\mathcal{B}) = \emptyset \neq aaaa^*$, i.e. this construction is not correct in general.

Ex. 3.20 shows the problem with concatenation of an AFA $\mathcal{A}$ with an AFA $\mathcal{B}$. It is impossible to guarantee that the moves from $\mathcal{A}$ to $\mathcal{B}$ are synchronised. In other words: different paths of a run tree of the concatenated automaton may split an input word differently into parts on which $\mathcal{A}$ operates, followed by a part from $\mathcal{B}$. This, however, does not correspond to the definition of the concatenation operation on languages: a word in LL' is such that it can be split in a unique position into two parts which belong to L and L' respectively.

A correct way to concatenate two AFA $\mathcal{A}$ and $\mathcal{B}$ is to first transform $\mathcal{A}$ into an NFA $\mathcal{A}'$ according to Thm. 3.11 and then to apply the concatenation construction. Having eliminated universal choices in the left automaton guarantees that the move into the right automaton will happen at a unique point in the input word. Note that it is not necessary to transform $\mathcal{B}$ into an NFA first.

3.4 Reachability Games

There is another, equivalent, way of explaining acceptance of a word by an AFA, namely in terms of reachability games. We first introduce the most important concepts of such games and then use them to develop the game-theoretic semantics of AFA in the next section.

3.4.1 Games, Plays and Strategies

Definition 3.21 A *reachability game* is a $\mathcal{G} = (V, V_0, V_1, v_I, E, F)$ s.t. (V, E) is a directed graph whose edge-relation is left-total, i.e. for every $u \in V$ there is a $v \in V$ s.t. $(u, v) \in E$. Moreover, V_0 and V_1 form a partition of V, i.e. $V_0 \cup V_1 = V$ and $V_0 \cap V_1 = \varnothing$; $v_I \in V$ is a designated initial node in the game, and $F \subseteq V$ is a designated set of end nodes.

In accordance with the way that we measure the size of an automaton we measure the size of a game in terms of the number of its nodes. Reachability games – and also other games studied later on – need not be finite, but the finite ones are of particular interest. Here we introduce games mainly as an alternative tool to explain acceptance of a word by an alternating automaton. These games can, however, also be used algorithmically to solve the word problem for alternating automata.

Intuitively, the game $\mathcal{G} = (V, V_0, V_1, v_I, E, F)$ is played between two players simply called 0 and 1 in the following way. The initial position is v_I. Whenever the game is in a position of the form $v_0 \ldots v_n$, here represented as a sequence of nodes, then we have $v_n \in V_p$ for a unique $p \in \{0, 1\}$, and it is player p's turn to make a move. I.e. they select some node $v_{n+1} \in V$ s.t. $(v_n, v_{n+}) \in E$, and the next position is $v_0 \ldots v_n v_{n+1}$.

When speaking about a particular player using pronouns, "she" will refer to player 0 and "he" will refer to player 1. An arbitrary player will be referred to neutrally as "they".

A sequence of positions that arises from playing according to these rules forms a *play* of the game. For brevity, we represent such a play simply as the sequence of nodes that have been selected successively, i.e. as $v_0, v_1, v_2, \ldots$ instead of $v_0, v_0 v_1, v_0 v_1 v_2, \ldots$ Clearly, each representation can easily be derived from the other.

Note that such a play need not be finite. However, as soon as it reaches a position $v \in F$, player 0 wins this play, and the game terminates. Player 1 wins a play that continues ad infinitum.

Definition 3.22 Let $\mathcal{G} = (V, V_0, V_1, v_I, E, F)$ be a reachability game. A function $\sigma_p : V^* V_p \to V$ that satisfies $(v, \sigma_p(\rho v)) \in E$ for all $v \in V_p$ is called a *strategy* for player p. Intuitively, a strategy for player p determines the next move whenever it is their turn to play.

A play $\rho = v_0, v_1, \ldots$ *conforms* to strategy σ_p if $v_{n+1} = \sigma_p(v_0 \ldots v_n)$ for all $n \geq 0$ with $v_n \in V_p$. I.e. in such a play, player p has always made the choices that were prescribed by σ_p.

Such a strategy σ_p is called *positional*, *memoryless* or *history-free*, if $\sigma_p(\rho v) = \sigma_p(\rho' v)$ for all $v \in V_p$, $\rho, \rho' \in V^*$. Thus, the choices prescribed by this strategy solely depend on the node that a play has reached, and not on the nodes that the play has previously visited, i.e. the history of that play. We will also consider such strategies simply to be of type $V_p \to V$ and write $\sigma_p(v)$ instead of $\sigma_p(\rho v)$ for arbitrary ρ.

The strategy σ_p is a *winning strategy* (for player p) if player p wins every play that conforms to this strategy. In other words, playing according to this strategy guarantees them to win any resulting play, regardless of the opponent's choices in the play.

3.4.2 Attractors

Reachability games are special two-player *zero-sum* games of *perfect information*. Perfect information refers to the fact that at any moment, both players have full knowledge of the state of the game – there are no concealed moves, and both players are always aware of the current position and a possible history of a play that is being played. In zero-sum (two-player) games, there is no simultaneous winning or losing for the players: a play is won by player p iff it is lost by player $1 - p$.

One of the most important concepts in the theory of two-player games is *determinacy*, describing the existence of winning strategies. Below, we will see that reachability games are in fact determined, and that positional strategies suffice. We will show this for a restricted class only, suited to our needs: henceforth we will assume that reachability games are finitely branching. We remark that all concepts and results can be extended to genuinely infinite reachability games as well, but this would need the introduction of ordinal numbers. The proof of Thm. 3.25 below would have to rely on the axiom of choice.

Definition 3.23 Let $\mathcal{G}$ be a game with node set V and edge relation E that is *finitely branching*, i.e. for every $v \in V$ we have $|vE| < \infty$.

Let $T \subseteq V$ be some set of nodes. The *T-attractor for player p* is

$$Attr_p(T) \;\; := \;\; \bigcup_{k \in \mathbb{N}} Attr_p^k(T)$$

where $Attr_p^0(T) := T$ and

$$Attr_p^{i+1}(T) \;\; := \;\; Attr_p^i(T) \;\cup\; \{v \in V_p \mid vE \cap Attr_p^i(T) \neq \varnothing\}$$
$$\cup \; \{v \in V_{1-p} \mid vE \subseteq Attr_p^i(T)\}$$

for $i \geq 0$ and both players p.

Intuitively, $Attr_p^i(T)$ consists of all the nodes from which player p can force every play to visit the set T in at most i moves. For $i = 0$ this is obviously only T. For $i > 0$, it contains, in particular, those nodes belonging to player p that have a successor from which player p can enforce a visit to T in $i - 1$ steps, and those belonging to the opponent whenever they cannot escape, i.e. whenever all those successor nodes belong to $Attr_p^{i-1}(T)$ already.

A strategy σ_p for player p that follows this definition is also called an *attractor strategy*, i.e. we have $\sigma_p(v) := u$ for some $u \in Attr_p^{i-1}(T)$ whenever $v \in V_p$ and

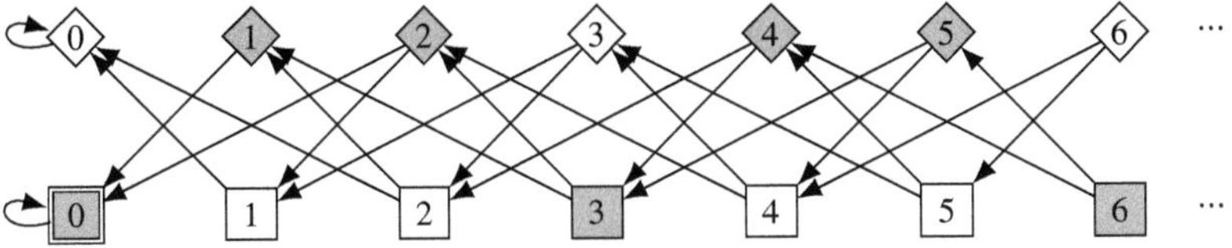

Fig. 3.6 Graphical representation of Nim as a reachability game.

$i := \min\{j \mid v \in Attr_p^j(T)\} > 0$, and $\sigma_p(v)$ arbitrary otherwise. Note that the minimality condition on i is important: it does not suffice to simply move to some successor that also belongs to the attractor. This could lead to cyclic plays that never reach the target T. Minimality guarantees that every time a step is taken according to this strategy, the play moves "one step closer to T."

The restriction to finitely-branching games is used in the third disjunct of the definition of $Attr_p^{i+1}(T)$ above: if the underlying game was not finitely-branching, then we could have a node owned by player $1 - p$ whose successors all belong to $Attr_p(T)$ in a way that there is no maximal i s.t. all successors belong to $Attr_p^i(T)$.

Note that a reachability game $\mathcal{G}$ or a target set T does not necessarily induce unique attractor strategies, but on every attractor $Attr_p(T)$ for T and player p there is at least some attractor strategy that guarantees player p to eventually visit T.

Example 3.24 A popular game that can indeed be seen as a reachability game, is Nim. Starting with a given arbitrary natural number, two players alternatingly choose to subtract either 1 or 2 from the current number. The player who cannot move anymore – because the play has reached the number 0 – loses. In other words, a player wins when they create a situation in which the other player has to move on 0.

We can model Nim as an infinite reachability game with nodes $V = \mathbb{N} \times \{0, 1\}$ where the first component of each pair contains the current value in the play, and the second indicates the player whose turn it is to move. Naturally, we then get $V_p = \mathbb{N} \times \{p\}$ for $p \in \{0, 1\}$. The possible moves are given as

$$\begin{aligned}
E \; &:= \; \{((n, p), (n - 1, 1 - p)) \mid n \geq 1, p \in \{0, 1\}\} \\
&\cup \; \{((n, p), (n - 2, 1 - p)) \mid n \geq 2, p \in \{0, 1\}\} \\
&\cup \; \{((0, p), (0, p)) \mid p \in \{0, 1\}\}.
\end{aligned}$$

The last moves are only added in order to adhere to the technical requirement that every node should have at least one successor. The winning target for player 0 is $\{(0, 1)\}$.

Fig. 3.6 introduces a graphical notation for such two-player games as a directed graph in which nodes in V_0 are shown in diamond shape and those in V_1 are shown in box shape. The content of each node (n, p) only displays the current value n for further subtraction, since the player p can be inferred from the node's shape. As with final states in an automaton, we mark the target set with double lines.

Note that the definition of a designated initial node is missing. We can see this infinite structure as a template for the reachability game Nim started in position (n, p) by any player p for arbitrary $n \geq 0$. In this case, one may simply delete all nodes that are not reachable from (n, p), and the game obviously becomes finite.

Fig. 3.6 also shows $Attr_0(\{(0, 1)\})$. The nodes belong to this attractor, i.e. those from which player 0 wins the reachability game when started there, are shown shaded in grey. A corresponding attractor strategy can easily be read off the graph: since edges are always strictly moving to the left, it suffices for player 0 to remain within grey nodes. Thus, we can see that player 0 wins Nim, when she is allowed to make the first move, and the game is started with an initial value $n \not\equiv 0 \bmod 3$, or her opponent begins to play and the initial value is some $n \equiv 0 \bmod 3$.

The following game shows that it is does generally not suffice to simply stay within the attractor as a strategy to win a reachability game.

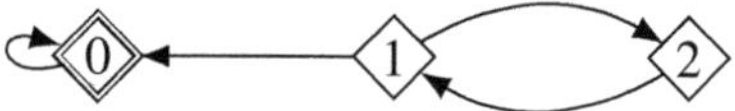

Here, all three nodes belong to the attractor for player 0 to reach node 0. Thus, any move keeps player 0 inside her attractor region. However, any strategy that does not make her eventually move from 1 to 0 is not a winning strategy even though it never takes her outside of the attractor region. Moreover, a positional strategy is only winning if it lets her move from node 0 to node 1 immediately.

3.4.3 Determinacy

Attractors can be used to prove the aforementioned result about positional determinacy.

Theorem 3.25 *Let $\mathcal{G}$ be a reachability game.*

a) Exactly one of the players has a winning strategy for $\mathcal{G}$.
b) A player has a winning strategy for $\mathcal{G}$ iff they have a positional winning strategy for $\mathcal{G}$.

Proof Let $\mathcal{G} = (V, V_0, V_1, E, v_I, F)$. Let $W_0 := Attr_0(F)$ and $W_1 := V \setminus W_0$. Clearly, (W_0, W_1) forms a partition of V, and it should be clear that player 0 wins the game $\mathcal{G}$ started in any node in W_0 using some attractor strategy for F. It remains to be seen that player 1 has a positional winning strategy for all the nodes in W_1, and both parts (a) and (b) are proven.

Define a positional strategy $\sigma_1 : V_1 \rightarrow V$ simply as follows. For any node $v \in V_1 \cap W_1$ let $\sigma_1(v)$ be some node $u \in vE$ s.t. $u \notin Attr_0(F)$, and $\sigma_1(v)$ be arbitrary for all $v \in V_1 \cap W_0$.

First note that for any $v \in V_1 \cap W_1$ there must be some successor not belonging to $Attr_0(F)$ because if all successors did belong to $Attr_0(F)$ then, by finiteness of the game, there would be a smallest $i \in \mathbb{N}$ s.t. $vE \subseteq Attr_0^i(F)$ and therefore $v \in Attr_0^{i+1}(F) \subseteq Attr_0(F)$ contradicting the assumption.

Next take a play $\rho = v_0 v_1 \ldots$ that conforms with strategy σ_1 and is started in some node $v_0 \in W_1$. We claim that $v_j \notin Attr_0(F)$ for all $j \geq 0$. For $j = 0$ this is the case by assumption. Suppose it is true for some j already. We distinguish two cases in order to show that it is also true for v_{j+1}.

- If $v_j \in V_1$ then $v_{j+1} = \sigma_1(v_j) \notin Attr_0(F)$ by the construction of σ_1 and the fact that ρ conforms to σ_1.
- If $v_j \in V_0$ then v_{j+1} is chosen by player 0, and suppose that $v_{j+1} \in Attr_0(F)$, i.e. there is some i s.t. $v_{j+1} \in Attr_0^i(F)$. By the definition of attractors we would have $v_j \in Attr_0^{i+1}(F) \subseteq Attr_0(F)$ contradicting the assumption that $v_j \notin Attr_0(F)$. Hence, we must also have $v_{j+1} \notin Attr_0(F)$.

So we know that, if player 1 plays according to strategy σ_1, he can steer any play that starts outside of $Attr_0(F)$ away from $Attr_0(F)$ forever. In particular, since $F = Attr_0^0(F) \subseteq Attr_0(F)$, he can avoid visiting F forever. But then σ_1 is a (positional) winning strategy for player 1.

Altogether, the partition (W_0, W_1) therefore divides the nodes of the game into two sets according to which player has a positional strategy to win the game started in this node. Then the membership of the designated starting node v_I in either W_0 or W_1 determines the player who has a positional winning strategy for $\mathcal{G}$. $\square$

3.4.4 Polynomial-Time Solvability

At last, we consider the most important algorithmic question regarding games in general, not necessarily just reachability games, namely the problem of *solving* the game:

> **given:** a reachability game $\mathcal{G}$
> **compute:** a (positional) winning strategy for either player to win $\mathcal{G}$

Sometimes we may consider a global variant of this problem, asking to determine winner and strategies for plays beginning in each of the game's nodes rather than just one designated starting node. It should be clear that these formulations are equivalent up to polynomial overheads: a solution to the global question includes one to the local question; and by solving the local problem $|V|$ many times one can obtain – not necessarily in the most efficient way – a solution to the global problem.

Theorem 3.26 *Reachability games can be solved in polynomial time.*

Proof According to Thm. 3.25 it suffices to compute the attractor for player 0 and the set of target nodes F in the game in order to obtain a partition of the game's nodes into the winning regions for players 0 and 1. It should also be clear that attractors can be computed naïvely in time $\mathcal{O}(|V| \cdot |E|)$ or more efficiently using a work-list-driven breadth-search backwards through the game graph in time $\mathcal{O}(|E|)$. Moreover, an attractor strategy for player 0 can easily be constructed along the way.

At last, once $Attr_0(F)$ has been found in this way, a strategy for player 1 can be constructed in time $\mathcal{O}(|E|)$ by selecting, for every node won by him, some successor not belonging to $Attr_0(F)$ as the proof of Thm. 3.25 suggests. $\qquad\square$

3.5 A Game-Theoretic Semantics

We make use of reachability games as an alternative characterisation of acceptance of a word by an AFA.

Definition 3.27 Let $\mathcal{A} = (Q, \Sigma, q_I, \delta, F)$ be an AFA and $w = a_0 a_1 \ldots a_{n-1} \in \Sigma^*$. The *acceptance game* for $\mathcal{A}$ and w is the reachability game $\mathcal{G}_{\mathcal{A},w} = (V, V_0, V_1, v_I, E, F')$ where

$$
\begin{aligned}
V_0 &:= \{(q,i) \mid q \in Q, 0 \le i < n\} \cup \{(q,n) \mid q \in Q \setminus F\}\,, \\
V_1 &:= \{(M,i) \mid M \subseteq Q, 1 \le i \le n\} \cup \{(q,n) \mid q \in F\}\,, \\
V &:= V_0 \cup V_1\,.
\end{aligned}
$$

The edge relation in this game is given as

$$
\begin{aligned}
E &:= \{((q,i),(M,i+1)) \mid M \vDash \delta(q,a_i), i < n\} \\
&\quad \cup \{((M,i),(q,i)) \mid q \in M, i \le n\}\,.
\end{aligned}
$$

The initial node is $(q_I, 0)$ and the reachability target for player 0 is $F' := F \times \{n\}$.

Hence, positions of this game are states or subsets of the AFA's state set, annotated with positions in the input word. The game begins in position $(q_I, 0)$, i.e. the initial state of the underlying AFA and position 0 in the word. In such a position, it is player 0's task to name a set of states that is a model of the Boolean formula obtained through the transition function applied to the state and the next input symbol in the word. Such a move is followed by a player-1 move who simply picks one of the states in the current set to continue with, and the play advances to the next position in the word. It is player 0's objective to end up in a position made up of an accepting state at the word's end.

Note that, strictly speaking, this definition violates the requirement that every node in a reachability game has at least one successor: positions of the form (q,n) where $n = |w|$ do not have successors. This could easily be fixed by simply letting the game loop in such states. Moreover, note that positive Boolean formulas cannot be unsatisfiable. Hence, every node of the form (q,i) has at least some successor $(M,i+1)$, and every such node has at least some successor $(q',i+1)$ because models of positive Boolean formulas over Q cannot be empty.

The following theorem shows that the game-theoretic semantics coincides with the runtree-based semantics of AFA.

Theorem 3.28 *Let $\mathcal{A}$ be an AFA over Σ and $w \in \Sigma^*$. Player 0 wins the acceptance game $\mathcal{G}_{\mathcal{A},w}$ iff $w \in L(\mathcal{A})$.*

Proof Let $\mathcal{A} = (Q, \Sigma, q_I, \delta, F)$, $w = a_0 \ldots a_{n-1}$ and $\mathcal{G}_{\mathcal{A},w} = (V, V_0, V_1, v_I, E, F')$.

"$\Leftarrow$" Suppose that $w \in L(\mathcal{A})$. According to Thm. 3.8 there is a memoryless run ρ of $\mathcal{A}$ on w. Remember that ρ consists of a layered DAG: its nodes reside on levels $0, \ldots, n$ and are labelled with states from Q. Memorylessness guarantees that every state occurs at most once on every level.

We define a positional strategy σ_0 for player 0 in $\mathcal{G}_{\mathcal{A},w}$ as follows. Take a node (q, i). To define $\sigma_0(q, i)$ we distinguish two cases.

- If the run ρ contains a node labelled q on level i and $i < n$, then let M be the collected labels of all its successors on level $i + 1$. Then let $\sigma_0(q, i) := (M, i + 1)$. We have $M \models \delta(q, a_i)$ by definition of ρ, hence, we have $((q, i), (M, i + 1)) \in E$ indeed.
- If $i = n$ or q does not occur on level i then let $\sigma_0(q, i)$ be chosen arbitrarily.

We claim that this is indeed a winning strategy for player 0 in $\mathcal{G}_{\mathcal{A},w}$. The following invariant holds for any play $(q_0, 0), (M_1, 1), (q_1, 1), (M_2, 2), \ldots, (q_n, n)$ that conforms to this strategy: for every $j = 0, \ldots, n$ there is a node on level j of ρ that is labelled with q_j; and for every $j = 1, \ldots, n$, M_j consists solely of node labels found on level j in ρ.

But then we must have, in particular, that for the last node (q_n, n) of the play there is a node on level n of ρ which is the last level. By the assumption $w \in L(\mathcal{A})$, this level only contains accepting states, hence, (q_n, n) is a target node in $\mathcal{G}$ and therefore, player 0 wins the play, i.e. σ_0 is indeed a winning strategy.

"$\Rightarrow$" Suppose that player 0 wins the acceptance game $\mathcal{G}_{\mathcal{A},w}$. Since it is a reachability game, we can assume that she wins it with an attractor strategy σ_0. We use this to construct a memoryless accepting run ρ of $\mathcal{A}$ on w in a surprisingly simple way: for every $(q, j) \in Attr_0(F')$ add a node labelled q on level j. Then introduce edges from any node on level j to any node on level $j + 1$ for $j = 0, \ldots, n$. It remains to be seen that this is indeed an accepting run of $\mathcal{A}$ on w – at least after removing every node on level 0 whose label is not q_I.

First consider ρ's last level n: note that we can only have $(q, n) \in Attr_0(F')$ if $(q, n) \in Attr_0^0(F')$ already because these are the target nodes in the game. Moreover, we then have $q \in F$ by construction of the game. Thus, ρ's final level contains accepting states only.

Next, since player 0 wins $\mathcal{G}_{\mathcal{A},w}$, we must have that $(q_I, 0) \in Attr_0(F')$. Hence, there is a node labelled q_I on ρ's first level.

For ρ to be an accepting run we only need to show that the labels on level $j + 1$ comprise a model of $\delta(q, a_j)$ for any label q occurring on level j and every $j \in [n]$. For simplicity, let Q_j denote the set of state labels occurring on level j. Now take any $j \in [n]$ and any $q \in Q_j$. Remember that by construction, we have $(q, j) \in Attr_0(F')$. Consider player 0's attractor strategy in this game node, i.e. $\sigma_0(q, j)$. According to the construction of $\mathcal{G}_{\mathcal{A},w}$ we have $\sigma_0(q, j) = (M, j + 1)$ for some $M \subseteq Q$ s.t. $M \models \delta(q, a_j)$. Moreover, since player 1 cannot escape the attractor region, we have $(q', j + 1) \in Attr_0(F')$ for any $q' \in M$. Thus, we have $M \subseteq Q_{j+1}$. Now note that models of positive Boolean formulas are upwards-closed, i.e. since $M \vDash \delta(q, a_j)$ so we have $Q_{j+1} \vDash \delta(q, a_j)$. But then ρ is in fact an accepting run of $\mathcal{A}$ on w. $\qquad\square$

This characterisation of the word problem for AFA as a reachability game is not optimal from a complexity point of view. The word problem for AFA can indeed be solved in polynomial time, but this does not follow with Thm. 3.26 because the reachability game, as it is defined here, is of exponential size. It is possible, though, to refine these games such that they are of polynomial size only, in which case the following follows from the polynomial-time decidability of the reachability problem. Working out the details is left as an exercise.

Theorem 3.29 *The word problem for AFA can be solved in polynomial time.*

Note that this also avoids a suboptimal solution to the word problem that one would obtain by translating an AFA into an NFA at an exponential blowup in the worst case first, and then appealing to polynomial-time solvability of the word problem for NFA.

Bibliographic Notes

Alternation as a generalisation to nondeterministic choice in a computational device was introduced and studied by Chandra and Stockmeyer and by Kozen at the same time [CKS81]. The focus in this work is on computational complexity, though, which implies results on expressiveness. Also, alternation is studied in the more general context of Turing Machines. The application of the techniques developed there to finite automata, which are essentially very restricted Turing Machines, is not difficult and one quickly obtains results like alternation elimination via a double powerset construction. The effect of the extension of nondeterminism to alternation on the expressive power of various kinds of restrictions of Turing has been an object of study since, cf. [Kin88, Hro85, FJY90]. Salomaa and Yu studied alternating finite automata to obtain a characterisation of star-free languages [SY00], the topic of the following chapter.

Sometimes, alternating finite automata are introduced differently in the literature with transition functions mapping states and symbols to sets of states as it is done for NFA here. The state set is then partitioned into existential and universal states, and the type of state determines whether the branching in the outgoing transitions is seen disjunctively or conjunctively. Clearly, this is a restriction of the model represented here. On the other hand, it is easy to see that it also captures NFA in that an NFA is an alternating automaton with existential states only in this sense. Hence, these two models of alternating automata are equi-expressive.

Alternation becomes more interesting when studied in the context of finite automata on infinite words (see Part II) or tree automata (see Part III of this book). This is also what the most notable work in the literature on alternating automata targets, and we refer to the bibliographic notes in the corresponding chapters of those parts for further pointers. Alternation has also been studied as an extension of finite (nondeterministic) pushdown automata [LSL84, LLS84, IJW92] but this is clearly leaving the realm of regular languages and therefore the focus of the presentation here.

Something similar can be said about the game-theoretic semantics of alternating automata. Reachability games on finite graphs are conceptually very simple, and it is only when extensions are considered, either by considering infinite game arenas or stronger winning conditions, that the study of games as a mechanism to explain acceptance by alternating automata has brought out the most notable work in the literature. We also refer to the bibliographic notes in the corresponding chapters of Parts II and III for pointers in that direction.

The concept of determinacy as a property of two-player games of perfect information and infinite duration was first studied by Gale and Stewart. The main goal in such work was to find topological properties of the winning sets that would guarantee determinacy. Gale and Stewart showed that this is true for open sets [GS53], and Martin extended this to all Borel sets [Mar75]. So determinacy for reachability games is an immediate consequence of the former already since the winning condition, given as a set of target nodes $F \subseteq V$, is just a representation of the open set $V^* F V^\omega$ of infinite plays won by player 0.

Exercises

Exercise 22 Let $f \in \mathbb{B}^+(Q)$ for some AFA's state set Q.

  a) Suppose $N \subseteq M \subseteq Q$ with $N \vDash f$. Show that $M \vDash f$ as well. *Hint:* Use induction on the structure of positive Boolean formulas.
  b) Argue whether or not it is possible that $\varnothing \vDash f$ holds.
  c) Argue whether or not it is possible that $Q \nvDash f$ holds.

Exercise 23 Let $M \subseteq Q$ for some AFA's state set Q. We call M a *minimal model* of $f \in \mathbb{B}^+(Q)$ if $M \vDash f$ and $N \nvDash f$ for all $N \subsetneq M$.

  a) Construct a positive Boolean formula that has more than one minimal model.
  b) An mAFA is defined syntactically like an AFA, but additionally, in their runtrees, the labels of successor nodes must form not just some but a minimal model of the transition function's formula at that point. Show that mAFA recognise exactly the regular languages.

Exercise 24 Construct an NFA with only two states that recognises the language L from Ex. 3.5.

Exercise 25   a) Construct an NFA which recognises the language L_{29393} from Ex. 3.12 and which has at most 29393 states.
  b) Show that L_{29393} cannot be recognised by any NFA with less than 29393 states. *Hint:* Suppose such an NFA did exist. Consider a long word in the language L

such that any accepting run must visit some state twice. Use this to construct an accepting run on a shorter word which does not belong to L. Conclude that this contradicts the assumption.

Exercise 26 Prove Thm. 3.13 by suitably generalising Ex. 3.12.

Exercise 27 Let $L_n = \{ww \mid w \in \{a, b\}^* \text{ and } |w| = n\}$ for each $n \geq 1$.

  a) Construct AFA $\mathcal{A}_n$ such that $L(\mathcal{A}_n) = L_n$ and $|\mathcal{A}_n| = \mathcal{O}(n)$.
  b) Draw an accepting run of $\mathcal{A}_3$ on $abaaba$.
  c) Show that every NFA for L_n needs to have at least 2^n many states.

Exercise 28 Prove Thm. 3.14. *Hint:* Use the following family of regular languages over $\Sigma = \{a, b\}$ as an example.

$$L_n := \Sigma^* a \Sigma^{P(n)}$$

where $P(n) := \prod_{i=1}^{n} \chi(i)$ and $\chi(i) = i$ if i is prime and $\chi(i) = 1$ otherwise. In other words, $P(n)$ is the product of all prime numbers up to n.

Construct small AFA $\mathcal{A}_n$ that recognise L_n using similar tricks as in Ex. 3.12. Then adjust the proof of the succinctness gap between NFA and DFA established in Exc. 6 to show that the smallest DFA recognising L_n must be of size doubly exponential in n.

Exercise 29 Prove Thm. 3.18.

Exercise 30 Give a formal description of the construction which takes an NFA $\mathcal{A}$ and an AFA $\mathcal{B}$ and produces an AFA $\mathcal{C}$ s.t. $L(\mathcal{C}) = L(\mathcal{A})L(\mathcal{B})$ and $|\mathcal{C}| = \mathcal{O}(|\mathcal{A}| + |\mathcal{B}|)$. Prove correctness of this construction.

Exercise 31 Give a construction of a reachability game that characterises the word problem for an AFA $\mathcal{A}$ and a word w whose size is only polynomial in $|\mathcal{A}|$ and $|w|$. Here, $|\mathcal{A}|$ can be assumed to be the collective length of all Boolean formulas occurring in $\mathcal{A}'s$ transition function. *Hint:* The nodes in this game should comprise of positions in w and subformulas of formulas in $\mathcal{A}$'s transition function. During the game, the two players then work their way through these formulas in order to establish whether or not there is a run of $\mathcal{A}$ on w.

Chapter 4
Star-Free Languages

A natural fragment of Monadic Second-Order Logic is First-Order Logic (FO), consisting of all MSO formulas that do not use second-order quantification over monadic predicates. Only first-order quantification over positions in a word is allowed. This chapter takes a closer look at FO over finite words, with a focus on two aspects.

First, while the expressiveness of MSO is reasonably well understood by now, matching the expressiveness of other regular formalisms like finite automata (from deterministic to alternating ones), the question after the expressive power of FO arises. It would be conceivable that this syntactic elimination does not limit the ability to formalise regular properties. This, however, is not the case as we will show: FO is strictly weaker than MSO over words. To show this, we develop a game-theoretic characterisation of the distinguishability of two words by an FO formula using limited resources. This can then be used to show that there are regular languages which cannot be defined in FO.

This then raises the question in turn, whether there are other characterisations of the class of FO-definable languages. One of the reasons for why the class of regular languages is well understood is the availability of many syntactic formalisms that can be used to represent its members: regular expressions, DFA, NFA, AFA, MSO, etc. We will show that the class of languages representable by formulas of FO has a neat algebraic characterisation in terms of so-called *star-free expressions*. These are comparable to regular expressions but do not contain the Kleene star as an operator. However, they cannot just be obtained from regular expressions by dropping the Kleene star as this would result in a characterisation of the class of all *finite* languages only. Instead, complementation needs to be added explicitly.

4.1 First-Order Logic

Recall that the syntax of *First-Order Logic* on finite words over an alphabet Σ and a reservoir of first-order variables $\mathcal{V}_1$ is given by

$$\varphi \; ::= \; x < y \mid a(x) \mid \varphi_1 \vee \varphi_2 \mid \neg\varphi \mid \exists x\, \varphi$$

where $x, y \in V_1$ and $a \in \Sigma$.

FO is therefore the fragment of MSO in which second-order quantification is not allowed. One could of course allow second-order variables X in formulas of the form $X(y)$ which would necessarily be free in any formula, and they can be seen as contributing to the underlying alphabet. However, technically it would be easier to then disallow formulas of the form $a(x)$ in order not to have to unify symbols a and X, i.e. not to work with words over an alphabet of the form $\Sigma \times 2^{V_2}$. Clearly, this would not change any of the results presented here; it would only introduce extra case distinctions in the proofs. We therefore adopt the clean way here and drop second-order variables entirely, i.e. the underlying words are constructed over an alphabet Σ that is not specified any further.

Other logical operators are introduced as abbreviations using deMorgan rules and the duality of existential and universal quantification for instance, see Chp. 2.

The semantics of FO is then completely determined by the semantics of MSO over words. For instance, the FO formula $\varphi = \forall x.a(x) \rightarrow \exists y.x{<}y \wedge b(y)$ defines the language

$$L(\varphi) \; = \; (a + b + c)^* b (b + c)^* + (b + c)^*$$

of all words in which every a is followed by a b (not necessarily directly).

Remember the first goal stated in the introduction to this chapter. We want to show that FO is strictly weaker in expressive power than MSO. Essentially we need to find some MSO formula φ and show that no FO formula is equivalent to it. Naïvely, one might expect that this could be done by constructing two words w and v which are distinguished by φ, e.g. $w \vDash \varphi$ and $v \nvDash \varphi$, but cannot be distinguished by any FO formula. This approach is doomed to fail. Clearly, w and v can only be distinguished by any φ if $w \neq v$. But then there is also an FO formula ψ that distinguishes them. We leave it as an exercise to formally prove this fact.

Note that this ψ would depend on w or v. A hypothetical FO formula that is equivalent to φ must of course not depend on the words that it is interpreted on. In other words, we need to show that for any FO formula ψ there is *some* pair of words w, v which is distinguished by φ but not by ψ. To establish this we introduce a measure on formulas such that the distinction of two words by an FO formula will require a large enough measure while, on the other hand, formulas with low measure cannot distinguish many pairs of words.

Definition 4.1 The *quantifier depth $qd(\varphi)$* of an FO formula φ is inductively defined as follows.

$$
\begin{aligned}
qd(x < y) \; = \; qd(a(x)) \; &:= \; 0 \\
qd(\varphi \vee \psi) \; &:= \; \max\{qd(\varphi), qd(\psi)\} \\
qd(\neg\varphi) \; &:= \; qd(\varphi) \\
qd(\exists x\, \varphi) \; &:= \; 1 + qd(\varphi)
\end{aligned}
$$

Hence, $qd(\varphi)$ measures the depth of nestings of quantifiers in φ. It equals the maximal number of quantifiers on a path in its syntax tree. The quantifier depth of $\varphi = \forall x.a(x) \rightarrow \exists y.x < y \wedge b(x)$ for instance is 2. The quantifier depth of $\forall x.a(x) \rightarrow (\exists y.x < y \wedge b(y)) \wedge \exists z.z < x \wedge b(z)$ is also 2 since the two existential quantifications appear on different branches of the formula's syntax tree.

Note that the abbreviations $x = y$, $x = 0$, $x < max$ or $x = max$, as introduced in Chp. 2, are definable in FO as they do not need second-order quantification. However, depending on how exactly they are defined, they may have non-zero quantifier depth already, even though the quantifier is not directly visible.

We state a rather obvious upper bound on the expressiveness of FO, obtained directly from the fact that FO is a fragment of MSO.

Theorem 4.2 *Let $\varphi \in FO$. Then $L(\varphi)$ is regular.*

Later on we will reason about FO formulas, and it will be convenient to assume them to be normalised in a certain way.

Definition 4.3 An FO formula over Σ is in *negation normal form* (NNF) if it is built from literals $a(x)$, $\neg a(x)$, $x < y$ and $\neg(x < y)$ using only the operators $\wedge$, $\vee$ and existential and universal quantification.

Lemma 4.4 *Let $k \geq 0$. For every FO formula φ of quantifier depth at most k there is a ψ in negation normal form of quantifier depth at most k s.t. $\psi \equiv \varphi$ and $|\psi| = \mathcal{O}(|\varphi|)$.*

Proof Using deMorgan Laws $(\neg(\varphi \wedge \psi) \equiv \neg\varphi \vee \neg\psi, \neg(\varphi \vee \psi) \equiv \neg\varphi \wedge \neg\psi)$, the duality between existential and universal quantifiers $(\neg\exists x\, \varphi \equiv \forall x\, \neg\varphi, \neg\forall x\, \varphi \equiv \exists x\, \neg\varphi)$ and double negation elimination $(\neg\neg\varphi \equiv \varphi)$ it is possible to push negation downwards in a formula to achieve the desired form. Since this does not create or delete quantifiers on any path of the syntax tree, quantifier depth is preserved. The number of nodes in the syntax tree is at most doubled. $\qquad\qquad\square$

4.2 Ehrenfeucht-Fraïssé Games

As mentioned above, FO is strictly weaker than full regularity. We will show that, in particular, there is no FO formula φ such that $L(\varphi) = (aa)^+$. In order to prove this we need a tool from finite model theory which characterises the indistinguishability of two structures – here: words – by formulas of FO in terms of winning strategies in simple 2-player games.

4.2.1 Word-Comparison Games

Let $k \geq 0$, Σ be a finite alphabet and $u, v \in \Sigma^*$. The k-round *Ehrenfeucht-Fraïssé game* (or EF game for short) $\mathcal{G}_k(u, v)$ is played between two players called *Spoiler*

(S) and *Duplicator* (**D**) on the two words u and v. It is helpful to imagine the words as being written down in two lines, one above the other. A *configuration* in the game is a sequence of pairs (i, j) with $0 \le i < |u|$ and $0 \le j < |v|$. We will use female pronouns to refer to **D** and male pronouns for **S**.

Each round consists of alternating moves; first **S** picks a position in one of the two words. Then **D** answers with a position in the other word. Intuitively this forms a straight line connecting these two positions. **D** has to make sure that the two letters at the positions selected in this round are the same and that the line formed in this way does not cross any previous line or share an endpoint with one of them. Otherwise she looses immediately. She wins if she manages to survive k rounds.

S is allowed to pick a position that has been previously selected. This is simply not wise as **D** can always answer with the position that it is connected to and thus survive one more round.

We say that **D** wins $\mathcal{G}_k(u, v)$ if she has a *strategy* which guarantees her to survive k rounds of the game, regardless of **S**'s moves. We leave it as an exercise to formally define EF games as reachability games in the sense of Sect. 3.4.

Example 4.5 Let $\Sigma = \{a, b\}$, $u = aabaacaa$, $v = aacaabaa$. **D** wins $\mathcal{G}_1(u, v)$ but looses $\mathcal{G}_2(u, v)$ since **S** has a winning strategy for this game.

Consider $\mathcal{G}_1(u, v)$ first. Player **D**'s strategy is simple: whatever **S** picks in his first move, pick a position that is labelled with the same letter. Since both words contain the same letters, this is always possible. It trivially does not create a situation in which **D** would lose. Hence, she can survive one round in this game.

Now consider $\mathcal{G}_2(u, v)$. The following strategy is winning for **S** for instance: in the first round, pick position 2 in u, in the second round pick position 5 in u. Since these are the only positions carrying b and c, respectively, **D**'s only choice is to answer with positions 5 and then 2 in v. Otherwise she would lose because she would have connected different letters. But then she loses because she has created a crossover:

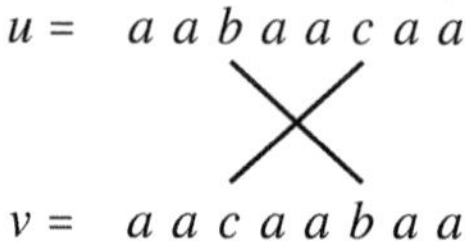

Being a 2-player game of finite duration and perfect information, the EF game enjoys *determinacy*: for every k, u, v, either **S** or **D** has a winning strategy for $\mathcal{G}_k(u, v)$. This is not too difficult to prove, especially not with the generalisation that we consider in the following as it enables inductive reasoning.

Definition 4.6 Let $u, v \in \Sigma^*$, $n \ge 0$, and $\mathbf{s} = (s_0, s_1, \ldots, s_{n-1})$ and $\mathbf{t} = (t_0, t_1, \ldots, t_{n-1})$ be sequences of positions in u, resp. v. Hence, we have $0 \le s_i < |u|, 0 \le t_i < |v|$ for all $i = 0, \ldots, n - 1$. We write $\mathbf{s}.i$ to denote the sequence that is obtained from $\mathbf{s}$ by appending the position i to it.

The *generalised EF game* $\mathcal{G}_k((u, \mathbf{s}), (v, \mathbf{t}))$ is played like the ordinary EF game on u and v with k rounds, assuming that the connections s_i—t_i have already been formed.

We say that $\mathbf{s}$ and $\mathbf{t}$ form a *partial isomorphism* if

- for all $i = 0, \ldots, n-1$: $u(s_i) = v(t_i)$, and
- for all i, j with $0 \leq i < j < n$: $s_i < s_j$ iff $t_i < t_j$.

The second condition also implies that $s_i = s_j$ iff $t_i = t_j$: if $s_i = s_j$ then neither $s_i < s_j$ nor $s_j < s_i$, so we neither have $t_i < t_j$ nor $t_j < t_i$ and therefore $t_i = t_j$, and vice-versa.

Note that $\mathbf{D}$ loses $\mathcal{G}_k((u,\mathbf{s}),(v,\mathbf{t}))$ unless $\mathbf{s},\mathbf{t}$ form a partial isomorphism, even if $k = 0$. Since the tuples of positions we consider here always arise from choices by the players in (generalised) EF games, and we already remarked that there is no gain for player $\mathbf{S}$ to choose a position that has already been chosen in a previous round, we can assume w.l.o.g. that these tuples always contain mutually different positions. I.e. if $\mathbf{s} = (s_0, \ldots, s_{n-1})$ then we assume that $s_i \neq s_j$ for all i, j with $0 \leq i < j < n$.

We list some facts about (generalised) EF games. The formal proofs are left as exercises.

Lemma 4.7 *Let $k \geq 0$, Σ be given, $u, v \in \Sigma^*$ and $\mathbf{s},\mathbf{t}$ be equal-length sequences of positions in u, resp. v.*

a) $\mathbf{D}$ *wins* $\mathcal{G}_k((u,\mathbf{s}),(v,\mathbf{t}))$ *iff* $\mathbf{S}$ *does not win* $\mathcal{G}_k((u,\mathbf{s}),(v,\mathbf{t}))$.

b) $\mathcal{G}_k(u,v)$ *is the same game as* $\mathcal{G}_k((u,()),(v,()))$. *In particular, they are won by the same players.*

c) $\mathbf{D}$ *wins* $\mathcal{G}_0((u,\mathbf{s}),(v,\mathbf{t}))$ *iff for all i, j with $0 \leq i, j < |\mathbf{s}|$: $s_i < s_j$ iff $t_i < t_j$, and for all i with $0 \leq i < |\mathbf{s}|$: $u(s_i) = v(t_i)$.*

d) $\mathbf{D}$ *wins* $\mathcal{G}_{k+1}((u,\mathbf{s}),v,\mathbf{t}))$ *iff for all $s < |u|$ there is $t < |v|$ and for all $t < |v|$ there is $s < |u|$ such that $\mathbf{D}$ wins $\mathcal{G}_k((u,\mathbf{s}.s),(v,\mathbf{t}.t))$.*

e) Let $m_u := |u| - 1$ and $m_v := |v| - 1$ be the last positions in u, resp. v. Suppose that $u(0) = v(0)$ and $u(m_u) = v(m_v)$, i.e. u and v agree on their first and last positions. Let $\mathbf{s}' = \mathbf{s}.0.m_u$ and $\mathbf{t}' := \mathbf{t}.0.m_v$. Then $\mathbf{S}$ wins $\mathcal{G}_k((u,\mathbf{s}'),(v,\mathbf{t}'))$ if he wins $\mathcal{G}_k((u,\mathbf{s}),(v,\mathbf{t}))$. I.e. there is no gain for him to choose the first or last position in this case.

f) Let σ be a permutation of n elements and $\mathbf{s}'$, resp. $\mathbf{t}'$ result from $\mathbf{s}$, resp. $\mathbf{t}$ by applying this same σ to them. Then $\mathbf{D}$ wins $\mathcal{G}_k((u,\mathbf{s}'),(v,\mathbf{t}'))$ iff she wins $\mathcal{G}_k((u,\mathbf{s}),(v,\mathbf{t}))$.

The following lemma will be useful later on in the proof of the fact that $(aa)^+$ is not definable in FO. It can also be seen as providing another example of an EF game, and how the extension to generalised EF games is helpful in reasoning about strategies. The lemma essentially says that $\mathbf{S}$'s ability to point out a length difference between (parts of) two words is limited to chunks of length that are at most exponential in the number of rounds to be played.

Lemma 4.8 *Let $k \geq 0$, $\Sigma = \{a\}$ and $u, v \in a^*$ such that $\min\{|u|, |v|\} > 2^k$. Then $\mathbf{D}$ wins $\mathcal{G}_k(u,v)$.*

Proof It should be clear that the statement is too weak to be proved by induction on k since, in a $(k+1)$- round EF game, one round does not take us into the initial position of a k-round EF game. However, it takes us into the initial position of a

k-round *generalised* EF game, and this is even true for generalised EF games. So we consider a stronger statement from which the statement of the lemma follows immediately.

Let k, Σ, u, v be as above. Furthermore, let $\mathbf{s} = (s_1, \ldots, s_n)$ and $\mathbf{t} = (t_1, \ldots, t_n)$ be tuples of positions in u, resp. v that form a partial isomorphism. We extend them to $\mathbf{s}' := (0, s_0, \ldots, s_n, |u| - 1)$ and $\mathbf{t}' := (0, t_0, \ldots, t_n, |v| - 1)$, assuming that they do not contain multiple occurrences of positions. Otherwise, extend them accordingly so that both contain the first and last positions in u, resp. v.

Claim. Now suppose that the following holds: for all i, j with $0 \leq i < j \leq n + 1$ we have $\min\{|s_j - s_i|, |t_j - t_i|\} \geq 2^k$ or $s_j - s_i = t_j - t_i$. We claim that $\mathbf{D}$ wins $\mathcal{G}_k((u, \mathbf{s}'), (v, \mathbf{t}'))$.

Before we move on to proving this claim, we remark that the original statement of the lemma follows from it: consider the case of $n = 0$ in this claim, i.e. the game $\mathcal{G}_k((u, (0, |u|-1)), (v, (0, |v|-1)))$. First of all, the assumption in the claim about the relative difference in the positions on both sides boils down to $\min\{|u|-1, |v|-1\} \geq 2^k$, i.e. $\min\{|u|, |v|\} > 2^k$. Next, if $\mathbf{D}$ wins $\mathcal{G}_k((u, (0, |u| - 1)), (v, (0, |v| - 1)))$ then by Lemma 4.7 (a) and (e), she also wins $\mathcal{G}_k((u, ()), (v, ()))$, i.e. $\mathcal{G}_k(u, v)$ by Lemma 4.7 (b).

Now the claim can easily be proved by induction. The case of $k = 0$ follows immediately from the assumption that $\mathbf{s}, \mathbf{t}$, and thus also $\mathbf{s}', \mathbf{t}'$ form a partial isomorphism, using Lemma 4.7 (c).

For the step case, we can apply Lemma 4.7 (f) to assume w.l.o.g. that $0 < s_0 < s_1 < \ldots < s_n < |u| - 1$ and likewise for $\mathbf{t}'$. Then the premise of the claim boils down to assuming that the difference between each two *successive* rather than arbitrary positions in $\mathbf{s}'$ and $\mathbf{t}'$ is either equal or larger than 2^k. Now consider the first round in the game $\mathcal{G}_{k+1}((u, \mathbf{s}'), (v, \mathbf{t}'))$. $\mathbf{S}$ picks a position which, by assumption, needs to lie somewhere in between two positions already chosen. Suppose he chooses some position s in u s.t. $s_i < s < s_{i+1}$ for some i. Now there are two cases.

- Case $s_{i+1} - s_i = t_{i+1} - t_i$. Then $\mathbf{D}$ can pick the unique position t in v s.t. $s_{i+1} - s = t_{i+1} - t$ and $s - s_i = t - t_i$, i.e. the position that has equal distances to both adjacent already chosen positions.
- Case $s_{i+1} - s_i \geq 2^k$ and $t_{t+1} - t_i \geq 2^k$. Then we must have $s_{i+1} - s \geq 2^{k-1}$ or $s - s_i \geq 2^{k-1}$ as it is impossible to divide an interval of length greater than 2^k into two parts without at least one of them having length greater than 2^{k-1}. If $s_{i+1} - s > s - s_i$ then $\mathbf{D}$ chooses the unique position t in v that has equal distance on the closer side, i.e. to s_i, obtaining $\min\{t_{i+1} - t, s_{i+1} - s\} \geq 2^{k-1}$ and $t - t_i = s - s_i$. If $s_{i+1} - s \leq s - s_i$ then $\mathbf{D}$ chooses accordingly s.t. $t_{i+1} - t = s_{i+1} - s$.

In both case, we get that $\mathbf{s}'.s$ and $\mathbf{t}'.t$ form a partial isomorphism and respect the assumption of the claim, now for the extended tuple of positions. The same holds analogously if $\mathbf{S}$ chose some position t in v first, in which case $\mathbf{D}$ would be able to respond with a corresponding s in u such that $\mathbf{s}'.s$ and $\mathbf{t}'.t$ equally preserve the claim's assumption. The induction hypothesis then yields that $\mathbf{D}$ wins $\mathcal{G}_k((u, \mathbf{s}'.s), (v, \mathbf{t}'.t))$. But then we can apply Lemma 4.7 (d) and obtain that $\mathbf{D}$ wins $\mathcal{G}_{k+1}((u, \mathbf{s}'), (v, \mathbf{t}'))$ which finishes the proof of the claim. $\qquad\square$

4.2.2 Indistinguishability through First-Order Formulas

The result we are aiming for next states that $\mathbf{D}$ wins the game $\mathcal{G}_k(u, v)$ iff u and v cannot be distinguished by first-order formulas of quantifier depth at most k. This means that there is no such formula φ with $u \vDash \varphi$ and $v \nvDash \varphi$. Since FO and each of its fragments of bounded quantifier depth is closed under negation there is then also no such formula that is satisfied by v but not by u.

In the following, when we speak of formulas we will always mean formulas of FO over predicate symbols of the form $x < y$ and $a(X)$ with $a \in \Sigma$, as defined in Sect. 4.1 above. Formulas like $x = y$ are definable without increasing the quantifier depth of the underlying formula. Formulas of quantifier depth 0 are then Boolean combinations of atomic formulas of the form $x < y$ and $a(x)$. Formulas of quantifier depth $k + 1$ can be regarded as Boolean combinations of formulas of the form $\exists x \, \varphi(x)$ where $\varphi(x)$ has quantifier depth k.

Now suppose that φ is a formula with n free first-order variables $x_0, \ldots, x_{n-1}$, u is a word over the corresponding alphabet, and $\mathbf{s} = (s_0, \ldots, s_{n-1})$ is an n-tuple of positions in u. We then write $u, \mathbf{s} \vDash \varphi$ if u satisfies φ under the variable assignment that interprets each first-order variable x_i by the position s_i. Alternatively, we write $u \vDash \varphi(\mathbf{s})$.

We formalise an equivalence relation on words $u, v \in \Sigma^+$: they are called k-*indistinguishable*, written $u \equiv_k v$ if for all formulas φ without free first-order variables and with $qd(\varphi) \leq k$ we have $u \vDash \varphi$ iff $v \vDash \varphi$.

While we are ultimately interested in exactly this notion of indistinguishability between two words, it is too weak to enable a proof by induction on the structure of formulas because a subformula of a closed formula need not be closed itself. For example, consider $\exists x \, a(x)$. It contains no free first-order variables but $a(x)$ clearly does. We therefore need to generalise this definition.

Definition 4.9 Let $k, n \geq 0$, $u, v \in \Sigma^+$ and $\mathbf{s} = (s_1, \ldots, s_n)$, $\mathbf{t} = (t_1, \ldots, t_n)$ be n-tuples of positions in u, resp. v. We say that $(u, \mathbf{s})$ and $(v, \mathbf{t})$ are (k, n)-*indistinguishable*, written $(u, \mathbf{s}) \equiv_{k,n} (v, \mathbf{t})$, if for all formulas φ with n free variables and $qd(\varphi) \leq k$ we have

$$u, \mathbf{s} \vDash \varphi \quad \text{iff} \quad v, \mathbf{t} \vDash \varphi \, .$$

It should be clear that the special case of $n = 0$ coincides with the notion of indistinguishability between two words as introduced above: $(u, ()) \equiv_{k,0} (v, ())$ iff $u \equiv_k v$.

We can now formulate the result known as the *Ehrenfeucht-Fraïssé Theorem*.

Theorem 4.10 *Let $k \geq 0$, $u, v \in \Sigma^+$. $\mathbf{D}$ wins the game $\mathcal{G}_k(u, v)$ iff $u \equiv_k v$.*

Proof As indicated above, it is helpful to generalise this statement in order to enable a proof by induction. So instead we will show the following stronger statement: let k, u, v be as above and additionally $n \geq 0$ be given and $\mathbf{s} = (s_1, \ldots, s_n)$ be positions in u and $\mathbf{t} = (t_1, \ldots, t_n)$ be positions in v. Then $\mathbf{D}$ has a winning strategy for $\mathcal{G}_k((u, \mathbf{s}), (v, \mathbf{t}))$ iff $(u, \mathbf{s}) \equiv_{k,n} (v, \mathbf{t})$. It should be clear that the theorem's statement follows from this immediately.

"⇒": By contraposition. Let $(u,\mathbf{s}), (v,\mathbf{t})$ be given and suppose there was a $\varphi(x_1,\ldots,x_n)$ with $qd(\varphi) \le k$ such that

$$(u,\mathbf{s}) \vDash \varphi \quad \text{iff} \quad (v,\mathbf{t}) \not\vDash \varphi . \tag{4.1}$$

We will construct a winning strategy for **S** in the game $\mathcal{G}_k((u,\mathbf{s}),(v,\mathbf{t}))$. This is done by a combined induction on k and the (Boolean) structure of φ.

In the base case, we have $qd(\varphi) = 0$ and φ does not feature Boolean operators at its top level. Hence, $\varphi = x_i < x_j$ for some i, j or $\varphi = a(x_i)$ for some i. In the latter case, assumption (4.1) yields $u(s_i) \ne v(t_i)$, since one of them must be a and the other must not. In the former case, we get $s_i < s_j$ and $t_i \ge t_j$, or vice-versa. In all cases, **S** wins $\mathcal{G}_k((u,\mathbf{s}),(v,\mathbf{t}))$ immediately according to Lemma 4.7 (c).

Now suppose that $\varphi = \psi_1 \vee \psi_2$. Then there is an $i \in \{1,2\}$ s.t. $(u,\mathbf{s}) \vDash \psi_i$ iff $(v,\mathbf{t}) \not\vDash \psi_i$, and **S** can simply use his winning strategy that is derived from ψ_i by the induction hypothesis.

Similarly, if $\varphi = \neg\psi$ then we have $(u,\mathbf{s}) \not\vDash \psi$ iff $(v,\mathbf{t}) \vDash \psi$ which is equivalent to saying that $(u,\mathbf{s}) \vDash \psi$ iff $(v,\mathbf{t}) \not\vDash \psi$. Since the truth values have flipped on each side, **S** cannot simply use the same strategy that is derived from ψ to win $\mathcal{G}_k((u,\mathbf{s}),(v,\mathbf{t}))$, but actually the one that is derived from ψ to win $\mathcal{G}_k((v,\mathbf{t}),(u,\mathbf{s}))$.

The only non-trivial case is that of $\varphi = \exists x_i \psi$. Note that $qd(\varphi) > 0$ in this case. According to (4.1) we either have (i) $(u,\mathbf{s}) \vDash \exists x_i \psi$ and $(v,\mathbf{t}) \not\vDash \exists x_i \psi$, or (ii) $(u,\mathbf{s}) \not\vDash \exists x_i \psi$ and $(v,\mathbf{t}) \vDash \exists x_i \psi$. Consider case (i) first. W.l.o.g. we can assume $i = n + 1$ where $n = |\mathbf{s}|$; otherwise one can simply re-arrange the tuple $\mathbf{s}.s$ in the following. From $(u,\mathbf{s}) \vDash \exists x_{n+1} \psi$ we get that there is some s with $0 \le s < |u|$ s.t. $(u,\mathbf{s}.s) \vDash \psi$. On the other hand, from $(v,\mathbf{t}) \not\vDash \exists x_i \psi$ we get that for all t with $0 \le t < |v|$ we have $(v,\mathbf{t}.t) \not\vDash \psi$. This provides **S** with the next step in the game $\mathcal{G}_k((u,\mathbf{s}),(v,\mathbf{t}))$: he chooses position s in u. Note that regardless of which position t in v **D** responds with, the resulting configuration in the game is given by the connections between $\mathbf{s}.s$ and $\mathbf{t}.t$ with $k - 1$ rounds left to play. By the induction hypothesis, **S** wins the game $\mathcal{G}_{k-1}((u,\mathbf{s}.s),(v,\mathbf{t}.t))$. Hence, by Lemma 4.7 (c), he also wins $\mathcal{G}_k((u,\mathbf{s}),(v,\mathbf{t}))$.

Case (ii) is entirely analogous with the only difference being that **S** needs to pick the position in v that witnesses $(v,\mathbf{t}) \vDash \exists x_{n+1} \psi$ instead.

"⇐": Likewise by contraposition. Now we assume that **S** has a winning strategy for $\mathcal{G}_k((u,\mathbf{s}),(v,\mathbf{t}))$ and we construct, by induction on k, a formula $\varphi(x_1,\ldots,x_n)$ with $qd(\varphi)$ that witnesses $(u,\mathbf{s}) \not\equiv_{k,n} (v,\mathbf{t})$.

In the base case, **S** wins $\mathcal{G}_k((u,\mathbf{s}),(v,\mathbf{t}))$ in $k = 0$ rounds, i.e. without making any moves. Hence, according to Lemma 4.7 (a) and (c), we either have $s_i < s_j$ iff $t_i \ge t_j$ for some i, j, or $u(s_i) \ne v(t_i)$ for some i. In the former case, take $\varphi := x_i < x_j$, and in the latter take $\varphi := a(x_i)$ where $a = u(s_i)$. By definition we then have $(u,\mathbf{s}) \vDash \varphi$ and $(v,\mathbf{t}) \not\vDash \varphi$.

In the step case we have $k > 0$, and **S** wins $\mathcal{G}_k((u,\mathbf{s}),(v,\mathbf{t}))$ by first picking a position in either u or v and **D** responding accordingly, and the game continuing just like $\mathcal{G}_{k-1}((u,\mathbf{s}.s),(v,\mathbf{t}.t))$ with s, t being the two selected positions. According to Lemma 4.7 (c), **S** also wins $\mathcal{G}_{k-1}((u,\mathbf{s}.s),(v,\mathbf{t}.t))$, and by the induction hypothesis, there is $\psi(x_0, \ldots, x_n)$ with $qd(\psi) = k - 1$ s.t., w.l.o.g. $(u, \mathbf{s}.s) \models \psi$ and $(v, \mathbf{t}.t) \not\models \psi$. Otherwise, simply continue with $\neg\psi$ instead.

Now suppose that **S** picked position s in u in his first move in $\mathcal{G}_k((u,\mathbf{s}),(v,\mathbf{t}))$. It is tempting to think that $\varphi := \exists x_n \psi$ reflects this on the logical side and can be used to distinguish $(u,\mathbf{s})$ from $(v,\mathbf{t})$. This is too simple, though. It does not suffice to just predict the existence of such a position that **S** chooses in the formula; it is additionally necessary to constrain it with respect to positions already chosen and the letter that is attached to this new position since both are relevant for **S** to win eventually. Hence, we take

$$\varphi(x_0, \ldots, x_{n-1}) \quad := \quad \exists x_n.(\bigwedge_{i \in I^<} x_i < x_n) \wedge (\bigwedge_{i \in I^>} x_n < x_i) \wedge (\bigwedge_{i \in I^=} x_i = x_n) \wedge$$

$$a(x_n) \wedge \psi(x_0, \ldots, x_n)$$

where $a = u(s)$, $I^< := \{i \mid 0 \le i \le n - 1, s_i < s\}$, $I^> := \{i \mid 0 \le i \le n - 1, s_i > s\}$ and $I^= := \{i \mid 0 \le i \le n - 1, s_i = s\}$.

Then we have $(u,\mathbf{s}) \models \varphi$. On the other hand, **S**'s move let him win regardless of **D**'s response with a position t in v. Hence, we have $(v,\mathbf{t}) \not\models \varphi$. Thus, φ distinguishes $(u,\mathbf{s})$ from $(v,\mathbf{t})$, and we clearly have $qd(\varphi) = k$.

The case where **S** picked the position t in v is, again, analoguous. Here, φ is simply constructed according to the letter that position t points to, and its relative position to the others in $\mathbf{t}$, and then negated in the end. $\qquad\qquad\square$

Example 4.11 Reconsider Ex. 4.5 with $u = aabaacaa$ and $v = aacaabaa$. **S** wins $\mathcal{G}_2(u,v)$ but loses $\mathcal{G}_1(u,v)$. Hence, there should be a formula of quantifier depth 2 that distinguishes the two, and it is not hard to construct one:

$$\exists x_1 \exists x_2.x_1 < x_2 \wedge b(x_1) \wedge c(x_2)$$

The formula that can be constructed along the lines of the proof of Thm. 4.10, assuming that **S** picks positions $2, 5$ in u in this order, is

$$\exists x_1.b(x_1) \wedge \exists x_2.x_1 < x_2 \wedge c(x_2)$$

which is clearly equivalent to the one above. Intuitively, it is also clear that no formula of quantifier depth at most one can distinguish u and v: such formulas are Boolean combinations of elementary assertions about the occurrence of particular letters, i.e. they can only distinguish words that differ in their set of occurring letters which is not the case for u and v here.

As a second example, consider $u = aaa$ and $v = aaaa$. Since $|\Sigma| = 1$ for the underlying alphabet Σ, **S** can never win by causing a connection between two positions labelled differently and, hence, we can discard subformulas of the form $a(x)$ from a distinguishing formula.

It is not hard to create such a distinguishing one, for example

$$\varphi \quad := \quad \exists x_1 \exists x_2 \exists x_2.x_1 < x_2 \wedge x_2 < x_3 \wedge \forall x_4.x_4 = x_1 \vee x_4 = x_2 \vee x_4 = x_3$$

demanding models to be of length 3 exactly. Clearly, $qd(\varphi) = 4$. This is not optimal though. Note that φ corresponds to **S**'s strategy to pick the positions $0, 1, 2$ in u and then to pick the one position in v that **D** has not selected in response to the first three moves. **D** then loses as she cannot respond with an unselected position in u.

There is a winning strategy for **S**, though, that leads to an earlier win. The trick is presented in Lemma 4.8 already: by selecting positions that successively halve the distances between word ends or already selected positions, **S** can bring out the difference between u and v in three moves. The corresponding formula of quantifier depth 3 is, for example,

$$\varphi' := \exists x_1 \forall x_2. \bigl(x_2 < x_1 \rightarrow \neg \exists x_3. x_2 < x_3 \wedge x_3 < x_1 \bigr) \wedge$$
$$\bigl(x_1 < x_2 \rightarrow \neg \exists x_3. x_1 < x_3 \wedge x_3 < x_2 \bigr)$$

stating that there is a point (in the middle) such that all points to the left or the right of it are directly adjacent to it. Even though φ' may look more complicated than φ, it is structurally simpler in that its quantifier depth is only 3. It can be obtained from **S**'s strategy as follows: pick position 1 in u. If **D** responds with an extremal position in v, then pick 0 or 2 in u, depending in whether **D** chose 0 or 4 in v. So assume that **D** responded with 1 or 2 in v. The two cases are entirely symmetrical, so assume that it is position 1 which she picked. Then **S** chooses position 3 in v to which **D** can only respond with position 2 in u without losing immediately. This creates the following situation.

Now it is clear that **S** should choose position 2 in v as there is no possible response for **D** without causing the crossing of two edges (at one end). Note how the choosing in u first and then twice in v corresponds to the $\exists \forall \forall$ quantifier structure on all paths of the syntax tree in φ' in negation normal form.

As an application of Thm. 4.10 we prove, as mentioned before, an inexpressibility result for FO.

Theorem 4.12 *The language $L = (aa)^+$ is not FO-definable.*

Proof Suppose L was FO-definable, i.e. there was some FO sentence φ s.t. $L(\varphi) = L$. Then φ would have some quantifier depth, say k. W.l.o.g. we can assume $k > 0$. Let $u = a^{2^k+1}$ and $v = a^{2^k+2}$. Note that $u \notin L$ but $v \in L$. However, according to Lemma 4.8, **D** wins $\mathcal{G}_k(u, v)$, and according to Thm. 4.10, we have $u \in L(\psi)$ iff $v \in L(\psi)$ for all ψ with $qd(\psi) \le k$, in particular for $\psi = \varphi$. But this contradicts the assumption that $L(\varphi) = L$. $\qquad\square$

4.3 Star-Free Expressions

The class of FO-definable languages forms a genuine subclass of the class of regular languages, according to Thm. 2.16 and 4.12. A question that arises, due to the rich variety of characterisations of the class of regular languages, asks for other characterisations of the class of FO-definable languages, for instance an algebraic one comparable to regular expressions.

Likewise, one could search for a restriction on NFA for example in order to obtain a computational model characterising this class. We do not pursue this any further here. Instead, we only remark that it is possible to restrict the model of AFA introduced in Chp. 3 in order to capture the class of FO-definable languages accordingly. We will elaborate on this later on in the context of automata on infinite words.

Definition 4.13 Let Σ be an alphabet. The class of *star-free languages* over Σ, written SF_Σ, is the smallest class of languages over Σ satisfying the following closure properties.

- $\emptyset, \{\varepsilon\}, \{a\} \in \mathrm{SF}_\Sigma$ for any $a \in \Sigma$.
- If $L, L_1, L_2 \in \mathrm{SF}_\Sigma$, then $L_1 L_2, L_1 \cup L_2, \overline{L} \in \mathrm{SF}_\Sigma$.

In other words, SF_Σ is the closure of the class of finite languages under concatenations, unions and complements, just like REG_Σ is its closure under concatenations, unions and Kleene iterations. It may be surprising to note that – with what is to be proved formally below – complementation turns out to be weaker than Kleene iteration with respect to expressive power, at least in the context of concatenation and union. Note though that the class of finite languages is closed under concatenations and unions. Hence, it is fair to say that complementation is weaker than iteration.

As usual, whenever Σ is clear from the context or irrelevant for some central message, we may simply write SF instead of SF_Σ.

As with regular languages, we introduce *star-free expressions* in order to neatly describe star-free languages, for example $\varepsilon + \overline{a\overline{\emptyset}}$ describing the language of all words not starting with an a. Note that here we explicitly introduce ε as an expression while it was only introduced as an abbreviation for regular expressions. The reason simply is that the abbreviation is $\varepsilon := \emptyset^*$, and the Kleene star is of course not available. However, it can also be abbreviated differently, see below.

Note that being star-free for a language L only means that there is *some* expression α that does not use the Kleene star (but perhaps the complementation operator), s.t. $L(\alpha) = L$. It clearly does not mean that *all* expressions describing the language L do not contain the Kleene star. In fact, there are star-free languages which are most naturally described using the Kleene star, for example Σ^*, because of $\Sigma^* = \overline{\emptyset}$. Finding a genuine star-free expression may be more difficult than finding one using the iteration operator.

Lemma 4.14 *If L_1, L_2 are star-free then so are $L_1 \cap L_2$ and $L_1 \setminus L_2$.*

Proof This holds simply because $L_1 \cap L_2 = \overline{\overline{L_1} \cup \overline{L_2}}$ by the deMorgan laws, and then $L_1 \setminus L_2 = L_1 \cap \overline{L_2}$.   □

In fact, SF is closed under all Boolean operators as it is well-known that each of them can be expressed using unions and complements only.

With the help of the lemma above we find that other regular languages are star-free as well.

Example 4.15 Let Σ be an alphabet.

- We have $\{\varepsilon\} = \Sigma^* \setminus \bigcup_{a \in \Sigma} a\Sigma^*$. Hence, there is also a star-free expression describing the language $\{\varepsilon\}$.
- Let $D \subseteq \Sigma$. Note that D in itself is a star-free language. Then D^* is also star-free since $D^* = \Sigma^* \setminus (\Sigma^*(\Sigma \setminus D)\Sigma^*)$.
- The language $(ab)^*$ is star-free since

$$(ab)^* = (((\Sigma^* \setminus b\Sigma^*) \setminus \Sigma^* aa\Sigma^*) \setminus \Sigma^* bb\Sigma^*) \setminus \Sigma^* a \,.$$

4.4 First-Order Equals Star-Freeness

The aim of this section is now to prove that FO over finite words and star-free expressions enjoy the same expressiveness. We start with the simpler part, namely that star-freeness does not exceed the expressive power of First-Order Logic.

4.4.1 From Expressions to Formulas

Remember the convention that logical formulas do not get interpreted over empty domains, in this case, over empty words. We therefore only consider star-free languages $L \subseteq \Sigma^+$ in the following. Again, this is not a restriction since, for any $L \subseteq \Sigma^*$ we have that $L \setminus \{\varepsilon\}$ is star-free iff L is star-free iff $L \cup \{\varepsilon\}$ is star-free. However, in order not to have to deal with ε at all, we have to remove the clause $\{\varepsilon\} \in \mathrm{SF}_\Sigma$, and this could of course be more restrictive than just removing ε from each star-free language, since it would also disallow $\{\varepsilon\}$ as part of the construction of a star-free language. The following technical lemma states that this can indeed be done without causing problems. Its proof is left as an exercise.

Lemma 4.16 *Let $L \subseteq \Sigma^+$ be star-free. Then there is a star-free expression α not using ε as a sub-expression such that $L(\alpha) = L$.*

Theorem 4.17 *Let L be star-free. Then L is FO-definable.*

Proof We construct, for any star-free expression α, an FO formula $\psi_\alpha(x, y)$ s.t. for all words u and positions i, j with $0 \le i \le j < |u|$:

$$u, \{x \mapsto i, y \mapsto j\} \models \psi_\alpha(x, y) \quad \text{iff} \quad u_i \, u_{i+1} \ldots u_j \in L(\alpha) \tag{4.2}$$

According to Lemma 4.16 we can assume α to be ε-free. Hence, the impossible case of $u_i \ldots u_j = \varepsilon$ is irrelevant.

Once $\psi_\alpha(x, y)$ is constructed, we can take $\varphi_\alpha := \psi_\alpha(0, max)$ and get that $u \models \varphi_\alpha$ iff $u \in L(\alpha)$, i.e. an FO sentence defining $L(\alpha)$ has been found.

We construct ψ_α by induction on the structure of α.

- Case $\alpha = \varnothing$. Let $\psi_\varnothing := \text{ff}$.
- Case $\alpha = a$ for some $a \in \Sigma$. Let $\psi_a := a(x) \wedge x = y$.
- Case $\alpha = \beta + \gamma$. Let $\psi_\alpha := \psi_\beta \vee \psi_\gamma$. Note that the two exist by the inductive hypothesis, and if they both satisfy (4.2), then so does ψ_α.
- Case $\alpha = \overline{\beta}$. Likewise, let $\psi_\alpha := \neg\psi_\beta$.
- Case $\alpha = \beta\gamma$. This is the only non-trivial case, and it is here where we need the generalisation of FO-definability of languages of subwords as stated in (4.2). Suppose $\psi_\beta(x, y)$ and $\psi_\gamma(x, y)$ are given by the inductive hypothesis. Let

$$\psi_\alpha(x, y) \; := \; \exists z. x \leq z \wedge z < y \wedge \psi_\beta(x, z) \wedge \psi_\gamma(succ(z), y)$$

where $\psi_\beta(x, z)$ results from $\psi_\beta(x, y)$ by uniformly replacing every free occurrence of y by z, and likewise for ψ_γ.

Note that ψ_α states that the part of a given word u from position x to position y can be split into a part from x to some z inclusively that belongs to the language of β, while the remaining part from z (exclusively) to y belongs to the language of γ. Hence, (4.2) is satisfied for ψ_α as well. $\qquad\square$

4.4.2 From Formulas to Expressions

To show that star-free expressions are as expressive as first-order formulas, we need to do a bit of preliminary work. Recall the relations $\equiv_{k,n}$ on words and interpretations like n-tuples of positions, denoting indistinguishability by FO formulas of quantifier depth at most k with n free variables. Also recall that the *index* of an equivalence relation is the number of its equivalence classes.

We call a formula of quantifier depth at most k and with at most n free variables a (k, n)-formula. The names of the free variables are in fact irrelevant since, in the end, we are only interested in their models as pairs $(u, \mathbf{s})$ of words $u \in \Sigma^+$ and n-tuples $\mathbf{s}$ of positions in u. Hence, it does not matter whether the positions are named $x, y, \ldots$ or $x_1, x_2, \ldots$ in the formula. We will therefore always assume that the free variables of a (k, n)-formula are $x_1, \ldots, x_n$. Note that it can contain other, namely bound variables.

Lemma 4.18 *Let $k, n \geq 0$. The relations $\equiv_{k,n}$ are equivalence relations of finite index.*

Proof It is easy to see that each $\equiv_{k,n}$ is an equivalence relation. The formal proof is left as an exercise.

We show by induction on k that for all $k, n \geq 0$, there are only finitely many mutually inequivalent (k, n)-formulas. The claim then follows from this, since the members of each $\equiv_{k,n}$-equivalence class are uniquely determined by the (k, n)-formulas that they satisfy. According to Lemma 4.4 we can assume formulas to be in negation normal form.

Let $k = 0$. Evidently, a $(0, n)$-formula cannot contain quantifiers. Hence, it is a Boolean combination of literals of the form $a(x_i)$, $\neg a(x_i)$, $x_i < x_j$ and $\neg(x_i < x_j)$ for some $a \in \Sigma$ and i, j with $1 \leq i, j \leq n$. By a standard argument, each such Boolean combination is equivalent to a formula in disjunctive normal form (DNF), i.e. a disjunction of conjunctions of literals of the above form. Now note that there are only finitely many such literals, namely $n_0 := 2 \cdot |\Sigma| \cdot n + 2 \cdot n^2$ many. Because of commutativity, associativity and idempotence of disjunctions, there are at most as many mutually inequivalent conjunctions of such literals as there are sets of such literals. The same then holds for disjunctions of such conjunctions. Hence, there are at most $f(0, n) := 2^{2^{n_0}}$ many $(0, n)$-formulas.

Now suppose there are at most $f(k, n)$ many mutually inequivalent (k, n)-formulas for some given k and n. We need to bound the number $f(k + 1, n)$ of mutually inequivalent $(k + 1, n)$-formulas. Note that a $(k + 1, n)$-formula with free variables $x_1, \ldots, x_n$ can be seen as a Boolean combination of formulas of the form $Qx_i \psi$ where $Q \in \{\exists, \forall\}$, ψ is a $(k, n + 1)$-formula, and $i \in \{1, \ldots, n + 1\}$. This includes the case of formulas of strictly lower quantifier rank, because the quantification may bind a variable that does not occur freely in ψ, as in $\exists x_3 \, x_1 < x_2$ for instance, which is then equivalent to $x_1 < x_2$ and therefore contains strictly less quantifiers.

Again, by a standard argument about propositional logic, such Boolean combinations can be transformed into DNF, leaving at most $f(k + 1, n) := 2^{2^{f(k, n+1)}}$ many mutually inequivalent combinations thereof. $\square$

We write $[(u, \mathbf{s})]_{k,n}$ for the $\equiv_{k,n}$-equivalence class of $(u, \mathbf{s})$, provided that $|\mathbf{s}| = n$.

Again, a (k, n)-formula describes a set of pairs $(u, \mathbf{s})$ of words with an n-tuple of positions in it, i.e. a set of elements of $\Sigma^+ \times \mathbb{N}^n$. We call such sets *generalised languages* when the length of the tuples of positions agrees for all its elements. We use the same notation $L(\varphi)$ as we use for ordinary languages defined by sentences. Note that this is indeed a suitable generalisation, since the generalised language of a $(k, 0)$-formula, i.e. a sentence, is then just its language.

Example 4.19 We analyse $\equiv_{1,1}$ through its equivalence classes over the alphabet $\Sigma = \{a, b\}$. We first enumerate all literals over two free variables, i.e. x_1, x_2 by convention. Since $\neg a(x_i) \equiv b(x_i)$ etc. we only get the following 8.

$$a(x_1), \; b(x_1), \; a(x_2), \; b(x_2), \; x_1 < x_2, \; x_1 \not< x_2, \; x_2 < x_1, \; x_2 \not< x_1$$

Obviously, some of them contradict each other: $a(x_1) \wedge b(x_1) \equiv \text{ff}$ for instance. Others can be simplified as one implies the other, for example $x_1 < x_2 \wedge x_2 \not<$

$x_1 \equiv x_1 < x_2$. Hence, there are strictly less than $2^8 = 256$ mutually inequivalent conjunctions that are not unsatisfiable, but still too many to list them all here. We pick out two.

$$\psi_1 \; := \; a(x_1) \wedge x_1 < x_2$$
$$\psi_2 \; := \; b(x_2) \wedge x_1 \not< x_2 \wedge x_2 \not< x_1$$

Note that unsatisfiability can also occur as a result of conjoining more than two literals. While ψ_2 is satisfiable, $\psi_2 \wedge a(x_1)$ is not since ψ_2 could also be written as $b(x_2) \wedge x_1 = x_2$.

The proof of Lemma 4.18 states that $\equiv_{0,2}$ is characterised by disjunctions of such conjunctions, and there are clearly too many to list them all here. We pick out three, based on ψ_1 and ψ_2 above, namely ψ_1, ψ_2 and $\psi_1 \vee \psi_2$. It is not too hard to describe the $\equiv_{0,2}$-equivalence classes that they induce.

- $L(\psi_1) = \{(uav, (|u|, j)) \mid u \in \Sigma^*, v \in \Sigma^+, |u| < j < |uav|\}$.
- $L(\psi_2) = \{(ubv, (|u|, |u|)) \mid u, v \in \Sigma^*\}$.

Clearly, $\psi_1 \vee \psi_2$ simply describes the union of these two sets.

Now consider $\equiv_{1,1}$. According to the proof of Lemma 4.18, it suffices to consider Boolean combinations of formulas of the form $Qx_i\,\psi$, where ψ is a $(0,2)$-formula (like those above), $Q \in \{\exists, \forall\}$ and $i \in \{1,2,3\}$. This yields – amongst many others – for instance

- $L(\exists x_1\,\psi_1(x_1, x_2)) = \{(uav, j) \mid u \in \Sigma^*, v \in \Sigma^+, |u| < j < |uav|\}$;
- $L(\forall x_1.x_1 \not< x_2 \vee a(x_2)) = \{(a^j w, j) \mid w \in \{a, b\}^+, j \geq 0\}$;
- $L(\forall x_1\,\psi_2(x_1, x_2)) = \{(b, 0)\}$. It is also equivalent to $\forall x_2\,\psi_2(x_1, x_2)$.

Again, in order to characterise $\equiv_{1,1}$ fully, one would then have to consider genuine Boolean combinations on top of these.

Lemma 4.20 *Let $k, n \geq 0$ and W be an equivalence class of $\equiv_{k,n}$. There is a (k,n)-formula χ_W such that $qd(\chi_W) = k$ and for all $(u, \mathbf{s})$ we have*

$$(u, \mathbf{s}) \vDash \chi_W \quad iff \quad (u, \mathbf{s}) \in W .$$

Proof Let k, n be given. According to Lemma 4.18 there are only finitely many (k, n)-formulas up to equivalence. Let $\Phi_{k,n}$ be the set of all these. Suppose W is an equivalence class of $\equiv_{k,n}$. Take an arbitrary representative $(u_0, \mathbf{s}_0) \in W$ and let

$$\chi_W \; := \; \bigwedge \{\varphi \in \Phi_{k,n} \mid u_0, \mathbf{s}_0 \vDash \varphi\} .$$

Since $\Phi_{k,n}$ is closed under negations (up to equivalence) it suffices to conjoin all formulas that are satisfied by $(u_0, \mathbf{s}_0)$, and it is not necessary to explicitly include the negations of those formulas that are not satisfied by $(u_0, \mathbf{s}_0)$.

Because of finiteness of $\Phi_{k,n}$ as well as independence of the exact choice of $(u_0, \mathbf{s}_0)$, χ_W is well-defined. Moreover, it should be clear that $qd(\chi_W) = k$ as it is a Boolean combination of formulas of quantifier depth at most k.

It remains to be seen that χ_W defines W in the sense of the lemma's statement.

"$\Rightarrow$" Suppose $(u,\mathbf{s}) \vDash \chi_W$. We need to see that $u,\mathbf{s} \equiv_{k,n} u_0,\mathbf{s}_0$. Suppose this was not the case. Then there would be some $\psi(\mathbf{x})$ with $qd(\psi) = k$ s.t. $u_0,\mathbf{s}_0 \vDash \psi(\mathbf{x})$ but $u,\mathbf{s} \nvDash \psi(\mathbf{x})$ (or vice-versa). According to Lemma 4.18, ψ is equivalent to some $\varphi \in \Phi_k$. I.e. we have $u_0,\mathbf{s}_0 \vDash \varphi$ but $u,\mathbf{s} \nvDash \varphi$. But then $u,\mathbf{s} \nvDash \chi_W$ since χ_W contains the conjunct φ, contradicting the initial assumption. The same holds if $u_0,\mathbf{s}_0 \nvDash \psi$ but $u,\mathbf{s} \vDash \psi$.

"$\Leftarrow$" Suppose $(u,\mathbf{s}) \in W$, i.e. $u,\mathbf{s} \equiv_{k,n} u_0,\mathbf{s}_0$. Hence, $u,\mathbf{s} \vDash \varphi$ for all $\varphi \in \Phi_{k,n}$ s.t. $u_0,\mathbf{s}_0 \vDash \varphi$. But then $u,\mathbf{s} \vDash \chi_W$. $\qquad\qquad\qquad\qquad\square$

Lemma 4.21 *Let $k,n \geq 0$ and $L \subseteq \Sigma^+ \times \mathbb{N}^n$ be a generalised language s.t. $L = L(\varphi)$ for some $\varphi \in \Phi_{k,n}$. Then L is a finite union of $\equiv_{k,n}$-equivalence classes.*

Proof Let $L = L(\varphi)$ for a (k,n)-formula φ and W be a $\equiv_{k,n}$-equivalence class. We observe that then either $W \subseteq L$ or $W \cap L = \varnothing$: take some $(u,\mathbf{s}) \in W$. Clearly, either $(u,\mathbf{s}) \in L$ and therefore $u,\mathbf{s} \vDash \varphi$, or $(u,\mathbf{s}) \notin L$ and therefore $u,\mathbf{s} \nvDash \varphi$.

Now take another $(s,\mathbf{t}) \in W$. By definition, we have $v,\mathbf{t} \equiv_{k,n} u,\mathbf{s}$, in particular $v,\mathbf{t} \vDash \varphi$ iff $u,\mathbf{s} \vDash \varphi$, i.e. $(v,\mathbf{t}) \in L$ iff $(u,\mathbf{s}) \in L$ and therefore $W \subseteq L$ if $(u,\mathbf{s}) \in L$, and $W \cap L = \varnothing$ if $(u,\mathbf{s}) \notin L$.

Since every $\equiv_{k,n}$-equivalence class is either contained in L entirely or disjoint from it, and there are only finitely many such equivalence classes according to Lemma 4.18, L is the necessarily finite union of those equivalence classes that are contained in it. $\qquad\qquad\qquad\qquad\square$

This is almost sufficient to show the converse of Thm. 4.17. In order to prove the following theorem by induction on the structure and quantifier depth of φ, we need to generalise the statement accordingly. As usual, subformulas of sentences may not be sentences themselves. Hence, the inductive invariant needs to take care of free variables. This is not a problem for the assumption in the theorem's statement. A formula $\varphi(\mathbf{x})$ over n free variables gets interpreted by a word and an n-tuple of positions, i.e. it defines a generalised language in the sense above.

We therefore need to generalise the concept on the conclusion side accordingly, i.e. we need a notion of star-freeness of sets $\{(u_0,\mathbf{s}_0),(u_1,\mathbf{s}_1),\dots\}$ where $|\mathbf{s}_i| = |\mathbf{s}_j|$ for all i,j. In order to obtain this, we can simply reuse the trick seen in the translation of MSO formulas into automata (see Sect. 2.2.2), accepting words that are enriched with extra tracks representing the evaluation of second-order variables. Likewise, we consider a generalised language of pairs of words u over Σ and a tuple $\mathbf{s} = (s_1,\dots,s_n)$ of n positions in this word as star-free, if the language of words that equip such u with n additional tracks of the form $0^{s_1} 10^{|u|-s_1-1}, 0^{s_2} 10^{|u|-s_2-1}, \dots, 0^{s_n} 10^{|u|-s_n-1}$ is star-free over $\Sigma \times \{0,1\}^n$.

For example, the pair $(aabaacaa,(5,2))$ consisting of a word over $\Sigma = \{a,b,c\}$ and two positions in it is encoded as the word

$$\begin{pmatrix}0\\0\\a\end{pmatrix}\begin{pmatrix}0\\0\\a\end{pmatrix}\begin{pmatrix}1\\0\\b\end{pmatrix}\begin{pmatrix}0\\0\\a\end{pmatrix}\begin{pmatrix}0\\0\\a\end{pmatrix}\begin{pmatrix}0\\1\\c\end{pmatrix}\begin{pmatrix}0\\0\\a\end{pmatrix}\begin{pmatrix}0\\0\\a\end{pmatrix}$$

over $\Sigma \times \{0,1\}^2$.

Clearly, not every element of $\Sigma \times \{0,1\}^n$ represents a valid encoding of a pair $(u, \mathbf{s})$. A *well-formed word* of this form is one in which every additional track contains the symbol 1 exactly once. Note that the set WF_n of well-formed representations of words with n positions is star-free, since it can be constructed as follows. Let Σ, n be given and define $\Delta := \Sigma \times \{0,1\}^n$ and $\Delta_{i=d} := \Sigma \times \{0,1\}^{i-1} \times \{d\} \times \{0,1\}^{n-i}$ for $i \in \{1, \ldots, n\}$, $d \in \{0,1\}$. Note that these are finite sets of alphabet symbols, hence, their Kleene iteration is star-free. Then we have

$$WF_n \;=\; \Delta^* \setminus \Big(\bigcup_{i=1}^{n} \Delta_{i=0}^* \Big) \setminus \Big(\bigcup_{i=1}^{n} \Delta^* \Delta_{i=1} \Delta^* \Delta_{i=1} \Delta^* \Big) .$$

Note that the operations on generalised languages suitably generalise the star-free operations on languages. Hence, a star-free generalised language of elements of the form $(u, ())$ is just a star-free language in the usual sense. However, concatenation extends the number of additional tracks in order to ensure well-formedness.

Theorem 4.22 *Let $\varphi \in FO$. Then $L(\varphi)$ is star-free.*

Proof We show, by induction on the structure and quantifier depth of φ, that any $\varphi(\mathbf{x}) \in FO$ defines a star-free (generalised) language over an enriched alphabet as shown above. We do not assume φ to be given in negation normal form but use the original syntax with negations and existential quantifications only. A sentence then defines an ordinary star-free language. Let Δ and $\Delta_{i=d}$ be defined as above for given Σ, n that will be clear from the context. Additionally, let $\Delta_a := \{a\} \times \{0,1\}^n$ for $a \in \Sigma$.

As usual, w.l.o.g. we can assume the free variables of φ to be $\mathbf{x} = (x_1, \ldots, x_n)$.

In the base case, we have $\varphi(\mathbf{x}) = a(x_i)$ or $\varphi(\mathbf{x}) = x_i < x_j$. They define, respectively, the generalised and star-free languages

$$
\begin{aligned}
L(a(x_i)) \;&=\; \{(uav, (s_1, \ldots, s_n)) \mid u, v \in \Sigma^*, s_i = |u|\} \\
&=\; \Big(\Delta \setminus \bigcup_{\substack{b \in \Sigma \\ b \neq a}} (\Delta_b \cap \Delta_{i=1}) \Big)^* \cap WF_n
\end{aligned}
$$

and

$$
L(x_i < x_j) \;=\; \{(u, (s_1, \ldots, s_n)) \mid u \in \Sigma^+, s_i < s_j\} \;=\; \Delta^* \Delta_{i=1} \Delta^* \Delta_{j=1} \Delta^* \cap WF_n \, .
$$

The cases of $\varphi(\mathbf{x}) = \psi_1(\mathbf{x}) \vee \psi_2(\mathbf{x})$ and $\varphi(\mathbf{x}) = \neg\psi(\mathbf{x})$ are covered by the fact that star-free languages are closed under unions and complementations.

The only interesting case is that of existential quantification. By renaming variables suitably, we can restrict attention to formulas of the form $\varphi(x_1, \ldots, x_n) = \exists x_{n+1} \, \psi(x_1, \ldots, x_{n+1})$. Suppose $qd(\varphi) = k + 1$ for some $k \geq 0$. According to the induction hypothesis, $\psi(x_1, \ldots, x_{n+1})$ defines a star-free language (over an alphabet with $n + 1$ additional tracks).

Claim. We have

$$L(\varphi) \;=\; L(\exists x_{n+1} \psi) \;=\; \{(uav, \mathbf{r}) \mid u, v \in \Sigma^*, a \in \Sigma, (uav, \mathbf{r}.|u|) \models \psi\}$$

$$= \bigcup_{a \in \Sigma} \bigcup_{m=0}^{n} \bigcup_{\substack{u,v,s,t \\ |s|=m, |t|=n-m \\ (uav, s.t.|u|) \models \psi}} [(u, \mathbf{s})]_{k,m} a [(v, \mathbf{t})]_{k, n-m}$$

Before we prove the claim, we note that this shows that $L(\varphi)$ is indeed star-free. By the hypothesis (on quantifier depth), $[u]_{k,n_1}$ and $[v]_{k,n_2}$ are star-free languages. This follows from Lemma 4.20 which states that these can be defined by characteristic formulas of quantifier depth k, i.e. smaller than that of φ. So we can apply the induction hypothesis to them and obtain their star-freeness. The first two unions are clearly finite, and the third one is finite by Lemma 4.18 stating that while there are infinitely many words u and v in general, there are only finitely many equivalence classes for them.

It remains to be seen that the claim is true.

"$\subseteq$" Suppose $(w, \mathbf{r}) \in L(\varphi)$, i.e. $w, \mathbf{r} \models \exists x_{n+1} \psi$. Hence, w must contain some position i s.t. $w, \mathbf{r}.i \models \psi$. But then w must be of the form uav for some $a \in \Sigma$, $u, v \in \Sigma^*$ s.t. $uav, \mathbf{r}.|u| \models \psi$. Let $\mathbf{r}$ be split into tuples $\mathbf{s}$ and $\mathbf{t}$ of positions less, respective greater than $|u|$, and of length n_1 and n_2 respectively, i.e. $n_1 + n_2 = n$. W.l.o.g. we assume $\mathbf{r} = \mathbf{s}.\mathbf{t}$. Then we have

$$w, \mathbf{r} \;\in\; \{(u, \mathbf{s})\}\{(a, 0)\}\{(v, \mathbf{t})\} \;\subseteq\; [(u, \mathbf{s})]_{k,n_1} \{a\} [(v, \mathbf{t})]_{k,n_2} \, .$$

"$\supseteq$" Suppose $(w, \mathbf{r}) \in [(u, \mathbf{s})]_{k,n_1} \{a\} [(v, \mathbf{t})]_{k,n_2}$ for some $a \in \Sigma$, $u, v \in \Sigma^*$ and m, resp. $n - m$ positions $\mathbf{s}, \mathbf{t}$ in u, resp. v, where $n = |\mathbf{r}|$, such that $uav, \mathbf{s}.\mathbf{t}.|u| \models \psi$. Hence, w must be of the form $u'av'$, and there must be tuples of positions $\mathbf{s}'$ in u' and $\mathbf{t}'$ in v' such that $u', \mathbf{s}' \equiv_{k,m} u, \mathbf{s}$ and $v', \mathbf{t}' \equiv_{k,n-m} v, \mathbf{t}$. We claim that $u'av', \mathbf{s}'.\mathbf{t}'.|u'| \models \psi$ as well.

Consider the generalised EF game $\mathcal{G}_k(uav, \mathbf{s}.\mathbf{t}.|u|, u'av', \mathbf{s}'.\mathbf{t}'.|u'|)$, in which there is an initial connection between position $|u|$ in uav and $|u'|$ in $u'av'$ that separates both words into their parts u, v, resp. u', v'. Moreover, the connections between $\mathbf{s}$ and $\mathbf{s}'$ are not crossing it, and neither are those between $\mathbf{t}$ and $\mathbf{t}'$. The assumptions that $u, \mathbf{s} \equiv_{k,m} u', \mathbf{s}'$ and $v, \mathbf{t} \equiv_{k,n-m} v', \mathbf{t}'$ yield that $\mathbf{D}$ has winning strategies for both the games $\mathcal{G}_k(u, \mathbf{s}, u', \mathbf{s}')$ and $\mathcal{G}_k(v, \mathbf{t}, v', \mathbf{t}')$ according to Thm. 4.10. It is then not hard to see that she also wins $\mathcal{G}_k(uav, \mathbf{s}.\mathbf{t}.|u|, u'av', \mathbf{s}'.\mathbf{t}'.|u'|)$: whenever $\mathbf{S}$ chooses a position in u or u', she responds with a corresponding move as if $\mathbf{S}$ had done his choice in the game $\mathcal{G}_k(u, \mathbf{s}, u', \mathbf{s}')$, and likewise for $\mathbf{S}$'s moves in v or v' (with indices shifted by $|u| + 1$, resp. $|u'| + 1$ accordingly). This way, she avoids crossing existing edges between $\mathbf{s}$ and $\mathbf{s}'$, resp. $\mathbf{t}$ and $\mathbf{t}'$ by copying her winning strategy moves in the games on the smaller words. She also avoids crossing the edge from $|u|$ in uav to $|u'|$ in $u'av'$ because she only ever responds with a position on the same side of that connection that $\mathbf{S}$ picked his position in. But then we can apply Thm. 4.10 again and obtain that $uav, \mathbf{s}.\mathbf{t}.|u| \equiv_{k,n} u'av', \mathbf{s}'.\mathbf{t}'.|u'|$ and, hence, we must have $u'av', \mathbf{s}'.\mathbf{t}'.|u'| \models \psi$ as well. Since $w = u'av'$ and $\mathbf{r} = \mathbf{s}.\mathbf{t}$ by assumption, we then get $w, \mathbf{r}.|u'| \models \psi$, resp. $w, \mathbf{r} \models \exists x_{n+1} \psi$ which was to be proved. $\square$

Bibliographic Notes

The class of star-free languages has attracted much attention, due to its natural definition that is very close to that of the class of regular languages, with complementation instead of Kleene iteration, and the intriguing result that, amongst the two, Kleene iteration is in fact stronger w.r.t. expressiveness.

There are many known different characterisations of the class of star-free languages besides the one presented here via First-Order Logic which is due to McNaughton and Papert [MP71], see also the book by Straubing [Str94] or the handbook article by Thomas [Tho97].

The model-distinguishing games known as Ehrenfeucht-Fraïssé games have been developed, as the name suggests, by Ehrenfeucht [Ehr61] and, earlier already but probably with lesser immediate outreach by Fraïssé [Fra54] as this was published in French. It is worth noting that EF-games are not restricted to words, let alone finite ones. They are an important tool not only in the theory of formal languages as presented here, but in overall finite model theory and descriptive complexity theory in order to characterise the expressive power of First-Order Logic over any kinds of structures like graphs, etc. EF games are covered widely in the literature, for instance in Immerman's book on descriptive complexity [Imm99], Thomas' handbook article [Tho97] or Kolaitis's article [Kol07] in the book on finite model theory by Grädel et al. [GKL$^+$07].

There is a part of the algebraic theory of formal languages and logic that is not covered in this book which characterises languages by their syntactic monoids, and languages classes by classes of monoids. This goes back to the otherwise (without necessarily coming across monoids) well-known *Myhill-Nerode Theorem* [Ner58], and is covered in a variety of works, for instance the aforementioned book by McNaughton and Papert [MP71]. Schützenberger showed that the star-free languages correspond exactly to the class of aperiodic monoids [Sch65]. This is also intuitively linked to characterisations via counter-free automata, cf. Wilke's comprehensive article [Wil99a].

For a detailed overview of various characterisations of star-free languages and further pointers into the literature, see also the article by Diekert and Gastin [DG08]. It deals not only with the case of finite words, as is done in this chapter, but also with star-free languages of and First-Order Logic on infinite words (as well as such generalisations of the other characterisations). Automata and logic on infinite words is the topic of the next part of this book, but we will not have a closer look at star-free languages of infinite words anymore. It has to be said that, not only is there a visible increase in combinatorial complexity in the study of First-Order Logic compared to Second-Order Logic, things become even more complex for First-Order Logic on infinite words, while the increase in difficulty for Monadic Second-Order Logic is much more manageable.

The study of star-free languages and First-Order Logic on infinite words is mainly due to Thomas [Tho79, Tho81] with contributions by Ladner [Lad77] and Perrin and Pin [PP86]. Again, the aforementioned overview article by Diekert and Gastin [DG08] surveys results in this area nicely.

Another logical characterisation of star-free languages, which is mainly interesting in the context of infinite words, is provided by Linear-Time Temporal Logic (LTL), cf. [Pnu77]. It is known to be equi-expressive to First-Order Logic and, while the embedding of LTL into FO is trivial, the other direction, due to Kamp [Kam68] and also Gabbay et al. [GPSS80], bears much of the aforementioned combinatorial difficulty of star-free languages on infinite words. LTL will be studied separately in Chp. 10.

Exercises

Exercise 32 Determine the minimal k for which **S** wins $\mathcal{G}_k(u, v)$ for the following words u and v.

a) $u = aabaabaaba$ and $v = abaabaabaa$,
b) $u = a^n ba^{n+1}$ and $v = a^{n+1} ba^n$ for some $n \in \mathbb{N}$.

Exercise 33 Let $w, v \in \Sigma^+$ s.t. $w \neq v$. Construct an FO formula that distinguishes the two, i.e. that is satisfied by one but not the other.

Exercise 34 a) Formally define the k-round EF game $\mathcal{G}_k(u, v)$ on words $u, v \in \Sigma^+$ as a reachability game in the sense of Sect. 3.4.
b) Let $u = aaa$ and $v = aaaa$. Construct the graph of the EF game $\mathcal{G}_2(u, v)$ as a reachability game.

Exercise 35 Prove Lemma 4.7.

Exercise 36 Transform the distinguishing formulas in Ex. 4.11 into prenex normal form, i.e. into the form $Q_n x_n \ldots Q_1 x_1 \psi$ for suitable variables $x_1, \ldots, x_n$, $Q_1, \ldots, Q_n \in \{\exists, \forall\}$ and ψ quantifier-free.
Do this transformation preserve the quantifier depth?

Exercise 37 Show that $L = (ab + ba)^*$ is star-free. *Hint:* Take the natural three-state DFA for L.

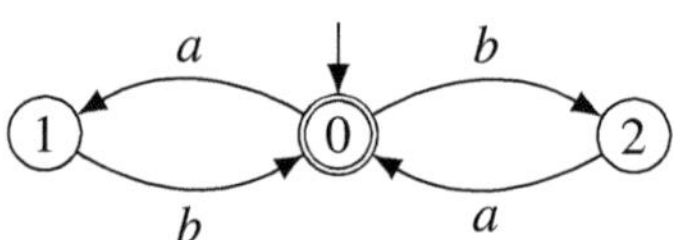

The key observation here is that it is the star-free languages $(ba)^* b$, resp. $(ab)^* a$ that take this automaton from state 1 to 2, resp. vice-versa, and that the automaton must be in state 1 after reading aa, resp. in state 2 after reading bb. Thus, take some $w \in (ab + ba)^*$, and suppose that $w = xaayaaz$ for some $x, y, z \in \Sigma^*$. Then y cannot be of the form $(ba)^* b$. An analogous consideration needs to be made for occurrences of bb. At last, w cannot begin or end with a repeated letter.

These observations can now be turned into restrictions in order to build a star-free expression of the form $\Sigma^* \setminus \ldots$ for the language in question.

Exercise 38 Show that $L = (aa + bb)^*$ is not star-free. *Hint:* Show that for any k there are words u, v with $u \in L$, $v \notin L$, s.t. **D** wins $\mathcal{G}_k(u, v)$. Then argue formally why this is sufficient to refute star-freeness of L.

Exercise 39 Prove Lemma 4.16.

Exercise 40 Show that $\equiv_{k,n}$ is an equivalence relation for any $k, n \geq 0$.

Exercise 41 Give an upper bound on the number of equivalence classes of $\equiv_{k,n}$ for $k, n \geq 0$, that is asymptotically as small as possible. *Hint:* Solve the recurrence for $f(k, n)$ in the proof of Lemma 4.18. Then argue that, despite each $\equiv_{k,n}$-equivalence class being determined by the *set* of (k, n)-formulas that are true on its members, the number of such classes is not exponential in $f(k, n)$ but is already bounded by $f(k, n)$.

Exercise 42 Determine all satisfiable conjunctions of the 8 literals from the beginning of Ex. 4.19.

Part II
Infinite Words

Chapter 5
Automata on Infinite Words

This second part is concerned with the definability of sets of *infinite* sequences of symbols using finite automata. The fact that an automaton should process an infinite word may seem unnatural at first, especially when using the intuition that the automaton works through the input symbols one by one starting from the beginning of the word. However, when we think of acceptance as of the existence of a run, i.e. a consistent decoration of input positions with states, then the generalisation from finite to infinite inputs is rather natural.

Moreover, finite sequences and their recognisability by automata have several applications in the theory of programming, most of all the following two: finite words can be seen as encodings of inputs to a program like the binary representation of a number or an adjacency list representation of a (finite) graph. Regularity on finite words then captures notions of well-formed inputs.

Secondly, words also occur as the observed behaviour of programs, for example by associating each step in a stepwise execution with a particular action like setting a particular bit, sending some data along some channel, etc. Clearly, terminating programs give rise to finite words in this sense, but – whereas non-termination may have been regarded as faulty behaviour in the early days of programming – it has long been seen as natural behaviour for many programs, for instance arising in reactive systems, operating systems, etc. Hence, a theory of definability of languages of infinite words by means of finite automata and logics provides the basis for methods in the specification and verification of reactive programs.

The step from finite to infinite words in terms of runs of finite automata is not such a big one. Clearly, acceptance cannot be explained anymore by what happens "at the end of the run" as there is no designated end moment. It is reasonable to complement the inherently local condition on the labelling of a word by automaton states, saying that it needs to follow the transition relation, by a global condition making demands on what happens "in the infinite", leading to what is called an *acceptance condition*.

A very natural one is the so-called *Büchi-condition*: a run is accepting if it keeps visiting designated states infinitely often. These states take over the role of the final or accepting states in an NFA, and it is now less appropriate to call them final as this may appeal too much to the notion of occurring "at the end". Hence, we will stick to

© The Author(s), under exclusive
license to Springer-Verlag GmbH, DE, part of Springer Nature 2025
M. Hofmann and M. Lange, *Automata Theory and Logic*,
https://doi.org/10.1007/978-3-662-72154-4_5

calling them *accepting*. Automata equipped with such an acceptance condition are called *Büchi automata*.

Many of the algorithmic problems considered in the context of finite automata on finite words carry over directly to the world of infinite words. For example, the emptiness problem is: given a Büchi automaton, does it accept some word? Note that the word itself need not be written down anywhere. Likewise, equivalence and inclusion problems between such automata are also well-defined.

The word problem does not carry over straightforwardly because here, a word is part of the input together with an automaton, and an infinite word cannot be represented finitely in general. It is possible, though, to restrict this for instance to infinite words of a specific, repetitive form that has natural finite presentations.

We start by defining infinite words formally and turn our attention to finite automata recognising languages thereof. We will see that the step from finite to infinite words introduces additional difficulties in the algorithmic treatment of the associated decision problems, and also that the results known from the world of finite words do not always carry over to the world of infinite words. However, the theory is rich enough to provide the algorithmic solutions for problems arising with logic, specifically Monadic Second-Order Logic again, this time naturally interpreted over infinite words.

5.1 Regular Languages of Infinite Words

5.1.1 Infinite Words

Let Σ be a finite alphabet, as usual. An *infinite word* (over Σ), or ω-word, is an infinite sequence $w = a_0 a_1 \ldots$ with $a_i \in \Sigma$ for all $i \in \mathbb{N}$. We write Σ^ω, in analogy to the notion Σ^*, for the set of all infinite words over Σ.

In ordinal set theory, the symbol ω is also used to denote the (ordered) natural numbers. Hence Σ^ω can be read as the set of all total functions from natural numbers to Σ, and each ω-word is in fact a representation of such a function and vice-versa. However, here it is more convenient to read X^ω as the infinite iteration of symbols in X through concatenation. For example, ba^ω is used to denote the infinite word that starts with b and has a at all following positions.

A subset $L \subseteq \Sigma^\omega$ is called an *ω-language*. We will often drop the explicit referral to ω and simply speak of words and languages when in fact we mean ω-words and ω-languages as these are the primary objects of interest in this entire Part II of this book. We will instead explicitly point out when words are supposed to be finite, or languages are sets of finite words. Note that these may well occur as building blocks for the corresponding ω-words and -languages.

Let $w \in \Sigma^\omega$ and $i \in \mathbb{N}$. As before, we write $w(i)$ for the i-th letter in w, i.e. $w = w(0)w(1)\ldots$. Let $a \in \Sigma$. We write $|w|_a$ for the number of occurrences of the letter a in w, and $|w|_a = \infty$ is of course possible. In fact, the pigeon-hole principle demands that for any $w \in \Sigma^\omega$ there is at least some $a \in \Sigma$ s.t. $|w|_a = \infty$.

Infinite words cannot be concatenated, intuitively because there is no end. So it is impossible to first traverse one word until its end, and then traverse the other. More formally, let $u, v \in \Sigma^\omega$. The concatenation of u with v should respect the orders of letters within each word, and additionally that all the letters in u occur before all the letters in v. Thus, the letter $v(0)$ would have to be placed at a position $i \in \mathbb{N}$, for which there are infinitely many positions $j < i$ providing space for the letters in u. But no such natural number i exists.

It is, however, possible to define the left-concatenation of an infinite word with a finite one. Let $v \in \Sigma^*$ and $w \in \Sigma^\omega$. Then vw is the unique ω-word defined by

$$
(vw)(i) \;=\; \begin{cases} v(i) & , \text{ if } i < |v|\,, \\ w(i - |v|) & , \text{ otherwise.} \end{cases}
$$

This can be extended to a left-concatenation of an ω-language with a language of finite words in the natural way: if $U \subseteq \Sigma^*$ and $L \subseteq \Sigma^\omega$, then $UL := \{uw \mid u \in U, w \in L\} \subseteq \Sigma^\omega$.

Likewise, given some $u \in \Sigma^+$, $u^\omega = uuu\ldots$ is the unique ω-word resulting from concatenating u infinitely often. Note that $\varepsilon^\omega \notin \Sigma^\omega$, and this is why we required $u \in \Sigma^+$.

Again, the operation of ω-iteration is lifted to languages in the natural way. Let $U \subseteq \Sigma^+$. Then $U^\omega := \{u_0 u_1 u_2 \ldots \mid u_i \in U \text{ for all } i \in \mathbb{N}\}$. This could even be made well-defined for $U \subseteq \Sigma^*$, provided that $U \neq \{\varepsilon\}$, but then we would have to additionally require $u_i \in U \setminus \{\varepsilon\}$ for infinitely many i.

Example 5.1 Let $\Sigma = \{a, b\}$. The set of all ω-words that contain infinitely many symbols b, such that in between each pair there is an even number of symbols a, can be described as $((aa)^* b)^\omega$. The notation is, strictly speaking, not defined. It appeals to the reader to take $(aa)^* b$ as a regular expression, i.e. a description of a language of finite words, in this case clearly non-empty. Then $((aa)^* b)^\omega$ can be read as the ω-language resulting from the infinite iteration of that language, and this clearly corresponds to the informal description given at the beginning.

Similarly, $(a^* b)^\omega \cap (b^* a)^\omega$ describes the set $\{w \in \Sigma^\omega \mid |w|_a = \infty = |w|_b\}$ where $\Sigma = \{a, b\}$. It can also be described as $\Sigma^\omega \setminus \Sigma^* (a^\omega \cup b^\omega)$.

5.1.2 ω-Regular Expressions

The class REG of regular languages undoubtedly forms an important and interesting object of study in the theory of formal languages because of its robustness, i.e. the fact that many natural algebraic, automata-theoretic, logical, etc. formalisms define exactly this class, and because of the fact that so many decision problems associated with such formalisms are decidable.

A natural question that arises concerns the ability to define an analogue of REG for infinite words, i.e. a class of *regular ω-languages*, often also called ω-regular languages. The answer is yes; we give a construction via so-called *ω-regular expressions*. Their structure may seem rather arbitrary at first sight, but it arises naturally in the following way.

A naïve attempt to define *ω*-regular expressions consists of extending ordinary regular expressions by introducing the infinite iteration operator $\cdot^{\omega}$. It is not hard to see, though, that this causes problems. For instance, α^{ω} is only well-defined when α describes a language of *finite* words that is not just $\{\varepsilon\}$. On the other hand, if α does this, then α^{ω} describes a language of *infinite* words. Thus, a simple extension by throwing in one more operator is unsuitable; one would at least have to distinguish two types of descriptions: those for finite and those for infinite words. This can easily be done. We then note that, while $\cdot^{\omega}$ turns something of type "finite" into something of type "infinite", there is nothing doing the opposite, at least no operation that immediately arises from the regular ones like union, concatenation and Kleene iteration. But we need to consider their effect on languages of type "infinite".

Clearly, the union of two *ω*-languages is, again, an *ω*-language. But concatenation is only meaningful when the left argument is a language of type "finite". Therefore, *ω*-languages can also not be iterated, neither by finite, let alone by infinite iteration. This leads to the following grammar for *ω*-regular expressions.

Definition 5.2 Let Σ be an alphabet. The set of *ω-regular expressions* over Σ is given by α in the following grammar.

$$\alpha \ ::= \ \varnothing \mid \alpha + \alpha \mid \beta\alpha \mid \beta^{\omega} \qquad\qquad \beta \ ::= \ a \mid \beta + \beta \mid \beta\beta \mid \beta^{*}$$

where $a \in \Sigma$. As before, we may also sometimes write $\alpha \cup \alpha'$ instead of $\alpha + \alpha'$ etc.

The separation into α and β realises the necessity of introducing two types. Note, though, that β does not derive expressions for all regular languages but only for those non-empty ones that do not contain ε. This avoids problems with ε in the infinite iteration. The price to pay is the shift of $\varnothing$ to the type of infinite languages.

Definition 5.3 Let Σ be an alphabet. The *language $L(\alpha)$* of an *ω*-regular expression α is defined recursively as follows, assuming that for each regular expression β of finite words, $L(\beta)$ is exactly that set of finite words described by β.

$$\begin{aligned}
L(\varnothing) &:= \varnothing & L(\alpha + \alpha') &:= L(\alpha) \cup L(\alpha') \\
L(\beta\alpha) &:= L(\beta)L(\alpha) & L(\beta^{\omega}) &:= (L(\beta))^{\omega}
\end{aligned}$$

An *ω*-language L is called *(ω)-regular* if there is an *ω*-regular expression α s.t. $L = L(\alpha)$. The class of all *ω*-regular languages over Σ is denoted $\omega\text{--REG}_{\Sigma}$. Again, if Σ is clear from context, we may simply write ω-REG.

We will also often write α instead of $L(\alpha)$, for instance as in $L = ((a + b)b)^{\omega}$, when it is clear whether we are referring to the expression α or the language that it defines.

It is not hard to see that *ω*-regular expressions enjoy a normal form.

Lemma 5.4 *Let $L \subseteq \Sigma^\omega$. Then L is ω-regular iff there are $n \geq 0$ and $U_1, \ldots, U_n$, $V_1, \ldots, V_n \in REG_\Sigma$ s.t. $\varepsilon \notin V_i$ for all $i = 1, \ldots, n$ and*

$$L = \bigcup_{i=1}^{n} U_i V_i^\omega .$$

Proof "$\Leftarrow$" It suffices to see that $\bigcup_{i=1}^{n} U_i V_i^\omega$ is essentially an ω-regular expression, provided that the U_i, V_i are given by regular expressions. Note that, if $\varepsilon \in U_i$ for some i, then we have $U_i V_i^\omega = V_i^\omega \cup (U_i \smallsetminus \{\varepsilon\}) V_i^\omega$, and this can be derived in the grammar of Def. 5.2.

"$\Rightarrow$" This makes use of the distributivity law $U(L \cup L') = UL \cup UL'$ and the associativity of concatenation, including the closure of regular languages of finite words under concatenations. With these at hand, anything that is derivable from α in the grammar above can be normalised into a (finite) union of left-concatenations of expressions of the form β^ω with a single regular expression. The case of $L = \varnothing$ is covered by any such finite union of zero disjuncts. $\square$

Example 5.5 Let $\Sigma = \{a, b, c\}$. The language $L = \{w \in \Sigma^\omega \mid$ if $|w|_a = \infty$ then $|w|_b = \infty\}$ is ω-regular. The key insight is a rewriting of the implication into a disjunction. Thus, L consists of all words that have finitely many occurrences of a only, or infinitely many occurrences of b (or both, of course). Then we have $L = L(\alpha)$ for

$$\alpha := (a + b + c)^* \big((a + c)^* b\big)^\omega + (a + b + c)^* (b + c)^\omega .$$

This description follows the general form defined in Lemma 5.4 already.

An immediate consequence of Lemma 5.4 is closure of ω-REG under certain operations.

Corollary 5.6 *The classes ω–REG_Σ are closed under finite unions and left-concatenations with regular languages from REG_Σ.*

For unions this is obvious, closure under left-concatenations with regular languages needs distributivity of concatenation over unions again.

Further closure properties are far less obvious, in particular closure under intersections and complementation. These hold as well but quite a bit more work is needed to prove them, in particular the latter. The key is the introduction of a computational model, namely the aforementioned Büchi automata.

5.2 Nondeterministic Büchi Automata

As informally described above, Büchi automata arise from NFA simply by reinterpreting the notion of acceptance to cater for infinite words. Syntactically they are indistinguishable from NFA.

Definition 5.7 A *nondeterministic Büchi automaton* (NBA) is an $\mathcal{A} = (Q, \Sigma, q_I, \delta, F)$ exactly as an NFA. Therefore, the *size* of an NBA is also defined as $|\mathcal{A}| := |Q|$.

A *run* of $\mathcal{A}$ on an ω-word $w = a_0 a_1 a_2 \ldots \in \Sigma^\omega$ is an infinite sequence $\rho = q_0, q_1, q_2, \ldots$ of states s.t. $q_0 = q_I$ and $q_{i+1} \in \delta(q_i, a_i)$ for all $i \geq 0$. For such a ρ, we let $\mathit{Inf}(\rho) := \{q \in Q \mid \forall i \exists j > i \text{ s.t. } q_j = q\}$ denote the set of all states that occur infinitely often in it. Note that $Q \supseteq \mathit{Inf}(\rho) \supsetneq \varnothing$ for any ρ by finiteness of Q. Such a run ρ is called *accepting* if $\mathit{Inf}(\rho) \cap F \neq \varnothing$, i.e. when at least some accepting state is visited infinitely often.

The *language* of the NBA $\mathcal{A}$ is $L(\mathcal{A}) := \{w \in \Sigma^\omega \mid \text{there is an accepting run of } \mathcal{A} \text{ on } w\}$. A language $L \subseteq \Sigma^\omega$ is called *Büchi-recognisable* or *NBA-recognisable*, resp. *-definable* if there exists an NBA $\mathcal{A}$ s.t. $L = L(\mathcal{A})$.

So the notion of acceptance and recognised languages are lifted straightforwardly to NBA from NFA, with the only difference being the arbitrary but natural convention that runs are considered to be accepting when they visit some accepting state infinitely often. Note that, because of finiteness of Q, a run visits the set F of accepting states infinitely often iff there is some state $q \in F$ that gets visited infinitely often.

Sometimes it will be more convenient to consider a run ρ on a word $w = a_0 a_1 \ldots$ to be an alternating sequence $q_0, a_0, q_1, a_1, \ldots$ of states and letters. We will make use of both notions of runs, and the context will make clear whether we only list states or states and letters.

Example 5.8 Let $\Sigma = \{a, b\}$ and $L_1 = (a^* b)^\omega$ be the language of all words that contain infinitely many symbols b. It is Büchi-recognisable; an NBA recognising it is the following for example.

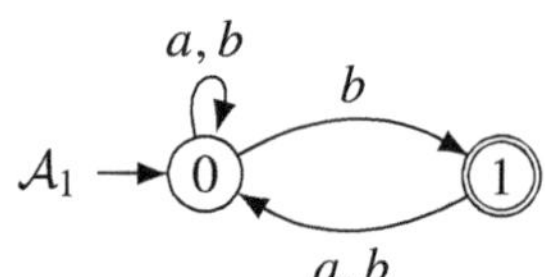

An accepting run of $\mathcal{A}_1$ on a word w containing infinitely many occurrences of the symbol b can be constructed as follows. Note that, if $|w|_b = \infty$ then w also contains infinitely many symbols b at positions that lie at least two steps apart (in the worst case, only taking every second of the infinitely many positions). Then an accepting run ρ can be built by moving from 0 to 1 at each of these positions and from 1 to 0 consequently when reading the letter right after that. The premise about distance two ensures that the run can move to state 1 infinitely often, i.e. it itself is of the form $(0^+ 1)^\omega$ and, hence, is accepting.

On the other hand, on every word that contains only finitely many symbols b, $\mathcal{A}$ will eventually have to remain in state 0 forever, i.e. any run on such a word must be of the form $(0 + 1)^* 0^\omega$ itself and is therefore not accepting. Hence, L_1 is NBA-recognisable.

Now let $\Sigma = \{a, b, c\}$ and L_2 be the language of all ω-words over Σ in which every b is eventually succeeded by some c. We have

$$L_2 \;=\; (a+c)^\omega + (a+b+c)^* c (a+c)^\omega + (a+b+c)^* (b(a+b+c)^* c)^\omega \,.$$

An NBA recognising L_2 is the following.

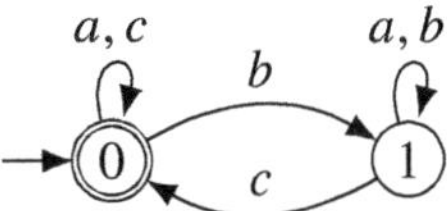

Intuitively, state 1 is used to remember that the symbol b has been seen but no subsequent c has been seen yet. State 0 can be interpreted as waiting for a potential b. It is accepting because, if no b occurs or several symbols b occur but there is at least some c after the last one, or there are infinitely many symbols b and c, then state 0 gets traversed infinitely often or even eventually only.

We remark that it would equally be possible to allow NBA to have more than one initial state. This model is no more expressive than the one with single initial states: the standard construction on NFA that adds a new initial state which simulates all original initial states can be applied here as well.

5.3 Closure Properties

The examples above show that there are ω-regular languages that can be recognised by Büchi automata and vice-versa. This is not a coincidence; a language is ω-regular iff it is NBA-recognisable. This correspondence between recognisability by finite automata and definability by regular operations is one of the properties that extends from the world of finite words to infinite words. Others do not, see for instance the following section on deterministic Büchi automata. In order to prove this correspondence formally, we investigate closure properties of NBA-definable languages.

5.3.1 Unions, Left-Concatenations and ω-Iterations

The proof of the following lemma is left as an exercise. It is done in exactly the same way as the corresponding construction for NFA.

Lemma 5.9 *Let $\mathcal{A}, \mathcal{B}$ be NBA over some Σ. There is an NBA $\mathcal{C}$ s.t. $L(\mathcal{C}) = L(\mathcal{A}) \cup L(\mathcal{B})$ and $|\mathcal{C}| \le |\mathcal{A}| + |\mathcal{B}| + 1$.*

In other words, the class of languages recognised by NBA is closed under finite unions. Clearly, we do not have closure under concatenations for NBA-recognisable languages, since the concatenation of two infinite words is no infinite word as argued above. However, the operation of left-concatenation with a finite word, resp.

a language of finite words, leads to another closure result. Again, the proof of the following lemma is left as an exercise since the construction is the same as the one proving concatenation-closure of the class of regular languages of finite words.

Lemma 5.10 *Let A be an NFA and B be an NBA, both over some Σ. There is an NBA C s.t. $L(C) = L(A)L(B)$ and $|C| \le |A| + |B|$.*

The last construction we need is not a closure property in the sense that it turns NBA for some languages into an NBA for a certain language. It is the pendant of the closure of regular languages of finite words under Kleene iteration; now we implement ω-iteration. This, of course, is an operation that turns (at most) a regular language into an ω-regular one.

Lemma 5.11 *Let A be an NFA over some Σ s.t. $\varepsilon \notin L(A)$. There is an NBA B s.t. $L(B) = (L(A))^\omega$ and $|B| \le |A| + 1$.*

Proof Let $A = (Q, \Sigma, q_I, \delta, F)$, and define $B := (Q \cup \{q_F\}, \Sigma, q_I, \delta', \{q_F\})$ for some $q_F \notin Q$, and

$$
\begin{aligned}
\delta' \ := \ &\delta \ \cup \ \{(q, a, q_F) \mid q \in Q, a \in \Sigma, \delta(q, a) \cap F \ne \varnothing\} \\
&\cup \ \{(q_F, a, p) \mid p \in \delta(q_I, a)\} \\
&\cup \ \{(q_F, a, q_F) \mid a \in \Sigma \text{ s.t. } \delta(q_I, a) \cap F \ne \varnothing\} \ .
\end{aligned}
$$

Hence, B is obtained from A by adding an extra state q_F and giving it the possibility to transition into this state instead of into a final state. Then, from this state, it can only do the same as from the initial state. This makes the claim on the size of B obvious. It remains to be seen that the construction is correct, i.e. that $L(B) = (L(A))^\omega$.

"$\supseteq$" Suppose $w \in (L(A))^\omega$, i.e. there are $u_0, u_1, \ldots$ s.t. $u_i \in L(A)$ for $i \in \mathbb{N}$, and $w = u_0 u_1 \ldots$. So there are runs $\rho_0, \rho_1, \ldots$ s.t. ρ_i is an accepting run of A on u_i. Since, by assumption, $u_i \ne \varepsilon$, we have $|\rho_i| > 1$ for every i. Let ρ'_i result from ρ_i by replacing the first (for $i \ge 1$) and the last state (for $i \ge 0$) with q_F. Note that this creates run fragments that are valid for the transition table δ' since B can always move to q_F instead of some final state, and from q_F it can do anything that it can do from q_I. We can now glue them together to a run ρ by merging the occurrences of q_F at the end of each ρ_i and the beginning of the subsequent ρ_{i+1}.

We claim that ρ is an accepting run of B on w: (I) it starts in the initial state q_I. (II) It obeys the transition relation δ' everywhere: inside each ρ_i it follows transitions from δ, and each step from the end of ρ'_{i-1} over into ρ'_i is done via the additional transitions through q_F. At last (III) the run is accepting since it visits q_F therefore infinitely often.

"$\subseteq$". Suppose $w = a_0 a_1 \ldots \in L(B)$, i.e. there is an accepting run $\rho = q_0, a_0, q_1, a_1, \ldots$ of B on w. Hence, there must be $0 = i_0 < i_1 < \ldots$ s.t. $q_{i_j} = q_F$ for all $j \ge 1$, and $q_h \ne q_F$ for all h not occurring in the sequence $i_0, i_1, \ldots$. This defines finite runs $\rho_j := q_{i_j}, a_{i_j}, \ldots, a_{i_{j+1}-1}, q_{i_{j+1}}$ on underlying words $u_j := a_{i_j} \ldots a_{i_{j+1}-1}$ for every $j \ge 0$. Next, we have $q_{i_j} \in F$ for all $j \ge 1$. Since $q_{i_0} = q_0 = q_I$ by construction, we have that ρ_0 is an accepting run of A on u_0. Likewise, we get that ρ_i is an accepting run of A on u_i for all $i \ge 1$. Since $w = u_0 u_1 \ldots$ we have $w \in L(A)^\omega$. $\square$

We can use these constructions to show that every ω-regular language is NBA-recognisable.

Theorem 5.12 *Let $L \subseteq \Sigma^\omega$. If L is ω-regular then L is Büchi-recognisable.*

Proof Suppose L is ω-regular. According to Lemma 5.4 we have $L = \bigcup_{i=1}^{n} U_i V_i^\omega$ for some n and regular languages U_i, V_i (with $\varepsilon \notin V_i$). According to Lemma 5.9–5.11 we can construct, making use of NFA for the U_i and V_i, an NBA for L. $\qquad\square$

The converse direction holds as well.

Theorem 5.13 *Let $L \subseteq \Sigma^\omega$. If L is Büchi-recognisable then L is ω-regular.*

Proof Suppose that L is Büchi-recognisable, i.e. there is some NBA $\mathcal{A} = (Q, \Sigma, q_I, \delta, F)$ s.t. $L = L(\mathcal{A})$. Given $p, q \in Q$, we write $L_{p,q}$ for $L(\mathcal{A}_{p,q})$ where $\mathcal{A}_{p,q}$ is the NFA $(Q, \Sigma, p, \delta, \{q\})$. Clearly, $L_{p,q}$ is a regular language of finite words by construction. We then claim that we have

$$L(\mathcal{A}) \;=\; \bigcup_{q \in F} L_{q_I,q}(L_{q,q} \setminus \{\varepsilon\})^\omega \tag{5.1}$$

which proves that L is ω-regular. Note that $L_{q,q} \setminus \{\varepsilon\}$ is regular and clearly does not contain ε. It remains to be seen that the claim made in (5.1) is true.

"$\supseteq$" Suppose $w \in \bigcup_{q \in F} L_{q_I,q}(L_{q,q} \setminus \{\varepsilon\})^\omega$. I.e. there is some $q \in F$ and there are $u \in \Sigma^*, v_0, v_1, \ldots \in \Sigma^+$ s.t. $w = u v_0 v_1 \ldots$ with $u \in L_{q_I,q}$ and $v_i \in L_{q,q}$ for all $i \geq 0$. Hence, there are accepting runs $\sigma = q_I, \ldots, q$ of $\mathcal{A}_{q_I,q}$ on u, and $\rho_i = q, \ldots, q$ of $\mathcal{A}_{q,q}$ on v_i for $i \geq 0$. Since $\mathcal{A}_{q_I,q}$ and $\mathcal{A}_{q,q}$ have the same transition table as $\mathcal{A}$, these runs can be concatenated to a run ρ that is obtained from $\sigma, \rho_0, \rho_1, \ldots$ by merging the double occurrences of state q at the beginning of each q_i with the end of the previous part. Then ρ is a run of $\mathcal{A}$ on w. It clearly starts in the initial states, and it visits state q infinitely often, namely at the beginning of each part ρ_i. Hence, it is an accepting run, and we therefore have $w \in L(\mathcal{A})$.

"$\subseteq$" Suppose $w = a_0 a_1 \ldots \in L(\mathcal{A})$, i.e. there is an accepting run $\rho = q_0, a_0, q_1, a_1, \ldots$ of $\mathcal{A}$ on w. We therefore have $q_0 = q_I$, and there must be some $q \in F$ s.t. $q_i = q$ for infinitely many i. In other words, there are $i_0 < i_1 < \ldots$ s.t. $q_{i_j} = q$ for all $j \geq 0$. This defines a decomposition of w into $u v_0 v_1 \ldots$ by $u := a_0 \ldots a_{i_0 - 1}$ and $v_j := a_{i_j} \ldots a_{i_{j+1} - 1}$ for $j \geq 0$. Then the prefix $q_0, \ldots, q_{i_0}$ of ρ is an accepting run of $\mathcal{A}_{q_I,q}$ because $q_0 = q_I$ and $q_{i_0} = q$. Hence, $u \in L_{q_I,q}$. Likewise, each infix $q_{i_j}, \ldots, q_{i_{j+1}}$ is an accepting run of $\mathcal{A}_{q,q}$ on v_i because $q_{i_j} = q = q_{i_{j+1}}$. Hence, $v_j \in L_{q,q}$ for all $j \geq 0$, and therefore $v_0 v_1 \ldots \in (L_{q,q})^\omega$. In fact, we even have $v_0 v_1 \ldots \in (L_{q,q} \setminus \{\varepsilon\})^\omega$ because $v_j \neq \varepsilon$ for each j which is a consequence of the fact that $i_j < i_{j+1}$. But then we have $w = u v_0 v_1 \ldots \in L_{q_I,q}(L_{q,q} \setminus \{\varepsilon\})^\omega$ which finishes the proof of the claim. $\qquad\square$

For the sake of completeness we state the combination of Thm. 5.12 and 5.13 explicitly. This result is also known as *Büchi's Theorem*.

Corollary 5.14 *Let $L \subseteq \Sigma^\omega$. L is Büchi-recognisable iff it is ω-regular.*

Thm. 5.13 suggests a simple procedure for determining non-emptiness of Büchi automata based on two nested graph reachability searches.

Theorem 5.15 *The nonemptiness problem for NBA is decidable in polynomial time.*

Proof Let $\mathcal{A} = (Q, \Sigma, q_I, \delta, F)$ be an NBA. The proof of Thm. 5.13 shows that $L(\mathcal{A}) \neq \varnothing$ if and only if there exists $q \in F$ such that q is reachable from q_I and q itself is reachable from q with a nonempty path. Using depth- or breadth-first search (DFS/BFS) we can first compute all accepting states that are reachable from the initial states. Then we can check, using DFS or BFS again, for each of them whether they are reachable from themselves in more than zero steps. Since DFS and BFS can be implemented to run in time that is linear in the number e of edges of the underlying graph, i.e. at most quadratic in the size n of the NBA measured in terms of number of nodes, the overall procedure takes at most time $\mathcal{O}(n \cdot e)$ or $\mathcal{O}(n^3)$. $\square$

This is not the tightest upper bound from a complexity-theoretic point of view. Reachability in graphs can be decided in nondeterministic logarithmic space. The nesting of two searches can be implemented in order not to exceed this asymptotically. Hence, the emptiness problem for NBA even belongs to the complexity class NLogSpace.

5.3.2 Intersections and Homomorphisms

Clearly, the closure properties of the class of Büchi-definable languages derived in Lemma 5.9–5.11 above carry over to ω-regular languages with the chracterisation of the latter via Büchi-recognisability. This, however, is of very little help since closure under union, left-concatenation with a regular language and under ω-iterations of regular languages is more or less a direct consequence of the construction of ω-regular languages. Nevertheless, Büchi automata can be used to provide further closure properties of this class, most notably closure under Boolean operations.

The construction showing closure under intersections is based on the product construction for NFA. However, for NBA it is more intricate. The reason is simple. Let $\mathcal{A}$ and $\mathcal{B}$ be NFA, and suppose we want to know whether they both accept a given word $w \in \Sigma^*$. This can be done in one traversal of the word by simulating both $\mathcal{A}$ and $\mathcal{B}$ at the same time, i.e. using a synchronous product construction. When arriving at the end, we need to check that both have reached an accepting state at that very same moment.

Now suppose that $\mathcal{A}$ and $\mathcal{B}$ are NBA, and $w \in \Sigma^\omega$. Again, using a product construction we can simulate both of them in parallel. However, we now need to accept if and only if both of them have seen their respective accepting states infinitely often, and this need not happen at the same time.

Example 5.16 The following shows three NBA $\mathcal{A}, \mathcal{B}, \mathcal{C}$ over $\Sigma = \{a\}$.

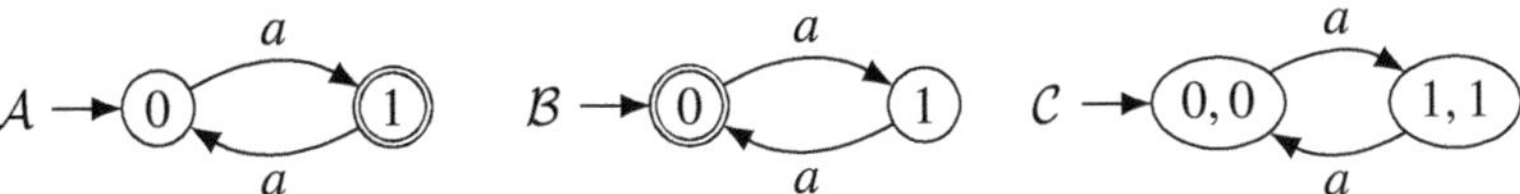

NBA $\mathcal{C}$ is obtained from $\mathcal{A}$ and $\mathcal{B}$ using the naïve product construction where a state pair becomes accepting when both its components are accepting in the respective underlying automata. Here, the only accepting pair would be $(1,0)$ but it is not reachable from the initial state $(0,0)$. Hence, we have $L(\mathcal{C}) = \varnothing$. On the other hand, we have $L(\mathcal{A}) = a^{\omega} = L(\mathcal{B})$ and, thus, $L(\mathcal{A}) \cap L(\mathcal{B}) = a^{\omega} \neq \varnothing$.

This example shows that a refinement of the product construction is needed to capture the intersection of two Büchi-definable languages. We need a mechanism that makes the product automaton hit an accepting state infinitely often if and only if the two underlying automata do this, and this may happen asynchronously. The trick relies on the following observation: suppose $\rho = p_0, p_1, \ldots$ and $\sigma = q_0, q_1, \ldots$ are accepting runs w.r.t. some sets F, F' of accepting states, i.e. $p_i \in F$ for infinitely many i, and $q_i \in F'$ for infinitely many i. Then for every i s.t. $p_i \in F$ there is some $j > i$ s.t. $q_j \in F'$, and vice-versa. The converse is true as well. This provides a simple recipe for detecting whether accepting states are seen infinitely often in both underlying runs in a product construction: simulate both runs until an accepting state is seen in the first component. Then continue simulating both runs until an accepting state is seen in the second component. Then accepting states are seen infinitely often in both components iff we change infinitely often from one waiting mode into the other.

Theorem 5.17 *Let $\mathcal{A}_i$ be NBA over some Σ for $i \in \{1,2\}$. There is an NBA $\mathcal{B}$ s.t. $L(\mathcal{B}) = L(\mathcal{A}_1) \cap L(\mathcal{A}_2)$ and $|\mathcal{B}| \leq 2 \cdot |\mathcal{A}_1| \cdot |\mathcal{A}_2|$.*

Proof Let $\mathcal{A}_i = (Q_i, \Sigma, q_I^i, \delta_i, F_i)$ for $i = 1, 2$. Define

$$\mathcal{B} := (Q_1 \times Q_2 \times \{1,2\}, \Sigma, (q_I^1, q_I^2, 1), \Delta, F_1 \times Q_2 \times \{1\})$$

where, for all $a \in \Sigma$, $p, q \in Q_1$, $p', q' \in Q_2$, $i, j \in \{1,2\}$ we have: $(q, q', j) \in \Delta((p, p', i), a)$ iff $q \in \delta_1(p, a)$, $q' \in \delta_2(p', a)$ and

$$j = \begin{cases} 1 & \text{, if } i = 1 \text{ and } p \notin F_1, \text{ or } i = 2 \text{ and } p' \in F_2 \\ 2 & \text{, otherwise.} \end{cases}$$

Thus, $\mathcal{B}$ simulates $\mathcal{A}_1$ and $\mathcal{A}_2$ in its first and second state components. The value i in the extra third component can be interpreted as $\mathcal{B}$ expecting to eventually see an accepting state of $\mathcal{A}_i$. Whenever this has happened, the value is flipped. So intuitively, in order to verify that both $\mathcal{A}_1$ and $\mathcal{A}_2$ have accepting runs on a given word, $\mathcal{B}$ simulates them both stepwise in parallel and verifies that there is an infinite sequence of alternating moments between them in which they traverse accepting states of theirs respectively.

The size claim on $\mathcal{B}$ is obvious. It remains to be seen that we have $L(\mathcal{B}) = L(\mathcal{A}_1) \cap L(\mathcal{A}_2)$.

"⊇" Suppose $w = a_0 a_1 \ldots \in L(\mathcal{A}_1) \cap L(\mathcal{A}_2)$, i.e. there are accepting runs $\rho = p_0, a_0, p_1, a_1, \ldots$ and $\rho' = q_0, a_0, q_1, a_1, \ldots$ of $\mathcal{A}_1$, resp. $\mathcal{A}_2$ on w. Let $\sigma := (p_0, q_0, c_0), a_0, (p_1, q_1, c_1), a_1, \ldots$ where $c_0 := 1$ and c_{i+1} is the unique value that, given p_i, q_i, c_i, ensures that $(p_{i+1}, q_{i+1}, c_{i+1}) \in \Delta((p_i, q_i, c_i), a_i)$. Note that Δ is indeed deterministic in its third component, i.e. this component in a successor state is uniquely determined by the previous state. Then σ is a run of $\mathcal{B}$ on w, and it clearly starts in $\mathcal{B}$'s initial state.

It is also an accepting run for the following reason. Starting with $c_0 = 1$, there must be some $i_0 \geq 0$ s.t. $p_{i_0} \in F_1$, because ρ contains infinitely many accepting states. Then we get $c_{i_0+1} = 2$. Likewise, there must be some $i_1 > i_0$ s.t. $q_{i_1} \in F_2$, because ρ' contains infinitely many accepting states. Hence, we have $c_{i_1+1} = 1$, and the argument can be iterated to construct an infinite sequence of positions in the run σ, namely $i_1, i_3, \ldots$, at which a state from $F_1 \times Q_2 \times \{1\}$, i.e. an accepting state, is seen.

"⊆" Analogously, the projection of an accepting run σ of $\mathcal{B}$ onto its first, resp. second component yields runs of $\mathcal{A}_1$, resp. $\mathcal{A}_2$ on the underlying word. Since σ is accepting, so must both projected runs be. Otherwise suppose that one of them would eventually not visit an accepting state from F_1, resp. F_2 anymore. Then the value in the third component of the states in ρ will eventually not flip anymore, and it will remain to be the index of the underlying NBA whose run does not visit accepting states anymore. So ρ will eventually only visit states in $(Q_1 \setminus F_1) \times Q_2 \times \{1\}$ or in $Q_1 \times (Q_2 \setminus F_2) \times \{2\}$. Neither of them is accepting in $\mathcal{B}$, though. Thus, if ρ is accepting, so are both the underlying runs in its components. $\square$

An obvious question concerns the closure of ω-REG under complementation. It is tempting to assume that the complement of an ω-regular language should be ω-regular as well, simply because of what is known about regular languages of finite words. This does not provide a sound mathematical argument, though, and at closer sight it is not so clear whether complementation closure holds as well. The following section investigates deterministic Büchi automata, and shows that they are useless for the question after the complementation closure of ω-REG: not only can they not be complemented, it is not even the case that they accept all languages in ω-REG. This is a surprising difference to the world of finite words, and it shows that the step to infinite words did introduce some extra combinatorial difficulty. Nevertheless, ω-REG is indeed closed under complements, and this extra difficulty becomes apparent when attempting to prove this. Because of this extra difficulty involved, the presentation of this result is deferred to its own section below, cf. Sect. 5.5.

At last, some later constructions need homomorphism closure which holds true for ω-regular languages as well. Here we state it in a slightly restricted form, namely for non-deleting homomorphisms only. Note that the notion of homomorphic image of a language of ω-words can become ill-defined in the context of homomorphisms that may delete letters. For instance, if $h(a) = \varepsilon$ and $h(b) = b$, then $\hat{h}((ab)^\omega) = b^\omega$ but $\hat{h}(a^\omega)$ is no longer an infinite word. The proof of the following lemma is left as an exercise.

Lemma 5.18 *Let* Σ, Δ *be alphabets,* $h : \Sigma \to \Delta^+$, $L \subseteq \Sigma^\omega$. *If* $L \in \omega\text{-}REG_\Sigma$ *then* $\hat{h}(L) \in \omega\text{-}REG_\Delta$.

5.4 Deterministic Büchi Automata

As with NFA and DFA, we can impose the restriction of determinism onto a Büchi automaton's transition relation.

Definition 5.19 A *deterministic Büchi automaton* (DBA) is an NBA $\mathcal{A} = (Q, \Sigma, q_I, \delta, F)$ s.t. $|\delta(q,a) \le 1|$ for all $q \in Q$, $a \in \Sigma$, just as determinism is defined for automata on finite words. Consequently, we call a language *deterministic Büchi-recognisable* or just *DBA-recognisable*, resp. *-definable* if it is the language of some DBA.

Example 5.20 Reconsider the language $L_1 = L((a^*b)^\omega)$ from Ex. 5.8 and the NBA $\mathcal{A}_1$ that recognises it. $\mathcal{A}_1$ is clearly not deterministic. The nondeterminism on b in state 0 is useless, though. There is no gain in taking the transition $(0, b, 0)$. Hence, it can be removed. This already leads to a DBA recognising L_1 as well. We give a slightly modified one.

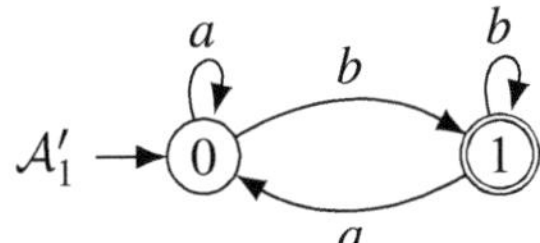

It is clearly deterministic as well. Additionally it has the property that any run takes $\mathcal{A}_1'$ into state 0 upon reading a and into state 1 upon reading b. A trivial consequence is that $L(\mathcal{A}_1') = L_1$; a run contains state 0 infinitely often iff the underlying word contains b infinitely often. Thus, L_1 is even DBA-recognisable.

Now consider $L_3 := (a+b)^* a^\omega$, i.e. the language of all words that contain b only finitely often. Clearly, we have $L_3 = \Sigma^\omega \setminus L_1$. First we note that we do not obtain a DBA for L_2 by employing the complementation construction for DFA on $\mathcal{A}_1'$, namely swapping accepting and non-accepting states. This results in a DBA that recognises the language of all words which contain infinitely many symbols a. This is a genuine superset of L_3; every word containing only finitely many symbols b necessarily has to contain infinitely many symbols a when the underlying alphabet is $\{a, b\}$, but there are also words that contain both letters infinitely often.

The fact that swapping accepting for non-accepting states in a DBA does not produce a DBA for the complement language is not surprising at closer inspection. A DBA accepts a word w if the unique run on it traverses accepting states infinitely often. Thus, a word is *not* accepted if the unique run on it traverses accepting states only *finitely* often, and this is stronger than visiting non-accepting states infinitely often.

Example 5.21 L_3 from Ex. 5.20 above is instead recognised by the following NBA.

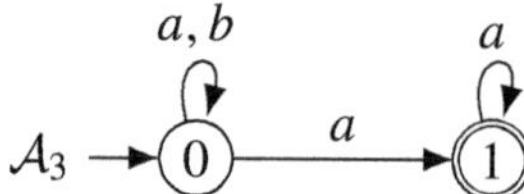

It makes proper use of nondeterminism. In order to confirm that the underlying word w only has finitely many symbols b, it reads an arbitrary prefix, essentially ignoring its content by simply looping around in state 0. This cannot be done forever, for such a run is clearly not accepting. Thus, $\mathcal{A}_3$ must eventually move to state 1 upon reading of a letter a. This can be interpreted as guessing that there will be no more symbols b in what follows since $\mathcal{A}_3$ would get stuck in state 1 upon reading another b.

The fact that $\mathcal{A}_3$ in this example is not a DBA but "only" an NBA for L_2 is not a coincidence. L_2 is an example of a language that is not DBA-recognisable, and this yields the first perhaps surprising deviation from the results in the theory of regular languages of finite words where every NFA-recognisable language is also DFA-recognisable. To prove this, we introduce a topological construction on infinite words.

Definition 5.22 Let $(w_n)_{n\geq 0}$ be an infinite sequence of ω-words. Its *limit*, denoted $\lim_{n\to\infty} w_n$ if it exists, is the ω-word defined by

$$\left(\lim_{n\to\infty} w_n \right)(i) \;:=\; \lim_{n\to\infty} w_n(i)$$

where $\lim_{n\to\infty} a_n = a$ for an infinite sequence $(a_n)_{n\geq 0}$, iff there is n_0 s.t. $a_n = a$ for all $n \geq n_0$.

The limit of a sequence $(w_n)_{n\geq 0}$ of words need not exist as the following example shows.

Example 5.23 Consider the infinite sequence of words $(w_n)_{n\geq 0}$ defined as follows.

$$w_0 \;:=\; a^{\omega} \;, \qquad w_{2n+1} := bw_{2n} \;, \qquad w_{2n+2} := aw_{2n+1}$$

for all $n \geq 0$. Then $\lim_{n\to\infty} w_n$ does not exist. Take any position i. The sequence of letters at position i in $(w_n)_{n\geq 0}$ is

$$\underbrace{a, \ldots, a}_{i+1}, b, a, b, a, b, a, \ldots$$

and clearly does not converge to a limit point, i.e. one single letter. Hence, the letter at any position of the supposed limit of $(w_n)_{n\geq 0}$ is undefined, and therefore this limit does not exist.

Now consider the sequence $(w_n')_{n\geq 0}$ defined by $w_n' := w_{2n}$, i.e. the subsequence of the one above obtained by dropping every second word. It is not hard to see that we have $w_0' = a^{\omega}$ and $w_{n+1}' = abw_n'$, hence, $w_n' = (ab)^n a^{\omega}$. The limit of this sequence does indeed exist, and we have $\lim_{n\to\infty} w_n' = (ab)^{\omega}$.

Note that the limit of $(w_n')_{n\geq 0}$ contains infinitely many symbols b even though every w_n' contains finitely many symbols b only.

Theorem 5.24 *There are NBA-definable languages that are not DBA-definable.*

Proof Take $L_3 = (a + b)^* a^\omega$ from Ex. 5.20 above. Ex. 5.21 shows that it is NBA-recognisable. Now suppose there was a DBA $\mathcal{A} = (Q, \Sigma, q_I, \delta, F)$ s.t. $L(\mathcal{A}) = L_3$. Here we denote a run as an infinite sequence $q_0, a_0, q_1, a_1, \ldots$ alternating between states and letters.

First consider the word $w_0 := ba^\omega$. Since $w_0 \in L_2$ there is an accepting run $\rho_0 = q_0^0, b, q_1^0, a, q_2^0, a, \ldots$ of $\mathcal{A}$ on w_0. Since it traverses accepting states infinitely often, there must be some $i_0 > 0$ s.t. $q_{i_0}^0 \in F$.

Now consider the word $w_1 := ba^{i_0-1}ba^\omega$. Again, we have $w_1 \in L_3$ and there must be an accepting run $\rho_1 = q_0^1, b, q_1^1, a, \ldots, a, q_{i_0}^1, b, q_{i_0+1}^1, a, \ldots$ The crucial insight here now is that, not only do we have $q_0^1 = q_0^0$ because both runs ρ_0 and ρ_1 start in the unique starting state, but in fact $q_j^1 = q_j^0$ for all $j \le i_0$. This is a consequence of $\mathcal{A}$'s determinism, namely that runs on two words that have a common prefix of some length m, have itself a common prefix of length $m + 1$ (purely counting states). Hence, we can drop the superscript indices and simply say that

$$\rho_0 = q_0, b, q_1, a, \ldots, a, q_{i_0}, a, q_{i_0+1}^0, a, \ldots ,$$
$$\rho_1 = q_0, b, q_1, a, \ldots, a, q_{i_0}, b, q_{i_0+1}^1, a, \ldots$$

Now this can be continued. Since ρ_1 is accepting, there must be some $i_1 > i_0$ s.t. $q_{i_1}^1 \in F$, yielding $w_2 := ba^{i_0-1}b^{i_1-i_0-1}a^\omega$ and an accepting run ρ_3 which, by the same argument appealing to $\mathcal{A}$'s determinism, must share a prefix with ρ_2 up to q_{i_1} at least. Continuing this yields the following sequence of runs.

$$\rho_0 = q_0, b, q_1, a, \ldots, a, q_{i_0}, a, q_{i_0+1}^0, \ldots$$
$$\rho_1 = q_0, b, q_1, a, \ldots, a, q_{i_0}, b, q_{i_0+1}, a, \ldots, a, q_{i_1}, a, q_{i_1+1}^1, \ldots$$
$$\rho_2 = q_0, b, q_1, a, \ldots, a, q_{i_0}, b, q_{i_0+1}, a, \ldots, a, q_{i_1}, b, q_{i_1+1}, a, \ldots, a, q_{i_2}, a, q_{i_2+1}^2, \ldots$$
$$\rho_3 = q_0, b, q_1, a, \ldots, a, q_{i_0}, b, q_{i_0+1}, a, \ldots, a, q_{i_1}, b, q_{i_1+1}, a, \ldots, a, q_{i_2}, b, q_{i_2+1}, \ldots$$
$$\vdots$$

Let $\rho := \lim_{n \to \infty} \rho_n$. Note that ρ exists because the ρ_n have growing common prefixes with all subsequent ρ_m. Next we note that ρ is a run of $\mathcal{A}$ on the word

$$w := ba^{i_0-1}ba^{i_1-i_0-1}ba^{i_2-i_1-i_0-1}b\ldots$$

which contains infinitely many symbols b. Thus, we have $w \notin L_3$. However, ρ is in fact an accepting run because it hits the states $q_{i_0}, q_{i_1}, q_{i_2}, \ldots$ which are all accepting. This contradicts the assumption that $\mathcal{A}$ is indeed a DBA for L_3. $\qquad\square$

Corollary 5.25 *The class of DBA-definable languages is not closed under complementation.*

Proof This is a direct consequence of the fact that the language L_2 which is shown not to be DBA-definable in the proof of Thm. 5.24 is in fact the complement of L_1 from Ex. 5.20 where this is shown to be DBA-definable. $\qquad\square$

5.5 Complementation Closure

As said before, the proof of complementation closure of the class of ω-regular languages is combinatorially more involved than the corresponding result for automata on finite words. One way of proving this uses a result from infinite combinatorics.

5.5.1 Ramsey's Theorem

For a set A we write $\binom{A}{2}$ to denote the set of subsets of A of size 2, i.e. $\binom{A}{2} = \{\{x,y\} \mid x,y \in A, x \neq y\}$. We are particularly interested in $\binom{\mathbb{N}}{2}$. In this case, $\binom{\mathbb{N}}{2}$ can be depicted as the set of edges in the following undirected graph.

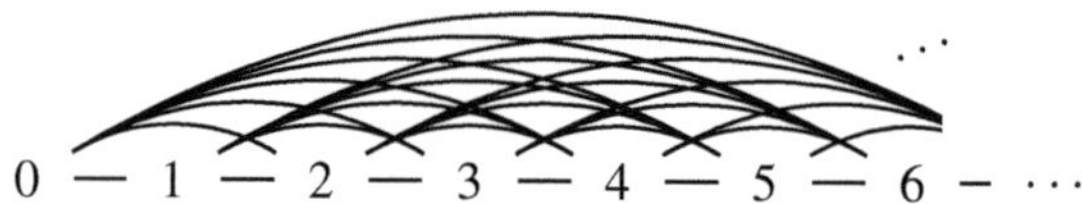

Given sets A, C, a *C-colouring* of A is a function $f : \binom{A}{2} \to C$. Usually we assume C to be finite here. Intuitively, the elements of C can be thought of as colours, and then f assigns a colour to each unordered pair of elements in A. Such a colouring f is called *constant* if $f(e) = f(e')$ for all $e, e' \in \binom{A}{2}$.

Now let $B \subseteq A$. Then the restriction of f to B, written $f|_B$ and simply defined as $f|_B(e) = f(e)$ for any $e \in \binom{B}{2}$, is clearly a C-colouring of B. Note that, if $B \subseteq A$ then $\binom{B}{2} \subseteq \binom{A}{2}$, and each C-colouring f of A uniquely determines a C-colouring $f|_B$ of B.

The following combinatorial result is known as *Ramsey's Theorem*.

Theorem 5.26 *Let A be an infinite set, C be a finite set and f be a C-colouring of A. Then there is an infinite subset $B \subseteq A$ such that $f|_B$ is constant.*

Proof W.l.o.g. we assume A to be countable. Otherwise one may restrict the following to a countable subset of A or rely on the axiom of choice. What is needed is just that we can always pick a "next" element from A.

We construct a sequence $(a_0, A_0, c_0), (a_1, A_1, c_1), (a_2, A_2, c_2), \ldots$ of triples from $A \times 2^A \times C$ such that

(I) $A_0 \supseteq A_1 \supseteq A_2 \supseteq \ldots$,
(II) $a_i \in A_{i-1} \setminus A_i$ for all $i \geq 1$, and, thus, $a_j \neq a_i$ for all $j > i$,
(III) $|A_i| = \infty$ for all $i \geq 0$ and
(IV) $f(\{a_i, x\}) = c_i$ for all $x \in A_i$.

We choose a_0 arbitrarily and c_0 as a colour that colours infinitely many pairs of the form $\{a_0, x\}$ for $x \in A \setminus \{a_0\}$. By finiteness of C and infiniteness of $A \setminus \{a_0\}$, some colour must be used infinitely often for sets containing a_0. We then put $A_0 := \{x \mid f(\{a_0, x\}) = c_0\}$. Note that $a_0 \notin A_0$.

Now suppose that the sequence has already been constructed up to the n-th element such that the properties (I)–(IV) hold accordingly. Then we choose a_{n+1} arbitrarily from A_n and construct A_{n+1}, c_{n+1} as in the case $n = 0$: pick a color c_{n+1} s.t. $f(\{a_{n+1}, x\}) = c_{n+1}$ for infinitely many $x \in A_n$. Note that here we restrict our attention to A_n rather than the full set A. Again, by finiteness of C and infiniteness of A_n, such a c_{n+1} must exist. Finally, let $A_{n+1} := \{x \in A_n \mid f(\{a_{n+1}, x\}) = c_{n+1}\}$.

Properties (I), (III) and (IV) are satisfied for $n + 1$ by construction. Property (II) also holds for $n + 1$ as well: we have $a_{n+1} \notin A_{n+1}$ because f is only defined on $\binom{A}{2}$ and $\{a_{n+1}, a_{n+1}\} = \{a_{n+1}\} \notin \binom{A}{2}$.

Now suppose that the infinite sequence $(a_0, A_0, c_0), (a_1, A_1, c_1), \ldots$ is given such that properties (I)–(IV) hold. Again, because of finiteness of C, there must be some $c \in C$ such that $c_i = c$ for infinitely many $i \in \mathbb{N}$, i.e. there are $i_0 < i_1 < \ldots$ s.t. $c_{i_j} = c$ for all $j \geq 0$. Let $B := \{a_{i_j} \mid j \geq 0\}$. We claim that B has the properties required in the theorem. Clearly, $|B| = \infty$ because of the conclusion in property (II). It remains to be seen that $f|_B$ is constant, in particular that $f(\{x, y\}) = c$ for any $\{x, y\} \in \binom{B}{2}$.

Take some $\{x, y\} \in \binom{B}{2}$. By construction, there must be $j, h \in \mathbb{N}$ such that $x = a_{i_j}$ and $y = a_{i_h}$. W.l.o.g. we assume that $j < h$ and therefore $i_j < i_h$. Thus, we have $a_{i_h} \in A_{i_j}$ by property (I) and $f(\{x, y\}) = f(\{a_{i_h}, a_{i_h}\}) = c_{i_j} = c$ by property (IV). $\square$

5.5.2 Büchi's Complementation Construction

Fix an NBA $\mathcal{A} = (Q, \Sigma, q_I, \delta, F)$. In the remainder of this section, n will always denote the size of $\mathcal{A}$, i.e. $n = |Q|$.

The goal is to construct an NBA $\mathcal{B}$ such that $L(\mathcal{B}) = \overline{L(\mathcal{A})}$. We define relations $\xrightarrow{u}, \xRightarrow{u} \subseteq Q \times Q$ for any finite word $u \in \Sigma^*$ as follows.

- We have $q \xrightarrow{u} q'$ if it is possible to reach state q' from state q in $\mathcal{A}$ while working off u. In other words, suppose that $u = a_0 \ldots a_{m-1}$. Then $q \xrightarrow{u} q'$ iff there are $q_0, \ldots, q_m \in Q$ s.t. $q_0 = q$, $q_m = q'$ and $q_{i+1} \in \delta(q_i, a_i)$ for all $i \in [m]$.
- The relation $\xRightarrow{u}$ is a refinement thereof. We have $q \xRightarrow{u} q'$ for $u = a_0 \ldots a_{m-1}$ if there are $q_0, \ldots, q_m \in Q$ s.t. $q_0 = q$, $q_m = q'$ and $q_{i+1} \in \delta(q_i, a_i)$ for all $i \in [m]$, and additionally $q_i \in F$ for some $i \in \{0, \ldots, m\}$.

The following properties are immediate from the definition of these two relations. If $q \xRightarrow{u} q'$ then $q \xrightarrow{u} q'$, too. If $q \xrightarrow{u} p$ and $p \xrightarrow{v} q'$ and $p \in F$ then $q \xRightarrow{uv} q'$.

We define an equivalence relation $\sim \subseteq \Sigma^+ \times \Sigma^+$ on *non-empty* finite words as follows.

$$u \sim v \quad \text{iff} \quad \forall q. \forall q'. (q \xrightarrow{u} q' \Leftrightarrow q \xrightarrow{v} q') \text{ and } (q \xRightarrow{u} q' \Leftrightarrow q \xRightarrow{v} q')$$

In other words, two words are considered to be equivalent if they induce the same reachability relation on $\mathcal{A}$, and also the same reachability-via-an-intermediate-accepting-state relation. Put even more intuitively, $u \sim v$ means that u and v cannot be distinguished by $\mathcal{A}$ when it only comes down to the question of which state changes the reading of a finite word induces in an NBA.

The following lemma collects a few useful observations about the relation $\sim$.

Lemma 5.27 *a) Let $u \in \Sigma^*$, $w \in \Sigma^\omega$ and $v, v' \in \Sigma^+$ s.t. $v \sim v'$. If $uvw \in L(\mathcal{A})$ then*
$uv'w \in L(\mathcal{A})$.

b) The relation $\sim$ is an equivalence relation of index at most 3^{n^2}.

Proof (a) Left as an exercise. (b) It is straightforward to see that $\sim$ is an equivalence relation. For the estimation of its index, remember that $n = |Q|$. Note that each equivalence class $[u] = \{v \mid v \sim u\}$ is uniquely determined by the pair of relations $\{(q,q') \mid q \xrightarrow{u} q'\}$ and $\{(q,q') \mid q \overset{u}{\Longrightarrow} q'\}$. Clearly, there are only 2^{n^2} many candidates for each such relations. This would result in $(2^{n^2})^2 = 4^{n^2}$ many possible pairs. However, since we have $\overset{u}{\Longrightarrow} \subseteq \xrightarrow{u}$ for any u, there are only three possibilities for any pair (q,q'): either it belongs to $\overset{u}{\Longrightarrow}$ (and therefore also to $\xrightarrow{u}$), or it belongs to $\xrightarrow{u} \setminus \overset{u}{\Longrightarrow}$, or it does not belong to $\xrightarrow{u}$. Hence, $|\{(\xrightarrow{u}, \overset{u}{\Longrightarrow}) \mid u \in \Sigma^+\}| \le 3^{n^2}$. This is then an upper bound on the index of $\sim$ because $u \sim v$ iff $(\xrightarrow{u}, \overset{u}{\Longrightarrow}) = (\xrightarrow{v}, \overset{v}{\Longrightarrow})$. □

We write $\Sigma^+/\!\sim$ for the set of all equivalence classes of $\sim$, i.e. $\Sigma^+/\!\sim \; := \{[u] \mid u \in \Sigma^+\}$. We need a few observations about such classes $U, V \in \Sigma^+/\!\sim$.

Lemma 5.28 *Let $U \in \Sigma^+/\!\sim$. There is an NFA $\mathcal{A}_U$ of size $2^{\mathcal{O}(n^3)}$ such that $L(\mathcal{A}_U) = U$.*

Proof Recall that $\mathcal{A} = (Q, \Sigma, q_I, \delta, F)$ and $n = |Q|$. For states $q, q' \in Q$ let $L_{q,q'} := \{u \mid q \xrightarrow{u} q'\}$ and $L^{\mathsf{F}}_{q,q'} := \{u \mid q \overset{u}{\Longrightarrow} q'\}$. Note that $L_{q,q'}$ is regular and recognisable by an NFA of size at most $n + 1$: if $q' \ne q$ then $L_{q,q'} = L(Q, \Sigma, q, \delta, \{q'\})$. If $q' = q$ then we need an extra state to ensure that the NFA only accepts non-empty words.

Regularity of $L^{\mathsf{F}}_{q,q'}$ follows from this because

$$L^{\mathsf{F}}_{q,q'} \;=\; \Big(\bigcup_{q'' \in F} L_{q,q''} L_{q'',q'} \Big) \cup \begin{cases} \{a \in \Sigma \mid q' \in \delta(q,a)\} & \text{, if } q \in F \text{ or } q' \in F, \\ \varnothing & \text{, otherwise.} \end{cases}$$

However, this may not lead to NFA of optimal size. It is possible, though, to construct NFA for the languages $L^{\mathsf{F}}_{q,q'}$ of size $2n$ by extending the state space of the NFA $(Q, \Sigma, q, \delta, \{q'\})$ with a 1-bit flag in order to remember whether a run has traversed through an accepting state. Details are left as an exercise.

Since $2n \ge n + 1$ for $n \ge 1$ we have that $L_{q,q'}$ and $L^{\mathsf{F}}_{q,q'}$ are recognisable by NFA of size at most $2n$, and their complements are recognisable by NFA of size at most 2^{2n}. Now the following equation holds for each $u \in \Sigma^+$.

$$[u] = \Big(\bigcap_{\substack{q,q'\in Q\\ q\xrightarrow{u} q'}} L_{q,q'}\Big) \cap \Big(\bigcap_{\substack{q,q'\in Q\\ q\xRightarrow{u} q'}} L^{\mathsf{F}}_{q,q'}\Big) \cap \Big(\bigcap_{\substack{q,q'\in Q\\ q\xnrightarrow{u} q'}} \overline{L_{q,q'}}\Big) \cap \Big(\bigcap_{\substack{q,q'\in Q\\ q\xnRightarrow{u} q'}} \overline{L^{\mathsf{F}}_{q,q'}}\Big)$$

Let R denote the right-hand side of this equation. Note that the statement "$u' \in R$" is merely a reformulation of the statement $u \sim u'$. It is then possible to use standard intersection constructions to obtain an NFA for $[u]$. Since the maximal number of conjuncts in this equation is $4n^2$, it is possible to construct an NFA of size $(2^{2n})^{4n^2} = 2^{\mathcal{O}(n^3)}$ for each equivalence class. $\qquad\square$

The key to the proof of complementation closure is the observation that these equivalence classes must be well-behaved w.r.t. the language $L(\mathcal{A})$ of infinite words. In particular, languages of the form UV^ω built from pairs of such equivalence classes must either be contained in or disjoint from $L(\mathcal{A})$.

Lemma 5.29 *Let U,V be equivalence classes of $\sim$ and let $w \in UV^\omega$. If $w \in L(\mathcal{A})$ then $UV^\omega \subseteq L(\mathcal{A})$.*

Proof We decompose w as $w = uv_0v_1v_2\ldots$ with $u \in U$ and $v_i \in V$ for $i \geq 0$ and consider an accepting run $\rho = q_0, q_1, \ldots$ of $\mathcal{A}$ on w. This yields a sequence of states $(q_{i_j})_{j\geq 0}$ such that $q_I \xrightarrow{u} q_{i_0}$ and $q_{i_j} \xrightarrow{v_j} q_{i_j+1}$ for $j \geq 0$. Moreover, we must have $q_{i_j} \xRightarrow{v_j} q_{i_j+1}$ for infinitely many j.

Now take some arbitrary $w' \in UV^\omega$. It remains to be seen that $w' \in L(\mathcal{A})$. As above, we decompose w' into $u'v'_0v'_1\ldots$ s.t. $u' \in U$ and $v'_i \in V$ for all $i \geq 0$. But then we have $u \sim u'$ and $v_i \sim v'_i$ for all $i \geq 0$ because U and V are equivalence classes of $\sim$. As a result, we have $q_I \xrightarrow{u'} q_{i_0}$ and $q_{i_j} \xrightarrow{v'_j} q_{i_j+1}$ for all $j \geq 0$ with, aditionally, $q_{i_j} \xRightarrow{v'_j} q_{i_j+1}$ for infinitely many j. Hence, it is possible to construct a run of $\mathcal{A}$ on w' that starts in q_I and then passes through q_{i_0} after reading u', and so on. The additional observation on the fact that infinitely many pairs (q_{i_j}, q_{i_j+1}) not only belong to $\xrightarrow{v_j}$ but even $\xRightarrow{v_j}$ for the respective indices j, means that this run is indeed accepting. $\qquad\square$

Lemma 5.30 *Let U, V be classes of $\sim$ and $w \in UV^\omega$. If $w \in \overline{L(\mathcal{A})}$ then $UV^\omega \subseteq \overline{L(\mathcal{A})}$.*

Proof Suppose for the sake of contradiction that there is some $w' \in UV^\omega$ with $w' \in L(\mathcal{A})$. Lemma 5.29 then shows that $w \in L(\mathcal{A})$, contradicting the assumption. $\square$

The next and final statement about the properties of equivalence classes may seem rather simple at first sight, stating that every ω-word belongs to some language built from equivalence classes. It is reminiscent of the decomposition of an ω-regular language into parts of the form UV^ω for regular languages U, V. Note, though, that this lemma makes a stronger statement about *all* ω-words. Moreover, one may be inclined to prove this via a standard decomposition of an infinite run of $\mathcal{A}$ which must necessarily revisit some state q infinitely often. However, since the lemma makes an assertion about all words, not just those in $L(\mathcal{A})$, such runs need not exist. And even if they exist, they would only yield a statement about the possibility to reach that state from itself, i.e. that $q \xrightarrow{v_i} q$ for infinitely many v_i. This is not sufficient to finally show that $\overline{L(\mathcal{A})}$ can be written as a union of languages of the form U, V for some regular languages U, V.

Lemma 5.31 *Let $w \in \Sigma^\omega$. There exist equivalence classes U, V of $\sim$ such that* $w \in UV^\omega$.

Proof Clearly, each non-empty finite word $u \in \Sigma^+$ lies in some class, namely its own class: $u \in [u]$. Now let $w = a_0 a_1 \ldots$ be given. We consider the following colouring $f : \binom{\mathbb{N}}{2} \to \Sigma^+/\sim$ defined by $f(\{i, j\}) := [a_i \ldots a_{j-1}]$ assuming, w.l.o.g., $i < j$. According to Thm. 5.26, there is some equivalence class $V \in \Sigma^+/\sim$ and an infinite $I \subseteq \mathbb{N}$ such that $f(\{i, j\}) = V$ for all $i, j \in I$. Let $i_0, i_1, i_2, \ldots$ be an enumeration of I in ascending order, i.e. $i_0 < i_1 < \ldots$. W.l.o.g. we can assume $i_0 > 0$ because any infinite subsequence of I is also sufficient for the rest of this argument.

Clearly, we have $w = a_0 \ldots a_{i_0-1} a_{i_0} \ldots a_{i_1-1} a_{i_1} \ldots$ and therefore

$$w \in \underbrace{\left[a_0 \ldots a_{i_0-1}\right]}_{U} \underbrace{\left[a_{i_0} \ldots a_{i_1-1}\right]}_{V} \underbrace{\left[a_{i_1} \ldots a_{i_2-1}\right]}_{V} \underbrace{\left[a_{i_2} \ldots a_{i_3-1}\right]}_{V} \ldots$$

which determines a class U in addition to the class V obtained above, and shows that $w \in UV^\omega$. $\qquad\square$

The essential combined statement of these three lemmas is the following: take an NBA $\mathcal{A}$ over some alphabet Σ, and its associated equivalence relation $\sim$ on Σ^+. Then Σ^ω is partitioned into segments of the form UV^ω for equivalence classes U, V. Moreover, the borderline between $L(\mathcal{A})$ and $\overline{L(\mathcal{A})}$ runs along the edges of such segments. Hence, both are unions of such segments, and finiteness of the index of $\sim$ even guarantees that they are finite unions. This allows us to prove complementation closure of the class of NBA-recognisable languages.

Theorem 5.32 *For every NBA $\mathcal{A}$ of size n there is an NBA $\mathcal{B}$ s.t. $L(\mathcal{B}) = \overline{L(\mathcal{A})}$ and* $|\mathcal{B}| = 2^{\mathcal{O}(n^3)}$.

Proof Suppose $\mathcal{A}$ is given. It induces the equivalence relation $\sim$ and its corresponding classes as studied above. We now claim that

$$\overline{L(\mathcal{A})} \;=\; \bigcup \{UV^\omega \mid U, V \in \Sigma^+/\sim \text{ and } UV^\omega \cap L(\mathcal{A}) = \varnothing\} \,. \tag{5.2}$$

It should be clear that $\overline{L(\mathcal{A})}$ then is ω-regular as a finite union of languages of the form UV^ω for languages U, V which are regular according to Lemma 5.28. Finiteness of this union is a consequence of Lemma 5.27 (b) stating that there are only finitely many equivalence classes, specifically at most 3^{n^2} many, i.e. at most 3^{2n^2} many pairs of them. Using standard constructions for the union, concatenation and ω-iteration on NFA (cf. Lemma 5.9, 5.10 and 5.11), we obtain an NBA of size $3^{2n^2} \cdot 2 \cdot 2^{\mathcal{O}(n^3)} = 2^{\mathcal{O}(n^3)}$ for the expression in (5.2) above.

It remains to be seen that (5.2) is true. "$\subseteq$" Suppose that $w \in \overline{L(\mathcal{A})}$. According to Lemma 5.31 there are equivalence classes U, V s.t. $w \in UV^{\omega}$. According to Lemma 5.30 we have $UV^{\omega} \subseteq \overline{L(\mathcal{A})}$ and therefore $UV^{\omega} \cap L(\mathcal{A}) = \varnothing$.

"$\supseteq$" It suffices to show that $UV^{\omega} \subseteq \overline{L(\mathcal{A})}$ for any pair of equivalence classes U, V such that $UV^{\omega} \cap L(\mathcal{A}) = \varnothing$. Let U, V be given with this property. Clearly, if $UV^{\omega} = \varnothing$ then the statement trivially holds true. Suppose therefore that there is some $w \in UV^{\omega}$ and assume, for the sake of contradiction, that $w \notin \overline{L(\mathcal{A})}$, i.e. $w \in L(\mathcal{A})$. According to Lemma 5.29, we then have $UV^{\omega} \subseteq L(\mathcal{A})$ contradicting the assumption that $UV^{\omega} \neq \varnothing$ and $UV^{\omega} \subseteq \overline{L(\mathcal{A})}$. $\qquad\square$

Example 5.33 Reconsider the language L_3 of all words over $\{a, b\}$ that contain finitely many symbols b only, recognised for example by the 2-state NBA $\mathcal{A}_3$ shown in Ex. 5.21. There are eight languages $L_{q,q'}$, resp. $L_{q,q'}^{\mathsf{F}}$ for $q, q' \in \{0, 1\}$ as follows. For brevity, we write $L_{qq'}$ instead of $L_{q,q'}$ etc.

$$
\begin{aligned}
L_{00} &= (a+b)^+ & L_{00}^{\mathsf{F}} &= \varnothing \\
L_{01} &= (a+b)^* a^+ & L_{01}^{\mathsf{F}} &= L_{01} \\
L_{10} &= \varnothing & L_{10}^{\mathsf{F}} &= \varnothing \\
L_{11} &= a^+ & L_{11}^{\mathsf{F}} &= L_{11}
\end{aligned}
$$

Note that only two of them are non-trivial, namely L_{01} and L_{11}. Their complements are as follows.

$$
\overline{L_{01}} := (a+b)^* b \qquad\qquad \overline{L_{11}} := (a+b)^* b (a+b)^*
$$

Without the observation on the triviality of some of these languages, i.e. them either being $\varnothing$ or $\{a, b\}^+$, we would have to consider 2^8 combinations of intersections of these, namely one for each choice of either L_{xy} or $\overline{L_{xy}}$, resp. L_{xy}^{F} or $\overline{L_{xy}^{\mathsf{F}}}$. However, here we only need to consider four combinations.

$$
\begin{aligned}
L_{01} \cap L_{11} &= a^+ = [a] \\
L_{01} \cap \overline{L_{11}} &= (a+b)^* b (a+b)^* a = [ba] \\
\overline{L_{01}} \cap L_{11} &= \varnothing \\
\overline{L_{01}} \cap \overline{L_{11}} &= (a+b)^* b = [b]
\end{aligned}
$$

Note that $UV^{\omega} \cap L_3 = \varnothing$ for $U, V \in \{[a], [ba], [b]\}$ iff $V = [b]$ or $V = [ba]$. We therefore have

$$
\begin{aligned}
\overline{L_3} &= [a][b]^{\omega} \cup [a][ba]^{\omega} \cup [b][b]^{\omega} \cup [b][ba]^{\omega} \cup [ba][b]^{\omega} \cup [ba][ba]^{\omega} \\
&= [b]^{\omega} \cup [ba]^{\omega}.
\end{aligned}
$$

because $[a][b] \subseteq [b]$, $[a][ba] \subseteq [ba]$, $[b][ba] \subseteq [ba]$ and $[ba][b] \subseteq [b]$.

According to this, $\overline{L_3}$ consists of all word of the form $((a + b)^*b)^\omega$ or $((a + b)^*b(a+b)^*a)^\omega$. Clearly, both contain infinitely many symbols b, and it is even the case that $((a + b)^*b(a + b)^*a)^\omega \subseteq ((a + b)^*b)^\omega$. Hence, $\overline{L_3} = ((a + b)^*b)^\omega$, and this is indeed pretty much the simplest ω-regular expression for the complement of the language of all infinite words that contain finitely many symbols b only.

5.6 Monadic Second-Order Logic on Infinite Words

Remember that effective complementation of NFA (via DFA) was the key to establishing decidability of MSO over finite words. Now we are in a similar situation with respect to infinite words, i.e. we have an automaton model in the form of NBA with effective procedures like complementation, that can serve as the basis for decision procedures of logics interpreted over infinite words.

We are mainly interested in Monadic Second-Order Logic (MSO) again. Its syntax is the same as that of MSO over finite words:

$$\varphi \ ::= \ x < y \mid X(x) \mid a(x) \mid \varphi_1 \vee \varphi_2 \mid \neg\varphi \mid \exists x\, \varphi \mid \exists X\, \varphi$$

where $a \in \Sigma, x, y \in \mathcal{V}_1$ are first-order variables, and $X \in \mathcal{V}_2$ is a second-order variable. Syntactic considerations like formula size, further operators as abbreviations etc. apply here as well.

Given a word $w \in \Sigma^\omega$, a matching variable assignment is an $I : (\mathcal{V}_1 \to \mathbb{N}) \cup (\mathcal{V}_2 \to 2^\mathbb{N})$ assigning arbitrary positions in w and sets thereof to the first-, respectively second-order variables in an MSO formula. The satisfaction of an MSO formula φ by a word w and an assignment I, written $w, I \models \varphi$, is defined in exactly the same way as for MSO over finite words.

Example 5.34 The difference in interpretation between finite and infinite words is best revealed by the formula $\exists x\, \forall y\, y \leq x$ which is not only satisfiable but in fact valid over finite words, but unsatisfiable over infinite words.

Likewise, $\varphi := \forall x\, \exists y.y \geq x \wedge a(y)$ states that the underlying word has infinitely many symbols a, i.e. we have $L(\varphi) = (\Sigma^*a)^\omega$. When interpreted over finite words it is not unsatisfiable but it says nothing about infinite occurrences which of course cannot happen on finite words anyway. There it only describes the language Σ^*a.

Formulas like

$$x < y \wedge \exists X.X(x) \wedge \neg X(y) \wedge \forall z.X(z) \leftrightarrow \neg X(succ(z))$$

however, express the same property – the distance between the positions x and y is odd – regardless of whether they are interpreted over finite or infinite words.

Henceforth, we will only speak of MSO instead of "MSO over infinite words" since this and the following chapters in Part II are concerned with infinite words, and MSO over finite words will play no active role here anymore.

Decidability of MSO follows the same line as in the case of finite words. We first observe that first-order variables can be eliminated by replacing them with suitable second-order variables and normalising formulas to be built from atomic formulas of the form $sing(X)$, $X \subseteq Y$, $X \subseteq a$ and $X < Y$.

Next, a word $w \in \Sigma^\omega$ together with an interpretation of k second-order variables $X_1, \ldots, X_k$ can again be regarded as a word $w_I \in (\Sigma \times (\{0,1\})^k)^\omega$. It is then possible to construct NBA for MSO formulas in the following sense.

Lemma 5.35 *Let $\varphi(X_1, \ldots, X_k)$ be a normalised MSO formula for some $k \geq 0$. It is possible to effectively construct an NBA $\mathcal{A}_\varphi$ over $\Sigma \times \{0,1\}^k$ such that $L(\mathcal{A}_\varphi) = \{w_I \mid w, I \vDash \varphi\}$.*

The proof is left as an exercise; it is done in exactly the same way as the translation from MSO over finite words into NFA. Here we rely on Thm. 5.32 to effectively handle negation in formulas by automata complementation.

Lemma 5.35 states the existence of an effective translation from MSO into NBA. The converse translation, showing that ω-regular languages are MSO-definable, is equally effective. It is done in the same way as for MSO over finite words (cf. Thm. 2.10). Details are left as an exercise.

Theorem 5.36 *A language is MSO-definable iff it is ω-regular.*

Decidability of MSO over infinite words is then obtained by combining Thm. 5.15 and Lemma 5.35.

Theorem 5.37 *The satisfiability problem for MSO is decidable.*

It should be clear that MSO over infinite words cannot be significantly easier to decide than MSO over finite words. Satisfiability of MSO over finite words can easily be reduced to that over infinite words. Remember that the non-elementary complexity of the satisfiability problem stems from the depth of alternations between existential quantification and negations in a formula. The translation presented in the proof of the following theorem does not decrease this measure. Hence, satisfiability of MSO over infinite words is also non-elementary.

Lemma 5.38 *For every MSO formula φ over finite words there is an equi-satisfiable MSO formula φ' over infinite words such that $|\varphi'| = \mathcal{O}(|\varphi|)$.*

Proof Let $\varphi \in$ MSO over finite words and z be a first-order variable not used in φ. The trick is to let ψ ask for some "maximal" position in an underlying word in the sense that everything that φ demands, needs to take place before that position. This can be done using quantifier relativisation. Let $\psi := \exists z.\varphi{\downarrow}_z$ where

$$(\exists x\, \chi){\downarrow}_z := \exists x.x < z \wedge \chi{\downarrow}_z \quad , \quad (\exists X\, \chi){\downarrow}_z := \exists X.(\forall x.X(x) \to x < z) \wedge \chi{\downarrow}_z$$

and $\cdot{\downarrow}_z$ distributes over Boolean operators and does not change atomic formulas.

Correctness of this construction is easily seen. Satisfiability of φ implies that of φ': for every $w \in \Sigma^*$ and matching interpretation with $w, I \vDash \varphi$ we have $wv, I[z \mapsto |w|] \vDash \varphi'$ for any $v \in \Sigma^\omega$.

The other direction holds because for every $w = a_0 a_1 \ldots \in \Sigma^\omega$ and matching interpretation I such that $w, I \vDash \varphi'$ we have $a_0 \ldots a_{I(z)-1}, I' \vDash \varphi$ where I' agrees with I on the first-order variables and $I'(X) := I(X) \cap \{0, \ldots, I(z) - 1\}$ for all second-order variables X. $\square$

Thus, the coarse estimation that deciding an MSO formula is roughly k-fold exponential in the depths k of alternations between existential quantifications and negation, resp. universal quantifications, is true here as well, both in terms of upper and lower bounds. The upper bound is obtained by inspection of the decision procedure; as in the case of finite words, every negation requires an exponential blowup. Note that here, complementation is more difficult, albeit only in terms of a higher polynomial degree inside an exponential.

Bibliographic Notes

Büchi automata were introduced – as the name suggests – by Büchi in order to obtain decidability of the logic often known as S1S, Second-Order Logic of One Successor [Büc62]. It can be understood as the variant of WS1S, as introduced in Sect. 2.4, where the restriction that second-order variables are interpreted as *finite* sets only, is lifted. Hence, an S1S formula is interpreted over the natural numbers with the ordering relation as the only binary predicate and arbitrary unary predicates, with first-order quantifiers ranging over arbitrary natural numbers and second-order quantifiers over arbitrary sets of natural numbers. This is easily seen to be just what MSO over infinite words does where the letters in each position can be seen as a combined interpretation of all unary predicates.

Büchi automata are such a natural, intuitive and computationally feasible model of computation for properties of infinite words that their prevalence in the literature is unsurprising. See for instance the handbook articles by Thomas [Tho97, Tho90] for an introduction into Büchi automata with a focus on their use in logical decision procedures.

Büchi automata have also proved to be a valuable tool in program verification, by providing – just as they do for MSO – a computational counterpart for denotational specification formalisms like Linear-Time Temporal Logic (LTL) [Pnu77]. This has been discovered and explored widely by Vardi and others [VW94, Var96]. The connection between Büchi automata and logics for infinite words is robust in the sense that extensions of the basic logic LTL can either be handled with Büchi automata directly, for instance general fixpoint quantifiers [BB89, Kai97], or Büchi automata can be extended elegantly whilst retaining similar algorithmic properties, to then capture the logic at hand. This is the case for the two-way extension for example, that can move in both directions on an input word. It corresponds nicely to temporal logics with past operators [Var88]. A historical overview of the development in logics for program specification and verification, together with its tight link to automata on infinite words, is given by Vardi [Var08].

The complementation problem for Büchi automata is, notably, the bottleneck for applications in which complementation is required in some form or other. The proof presented here is based on Büchi's work [Büc62], used to obtain decidability of S1S, making use of Thm. 5.26 – the combinatorial result known as *Ramsey's Theorem* [Ram30]. It is worth noting, though, that this is Ramsey's Theorem for infinite graphs, and the term "Ramsey's Theorem" is also used for a combinatorial result on finite graphs which is not of significant relevance to the work on automata and logics presented here. This is why we simply refer to the result used by Büchi as "Ramsey's Theorem".

Other applications of Büchi complementation with more practical relevance have created a demand for better efficiency, and this has led to a variety of contributions on the complementation problem. McNaughton showed that ω-regular languages can be recognised by deterministic automata using a richer acceptance condition [McN66], see the following chapter, from which complementation closure can be derived. Safra provided a solution using determinisation [Saf88] which is discussed in detail in a later chapter. Klarlund found a procedure that is based not on Ramsey's Theorem as the combinatorial backbone, but on progress measures which are sophisticated counters used to track combinations of infinite and finite behaviour [Kla91]. Kupferman and Vardi went through alternating automata on infinite words, based on work by Muller and Schupp [MS87, MSS88] and to be studied in a later chapter, to obtain a complementation procedure [KV01].

It is fair to summarise the situation as follows: complementation of Büchi automata remains to be an inherently intricate problem, and no single suggestion of a solution is commonly accepted to yield a satisfactory procedure in practice.

The combinatorial difficulty is also made apparent by studying lower bounds on the size of Büchi automata for the complements of given ω-regular languages. Michel was the first to provide an example which shows that Büchi complementation requires a greater blowup of $\Omega(n!)$ than the $\Omega(2^n)$-blowup for NFA [Mic88]. A more detailed discussion on the history and state-of-the-art in the asymptotic complexities of procedures for Büchi complementation is given by Schewe [Sch09a], following an equal-directed earlier study by Friedgut et al. [FKV06].

Exercises

Exercise 43 Let $\Sigma = \{0, 1\}$. Show that Σ^* is countable but Σ^ω is uncountable. *Hint:* Construct an injective function $f : [0, 1) \to \Sigma^\omega$ where $[0, 1) = \{x \in \mathbb{R} \mid 0 \leq x < 1\}$. Simply for the purpose of interest and insight, try to construct f such that it is bijective. This is a bit harder, though.

Exercise 44 Let $u \in \Sigma^+$. Define u^ω formally in the form $(u^\omega)(i) = \ldots$ for $i \in \mathbb{N}$.

Exercise 45 Let $U \subseteq \Sigma^*$. Is it the case that every $w \in U^\omega$ has a unique representation as $w = u_0 u_1 \ldots$ with $u_i \in U$ for all $i \in \mathbb{N}$? If so, prove it. If not, work out a non-trivial property on such languages of finite words such that the proposition becomes true at least for such languages U that satisfy this property.

Exercise 46 Construct NBA for the following languages.

a) $\{w \in \{a,b\}^\omega \mid \forall n \geq 0 : w(3n) = a\}$.
b) $\{w \in \{a,b\}^\omega \mid \forall n \geq 0 : w(n) = a$ iff $n \equiv 0 \bmod 3\}$.
c) The set of all words over $\{a,b,c\}$ s.t. between every two positions that carry a b and have no further b in between, there is an odd number of occurrences of the symbol c.
d) The set of all words over $\Sigma_k = [k]$ s.t. the largest number that occurs infinitely often in this word is even.
e) The set of all ω-words over Σ that contain at least one occurrence of a given word $u \in \Sigma^+$.
f) The set of all ω-words over Σ that contain infinitely many occurrences of a given word $u \in \Sigma^+$.
g) The set of all ω-words over Σ that contain only finitely many occurrences of a given word $u \in \Sigma^+$.

Exercise 47 Formally define NBA with possibly more than one initial state and show that they are equi-expressive to the model of NBA with a single initial state.

Exercise 48 Let $\Sigma = \{+, -, 0, 1, .\}$. Note that an ω-word w over Σ that is of the form $(+ \cup -)(0 + 1(0 \cup 1)^*).(0 \cup 1)^\omega$ naturally represents a real number x_w as follows. Let $w = sd_n \ldots d_0.f_0 f_1 f_2 \ldots$. Then

$$x_w \; := \; s' \cdot \left(\left(\sum_{i=0}^{n} d_i \cdot 2^i\right) + \left(\sum_{i=0}^{\infty} f_i \cdot 2^{-(i+1)}\right)\right)$$

where $s' = 1$ if $s = +$ and $s' = -1$ if $s = -$.

For example, $w = -1010.1(110)^\omega$ represents $-10\frac{13}{14}$ because $\frac{13}{14} = \frac{1}{2} + \frac{3}{7}$. The contribution of the periodic part $(110)^\omega$ with its first digit stating the contribution of $\frac{1}{4}$ is $\frac{3}{7}$ as the following calculation shows.

$$1 \cdot \frac{1}{4} + 1 \cdot \frac{1}{8} + 0 \cdot \frac{1}{16} + 1 \cdot \frac{1}{32} + 1 \cdot \frac{1}{64} + 0 \cdot \frac{1}{128} + 1 \cdot \ldots \; =$$

$$\frac{3}{8} + \frac{3}{64} + \frac{3}{512} + \ldots \; = \; \sum_{i=1}^{\infty} 3 \cdot \frac{1}{2^{3n}} \; = \; 3 \cdot \sum_{i=1}^{\infty} \left(\frac{1}{8}\right)^n \; = \; 3 \cdot \frac{\frac{1}{8}}{1 - \frac{1}{8}} \; = \; \frac{3 \cdot 8}{7 \cdot 8} \; = \; \frac{3}{7}$$

Likewise, an ω-word over Σ^k for some $k \geq 1$ represents a k-tuple of real numbers; the representation of the i-th number in this tuple is given in the i-th track of this word. We will only consider words of the form $(+ \cup -)^k((0 \cup 1)^k)^*(.)^k((0 \cup 1)^k)^\omega$, though, i.e. those where the decimal points are aligned (at the expense of possible leading zeros in any of the tracks). Note that a language of such k-track words can be seen as a k-ary relation on the reals.

a) Construct an NBA $\mathcal{A}^2_{add}$ over Σ^3 that accepts a word iff it represents a triple (x, y, z) s.t. $x + y = z$. *Hint:* Consider the case of w starting with $(+, +, +)$ first. Then determine which other tuples of sign symbols can occur at all, and make use of equivalences like $x - y = z$ iff $x = y + z$.

b) Let $k > 2$. Construct NBA $\mathcal{A}^k_{add}$ over Σ^{k+1} that recognise the relation $\{(x_1, \ldots, x_k, y) \mid y = \sum_{i=1}^{k} x_i\}$ in generalisation of part (a). *Hint:* Use product and projection constructions on NBA.

c) Let $n \geq 0$. Construct an NBA $\mathcal{A}^n_{shift}$ that recognises the relation $\{(x, y) \mid y = x \cdot 2^n\}$. *Hint:* Multiplication of a number in binary representation by 2^n is simply realised by shifting the decimal point n positions to the left.

d) Let $p \in \mathbb{Z}$. Construct an NBA $\mathcal{A}^p_{imult}$ that recognises the relation $\{(x, y) \mid y = p \cdot x\}$. *Hint:* This can be realised by employing the construction in part (c) several times. The key is to consider the binary representation of p. In other words, p can be decomposed into a sum of powers of 2. By distributivity of multiplication over addition, multiplication by p can be realised by successive additions of multiples of p by powers of 2.

e) Let $q \in \mathbb{Q}$. Construct an NBA $\mathcal{A}^q_{rmult}$ that recognises the relation $\{(x, y) \mid y = q \cdot x\}$. *Hint:* Each q can be written as $\frac{p}{n}$ with $p \in \mathbb{Z}$ and $n \in \mathbb{N} \setminus \{0\}$. Now note that $y = \frac{p}{n} \cdot x$ iff $n \cdot y = p \cdot x$. By using a product of two NBA from part (d) it is possible to recognise the relation of quadruples (x, y, px, ny). This automaton then only needs to be intersected with one that checks for equality in the third and fourth track, and by alphabet projection to the first two tracks, we obtain an NBA for the target relation.

Exercise 49 Prove Lemma 5.9.

Exercise 50 Prove Lemma 5.10.

Exercise 51   a) Prove Lemma 5.18.

b) Let $h : \Sigma \to \Delta^*$ be a morphism that is potentially deleting. Provide a well-defined notion of homomorphic image of a Σ-language as a Δ-language that preserves ω-regularity.

Exercise 52 Prove part (a) of Lemma 5.27, and show that $\sim$ is indeed an equivalence relation.

Exercise 53 Let $\mathcal{A}$ be some NBA with state set Q and $q, q' \in Q$. Construct an NFA for the language $L^F_{q,q'}$ whose size does not exceed $2 \cdot |Q|$, cf. Lemma 5.28.

Exercise 54 Construct NBA for the complements of the following languages, using Büchi's complementation construction along the lines of Ex. 5.33.

a) $L_1 = (ab)^\omega$ over $\{a, b\}$,
b) $L_2 = (a(a + b))^\omega$ over $\{a, b\}$,
c) $L_3 = \{w \in \{a, b\}^\omega \mid |w|_b = \infty\}$,
d) $L_4 = (a + b)^* aa(a + b)^\omega$ over $\{a, b\}$.

Hint: Start by constructing NBA for these languages that lead to a smallest number of languages $L_{q,q'}$, resp. $L^F_{q,q'}$.

Exercise 55 Write down MSO formulas for the four languages specified in Exc. 54.

Exercise 56 Prove Lemma 5.35.

Exercise 57 Prove the direction from right-to-left in Thm. 5.36.

Chapter 6
Acceptance Conditions

The acceptance condition leading to the notion of Büchi automaton – traversing certain states infinitely many times – is a natural extension of the acceptance of finite words by reaching an accepting state at the end of run. It is by no means the only way to make a distinction between accepting and non-accepting infinite runs.

In this chapter we study further acceptance conditions and the expressiveness of the automata models that arise from these. As it turns out, all of them give rise to the same class of languages, i.e. the so-called Rabin, Streett, parity and Muller automata do not exceed ω-regularity in expressive power. However, Büchi acceptance stands out as a weaker one in the sense that the others allow determinisation which is studied in the following chapter.

Moreover, remember that one of the reasons for why NBA cannot easily be complemented via DBA is the fact that the Büchi acceptance condition is not self-dual, i.e. the complement of a Büchi condition is not a Büchi condition itself. As we will see, there is sufficient self-duality in this respect amongst the other acceptance conditions. At the end, we explicitly study the complement of a Büchi acceptance condition – visiting designated states only finitely often – as another separate acceptance condition leading to yet another automaton model operating on infinite words. This one will turn out to be strictly weaker in expressiveness, though.

6.1 Rabin- and Streett-Automata

Recall that, for an infinite sequence $\rho = q_0, q_1, \dots$ of elements from a finite set, we write $Inf(\rho)$ to denote the set of such elements that occur infinitely often in ρ, i.e. $Inf(\rho) = \{q \mid \forall i \in \mathbb{N} \, \exists j \geq i \text{ s.t. } q_j = q\}$. This was used in Def. 5.7 for instance to define acceptance by an NBA. The additional acceptance conditions discussed here and below will also refer to $Inf(\rho)$ for runs ρ. The reason simply is that any finitary condition like "reaching a designated state after the first 1000 letters" can easily be encoded in the state set and transition relation. Hence, the acceptance conditions should only be concerned with infinite occurrences of states in a run.

© The Author(s), under exclusive
license to Springer-Verlag GmbH, DE, part of Springer Nature 2025
M. Hofmann and M. Lange, *Automata Theory and Logic*,
https://doi.org/10.1007/978-3-662-72154-4_6

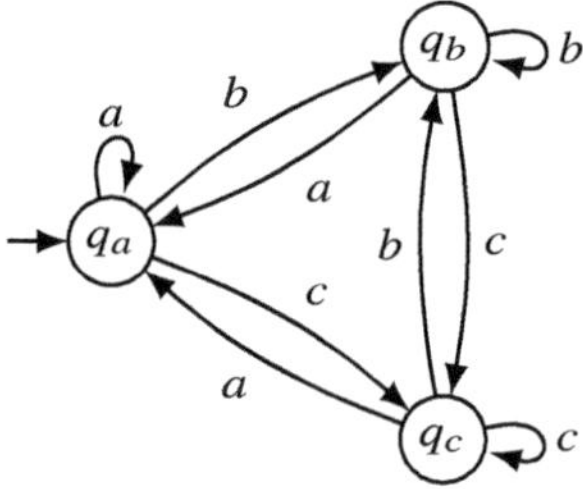

Fig. 6.1 Transition function of a finite automaton that uses its state set to only remember the letter from $\{a, b, c\}$ that has just been read.

Definition 6.1 A *nondeterministic Rabin automaton* (NRA) is an $\mathcal{A} = (Q, \Sigma, q_I, \delta, \mathcal{F})$ where Q, Σ, q_I, δ are the states, alphabet, initial state and transition relation just as in an NBA. The acceptance condition is $\mathcal{F} = \{(G_1, F_1), \ldots, (G_k, F_k)\}$ where $G_i, F_i \subseteq Q$ for some k and all $i = 1, \ldots, k$.

As usual, a *deterministic Rabin automaton* (DRA) is an NRA such that $|\delta(q, a)| \leq 1$ for all $q \in Q$ and $a \in \Sigma$. Note that determinism is purely a property of the transition function, not the acceptance condition.

A *run* of an NRA on a word $w = a_0 a_1 \ldots$ is, as usual, an infinite sequence $\rho = q_0, q_1, \ldots$ such that $q_0 = q_I$ and $q_{i+1} \in \delta(q_i, a_i)$ for all $i \geq 0$. It is *accepting* if there is an $i \in \{1, \ldots, k\}$ such that $Inf(\rho) \cap G_i \neq \varnothing$ and $Inf(\rho) \cap F_i = \varnothing$. As before, we may sometimes denote a run on w as an alternating sequence $q_0, a_0, q_1, a_1, \ldots$.

As usual, the language $L(\mathcal{A})$ of an NRA $\mathcal{A}$ is the set of all ω-words over Σ for which there is an accepting run. A language L is called *Rabin-recognisable* or *NRA-recognisable* if there is an NRA $\mathcal{A}$ such that $L(\mathcal{A}) = L$. DRA-recognisability is defined analogously.

The *size* of an NRA is measured, as with the other automata, as the size of its state set: $|\mathcal{A}| := |Q|$. Note that this is not necessarily a complete measure of the space needed to represent an NRA, notwithstanding the fact that the transition function may be (quadratically) bigger than that. Here, the acceptance condition $\mathcal{F}$ may be unbounded in $|Q|$, so we introduce a second measure. The *index* of the NRA $\mathcal{A} = (Q, \Sigma, q_I, \delta, \mathcal{F})$ is $|\mathcal{F}|$.

Hence, Rabin automata syntactically differ from Büchi automata in that their acceptance condition does not just designate a set of states that are to be visited infinitely often. They provide several alternatives of pairs of state sets with one component to be visited infinitely often, and the other one consisting of states that, at the same time, must not be visited infinitely often. Note that, for a so-called Rabin pair (G, F) from an NRA $\mathcal{A}$'s acceptance condition and a run ρ of $\mathcal{A}$, we have $Inf(\rho) \cap G \neq \varnothing$ iff *some* state in G is visited infinitely often, and $Inf(\rho) \cap F = \varnothing$ iff *all* states in F are visited finitely often only.

Example 6.2 Let $\Sigma = \{a, b, c\}$ and consider the language $L := \{w \in \Sigma^\omega \mid |w|_a = \infty \Rightarrow |w|_b = \infty\}$. The NRA in Fig. 6.1 simply remembers in its state what the last letter was that it read. The aim is to equip this automaton with a suitable Rabin acceptance condition to turn it into an NRA accepting L. For this, it suffices to note that a word w belongs to L iff $|w|_a < \infty$ or $|w|_b = \infty$. Hence, there are two possibilities for a word to be accepted: it contains finitely many symbols a or infinitely many symbols b. This is captured directly by two Rabin pairs, the former by $(\{q_b, q_c\}, \{q_a\})$, the latter by $(\{q_b\}, \varnothing)$.

Hence, we have $L = L(\mathcal{A})$ for the NRA $\mathcal{A} = (\{q_a, q_b, q_c\}, \{a, b, c\}, q_a, \delta, \mathcal{F})$ where δ is as shown in Fig. 6.1 and $\mathcal{F} = \{(\{q_b, q_c\}, \{q_a\}), (\{q_b\}, \varnothing)\}$. $\mathcal{A}$ is in fact even a DRA. Moreover, any of its states can be used as the initial state because all three recognise the same language.

The fact that two states in an automaton operating on infinite words recognise the same language does not mean that these can be collapsed into a single state, as it is possible for NFA. It should be clear that no 1-state NRA can recognise the language L from the example above.

As with the Büchi condition whose lack of self-duality was mentioned above, the Rabin acceptance condition also lacks (obvious) self-duality. That is, the natural complement of the assertion *"there is i such that $Inf(\rho) \cap G_i \neq \varnothing$ and $Inf(\rho) \cap F_i = \varnothing$"* is *"for all i we have $Inf(\rho) \cap G_i = \varnothing$ or $Inf(\rho) \cap F_i \neq \varnothing$."* This can be rephrased as *"for all i: if $Inf(\rho) \cap G_i \neq \varnothing$ then $Inf(\rho) \cap F_i \neq \varnothing$."*

First of all, it is unclear that this universal statement should be equivalent to an existential one which the Rabin condition is. Later we will see that the complement of a Rabin-recognisable language is also Rabin-recognisable, but this generally involves a non-trivial blowup. Hence, it is possible to rephrase "there is *no i* such that $Inf(\rho) \cap G_i \neq \varnothing$ and $Inf(\rho) \cap F_i = \varnothing$" as "there is i such that $Inf(\rho) \cap G_i' \neq \varnothing$ and $Inf(\rho) \cap F_i' = \varnothing$" for a different set of Rabin pairs (G_i', F_i'). In particular, when the underlying NRA is in fact deterministic, we cannot simply invert the acceptance condition in order to obtain a DRA for the complement language. We can help ourselves, though, by simply introducing the complement of a Rabin condition as an acceptance condition in its own right.

Definition 6.3 A *nondeterministic Streett automaton* (NSA) is an $\mathcal{A} = (Q, \Sigma, q_I, \delta, \mathcal{F})$ just like an NRA. The notions of size, index and deterministic Street automaton (DSA) are defined in the same way.

The only difference is in the interpretation of the acceptance condition $\mathcal{F} = \{(G_1, F_1), \ldots, (G_k, F_k)\} \subseteq 2^Q \times 2^Q$ as a Street-condition: a *run* $\rho = q_0, q_1, \ldots$ of such an NSA is *accepting* if for all $i = 1, \ldots, k$ we have that $Inf(\rho) \cap G_i \neq \varnothing$ implies $Inf(\rho) \cap F_i \neq \varnothing$.

Again, the notions of language of an NSA, Streett-recognisability, etc. are defined as usual.

Thus, the Streett-acceptance condition formalises dependencies of the form that certain states need to be visited infinitely often if certain (other) states are being visited infinitely often.

Example 6.4 Reconsider the language $L = \{w \in \{a, b, c\}^\omega \mid |w|_a = \infty \Rightarrow |w|_b = \infty\}$ from Ex. 6.2. It is not only Rabin-recognisable but also Streett-recognisable on the basis of the same deterministic automaton shown in Fig. 6.1 that signals the last seen letter in its state set. In particular, whenever it reads an a it moves to state q_a from anywhere, and likewise for b. Moreover, it moves out of state q_a, resp. q_b upon reading a letter that is different to a, resp. b. Hence, it visits state q_a infinitely often iff the word it reads contains infinitely many symbols a and likewise for b. Then the condition in the definition of L immediately translates into a Streett-acceptance condition with a single Streett pair: $\mathcal{F} = \{((\{q_a\}, \{q_b\}))\}$.

A natural question to consider concerns the expressiveness of Rabin and Streett automata in comparison to the class of ω-regular, i.e. Büchi-recognisable languages. It is not hard to see that Rabin- and Streett-recognisability is not weaker than that.

Theorem 6.5 *For every NBA $\mathcal{A}$ of size n there is an NRA, resp. NSA $\mathcal{B}$ of size n and index 1 such that $L(\mathcal{B}) = L(\mathcal{A})$.*

Proof Let $\mathcal{A} = (Q, \Sigma, q_I, \delta, F)$. It is easy to see that the Büchi acceptance condition F is equivalent to the Rabin-acceptance condition $\mathcal{F} = \{(F, \varnothing)\}$ and the Streett-acceptance condition $\mathcal{F} = \{(Q, F)\}$. Hence, $L(\mathcal{A})$ is recognisable by an NRA or NSA with the same transition graph as $\mathcal{A}$. $\qquad\square$

The more interesting direction is the converse of this: are there non-regular but Rabin- or Streett-recognisable languages, i.e. does the more elaborate acceptance condition lead to greater expressiveness? The answer is no, but we will continue to study further acceptance conditions including the so-called Muller condition that the Rabin- and Streett conditions easily embed into, and then show that these automata only recognise ω-regular languages. This minimises the effort needed to study expressiveness, i.e. we avoid comparing each two models of automata directly.

We do compare, though, the expressiveness of deterministic Rabin- and Streett automata with each other because of the way that these conditions have been introduced as dual ones.

Theorem 6.6 *Let $L \subseteq \Sigma^\omega$. If L is recognisable by a DRA, resp. DSA of size n and index k then $\Sigma^\omega \setminus L$ is recognisable by a DSA, resp. DRA of size n + 1 and index k + 1.*

Proof This is based on the observation that a run ρ is accepting w.r.t. the Rabin-acceptance condition $\mathcal{F}$ iff it is rejecting w.r.t. the Streett-acceptance condition $\mathcal{F}$ for the very same $\mathcal{F}$. The result then follows with the usual argument that runs of deterministic automata on given words are unique. The blowup with a possible extra state is needed in case the original DRA, resp. DSA is not complete, i.e. there are words that do not have infinite runs. This can be fixed with the usual trick of adding an extra state q that acts as a trap for those runs. When turning a DSA into a DRA for the complement language, one extra Rabin pair $(\{q\}, \varnothing)$ is needed. When turning a DRA into a DSA, the trap state q needs to be added to every F in a Streett pair (G, F). $\qquad\square$

Note that determinism is an important premise in this statement: one cannot simply complement an NRA by declaring it to be an NSA. This fails because NRA and NSA may have more than one run and thus complementation requires the universal quantification over all runs to be rephrased as an existential one. This is not possible without the aforementioned non-trivial blowup in the state space.

6.2 Parity Automata

The lack of self-duality of each of the Rabin and Streett conditions, resp. the fact that they are dual to each other, raises the question after the construction of an acceptance condition that sits in-between the two and is self-dual. This is what the parity condition, to be studied in this section, is and does. It is more abstract than the two in the way that it is presented: it does not directly make a requirement on the infinite occurrence of states. Instead, each state gets assigned a natural number that we call its *priority*, and then the parity condition makes an assertion on the infinite occurrence of priorities.

6.2.1 Priorities for Acceptance and Rejection

Definition 6.7 Let Σ be an alphabet as usual. A *nondeterministic parity automaton* (NPA) is an $\mathcal{A} = (Q, \Sigma, q_I, \delta, \Omega)$ where Q, Σ, q_I, δ are as with NBA, NRA or NSA, and the acceptance condition is given by the priority mapping $\Omega : Q \to \mathbb{N}$ on states. The size of an NPA is measured as the number of its states, as usual. The *index* of $\mathcal{A}$ is $|\Omega(Q)|$ where $\Omega(Q) := \{\Omega(q) \mid q \in Q\}$, i.e. the number of different priorities assigned to its states.

For certain considerations on expressiveness, this measure is too coarse. We therefore sometimes measure the index of an NPA as an interval, and say that $\mathcal{A}$ is of index $[k, m]$ for $k \le m$, if $\Omega(Q) \subseteq [k, m] := \{k, \ldots, m\}$.

We use $\equiv_2$ to denote equivalence modulo even/odd parity, i.e. $x \equiv_2 y$ iff $x \bmod 2 = y \bmod 2$ for $x, y \in \mathbb{N}$. A run $\rho = q_0, q_1, \ldots$ of the NPA $\mathcal{A}$ is *accepting* if $\max\{\Omega(q) \mid q \in Inf(\rho)\} \equiv_2 0$, i.e. it is even.

A *deterministic parity automaton* (DPA) is, as usual, an NPA with a deterministic transition function.

The notions of language of an NPA, NPA-/DPA-recognisability, resp. -definability are defined in the usual way.

Thus, NPA runs are accepting when the highest priority that is seen infinitely often in the run is even. This seems arbitrary in two ways. The reason for the fact that it is only the priorities that do or do not occur infinitely often in a run that determine acceptance is as before: the effect of a priority seen at some fixed n-th position in a run could easily be encoded in the state space. Thus, the question is: why the largest, and why even? There is in fact no particular reason for this convention. The expressiveness of NPA models that accept through odd priorities or minimal ones is the same. In fact, while there is general agreement in the literature that evenness should be associated with acceptance and consequently oddness with rejection, one often sees NPA acceptance being defined by evenness of the *least* priority seen infinitely often. As said before, this is purely a matter of convention and makes no difference for the expressiveness. Sometimes, these two variants of NPA are called *max-parity* and *min-parity* respectively, but the only purpose of this distinction is to fix the definition of acceptance. In this respect, we will be dealing with max-parity NPA exclusively, and all the results can be transferred straightforwardly to min-parity NPA.

Example 6.8 Let $\Sigma = \{a, b, c\}$. Reconsider the language $L = \{w \in \Sigma^\omega \mid |w|_a = \infty \Rightarrow |w|_b = \infty\}$ of Ex. 6.2 above. The automaton shown in Fig. 6.1 that has been equipped with a Rabin- and a Streett-condition in order to accept L, can also be equipped with a parity condition in order to accept L.

The trick here is to note that the condition $|w|_a = \infty \Rightarrow |w|_b = \infty$ can be enforced by the automaton under consideration that remembers the last seen letter in its state space, by signalling hierarchical values: seeing a b is obviously good in terms of this happening infinitely often because it makes the condition satisfied. Seeing an a infinitely often is bad unless a b is also seen infinitely often. Hence, it should signal something good, i.e. an even value, when seeing a b, and something bad and less relevant, i.e. an odd and smaller value, when seeing an a. Finally, seeing a c infinitely often is good for as long as no a is seen infinitely often. So seeing a letter c should result in the signalling of a good value that is even less relevant than the one for a. This leads to an NPA, in fact a DPA, for L by equipping the automaton from Fig. 6.2 with the parity acceptance condition $\Omega : \{q_a, a_b, a_c\} \to [0, 2]$ where

$$\Omega(q_a) := 1 \quad , \quad \Omega(q_b) := 2 \quad , \quad \Omega(q_c) := 0 .$$

To see that this is correct, take a run $\rho = q_I, q_{x_0}, q_{x_1}, \ldots$ on the word $w = x_0 x_1 \ldots$ and suppose that it is accepting, i.e. $m := \max\{\Omega(q_{x_i}) \mid i \geq 0\}$ is even. Since $\Omega(\{q_a, q_b, q_c\}) = \{0, 1, 2\}$ there are only two possibilities.

- Case $m = 2$, i.e. $q_b \in \mathit{Inf}(\rho)$. Then $|w|_b = \infty$ and therefore $w \in L$.
- Case $m = 0$, i.e. $\{q_c\} = \mathit{Inf}(\rho)$ because $\Omega(q_a) > 0$ and $\Omega(q_b) > 0$. But then $|w|_c = \infty$ and, moreover, $|w|_a \neq \infty \neq |w|_b$. Thus, $w \in (a + b + c)^* c^\omega$ and, again, $w \in L$.

The converse direction is shown in the same way. So we have that L is indeed recognisable by an NPA of index 3 or, more precisely, of index $[0, 2]$.

Self-duality of the parity acceptance condition is a consequence of the fact that $\max\{\Omega(q) \mid q \in \mathit{Inf}(\rho)\}$ is unique for any run ρ, and that it is even iff it is not odd, and there is a simple way of transposing priorities to swap their parity whilst keep their internal total ordering.

The next lemma formalises the intuitive idea that the absolute values of states' priorities are irrelevant; instead it is their relative ordering – being greater or smaller – and their parities – being even or odd – that is only relevant for determining acceptance of a run.

Lemma 6.9 $\mathcal{A} = (Q, \Sigma, q_I, \delta, \Omega)$ *be an NPA and* $\mathcal{A}' = (Q, \Sigma, q_I, \delta, \Omega')$ *be an NPA that differs from* $\mathcal{A}$ *at most in the priority assignment. Suppose we have*

(i) $\Omega(q) \le \Omega(q')$ *iff* $\Omega'(q) \le \Omega'(q')$ *for all* $q, q' \in Q$, *and*
(ii) $\Omega(q) \equiv_2 0$ *iff* $\Omega'(q) \equiv_2 0$ *for all* $q \in Q$.

Then we have $L(\mathcal{A}') = L(\mathcal{A})$.

Proof Suppose that ρ is a run of $\mathcal{A}$, resp. $\mathcal{A}'$ on some word w. We get that $\max\{\Omega(q) \mid q \in \mathit{Inf}(\rho)\}$ is even iff $\max\{\Omega'(q) \mid q \in \mathit{Inf}(\rho)\}$ is even; (i) ensures that it is the same state $q \in \mathit{Inf}(\rho)$ that attains the maximal priority in the respective set, and (ii) ensures that it is either even in both cases or odd in both. Thus, an accepting run in $\mathcal{A}$ is an accepting run in $\mathcal{A}'$ and vice-versa. $\qquad\Box$

As a consequence, we can make some assumptions on the indices of NPA, namely that the priorities are as small as possible, with the smallest being 0 or 1, and that they do not leave gaps. The formal proof, based on (possibly multiple) applications of Lemma 6.9 is left as an exercise.

Corollary 6.10 *Let* $L \subseteq \Sigma^\omega$. *Suppose that* $L = L(\mathcal{A})$ *for an NPA* $\mathcal{A} = (Q, \Sigma, q_I, \delta, \Omega)$ *with* $\Omega : Q \to [k, m]$. *Then* $L = L(\mathcal{A}')$ *where* $\mathcal{A}' = (Q, \Sigma, q_I, \delta, \Omega')$ *such that* $\Omega' : Q \to [k', m']$ *for some* $k', m' \in \mathbb{N}$, *and the following two properties are satisfied.*

a) $k' \in \{0, 1\}$,
b) for every $p \in [k', m']$ *there is some* $q \in Q$ *such that* $\Omega'(q) = p$.

It should be clear with Lemma 6.9 that shifting all priorities uniformly by an even amount does not change the language of an NPA. Shifting them uniformly by an odd amount does change the language in general, as it turns an even maximal priority occurring infinitely often in a run into an odd one and vice-versa. This simple construction can be used to complement the language of a DPA.

Theorem 6.11 *For every DPA* $\mathcal{A}$ *of size* n *and index* $[k, m]$ *there is a DPA* $\overline{\mathcal{A}}$ *of size at most* $n + 1$ *and index* $[k + 1, m + 1]$ *such that* $L(\overline{\mathcal{A}}) = \Sigma^\omega \setminus L(\mathcal{A})$.

Proof Let $\mathcal{A} = (Q, \Sigma, q_I, \delta, \Omega)$ be a DPA of size n and index $[k, m]$. By adding at most one extra state we can make its transition function complete so that every word has exactly one run. It can receive an arbitrary odd priority. Then define $\overline{\mathcal{A}} := (Q, \Sigma, q_I, \delta, \overline{\Omega})$ where, for any $q \in Q$, $\overline{\Omega}(q) := \Omega(q) + 1$.

It should be clear that $\overline{\mathcal{A}}$ is a DPA of size at most $n + 1$ and index $[k + 1, m + 1]$. For correctness of the construction take an arbitrary $w \in \Sigma^\omega$ and let ρ be $\mathcal{A}$'s unique run on w. Note that ρ is then also the unique run of $\overline{\mathcal{A}}$ on w. The simple but key observation is that we have $\max\{\Omega(q) \mid q \in \mathit{Inf}(\rho)\} \equiv_2 0$ iff $\max\{\overline{\Omega}(q) \mid q \in \mathit{Inf}(\rho)\} \equiv_2 1$. Thus, $w \in L(\mathcal{A})$ iff $w \notin L(\overline{\mathcal{A}})$. $\qquad\Box$

Note that this simple complementation construction again heavily relies on determinism, namely the fact that runs are unique.

6.2.2 Parity vs. Büchi Acceptance

In accordance with the corresponding result for Rabin- and Streett-automata it is not hard to see that parity automata are at least as expressive as Büchi automata, i.e. they can recognise all ω-regular languages.

Theorem 6.12 *For every NBA $\mathcal{A}$ of size n there is an NPA $\mathcal{B}$ of size n and index $[1,2]$ such that $L(\mathcal{B}) = L(\mathcal{A})$.*

Proof Let $\mathcal{A} = (Q, \Sigma, q_I, \delta, F)$. Define $\mathcal{B} := (Q, \Sigma, q_I, \delta, \Omega)$ with

$$
\Omega(q) \ := \ \begin{cases} 2 & , \text{ if } q \in F, \\ 1 & , \text{ otherwise.} \end{cases}
$$

The statements on the size and index of $\mathcal{B}$ are obviously satisfied.

For a run ρ of $\mathcal{A}$ or, likewise, $\mathcal{B}$ on some $w \in \Sigma^\omega$ we then have $Inf(\rho) \cap F \neq \varnothing$ iff $\max\{\Omega(q) \mid q \in Inf(\rho)\} = 2$. Hence, $w \in L(\mathcal{A})$ iff $w \in L(\mathcal{B})$. $\qquad\square$

We remark that the construction preserves determinism, i.e. a DBA can equally be seen as a DPA with priorities in $[1,2]$.

The simplicity of the constructions in Thm. 6.5 and 6.12 is not very surprising, given that Rabin-, Streett- and parity automata clearly allow for more elaborate conditions for determining acceptance. We now turn to the more interesting part of the study of their expressiveness and show that parity automata in fact only recognise ω-regular languages. We show how to translate an NPA "back" into an NBA. This requires a slightly more elaborate construction, though. In particular, this involves a blowup of the state space in general.

The transformation makes use of the fact that the maximal priority occurring in a run $\rho = q_0, q_1, \ldots$ of an NPA is even iff there is an even priority p and some $\ell \in \mathbb{N}$, s.t. priority p is seen infinitely often in the suffix $q_\ell, q_{\ell+1}, \ldots$ and no greater priority is seen at all. This is a simple consequence of the fact that all priorities greater than p will only be seen finitely often, for otherwise p would not be the greatest that is being seen infinitely often. Seeing something infinitely often can be formulated as a Büchi condition, and not seeing particular states at all can be implemented in an NBA's transition function. The existential quantification over finitely many even priorities can be realised by essentially a union construction, and the existential quantification over the moment ℓ can be realised in the transition function again, both requiring nondeterminism. Hence, the following construction does not preserve determinism, and this is not a surprise, for otherwise it would contradict the result that DBA are strictly weaker than NBA, cf. Thm. 5.24.

Theorem 6.13 *For every NPA $\mathcal{A}$ of size n and index k there is an NBA $\mathcal{B}$ of size at most $n \cdot (\lceil \frac{k}{2} \rceil + 1)$ such that $L(\mathcal{B}) = L(\mathcal{A})$.*

Proof Let $\mathcal{A} = (Q, \Sigma, q_I, \delta, \Omega)$. According to Cor. 6.10 we can assume that $\mathcal{A}$ uses at most $k' \leq \lceil \frac{k}{2} \rceil$ many even priorities. Otherwise $\Omega(Q)$ would contain two even priorities $p < p'$ s.t. $p'' \notin \Omega(Q)$ for all odd p'' with $p < p'' < p'$.

We construct an NBA $\mathcal{B}$ that intuitively works as follows. It has $1 + k'$ many components. The first one is simply a copy of $\mathcal{A}$ as a Büchi automaton with no accepting states. By traversing through this component, $\mathcal{B}$ can simulate the reading of an arbitrary prefix of a word by $\mathcal{A}$. It cannot accept the underlying word by continuing in this part since there are no accepting states. The other k' components – one for each even priority p – also simulate $\mathcal{A}$, but the one for p has all states of priority p as accepting states, and all states of greater priority than p have been removed, resp. made inaccessible. From the first component, when visiting a state with even priority p, it is possible to switch over to the component for p in order to confirm that p is indeed the maximal priority that occurs infinitely often. From then on, no further component change is possible anymore.

Formally, let $p_1, \ldots, p_{k'}$ be the even priorities used in $\Omega(Q)$. We define $\mathcal{B} :=$ $(Q \cup Q \times \{p_1, \ldots, p_{k'}\}, \Sigma, q_I, \Delta, F)$ where

$$\Delta(q, a) \;:=\; \delta(q, a) \cup \begin{cases} \{(q', \Omega(q)) \mid q' \in \delta(q, a)\} & , \text{if } \Omega(q) \equiv_2 0, \\ \varnothing & , \text{otherwise,} \end{cases}$$

for $q \in Q$ and $a \in \Sigma$ are the transitions within the component described first as well as those used to switch over to another component for confirming acceptance by some priority p_i. Then, for $i \in \{1, \ldots, k'\}$,

$$\Delta((q, p_i), a) \;:=\; \{(q', p_i) \mid q' \in \delta(q, a), \Omega(q') \le p_i\}$$

for states from $Q \times \{p_1, \ldots, p_{k'}\}$, and $a \in \Sigma$ consists of the transitions inside the component for p_i.

The set of accepting states is $F := \bigcup_{i=1}^{k'} \{(q, p_i) \mid \Omega(q) = p_i\}$. Thus, a run of $\mathcal{B}$ is accepting if it visits states of priority p_i in the respective component for p_i infinitely often. The size estimation on $\mathcal{B}$ should be clear. It remains to be seen that the construction is correct, i.e. that we have $L(\mathcal{B}) = L(\mathcal{A})$.

"$\subseteq$" The key is the observation that a run will eventually get trapped in either the component based on Q (but then it is not accepting) or in a component based on $Q \times \{p_i\}$ for some i, and then it is accepting iff it visits states of priority p_i infinitely often, and it cannot visit any state of greater priority at all because no transition can lead to such a state in the respective components.

So suppose that $w = a_0 a_1 \ldots \in L(\mathcal{B})$, i.e. there is an accepting run ρ of $\mathcal{B}$ on w. By the aforementioned key observation, ρ must be of the form

$$q_0, a_0, q_1, a_1, \ldots, q_\ell, a_\ell, (q_{\ell+1}, p_i), a_{\ell+1}, (q_{\ell+2}, p_i), \ldots$$

with $q_0 = q_I$ and some even priority p_i. Moreover, by the construction of Δ, we have $q_{j+1} \in \delta(q_j, a_j)$ for all $j \ge 0$. Thus,

$$\rho' \;:=\; q_0, a_0, q_1, \ldots, q_\ell, a_\ell, q_{\ell+1}, a_{\ell+1}, q_{\ell+2}, \ldots$$

is a run of $\mathcal{A}$ on w. We also have that $\max\{\Omega(q) \mid q \in \mathit{Inf}(\rho')\}$ is even: we have $\mathit{Inf}(\rho) \cap F \ne \varnothing$ because ρ is accepting, but ρ eventually contains only states from

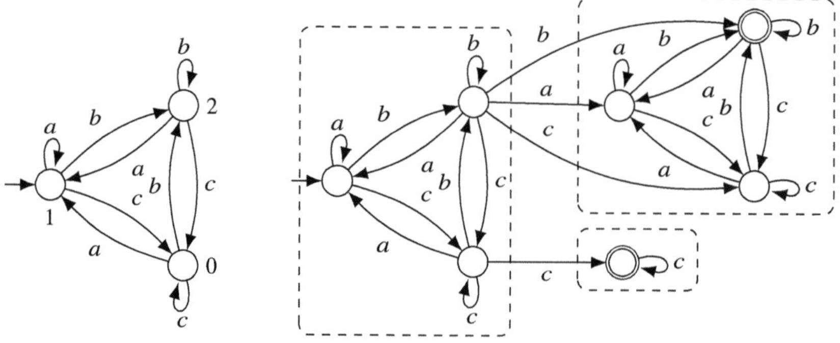

Fig. 6.2 DPA for the language from Ex. 6.2 and its translation into an NBA according to Thm. 6.13.

$Q \times \{p_i\}$, and $F \cap (Q \times \{p_i\})$ contains only states of the form (q, p_i) such that $\Omega(q) = p_i$. Thus, there is at least some such state q with $q \in Inf(\rho')$, i.e. the priority p_i occurs infinitely often in ρ'. At last, no priority greater than p_i can occur in ρ' infinitely often, for otherwise it would have to occur after the transition from q_ℓ to $(q_{\ell+1}, p_i)$ in ρ, but this part does not contain transitions to states with priorities greater than p_i anymore, cf. the construction of Δ. Thus, we get that $\max\{\Omega(q) \mid q \in Inf(\rho')\} = p_i$ which is even, and therefore ρ' is an accepting run of $\mathcal{A}$ on w which yields $w \in L(\mathcal{A})$.

"$\supseteq$" Suppose that $w = a_0 a_1 \ldots \in L(\mathcal{A})$, i.e. there is an accepting run $\rho = q_0, a_0, q_1, a_1, \ldots$ of $\mathcal{A}$ on w, i.e. $\max\{\Omega(q) \mid q \in Inf(\rho)\}$ is even. Thus, there is some $i \in \{1, \ldots, k\}$ such that $\max\{\Omega(q) \mid q \in Inf(\rho)\} = p_i$. Then there are $j_0 < j_1 < \ldots$ such that $\Omega(q_{j_h}) = p_i$ for all $h \geq 0$ and $\Omega(q_j) \leq p_i$ for all $j \geq j_0$. I.e. when priority p_i is the one that determines whether ρ is accepting or not, then there must be some point after which no greater priority occurs at all, and p_i occurs infinitely often. Then consider the run

$$q_0, a_0, q_1, \ldots, q_{j_0-1}, a_{j_0}, q_{j_0}, a_{j_0+1}, (q_{j_0+1}, p_i), \ldots, (q_{j_1}, p_i), \ldots, (q_{j_2}, p_i), \ldots$$

It can easily be checked that ρ' is indeed a run of $\mathcal{B}$ on w since all the transitions are valid w.r.t. its transition function Δ. Moreover, it is accepting because $(q_{j_h}, p_i) \in F$ for all $h \geq 0$. Thus, $w \in L(\mathcal{B})$. $\qquad\square$

Example 6.14 Reconsider the DPA $\mathcal{A}$ constructed in Ex. 6.8 for the language $L = \{w \in \{a, b, c\}^\omega \mid |w|_a = \infty \Rightarrow |w|_b = \infty\}$ from Ex. 6.2. It is shown again in Fig. 6.2 on the left. The right-hand side shows the NBA $\mathcal{B}$ resulting from $\mathcal{A}$ under the translation given in the proof of Thm. 6.13.

The three-component structure, arising from the fact that $\mathcal{A}$ uses two even priorities, is marked and also clearly visible, as well as $\mathcal{B}$'s functionality simulating $\mathcal{A}$ and guessing both the even maximal priority occurring infinitely often as well as the moment after which no greater priority will be seen anymore. The two components with accepting states quite clearly accept words that contain infinitely many symbols b, as well as those that eventually only contain the symbol c.

It is easy to see that $\mathcal{B}$ obtained in this way is not optimal in terms of minimal size, even though $\mathcal{A}$ was minimal as a DPA. A smaller NBA can be obtained immediately by collapsing all three states in the left component into one, and the two non-accepting states in the right upper component into one as well, leading to the following NBA.

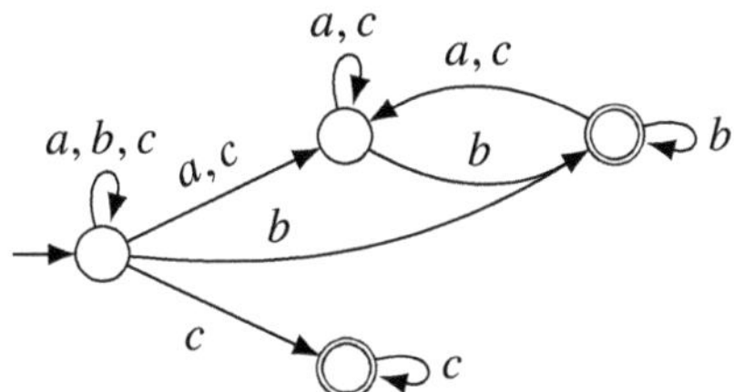

It is still possible to reduce the size further, but this will destroy the three-component structure still visible in this NBA where the left state is only used to traverse a prefix of an input word, the transitions going out of it to the right realise the guessing of a moment after which one can see symbols c only (state below right) or infinitely many symbols b (states above right).

A similar principle can be used to translate an NRA $\mathcal{A}$ with acceptance condition $\mathcal{F} = \{(G_1, F_1), \ldots, (G_k, F_k)\}$ into an NBA $\mathcal{B}$. Remember that Rabin acceptance is an existential condition: for some i, some state in G_i is seen infinitely often while no state on F_i is seen infinitely often. This can be simulated by $\mathcal{B}$ as follows: it first reads off an arbitrary prefix whilst changing states as $\mathcal{A}$ would. Then it guesses some $i \in \{1, \ldots, k\}$ and proceeds into a separate component in which it verifies through its Büchi acceptance condition that G_i is visited infinitely often. Likewise, states from F_i are removed or made inaccessible to ensure that none of these is seen anymore. Working out the formal details of this translation is left as an exercise.

Simulating an NSA with an NBA is more difficult because the acceptance condition is universal. Here, the NBA cannot simply guess some part (G, F) of the acceptance condition and verify this. It would have to keep track of the infinite occurrence of states w.r.t. *all* such G and F. The simulation is still possible but it becomes conceptually much simpler when it takes the detour via Muller automata which are studied in the next section.

6.2.3 Parity vs. Rabin and Streett Acceptance

While it is not a mystery that a Büchi condition can be translated directly into a parity condition but the converse can only be done with a blowup in the state space in general, it is not immediately clear whether there is a similar relationship between the parity condition on one hand and the Rabin or Streett condition on the other hand. The last theorem in this section shows that the latter are the more general ones in the sense that a parity condition can be expressed directly as a Rabin and as a Streett condition.

Theorem 6.15 *For every NPA $\mathcal{A}$ of size n and index k there is an NRA $\mathcal{B}$, resp. NSA $\mathcal{B}'$ of size n and index $\lceil \frac{k}{2} \rceil$ such that $L(\mathcal{B}) = L(\mathcal{A}) = L(\mathcal{B}')$.*

Proof Let $\mathcal{A} = (Q, \Sigma, q_I, \delta, \Omega)$. We construct an equivalent NRA with the required properties first.

Using Cor. 6.10 we can assume that there are at most $k' := \lceil \frac{k}{2} \rceil$ many even priorities in $\Omega(Q)$, and that these are $p_1, \ldots, p_{k'}$. Note that the following two conditions are equivalent for a run ρ.

(ɪ) $\max\{\Omega(q) \mid q \in \mathit{Inf}(\rho)\} \equiv_2 0$,

(ɪɪ) there are $i \in \{1, \ldots, k'\}$ and $q \in Q$ with $\Omega(q) = p_i$ such that $q \in \mathit{Inf}(\rho)$ and $q' \notin \mathit{Inf}(\rho)$ for every $q \in Q$ with $\Omega(q') > p_i$.

Condition (ɪ) is of course just the well-known parity condition for Ω. Condition (ɪɪ) can be expressed as the Rabin condition $\mathcal{F} := \{(G_1, F_1), \ldots, (G_{k'}, F_{k'}\}$ where $G_i := \{q \in Q \mid \Omega(q) = p_i\}$ and $F_i := \{q \in Q \mid \Omega(q) > p_i\}$ for $i = 1, \ldots, k'$. Hence, $\mathcal{B} := (Q, \Sigma, q_I, \delta, \mathcal{F})$ is an NRA with the required properties.

The construction of an NSA is analogous. With Cor. 6.10 we can equally bound the number of odd priorities to be at most k'. Suppose they are $p'_1, \ldots, p'_{k'}$. We then observe that there is a third formulation that is equivalent to (ɪ) and (ɪɪ) above, namely the following one.

(ɪɪɪ) for every $i \in \{1, \ldots, k'\}$ and $q \in Q$ with $\Omega(q) = p'_i$ and $q \in \mathit{Inf}(\rho)$ there is $q' \in \mathit{Inf}(\rho)$ with $\Omega(q') > p_i$.

I.e. the largest priority seen infinitely often is even iff for every odd priority seen infinitely often there is a greater one that is also seen infinitely often. One is tempted to require that the greater one needs to be even, but this is in fact not necessary, and the formulation (ɪɪɪ) is then entirely dual to (ɪɪ). This is also why it is easily seen to be phrasable as the Streett condition $\mathcal{F}' = \{(G'_1, F'_1), \ldots, (G'_{k'}, F'_{k'})\}$ where $G'_i := \{q \in Q \mid \Omega(q) = p'_i\}$ and $F'_i := \{q \in Q \mid \Omega(q) > p'_i\}$. This appears to be the same as the Rabin condition $\mathcal{F}$ defined above but it is not because it is based on the odd priorities p'_i rather than the even ones p_i. Again, $\mathcal{B}' := (Q, \Sigma, q_I, \delta, \mathcal{F}')$ is then an NSA equivalent to $\mathcal{A}$.   □

Since the constructions in the proof above translate acceptance conditions rather than automata, i.e. not blowing up state spaces, the corresponding translation on automata that only exchange the acceptance condition preserve determinism again.

Corollary 6.16 *For every DPA $\mathcal{A}$ of size n and index k there is a DRA $\mathcal{B}$, resp. DSA $\mathcal{B}'$ of size n and index $\lceil \frac{k}{2} \rceil$ such that $L(\mathcal{B}) = L(\mathcal{A}) = L(\mathcal{B}')$.*

The parity acceptance condition is also sometimes known as the *Rabin chain condition*, and it may not be immediate that there are chains involved in the construction above. However, reconsider the Rabin acceptance condition $\mathcal{F}$, where G_i, resp. F_i consist of all states of priority p_i, resp. of priority greater than p_i. Clearly, we have

$F_1 \supseteq F_2 \supseteq \ldots \supseteq F_{k'}$, i.e. the second components do indeed form a descending chain. Moreover, one could equally define the G_i as the sets of states that have even priority *at most* p_i. Then we get $G_1 \subseteq G_2 \subseteq \ldots \subseteq G_{k'}$ and the first components form an ascending chain in the same order. By the same reasoning, the translation into NSA can of course also be amended to yield pairs that form two opposing chains.

6.3 Muller Automata

The previous sections have studied three ways to significantly extend the Büchi acceptance condition into Rabin-, Streett- and parity conditions. Yet, finite automata accepting infinite words with either of them still only recognise ω-regular languages. For parity automata, this has been shown in Thm. 6.13, for Rabin automata this is done in a very similar way, and Streett automata can also be translated into NBA but this is more difficult to do directly, and it will follow immediately from constructions in this section where we study the question: is it possible at all to build an acceptance condition based on the infinite occurrence of states such that the expressive power of the corresponding automaton model exceeds that of ω-regularity? The answer is no.

6.3.1 The Most General Acceptance Condition

Definition 6.17 A *nondeterministic Muller automaton* (NMA) is an $\mathcal{A} = (Q, \Sigma, q_I, \delta, \mathcal{F})$ where Q, Σ, q_I, δ are as with all the other finite automata studied before, and the acceptance condition $\mathcal{F} \subseteq 2^Q$ is a set of sets of states.

The notions of *size, deterministic Muller automata* (DMA), *run, language*, NMA-/DMA-recognisability etc. are defined as usual, the latter of course based on the following definition. A run $\rho = q_0, q_1, \ldots$ of an NMA is *accepting* if $Inf(\rho) \in \mathcal{F}$. The *index* of $\mathcal{A}$ is $|\mathcal{F}|$, i.e. the number of acceptance sets in the acceptance condition.

So a Muller acceptance condition simply lists all the state sets which are allowed to occur infinitely often for a run to be seen as accepting. In a sense, this is a brute-force method of defining acceptance based on infinite occurrences of states.

Example 6.18 We consider, yet again, the language $L = \{w \in \{a, b, c\}^\omega \mid |w|_a = \infty \Rightarrow |w|_b = \infty\}$ initially introduced in Ex. 6.2. Again, the three-state deterministic automaton (skeleton) shown in Fig. 6.1 that simply records the last seen letter in its state space, can be turned into an NMA recognising L. For this, we equip it with the Muller acceptance condition

$$\{\{q_b\}, \{q_c\}, \{q_a, q_b\}, \{q_b, q_c\}, \{q_a, q_b, q_c\}\} \, .$$

Note that this contains exactly those non-empty sets $M \subseteq \{q_a, q_b, a_c\}$ that satisfy: if $q_a \in M$ then $q_b \in M$. I.e. the acceptance condition is obtained by a straightforward translation from the predicate defining L.

The empty set clearly also fulfills this condition but it can never cause acceptance because every infinite run must contain at least some state infinitely often.

The next goal is to justify the claim that the Muller condition is the most general condition based on infinite occurrences of states. This is not necessarily a statement about the expressive power of NMA, at least not a statement about some increase in expressiveness. It merely says that the other acceptance conditions can be seen as special cases of the Muller condition, just as a Büchi condition is a special case of a parity condition which is a special case of a Rabin and a Streett condition.

To formalise the claim we introduce a symbolic acceptance condition based on propositional logic.

Definition 6.19 Let Q be the finite state set of some automaton. *Acceptance formulas* over Q are given by the grammar

$$\Phi \ ::= \ q \mid \neg\Phi \mid \Phi \vee \Phi$$

where $q \in Q$. The *size* $|\Phi|$ of an acceptance formula Φ is inductively defined by

$$|q| \ := \ 1 \quad , \quad |\neg\Phi| \ := \ 1 + |\Phi| \quad , \quad |\Phi \vee \Psi| \ := \ 1 + |\Phi| + |\Psi| \,.$$

Other Boolean operators like $\wedge$, $\rightarrow$, $\leftrightarrow$ etc. are allowed as abbreviations but we do not require them to be spelled out when measuring the size. For example, $q_1 \wedge q_2$ can be counted to have size 3 rather than size 6 via $\neg(\neg q_1 \vee \neg q_2)$.

A set $M \subseteq Q$ *satisfies* the acceptance formula Φ or, simply, is accepting w.r.t. Φ, if $M \vDash \Phi$ holds according to the following straightforward inductive definition.

$$
\begin{aligned}
M &\vDash q   &&\text{iff} \quad q \in M \\
M &\vDash \neg\Phi   &&\text{iff} \quad M \nvDash \Phi \\
M &\vDash \Phi \vee \Psi &&\text{iff} \quad M \vDash \Phi \text{ or } M \vDash \Psi
\end{aligned}
$$

A *symbolic Muller automaton* (sNMA) is an $\mathcal{A} = (Q, \Sigma, q_I, \delta, \Phi)$ as with all the other finite automata, but Φ is an acceptance formula over Q. Its size is $|Q|$ as usual, and its index is $|\Phi|$. A run ρ is accepting iff $Inf(\rho) \vDash \Phi$.

All the acceptance conditions discussed so far can be rephrased in terms of acceptance formulas.

Lemma 6.20 *For every NBA / NPA / NRA / NSA $\mathcal{A}$ of size n and index k (where applicable) there is an sNMA $\mathcal{B}$ of size n and index $\mathcal{O}(n) \, / \, \mathcal{O}(n^2) \, / \, \mathcal{O}(kn)$ such that $L(\mathcal{B}) = L(\mathcal{A})$.*

Proof All translations preserve the automaton's state space and transition function. Only the acceptance condition is changed.

An NBA with acceptance condition F is an sNMA for $\Phi_F := \bigvee_{q \in F} \inf(q)$. Its index is $\mathcal{O}(n)$.

An NRA with acceptance condition $\mathcal{F} = \{(G_1, F_1), \ldots, (G_k, F_k)\}$ is an sNMA for the acceptance formula

$$\Phi_{\mathcal{F}} := \bigvee_{i=1}^{k} \Big(\bigvee_{q \in G_i} q \Big) \wedge \Big(\bigwedge_{q \in F_i} \neg q \Big) .$$

Likewise, an NSA with this acceptance condition is an sNMA for

$$\Phi_{\mathcal{F}} := \bigwedge_{i=1}^{k} \Big(\bigwedge_{q \in G_i} \neg q \Big) \vee \Big(\bigvee_{q \in F_i} q \Big) .$$

The sizes of these formulas are $\mathcal{O}(kn)$ in both cases.

An NPA with state set Q and acceptance condition $\Omega : Q \to \mathbb{N}$ is an sNMA for

$$\Phi_{\Omega} := \bigvee_{\substack{q \in Q \\ \Omega(q) \text{ even}}} q \wedge \bigwedge_{\substack{q' \in Q \\ \Omega(q') > \Omega(q)}} \neg q' \quad \text{or} \quad \Phi_{\Omega} := \bigwedge_{\substack{q \in Q \\ \Omega(q) \text{ odd}}} q \to \bigvee_{\substack{q' \in Q \\ \Omega(q') > \Omega(q)}} q'$$

whose sizes are $\mathcal{O}(n^2)$. $\qquad\square$

The following lemma shows why the Muller condition can be seen as most general, as it covers any case of an acceptance formula.

Lemma 6.21 *Let $L \subseteq \Sigma^{\omega}$.*

 a) *If L is recognisable by an NMA of size n and index k then L is recognisable by an sNMA of size n and index at most $3 \cdot k \cdot n$.*
 b) *If L is recognisable by an sNMA of size n and index k then L is recognisable by an NMA of size n and index at most 2^{2^n-1}.*

Proof For both parts, the underlying automaton remains the same, in particular its state set Q, just the acceptance condition gets translated.

(a) Let $\mathcal{F}$ be the NMA's acceptance condition. It is equivalent to the acceptance formula

$$\Phi_{\mathcal{F}} := \bigvee_{F \in \mathcal{F}} \Big(\bigwedge_{q \in F} q \Big) \wedge \Big(\bigwedge_{q \notin F} \neg q \Big)$$

Each disjunct has size at most $3 \cdot |Q|$, hence the size of the entire formula is bounded by $|\mathcal{F}| \cdot 3 \cdot |Q|$. Moreover, we have $\mathit{Inf}(\rho) \vDash \Phi_{\mathcal{F}}$ iff $\mathit{Inf}(\rho) \in \mathcal{F}$ which proves the lemma's statement.

(b) Let Φ be the acceptance condition of the given sNMA. It is equivalent to the NMA condition $\mathcal{F}_{\Phi} := \{M \subseteq Q \mid M \neq \varnothing \text{ and } M \vDash \Phi\}$. Clearly, we have $\mathcal{F}_{\Phi} \subseteq 2^Q \setminus \{\varnothing\}$ and therefore $|\mathcal{F}| \leq 2^{2^{|Q|}-1}$. Again, we immediately have $\mathit{Inf}(\rho) \in \mathcal{F}_{\Phi}$ iff $\mathit{Inf}(\rho) \vDash \Phi$ $\qquad\square$

As an immediate consequence we obtain that Büchi-, Rabin-, Streett- and parity conditions can directly be translated into Muller conditions.

Corollary 6.22 *For every NBA, NRA, NSA, NPA $\mathcal{A}$ of size n there is an NMA $\mathcal{B}$ of size n such that $L(\mathcal{B}) = L(\mathcal{A})$.*

Another consequence of Lemma 6.21 concerns closure properties. Closure of Muller-recognisable languages under unions should be clear: because of availability of nondeterminism, the disjoint union of two NMA $\mathcal{A}_1$ and $\mathcal{A}_2$ – equipped with an additional single starting state that simulates both original starting states – recognises the union of the two languages at hand. The acceptance condition simply is the union of the two underlying acceptance conditions $\mathcal{F}_1$ and $\mathcal{F}_2$. A more interesting question concerns the closure under intersections for example.

Theorem 6.23 *Let $\mathcal{A}_i$ be NMA of size n_i and index k_i for $i \in \{1,2\}$. There is an NMA $\mathcal{B}$ of size at most $n_1 \cdot n_2$ and index at most $\min\{k_1 \cdot 2^{n_2}, k_2 \cdot 2^{n_1}\}$ such that $L(\mathcal{B}) = L(\mathcal{A}_1) \cap L(\mathcal{A}_2)$.*

Proof Using Lemma 6.21 we can assume both $\mathcal{A}_i$ to be given as sNMA $(Q_i, \Sigma, q_I^i, \delta_i, \Phi_i)$ such that $|Q_i| = n_i$ for $i \in \{1,2\}$. We employ the usual product construction to obtain an sNMA $\mathcal{B} = (Q_1 \times Q_2, \Sigma, (q_I^1, q_I^2), \Delta, \Phi)$ where

$$\Delta((q_1, q_2), a) \ := \ \{(q_1', q_2') \mid q_1' \in \delta_1(q_1, a), q_2' \in \delta_2(q_2, a)\} \ .$$

The reason for taking the detour via the symbolically represented acceptance conditions is that conjunctions are obviously available. Intuitively, the acceptance formula $\Phi_1 \wedge \Phi_2$ expresses that both $\mathcal{A}_1$ and $\mathcal{A}_2$ need to accept, but this obviously cannot work because this is not a formula over $\mathcal{B}$'s state set $Q_1 \times Q_2$. However, it can easily be turned into the right one by taking $\Phi := rlx_2(\Phi_1) \wedge rlx_1(\Phi_2)$ where $rlx_i(\Psi)$ relaxes the requirement Ψ on the infinite occurrences of states in Q_{3-i} to the corresponding set in $Q_1 \times Q_2$. It can easily be defined inductively as

$$rlx_1(q_2) \ := \ \bigvee_{q_1 \in Q_i} (q_1, q_2) \qquad\qquad rlx_i(\neg\Psi) \ := \ \neg rlx_i(\Phi)$$

$$rlx_2(q_1) \ := \ \bigvee_{q_2 \in Q_i} (q_1, q_2) \qquad\qquad rlx_i(\Psi_1 \vee \Psi_2) \ := \ rlx_i(\Psi_1) \vee rlx_i(\Psi_2)$$

for $i \in \{1,2\}$.

Correctness of this follows from the observation that for any run $\rho = (q_0^1, q_0^2)$, $(q_1^1, q_1^2), \ldots$ and its projections onto the first and second components $\rho_i = q_0^i, q_1^i, \ldots$ for $i \in \{1,2\}$ we have $Inf(\rho) \vDash rlx_2(\Phi_1) \wedge rlx_1(\Phi_2)$ iff $Inf(\rho_1) \vDash \Phi_1$ and $Inf(\rho_2) \vDash \Phi_2$.

Obviously, we have $|\mathcal{B}| \leq n_1 \cdot n_2$. Lemma 6.21 would only yield a bound of $2^{2^{n_1 \cdot n_2} - 1}$ on the index of $\mathcal{B}$ which is not optimal as it is simply the maximally possible size of a Muller acceptance condition in an NMA with $n_1 \cdot n_2$ many states. It is, however, possible to transfer the relaxation operation carried out on formulas above onto sets via $rlx_1(F_2) := \{(q_1, q_2) \mid q_1 \in Q_1, q_2 \in F_2\}$ for $F_2 \subseteq Q_2$ and likewise for rlx_2. Then $\mathcal{B}$'s explicit acceptance condition can be given as

$$\mathcal{F} \ := \ \{F \subseteq Q_1 \times Q_2 \mid \exists F_1 \in \mathcal{F}_1, \exists F_2 \in \mathcal{F}_2 \text{ s.t. } rlx_2(F_1) = F = rlx_1(F_2)\}$$

with which $\mathcal{B}$ accepts exactly $L(\mathcal{A}_1) \cap L(\mathcal{A}_2)$. Note that $|\mathcal{F}|$ is naturally bounded by $k_1 \cdot 2^{n_2}$ and by $k_2 \cdot 2^{n_1}$: every set $F \in \mathcal{F}$ must be such that its projection onto the first components of the state pairs in F yields some $F_1 \in \mathcal{F}_2$, and the projection onto the second components yields some $F_2 \in \mathcal{F}_2$. $\qquad\square$

6.3.2 Muller vs. Büchi Acceptance

Nevertheless, despite this very general acceptance mechanism, Muller automata still only recognise ω-regular languages. Büchi automata can make up for their lack in elaborateness of their acceptance condition through additional states in order to recognise Muller-definable languages.

The construction of an NBA that is equivalent to a given NMA is based on the same idea underlying the translation of NPA or NRA to NBA: the NBA guesses the moment after which all states that only occur finitely often will not be seen anymore, as well as the acceptance set $F \in \mathcal{F}$ that determines acceptance. Now the construction becomes a little bit trickier because the NBA has to verify that exactly those states in F occur infinitely often. The key here is to take an arbitrary ordering of F, say $\{f_0, \ldots, f_{m-1}\}$. Note that all states in F are seen infinitely often iff eventually f_0 is seen, then eventually after this f_1 is seen, etc., until after f_{m-1} we require to see f_0 again and so on. An NBA can check that this is the case by employing an additional counter with values from $[m]$ that is increased by one when its value is i and state f_i is just being visited. At the end, when the value is $m-1$ and f_{m-1} is seen, it goes back to 0. Thus, any value in this extra component, for instance 0, is seen infinitely often iff all states in F are being visited infinitely often.

Theorem 6.24 *For every NMA $\mathcal{A}$ of size n and of index k there is an NBA $\mathcal{B}$ of size at most $n + k \cdot n^2$ such that $L(\mathcal{B}) = L(\mathcal{A})$.*

Proof Let $\mathcal{A} = (Q, \Sigma, q_I, \delta, \mathcal{F})$ be an NMA such that $|Q| = n$ and $\mathcal{F} = \{F_1, \ldots, F_k\}$. Let $\mathcal{B} := (Q', \Sigma, q_I, \Delta, F)$ with

$$Q' := Q \cup \bigcup_{i=1}^{k} \{i\} \times F_i \times \{0, \ldots, |F_i| - 1\} \, .$$

There are three kinds of transitions. The component based on Q simulates $\mathcal{A}$ and allows transitions into any component for an acceptance set F_i, recognisable by states of the form (i, q', c) for some q', c, at any time. We have

$$\Delta(q, a) := \delta(q, a) \cup \{(i, q', 0) \mid i \in \{1, \ldots, k\}, q' \in \delta(q, a) \cap F_i\}$$

for every $q \in Q$ and $a \in \Sigma$.

The third kind consists of transitions within each of these components. They can be defined uniformly as follows. Fix $i \in \{1, \ldots, k\}$ and let $m := |F_i|$ and $F_i = \{f_0, \ldots, f_{m-1}\}$. Then we have, for every $c, j \in [m]$ and every $a \in \Sigma$:

$$\Delta((i, f_j, c), a) \; := \; \{(i, f_h, c') \mid f_h \in F_i \cap \delta(f_j, a)\}$$

where, in each case,

$$c' \; := \; \begin{cases} c + 1 \bmod m & \text{, if } j = c, \\ c & \text{, otherwise.} \end{cases}$$

In order to define the Büchi acceptance condition, let f_0^i denote the first state in F_i according to the total orders fixed above, for $i = 1, \ldots, k$. Then let $F := \{(i, f_0^i, 0) \mid i \in \{1, \ldots, k\}\}$.

It should be clear that the size of $\mathcal{B}$ is bounded by $n + k \cdot n \cdot n$ since n is a bound on the size of each acceptance set F_i. It remains to be seen that $L(\mathcal{B}) = L(\mathcal{A})$.

"$\supseteq$" Suppose that $w = a_0 a_1 \ldots \in L(\mathcal{A})$, i.e. there is a run $\rho = q_0, q_1, \ldots$ on w such that $Inf(\rho) \in \mathcal{F}$, i.e. $Inf(\rho) = F_i$ for some $i \in \{1, \ldots, k\}$. Then there is some $\ell > 0$ such that $q_h \in F_i$ for all $h \geq \ell$ and, additionally, for every $q \in F_i$ there are infinitely many h such that $q_h = q$. We can construct a run ρ' of $\mathcal{B}$ on w as

$$q_0, q_1, \ldots, q_{\ell-1}, (i, q_\ell, 0), (i, q_{\ell+1}, c_{\ell+1}), (i, q_{\ell+2}, c_{\ell+2}), \ldots$$

Clearly, this is not fully specified yet since we have not given concrete values $c_{\ell+1}, c_{\ell+2}, \ldots$. Note that Δ is deterministic in the first and third part of triples making up states, i.e. in a transition from (i, q, c) to (i', q', c'), the values of i' and c' are uniquely determined by i, resp. by q and c. The former is irrelevant and only stated for completeness, but the determination of the counter values means that the run ρ' as listed above is indeed fully specified because the counter value at position ℓ is set to 0, and the states at all positions are known, so all the counter values at positions past ℓ are also known.

What is important to note now is that for every $h \geq \ell$ there is some $h' \geq h$ such that $q_{h'} = f_{c_h}$ where f_{c_h} is the c_h-th state in F_i according to some enumeration of the states therein. In other words, whenever at some moment h in ρ' the counter value c_h names some particular state in F_i, then at some point later this state will be visited. Consequently, the counter value will then point to the next state in the underlying enumeration of F_i, and the argument can be repeated. Moreover, the counter is cyclic, i.e. once it reaches value $|F_i| - 1$ and later the last state in this enumeration is visited, the process restarts with counter value 0 in the next step. Hence, the counter value will be 0 infinitely often which means that ρ' visits accepting states infinitely often. Thus, $w \in L(\mathcal{B})$.

"$\subseteq$" This direction is analogous. In fact, the reasoning for the previous direction can be reversed: whenever $\mathcal{B}$ visits a state of the form $(i, q, 0)$ (apart from the first time), then the run must have contained all states from F_i since the last time that the counter value was 0. Hence, if the counter value is 0 infinitely often, then all states from the corresponding F_i must have been visited infinitely often. A projection of an accepting run of $\mathcal{B}$ onto the Q-components of the triple states therefore yields an accepting run of $\mathcal{A}$ on the same word. $\qquad\square$

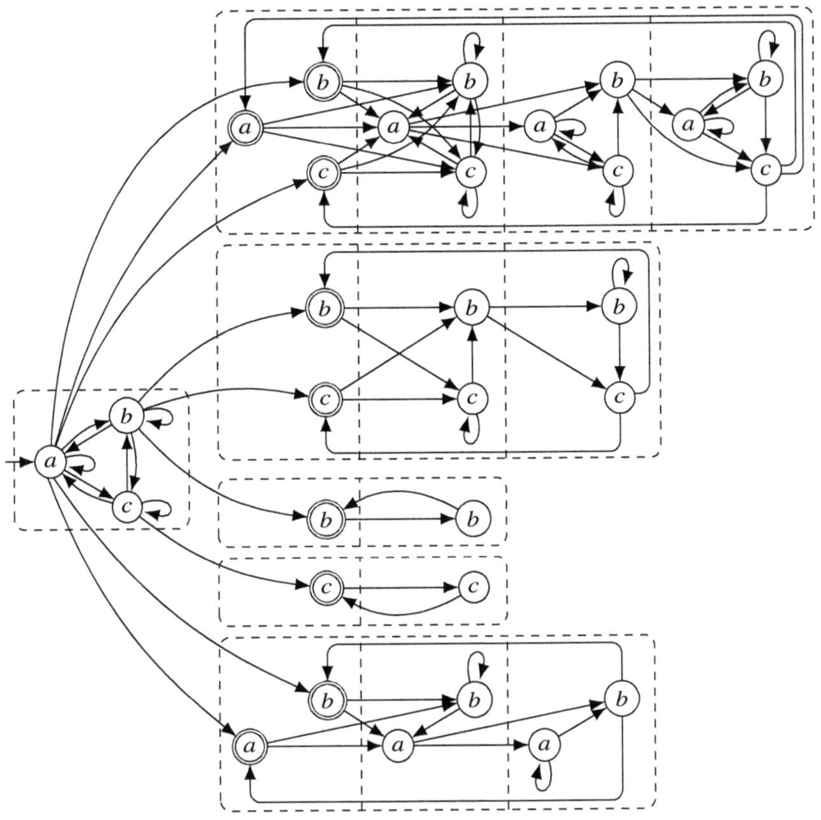

Fig. 6.3 NBA resulting from the NMA in Ex. 6.18. See Ex. 6.25 for an explanation regarding the transitions from the left component into those on the right-hand side.

Example 6.25 Let $\Sigma = \{a, b, c\}$ and consider the DMA $\mathcal{A}$ constructed in Ex. 6.18 for the running example of the language $L = \{w \in \Sigma^\omega \mid |w|_a = \infty \Rightarrow |w|_b = \infty\}$. It was obtained by equipping the deterministic automaton depicted in Fig. 6.1 with the Muller condition

$$\{\{q_a, q_b, q_c\}, \{q_b, q_c\}, \{q_b\}, \{q_c\}, \{q_a, q_b\}\}$$

of index 5.

An NBA for this language is shown in Fig. 6.3. In order to avoid clutter, transition labels and state names have been left out. Instead, the alphabet symbols that are shown inside each state are the labels of the transitions that lead into each such state.

The NBA's component structure that it received in the construction in the proof of Thm. 6.24 is clearly visible. The component on the left does a simulation of $\mathcal{A}$ only to read off a prefix of an input word. On the right, the components, from top to bottom, correspond to the acceptance sets given in the order above, and accept words of the form

- $\Sigma^*(a(a+c)^*b(a+b)^*c(b+c)^*)^\omega$, corresponding to the acceptance set $\{q_a, q_b, q_c\}$,
- $\Sigma^*(b^+c^+)^\omega$, corresponding to the acceptance set $\{q_b, q_c\}$,
- Σ^*b^ω, corresponding to the acceptance set $\{q_b\}$,
- Σ^*c^ω, corresponding to the acceptance set $\{q_c\}$,
- $\Sigma^*(a^+b^+)^\omega$, corresponding to the acceptance set $\{q_a, q_b\}$.

Furthermore, the counter structure in each of the components on the right-hand side has been made visible as well. Note how each component's acceptance set F is divided into $|F| + 1$ parts, and transitions only remain within each part (when the counter is not increased) or move over to the next part (when it is increased). Büchi acceptance states are then seen to be those in which the counter value is 0.

Note that the NBA shown in Fig. 6.3 is missing some transitions according to the construction in the proof of Thm. 6.24. These would link states in the left component with states at the beginning of each of the components on the right, and they have omitted here to avoid cluttering, but also because they can be left out without changing the NBA's language and intuitive behaviour: it should be clear that, in general, the constructed NBA $\mathcal{B}$ need not have the possibility to switch into any of the components checking infinite occurrence of some acceptance set F *at any time*. Instead it suffices to give it the possibility to do so *ever again*. In the general construction, it is easier to implement this possibility at any time, leading to more transitions. In a particular case, when the structure of the underlying NMA can be inspected to see that having transitions at particular moments only suffices to guarantee that switches into these components may eventually occur, it may be easier to implement fewer transitions. This is what has been done for the NBA in Fig. 6.3: such component-switching transitions from some state q to a state $(i, q', 0)$ are only available for one particular state $q \in F_i$, rather than all.

6.3.3 Muller vs. Parity Acceptance

The composition of the construction of Thm. 6.24, translating an NMA into an NBA, and the rather trivial construction of Thm. 6.12, showing that an NBA can be seen as an NPA, clearly yields a translation from NMA into NPA. One may ask for a more direct way to get there because of the following reason. While the translation in Thm. 6.12 preserves determinism, since it only translates the Büchi condition into a parity condition, the one in Thm. 6.24 genuinely introduces nondeterminism. Thus, even when starting with a DMA, the route through these two theorems does not yield a DPA in the end, but only an NPA in general.

On the other hand, the self-duality of the parity condition and its slightly more abstract nature make it an ideal ground for further algorithmic investigations, in particular later in Part III where we study automata operating on infinite trees rather than words. We therefore give yet another translation. It sits halfway in between being a translation purely on acceptance conditions and a translation on automata: it does not simply translate a Muller condition into a parity condition (which is also not possible in general) but it can be realised with a factor, known as a *latest appearance record*, in an automaton's state space that acts entirely deterministically. Hence, this translation, formulated for nondeterministic automata below, preserves determinism and therefore immediately yields a translation from DMA to DPA as well.

Definition 6.26 Let $Q = \{q_0, \ldots, q_{n-1}\}$ be a finite set of states of an automaton. A *permutation* of Q is a bijection $\pi : [n] \to Q$. Note that its inverse $\pi^{-1} : Q \to [n]$ exists. We write $Q!$ for the set of all permutations of Q.

A *latest appearance record* (LAR) is a pair (π, m) where π is a permutation of Q, and $m \in [n]$ points to one position in this list. We write the LAR (π, m) also as

$$[\pi(0), \ldots, \pi(m-1), \underline{\pi(m)}, \pi(m+1), \ldots, \pi(n-1)]$$

with the marker position m underlined, starting at index 0. Note that $\pi^{-1}(q)$ then denotes the unique position of state q in this list.

The *update* of the LAR (π, m) w.r.t. some $q \in Q$ is the LAR $upd_q(\pi, m) := (\pi', \pi^{-1}(q))$ where

$$\pi'(i) := \begin{cases} q & \text{, if } i = 0, \\ \pi(i-1) & \text{, if } 0 < i \leq \pi(q), \\ \pi(i) & \text{, otherwise.} \end{cases}$$

An LAR provides information about – as the name suggests – the occurrences of states from Q in latest times. I.e. one should imagine an LAR as being manipulated along the run of an underlying automaton. States at the beginning in its list representation should be those that have been visited more recently than those towards the end of that list.

The update $upd_q(\Lambda)$ of some LAR Λ w.r.t. q removes q from the list and prepends it to its beginning, consequently shifting all states that occurred before q further back by one position. Those that occurred after q remain where they were. Clearly, this preserves the property of being a permutation. The appearance marker is set to the position from which q was taken. Thus, updating the LAR $\Lambda = [q_1, \ldots, \underline{q_m}, \ldots, q_n]$ w.r.t. some state q_j results in the LAR

$$upd_{q_j}(\Lambda) := [q_j, q_1, \ldots, \underline{q_{j-1}}, q_{j+1}, \ldots, q_n] .$$

Note that the position of the marker in the previous moment was irrelevant, at least momentarily. However, when used consecutively, then this marker serves an interesting purpose in the infinite.

Lemma 6.27 *Let Q be a finite set of states and $\rho = q_0, q_1, \ldots$ be a run. Let $\Lambda_0, \Lambda_1, \ldots$ with $\Lambda_i = (\pi_i, m_i)$ for all $i \geq 0$ be a sequence of LAR such that, for* all $i \geq 1$, $\Lambda_i := upd_{q_{i-1}}(\Lambda_{i-1})$. *Let* $m := \limsup (m_i)_{i \geq 0}$. *Then* $Inf(\rho) = \{q \in Q \mid \limsup (\pi_i^{-1}(q))_{i \geq 0} \leq m\}$.

Proof First of all, we recall two properties of a value $x = \limsup (x_i)_{i \geq 0}$ for a sequence $(x_i)_{i \geq 0}$ with $x_i \in [n]$ for some n and all $i \geq 0$. (I) Eventually, x is an upper bound for all x_i: there must be some i_0 s.t. $x_i \leq x$ for all $i \geq i_0$. (II) The limes superior is met infinitely often: for every $i \geq 0$ there is some $i' \geq i$ such that $x_{i'} = x$. Now we proceed with the proof of the lemma's claim.

"$\subseteq$" We make use of (I) for the sequence $(m_i)_{i \geq 0}$ to obtain some index i_0 s.t. $m \geq m_i$ for all $i \geq i_0$. Take some $q \in Inf(\rho)$ and suppose, for the sake of contradiction, that $\limsup (\pi_i^{-1}(q))_{i \geq 0} > m$. We make use of property (II) for the sequence $(\pi^{-1}(q))_{i \geq 0}$ and i_0 to obtain some $i' \geq i_0$ s.t. $\pi_{i'}^{-1}(q) > m$. Now consider the LAR at position $i' + 1$. We have $\Lambda_{i'+1} = (\pi_{i'+1}, m_{i'+1})$ by assumption and $\Lambda_{i'+1} = upd_q(\pi_{i'}, m_{i'}) = (\pi_{i'+1}, \pi_{i'}^{-1}(q))$ by construction. Hence, we have $m \geq m_{i'+1} = \pi_{i'}^{-1}(q) > m$ which is impossible.

"$\supseteq$" Take some $q \notin Inf(\rho)$. We will show that $\limsup (\pi_i^{-1}(q))_{i \geq 0} > m$. Take some i_0 s.t. $q_i \neq q$ for all $i \geq i_0$. In a step from $\Lambda_i = (\pi_i, m_i)$ to $\Lambda_{i+1} = upd_{q_i}(\Lambda_i) = (\pi_{i+1}, m_{i+1})$, we have $\pi_{i+1}^{-1}(q') \geq \pi_i^{-1}(q')$ for all $q' \neq q_i$, and therefore in particular for q if $i \geq i_0$. In other words, after moment i_0, q can only move further towards the end of the LAR list.

Moreover, suppose there is some $i \geq i_0$ s.t. $m_i \geq \pi_i^{-1}(q)$. Then we have $\pi_{i+1}^{-1}(q) > \pi_i^{-1}(q)$, i.e. if some update is done with respect to a state q' that resides behind q in the current LAR, then q's position is shifted towards the end of the list. Clearly, this cannot happen infinitely often. Thus, there must be some $i_1 \geq i_0$ such that $m_i < \pi_i^{-1}(q)$ for all $i \geq i_1$. But then $\limsup (\pi_i^{-1}(q))_{i \geq 0} > \limsup (m_i)_{i \geq 0} = m$ which proves the claim. $\qquad\square$

Theorem 6.28 *For every NMA* $\mathcal{A}$ *of size n there is an NPA* $\mathcal{B}$ *of size at most* $n^2 \cdot n!$ *and index at most 2n such that* $L(\mathcal{B}) = L(\mathcal{A})$.

Proof Let $\mathcal{A} = (Q, \Sigma, q_I, \delta, \mathcal{F})$ be an NMA with $|Q| = n$. Pick an arbitrary permutation π_0 of Q and let $\Lambda_0 := (\pi_0, 0)$. We define the NPA $\mathcal{B} := (Q \times (Q! \times [n]), \Sigma, (q_I, \Lambda_0), \Delta, \Omega)$ where

$$\Delta((q, \Lambda), a) := \{(q', upd_q(\Lambda)) \mid q' \in \delta(q, a)\}.$$

In other words, $\mathcal{B}$ runs a simulation of $\mathcal{A}$ in which it uses an LAR to track the occurrences of states in any run. The claim on the size of $\mathcal{B}$ should be clear.

The parity acceptance condition remains to be defined. We set

$$\Omega(q, (\pi, m)) := \begin{cases} 2 \cdot m + 2 & \text{, if } \{\pi(0), \ldots, \pi(m)\} \in \mathcal{F}, \\ 2 \cdot m + 1 & \text{, otherwise.} \end{cases}$$

Hence, a state's priority solely depends on the LAR in that state. It is higher with greater marker positions, and it is even whenever the set of states up to and including the marker position forms a Muller acceptance set. Otherwise it is odd. This reflects the fact that along some run, the marker position will eventually oscillate below and up to its limes superior m. The states that reside on positions up to and including m are exactly those that are seen infinitely often.

For the claim on the index of $\mathcal{B}$ note that the minimal and maximal value for the marker position are 0 and $n-1$, respectively. Hence, minimal and maximal priorities used in Ω are 1 and $2(n-1)+2$, respectively, and so there are at most $2n$ many different ones.

It remains to be seen that we have $L(\mathcal{B}) = L(\mathcal{A})$.

"$\supseteq$" Let $\rho = q_0, q_1, \ldots$ be an accepting run of $\mathcal{A}$ on some word $w \in \Sigma^\omega$, i.e. $\mathit{Inf}(\rho) \in \mathcal{F}$. It gives rise to a run $\rho' = (q_0, \Lambda_0), (q_1, \Lambda_1), \ldots$ on the same w where Λ_0 is as defined above and $\Lambda_{i+1} := \mathit{upd}_{q_i}(\Lambda_i)$ for all $i \geq 0$. We need to show that the maximal priority occurring infinitely often in ρ' is even.

Let $\Lambda_i = (\pi_i, m_i)$ for all $i \geq 0$, and let $m := \limsup (m_i)_{i \geq 0}$ be the limes superior of the marker positions in the sequence of LAR constructed in this way. According to Lemma 6.27 we have $\mathit{Inf}(\rho) = \{ q \in Q \mid \limsup (\pi_i^{-1}(q))_{i \geq 0} \leq m \}$. Since $\mathit{Inf}(\rho)$ is given, Lemma 6.27 dictates that there is some i_0 such that for all $i \geq i_0$ we have $\pi_i^{-1}(q) \leq m$ iff $q \in \mathit{Inf}(\rho)$. Moreover, there must be infinitely many i such that $m_i = m$. Hence, the greatest priority occurring infinitely often must be $2m+2$ or $2m+1$, depending on the sets $\{\pi_i^{-1}(0), \ldots, \pi_i^{-1}(m)\}$ at such positions i. Since this equals $\mathit{Inf}(\rho)$, the exact priority is determined by the question of whether or not $\mathit{Inf}(\rho) \in \mathcal{F}$. Since this is the case by assumption, the maximal priority occurring infinitely often in ρ' is $2m+2$ which is clearly even.

"$\subseteq$" Now take a run $\rho' = (q_0, \Lambda_0), (q_1, \Lambda_1), \ldots$ on some $w \in \Sigma^\omega$ with $\Lambda_i = (\pi_i, m_i)$ and suppose that it is accepting, i.e. $\limsup (\Omega(q_i, \Lambda_i))_{i \geq 0}$ is even. Then it must be of the form $2m+2$, and this is because $\limsup (m_i)_{i \geq 0} = m$ and there are infinitely many i such that $\{\pi_i^{-1}(0), \ldots, \pi_i^{-1}(m)\} \in \mathcal{F}$. By finiteness of $\mathcal{F}$ and the pigeon hole principle, we even have some $F \in \mathcal{F}$ such that $\{\pi_i^{-1}(0), \ldots, \pi_i^{-1}(m)\} = F$ for all such i. We can then use Lemma 6.27 again to obtain that $F = \mathit{Inf}(\rho)$ for the projection ρ of ρ' onto its first components. This is then not only a run of $\mathcal{A}$ on w but in fact also an accepting one. $\qquad\square$

Note that the initial LAR that the simulation of the NPA starts with, is irrelevant. This is of course not the same as letting the automaton choose some LAR nondeterministically. This would not change the language but it would kill the property that a DMA becomes a DPA under this construction which is easily verified.

Corollary 6.29 *For every DMA $\mathcal{A}$ of size n there is a DPA $\mathcal{B}$ of size at most $n^2 \cdot n!$ and index at most $2n$ such that $L(\mathcal{B}) = L(\mathcal{A})$.*

6.4 Co-Büchi Automata

Cor. 6.22 and Thm. 6.24 show that, at least for the nondeterministic variant, Büchi, Rabin, Streett, parity and Muller automata all have equal expressiveness, recognising exactly the ω-regular languages. We already know from Chp. 5 that, at least for Büchi automata, the deterministic variant is less expressive. Chp. 7 will show that this is not the case for the other models based on the richer Rabin, Streett, parity and Muller acceptance conditions.

Moreover, we have seen that Rabin and Streett conditions are dual to each other, while the parity and the Muller condition is self-dual in the sense that an automaton of the respective type can easily be obtained for the complement of the language of a deterministic automaton. For Büchi automata this is not the case: the complement of a Büchi acceptance condition "F infinitely often" is "$Q \setminus F$ only *finitely often*". While this can generally be expressed by a Büchi automaton, making use of nondeterminism, it does not help for a simple complementation construction on deterministic automata as we have seen based on the dualities mentioned above. In order for this to work, we simply introduce the complement of Büchi acceptance formally as yet another automaton model for languages of ω-words and study its expressiveness.

Definition 6.30 A *nondeterministic co-Büchi automaton* (NcoBA) is an $\mathcal{A} = (Q, \Sigma, q_I, \delta, F)$ just like an NBA. In particular, we have $F \subseteq Q$, and this is also said to be the set of accepting states. The notion of size is as usual, and so is that of determinism in the transition function, leading to the model of a *deterministic co-Büchi automaton* (DcoBA).

An infinite run $\rho = q_0, q_1, \ldots$ of the NcoBA $\mathcal{A}$ is *accepting* if there is some $i \in \mathbb{N}$ such that $q_j \in F$ for all $j \geq i$. I.e. co-Büchi acceptance is equivalent to seeing non-accepting states only finitely often.

The notions of language of an NcoBA, NcoBA-, resp. DcoBA-recognisability, etc. are defined as usual.

It is important to state explicitly that accepting runs need to be of infinite length, since the requirement of seeing non-accepting states only finitely often would trivially apply to any finite run.

Sometimes, acceptance of an NcoBA is defined differently in the literature, namely via $Inf(\rho) \subseteq Q \setminus F$, i.e. the designated set of states F is not what needs to be seen eventually only, but what should only be seen finitely often. This is clearly not an essential difference, though, as the co-Büchi acceptance condition in Def. 6.30 demands $Inf(\rho) \subseteq F$. Hence, it is just a matter of taste whether the states in F are seen as accepting or as non-accepting. We stick to the former view as it fits better with the intuition behind the other acceptance conditions as primarily demanding what needs to happen rather than what must not happen.

Co-Büchi acceptance is of course made for languages that are specified via finite occurrences of certain patterns in an ω-word only.

Example 6.31 The following NcoBA $\mathcal{A}$ recognises the language $L = \{w \in \{a, b\}^\omega \mid |w|_b < \infty\}$.

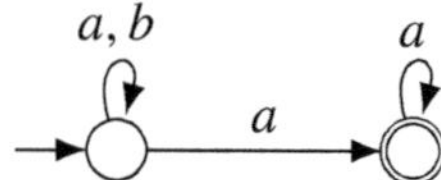

When interpreted as an NBA, its language is L is as well. The reason is that no non-accepting state is reachable from an accepting state. Hence, any infinite run of such an automaton will visit accepting states infinitely often iff it visits non-accepting states only finitely often.

The difference between Büchi acceptance and co-Büchi acceptance is made apparent with the following automaton.

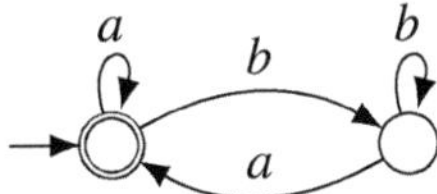

When regarded as an NcoBA its language is also L. When regarded as an NBA, its language is $L' := \{w \in \{a, b\}^\omega \mid |w|_a = \infty\}$, though. Note that these two languages differ on all words w such that $|w|_a = \infty$ and $|w|_b = \infty$.

The language of an NBA is always a superset of the language of the same automaton regarded as an NcoBA. This is a simple consequence of the fact that any infinite run that eventually sees accepting states only, must visit accepting states infinitely often. The converse is not true, as the previous example shows.

The constructed duality between the Büchi and the co-Büchi acceptance condition can then be used to easily complement deterministic automata into those of the other type.

Theorem 6.32 *For every DBA, resp. DcoBA $\mathcal{A}$ over Σ of size n there is a DcoBA, resp. DBA $\mathcal{B}$ of size at most $n + 1$ such that $L(\mathcal{B}) = \Sigma^\omega \setminus L(\mathcal{A})$.*

Proof As usual, by potentially adding one extra non-accepting state that acts like a trap it is possible to eliminate rejecting finite runs making sure that every word has exactly one run and that is infinite. It is then easy to see that the complement of the language of the DBA $(Q, \Sigma, q_I, \delta, F)$ is the language of the DcoBA $(Q, \Sigma, q_I, \delta, Q \setminus F)$ and vice-versa. $\qquad\square$

There is an essential combinatorial difference between Büchi and co-Büchi acceptance that will show up in the next chapters: while determinisation of Büchi automata requires an elaborate construction that genuinely goes beyond the techniques used for automata on finite words and has to result in automata with a richer acceptance condition, determinisation of co-Büchi automata is possible with a surprisingly simple and elegant extension of the well-known powerset construction. Moreover, it turns an NcoBA into a DcoBA, i.e. it does not rely on richer acceptance conditions.

We state determinisability of co-Büchi automata here without a proof and remark that the very same construction used in the proof of Thm. 9.17 to turn an alternating Büchi automaton into a nondeterministic one, can be used here as well.

Proposition 6.33 *For every NcoBA $\mathcal{A}$ of size n there is a DcoBA $\mathcal{B}$ of size at most 3^n such that $L(\mathcal{B}) = L(\mathcal{A})$.*

At last, we study the expressive power of Büchi and co-Büchi automata. It is not hard to see that co-Büchi automata, just like Büchi automata, are special parity, Rabin and Streett automata. Formulating the corresponding acceptance conditions is left as an exercise.

Thm. 6.32 may suggest that co-Büchi and Büchi automata are incomparable in terms of expressiveness but this is immediately seen not to be true. Thm. 6.32 states that the deterministic variants are linked through complements, i.e. L is DBA-recognisable iff $\overline{L}$ is DcoBA-recognisable. We already know that NBA recognise exactly the ω-regular languages and they are closed under complements. Hence, if a language L was NBA-recognisable iff its complement $\overline{L}$ was NcoBA-recognisable, then NcoBA would recognise all ω-regular languages as well. It is not clear, though, how an NcoBA could be built for a simple ω-regular language like $\{w \in \{a,b\}^{\omega} \mid |w|_b = \infty\}$, though. This suggests that NcoBA are weaker than NBA, and this is in fact the case as the next two theorems show.

Theorem 6.34 *For every NcoBA $\mathcal{A}$ of size n there is an NBA $\mathcal{B}$ of size at most $2n$ such that $L(\mathcal{B}) = L(\mathcal{A})$.*

Proof Let $\mathcal{A} = (Q, \Sigma, q_I, \delta, F)$. Then $\mathcal{B} := (Q', \Sigma, (q_I, 0), \Delta, F')$ where $Q' = Q \times \{0\} \cup F \times \{1\}$ and $F' = F \times \{1\}$. Hence, $\mathcal{B}$ consists of two copies of $\mathcal{A}$ and starts in the first one. The second one only consists of accepting states of $\mathcal{A}$, though, and these are also the accepting states of $\mathcal{B}$. It is better to consider this conversely: all non-accepting states in the second component have been removed.

There are three kinds of transitions: $\mathcal{B}$ can simulate $\mathcal{A}$ in its first component, it can nondeterministically move to its second component, and it can continue to simulate $\mathcal{A}$ there, provided that it does not get stuck because of lack of non-accepting states there. We have

$$\Delta((q,0),a) := \{(q',0) \mid q' \in \delta(q,a)\} \cup \{(q',1) \mid q' \in \delta(q,a) \cap F\},$$
$$\Delta((q,1),a) := \{(q',1) \mid q' \in \delta(q,a) \cap F\}.$$

It should be clear that $\mathcal{B}$'s size is at most $2n$. It remains to be seen that it is correct, i.e. that $L(\mathcal{B}) = L(\mathcal{A})$.

"$\supseteq$" Suppose $\rho = q_0, q_1, \ldots$ is an accepting run of the NcoBA $\mathcal{A}$ on some $w \in \Sigma^{\omega}$. Thus, there is an $i \geq 1$ s.t. $q_j \in F$ for all $j \geq i$. Consider

$$\rho' := (q_0,0), \ldots, (q_{i-1},0), (q_i,1), (q_{i+1},1), \ldots$$

which is easily seen to be a run of $\mathcal{B}$ on the same w, even an accepting one. Thus, $w \in L(\mathcal{B})$.

Note that for this direction, no argument about the separate components is needed. This is because of the observation made above that co-Büchi acceptance implies Büchi-acceptance but not vice-versa. Hence, the other direction can be expected to make use of the two-component construction.

"$\subseteq$" Suppose that $w \in L(\mathcal{B})$, i.e. there is an accepting run $\rho' = (q_0, i_0), (q_1, i_1), \ldots$ of $\mathcal{B}$ on w. By inspection of Δ we see that $i_0 = 0$ and $i_{j+1} \geq i_j$ for all $j \geq 0$. Since only states of the form $(q,1)$ are accepting, the run is indeed of the form

$$\rho' = (q_0, 0), \ldots, (q_{i-1}, 0), (q_i, 1), (q_{i+1}, 1), \ldots$$

for some $i \geq 1$, i.e. $\rho' \in (Q \times \{0\})^+ (F \times \{1\})^\omega$. But then we must have $q_j \in F$ for all $j \geq i$. Hence, the projection $\rho = q_0, q_1, \ldots$ onto the first components is a run of $\mathcal{A}$ on w that satisfies the co-Büchi acceptance condition F, and we have $w \in \mathcal{A}$. $\square$

The converse direction is not true; NBA are indeed more expressive than NcoBA. The language $L = \{w \in \{a, b\}^\omega \mid |w|_b = \infty\}$ mentioned just before Thm. 6.34 is an example.

Theorem 6.35 *There are ω-regular languages that cannot be recognised by an NcoBA.*

Proof Take the language $L = \{w \in \{a, b\}^\omega \mid |w|_b = \infty\}$. Clearly, it is ω-regular. Suppose we had $L = L(\mathcal{A})$ for some NcoBA $\mathcal{A} = (Q, \{a, b\}, q_I, \delta, F)$. Let $n := |Q|$ and consider the word $w = (a^n b)^\omega$. Obviously, $w \in L$ so there is an accepting run $\rho = q_0, q_1, \ldots$ of $\mathcal{A}$ on w. According to co-Büchi acceptance, there is an $i \in \mathbb{N}$ s.t. $q_j \in F$ for all $j \geq i$.

W.l.o.g. we can assume that $i = 1 + (n + 1) \cdot k$ for some k; simply choose i to be large enough. Thus, we have $\rho =$

$$q_0, a, q_1, \ldots, q_{i-1}, b, q_i, a, q_{i+1}, \ldots, q_{i+n-1}, a, q_{i+n}, b, q_{i+n+1}, a, q_{i+n+2}, \ldots$$

Since $(i + n) - i + 1 = n + 1 > n$ there must be j, h such that $i \leq j < h \leq i + n$ and $q_j = q_h$. Since between q_j and q_h, $\mathcal{A}$ has only been reading symbols a, and all states are accepting by assumption, we can use a pumping argument to construct an accepting run $\rho' =$

$$q_0, a, q_1, \ldots, q_{i-1}, b, q_i, \ldots, q_j \big(, a, q_{j+1}, \ldots, a, q_h \big)^\omega$$

on a word of the form $(a + b)^* a^\omega$, contradicting the assumption that $L(\mathcal{A}) = L$. $\square$

There is also another argument for the claim in Thm. 6.35 that relies on the stated, but yet formally unproven determinisability of NcoBA. Suppose that $L = \{w \in \{a, b\}^\omega \mid |w|_b = \infty\}$ was NcoBA-recognisable. So it would also be DcoBA-recognisable. According to Thm. 6.32, its complement would be DBA-recognisable, but the complement is $\overline{L} = \{w \in \{a, b\}^\omega \mid |w|_b < \infty\}$ and this is not DBA-recognisable according to Thm. 5.24.

Since $\overline{L}$ is clearly NcoBA-recognisable, the class of NcoBA-recognisable languages is not closed under complements. Since it is defined via a nondeterministic automaton model, it is easily seen to be closed under unions. Closure under intersections also holds, and the construction is, again, simpler than the corresponding one for NBA. The proof is left as an exercise.

Theorem 6.36 *Let $\mathcal{A}_i$ be NcoBA of size n_i for $i \in \{1, 2\}$.*

a) There is an NcoBA $\mathcal{B}_1$ of size at most $n_1 + n_2 + 1$ such that $L(\mathcal{B}_1) = L(\mathcal{A}_1) \cup L(\mathcal{A}_2)$.
b) There is an NcoBA $\mathcal{B}_2$ of size at most $n_1 \cdot n_2$ such that $L(\mathcal{B}_2) = L(\mathcal{A}_1) \cap L(\mathcal{A}_2)$.

Sometimes it is worth considering closure properties for different kinds of automata. Suppose some language L was described as the intersection between two languages L' and L'', and the task is to construct an automaton for L. Assume furthermore that L'' was easily seen to be co-Büchi-recognisable. With a result stating that the intersection of a co-Büchi-recognisable language with a language of some other type can be recognised by an automaton of that other type, we may be able to construct an automaton for L modularly.

This possibility is of course not restricted to co-Büchi automata, and a properly exhaustive study would have to tell, for each (binary) Boolean operation and each three automaton types, what the simplest construction is for an automaton of the third type, given automata of the first and second types.

Here we only consider one such case, namely that of the intersection of a parity-recognisable language with a co-Büchi-recognisable one. The reason simply is that this is needed later on in Chp. 13. Proof details are left as an exercise.

Lemma 6.37 *For every NPA $\mathcal{A}$ of size n and index k and NcoBA $\mathcal{B}$ of size m there is an NPA $\mathcal{C}$ of size nm and index at most $k + 1$ such that $L(\mathcal{C}) = L(\mathcal{A}) \cap L(\mathcal{B})$.*

6.5 Transition-Based Acceptance

A natural variant of acceptance by infinite occurrence is concerned with transitions in runs rather than states. We briefly investigate automata models that use such acceptance conditions to see that their expressive power remains the same.

It is convenient to see the transition table of a finite automaton as a relation $\delta \subseteq Q \times \Sigma \times Q$ rather than a function $\delta : Q \times \Sigma \to 2^Q$. Mathematically, there is of course no conceptual difference but the former allows us to easily speak about sets of transitions, simply as subsets of the transition relation.

Definition 6.38 A *nondeterministic Büchi-edge automaton* (NBA$_e$) is an $\mathcal{A} = (Q, \Sigma, q_I, \delta, F)$ just like an NBA but with $F \subseteq \delta$. A run of an NBA$_e$ on a word $w = a_0 a_1 \ldots \in \Sigma^\omega$ is an infinite sequence $\rho = q_0, a_0, q_1, a_1, \ldots$ as usual. We write $\mathit{Inf}_e(\rho)$ for the set of *transitions* being used infinitely often in ρ, i.e.

$$\mathit{Inf}_e(\rho) := \{(q, a, p) \in \delta \mid \forall i \geq 0 \exists j \geq i.q = q_i, a = a_i, p = q_{i+1}\} \,.$$

Such a run ρ is *accepting* if $\mathit{Inf}_e(\rho) \cap F \neq \emptyset$.

The *language* of an NBA$_e$ is, as usual, the set of words for which there is an accepting run. Other notions like size etc. apply here equally.

Example 6.39 Consider the language $L = \{w \in \{a, b\}^\omega \mid |w|_a = \infty = |w|_b\}$. Note that a word over $\{a, b\}$ contains both a and b infinitely often iff it contains infinitely many subwords of the form ab or ba. In fact, it suffices to demand that only one of them occurs infinitely often. L is accepted by the NBA$_e$

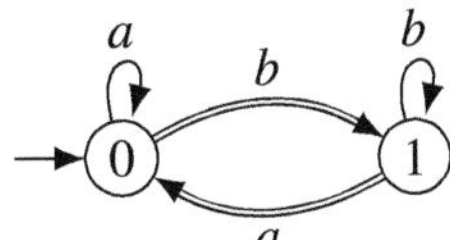

where double arrows are used to denote accepting transitions.

Ex. 6.39 shows a potential appeal of edge-based acceptance conditions. The language L from this example is recognised by an NBA_e of size 2. This is smaller than any NBA for this language.

There is of course no reason not to transfer all the other acceptance conditions based to the setting in which the infinite occurrence of edges determines whether or not a run is accepting. A *nondeterministic co-Büchi-edge automaton* ($NcoBA_e$) is an $\mathcal{A} = (Q, \Sigma, q_I, \delta, F)$ just like an NBA_e, but a run $\rho = q_0, a_0, q_1, a_1, \ldots$ is *accepting* if $Inf_e(\rho) \subseteq F$. A *nondeterministic parity-edge automaton* (NPA_e) is an $\mathcal{A} = (Q, \Sigma, q_I, \delta, \Omega)$ with $\Omega : \delta \to \mathbb{N}$, and accepting runs are those in which $\max\{\Omega(e) \mid e \in Inf_e(\rho)\}$ is even. Nondeterministic Rabin-edge, Streett-edge and Muller-edge automata (NRA_e / NSA_e / NMA_e) and their accepting runs are defined analogously. The *index* measures the size of the acceptance condition again.

6.5.1 From States to Edges

Automata with edge-based acceptance conditions may be more succinct than those with state-based acceptance conditions, but their expressiveness does not exceed that of ω-regularity. In fact, there are conceptually simple transformations between the two variants for each acceptance condition. We start with the even simpler one, turning a state-based condition into an edge-based on. It is based on the observation that in a finite automaton over a finite alphabet, every state can only have a bounded number of outgoing transitions. It is then possible to shift the acceptance condition from states to edges going out of the respective states. It should be clear that a run visiting some state q infinitely often must necessarily see some transition (q, a, p) infinitely often for some $a \in \Sigma$ and state p. However, note that it need not see *all* of them infinitely often.

Theorem 6.40 *For every NcoBA / NBA / NPA / NRA / NSA $\mathcal{A}$ of size n and index k (where applicable) there is an $NcoBA_e$ / NBA_e / NPA_e / NRA_e / NSA_e $\mathcal{B}$ of size n and index k such that $L(\mathcal{B}) = L(\mathcal{A})$.*

Proof We carry this out for the case of NRA and remark that the construction, when restricted to NPA, NBA and NcoBA that can be seen as special NRA, yields NPA_e, resp. NBA_e or $NcoBA_e$. Moreover, the construction for the dual model of NSA is done analogously.

Let $\mathcal{A} = (Q, \Sigma, q_I, \delta, \mathcal{F})$ be an NRA with $\mathcal{F} = \{(G_1, F_1), \ldots, (G_k, F_k)\}$. Define $\mathcal{B} := (Q, \Sigma, q_I, \delta, \mathcal{F}')$ with $\mathcal{F}' := \{(G'_1, F'_1), \ldots, (G'_k, F'_k)\}$ and

$$G_i' := \{(q,a,p) \in \delta \mid q \in G_i\},$$
$$F_i' := \{(q,a,p) \in \delta \mid q \in F_i\}.$$

The claims on the size and index of $\mathcal{B}$ are clear. It remains to be seen that we have $L(\mathcal{B}) = L(\mathcal{A})$.

"$\supseteq$" Let $\rho = q_0, a_0, q_1, a_1, \ldots$ be an accepting run of $\mathcal{A}$ on $w = a_0 a_1 \ldots$, i.e. there is some $i \in \{1, \ldots, k\}$ such that $Inf(\rho) \cap G_i \neq \varnothing$ and $Inf(\rho) \cap F_i = \varnothing$. Hence, there is $q \in G_i$ such that $q \in Inf(\rho)$.

Clearly, ρ is also a run of $\mathcal{B}$ on w. Moreover, $|\{(a,p) \in \Sigma \times Q \mid (q,a,p) \in \delta\}| < \infty$. Thus, if $q = q_j$ for infinitely many j then there must be a, p such that $(q_j, a_j, q_{j+1}) = (q,a,p)$ for infinitely many j, i.e. $(q,a,p) \in Inf_e(\rho)$, and $(q,a,p) \in G_i'$ by construction. Hence, $Inf_e(\rho) \cap G_i' \neq \varnothing$.

On the other hand, suppose there was some $(q,a,p) \in F_i' \cap Inf_e(\rho)$. Then we would have $q \in Inf(\rho) \cap F_i$. Hence, through the assumption $Inf(\rho) \cap F_i = \varnothing$ we get $Inf_e(\rho) \cap F_i' = \varnothing$ which shows that ρ is also an accepting run of $\mathcal{B}$ on w.

"$\subseteq$" Take a run $\rho = q_0, a_0, q_1, a_1, \ldots$ and suppose there is an $i \in \{1, \ldots, k\}$ such that $Inf_e(\rho) \cap G_i' \neq \varnothing$ and $Inf_e(\rho) \cap F_i' = \varnothing$. Analogously to the part above, we get that there must be some $q \in Inf(\rho)$ with $q \in G_i$, and also $Inf(\rho) \cap F_i = \varnothing$, showing that ρ is also an accepting run of $\mathcal{A}$ on the same underlying word.   □

Note that NMA were not mentioned in the previous theorem. It is not that the corresponding result does not hold for Muller automata. We state it separately simply because the construction does not preserve the automaton's index.

Theorem 6.41 *For every NMA $\mathcal{A}$ of size n there is an NMA$_e$ $\mathcal{B}$ of size n such that $L(\mathcal{B}) = L(\mathcal{A})$.*

As stated above, infinite traversal of a state does not imply infinite traversal of *all* its outgoing transitions. Remember that a Muller condition is not necessarily closed under supersets or subsets. Hence, we may have to list every possibility to traverse outgoing transitions from some state separately. However, we can make use of the fact that a Muller-accepting run will eventually only see transitions between states of the same acceptance component. Details of a formal construction are left as an exercise.

6.5.2 From Edges to States

So transition-based acceptance is at least as powerful as state-based acceptance. We now turn to the other part of the expressiveness study, showing that transition-based acceptance is not more powerful.

It should be clear that the naïve approach of splitting every transition into two, inserting an intermediate state that is uniquely traversed by the two halves of that transition, cannot work as this would require the automaton with the state-based acceptance condition to simulate the transition-based acceptance condition with

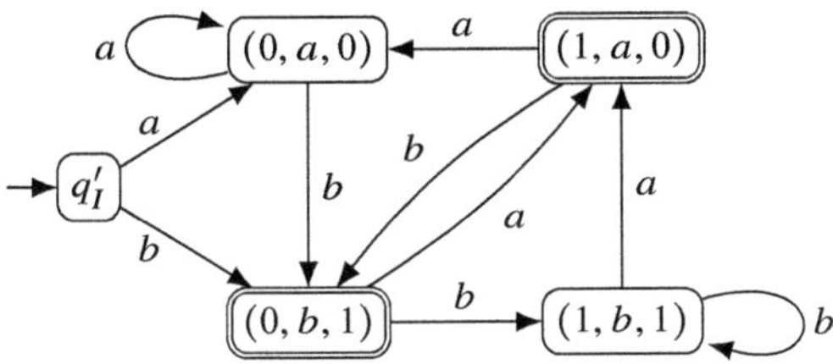

Fig. 6.4 NBA obtained from an NBA$_e$ for the language described in Ex. 6.44.

unbounded delays. Instead, the trick is to shift transitions by one half, regarding a run $q_0, a_0, q_1, a_1, \ldots$ as an infinite sequence $(q_0, a_0, q_1), (q_1, a_1, q_2), \ldots$ of transitions.

Again, we formulate the corresponding translation result for one acceptance condition, namely the Rabin one, and leave it as an exercise to prove a corresponding statement for the other acceptance conditions.

Theorem 6.42 *For every NRA$_e$ $\mathcal{A}$ of size n and index k with e many transitions there is an NRA $\mathcal{B}$ of size $e + 1$ and index k such that $L(\mathcal{B}) = L(\mathcal{A})$.*

Proof Let $\mathcal{A} = (Q, \Sigma, q_I, \delta, \mathcal{F})$ be an NRA$_e$ with $\mathcal{F} = \{(G_1, F_1), \ldots, (G_k, F_k)\}$ and $G_i, F_i \subseteq \delta$ for all $i = 1, \ldots, k$. Let $\mathcal{B} := (\delta \cup \{q_I'\}, \Sigma, q_I', \Delta, \mathcal{F})$ where, for all $(q, a, p), (q', b, p') \in \delta$ and $c \in \Sigma$ we have

$$\big((q, a, p), c, (q', b, p')\big) \in \Delta \quad \text{iff} \quad p = q' \text{ and } c = b$$

and for all $(q_I, a, p) \in \delta$ we have $(q_I', a, (q_I, a, p)) \in \Delta$.

Correctness of this construction follows immediately from the observation that $\rho = q_0, a_0, q_1, \ldots$ (with $q_0 = q_I$) is an accepting run of $\mathcal{A}$ on $w = a_0 a_1 \ldots$ iff

$$\rho' = q_I', a_0, (q_I, a_0, q_1), a_1, (q_1, a_2, q_2), \ldots$$

is an accepting run of $\mathcal{B}$ on the same w, because $Inf(\rho') = Inf_e(\rho)$ and therefore, for any $i \in \{1, \ldots, k\}$ we have

$$Inf_e(\rho) \cap G_i \neq \varnothing \text{ and } Inf_e(\rho) \cap F_i = \varnothing \text{ iff } Inf(\rho') \cap G_i \neq \varnothing \text{ and } Inf(\rho') \cap F_i = \varnothing .$$

The claims on size and index are obvious.   □

Note that this construction preserves determinism, i.e. it turns a deterministic automaton with a transition-based Rabin acceptance condition into a deterministic Rabin automaton.

Corollary 6.43 *For every deterministic NRA$_e$ $\mathcal{A}$ of size n and index k with e many transitions there is a DRA $\mathcal{B}$ of size $e + 1$ and index k such that $L(\mathcal{B}) = L(\mathcal{A})$.*

Example 6.44 Remember that a Büchi acceptance condition F is a Rabin acceptance condition $\{(F, \varnothing)\}$, and this holds regardless of whether F is a set of states or set of transitions. Hence, we can regard the $\text{NBA}_\ominus$ from Ex. 6.39 as an $\text{NRA}_\ominus$ and translate it into the NRA shown in Fig. 6.4 that equally happens to be an NBA, recognising the language L of all words over $\{a, b\}$ that contain both a and b infinitely often.

To see that this NBA correctly accepts the designated language note that any path from any accepting state to itself needs to read both the letter a and the letter b. Hence, it can only accept words that contain infinitely many symbols a and infinitely many symbols b. On the other hand, each state has an a- and a b-successor. Hence, every word from $\{a, b\}^\omega$ can fully be processed by this NBA, so it does not just accept a subset of L.

As the example suggests, the translation can be specialised to Büchi- and parity automata. It can also be used to transform transition-based Streett-automata into state-based ones, and it can be used to do the same for Muller conditions as well. Details are left as an exercise.

6.6 Expressiveness of Finite Automata on Infinite Words

The essence of this chapter can be summarised as follows: the class of ω-regular languages is very robust under any choice of acceptance condition. Any model of finite automata with an acceptance condition based on the infinite occurrence of states (or in fact transitions) recognises the ω-regular languages, with one exception: co-Büchi automata are strictly weaker. With the respective results on the other automaton models we collectively obtain the following equi-expressiveness result.

Corollary 6.45 *Let $L \subseteq \Sigma^\omega$. The following statements are equivalent.*

a) L is ω-regular.   *g) L is $\text{NBA}_\ominus$-recognisable.*
b) L is NBA-recognisable.   *h) L is $\text{NPA}_\ominus$-recognisable.*
c) L is NPA-recognisable.   *i) L is $\text{NRA}_\ominus$-recognisable.*
d) L is NRA-recognisable.   *j) L is $\text{NSA}_\ominus$-recognisable.*
e) L is NSA-recognisable.   *k) L is $\text{NMA}_\ominus$-recognisable.*
f) L is NMA-recognisable.

Equivalence between (a) and (b) was shown in Cor. 5.14. The way that equivalence amongst these and the other statements is achieved is shown in Fig. 6.5.

Bibliographic Notes

Clearly, three of the automata models discussed here – besides Büchi automata – are also named after their inventors. Rabin needed a richer acceptance condition than

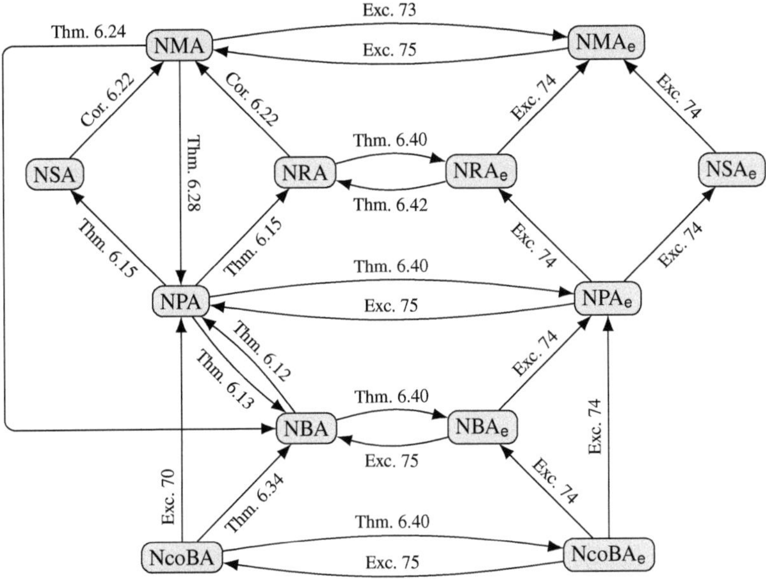

Fig. 6.5 Expressiveness of models of finite automata on infinite words.

Büchi's in the context of finite automata accepting languages of trees rather than words [Rab69]. As we will see later, Rabin automata are in fact more expressive there than Büchi automata. The motivation came, as in Büchi's case, from logic: Rabin proved complementation closure of Rabin tree automata which was the key part in a decidability result for a version of Monadic Second-Order Logic interpreted over trees.

Streett automata were also introduced as a tool for deciding formal logics [Str82], but there the logic under foremost consideration was Propositional Dynamic Logic (PDL). As it turns out, PDL [FL79] and related formalisms, i.e. temporal logics like CTL [EC82] and CTL* [EH86], or modal fixpoint logics like the modal μ-calculus [Koz83], used primarily for purposes of program specification and verification, are (relatively) easily seen to be fragments of MSO interpreted over trees, cf. Chp. 14. Hence, it is not too surprising that Streett automata also fall into the categories studied in this context.

The conceptual hierarchy given by the translations of one acceptance condition into another suggests that the corresponding automata models may have been introduced in the same chronological order, starting from the simplest and most natural one and progressing on to richer ones. This is not true, though. Muller automata were introduced before Rabin and Streett automata, for example, in the context of specifications of the behaviour of digital circuits [Mul63]. The relative richness of certain acceptance conditions compared to others has been used and observed over the years, though. For example, McNaughton showed that Büchi automata could be determinised into Muller automata [McN66]. Determinisation will explicitly be studied in the next chapter; we therefore also refer to the bibliographic notes there, since the issue of determinisation is tightly linked to questions concerning acceptance conditions.

There is also plenty of work that gives an overview of automata constructions transforming between different models or studies them in detail, cf. the corresponding chapter in the book by Esparza and Blondin [EB23, Chp. 10], the handbook articles by Thomas [Tho97] and Kupferman [Kup18], or overview articles by Farwer [Far02] and Boker [Bok18].

Exercises

Exercise 58 Show that merging states of an NRA that recognise the same language does not generally preserve the language of the NRA. *Hint:* Consider the language L of all words over $\{a, b\}$ that contain infinitely many symbols b. It is easy to construct a two-state NRA $\mathcal{A}$ such that $L(\mathcal{A}) = L$, regardless of which one of them is the initial state. Now suppose that these would be merged. List possible Rabin pairs and analyse each possibility to build a Rabin acceptance condition from them.

Exercise 59 Show how to translate an NRA directly into an NBA without taking a detour via NMA. *Hint:* Amend the translation from NPA to NBA accordingly.

Exercise 60 A *min-parity automaton* is an $\mathcal{A} = (Q, \Sigma, q_I, \delta, \Omega)$ just like a max-parity NPA considered here. A run $\rho = q_0, q_1, \ldots$ of such a min-parity NPA is accepting if $\min\{\Omega(q) \mid q \in \mathit{Inf}(\rho)\}$ is even.

  a) Show that a language is recognisable by a max-parity NPA of size n and index k iff it is recognisable by a min-parity NPA of size n and index k.
  b) Refine the statement of part (a) and prove it, so that it yields a bound on the finer measure of indices as intervals $[k, m]$. I.e. if L is accepted by a max-parity NPA of index $[k, m]$, what can be said about the index $[k', m']$ of a min-parity NPA recognising L, and vice-versa?

Exercise 61 Prove Cor. 6.10 by making use of Lemma 6.9, possibly multiple times.

Exercise 62 Construct a three-state NBA for the language L used in Ex. 6.14 by collapsing states in the four-state NBA at the end of this example. Explain why such a collapse is possible without changing the NBA's language.

Exercise 63 Prove the converse of Lemma 6.21, i.e. show that any Muller condition $\mathcal{F} \subseteq 2^Q$ for some finite state set Q can be expressed as an acceptance formula $\Phi_{\mathcal{F}}$.

Exercise 64 Reduce the state space of the NBA shown in Fig. 6.3 by successively merging states. Argue in each case why this merging does not change the language, even though merging states of NBA does not preserve an NBA's language in general. As a second measurement, remove parts whenever this only deletes redundant accepting paths.

Exercise 65 Let $\mathcal{A}$ be a DMA of size n and index k recognising $L \subseteq \Sigma^\omega$. Construct a DMA recognising $\Sigma^\omega \setminus L$ and state bounds on its size and index.

Exercise 66 For $n \geq 2$ let $\Sigma_n := \{a_1, \ldots a_n, b_1, \ldots, b_n\}$ and

$$L_n := \left\{ w \in \Sigma_n^\omega \mid |\{i \mid a_i \in Inf(w)\}| = \lceil \tfrac{n}{2} \rceil \text{ and } |\{i \mid b_i \in Inf(w)\}| = \lfloor \tfrac{n}{2} \rfloor \right\}.$$

a) Build an NMA for L_3 using the construction in the proof of Thm. 6.23. Determine, in particular, its index.

b) Do the same for L_n for arbitrary $n \geq 2$.

Exercise 67 Explain how to obtain an automaton recognising the intersection of the languages of two given automata, for NPA, NRA and NSA, respectively. *Hint:* Start with NSA for which this can be done similarly to the construction for NMA. For NRA and NPA one may have to take a detour through other models.

Exercise 68 Is the language of all words over $\{a, b\}$ that contain the subword ab infinitely often or contain the subword ba infinitely often, NcoBA-recgnisable? If so, construct a corresponding automaton. Otherwise prove that this is impossible.

Exercise 69 Prove Thm. 6.36.

Exercise 70 Show how a co-Büchi acceptance condition can be seen as a special case of each of a parity, Rabin, Streett and Muller condition. In each case, determine the minimal index of the target model when translating co-Büchi automata into it.

Exercise 71 a) Prove Lemma 6.37. *Hint:* A simple product construction suffices. All that is needed is an assignment of priorities to state pairs which essentially preserves the priorities of the underlying NPA but only makes them count when the underlying NcoBA eventually only traverses through accepting states.

b) Give a direct construction for the intersection of an NPA- and an NBA-recgnisable language. *Hint:* A pure product construction does not suffices. However, it can be extended in order to remember the greatest priority seen by the underlying NPA on each segment of a word between accepting states of the NBA.

c) Explain whether the constructions in (a) and (b) preserve determinism, i.e. yield DPA when applied to a DPA and a DcoBA, resp. DBA.

Exercise 72 Show that there is no NBA of size 2 that recognises $L = \{w \in \{a, b\}^\omega \mid |w|_a = \infty = |w|_b\}$.

Exercise 73 Prove Thm. 6.41, i.e. show how to translate an NMA into an equivalent NMA_e. Give an upper bound on the blowup in index.

Exercise 74 Prove that

a) every NcoBA_e-recognisable language is NBA_e-recognisable,

b) every NBA_e- or NcoBA_e-recognisable language is NPA_e-recognisable,

c) every NPA_e-recognisable language is both NRA_e- and NSA_e-recognisable, and
d) every NRA_e- or NSA_e-recognisable language is NMA_e-recognisable.

Hint: Simply check that the corresponding embeddings of the state-based acceptance conditions can be reused for transition-based ones.

Exercise 75 Give translations from transition-based Büchi, co-Büchi, parity, Streett and Muller automata into the corresponding state-based ones, along the lines of Thm. 6.42. Estimate the incurring blowup in size and index.

Chapter 7
Determinisation

This title's chapter may seem paradoxical in the context of Chapter 5 where is was shown that deterministic Büchi automata are strictly weaker than nondeterministic ones. In particular, the language $(a + b)^* a^\omega$ cannot be recognised by a DBA, cf. Thm. 5.24. Thus, there is no determinisation procedure for NBA, at least none that yields equivalent DBA. While equivalence of the resulting automaton with regards to the original one is usually the entire purpose of any transformation like a determinisation procedure, Chp. 6 provides us with several other models of finite automata on infinite words for which the example of the non-DBA-definable language $(a + b)^* a^\omega$ fails. It is easy to construct deterministic parity, Rabin, Streett and Muller automata that recognise this language. Hence, it is reasonable to ask whether determinisation for NBA may indeed be possible at the expense of employing a richer acceptance condition on the deterministic side. The answer is yes. This chapter presents a construction that is based on the famous so-called *Safra construction* which solved the long-standing open problem of NBA determinisation.

7.1 The Inadequacy of Powerset-Based Determinisation

Reconsider the example of the non-DBA-definable language $(a + b)^* a^\omega$ mentioned above. It is recognised by the NBA shown on the left below, and it may be tempting, or at least informative, to simply "determinise" it via the powerset construction into the finite-state automaton shown on the right below.

It is obviously deterministic, and it should be clear that none of the four possible acceptance sets $\varnothing, \{0\}, \{01\}, \{0, 01\}$ makes it accept $(a + b)^* a^\omega$ as a DBA.

© The Author(s), under exclusive
license to Springer-Verlag GmbH, DE, part of Springer Nature 2025
M. Hofmann and M. Lange, *Automata Theory and Logic*,
https://doi.org/10.1007/978-3-662-72154-4_7

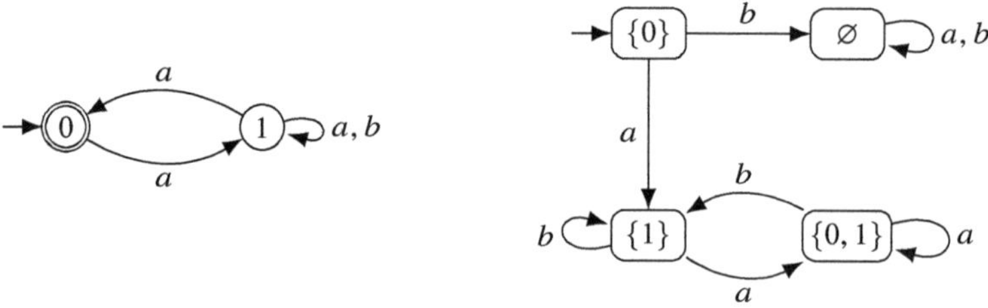

Fig. 7.1 NBA (left) and its powerset automaton (right).

However, it can be given a parity acceptance condition, for instance $\Omega(0) = 1$, $\Omega(01) = 0$ (and therefore also a Rabin or Muller condition) to accept this language. It is not even difficult to give it a Streett condition, namely $\{(\{0\},\varnothing)\}$, for that purpose.

Can the powerset construction be refined by equipping it with a parity, Rabin, Streett or Muller condition so that it yields equivalent deterministic automata in general? Note that while automata with any of these acceptance conditions can be turned into any others, and this even preserves determinacy, it is only the transformations from parity into Rabin or Streett, and from these into Muller automata that do not involve a blowup in the state space. This is relevant for the question under consideration here. For instance, perhaps it was possible to define a Rabin acceptance condition on the basis of the pure powerset construction but not a parity condition. In other words, if the answer to this question was positive, the strongest result would be given by a powerset-based translation from NBA to DPA. But a negative answer is strongest in terms of a Muller condition. It is indeed possible to answer this question to the negative in this form. We give an example of an NBA such that no Muller condition on the powerset automaton yields a DMA that is equivalent to the original NBA. Consequently, there is also no way to equip this powerset automaton with a parity, Rabin or Streett condition without changing its language.

Theorem 7.1 *There is an NBA $\mathcal{A}$ such that for every DMA $\mathcal{B}$ whose state space and transition graph results from $\mathcal{A}$ using the powerset construction, we have $L(\mathcal{B}) \neq L(\mathcal{A})$.*

Proof Consider the NBA $\mathcal{A}$ shown in Fig. 7.1 on the left. The part on the right shows the automaton that is obtained from $\mathcal{A}$ via the powerset construction. All that remains to be done is to see that no Muller condition, in terms of a set of subsets of its state space $2^{\{0,1\}}$ yields a DMA that is equivalent to $\mathcal{A}$. Note that $L(\mathcal{A}) = (a(a+b)^*a)^\omega$ consists only of words that contain the pattern aa infinitely often.

So let $\mathcal{B}$ be a DMA with state space and transitions as shown in Fig. 7.1 on the right with a fictitious Muller acceptance set $\mathcal{F}$. Now consider $w = a(aab)^\omega$. We have $w \in L(\mathcal{A})$. Thus, $\mathcal{B}$ must have an accepting run on w. Since it is deterministic and complete, there is exactly one run of $\mathcal{B}$ on w, and this one visits states $\{1\}$ and

$\{0, 1\}$ infinitely often. So we have $\{\{1\}, \{0, 1\}\} \in \mathcal{F}$. But then we would also get $a(ab)^\omega \in L(\mathcal{B})$, even though $a(ab)^\omega \notin L(\mathcal{A})$.   □

Thus, NBA not only cannot be transformed into DBA by the powerset construction but such a transformation also fails for all other known acceptance conditions. While the example used in the previous theorem is sufficient to prove such a strong statement, it does not exemplify well what the problem with the powerset construction really is. In order to examine this closer we remark that the powerset construction always yields an overapproximation to the language of an NBA. Thus, it is complete but unsound in the sense that the resulting automaton accepts all the words that need to be accepted but possibly more. To analyse in more detail what is going wrong we consider another example.

Example 7.2 Let $\mathcal{A}_1$ and $\mathcal{A}_2$ be NBA over the unary alphabet $\Sigma = \{a\}$ as follows.

Obviously, we have $L(\mathcal{A}_1) = \{a^\omega\}$ and $L(\mathcal{A}_2) = \emptyset$ since no run in $\mathcal{A}_2$ can see accepting states infinitely often.

The key insight here is that both lead to the same automaton $\mathcal{B}$ under the powerset construction, namely the following.

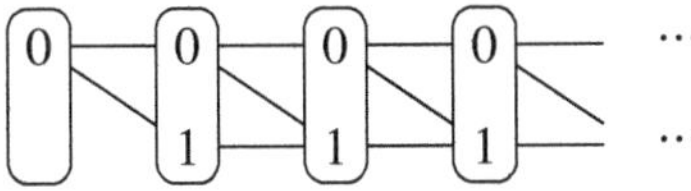

In order to disambiguate language when speaking about states in an NBA and in a corresponding powerset automaton, we also use the terms *microstate* for states of the NBA and *macrostate* for states of the powerset automaton.

When tracing the origins of each microstate through a sequence of macrostates forming a run of the powerset automaton, it becomes apparent that the powerset automaton is not refined enough to distinguish between sequences of microstates that form runs and those that do not. Clearly, there is only one run of $\mathcal{B}$ on a^ω, and it is $\{0\}(\{0, 1\})^\omega$. However, when revealing the structure of the macrostates in this run in terms of the origins of each of the microstates contained in them, we notice a difference. When the underlying NBA is $\mathcal{A}_1$ then this run is the following, called ρ_1 for future reference.

If, however, the underlying NBA is $\mathcal{A}_2$ then there are fewer connections between the microstates because now the only reason for microstate 1 to be included in macrostate $\{0, 1\}$ is the fact that it is an a-successor of microstate 0, whereas before it was an a-successor of both 0 and 1. This forms the following run ρ_2.

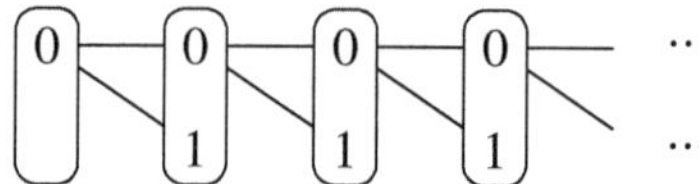

While ρ_1 and ρ_2 are the same run of $\mathcal{B}$ in terms of a sequence of macrostates, their difference is that ρ_2 contains only a single infinite run of microstates, namely 0^ω and that is not accepting. On the other hand, ρ_1 contains infinitely many runs of microstates, namely 0^ω (which is not accepting) and $0^n 1^\omega$ for any $n \geq 1$ which are all accepting.

This example, together with the observation stated above about the pure powerset construction yielding on overapproximation to the language of the underlying NBA, suggests that a determinisation procedure could be built by refining the powerset construction in a way that reveals the inner structure of connections between microstates. In other words, macrostates must not simply be sets of microstates but be built using some more advanced data structure which records the origins of microstates in the deterministic automaton's transitions so that acceptance in this automaton can be linked to the existence of an accepting run of microstates through the corresponding sequence of macrostates. The key in the Safra construction – to be presented next – is exactly the choice of a suitable tree-like data structure that refines simple sets of microstates accordingly.

7.2 Trees and Kőnig's Lemma

7.2.1 A Formal Model of Trees

Trees will play an important role not only as the basis of a refinement of sets in the forthcoming presentation of a determinisation construction for NBA. In Part III of this book we study automata and logic on trees as extensions of words. We therefore formalise the intuitive notion of a tree. For this, we write $\mathbb{N}^*$ to denote the set of all finite sequences of natural numbers, slightly abusing the notion of Σ^* for a finite alphabet Σ. However, all we use it for is to conveniently speak about sequences, prefixes, extensions, etc. We do not attempt to lift any results from the theory of regular languages over finite alphabets to infinite alphabets.

Definition 7.3 An ordered *tree* is a $T \subseteq \mathbb{N}^*$ that satisfies the following two properties.

- *Parent closure*: For every $ui \in T$ with $u \in \mathbb{N}^*$, $i \in \mathbb{N}$ we have $u \in T$.
- *Left-sibling closure*: For every $u(i+1) \in T$ with $u \in \mathbb{N}^*$, $i \in \mathbb{N}$ we have $ui \in T$.

Let Λ be some set. A Λ-labelled tree is a (T, t) such that T is an ordered tree and $t : T \to \Lambda$ labels the *nodes* with elements from Λ.

In the following, trees are always ordered. Hence, we only speak of trees rather than ordered trees.

The intuition behind this definition of trees is the following. Each node in a tree is identified by a sequence $u \in \mathbb{N}^*$ that encodes the unique path from the root to node u. Hence, T only contains the nodes, and the edges in the tree are given implicitly.

The root is ε since there is no direction to be taken from the root to arrive at the root. A node ui is the $(i + 1)$-th successor of node u, also known as the $(i + 1)$-th *child* of node u, where the first one is given direction 0, the second one direction 1, etc. The necessity for the two closure properties is the following.

- Parent closure requires every node, apart from the root, to have a parent in the tree, and the parent node is given by the maximal proper prefix of the node itself.
- Left-sibling closure simply states that every node which is not of the form $u0$, i.e. which is not the first child of its parent but the $(i + 1)$-th for some $i \geq 0$, must have a left sibling which is the i-th child of the parent node. The root node forms an exception since it has no parent, and it is therefore not the i-th child of a node for any i.

Note that in this formalisation, resp. representation of trees, it is easy to read off the levels of a tree T: level 0 consists of the root node ε only, i.e. all node names of length 0. Its children form level 1, and their names all have length 1, and so on.

Likewise, paths (from the root node) also have natural representations. Such a path can be given as a sequence of directions $i_1, i_2, i_3, \ldots$, and it traverses the nodes $\varepsilon, i_1, i_1 i_2, i_1 i_2 i_3, \ldots$ This works both for finite and infinite paths. A finite path taking directions $i_1, \ldots, i_n$ goes from ε via i_1, $i_1 i_2$, etc. to $i_1 \ldots i_n$, which shows clearly that a node's name is simply given as the unique sequence of directions to be taken from the root to that node.

We need a few more technical definitions about trees.

Definition 7.4 The *length* of a finite path from the root to node v in a tree T is $|v| + 1$. T has *paths of unbounded length* if it has a path of length n for every $n \in \mathbb{N}$.

A *descendant* of node u is every node v that is either u itself or a descendant of one of its children. Hence, v is a descendant of u iff there is a $w \in \mathbb{N}^*$ such that $v = uw$. The *branching degree* of a node u in T is $deg(u) := \sup\{i \mid ui \in T\}$ where $\sup \mathbb{N} = \infty$. We say that T has *infinite branching* if there is some $u \in T$ such that $deg(u) = \infty$. Otherwise it is said to be *finitely branching*. It has *bounded branching* if there is some $d \in \mathbb{N}$ such that $deg(u) \leq d$ for all nodes $u \in dom(t)$.

The branching degree of a tree simply measures how many children a node in the tree has maximally. Note that nothing forbids a node to have infinitely many children, hence the branching degree needs to be measured as a supremum, not a maximum.

Example 7.5 Fig. 7.2 shows three examples of (infinite) trees. We have $T_0 = 0^*$, and it is easily seen from the regular expression for this language that 0^* satisfies parent and left-sibling closure, the latter trivially.

The entire set of nodes of T_1 is less obviously derived from the picture showing only its first five levels. The picture suggests that T_1 also has paths of unbounded length, but unlike T_1 these need not be extensions of each other. For instance, a path of length 2 is $\pi_2 = \varepsilon, 2$, and a path of length 4 is $\pi_3 = \varepsilon, 0, 01$. Clearly, it does not

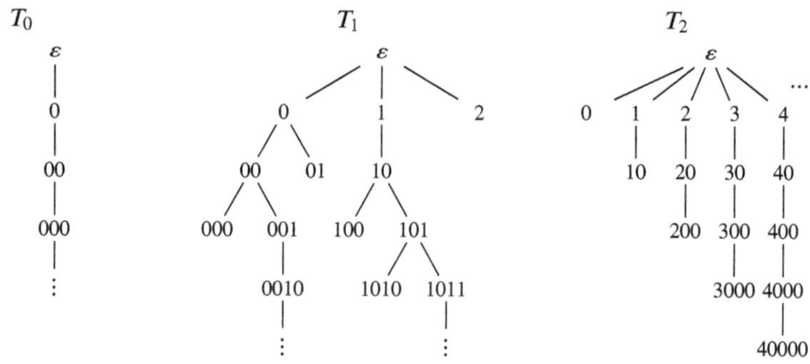

Fig. 7.2 Example trees with bounded or infinite branching, all with paths of unbounded lengths.

extend π_2. On the other hand, each path of length n of course also defines paths of length m for all $m < n$. For example, $\pi_2' = \varepsilon, 0$ is a path of length 2, and it is extended by π_3.

T_2 has node set $\{\varepsilon\} \cup \{n0^j \mid n \in \mathbb{N}, 0 \le j \le n\}$ which makes it the only example here of infinite branching. It also has paths of unbounded length: $\varepsilon, n, n0, n00, \ldots, n0^n$ is a path of length $n + 2$ for example.

7.2.2 Infinite Paths in Trees

Kőnig's Lemma connects the existence of paths of unbounded length with that of infinite paths. The trees T_1 and T_2 from the previous example present the essential difference that finite vs. infinite branching degree makes: T_2 has paths of unbounded length but no infinite path. T_1, however, when imagined to be continued in the same spirit as shown on the first few levels, in particular being of finite branching degree, will either have to stop at some level in which case it does not have paths of unbounded length, or it will have to have an infinite path.

Lemma 7.6 *A tree T with bounded branching has paths of unbounded length iff* $|T| = \infty$.

Proof "$\Rightarrow$" This direction does not even need the requirement regarding bounded branching. Suppose T has paths of unbounded length. I.e. for every $n \in \mathbb{N}$ there is a path of length n. The end node on this path must be some u_n such that $|u_n| = n$. Hence, $T \cap \mathbb{N}^n \ne \varnothing$ for every $n \in \mathbb{N}$, and therefore $|T| = \infty$.

"$\Leftarrow$" We first show, by induction on n, that $|T \cap \mathbb{N}^n| < \infty$ for every $n \in \mathbb{N}$. The claim is obvious for $n = 0$ because $|T \cap \mathbb{N}^0| = |\{\varepsilon\}| = 1$.

Suppose n is given and $|T \cap \mathbb{N}^n| = k < \infty$, i.e. there are k nodes on level n. Let $m := \max\{deg(u) \mid u \in T \cap \mathbb{N}^n\}$ be the maximal branching degree of nodes on this level. Because of the assumption of T having bounded branching, m exists. Now, every node on level $n + 1$ is a successor of a node on level n, and the k

nodes on level n can have at most $k \cdot m$ many successors. Otherwise one would have to have more successors than the maximal branching degree on that level. Thus, $|T \cap \mathbb{N}^{n+1}| \le k \cdot m < \infty$.

This proves the claim about each level having finitely many nodes only. Now, since $T = \bigcup_{n \ge 0} T \cap \mathbb{N}^n$, and each $T \cap \mathbb{N}^n$ is finite, there must be $n_0 < n_1 < \ldots$ such that $T \cap \mathbb{N}^{n_i} \ne \varnothing$ for every $i \ge 0$. Because of parent closure, we even have $T \cap \mathbb{N}^n \ne \varnothing$ for every $n \ge 0$. Each node v on level n defines a path of length $n + 1$, namely the unique path from the root to v. Thus, T contains paths of unbounded length. $\qquad\square$

The following is then known as *Kőnig's Lemma*.

Theorem 7.7 *Let T be a tree of finite branching degree. If T has paths of unbounded length then it has an infinite path.*

Proof Let T be a tree of finite branching degree that has paths of unbounded length. According to Lemma 7.6, we have $|T| = \infty$. We will now construct two sequences $v_0, v_1, \ldots$ and $T_0, T_1, \ldots$ such that

- $v_0, v_1, \ldots$ is an infinite path through T,
- $T_i = \{v \mid v$ is a descendant of $v_i\}$ and $|T_i| = \infty$ for all $i \ge 0$.

We start with $v_0 := \varepsilon$ and $T_0 := T$. By the observation using Lemma 7.6 we have $|T_0| = \infty$. Moreover, T_0 clearly consists of all descendants of the root node v_0.

Now suppose that v_i and T_i have been constructed already. Since T is of bounded branching, let $d := deg(v_i)$. By hypothesis, $|T_i| = \infty$, i.e. there are infinitely many nodes reachable from v_i, but it only has d many children. Hence, v_i must have some child node u so that infinitely many descendants of v_i are also descendants of u. Then simply take $v_{i+1} := u$ which guarantees that $|T_{i+1}| = \infty$.

Since each v_{i+1} was chosen as a child node to v_i, we have that $v_0, v_1, \ldots$ forms a path of infinite length through T. $\qquad\square$

Kőnig's Lemma is presented here because it is used in the combinatorics of the correctness proof of the Safra construction for the determinisation of NBA.

7.3 The Safra Construction

Fix an NBA $\mathcal{A} = (Q, \Sigma, q_I, \delta, F)$ for the rest of this section. W.l.o.g. we assume that it is total in the sense that for every $q \in Q$ and $a \in \Sigma$ there is at least one $p \in Q$ with $(q, a, p) \in \delta$. It should be clear that it is always possible to guarantee this by adding at most one state.

We discuss the general construction of a deterministic finite-state automaton $\mathcal{B}$ with respect to this NBA. We will use the terms *microstate* and *macrostate* again to refer to the states of $\mathcal{A}$, resp. $\mathcal{B}$.

7.3.1 Refining the Powerset Construction

In the end, we will make use of the results of Chp. 6, in particular Cor. 6.43, stating that a deterministic automaton with a transition-based Rabin acceptance condition can easily be transformed into a deterministic Rabin automaton, i.e. one that uses the more traditional state-based acceptance. Hence, it suffices to construct $\mathcal{B}$ as a finite-state automaton with a transition-based Rabin acceptance condition.

The states of $\mathcal{B}$, i.e. the macrostates, are finite trees whose nodes are labelled with sets of microstates from Q.

Definition 7.8 A *history tree* is a finite tree T whose nodes are labelled by a function $t : T \to 2^Q \setminus \{\varnothing\}$ with sets of states from Q such that the following conditions are met for all $v \in T$:

- $t(vi) \cap t(vj) = \varnothing$ for all $vi, vj \in T$ with $i \neq j$,
- $\bigcup_{i=0}^{d-1} t(vi) \subsetneq t(v)$ where $d = deg(v)$.

In the following, we will often identify a pair (T, t) consisting of a tree and a labelling function t simply with t, since the tree T can implicitly be derived as the domain of t.

So the nodes in a history cannot be labelled arbitrarily with sets of microstates. Instead, the label of any node gets distributed over its children (provided there are any), with at least one microstate being left out. This also restricts the number of possible history trees for a given Q.

A rather crude upper bound on the number of different possible history trees for a set Q of n microstates can be obtained as follows. First observe that the branching degree of every node in a history tree is at most $n - 1$: the label of a node can contain at most n microstates, and the combined label of all its children must form a genuine subset thereof. This also restricts the possible depth of a history tree to n since the label of each node must be a genuine subset of the label of its parent. At last, it should be clear that there are only finitely many trees of branching degree at most n and depth at most n, and then for each of them there are only finitely many possibilities to attach labels as subsets of n states to its nodes. A better estimation can be obtained as follows, though.

Lemma 7.9 *There are at most* $2^{\mathcal{O}(n \log n)}$ *many history trees for an NBA of size n.*

Proof First note that a history tree t defines, for each microstate $q \in Q$, a unique deepest node v in t such that $q \in t(v)$. Any microstate contained in the label of some node must also occur in the labels of its parent, the parent of the parent, etc. up to the root. Since sibling nodes are required to have disjoint labels, q cannot occur on a second path in the tree. Hence, each history tree can contain at most n nodes.

Now there is a one-to-one correspondence between finite trees with arbitrary branching degree and n nodes on one hand, and binary trees with $n + 1$ nodes on the other, known as the first-child-next-sibling encoding. It actually suffices to consider the number of binary trees with n nodes only, since one particular node – the right child of the root – is always fixed in these encodings. The number of such trees is given by the Catalan number $C_n = \frac{1}{n+1} \cdot \binom{2n}{n} \leq 2^n \cdot n^n = 2^{\mathcal{O}(n \log n)}$.

A history tree is then given by a pair of one of these trees plus an assignment of microstates to its n nodes. The number of such assignments is at most $n! = 2^{\mathcal{O}(n \log n)}$ which means that the number of different history trees can be estimated as $(2^{\mathcal{O}(n \log n)})^2 = 2^{\mathcal{O}(n \log n)}$. $\qquad\qquad\square$

Let $\mathcal{H}$ denote the set of all history trees for $\mathcal{A}$. It will serve as the state set for $\mathcal{B}$. Its initial state is simply the history tree t_I with $dom(t_I) = \{\varepsilon\}$ and $t_I(\varepsilon) = \{q_I\}$. This is comparable to what is happening in the powerset construction where the initial macrostate is given as the *set* containing the initial microstate. Here, the data structure used to build macrostates is not just a set but a history tree, so the initial macro state consists of the most obvious history tree that contains the initial microstate.

Next we turn to the transition function Δ in $\mathcal{B}$. Given an arbitrary history tree, i.e. a macrostate $t \in \mathcal{H}$, and some alphabet letter $a \in \Sigma$, we need to determine the macrostate $\Delta(t, a)$, i.e. the successor of t under a. This is done in six steps: given t and a as required, we define a sequence of trees $t_1, \dots, t_6$ in which $t_1, \dots, t_5$ are generally not history trees but t_6 is. Moreover, we then have $\Delta(t, a) := t_6$.

Step 1, powerset construction: t_1 results from t by replacing all labels by their joint successors under the transition relation δ of $\mathcal{A}$: we have $dom(t_1) = dom(t)$ and

$$t_1(v) \;:=\; \bigcup_{q \in t(v)} \{p \mid (q, a, p) \in \delta\} \;.$$

for any $v \in dom(t_1)$. Note that this may violate the conditions of being a history tree: while it is guaranteed that the joint labels of a node's children still form a subset of the parent's label, this may not be a proper subset anymore.

Step 2, spawning off accepting states: t_2 results from t_1 by potentially adding new nodes. For every node $v \in dom(t_1)$ such that $t_1(v) \cap F \neq \varnothing$, add node vd to $dom(t_2)$ where $d = deg(v)$. Its label is $t_2(v) := t_1(v) \cap F$. All other nodes retain their label from t_1.

In addition to the potential violations of the conditions for history trees that may happen in step 1, this step may cause violations of the requirement on siblings. It can create nodes with labels that contain microstates which are already contained in older siblings. This could be avoided right away because later steps clear this up anyway.

Step 3, horizontal cleaning: we write $u \rceil v$ if there is a node $w \neq u$ that is a sibling of u further right in the tree, and v is a descendant of w. The case of $w = v$ is allowed in which case u is simply a left sibling of v. We then have $dom(t_3) = dom(t_2)$ but

$$t_3(v) \;:=\; \{q \in t_2(v) \mid \forall u : u \rceil v \Rightarrow q \notin t_2(u)\} \;.$$

In other words, we delete all microstates from labels that already occur in siblings further left, and also remove them from any descendants.

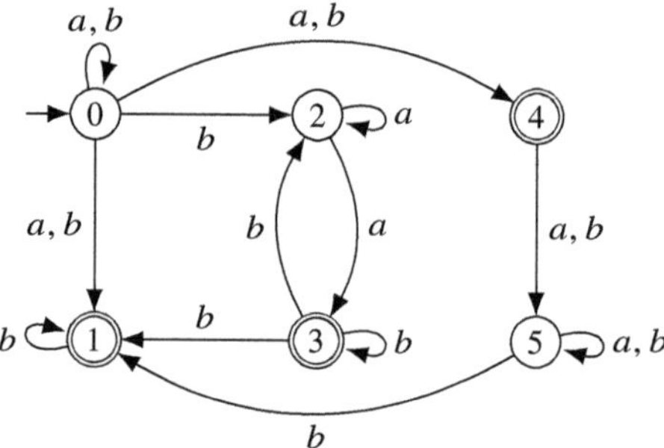

Fig. 7.3 NBA used to exemplify the construction of an equivalent deterministic automaton.

While this trivially ensures the property of disjointness of children's labels in a history tree, it may violate another condition, namely that of nodes carrying non-empty labels.

Step 4, removal of empty nodes: simply let

$$dom(t_4) \;:=\; \{v \in dom(t_3) \mid t_3(v) \neq \varnothing\}$$

and $t_4(v) := t_3(v)$ for all remaining nodes v. Technically, t_4 is not a tree according to our definition because it does not satisfy left-sibling closure anymore. We refrain from inventing a new name for such structures and simply call it a tree for the moment since left-sibling closure is not relevant for what happens here or in the next step. The last step in this sequence will ensure that it is a proper tree again.

Step 5, vertical cleaning: let

$$dom(t_5) \;:=\; \{v \in dom(t_4) \mid \forall u \in \mathbb{N}^*, w \in \mathbb{N}^+ : v = uw \Rightarrow t_4(u) \neq \bigcup_{i=0}^{deg(u)-1} t_4(ui)\}$$

and $t_5(v) := t_4(v)$ for all remaining v. Hence, in this step we remove the children (and their descendants) of all nodes whose children have joint labels that equal that of the parent node.

It should be clear that this recovers the potential violation on the requirement that the label of a parent's node is always a genuine superset of the labels of its children.

Step 6, left shifting: at last, we restore a proper tree structure by shifting nodes further left. For as long as left-sibling closure is not satisfied, i.e. there is a node $u(i + 1)$ but no node ui for some $u \in \mathbb{N}^*$, $i \in \mathbb{N}$, shift all nodes of the form $u(i + 1)w$ to uiw for any $w \in \mathbb{N}^*$, retaining their labels. When left-sibling closure is restored entirely, the final tree t_6 is obtained.

Example 7.10 Let $\mathcal{A}$ be the NFA over $\Sigma = \{a, b\}$ from Fig. 7.3. It is not complete but this does not invalidate the following considerations as we are only constructing a particular successor of the following history tree t.

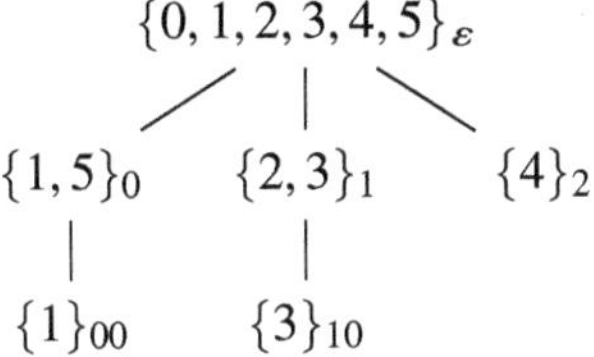

For clarity, the nodes' names are shown as indices to the labels.

We show how to obtain $\Delta(t, b)$. First, we perform the powerset construction in every node, obtaining t_1 as follows.

$$
\{0, 1, 2, 3, 4, 5\}_\varepsilon
$$

with children $\{1, 5\}_0$, $\{1, 2, 3\}_1$, $\{5\}_2$, and below them $\{1\}_{00}$ and $\{1, 2, 3\}_{10}$.

It is noteworthy that all microstates $1, 2, 3$ in node 1 are obtained as b-successors of microstate 3, whereas microstate 2 does not contribute anything in this step.

The tree is clearly not a history tree. Next we need to spawn off new children carrying accepting states. Theoretically, node ε would receive a new child 3 with label $\{1, 3, 4\}$ but microstates 1 and 3 are already included in the labels of older siblings. So they would get removed in the next step anyway. Hence, it suffices to introduce a new node 3 with label $\{4\}$ only. Similar considerations lead to the introduction of a new node 11 as a child of node 1 with label $\{1\}$ only. Likewise, node 00 has a single accepting state in its label. Theoretically, we could add a new child 000 with the same label, but this node would get deleted in the subsequent vertical clearance step. This is why we only introduce new children when the parent contains accepting states that are not contained in already existing children, and the parent's label does not consist of accepting states only. This then yields the following tree t_2.

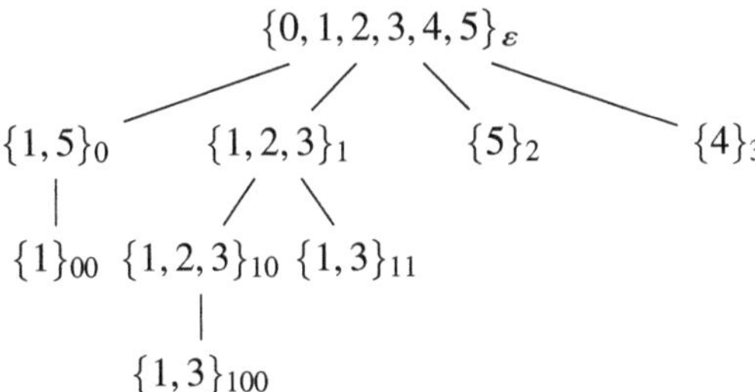

Next we perform horizontal cleaning, i.e. we remove every microstate from a label that is already contained in the label of a left (and therefore older, resp. non-younger) sibling. This leads to the following tree t_3.

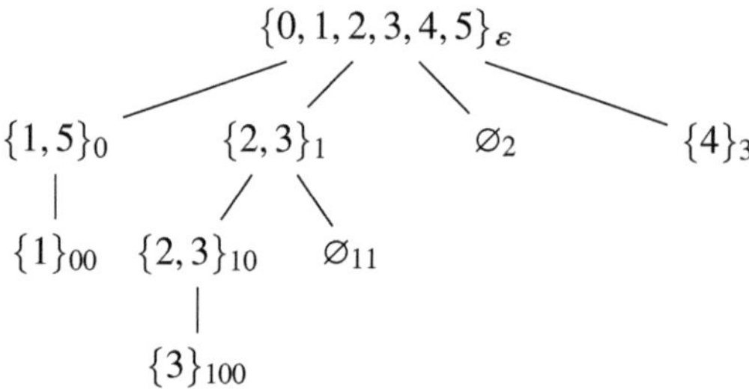

Microstate 1 gets removed from the label of node 100 even though this node has no left siblings. But microstate 1 needs to be removed from the label of node 1 because it is also contained in the label of node 0. It then also gets removed from all descendants in order to eventually turn the tree into a history tree again, in particular to ensure the invariant that the labels of children form a subset of the parent's label.

In the next step we simply remove nodes with empty labels, resulting in the following tree-like structure t_4.

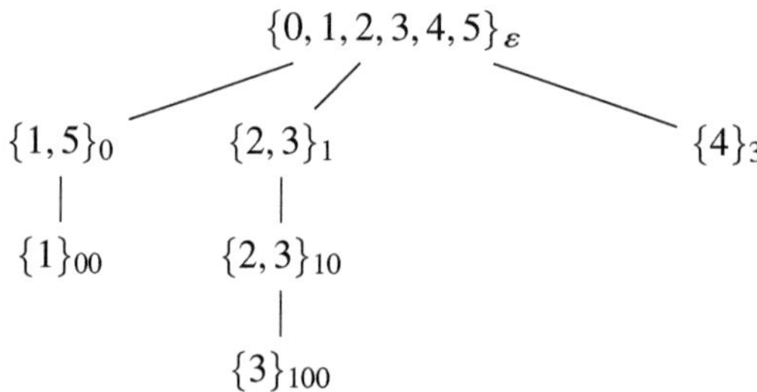

Then we perform vertical cleaning. There is one node whose label is the same as the joint labels of all its children, of which there is only one: nodes 1 and 10 both have the label $\{2, 3\}$. We therefore delete the child and all its descendants, which results in the following tree t_5.

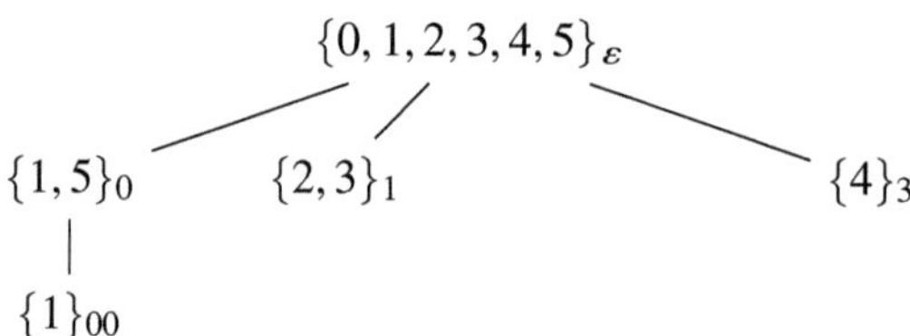

This is not yet a history tree, simply because it is not a tree strictly speaking since the deletion of node 2 has led to the violation of left-sibling closure. This is then easily fixed in the last step which shifts nodes as far left as possible, eliminating such gaps in the tree's domain. The result is the following tree t_6 which is then also the successor of the original tree t under the letter b in the transition function of the deterministic automaton $\mathcal{B}$.

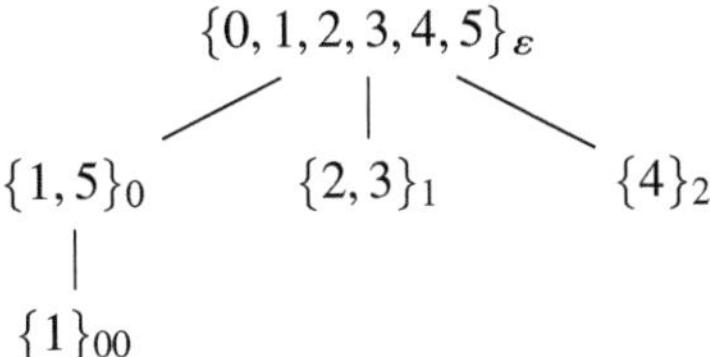

The entire deterministic finite-state automaton $\mathcal{B}$, resulting from the NBA in Fig. 7.3 is too big to be shown completely, but Fig. 7.4 shows an initial part of its run on the word *abbabb* . . .

Next we need to discuss the acceptance condition for the deterministic automaton $\mathcal{B}$. For this it is helpful to analyse the purpose of the nodes in a history tree, and to remember the discussion above on the fundamental problem with powerset-based constructions for the determinisation of Büchi automata: it is an overapproximation in the sense that runs through the microstates are contained in runs of the macrostates but a simple powerset construction alone is too coarse to determine whether the sequence of macrostates contains a run that traverses through accepting microstates infinitely often. Note that node ε in all runs contains the sets of microstates as one would obtain them through an ordinary powerset construction.

The interesting point is then the spawning off of new nodes that contain accepting microstates only. This can be seen as a refinement of the powerset construction in the sense that a special focus is being put on these accepting microstates at the current point. Remember that in a sequence of macrostates obtained by powerset construction, one knows that any microstate can be traced back to some microstate in an earlier macrostate. This is what happens in the root of the history trees: any of the microstates $0, 1, 2, 3, 4, 5$ in node ε in t_6 of Fig. 7.4 can be traced back to microstate 0 in node ε in t_0 in the sense that there is a run in $\mathcal{A}$ on the underlying word that starts in 0 and hits the desired microstate from the label of node ε in t_6.

Now consider node 1 in t_6 instead with its two microstates $2, 3$. What happens in a child node can be seen as the powerset construction (happening in the parent node) with a special focus on some microstates. So $2, 3$ can surely be traced back to microstates $2, 3$ in node 1 of t_5 and also to $1, 3, 4$ in node 1 in t_4. Remember that a new node is only every created with a label consisting of accepting microstates only. Hence, when we trace a microstate's origin back through some particular (child) node, we eventually trace it back to an accepting state.

We cannot go back arbitrarily, though. It is wrong to assume that the microstates $2, 3$ in node 1 of t_6 could be traced back to microstate 4 in node 1 in t_2. The reason simply is that node 1 died out in the transition from t_2 to t_3, and has been recreated with a new label in the transition from t_3 to t_4. So in determining whether the underlying nondeterministic automaton $\mathcal{A}$ has a run that visits accepting microstates infinitely often we need to consider the continuous evolution of particular nodes in the history trees. This leads us to the notion of a node being *stable* in a particular transition, to be defined precisely below.

Moreover, it is not sufficient to determine whether all microstates in a node can be traced back to some accepting microstate. This needs to happen infinitely often.

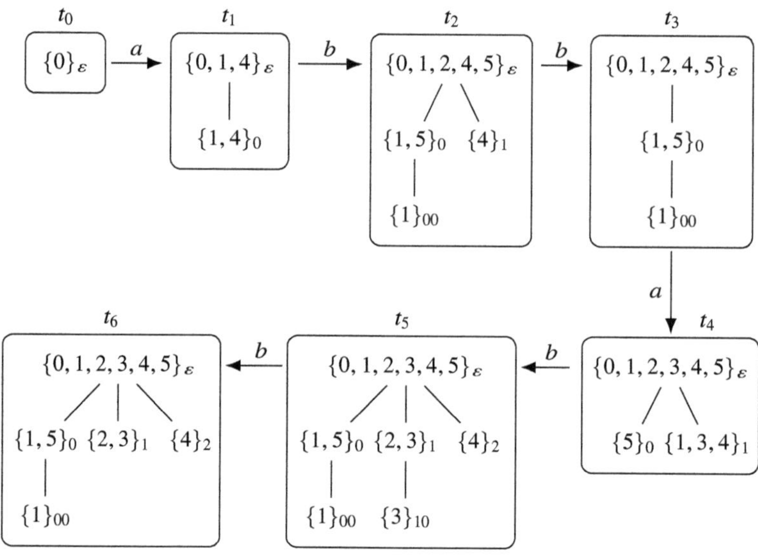

Fig. 7.4 The history trees in a run of the deterministic automaton obtained from the NBA in Fig. 7.3 with the underlying word being *abbabb*...

And this is what the deletion of nodes in a history tree comes in for: take node 10 in t_5 and note that it gets removed in a vertical cleaning step in t_6. The reason is that label $\{3\}$ in t_5 gets replaced by $\{1, 2, 3\}$ in the powerset construction step, then microstate 1 gets deleted because it is contained in a left sibling of the parent node. The remaining label $\{2, 3\}$ is then the same as the label of the parent node 1. We can then not only conclude that both 2 and 3 (in node 1 of t_6) can be traced back to any of 2 or 3 (in node 1 in t_5) but in fact more: since the label $\{2, 3\}$ of node 1 in t_6 equals the joint labels of all its children (here: its only child), and the microstates in child nodes can always be traced back to accepting microstates, we additionally know that both 2 and 3 can be traced back to microstate 3. Thus, when this happens infinitely often, we can conclude that there is indeed a run of $\mathcal{A}$ that traverses through accepting microstates infinitely often. The key concept here is that of a node being *successful*.

Definition 7.11 Let t, t' be history trees of $\mathcal{A}$ such that there is some $a \in \Sigma$ with $t' = \Delta(t, a)$. Let v be a node name. We say that v is *stable* in the transition from t to t' if $v \in dom(t)$, $v \in dom(t')$ and v did not get removed in steps 3 (horizontal cleaning), 4 (removal of empty nodes), 5 (vertical cleaning) and did not get shifted in step 6 of the construction of t' from t.

We say that v is *successful* in the transition from t to t' if all its children got removed in step 5 (vertical cleaning).

This allows us to define an acceptance condition on $\mathcal{B}$ as a transition-based Rabin condition: intuitively, a run of $\mathcal{B}$ is accepting if there is some node v that is eventually stable and infinitely often successful. To see that this is indeed definable as a Rabin condition, all we need is the observation that there are only finitely many possible node names in a history tree for $\mathcal{A}$. This is of course an immediate consequence of the argumentation above that the depth and the branching degree of a history tree are both bounded by the number of microstates.

Formally, we therefore have $\mathcal{B} := (\mathcal{H}, \Sigma, t_I, \Delta, \mathcal{F})$ where t_I is the initial history tree, Δ is the transition function as explained above and $\mathcal{F} := \{(G_v, F_v) \mid v \text{ is a node name }\}$ where

$$G_v := \{(t, a, t') \mid t' = \Delta(t, a) \text{ and } v \text{ is successful in the transition from } t \text{ to } t'\},$$
$$F_v := \{(t, a, t') \mid t' = \Delta(t, a) \text{ and } v \text{ is unstable in the transition from } t \text{ to } t'\}.$$

This completes the construction of the DRA_e $\mathcal{B}$ from the NBA $\mathcal{A}$. It remains to be seen that it accepts the same language.

7.3.2 Correctness of the Construction

We consider soundness and completeness separately in the following lemmas.

Lemma 7.12 *Let $\mathcal{A}$ be an NBA and $\mathcal{B}$ be the DRA_e resulting from it according to the construction above. Then we have $L(\mathcal{B}) \subseteq L(\mathcal{A})$.*

Proof Let $t_0, t_1, \ldots$ be an accepting run of $\mathcal{B}$ on some word $w = a_0 a_1 \ldots \in \Sigma^\omega$. There must be some node name v and some $n \in \mathbb{N}$ such that v is stable in the transitions from t_i to t_{i+1} for all $i \geq n$ and infinitely often successful, i.e. there are $i_0, i_1, \ldots$ such that, w.l.o.g. $0 < n = i_0 < i_1 < \ldots$ and node v is successful in the transition from t_{i_j-1} to t_{i_j} for all $j \geq 1$.

We now construct a tree as follows. Its nodes are $Q \times \{0, i_0, i_1, i_2, \ldots\}$. We distinguish two cases for the definition of the edges between them.

- For each $q \in Q$ that occurs in the label of node v in t_{i_0}, draw an edge from $(q_I, 0)$ to (q, i_0). Note that q also occurs in t_{i_0}'s root node and therefore $q_I \xrightarrow{a_0 \ldots a_{i_0-1}} q$ in $\mathcal{A}$ where $p \xrightarrow{v} q$ for any $p, q \in Q$ and $v \in \Sigma^*$ is used to denote the existence of a path from p to q with edge labels forming the word v.
- For each $j > 0$ and $q \in Q$ that occurs in the label of node v in t_{i_j}, draw an edge from (q', i_{j-1}) to (q, i_j) for some q' in the label of node v in $t_{i_{j-1}}$ such that $q' \xrightarrow{a_{i_{j-1}} \ldots a_{i_j-1}} q$ in $\mathcal{A}$. By stability of v, such a q' must exist. Moreover, since v is successful in the transition to t_{i_j}, we know that the partial run in $\mathcal{A}$ witnessing this can be chosen such that it traverses through a final state.

This structure is not a tree in general but a DAG. However, it can easily be unfolded into a tree by introducing new copies of nodes that are successors of multiple nodes in the DAG. In any case, this tree has paths of unbounded length, because the labels of node v in each t_{i_j} are non-empty, i.e. on every level there is a node that is connected to a node on the previous level, which in turn is connected to a node on the level before that, etc. Each such connection can be traced back to q_I on the DAG's first level.

According to Kőnig's Lemma, we can also find an infinite path through this tree or DAG. I.e. there is an infinite sequence of microstates $q_{i_0}, q_{i_1}, \ldots$ such that

$$q_I \xrightarrow{a_0 \ldots a_{i_0-1}} q_{i_0} \xrightarrow{a_{i_0} \ldots a_{i_1-1}} q_{i_1} \xrightarrow{a_{i_1} \ldots a_{i_2-1}} \ldots$$

This forms a run of $\mathcal{A}$ on w. Moreover, since each part between q_{i_j} and $q_{i_{j+1}}$ traverses through an accepting state, the run is accepting, showing that $w \in L(\mathcal{A})$. $\square$

Lemma 7.13 *Let $\mathcal{A}$ be an NBA and $\mathcal{B}$ be the DRA_e resulting from it according to the construction above. Then we have $L(\mathcal{B}) \supseteq L(\mathcal{A})$.*

Proof Let $\rho = q_0, q_1, q_2, \ldots$ be an accepting run of $\mathcal{A}$ on some word $w = a_0 a_1 \ldots \in \Sigma^\omega$. In particular, we have $q_i \in F$ for infinitely many i. Since $\mathcal{B}$ is deterministic, it has a unique run $t_0, t_1, \ldots$ on w.

We say that some history tree node v *captures* the run ρ, if there is some $n \geq 0$ such that v is stable in the transition from t_i to t_{i+1} and $q_i \in t_i(v)$ for all $i \geq n$. Note that ε captures ρ. In other words, the run ρ can be found within the sets $t_0(\varepsilon), t_1(\varepsilon), \ldots$

We now claim that the following is true: if node v captures ρ but is not successful infinitely often, then it has a child v' that captures ρ. Once this is shown, the statement of the lemma is proved: since history trees are of finite depth, there must be a deepest node that captures ρ and it must also be successful infinitely often because it has no child that captures ρ. Hence, the Rabin acceptance condition is satisfied by the run $t_0, t_1, \ldots$ and we therefore have $w \in L(\mathcal{B})$.

To prove the claim suppose that v is a node that is eventually stable but successful at most finitely often. Let i_0 be such that $q_{i_0} \in F$ but node v is not successful in a transition from t_{i_0-1} to t_{i_0} or afterwards. Since $q_{i_0} \in \delta(q_{i_0-1}, a_{i_0-1})$, we get that q_{i_0} is contained in the label of node v after step 1 (powerset construction) in the transition from t_{i_0-1} to t_{i_0}. For simplicity we will simply refer to the resulting trees as t_{i_0} and explicitly mention the step of the construction we are considering. Since $q_{i_0} \in t_{i_0}(v) \cap F$ at this point, step 2 (spawning off accepting states) creates a new child for node v that contains q_{i_0}. It is of course possible that q_{i_0} is already contained in a child further to the left in which case this new child node gets deleted in step 3 (horizontal cleaning). In either case, the child $v j$ containing q_{i_0} does not get removed in steps 4 (removal of empty nodes) for trivial reasons. It also does not get removed in step 5 (vertical cleaning) as this would cause v to be successful in this step which it is not by assumption.

This argumentation can now be repeated to see that this node $v j$ persists. It can of course be shifted to the left in subsequent steps 6 of the constructions. But this can happen at most j many times, so eventually there is a stable node that is deeper in the tree than v and which captures the run ρ. $\square$

The following is then obtained immediately from Lemma 7.9, 7.12 and 7.13.

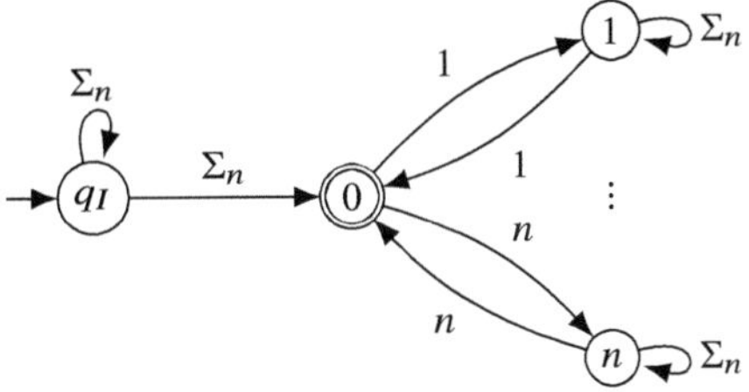

Fig. 7.5 NBA $\mathcal{A}_n$ for a language whose complementation requires a blowup of $\Omega(n!)$.

Theorem 7.14 *For every NBA $\mathcal{A}$ of size n there is a DRA_e $\mathcal{B}$ of size $2^{\mathcal{O}(n\log n)}$ and index $\mathcal{O}(n)$ such that $L(\mathcal{B}) = L(\mathcal{A})$.*

Moreover, Cor. 6.43 states that deterministic automata with a transition based Rabin acceptance condition can easily be converted into ordinary deterministic Rabin automata. Cor. 6.22 states that Rabin automata are special cases of Muller automata. Combining these with Thm. 7.14 we easily obtain the possibility to determinise nondeterministic Büchi automata into Rabin or Muller automata.

Corollary 7.15 *For every NBA $\mathcal{A}$ of size n there is a DRA of size $2^{\mathcal{O}(n\log n)}$ and index $\mathcal{O}(n)$ such that $L(\mathcal{B}) = L(\mathcal{A})$.*

7.3.3 A Lower Bound on Complementation and Determinisation

Determinisation yields an alternative approach to the decidability of MSO over infinite words, since deterministic automata – in particular DMA – can easily be complemented, and complementation is needed in an inductive translation from MSO formulas into automata. However, existential quantification then needs to be handled by alphabet projection which yields nondeterministic automata again.

Conversely, we can use the determinisation construction to complement NBA. The following is a direct consequence of Cor. 7.15 and Thm. 6.24 showing how to translate NMA (and therefore also DRA) into equivalent NBA at a polynomial blowup only.

Corollary 7.16 *For every NBA $\mathcal{A}$ of size n there is an NBA $\overline{\mathcal{A}}$ of size $2^{\mathcal{O}(n\log n)}$ such that $L(\overline{\mathcal{A}}) = \overline{L(\mathcal{A})}$.*

This is asymptotically optimal. It is not possible to reduce the index and number of states of the DRA resulting from an NBA significantly further so that it leads to an asymptotically better procedure for complementing NBA. In the following, we will create a family of ω-regular languages that require such a blowup in complementation.

For $n \geq 1$ let $\Sigma_n := \{\#, 1, \ldots, n\}$, $\mathcal{A}_n$ be the NBA over state space $\{q_I, 0, 1, \ldots, n\}$ shown in Fig. 7.5 and $L_n := L(\mathcal{A}_n)$. Consider a word $w \in \Sigma_n^\omega$. We say that it contains a *cycle* if there is some $k \geq 1$ and $x_1, \ldots, x_k \in \{1, \ldots, n\}$ such that w has infinitely many occurrences of the k two-letter subwords $x_1 x_2, x_2 x_3, \ldots, x_k x_1$.

Example 7.17 Let $n = 4$ and consider $(1423\#2431\#)^{\omega}$. It contains a cycle, witnessed by the occurrences of $14, 42, 24, 43, 31$. Clearly, it also contains a shorter cycle as well, namely $42, 24$. On the other hand, neither $(1423\#)^{\omega}$ nor $(2431\#)^{\omega}$ contain cycles. Note that between each two consecutive occurrences of # in these words, there is the same fixed pattern of symbols that can be used to form cycles. Moreover, these patterns only contain each symbol $1, \ldots, 4$ at most once. Hence, every sequence $x_1 x_2, x_2 x_3, \ldots$ of two-letter subword in those parts invariably would have to contain the symbol # before the cycle can be closed. But this is forbidden according to the definition of a cycle.

The property of containing a cycle is exactly what defines L_n.

Lemma 7.18 *Let $n \geq 1$ and $w \in \Sigma_n^{\omega}$. Then $w \in L_n$ iff w contains a cycle.*

Proof "$\Leftarrow$" Suppose that w contains a cycle $x_1 x_2, \ldots, x_k x_1$. It is easy to construct an accepting run of $\mathcal{A}_n$ on w. It stays in state q_I whilst reading the prefix of w up to the last letter before the first occurrence of $x_1 x_2$. With these two letters it moves to state x_2 via state 0. It remains there up to the next occurrence of $x_2 x_3$. Upon reading this two-letter subword, it moves to state x_3 via state 0. This is continued ad infinitum. The run is obviously accepting because it traverses state 0 infinitely often.

"$\Rightarrow$" Suppose there is an accepting run ρ of $\mathcal{A}_n$ on w. Clearly, ρ must eventually leave state q_I and move to some state $q_1 \in \{1, \ldots, n\}$. It cannot stay there forever because these are not accepting. Hence, it must eventually move to some state $q_2 \in \{1, \ldots, n\}$ via state 0, and so on. Since there are only $n^2 < \infty$ many pairs of such states, a two-step transition from some state x_1 to some state x_2 must be taken infinitely often. Let $(x_1, y_1), \ldots, (x_m, y_m)$ be all the pairs of states such that ρ contains infinitely many two-step transitions from x_i to y_i. Note that w must contain the two-letter subwords $x_1 y_1, \ldots, x_m y_m$ infinitely often.

It remains to be seen that there is a cycle amongst these. W.l.o.g. we can assume them to be chosen minimal, i.e. if there is a cycle amongst them then all pairs participate in its formation. Note then that there is a cycle iff for every $i = 1, \ldots, m$ there is a $j \in \{1, \ldots, m\}$ such that $y_i = x_j$. So suppose that this was not the case, i.e. there is some y_i that does not equal any x_j. But then the run ρ contains infinitely many transitions from state y_i to state 0 without infinitely many transitions from state 0 to any state $x_j \in \{1, \ldots, n\}$. This is clearly impossible. $\square$

Lemma 7.18 immediately gives us a characterisation of $\overline{L_n}$ as the set of words that do not contain a cycle. For the remainder of the argument it suffices to spell out particular words with this property. Let $n \geq 1$ be given. A word $u \in \Sigma_n^n$ is called a *permutation* if it contains each symbol of $\{1, \ldots, n\}$ exactly once. Let Π_n be the set of all permutations. Clearly, we have $n! = |\Pi_n|$.

The next lemma just generalises the observations made in the example above. Proof details are left as an exercise.

Lemma 7.19 *Let $n \geq 1$.*

a) For all $u \in \Pi_n$ we have $(u\#)^\omega \in \overline{L_n}$.

b) For all $u, v \in \Pi_n$ such that $u \neq v$ and all $w \in \Sigma_n^\omega$ that contain both u and v infinitely often we have $w \in L_n$.

We can then show that the complements of the languages L_n do indeed require NBA of size $\Omega(n!)$.

Theorem 7.20 *Let $n \geq 1$ be given and $\mathcal{B}$ be an NBA such that $L(\mathcal{B}) = \overline{L_n}$. Then $n! \leq |\mathcal{B}|$.*

Proof Let $\mathcal{B} = (Q, \Sigma_n, q_I, \delta, F)$. Take any $u \in \Pi_n$. According to Lemma 7.19 (a) we have $(u\#)^\omega \in \overline{L_n} = L(\mathcal{B})$. Hence, there is a run of $\mathcal{B}$ on $(u\#)^\omega$ that visits accepting states infinitely often. In particular, there must be some state $f_u \in F$ such that $f_u \xrightarrow{\Sigma_n^* u \Sigma_n^*} f_u$, i.e. f_u is reachable from itself under a word that contains u. This is simply a consequence of the fact that $(u\#)^\omega$ contains infinitely many occurrences of u, and the accepting run contains infinitely many occurrences of f_u.

Note that each such f_u need not be unique. An accepting run on $(u\#)^\omega$ may of course contain several accepting states infinitely often. Moreover, there can be more than one accepting run. It suffices to pick an arbitrary f_u with the required property for each $u \in \Pi_n$.

Now suppose that, for the sake of contradiction, we have $n! > |Q|$. We will show that $L(\mathcal{B}) \neq \overline{L_n}$ in this case.

Since $F \subseteq Q$ but there are $n!$ many permutations, there must be $u, v \in \Pi_n$ such that $u \neq v$ but $f_u = f_v =: f$, i.e. some accepting runs on $(u\#)^\omega$ and on $(v\#)^\omega$ traverse through a common accepting state infinitely often. Clearly, f is reachable from the initial state q_I under some word in Σ_n^*. So we have

$$q_I \xrightarrow{\Sigma_n^*} f \xrightarrow{\Sigma_n^* u \Sigma_n^*} f \xrightarrow{\Sigma_n^* v \Sigma_n^*} f \xrightarrow{\Sigma_n^* u \Sigma_n^*} f \xrightarrow{\Sigma_n^* v \Sigma_n^*} \ldots$$

I.e. we get an accepting run of $\mathcal{B}$ on a word w that contains the two different permutations u and v infinitely often. According to Lemma 7.19 (b) we have $w \notin \overline{L_n}$ which contradicts the assumption that $L(\mathcal{B}) = \overline{L_n}$. $\square$

So we have indeed exposed a family of ω-regular languages that can be recognised by NBA of linear size and whose complements require NBA of size that asymptotically matches the upper bound we get through determinisation via the Safra construction.

Corollary 7.21 *There is a family of ω-regular languages $(L_n)_{n \geq 1}$ that are recognisable by NBA of size $\mathcal{O}(n)$ such that every NBA recognising $\overline{L_n}$ needs to be of size $n!$ at least.*

The lower bound on complementation then carries over to a lower bound on determinisation. The next statement follows from the fact that DRA can be complemented into DSA incurring no blowup, and these can be translated into NBA at a polynomial blowup only. So any determinisation procedure that is asymptotically better than the one presented here would contradict the lower bound on complementation in Cor. 7.21.

Corollary 7.22 *There is a family* $(\mathcal{A}_n)_{n \geq 1}$ *of NBA with* $\mathcal{O}(n)$ *many states such that every equivalent DRA must have* $2^{\Omega(n \log n)}$ *many states and index* $\Omega(n)$.

7.3.4 From NBA to DPA

Cor. 7.15 yields a deterministic counterpart to an arbitrary nondeterministic Büchi automaton in the form of a Rabin or Muller automaton. For algorithmic purposes it is sometimes more desirable, though, to obtain a deterministic parity automaton. This is achievable with the constructions seen so far:

a) From a given NBA $\mathcal{A}$, construct a DMA using Cor. 7.15.
b) Turn the DMA into a DPA using the latest-appearance-record construction of Thm. 6.28, observing that it preserves determinism, i.e. it turns a DMA into a DPA.

This is not optimal, though. The blowup incurring in step (1) is $2^{\mathcal{O}(n \log n)}$ in size; the index is irrelevant for what follows. The construction of Thm. 6.28 turns a DMA of size n into a DPA of size $n^2 \cdot n!$ in the worst case. Since $n! \in 2^{\Omega n}$ we obtain a DPA of doubly exponential size in this way.

It is possible, though, to obtain DPA of singly exponential size by internalising the LAR construction. Again, we construct an automaton with a transition-based acceptance condition and then refer to the general construction to turn this into an automaton with a state-based acceptance condition of the same kind, see Thm. 6.42 for how this is done in case of Rabin conditions. We need a small technical definition.

Definition 7.23 Let t be a history tree and v be one of its nodes. The *seniority* $s(v)$ of v (in t) is the number of nodes ahead of v in a preorder traversal of the tree, i.e. the number of nodes that are above or further left of v.

Example 7.24 Take the history tree t_5 shown in Fig. 7.4. A preorder traversal of this tree yields the node list $\varepsilon, 0, 00, 1, 10, 2$, so the seniority values of these nodes are $s(\varepsilon) = 0$, $s(0) = 1$, $s(00) = 2$, $s(1) = 3$, $s(10) = 4$ and $s(2) = 5$.

Theorem 7.25 *For every NBA* $\mathcal{A}$ *of size* n *there is a* DPA_e $\mathcal{B}$ *of size* $2^{\mathcal{O}(n \log n)}$ *and index* $\mathcal{O}(n)$ *such that* $L(\mathcal{B}) = L(\mathcal{A})$.

Proof Let $\mathcal{A} = (Q, \Sigma, q_I, \delta, F)$ be an NBA and $\mathcal{B} = (\mathcal{H}, \Sigma, t_I, \Delta, \mathcal{F})$ be the corresponding DRA_e that accepts the same language according to Thm. 7.14. We modify this into a DPA_e $\mathcal{B}' := (\mathcal{H} \times \mathcal{L}, \Sigma, (t_I, \Lambda_0), \Delta', \Omega)$ as follows, where $\mathcal{L}$ is the set of all latest appearance records that contain the nodes of a history tree from $\mathcal{H}$. The initial LAR Λ_0 is $([\varepsilon], 0)$.

The transition function Δ' is obtained by extending Δ appropriately to update the LARs as follows: $\Delta'((t,\Lambda),a) := (\Delta(t,a),\Lambda')$ where Λ' is obtained from Λ as follows. Let $\Lambda = (\pi,m)$. Then $\Lambda' := (\pi',m')$ where

- π' is obtained from π by deleting those nodes that are unstable in the transition from t to t', and then adding the (new names of these) unstable nodes as well as any new nodes created in the transition from t to t' at the end of the queue in some arbitrary but fixed order;
- m' is the maximal length of a prefix of stable nodes in π.

Then Ω can assign a priority to every transition $((t,(\pi,m)),a,(t',(\pi',m'))) \in \Delta'$ with $\pi = [v_1,\ldots,v_k]$ as follows.

$$
\Omega((t,\Lambda),a,(t',\Lambda')) \;:=\; \begin{cases} 2\cdot m + 2, & \text{if some } v_j \text{ with } j \in \{1,\ldots,m\} \text{ is} \\ & \text{successful in the transition from } t \text{ to } t', \\ 2\cdot m + 1, & \text{otherwise}. \end{cases}
$$

We leave it as an exercise to argue for correctness of this construction and for the fact that this only yields a singly exponential blowup from $\mathcal{A}$ to $\mathcal{B}'$. $\qquad\square$

As stated above, a $\mathrm{DPA_e}$ can be turned into a DPA using the same construction as in Thm. 6.42 which only incurs a mild blowup. This then completes the argument that nondeterministic Büchi automata can be determinised into parity automata.

Corollary 7.26 *For every NBA $\mathcal{A}$ of size n there is a DPA $\mathcal{B}$ of size $2^{\mathcal{O}(n\log n)}$ and index $\mathcal{O}(n)$ such that $L(\mathcal{B}) = L(\mathcal{A})$.*

Bibliographic Notes

The problem of determinisation of a Büchi automaton clearly arose with their introduction and was solved not too long afterwards by McNaughton [McN66] who came up with a construction of a deterministic Muller automaton of doubly exponential size compared to the original nondeterministic Büchi automaton. The form of the Muller acceptance condition used in this construction instigated the introduction of an explicitly different and more specialised kind, later known as a Rabin condition [Rab69].

The doubly exponential blowup was seen as non-optimal which caused the search for better determinisation procedures. Some alternatives were suggested in the following years [Rab72, Büc73, TB73, Sch72, Cho74, Eil74, Tho81] but none of them broke the doubly exponential barrier, some were even triply exponential. A singly exponential construction was eventually found by Safra in the late 80's only [Saf88, Saf89] and was celebrated accordingly.

The construction in the form that is presented here, is – strictly speaking – not Safra's, even though it is called "the Safra construction" here. Safra's original construction yielded the essentials, in particular regarding the refinement of the powerset construction using a tree-like data structure. Safra did not use history trees as they are called here. In his original work, nodes carry names from a finite name space and have the ability to signal what we call here being successful. Such minor differences in the underlying data structures as well as the separation of the determinisation into automata with a transition-based acceptance condition from the subsequent transformation into a state-based one are of course not essential.

The details of the construction in the form presented here, including the use of history trees, are due to Schewe [Sch09b]. His construction falls into a line of work that examines possibilities to improve the original Safra construction with the aim of closing the gap between lower and upper bounds in the area of $n!$, resp. $2^{\mathcal{O}(n\log n)}$, narrowing it down to the intersection of $\Omega((1.64n)^n)$ and $o((1.65n)^n)$ [CZ09].

The lower bound on complementation presented here, giving also a lower bound on the blowup needed in determinisation is from unpublished work by Michel [Mic88]. Löding has provided further bounds on the transformations of automata on infinite words [Löd99].

The determinisation of Büchi automata into parity automata, internalising an otherwise non-optimal transformation of the Rabin condition into a parity condition, is due to Piterman [Pit06]. Likewise, one may be interested in the determinisation of other types of automata on ω-words, even though they can be translated into NBA. This has extensively been studied as well, for instance for generalised Büchi automata [SV12] but most of all for Streett automata [Saf92, Sch02, Pit06, TWD20] since they require a greater blowup when first translated into Büchi automata.

It seems like Safra's original determinisation construction is without real alternatives when it comes to an asymptotically optimal determinisation of automata on ω-words in the sense that it yields the essential ingredients for all subsequent constructions. Likewise, all subsequent constructions – even for extensions of Büchi automata – can be seen as refinements and optimisations of Safra's original construction. This is why we chose to stick to the name "Safra construction" here even though the presented details deviate slightly from the original construction.

Exercises

Exercise 76 Let $\mathcal{A} = (Q, \Sigma, q_I, \delta, F)$ be an NBA and $\mathcal{B} = (2^Q, \Sigma, \{q_I\}, \Delta, \mathcal{F})$ be the DBA resulting from it via the powerset construction, i.e. $\mathcal{F} = \{S \subseteq Q \mid S \cap F \neq \varnothing\}$ and

$$\Delta(S, a) := \bigcup_{q \in S} \{p \mid (q, a, p) \in \delta\}$$

for every $S \in 2^Q$ and $a \in \Sigma$. Show that $L(\mathcal{B}) \supseteq L(\mathcal{A})$.

Exercise 77 Construct the run of the deterministic automaton from Fig. 7.3 on the word $(abb)^{\omega}$ up to the point where a loop is closed. Which nodes of the history trees occurring in this run are stable on the looping part, which ones are successful in which transitions?

Exercise 78 Prove Lemma 7.19.

Exercise 79 Complete the missing details of the proof of Thm. 7.25, i.e. show that

a) $|\mathcal{B}'| \in 2^{\mathcal{O}(n \log n)}$ where $n = |\mathcal{A}|$, and
b) $L(\mathcal{B}') = L(\mathcal{A})$. *Hint:* It suffices of course to show that $L(\mathcal{B}') = L(\mathcal{B})$.

Exercise 80 Construct the automaton obtained by applying the determinisation construction to the NBA $\mathcal{A}_3$ from Fig. 7.5. It suffices to start with the initial state and only construct those states that are reachable in a run on the word $w := (123\#)^\omega$ or $w' := (123\#132\#)^\omega$. Explain, using the notions of stable and successful transitions, why it accepts w' but rejects w.

Chapter 8
Decision Problems

Automata are used for an algorithmic approach to logical decision problems, in particular the *satisfiability problem*: does a given φ have a model? Other equally fundamental problems like the *validity problem* (is a given formula φ true in all possible interpretations?) or the *equivalence problem* (do two given formulas φ and ψ express the same property?) can easily be reduced to the satisfiability problem, at least when the logic provides negation.

This chapter examines algorithmic problems for automata on infinite words. First we address the *non-emptiness problem*: is $L(\mathcal{A}) \neq \varnothing$ for a given automaton $\mathcal{A}$ of some particular kind? It corresponds directly to the satisfiability problem in logic when there is an automaton $\mathcal{A}_\varphi$ for each logical formula φ under consideration that accepts exactly the models of φ, i.e. when there is an equivalence-preserving mapping from formulas to automata. This is of course the case for MSO and NBA for example, as was shown in Chp. 5, and also for MSO over finite words and NFA.

Chp. 10 will introduce linear-time temporal logic which can be seen as a restriction of MSO with a perhaps more readable syntax. Its use in program specification and verification heavily relies on such equivalence-preserving translations from formulas into automata as well, and the non-emptiness problem for NBA therefore plays an important role in the algorithmics of program verification.

We also address the *universality problem* (is $L(\mathcal{A}) = \Sigma^\omega$ for some given automaton $\mathcal{A}$ over alphabet Σ?) and its generalisation, the *subsumption* or *inclusion problem* (is $L(\mathcal{A}) \subseteq L(\mathcal{B})$ for two given automata $\mathcal{A}, \mathcal{B}$?). It should be clear that universality is the counterpart of logical validity on the automata side, again assuming that formulas can be translated into equivalent automata. The subsumption problem then corresponds directly to an implication problem on the logical side: given φ, ψ, is $\varphi \to \psi$ valid? Thus, not surprisingly, it is closely related to universality, albeit more general, but we will show how algorithms for universality can also be used to decide subsumption. Moreover, subsumption covers equivalence: we have $\varphi \equiv \psi$ iff $L(\mathcal{A}_\varphi) \subseteq L(\mathcal{A}_\psi)$ and $L(\mathcal{A}_\psi) \subseteq L(\mathcal{A}_\varphi)$ where $\mathcal{A}_\varphi$ and $\mathcal{A}_\psi$ are assumed to be automata equivalent to the logical formulas φ and ψ.

Thus, the decision problems on logics on one hand or automata on the other fall into two groups: non-emptiness being one of them and universality, subsumption

© The Author(s), under exclusive
license to Springer-Verlag GmbH, DE, part of Springer Nature 2025
M. Hofmann and M. Lange, *Automata Theory and Logic*,
https://doi.org/10.1007/978-3-662-72154-4_8

and equivalence forming the other. The reason for the distinction is that, whilst all of the latter can be reduced to the former, this requires complementation. Even though we have complementation closure of ω-regular languages and at least two explicit procedures for complementing NBA, both incur an exponential blowup. This is why we address the problems of the second group separately. This does not avoid the extra complexity – non-emptiness for NBA is NLogSpace-complete, universality etc. is PSpace-complete – but it can avoid the explicit construction of exponentially large automata at the expense of applying an exponential algorithm to small input rather than a polynomial algorithm to some input that is exponentially larger.

8.1 Automata Non-Emptiness

The decidability of the non-emptiness problem for NBA has been discussed in Chp. 5 already in the context of the decidability of satisfiability of MSO over infinite words. The basis was Büchi's characterisation of ω-regular languages as finite unions of the form $\bigcup_{i=1}^{n} U_i V_i^{\omega}$ for regular languages U_i, V_i, cf. Thm. 5.13. This, together with the observation that these languages of finite words are recognisable by NFA obtained from the same transition graph as the ω-regular languages, led to a simple algorithm for deciding NBA non-emptiness: find an accepting state that is reachable from the initial state and that is on a non-trivial cycle.

These are in fact the two main concepts – reachability and cycles in directed graphs – that are needed for deciding non-emptiness of various kinds of automata over infinite words. We will briefly discuss them before continuing to devise non-emptiness checks for other kinds of automata besides NBA.

8.1.1 Graphs and Strongly Connected Components

We assume familiarity with the basics of directed graphs.

Definition 8.1 Let $\mathcal{G} = (V, E)$ with $E \subseteq V \times V$ be a directed graph. The *reflexive-transitive closure* of E is defined as $E^* := \bigcup_{i \in \mathbb{N}} E^i$ where

$$
\begin{aligned}
E^0 &:= \{(v, v) \mid v \in V\} \\
E^{i+1} &:= \{(v, w) \mid \exists u \in V . (v, u) \in E^i \text{ and } (u, w) \in E\}
\end{aligned}
$$

The *transitive closure* is the relation $E^+ := \bigcup_{i \geq 1} E^i$.

Note that the relation E^i in a graph $\mathcal{G}$ consists of all pairs (u, v) of nodes for which there is a path from u to v of length i. Here, the length of a path is measured as the number of edges that make up the path. Hence, a path of length 0 consists of a single node only that is both the start and the end of the path.

Then E^*, resp. E^+ consist of all pairs (u, v) for which there is a path of some arbitrary length, resp. some arbitrary non-zero length from u to v. In other words, $(u, v) \in E^*$ iff v is *reachable* from u along the edges of the underlying graph. Likewise, $(u, v) \in E^+$ iff v is reachable from u along a path that takes at least one edge. Note that this is does not entail $u \neq v$. Clearly, a node can be reachable from itself on a path of non-zero length. This is exactly the case when the underlying graph contains a cycle.

Definition 8.2 A *strongly connected component* (SCC) of a directed graph $\mathcal{G} = (V, E)$ is a $C \subseteq V$ such that for all $v, w \in C$ we have $(v, w) \in E^*$. An SCC C is *maximal* if for all C' with $C \subsetneq C' \subseteq V$ we have that C' is not an SCC.

An SCC C is called *non-trivial* if it contains at least one edge, i.e. if $C \times C \cap E \neq \varnothing$.

Example 8.3 Consider the following directed graph $\mathcal{G}$.

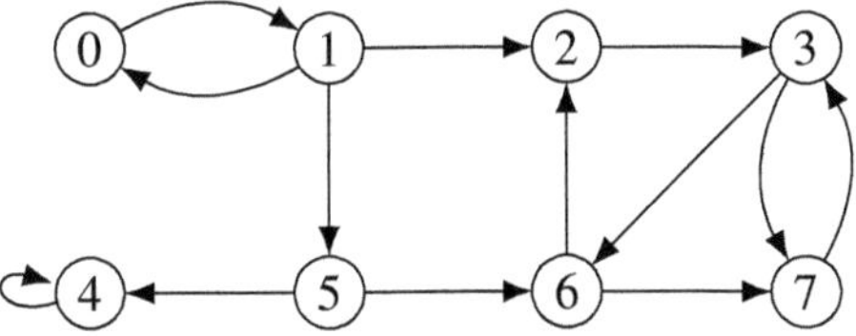

The set $\{0, 1\}$ forms an SCC since both 0 and 1 clearly are reachable from one another. Note that every node is always reachable from itself. Hence, in order to determine whether C is an SCC, it suffices to only check that $(u, v) \in E^*$ for all $u, v \in C$ with $u \neq v$.

Likewise, $\{3, 7\}$ is an SCC for the same reason. However, while $\{0, 1\}$ is a maximal SCC, $\{3, 7\}$ is not, because its superset $\{3, 6, 7\}$ also has the property that all nodes in it are reachable from one another. It is still not a maximal one because $\{2, 3, 6, 7\}$ is also an SCC, and this one is maximal.

Both $\{4\}$ and $\{5\}$ are SCCs, even maximal ones. Here the difference is non-triviality: while $\{4\}$ is a non-trivial one because there is a path of length 1 from 4 to 4, $\{5\}$ is a trivial one: 5 is only reachable from itself on a path of length 0.

A fundamental and relatively simple result in graph theory states that every directed graph can be decomposed uniquely into maximal SCCs. An *SCC decomposition* of a graph $\mathcal{G} = (V, E)$ is a set of maximal SCCs $\{C_1, \ldots, C_m\}$ such that $\bigcup_{i=1}^{m} C_i = V$. Necessarily we have $C_i \cap C_j = \varnothing$ whenever $i \neq j$ because no node can belong to two different maximal SCCs. An immediate consequence of this is the fact that the decomposition of a directed graph into maximal SCCs is unique.

Here and henceforth, when estimating complexities, we will stick to the convention that n denotes the number of nodes in the graph, and e denotes its number of edges. We will also assume that $e \in \Omega(n)$, i.e. there are essentially not fewer edges than nodes. This excludes degenerate cases of graphs with many isolated nodes.

Clearly, the SCC decomposition of a graph $\mathcal{G} = (V, E)$ can be computed naïvely by checking for each pair $u, v \in V$ whether $\{(u, v), (v, u)\} \in E^*$ using two graph searches. When this information is obtained for each pair, assembling the maximal SCCs boils down to a simple lookup procedure on this information.

It is known that reachability of a node from another can be done in time $\mathcal{O}(e)$ using breadth-first or depth-first search for instance. This leads to an overall time complexity of $\mathcal{O}(n^2 \cdot e)$ which can be estimated as $\mathcal{O}(n^4)$ since $e \leq n^2$ in general.

It should be clear that this is not optimal, though, as this naïve procedure recalculates reachability information multiple times. Take the graph in Ex. 8.3 for instance. Suppose we already know that 7 is reachable from 1. Then we do not need to explore an entire path from 0 to 7 to work out whether 7 is also reachable from 0. Instead, it suffices to see that there is a (short) path from 0 to 1.

This is a classic situation for employing so-called dynamic programming, i.e. to compute and store the results of subtasks in order to use them efficiently for the computation of supertasks. In this case, this simply boils down to the question of whether the relation E^* can be computed from E. This is clearly possible but in order to beat the bound of $\mathcal{O}(n^4)$ in the end, this needs to be done in a clever way.

Lemma 8.4 *Given a directed graph $\mathcal{G} = (V, E)$, its reflexive-transitive closure E^* can be computed in time $\mathcal{O}(n^3)$.*

Proof We sketch an algorithm that maintains a queue Q and gradually assembles the edges in E^*. At the beginning, E^* is initialised to be $\{(u, u) \mid u \in V\}$, and Q contains all edges in an arbitrary order. We also assume that, given a node u, we can obtain the list of all of its successors in constant time.

For as long as the queue Q is not empty, take the first edge (u, v) from Q, add it to E^*, take the list $w_1, \ldots, w_k$ of v's successors and add each (u, w_i) to the end of the queue for all $i = 1, \ldots, k$, unless it belongs to E^* already.

It should be clear that this algorithm terminates because there are only finitely many pairs $(u, v) \in V^2$ and none can be processed twice. It is also easy to see that it is correct in the sense that it computes a set E^* of pairs of nodes (u, v) such that v is reachable from u.

It is also complete in the sense that whenever v is reachable from u then the pair (u, v) gets added to E^* eventually. This can be shown by induction on the length ℓ of a shortest path from u to v. In case of $\ell = 0$ we have $v = u$ and (u, u) is added to E^* at the beginning. In case of $\ell = 1$ we have $(u, v) \in E$ and this edge is put into Q at the beginning, so it will eventually be removed from there and added to E^*. If $\ell > 1$ then there is some node w such that w is reachable from u in $\ell - 1$ steps. By induction, the pair (u, w) gets added to E^* eventually. But then it must have been processed in the queue. At this point, since $(w, v) \in E$, the pair (u, v) gets added to the queue and then eventually ends up in E^*.

At last, the complexity of this procedure remains to be analysed. There are at most n^2 potential edges in E^* that get processed in the queue. Processing an edge (u, v) requires obtaining the list of successors of v, assumed to be possible in constant time, but then also traversing that list which may contain up to n elements. Hence, processing a pair requires time $\mathcal{O}(n)$, leading to the overall time complexity of $\mathcal{O}(n^3)$. $\qquad\qquad\square$

This is not the most efficient way to compute an SCC decomposition of a directed graph, though. There is a clever algorithm known as *Tarjan's algorithm* which does this in linear time.

Proposition 8.5 *The SCC decomposition of a directed graph can be computed in time $\mathcal{O}(e)$.*

We refer to the literature for a proof, resp. an explanation of how this is done using two depth-first searches on the graph and its transposed graph. To be precise, time $\mathcal{O}(e)$ is generally not sufficient to output an SCC decomposition by stating for each pair of nodes whether they are mutually connected or not. Tarjan's algorithm computes a value for each node, so that two nodes belong to the same SCC iff they obtain the same value. These values can be seen as a symbolic representation of the SCC decomposition in the sense that from this data, we can decide in constant time whether two nodes belong to the same maximal SCC.

In the light of the abstract graph-theoretic view on the algorithmic side of decision problems on automata, we can rephrase the non-emptiness problem for an NBA $\mathcal{A} = (Q, \Sigma, q_I, \delta, F)$ as follows. $L(\mathcal{A}) \neq \varnothing$ iff there is a node $q \in F$ in some maximal, non-trivial SCC that is reachable from q_I in the graph $\mathcal{G}_\mathcal{A} = (Q, E)$ where $E = \{(p, q) \mid \exists a \in \Sigma \text{ s.t. } (p, a, q) \in \delta\}$.

So the directed graph to be analysed for reachability and maximal SCCs is just the transition graph of the automaton with transition labels being ignored. This is justified because in order to decide non-emptiness we are only interested in the existence of some word but not its exact letter structure. Hence, the labels on the transitions become irrelevant for the question whether some (here: ultimately periodic) word induces a run that connects the initial state to some accepting state and this one back to itself on a proper loop.

8.1.2 Rabin and Parity Automata

In line with the considerations above, when determining the complexity of some procedure operating on an automaton we will use n to denote its number of states, e to denote its number of transitions and, whenever applicable, k to denote its index, i.e. the number of Rabin / Streett pairs, the number of priorities being used etc.

We begin with the non-emptiness problem for Rabin automata.

Theorem 8.6 *The non-emptiness problem for NRA of size n and index k is solvable in time $\mathcal{O}(n^2 \cdot k)$.*

Proof Let $\mathcal{A} = (Q, \Sigma, q_I, \delta, \{(G_1, F_1), \ldots, (G_k, F_k)\})$ be an NRA and $\mathcal{G}_\mathcal{A}$ be the directed graph obtained from it with states as nodes and edges as unlabelled transitions, as done above for NBA.

We have $L(\mathcal{A}) \neq \varnothing$ iff there is an $i \in \{1, \ldots, k\}$ and some $q \in G_i$ such that q is reachable from q_I and reachable from itself on a non-empty path that does not contain any node from F_i.

To decide this condition we can proceed as follows. W.l.o.g. we can assume that $\mathcal{G}_\mathcal{A}$ does not contain states that are unreachable from q_I. This can be ensured using a simple reachability analysis in time $\mathcal{O}(e)$. We then iterate through all $i = 1, \ldots, k$, doing the following.

1) Let $\mathcal{G}_{\mathcal{A}}^i$ result from $\mathcal{G}_{\mathcal{A}}$ by removing all states from F_i including their incident edges. This can be done in time $\mathcal{O}(e)$.

2) Compute the SCC decomposition of $\mathcal{G}_{\mathcal{A}}^i$ in time $\mathcal{O}(e)$.

3) Check whether there is a state $q \in G_i$ that belongs to a non-trivial maximal SCC. This can be done in time $\mathcal{O}(n)$ simply by traversing through all states to find one in G_i. It then only remains to see whether it has a successor that belongs to the same SCC. Altogether this requires time $\mathcal{O}(n^2)$.

Since $e \leq n^2$ we obtain an overall running time of $\mathcal{O}(n^2 \cdot k)$.

Correctness of this procedure follows from the characterisation of non-emptiness above. Suppose there is some $i \in \{1, \ldots, k\}$ and some $q \in G_i$ that is reachable from q_I and reachable from itself without seeing a state in F_i in between. It survives the removal of all states that are not reachable from q_I. Conversely, after this step, every remaining state is reachable from q_I so this does not need to be checked any further. At last, if q is reachable from itself on a path not visiting states from F_i then it must belong to a non-trivial SCC in the directed graph obtained after removing all nodes from F_i, and vice-versa. $\qquad\square$

It is fair to ask whether this is in any way beneficial over the approach that transforms an NRA into an equivalent NBA first, possibly regarding it as a Muller automaton in between (Thm. 6.5 and 6.24). The detour via Muller automata definitely creates an avoidable overhead. Instead, one can translate an NRA directly into an NBA using the same principle as used in the translation from Muller automata: the resulting NBA simulates the NRA and guesses the Rabin pair (G, F) as well as the moment after which no more states in F will be seen. This is realised by a separate component for each such Rabin pair which is obtained as a copy of the NRA's transition graph with states from F missing and states from G being accepting.

Note that the translation from Rabin into Muller automata does not preserve the index. In general the index of the Muller automaton is much higher. This is why this direct translation into NBA that creates k many components, where k is the index of the Rabin or Muller automaton, is more efficient than going through Muller automata.

The second aspect to note here is that this sketched translation uses the same principles as the algorithm in the proof of Thm. 8.6, most notably the removal of states from the F-component of a Rabin pair. It is in fact true that the algorithm from Thm. 8.6 is obtained from the algorithm for NBA non-emptiness when run on the NBA translated from the input NRA in the way sketched above. Hence, there is no time-efficiency gain in this algorithm when compared to the method that reduces NRA non-emptiness to NBA non-emptiness. However, the algorithm of Thm. 8.6 is more space efficient because it avoids the explicit construction of an automaton that contains multiple copies, each of which is obtained from a given automaton's transition graph with certain nodes missing.

The same principles can then be applied to obtain an algorithm for deciding the non-emptiness problem for parity automata.

Corollary 8.7 *The non-emptiness problem for NPA of size n and index k is solvable in time $\mathcal{O}(n^2 \cdot k)$.*

Again, it is more space efficient to avoid the explicit construction of an NBA from an NPA but to iterate through all even priorities, computing SCC decompositions several times in order to find a node of that priority that can reach itself on a path not traversing through nodes of greater odd priority. We leave it as an exercise to devise a non-emptiness check for Muller automata.

8.1.3 Streett Automata

While Streett automata are equi-expressive to Rabin automata, for instance through a translation via Muller and then Büchi automata, this is not advisable for a non-emptiness check for NSA as this involves two blowups: the translation from Streett to Muller automata can be done on the same transition graph but at a general increase in its index which can become exponential in the size of the underlying automaton. Then this Muller index becomes a factor in the subsequent translation into Büchi automata.

Moreover, there is a conceptual difference between Streett and Rabin automata which justifies considering the former separately as their non-emptiness test is conceptually more difficult. The reason is that a Rabin condition is a disjunction: an NRA accepts a word if it has a run that satisfies *some* Rabin pair. Disjunctions are harmless for non-emptiness checks because non-emptiness is an existential property.

A Streett condition, on the other hand, is conjunctive: a word is accepted by an NSA if it has a run that satisfies *all* Streett pairs. It should be clear that this excludes a simple handling of the Streett pairs by separate consideration as it is done in the case of Rabin automata.

We need a technical observation in order to study the non-emptiness problem for NSA.

Definition 8.8 Let $\mathcal{A}$ be an automaton over ω-words and $\rho = q_0, q_1, q_2, \ldots$ be a run of it on some word. The run is called *ultimately periodic* if there is some $i \geq 0, n \geq 1$ such that for all $j \geq i$ we have $q_j = q_{j+n}$. Thus, it eventually traverses a particular loop forever.

A fundamental result in the theory of ω-regular languages states that an NBA accepts some word iff it has an ultimately periodic run. This is easily seen to be an immediate consequence of Thm. 5.13: an ω-regular language is of the form $\bigcup_{i=1}^{n} U_i V_i^{\omega}$ for regular languages of finite words $U_1, \ldots, U_n, V_1, \ldots, V_n$ such that $\varepsilon \notin V_i$ for all $i = 1, \ldots, n$. Hence, it must contain a word of the form uv^{ω}, and this clearly has an ultimately periodic accepting run. Note that this result has also been used in Büchi's proof of complementation closure for ω-regular languages.

Ultimate periodicity is a property of runs and therefore depends on the underlying automaton. It is not a property of a language, for otherwise it would be trivial to lift this to Streett-recognisable languages since they are just the ω-regular ones. However, it is also not very difficult to show that Streett automata have ultimately periodic accepting runs as well.

Algorithm 1 finding SCCs that contain a run satisfying all Streett pairs.

```
 1: procedure StAux((G = (V, E), {(G_1, F_1), ..., (G_k, F_k)}))
 2:     let C_1, ..., C_m be the non-trivial, maximal SCCs of G
 3:     if ∃i ∈ {1, ..., m}.∀j = 1, ..., k. C_i ∩ F_j ≠ ∅ then
 4:         return true
 5:     else
 6:         for i = 1, ..., m do
 7:             J ← {j | C_i ∩ F_j = ∅}
 8:             V' ← C_i ∖ ⋃{G_j | j ∈ J}
 9:             E' ← E ∩ V' × V'
10:             G' ← (V', E')
11:             S' ← {(G_j, F_j) | j ∉ J}
12:             if StAux(G', S') = true then
13:                 return true
14:         return false
```

Lemma 8.9 *Let $\mathcal{A}$ be an NSA. We have $L(\mathcal{A}) \neq \emptyset$ iff there is an accepting, ultimately periodic run in $\mathcal{A}$.*

Proof The direction "$\Leftarrow$" is trivial. For the "$\Rightarrow$"-direction let $\mathcal{A} = (Q, \Sigma, q_I, \delta, \mathcal{F})$ with $\mathcal{F} = \{(G_1, F_1), ..., (G_k, F_k)\}$ and assume that $w \in L(\mathcal{A})$. I.e. there is an accepting run $\rho = q_0, q_1, ...$ of $\mathcal{A}$ on w. By definition, we have $\inf \rho \cap G_i = \emptyset$ or $\inf \rho \cap F_i \neq \emptyset$ for all $i = 1, ..., k$.

Since $|Q| < \infty$, there is an earliest and shortest infix $q_j, ..., q_m$ for some $0 \leq j < m$ such that $q_m = q_j$ and for all $i = 1, ..., k$ we have $G_i \cap \{q_j, ..., q_{m-1}\} = \emptyset$ or $F_i \cap \{q_j, ..., q_{m-1}\} \neq \emptyset$. Note that q_j is a successor or q_{m-1}. Hence,

$$\rho' := q_0, ..., q_{j-1}, q_j, ..., q_{m-1}, q_j, ..., q_{m-1}, ...$$

is clearly an ultimately periodic run of $\mathcal{A}$. It is also accepting because, for every $i = 1, ..., k$ it either does not contain any state from G_i anymore after the first occurrence of q_j, or it contains infinitely many occurrences of some state in F_i because ultimate periodicity entails that each state on the looping part occurs infinitely often and those outside of the looping part only occur finitely often. □

Given a directed graph $\mathcal{G} = (V, E)$, a maximal SCC $C \subseteq V$ and a set $\mathcal{F} = \{(G_1, F_1), ..., (G_k, F_k)\}$ of pairs of sets of nodes, here also called a *Streett condition*, we say that C satisfies $\mathcal{F}$ if C contains a path $v_0, v_1, ..., v_m$ for some $m \geq 0$ such that

- $(v_j, v_{j+1}) \in E$ for all $j = 0, ..., m - 1$, and $(v_m, v_0) \in E$, i.e. $(v_0, ..., v_m)^\omega$ is an infinite periodic path within C,
- for all $i = 1, ..., k$ we have that $G_i \cap \{v_0, ..., v_m\} = \emptyset$ or $F_i \cap \{v_0, ..., v_m\} \neq \emptyset$.

Next we present an algorithm StAux that takes as input a directed graph $\mathcal{G} = (V, E)$ and a Streett condition $\mathcal{F}$ and decides whether $\mathcal{G}$ contains a non-trivial maximal SCC that satisfies $\mathcal{F}$.

The algorithm works recursively over the number of Streett pairs as follows. First we decompose the given graph into SCCs and discard the trivial ones. If there is a non-trivial SCC C such that $C \cap F_i \neq \varnothing$ for all $i = 1, \ldots, k$ then we can return *true*, because in an SCC we can find paths from every node to every other node. Hence, we can create a path that traverses nodes from each F_i in some arbitrary but fixed order all over again.

If this is not the case, then the graph $\mathcal{G}$ may still have an SCC containing the looping part of an ultimately periodic path that satisfies all Streett pairs. Suppose such an SCC C_i is disjoint from the set F_j in a Streett pair (G_j, F_j). In this case we need to check whether G_j can be avoided inside this SCC whilst still repeatedly hitting states from other Streett pairs. This is done by removing all states from G_j for any Streett pair (G_j, F_j) for which F_j is disjoint from C_i, and then calling the algorithm recursively on the potentially reduced graph and the remaining Streett pairs whose F-component still has an intersection with this SCC. The second argument is then guaranteed to be smaller now.

Lemma 8.10 *Algorithm* STAUX *correctly decides for a graph $\mathcal{G} = (V, E)$ and Streett condition $\mathcal{F}$ whether $\mathcal{G}$ contains a non-trivial SCC C that satisfies $\mathcal{F}$.*

Proof Correctness is argued for along the same lines as explained above: if some recursion branch eventually yields *true*, then by successive SCC decompositions a maximal SCC of the original graph has been found in which a cyclic path can be constructed that either traverses F eventually or avoids G entirely for every original Streett pair (G, F). This SCC must necessarily be non-trivial because trivial ones are not considered and do not contribute to a return value *true*.

Likewise, if $\mathcal{G}$ contains a non-trivial SCC C with the desired properties than algorithm STAUX wil eventually return *true*, depending on how C fulfills all Streett pairs. If it has a non-empty intersection will all Streett pairs then algorithm STAUX returns *true* immediately in line 4. $\square$

Another interesting question concerns its running time.

Lemma 8.11 *Algorithm* STAUX *terminates on input* $(\mathcal{G}, \mathcal{F})$ *in time* $\mathcal{O}(ek^2)$ *where* e *is the number of edges in* $\mathcal{G}$ *and* $k = |\mathcal{F}|$.

Proof Termination is guaranteed because the condition in line 3 is trivially true when $S = \varnothing$, and in every iteration of the for-loop in lines 6ff, we have $J \subsetneq \{1, \ldots, k\}$ for otherwise the condition in line 3 would have been true already. Hence, the recursion depth is limited by the number of Streett pairs in the initial argument.

Estimating the running time requires a refined consideration. According to Prop. 8.5 the SCC decomposition can be computed in time $\mathcal{O}(e)$. We can write a recurrence equation for the worst-case running time depending on the number of nodes n, the number of edges e and the size of the Streett condition k as follows.

$$T(n, 0) \;=\; \mathcal{O}(1)$$

$$T(n, k) \;=\; \mathcal{O}(e) + \mathcal{O}(k \cdot n) + \sum_{i=1}^{m} \mathcal{O}(e) + T(|C_i|, k-1) \;\leq\; \mathcal{O}(e \cdot k) + T(n, k-1)$$

The inequation holds because we can assume $n \leq e$ and that $T(n, k)$ is at least linear in its first argument. This is the case because otherwise it would not have time to consider the graph given as its input. One can then check that $T(n, k) = \mathcal{O}(ek^2)$ solves this recurrence. □

We can the use this auxiliary algorithm on plain directed graphs to solve the non-emptiness problem for Streett automata.

Theorem 8.12 *The non-emptiness problem for NSA with e transitions and index k is solvable in time $\mathcal{O}(ek^2)$.*

Proof Let $\mathcal{A} = (Q, \Sigma, q_I, \delta, \mathcal{F})$ be an NSA with $|\mathcal{F}| = k$ and $|\delta| = e$. According to Lemma 8.9 it suffices to search for ultimately periodic runs that satisfy the Streett condition $\mathcal{F}$ in order to decide whether $L(\mathcal{A}) \neq \emptyset$. Hence, we have $L(\mathcal{A}) \neq \emptyset$ iff there is an SCC $C \subseteq Q$ that is reachable from q_I and which contains a cyclic path that satisfies $\mathcal{F}$. According to Lemma 8.11 this can be decided in time $\mathcal{O}(ek^2)$ by running algorithm STAUX on transition graph of $\mathcal{A}$ with the Streett condition $\mathcal{F}$ after the removal of states that are not reachable from q_I. □

It is important not to apply algorithm STAUX directly to the transition graph of the NSA but to remove non-reachable states first, as STAUX does not check for reachability itself. In essence, algorithm STAUX only determines the existence of the looping part of an ultimately periodic run, and by ensuring that it only operates on reachable states, this looping part can always be extended with a prefix to form an ultimately periodic and accepting run starting in the automaton's initial state.

8.2 Universality and Subsumption

As argued above, problems other than non-emptiness, in particular universality, subsumption and equivalence, are different in their nature in that they involve complementation when reduced to non-emptiness. Since complementation is combinatorially not without certain difficulties, it is worth considering direct approaches to these problems that avoid explicit complementation.

8.2.1 From Subsumption to Universality

It should be clear that the subsumption problem is the most general problem of the three mentioned above, in the sense that the others easily reduce to it.

Lemma 8.13 *Any algorithm for the subsumption problem for NBA / NcoBA / NPA / NRA / NSA / NMA can be used to solve the universality and equivalence problem for these kinds of automata as well.*

Proof For the equivalence problem this simply follows from the fact that $L(\mathcal{A}) = L(\mathcal{B})$ iff $L(\mathcal{A}) \subseteq L(\mathcal{B})$ and $L(\mathcal{B}) \subseteq L(\mathcal{A})$. Thus, an equivalence checker can be built from two calls to a subsumption checker.

For the universality problem this is a simple consequence of the fact that the universal language Σ^ω is recognisable with each of the mentioned automata. In fact, a one-state automaton suffices in each case. Moreover, we have $L(\mathcal{A}) = \Sigma^\omega$ iff $\Sigma^\omega \subseteq L(\mathcal{A})$. Hence, universality of automaton $\mathcal{A}$ can be determined by checking for subsumption between an automaton recognising Σ^ω and $\mathcal{A}$. $\qquad\square$

Nevertheless, the universality problem is a little bit simpler to study from a technical point of view, without missing any essentials that would be necessary for subsumption. The question therefore arises whether subsumption can be reduced to universality as well. The answer is yes, and this follows from complexity-theoretic considerations already: both subsumption and universality for NFA and therefore also all kinds of automata over ω-words are PSpace-complete, so (polynomial-time) reductions between them exist in either direction. However, this argument is not immediately constructive, and even when considering this in detail, one may end up with an NBA encoding runs of Turing Machines that solve the subsumption problem for NBA for instance. So the question really is: is there a direct reduction from subsumption to universality? The answer is still yes, and the trick that is needed when constructing an NBA $\mathcal{C}$ from two NBA $\mathcal{A}$ and $\mathcal{B}$ so that the language of $\mathcal{C}$ is universal iff $L(\mathcal{A}) \subseteq L(\mathcal{B})$, is to allow $\mathcal{C}$ to work over a different alphabet than $\mathcal{A}$ and $\mathcal{B}$.

Theorem 8.14 *For all NBA $\mathcal{A}, \mathcal{B}$ over some common alphabet Σ there is an NBA $\mathcal{C}$ of size at most $\mathcal{O}(|\mathcal{A}| + |\mathcal{B}|)$ over an alphabet Δ such that $L(\mathcal{C}) = \Delta^\omega$ iff $L(\mathcal{A}) \subseteq L(\mathcal{B})$.*

Proof Let $\mathcal{A} = (Q, \Sigma, q_I, \delta, F)$ and $\mathcal{B} = (Q', \Sigma, q'_I, \delta', F')$. W.l.o.g. we can assume them to be total, i.e. runs are always infinite, and they never get stuck on any letter.

We have $L(\mathcal{A}) \subseteq L(\mathcal{B})$ iff for every word $w \in \Sigma^\omega$ and every accepting run $\rho \in Q^\omega$ of $\mathcal{A}$ on w there is an accepting run ρ' of $\mathcal{B}$ on w. This can be reformulated as follows. For every sequence $\rho \in Q^\omega$ one of three cases holds:

(I) ρ is not a run of $\mathcal{A}$ on some word in Σ^ω,

(II) ρ is a run of $\mathcal{A}$ on some word in Σ^ω but it is not an accepting run,

(III) ρ is a run of $\mathcal{A}$ on some word $w \in \Sigma^\omega$ and there is an accepting run of $\mathcal{B}$ on w.

This reformulation with a universal quantification over all ω-sequences of states is now what allows us to view this as a universality problem. The first condition is even easier to check when we do not regard a run as a sequence $q_0, q_1, \ldots$ of states but – as we have sometimes done before – as an alternating sequence $q_0, a_0, q_1, a_1, \ldots$ of states and alphabet letters. This could mean choosing $Q \cup \Sigma$ as the alphabet for the NBA $\mathcal{C}$, and clearly not every sequence over this alphabet is a run in this form. Instead, we choose $\Delta := \delta$ as the new alphabet and regard such a run as a sequence of transitions $(q_0, a_0, q_1), (q_1, a_1, q_2), \ldots$

We can then build three NBA $\mathcal{C}_1, \mathcal{C}_2, \mathcal{C}_3$ that check the three conditions respectively. The desired NBA $\mathcal{C}$ is then obtained from these three via a standard union construction, cf. Lemma 5.9.

Note that a sequence $(q_0, a_0, p_0), (q_1, a_1, p_1), \ldots$ is not a run of $\mathcal{A}$ if $q_0 \neq q_1$ or $p_i \neq q_{i+1}$ for some $i \geq 0$. It is easy to construct an NBA, in fact a DBA, that keeps remembering the third component of the last triple it read and accepts as soon as this does not agree with the first component of the next triple. The details of the construction of $\mathcal{C}_1$ are left as an exercise.

Next, it is even easier to check that such a sequence $(q_0, a_0, p_0), (q_1, a_1, p_1), \ldots$ is not accepting since we do not need to check anymore whether it is a run or not. We only need to check that eventually none of the q_i and p_i are accepting states, i.e. that eventually we only ever see transitions from $((Q \setminus F) \times \Sigma \times (Q \setminus F)) \cap \delta$. This can easily be done with a two-state DcoBA or a two-state NBA. Again the details of the construction of $\mathcal{C}_2$ are left as an exercise.

At last, $\mathcal{C}_3$ needs to simulate, given such a sequence $\rho = (q_0, a_0, p_0), (q_1, a_1, p_1), \ldots$, an accepting run of $\mathcal{B}$ on ρ. Again, we do not need to be concerned with the question of whether ρ is indeed a run or not. All that is relevant for $\mathcal{C}_3$ to be correct according to its specification, is the projection of ρ onto Σ, i.e. the sequence $a_0, a_1, \ldots$ forming the underlying word.

This can easily be done by extending $\mathcal{B}$'s transition relation as follows: whenever $\mathcal{B}$ can take an a-transition from q to p, we allow it to take a transition from q to p with any letter (q', a, p') of the new alphabet Δ whose second component is still a. Accepting states are exactly those that are accepting in $\mathcal{B}$. This way, $\mathcal{C}_3$ accepts such a sequence iff $\mathcal{B}$ accepts the Σ-word embedded in this sequence. Again, writing down the technical details of this construction is left as an exercise. $\qquad\square$

Hence, the subsumption problem for two NBA $\mathcal{A}, \mathcal{B}$ can be solved by constructing the NBA $\mathcal{C}$ as explained above, and then checking this one for universality.

We finish this section with the observation, already mentioned above, that the universality problem is decidable using a reduction to the emptiness problem.

Corollary 8.15 *The universality problem for NBA of size n is solvable in time* $2^{\mathcal{O}(n \log n)}$.

Proof Let $\mathcal{A}$ be an NBA with n states over alphabet Σ. According to Cor. 7.26 it can be translated into a DPA of size $2^{\mathcal{O}(n \log n)}$ and index $\mathcal{O}(n)$. A close inspection shows that the size of the resulting automaton is the dominating factor in the time complexity here. DPA can easily be complemented at no blowup according to Thm. 6.11. The resulting DPA can be turned into an equivalent NBA $\overline{\mathcal{A}}$ of size $\mathcal{O}(n) \cdot 2^{\mathcal{O}(n \log n)} = 2^{\mathcal{O}(n \log n)}$ according to Thm. 6.13, so we have $L(\overline{\mathcal{A}}) = \overline{L(\mathcal{A})} = \Sigma^\omega \setminus L(\mathcal{A})$.

Now we can apply the usual reasoning for converting emptiness into universality and vice-versa: we have $L(\mathcal{A}) = \Sigma^\omega$ iff $\overline{L(\mathcal{A})} = L(\overline{\mathcal{A}}) = \varnothing$.

Since non-emptiness can be decided in polynomial time, so can emptiness, and so the worst-case time needed for this universality check is indeed $2^{\mathcal{O}(n \log n)}$. $\qquad\square$

The reason for stating this here explicitly is mainly to put it in contrast with what comes next. We devise a conceptually simpler universality check that turns out not to be asymptotically optimal. However, it avoids much of the intrinsic combinatorial difficulties that arise with the use of the Safra construction for complementation.

8.2.2 Universality as a Search Problem in Monoids

We study the universality of the language accepted by an NBA using an abstract search problem in finite monoids. Recall that a monoid is a structure $\mathcal{M} = (M, \circ, e)$ where M is the set of elements of the monoid, and $\circ : M \times M \to M$ is a binary function on it that is associative. At last, $e \in M$ is neutral for $\circ$, i.e. we have $e \circ m = e = m \circ e$ for all $m \in M$.

This method for determining universality is based in Büchi's complementation proof, especially the characterisation of non-universality of $\mathcal{A}$ over Σ as the existence of two words $u \in \Sigma^*$, $v \in \Sigma^+$ so that $uv^\omega \notin L(\mathcal{A})$ and therefore two equivalence classes $[u], [v]$ such that $[u][v]^\omega \notin L(\mathcal{A})$. It is the fact that there are only finitely many such equivalence classes which allows this to be used in a decision procedure.

So non-universality can therefore be checked in principle by computing all equivalence classes and checking for each pair $[u], [v]$ of them whether $uv \notin L(\mathcal{A})$. The main contribution of this section is then to introduce a data format for such equivalence classes and a method to compute them without enumerating words etc.

For the remainder of this section we fix an NBA $\mathcal{A} = (Q, \Sigma, q_I, \delta, F)$ and show how its universality can be decided. Recall that for $u, v \in \Sigma^*$ we have

$$u \sim v \quad \text{iff} \quad \forall q. \forall q'. (q \xrightarrow{u} q' \Leftrightarrow q \xrightarrow{v} q') \text{ and } (q \xRightarrow{u} q' \Leftrightarrow q \xRightarrow{v} q')$$

where $q \xrightarrow{u} q'$ if q' is reachable from q in $\mathcal{A}$'s transition graph along some path labelled with u, and $q \xRightarrow{u} q'$ likewise but the path is additionally required to visit some accepting state. As usual, we write $[w]$ for the equivalence class of w under $\sim$.

Given a word $w \in \Sigma^*$, we associate with it two sets of pairs of states:

- the set R_w of all pairs (q, q') such that $q \xrightarrow{w} q'$, and
- the set R_w^F of all pairs (q, q') such that $q \xRightarrow{w} q'$.

Note that $R_w, R_w^F \subseteq Q \times Q$ for all $w \in \Sigma^*$, i.e. they are binary relations on the NBA's state space Q. Recall the definition of the composition of relations $R, S \subseteq Q \times Q$ via

$$R \circ S \; := \; \{(q, q') \mid \exists q'' \in Q \text{ with } (q, q'') \in R \text{ and } (q'', q') \in S\} \, .$$

It should be clear that for two words $u, v \in \Sigma^*$ with $u \sim v$ we have $R_u = R_v$ and $R_u^F = R_v^F$. Hence, these sets of pairs of states do not depend on the exact form of a word w but only its equivalence class $[w]$, and we therefore denote them as $R_{[w]}$ and $R_{[w]}^F$ instead.

So, while the equivalence class $[w]$ of a word, when seen as the set $\{v \in \Sigma^* \mid v \sim w\}$, is an infinite set and therefore not very useful for algorithmic purposes, the pair (R_w, R_w^F) is a finite object (as there are only finitely many state pairs) and can therefore serve as a data structure for the representation of such equivalence classes. Remember that $R_w^F \subseteq R_w$ for any $w \in \Sigma^*$ which is why there are at most 3^{n^2} many different equivalence classes $[w]$ for an NBA with n states.

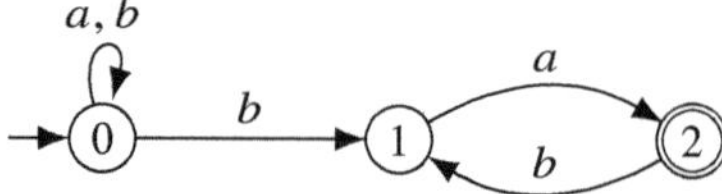

Fig. 8.1 Example NBA for the construction of boxes and the test for non-universality.

The next lemma essentially states that R_w and R_w^F can be computed by induction on the length of w. The proof is left as an exercise.

Lemma 8.16 *Let* $u, v \in \Sigma^*$, $a \in \Sigma$. *The following statements are true.*

a) $R_{[\varepsilon]} = \{(q, q) \mid q \in Q\}$ *and* $R_{[\varepsilon]}^F = \{(q, q) \mid q \in F\}$.

b) $R_{[a]} = \{(q, q') \mid q' \in \delta(a, q)\}$ *and* $R_{[a]}^F = \{(q, q') \mid q' \in \delta(a, q)$ *and* $\{q, q'\} \cap F \neq \varnothing\}$.

c) $R_{[uv]} = R_{[u]} \circ R_{[v]}$ *and* $R_{[uv]}^F = R_{[u]}^F \circ R_{[v]} \cup R_{[u]} \circ R_{[v]}^F$.

Using the induction principle from this lemma it is possible to finitely enumerate all equivalence classes $[w]$ for $w \in \Sigma^*$ as follows, where computing $[w]$ simply means constructing $R_{[w]}$ and $R_{[w]}^{\text{fin}}$.

a) Construct $[\varepsilon]$ and $[a]$ for $a \in \Sigma$ directly from $\mathcal{A}$'s transition table.

b) Starting with the set of all $[a]$ for $a \in \Sigma$, compute $[uv]$ for any equivalence classes $[u], [v]$ already computed until no more new classes can be found.

Before we carry this out on an example NBA we introduce a graphical notion for such pairs of relations (R_w, R_w^F) which is nothing more than the straightforward interpretation of an object of type 3^{Q^2}. These can be regarded as boxes with inputs (on the left) and outputs (on the right), one for each state $q \in Q$. Internally, such a box connects the input state q with the output state q' if $(q, q') \in R_w$. This connection is marked if, additionally, $(q, q') \in R_w^F$.

Example 8.17 Consider the NBA shown in Fig. 8.1. The basic boxes arising from its transition table are the following three.

$$[\varepsilon] = \qquad [a] = \qquad [b] =$$

Since the states represented by an input or output port are given by the numerical order of the states in this case we will drop the annotations in the computation of further boxes.

We can then compute the equivalence classes $[u]$ for words of length 2 using the composition principle from Lemma 8.16 and the boxes for equivalence classes of words of length 1. The composition of two relations represented as boxes can easily be obtained by putting them side-by-side and merging them into one. For instance, we have

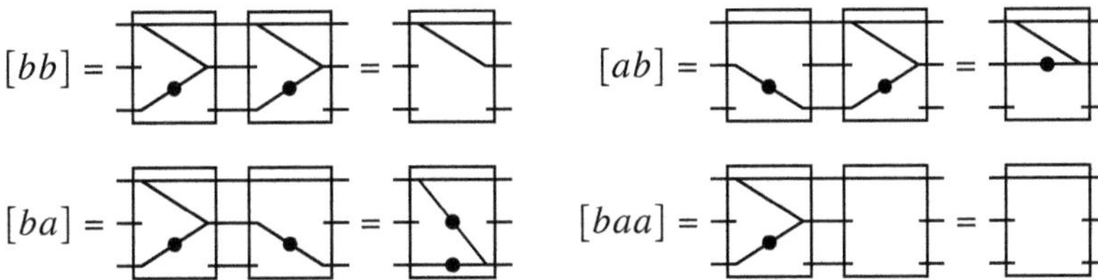

In general, the box $[uv]$ has a line from input port q to output port q' if a line can be traced from input port q in $[u]$ to some output port, and from the corresponding input port in box $[v]$ to its output port q'. The resulting line is marked if one of the two segments was marked. So likewise we get the following boxes for other equivalence classes of words.

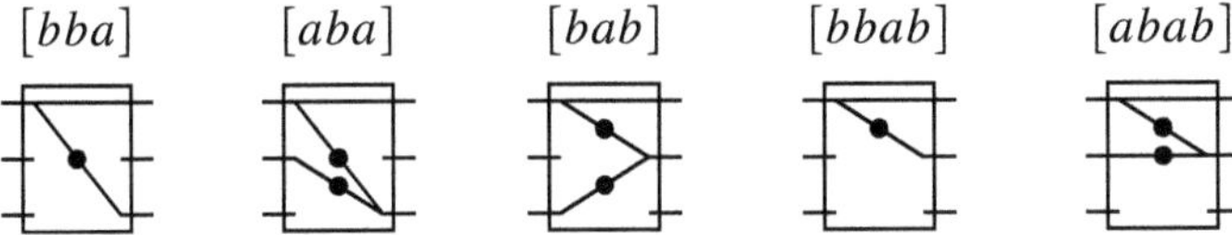

The last equation shows that $[baa] = [aa]$. An exhaustive search reveals five more boxes, namely the following ones.

$$[bba] \qquad [aba] \qquad [bab] \qquad [bbab] \qquad [abab]$$

Composing one of these with any other one yields a box that has been discovered already, for instance

$$[ba] \circ [abab] \; = \; \cdots \; \circ \; \cdots \; = \; \cdots \; = \; [bbab]$$

which can also be obtained algebraically as

$$[ba] \circ [abab] = [ba] \circ ([ab] \circ [ab]) = ([ba] \circ [ab]) \circ [ab] = [bb] \circ [ab]$$
$$= [bbab]$$

once we have established by direct calculation that $[ba] \circ [ab] = [bb]$.

The next theorem then establishes the use of equivalence classes in a decision procedure for universality. Recall that a monoid element m is called *idempotent* if $m \circ m = m$.

Theorem 8.18 *Let* $\mathcal{A} = (Q, \Sigma, q_I, \delta, F)$ *be an NBA. We have* $L(\mathcal{A}) = \Sigma^\omega$ *iff for all* $u \in \Sigma^*$ *and* $v \in \Sigma^+$ *such that* $[v]$ *is idempotent and* $[uv] = [u]$, *there is some* $q \in Q$ *such that* $(q_I, q) \in R_{[u]}$ *and* $(q, q) \in R^F_{[v]}$.

Proof "$\Rightarrow$" Assume that $L(\mathcal{A}) = \Sigma^\omega$. Take two arbitrary equivalence classes $[u], [v]$ such that $v \neq \varepsilon$, $[vv] = [v]$ and $[uv] = [u]$. Since $v \neq \varepsilon$ we have $uv^\omega \in \Sigma^\omega$. Since $L(\mathcal{A}) = \Sigma^\omega$ there must be an accepting run of $\mathcal{A}$ on uv^ω. For $i \geq 0$ let q_i be the state in this run that $\mathcal{A}$ reaches after reading uv^i. Hence, we have $q_I \xrightarrow{uv^0} q_0$ and $q_{i-1} \xrightarrow{v} q_i$ for all $i \geq 1$. Since $|Q| < \infty$ there must be some $q \in Q$ such that

$$q_I \xrightarrow{uv^m} q \xrightarrow{v^{k_0}} q \xrightarrow{v^{k_1}} \dots$$

for some $m \geq 0$ and $k_j \geq 1$ for all $j \in \mathbb{N}$. So we have $(q_I, q) \in [uv^m]$. If $m = 0$ then we trivially also get $(q_I, q) \in R_{[u]}$. If $m > 0$ then we make use of the fact that $[v]$ is idempotent, so we have $[uv^m] = [u] \circ [v]^m = [u] \circ [v] = [u]$ by assumption.

Likewise, we have $(q, q) \in [v^{k_j}]$ for all $j \in \mathbb{N}$ and since $[v]$ is idempotent we also have $(q, q) \in R_{[v]}$. At last, since the run is accepting, it contains infinitely many accepting states, so we have $(q, q) \in R_{[v]}^{\mathsf{F}}$ in fact.

"$\Leftarrow$" Now assume that $L(\mathcal{A}) \neq \Sigma^\omega$, i.e. there is some $w = a_0 a_1 \dots \in \Sigma^\omega$ such that all runs of $\mathcal{A}$ on w contain finitely many accepting states only. As in the proof of Lemma 5.31 this determines a colouring f of $\binom{\mathbb{N}}{2}$ via $f(i, j) = [a_i \dots a_{j-1}]$ with a finite number of colours, and Ramsey's Theorem yields an infinite sequence of indices $i_0 < i_1 < \dots$ and a colour – in this case an equivalence class – that is the same for all pairs of indices in this sequence. In other words, it yields a class $[v]$ such that not only $[v] = [a_{i_j} \dots a_{i_{j+1}-1}]$ for all $j \geq 0$, but even $[v] = [a_{i_j} \dots a_{i_{j'}-1}]$ for all $0 \leq j < j'$. Since

$$[v] = [a_{i_1} \dots a_{i_3-1}] = [a_{i_1} \dots a_{i_2-1}] \circ [a_{i_2} \dots a_{i_3-1}] = [v] \circ [v]$$

we have that $[v]$ is indeed idempotent.

It is tempting to choose $u := a_0 \dots a_{i_0-1}$ but then we do not necessarily have $[uv] = [u]$. So instead let $u' := a_0 \dots a_{i_0-1}$ and $u := a_0 \dots a_{i_1-1}$. Then we have $[u] = [u'v]$ and therefore $[uv] \circ [v] = [u'vv] = [u'v] = [u]$ by idempotency of $[v]$.

At last, take any $q \in Q$ such that $(q_I, q) \in R_{[u]}$, i.e. $q_I \xrightarrow{u} q$. Suppose that also $(q, q) \in R_{[v]}^{\mathsf{F}}$. Then we have $uv^\omega \in L(\mathcal{A})$ because it is easy to construct an accepting run of $\mathcal{A}$ on uv^ω by concatenating a finite path from q_I to q on u with a looping path from q back to q on v that visits an accepting state in between. However, since $a_0 \dots a_{i_1-1} \sim u$ and $a_{i_j} \dots a_{i_{j+1}-1} \sim v$ for all $j \geq 1$ we also have

$$q_I \xrightarrow{a_0 \dots a_{i_1-1}} q \xRightarrow{a_{i_1} \dots a_{i_2+1-1}} q \xRightarrow{a_{i_2} \dots a_{i_3+1-1}} \dots$$

which contradicts the assumption that $w \notin L(\mathcal{A})$. $\qquad\square$

Thm. 8.18 yields the basis for a simple algorithm that checks for universality of a given NFA $\mathcal{A}$: starting with the classes $[a]$ for every $a \in \Sigma$, represented as boxes, form classes $[u]$ for $u \in \Sigma^*$ with $|u| > 2$ by composing existing boxes. For every new box $[v]$ resulting in this way, check whether it is idempotent and whether there is a class $[u]$ such that $[uv] = [u]$. Once such a pair is found, we know that $L(\mathcal{A}) \neq \Sigma^\omega$. Otherwise the search will terminate eventually when no more new boxes arise, and we know that $L(\mathcal{A}) = \Sigma^\omega$.

Example 8.19 Reconsider the NBA from Fig. 8.1. Its language is not universal. Its idempotent boxes are $[aa], [bb], [ba], [bba], [bbab]$ and $[abab]$.

Now take, for instance, $v := aa$ and $u := baa$. Then we have $[u] = [v]$ according to the development in Ex. 8.17, and therefore $[uv] = [u]$. At last, there is only one state $q \in \{0, 1, 2\}$ s.t. $(0, q) \in R_{[u]}$, namely 0 itself. But then we have $(0, 0) \notin R^F_{[v]}$, witnessing this NBA's non-universality.

We remark that, in order to decide inclusion between the languages of two NBA, there is a more direct way than laid out in the reduction from subsumption to universality. It is possible to extend the algorithm for universality to one for subsumption as follows.

Let $\mathcal{A} = (Q, \Sigma, q_I, \delta, F)$ and $\mathcal{B} = (Q', \Sigma, q_I', \delta', F')$ be given. A box is no longer an object of type 3^{Q^2}, resp. $3^{Q'^2}$, but it is now an object of type $Q^2 \times \{0, 1\} \times 3^{Q'^2}$. This can be seen as a box like the ones above that is additionally equipped with an in-type and an out-type and a flag. Composition is only possible when the out-type of the left box matches the in-type of the right box. The operation on the flag in composition is just the maximum. Thus, we have, for instance the following equalities where the additional flag is shown by a dot on the top side of the box's rectangle.

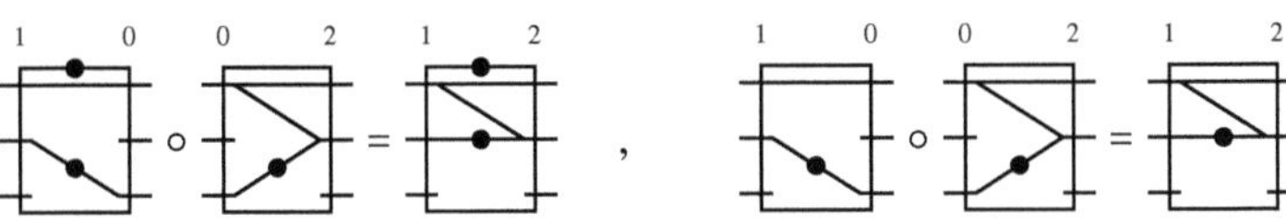

On the other hand, we also have

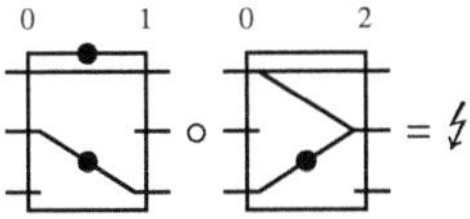

because the out-type 1 of the left box does not match the in-type 0 of the right box.

Remember that in the non-universality checks, a box represents an equivalence class $[u]$ for some word $u \in \Sigma^*$ which, again, can be seen as the collected information of all the consecutive transitions that the underlying NBA can do when reading u, especially with regards to the visiting of accepting states. Now such an extended box does this for the automaton $\mathcal{B}$, and additionally carries information about the possibility to go from the in-type state in $\mathcal{A}$ to the out-type state when reading u, on a path that visits an accepting state there or not. This is what the additional flag is for. It is then possible to characterise non-inclusion between the languages of two NBA via the existence of a witnessing pair of extended boxes as follows.

Theorem 8.20 *Let $\mathcal{A}, \mathcal{B}$ be NBA over the same alphabet Σ. We have $L(\mathcal{A}) \nsubseteq L(\mathcal{B})$ iff there is a pair of extended boxes $[u], [v]$ such that $[v]$ is idempotent, $[u] \circ [v] = [u]$, $v \neq \varepsilon$, the extra flag on $[v]$ is set, and all edges in $[v]$ of the form (q', q') for some of $\mathcal{B}$'s states q' with $(q_I', q') \in [u]$ are unmarked.*

Idempotency of $[v]$ implies that its in-type equals its out-type. Proof details for this theorem are left as an exercise. Note that, if the condition stated in this theorem is met, then there is an accepting run of $\mathcal{A}$ on uv^ω but every run of $\mathcal{B}$ on uv^ω does not traverse accepting states infinitely often. Not surprisingly, this shows that non-subsumption between two NBA is also witnessed by an ultimately periodic word.

8.3 An Application: Size-Change Termination

We consider an application of NBA subsumption (and therefore also universality) from the area of termination analysis for recursive programs. We assume the reader to be familiar with recursion in a standard programming language, and the issue of termination that routinely arises with it. The question under consideration is: does a given recursive program terminate for all inputs? It should be clear that this is undecidable in general but potentially decidable for restricted forms of recursion.

We do not develop a model of a programming language with data types and a proper semantics but appeal to the intuitive understanding of termination for recursive programs over natural numbers. This is to be seen as an abstraction. Take for instance any well-known recursive sorting algorithm like Mergesort. It operates on lists or arrays of ordered data, but in order to argue that it terminates it typically suffices to regard the length of its arguments only. This abstracts the problem into one for recursive programs over natural numbers.

8.3.1 Recursive Programs

We define recursive programs abstractly as collections of functions.

Definition 8.21 Let $F = \{f_1, f_2, \dots, f_n\}$ be a finite set of function symbols, each of which has an arity $ar(f_i)$.

A *recursive program* is a system of equations of the form

$$f_1(x_1, \dots, x_{k_1}) \;=\; f_{1,1}(\mathbf{t}_{1,1}), \dots, f_{1,m_1}(\mathbf{t}_{1,m_1})$$

$$\vdots$$

$$f_n(x_1, \dots, x_{k_n}) \;=\; f_{n,1}(\mathbf{t}_{n,1}), \dots, f_{n,m_n}(\mathbf{t}_{1,m_n})$$

where $f_{1,1}, \dots, f_{n,m_n}$ are function symbols from F, the x_i are parameter variables so that $ar(f_i) = k_i$ for all $i = 1, \dots, n$. Each $\mathbf{t}_{i,j}$ is a vector of terms of the form $x_{i,h}$ or $x_{i,h} - 1$ for some $h \in \{1, \dots, k_i\}$, so that $|\mathbf{t}_{i,j}| = ar(f_{i,j})$ for $1 \le i \le n$, $1 \le j \le m_i$.

Such programs abstract away from concrete recursive programs in the following sense: the list of function applications to terms on the right-hand side of the equation for f_i contains all the recursive calls that have to be made when executing f_i on parameter values $(x_{i,1}, \dots, x_{i,k_i})$. The order of these recursive calls is irrelevant; a function call terminates when all its recursive subcalls terminate.

Each argument to a recursive call is either one of the parameter values of the parent call, or it is such a value decreased by 1. Again, the exact (positive) amount by which a value gets decreased is irrelevant when considering the question of termination for all input values.

Example 8.22 Consider the following program for computing multiplication recursively, written in (functional) pseudocode.

$$\mathsf{mult}(x, 0, z) = z \qquad\qquad\qquad \mathsf{add}(x, 0) = x$$
$$\mathsf{mult}(x, y, z) = \mathsf{mult}(x, y - 1, \mathsf{add}(x, z)) \qquad \mathsf{add}(x, y) = \mathsf{add}(x + 1, y - 1)$$

Here we generalised the problem slightly into a ternary operation $\mathsf{mult}(x, y, z)$ that is supposed to compute $x \cdot y + z$. This enables a tail-recursive description of the algorithm.

This program can now be abstracted into the following, bearing in mind that we are only interested in its termination. We simply consider recursive calls on an argument that is zero to be terminating immediately. This allows us to discard the first two clauses of the two functions, and we are left with the following.

$$\mathsf{mult}(x, y, u) \;=\; \mathsf{add}(x, u), \mathsf{mult}(x, y - 1, u)$$
$$\mathsf{add}(x, y) \;=\; \mathsf{add}(x, y - 1)$$

Unlike above, the right-hand side of the equation does not contain a term describing how to compute the return value, but it simply contains a list of recursive calls. So the symbol '=' does not denote equality of values but equality with respect to termination, and the commas are conjunctions.

The call parameters are slightly changed in comparison to the original function definition above. In function mult we replaced z with u, simply because the third parameter in the recursive call to mult may obtain an arbitrarily high value. It should be clear that the introduction of the parameter u models this because we are interested in termination for all parameter values, including those for u that are that arbitrarily high.

Something similar is done with the first argument for add. Here we replaced $x + 1$ by x. Again, since only the decreasing of values is what we consider to lead to termination, the resulting program is termination-equivalent to the original one.

Example 8.23 As a second example consider the Ackermann function, known from recursion or computability theory. It can be modelled using a ternary function symbol as follows.

$$\mathsf{ack}(x, y, u) \;=\; \mathsf{ack}(x - 1, u, u), \mathsf{ack}(x, y - 1, u)$$

The Ackermann function obtains its enormous growth rate from the clever nesting of a recursive call in the argument position of a second recursive call. This is not anything that can be modelled in the formalism introduced here where recursive calls appear to be "flat". Again, for pure termination considerations this suffices because non-termination is then given by some non-terminating recursion path, and there is no relevance to how the non-existing return-values would be used in further paths in the recursion tree.

Let P be a recursive program over $F = \{f_1, \ldots, f_n\}$ with defining equations as in Def. 8.21. It defines a set of n partial functions $f_i : \mathbb{N}^{ar(f_i)} \to D$ for some arbitrary non-empty co-domain D. Note that recursive functions in the form defined here do not specify return values. Hence, we can simply regard them as partial functions of type $f_i : \mathbb{N}^{ar(f_i)} \to \{\top\}$ or total functions of type $f_i : \mathbb{N}^{ar(f_i)} \to \{\top, \bot\}$. We do not distinguish notationally between a function symbol $f_i \in F$ and its associated function.

By definition, we say that $f_i(x_1, \ldots, x_{ar(f_i)}) = \top$ if $x_i = 0$ for some $i \in \{1, \ldots, ar(f_i)\}$. I.e. recursive calls are assumed to terminate when some parameter has become zero.

For other parameter values the functions' return values are given by their defining equations. We have

$$f_i(\mathbf{x}) = \top \quad \text{iff} \quad f_{i,j}(\mathbf{t}_{i,j}) = \top \text{ for all } j = 1, \ldots, m_i.$$

This means that a call to function f_i with parameter values $\mathbf{x}$ all different from 0 does not terminate if some recursive call to one of the functions $f_{i,j}$ with corresponding parameter values $\mathbf{t}_{i,j}$ does not terminate.

8.3.2 Termination Analysis as Büchi Inclusion

Let P be a recursive program of the form

$$f_1(x_1, \ldots, x_{k_1}) \;=\; f_{1,1}(\mathbf{t}_{1,1}), \ldots, f_{1,m_1}(\mathbf{t}_{1,m_1})$$
$$\vdots$$
$$f_n(x_1, \ldots, x_{k_n}) \;=\; f_{n,1}(\mathbf{t}_{n,1}), \ldots, f_{n,m_n}(\mathbf{t}_{1,m_n})$$

for function symbols from $F = \{f_1, \ldots, f_n\}$. Let $m := \max\{m_i \mid 1 \le i \le n\}$ be the maximal number of recursive function calls in right-hand sides in P.

We consider the alphabet $\Sigma := F \times \{1, \ldots, m\}$ and define the language of ω-words $L_{\mathsf{call}} \subseteq \Sigma^\omega$ to be the set of all possible call sequences. I.e. we have $(f_0, d_0)(f_1, d_1)(f_2, d_2) \ldots \in L_{\mathsf{call}}^P$ iff $f_{i+1} = f_{i,d_i}$ for all $i \ge 0$. For simplicity we omit parentheses and commas and simply write such a call sequence as $f_0 d_0 f_1 d_1 \ldots$. The following is very easy to see.

Lemma 8.24 *Let P be a recursive program over F. Then L_{call}^P can be recognised by a DcoBA with $|F| + 1$ states.*

Clearly, L_{call}^P is then also ω-regular for any P.

Example 8.25 Let P_1 be the following recursive program over ternary functions f, g, h, i, k, defined as follows.

$$f(x,y,z) \;=\; g(x,x,y) \qquad\qquad i(x,y,z) \;=\; k(x,y-1,z-1)$$
$$g(x,y,z) \;=\; h(x,y-1,z-1) \qquad k(x,y,z) \;=\; f(x,y-1,z-1)$$
$$h(x,y,z) \;=\; i(x,y-1,z-1)$$

Then $L^{P_1}_{\text{call}}$ contains a few words only, namely the following five.

$$w_f \;:=\; (f1g1h1i1k1)^\omega \qquad\qquad w_i \;:=\; i1w_k$$
$$w_g \;:=\; g1w_h \qquad\qquad\qquad w_k \;:=\; k1w_f$$
$$w_h \;:=\; h1w_i$$

There is no designated starting symbol in a recursive program, comparable to a "main" function. It is simply not necessary to single out one of these symbols; we consider the program non-terminating when any of its functions is non-terminating. This is of course also the reason for the extra state needed in Lemma 8.24. If, say, f was the designated entry point into the program in Ex. 8.25, and we would only consider its termination, then a DcoBA with five states would suffice to recognise $L^{P_1}_{\text{call}}$, and this language would contain a single word only. On the other hand, this example shows nicely that termination of a particular function is in general not different to termination of all functions.

Example 8.26 Let P_2 be the recursive program

$$t(x,y,z,w) \;=\; t(x,x,z,w-1), t(x-1,z,w-1,y-1), t(z,x-1,y,w-1)$$

for the single function t of arity four. Then $L^{P_2}_{\text{call}} = (t1 + t2 + t3)^\omega$.

A call sequence is terminating if there is a parameter that gets decremented over and over again in this sequence. In such a case, no matter what the value of that parameter at the start was, it will eventually be reduced down to zero, causing termination of this sequence. For termination of the entire program to hold we need to demand termination of every call sequence in this respect. Note that different parameters can be responsible for termination of different call sequences. In order to address this formally we define a second language associated with a recursive program P, namely the language L^P_{term} of all call sequences that are terminating in this sense.

Example 8.27 Take the recursive program P modelling multiplication in Ex. 8.22. We have $(\text{mult2})^\omega \in L^P_{\text{term}}$ since variable y gets decremented over and over again in recursive calls through function mult. Other call sequences of the form $(\text{mult2})^* \text{mult1}(\text{add1})^\omega$ are also terminating because of variable y as well. This is a different variable y, though. When control flow passes from mult to add, the value of mult's parameter u gets written into add's parameter y. Still, the same reasoning applies here: regardless of what value this variable y had, either initially or finitely many steps later when the call sequence moves into function add, it will eventually reach value zero.

Take the program P_2 from Ex. 8.26. Here we have $(\text{t1})^\omega \in L^{P_2}_{\text{term}}$, even $(\text{t1}+\text{t3})^\omega \subseteq L^{P_2}_{\text{term}}$. On the other hand, we have $(\text{t2t3t1t3t1t3})^\omega \notin L^{P_2}_{\text{term}}$.

Termination, resp. non-termination is not always that easy to see, though.

Example 8.28 We write $f(\mathbf{x}) \rightsquigarrow g(\mathbf{y})$ to indicate that a call to f with parameters $\mathbf{x}$ entails a call to function g on parameters $\mathbf{y}$. Reconsider the recursive program P_1 from Ex. 8.25 now. We have

$$
\begin{aligned}
&\mathsf{f}(10,10,10) \rightsquigarrow \mathsf{g}(10,10,10) \rightsquigarrow \mathsf{h}(10,9,9) \rightsquigarrow \mathsf{i}(10,8,8) \rightsquigarrow \mathsf{k}(10,7,7) \rightsquigarrow \\
&\mathsf{f}(10,6,6) \quad\; \rightsquigarrow \mathsf{g}(10,10,6) \;\; \rightsquigarrow \mathsf{h}(10,9,5) \rightsquigarrow \mathsf{i}(10,8,4) \rightsquigarrow \mathsf{k}(10,7,3) \rightsquigarrow \\
&\mathsf{f}(10,6,2) \quad\; \rightsquigarrow \mathsf{g}(10,10,6) \;\; \rightsquigarrow \ldots
\end{aligned}
$$

so $\mathsf{f}(10,10,10)$ is not defined, and neither is a call to f on larger parameter values. On the other hand, it is possible to find smaller instances on which the call terminates.

Analysing the termination behaviour of the recursive program P_2 from Ex. 8.26 reveals some combinatorial intricacies. We have

$$
\begin{aligned}
&\mathsf{t}(3,10,11,4) \rightsquigarrow \mathsf{t}(2,11,3,9) \;\; \rightsquigarrow \mathsf{t}(3,1,11,8) \;\; \rightsquigarrow \mathsf{t}(3,3,11,7) \rightsquigarrow \\
&\mathsf{t}(11,2,3,6) \;\; \rightsquigarrow \mathsf{t}(11,11,3,5) \rightsquigarrow \mathsf{t}(3,10,11,4) \rightsquigarrow \ldots
\end{aligned}
$$

which shows that $\mathsf{t}(3,10,11,4)$ is not defined. However, $\mathsf{t}(10,10,10,10)$ is defined.

The way that termination of recursive programs reduces to inclusion checking between regular languages should slowly become visible: program P terminates iff $L^P_{\text{call}} \subseteq L^P_{\text{term}}$, i.e. all valid call sequences are terminating in the respect above. It remains to be seen that L^P_{term} is also ω-regular. The following lemma does not provide an NBA for L^P_{term} but for an overapproximation of that language. The reason is not that it is not ω-regular, but only that it is much simpler and also sufficient to let the NBA also potentially accept non-valid call sequences.

Lemma 8.29 *Let P be a recursive program over F with $m := \max\{ar(f) \mid f \in F\}$. There is an NBA $\mathcal{A}^P_{\text{term}}$ with at most $2m+1$ states such that $L(\mathcal{A}^P_{\text{term}}) \cap L^P_{\text{call}} = L^P_{\text{term}}$.*

Proof For simplicity we assume that $ar(f) = m$ for all $f \in F$, not just $ar(f) \leq m$. This can be achieved for example by introducing dummy variables that simply get passed through to recursive calls without decrements. So let $F = \{f_1, \ldots, f_n\}$ and

$$
f_i(x_{i,1}, \ldots, x_{i,m}) = g_{i,1}(t^1_{i,1}, \ldots, t^m_{i,1}), \ldots, g_{i,k}(t^k_{i,1}, \ldots, t^k_{i,m})
$$

be the definition for function symbol f_i in P for every $i = 1, \ldots, n$ where each $t^d_{i,k}$ is either $y^d_{i,k}$ or $y^d_{i,k} - 1$ for some variable $y^d_{i,k}$.

We construct an NBA $\mathcal{A}^P_{\text{term}} := (Q \cup \{q_I\}, \Sigma, q_I, \delta, F)$ as follows. Its states, except one, are pairs consisting of a parameter index and a flag: $Q := (\{1, \ldots, m\} \times \{0,1\}) \cup \{q_I\}$. Intuitively, $\mathcal{A}^P_{\text{term}}$ guesses a parameter (represented by an index between 1 and m) and then follows the evolution of values initially stored in this parameter through a call sequence. Whenever it observes a decrement operation, it signals this with its flag. Thus,

$$\delta\big((j,b),(f_i,d)\big) \ := \ \{(h,0) \mid t_{i,h}^d = x_{i,j}\} \cup \{(h,1) \mid t_{i,h}^d = x_{i,j} - 1\}$$

for any state (j,b) and any alphabet symbol (f_i,d). Accepting states are traversed whenever a decrement of the parameter that is followed has been encountered: $F := \{1,\ldots,m\} \times \{1\}$.

By a standard construction, q_I is given transitions to mimic the behaviour of all other states, thus obtaining an NBA with a unique initial state that uses its nondeterminism to guess, initially, the parameter that gets decreased infinitely often. Note that this is not the only form of nondeterminism used in δ. Each parameter can potentially be used multiple times in any recursive call, and $\mathcal{A}_{\text{term}}^P$ can guess which occurrence to follow.

It should be clear that $\mathcal{A}_{\text{term}}^P$ accepts a valid call sequence from L_{call}^P iff it is possible to trace some parameter value through this call sequence whilst seeing infinitely many decrement operations on this parameter, i.e. iff the call sequence is terminating. Likewise, the statement on its size is easily seen to be true as well. □

Example 8.30 Reconsider the recursive program P from Ex. 8.22 modelling multiplication. The corresponding NBA according to Lemma 8.29 has the following transitions.

$$\begin{aligned}
\delta\big((1,_),(\mathsf{add},1)\big) &= \{(1,0)\} & \delta\big((2,_),(\mathsf{add},1)\big) &= \{(2,1)\} \\
\delta\big((1,_),(\mathsf{mult},1)\big) &= \{(1,0)\} & \delta\big((2,_),(\mathsf{mult},1)\big) &= \varnothing \\
\delta\big((3,_),(\mathsf{mult},1)\big) &= \{(2,0)\} & \delta\big((1,_),(\mathsf{mult},2)\big) &= \{(1,0)\} \\
\delta\big((2,_),(\mathsf{mult},2)\big) &= \{(2,1)\} & \delta\big((3,_),(\mathsf{mult},2)\big) &= \{(3,1)\}
\end{aligned}$$

An immediate consequence of Lemma 8.24 and 8.29 is the decidability of the size-change termination problem, i.e. the problem of deciding termination for recursive programs of the simple form considered here.

Theorem 8.31 *The size-change-termination problem is decidable in exponential time.*

Proof Let P be a recursive program P, and $\mathcal{A}_{\text{call}}^P$, $\mathcal{A}_{\text{term}}^P$ be the DcoBA, resp. NBA for it according to Lemma 8.24 and 8.29. Then P is terminating iff $L(\mathcal{A}_{\text{call}}^P) \subseteq L(\mathcal{A}_{\text{term}}^P)$. Note that this holds even though $L(\mathcal{A}_{\text{term}}^P) \supseteq L_{\text{term}}^P$ in general.

Both automata are of size linear in $|P|$, and a DcoBA can easily be transformed into an NBA under a linear blowup only. Hence, size-change termination can be decided by a linear reduction to the subsumption problem for NBA, which is decidable in exponential time: Thm. 8.14 reduces it polynomially to universality and Cor. 8.15 states that it is decidable in exponential time. □

The nature of the size-change termination problem allows a short-cut to be taken. For two ω-languages $L_1, L_2 \subseteq \Sigma^\omega$ we do not only have $L_1 \subseteq L_2$ iff $L_1 \cap \overline{L_2} = \varnothing$ but also, by simple reasoning using deMorgan rules, $L_1 \subseteq L_2$ iff $\overline{L_1} \cup L_2 = \Sigma^\omega$. Now, in this particular case, L_{call}^P is DcoBA-recognisable according to Lemma 8.24. Hence, its complement is DBA-recognisable according to Thm. 6.32 and therefore clearly also NBA-recognisable. NBA-recognisable languages are closed under unions according to Lemma 5.9. Thus, it is easy to obtain an NBA directly for the language $L(\mathcal{A}^P_{\text{call}}) \cup L(\mathcal{A}^P_{\text{term}})$, and this can be checked for universality directly instead of checking subsumption between $L(\mathcal{A}^P_{\text{call}})$ and $L(\mathcal{A}^P_{\text{term}})$.

We finish with a remark on the applicability of finite automata on ω-words for problems like size-change termination. Not only can simple program termination questions be reduced to NBA subsumption, resp. universality. Termination checking also arises in automatic theorem proving where proofs are only valid when they are well-founded, i.e. they derive statements from previously proved statements. Thus, a proof construction process needs to be terminating in a very similar sense to the notion of program termination studied here.

Bibliographic Notes

Decidability of emptiness for Büchi automata is a direct consequence of Büchi's Theorem characterising ω-regular languages as finite unions of concatenations between a regular language and the infinite iteration of a regular language. It is easy to observe that emptiness of an NBA is answered by two nested graph reachability analyses. Thus, decidability of the NBA emptiness problem was answered in Büchi's seminal work within the context of establishing decidability of S1S, the monadic theory of the natural numbers with a successor relation [Büc62].

Basic algorithms on directed graphs starting from depth-first and breadth-first search and also including algorithms to compute SCC decompositions are routinely covered in courses and textbooks on algorithms and data structures, cf. [CLRS22, SW11, AHU83]. Tarjan's algorithm [Tar72] is just one example of a linear-time algorithm to compute an SCC decomposition. Another one is Kosaraju-Sharir's algorithm [Sha81], using similar observations about the use of the transposed graph for this purpose.

The textbook by Esparza and Blondin [EB23] sheds a light onto automata theory from a particular algorithmic perspective and therefore considers problems like non-emptiness for Büchi automata in a more in-depth way than it is done here.

Universality and subsumption are of course the more interesting problems from a computational perspective, and this is also reflected in the literature containing work on these problems. The presentation in this chapter does not follow the historical development. Decidability of these two problems was of course established in theory by Büchi's proof of complementation closure of ω-regular languages [Büc62], but it was not necessarily seen as a practically viable procedure. Subsequent work on the determinisation problem did not change this until Safra presented a determinisation (and consequently complementation) procedure that runs in time $2^{o(n^2)}$ [Saf88]. Still, it turned out not to be very practical and the search for other algorithms continued.

Unlike it is presented here, size-change termination was not developed as an application of NBA subsumption. The problem was considered interesting in program analysis, and easily seen to be solvable by a reduction to NBA subsumption, resp.

universality. However, at the time algorithms for the latter were only considered to be of theoretical interest and not of practical viability. Jones et al. then developed the method that is presented here for NBA universality as an approach for program termination that avoids the use of Büchi automata and explicit complementation thereof [LJBA01]. The method – also often called *Ramsey-based* because of the use of Ramsey's Theorem in the correctness proof – has only then become popular as a practical approach for problems in the area of automata theory and logic that avoids explicit complementation. Dax et al. [DHL06] were the first to use it in a decision procedure for a temporal logic, namely the so-called linear-time μ-calculus [BB89, Var88]. It exceeds the expressiveness of the popular temporal logic LTL (see Chp. 10) and is in fact expressively equivalent to Büchi automata.

Ramsey-based universality checking was then finally accepted as a practically viable algorithmic approach to decision problems on Büchi automata [FV10], its origin in the size-change termination problem was duly noted [FV12], and its use in universality and subsumption checking [ACC$^+$10, ACC$^+$11] as well as explicit complementation [BLO12] was studied intensively. The Ramsey-based method has also been extended to parity automata [FL12a] and even to automata models beyond the expressiveness of ω-regular languages [FKL15].

The success that Ramsey-based methods have had in universality and subsumption checking may have put explicit complementation constructions out of competition for good which are generally being avoided by modern approaches [DGPR21, DGW24].

Another general method that has proven to be very useful in checking language inclusion and related problems and which is not covered here, is the so-called *anti-chain method*. It can be seen as an on-the-fly symbolic powerset construction, and it is best understood as a method for NFA universality testing [WDHR06, DR10]. Nevertheless, it has successfully been extended to yield practically efficient algorithms for problems in program verification that essentially boil down to Büchi automata subsumption checking [WDMR08, DR09].

Exercises

Exercise 81 Let $\mathcal{G} = (V, E)$ be a directed graph.

  a) Let C, C' be two maximal SCCs in $\mathcal{G}$. Show that $C = C'$ or $C \cap C' = \emptyset$.
  b) Conclude from part (a) that the SCC decomposition of $\mathcal{G}$ is unique.

Exercise 82 Show how to compute the transitive closure of a directed graph in time $\mathcal{O}(n^3)$.

Exercise 83 Give an algorithm for deciding non-emptiness for NMA by internalising the translation from an NMA into an NBA (cf. Thm. 6.24) followed by a non-emptiness check for NBA.

Exercise 84 Explain how to solve the non-emptiness problem for nondeterministic co-Büchi automata.

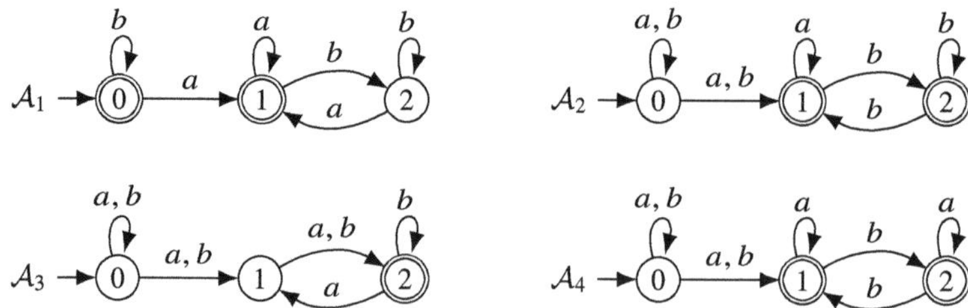

Fig. 8.2 Four NBA to test for non-universality in Exc. 91.

Exercise 85 Complete the missing details in the proof of Thm. 8.14, i.e. give the technical details of the construction of the NBA C_1, C_2, C_3.

Exercise 86 Explain what modifications are needed in the reduction from the subsumption problem to the universality problem for NBA (proof of Thm. 8.14) in order to obtain reductions from subsumption to universality for NcoBA, NPA, NRA, NSA and NMA.

Exercise 87 Show that the universality problem for deterministic Streett automata with e many transitions and index k can be solved in time $\mathcal{O}(ek)$. *Hint:* Use Thm. 8.6.

Exercise 1 Determine emptiness of the language of the following Streett automaton with acceptance condition

$$\mathcal{F} = \{(\{1\}, \{4, 5\}), (\{7, 8\}, \{2, 3\}), (\{4\}, \{6\})\}$$

using the algorithm underlying Thm. 8.12.

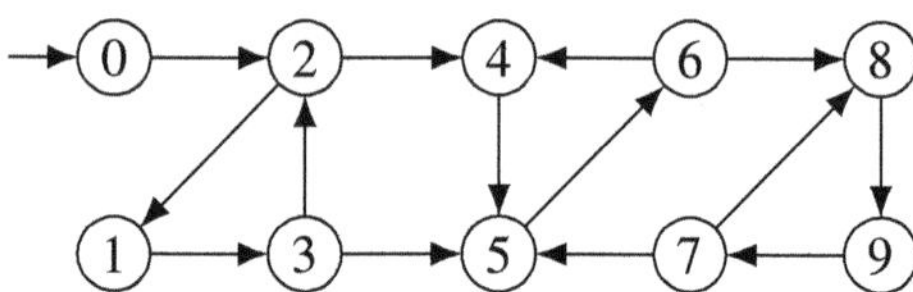

Transition labels have been left out since they are not relevant for language emptiness.

Exercise 88 Prove Lemma 8.16.

Exercise 89 Write down the entire multiplication table for the monoid of the equivalence classes $[w]$ for the NBA shown in Fig. 8.1 that are listed in Ex. 8.17.

Exercise 90 Consider all idempotent boxes $[v]$ other than $[aa]$ in Ex. 8.19, and determine for each of them whether there is a box $[u]$ such that the pair satisfies the conditions laid out in Thm. 8.18.

Exercise 91 Use Thm. 8.18 to decide whether $L(\mathcal{A}_i) = \{a, b\}^\omega$ for each of the NBA $\mathcal{A}_i$, $i = 1, \ldots, 4$, shown in Fig. 8.2. In each case, construct the finite set of boxes arising as the composition closure of $\{[a], [b]\}$ for this NBA, select the idempotent ones and determine whether they can be used as a witness for non-universality according to the characterisation in Thm. 8.18.

Exercise 92 Prove Thm. 8.20.

Exercise 93 Give a characterisation of universality for nondeterministic parity automata as a search problem in a finite monoid along the lines of Thm. 8.18. *Hint:* Extend the notion of a box as follows. A line from an in-port to an out-port is not just unmarked or marked, but it carries a priority. A line from p to q with label m in the box $[w]$ is supposed to say that the best priority that can be achieved (in terms of an accepting run) when reading w in state p and ending in state q, is m. The composition of two such boxes needs to be explained in detail. In particular, when composing two boxes there can be multiple paths from q to q'' via different intermediate states q'. Composition needs two different orders on priorities: one is used to determine what the significant priority is when composing two paths, the other is used to determine what the best composed path is when there are several ones. In the case of NBA, both operations degenerate to simple disjunctions: a path visits an accepting state if one of its parts does, and amongst several paths from one state to another the best is the one that visits an accepting state.

Exercise 94 Consider the recursive program of Ex. 8.25 and determine the largest values for x, y, und z such that $f(x, y, z)$ is defined.

Exercise 95 Consider the following recursive program P over $\{f, g, h\}$.

$$
\begin{aligned}
f(x, y, z) &= f(x, x, z - 1), g(z, y, x) \\
g(x, y, z) &= f(x, y - 1, z), h(z, x, y) \\
h(x, y, z) &= f(x - 1, y, z)
\end{aligned}
$$

a) Construct a DcoBA $\mathcal{A}^P_{\text{call}}$ such that $L(\mathcal{A}^P_{\text{call}}) = L^P_{\text{call}}$.
b) Construct an NBA $\mathcal{A}^P_{\text{term}}$ such that $L(\mathcal{A}^P_{\text{term}}) \cap L^P_{\text{call}} = L^P_{\text{term}}$.
c) Construct an NBA $\mathcal{A}^P$ such that $L(\mathcal{A}^P) = \overline{L^P_{\text{call}}} \cup L^P_{\text{term}}$.
d) Use the Ramsey-based method to determine whether P terminates for all values of its parameters by checking $L(\mathcal{A}^P)$ for universality.

Exercise 96 a) Prove Lemma 8.24.
  b) Construct the DcoBA for the languages L^P_{call} for the recursive programs P from Ex. 8.22, 8.23, 8.25 and 8.26.

Exercise 97 Reconsider the recursive program from Ex. 8.26. Show that the value of $t(3, 10, 11, 4)$ is defined, i.e. that all call sequences starting on this call terminate. *Hint:* Write a program that uses dynamic programming to answer this question.

Exercise 98 Construct the NBA $\mathcal{A}^{P_1}_{\text{term}}$ according to Lemma 8.29 for the recursive program P_1 from Ex. 8.25.

Chapter 9
Alternating Büchi Automata

In Chapter 3 we introduced alternating automata as an extension of nondeterministic finite automata operating on finite words. They turned out not to be more expressive than NFA but generally more succinct, i.e. there are languages that can be recognised by AFA which are exponentially smaller than the smallest equivalent NFA.

There is no reason why the concept of alternation with its two modes of branching – nondeterministic and universal – should be restricted to automata operating on finite words only. In this chapter we consider alternating automata operating on infinite words as an extension of Büchi automata just in the same way as AFA extend NFA. An obvious question that arises with this is that of expressiveness: do alternating Büchi automata exceed the power of nondeterministic Büchi automata to recognise more than ω-regular languages? The answer will be negative again. While the possibility to translate NFA into DFA does not extend to Büchi automata, the possibility to eliminate alternation does extend to Büchi automata. However, the construction is a little bit more complicated than the simple powerset construction turning AFA into NFA. On the other hand, it is much simpler than the translation from NBA into DRA or DPA studied in Chp. 7.

This chapter is mainly concerned with alternating automata that recognise words via the Büchi condition. Co-Büchi automata will also play a role as they provide the means for simple complementation constructions. It is possible to study alternating automata with any of the other acceptance conditions introduced in Chapter 6, i.e. alternating parity, Rabin, Streett and Muller automata. Details of such investigations, in particular the possibility to eliminate alternation, are left as exercises. Here we only remark that none of these combinations exceeds the limits of ω-regularity in expressiveness either.

9.1 Alternating Automata on Infinite Words

9.1.1 Syntax and Semantics

Just as NBA cannot be distinguished syntactically from NFA, alternating Büchi automata are no different to AFA syntactically. In particular, their transition functions map pairs of states and alphabet letters to positive Boolean combinations of states. Conjunctions in there can be interpreted again as the automaton reading the rest of the word from multiple states in parallel. In order to facilitate this, runs are trees again. However, these trees are now infinite in general, since so are the underlying words.

Definition 9.1 An *alternating Büchi automaton* (ABA) is an $\mathcal{A} = (Q, \Sigma, q_I, \delta, F)$ just like an AFA. In particular, we have $q_I \in Q$, $\delta : Q \times \Sigma \to \mathbb{B}^+(Q)$ and $F \subseteq Q$. The size of an ABA is measured in terms of the number of its states as usual.

A run of the ABA $\mathcal{A}$ on a word $w = a_0 a_1 \ldots \in \Sigma^\omega$ is an infinite Q-labelled tree ρ with the following properties.

- The root node v_0 is labelled with the initial state: $\rho(v_0) = q_I$.
- Let v be a node on level i (with the root node being on level 0), and let $v_1, \ldots, v_m$ be all its successors (necessarily on level $i + 1$). Then we have

$$\{\rho(v_i) \mid i \in \{1, \ldots, m\}\} \models \delta(\rho(v), a_i)$$

Such a run is *accepting* if for every (necessarily infinite) branch $v_0, v_1, v_2, \ldots$ there are infinitely many i such that $\rho(v_i) \in F$.

As usual, the language of the ABA $\mathcal{A}$ is $L(\mathcal{A}) := \{w \in \Sigma^\omega \mid$ there is an accepting run of $\mathcal{A}$ on $w\}$.

It is easy to see that ABA are at least as expressive as NBA. The proof of the following theorem is left as an exercise.

Theorem 9.2 *For every NBA $\mathcal{A}$ with n states there is an ABA $\mathcal{B}$ with at most $n + 1$ states such that $L(\mathcal{B}) = L(\mathcal{A})$.*

The construction is entirely analogous to the one that embeds NFA into AFA, cf. Thm. 3.10, simply expressing nondeterminism in terms of disjunctions in Boolean formulas in the transition table. The construction requires the transition table of the underlying NBA to be total, i.e. there being at least one successor for every state under any alphabet symbol. This could be avoided if Boolean functions in an ABA's transition table were allowed to include the constants *true* and *false*. Then getting stuck in an NBA could be modelled using *false*. But then runs could have finite branches, and those that end with a transition to *true* would have to count for acceptance as well. For general simplicity in the constructions on alternating automata, we omit these Boolean constants.

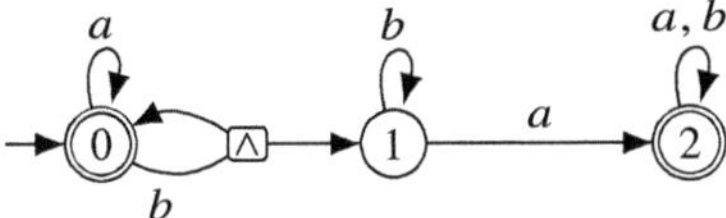

Fig. 9.1 ABA $\mathcal{A}$ for the language $\{w \in \{a, b\}^\omega \mid |w|_a = \infty\}$.

Example 9.3 Consider the ω-regular language $L = \{w \in \{a, b\}^\omega \mid |w|_a = \infty\}$. It is a standard exercise to construct a two-state NBA recognising L. With Thm. 9.2 we immediately obtain an ABA for L, too. This degenerate ABA – not making use of proper alternation at all – does not shed any real insight into the usefulness of alternation for recognising ω-regular languages, or onto their conceptual difference to NBA.

It is possible, though, to construct a genuine ABA recognising L, i.e. one that makes use of universal branching. The underlying idea here is that in linear structures, "infinitely often" is the same as "always eventually", i.e. an ω-word contains infinitely many symbols a iff for every position i there is some position $j \geq i$ such that $w(j) = a$.

We make use of this correspondence to construct an ABA for L that works as follows. It successively reads the next symbol from an input word w. If it is an a then the ABA can simply continue with the next letter. When it is not an a, then it employs universal branching. One part continues with the next letter, the other part reads symbols until it has found an a at some point in the future.

The ABA $\mathcal{A} := (\{0, 1, 2\}, \Sigma, 0, \delta, \{0, 2\})$ with

$$\delta(0, a) = 0 \qquad \delta(1, a) = 2 \qquad \delta(2, x) = 2 \ \text{ for } x \in \{a, b\}$$
$$\delta(0, b) = 0 \wedge 1 \qquad \delta(1, b) = 1$$

is shown in Fig. 9.1. We depict alternation in the transition function naturally with intermediate nodes for universal ($\wedge$) or existential ($\vee$) branching.

A run of $\mathcal{A}$ on the word $(abb)^\omega$ is shown in Fig. 9.2. The nodes' labels are shown inside the nodes. The fact that it is an accepting run and, moreover, that $L(\mathcal{A}) = L$, can be seen as follows. On any word, each run will have a branch of the form $0, 0, 0, \ldots$ – here shown as the leftmost one. The i-th node on this branch has a single child (which is necessarily labelled 0 as well) if the i-th letter (starting from 0) of the underlying word is a. Otherwise, if it is b, then this node has two children: one on this path with all nodes labelled 0, and another starting a path with labels of the form 1^+2^ω or 1^ω. The number of occurrences of 1 on this path is determined by the distance from position i to the next a in the underlying word.

In particular, if the underlying word is of the form $(a + b)^* b^\omega$, then the run will have a branch of the form $0^* 1^\omega$, containing only finitely many accepting states, namely state 0. On the other hand, on a word of the form $((a + b)^* a)^\omega$, there is one branch of the form 0^ω, obviously containing infinitely many accepting states, and all other branches are of the form $0^+ 1^+ 2^\omega$, and these also contain infinitely many accepting states, namely state 2.

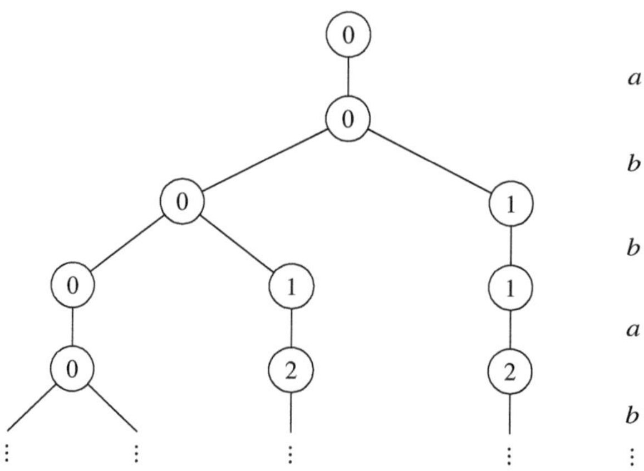

Fig. 9.2 Run of the ABA from Ex. 9.3 on the word $(abb)^{\omega}$.

The analysis of the general functionality of $\mathcal{A}$ from this example shows that it would also accept the language of all words having infinitely many symbols a, if seen as an alternating co-Büchi automaton. Branches of any run that contain infinitely many accepting states will necessarily eventually see accepting states only.

It is reasonable to question the usefulness of ABA over NBA, based on this example, where the "genuine" ABA recognising the given language is larger than the standard NBA. However, it has an interesting structural property that NBA do not possess: it is a *weak* alternating automaton. We will study weakness in detail later on in Sect. 9.5. Here we remark that the possibility to see $\mathcal{A}$ above as an alternating co-Büchi automaton without changing its language is not a coincidence; instead, it is essentially what weakness is: the irrelevance of a distinction between Büchi and co-Büchi acceptance.

9.1.2 Memoryless Runs

A *memoryless run* is defined as it is for AFA: two nodes on the same level that are labelled with the same state cannot be the roots of two different subtrees. The run shown in Fig. 9.2 is memoryless. In fact, all runs of the ABA $\mathcal{A}$ from Ex. 9.3 are always memoryless. This is a consequence of the simplicity of this ABA: starting in any state, the run on any input word is uniquely determined. This is a property of this particular ABA, though, and not of ABA in general as the following example shows.

Example 9.4 Reconsider the language L of words having infinitely many symbols a from Ex. 9.3. It is also recognised by the ABA $\mathcal{B}$ shown in Fig. 9.3. It differs from the ABA $\mathcal{A}$ from Ex. 9.3 in that, upon reading an a in state 1, it does not have to go

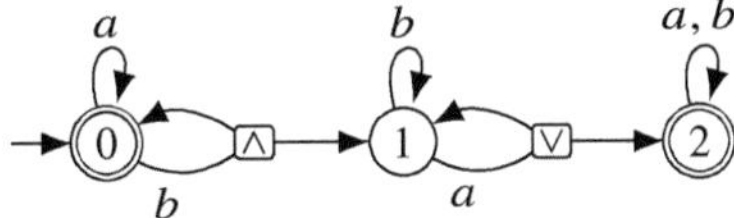

Fig. 9.3 ABA $\mathcal{B}$ for the language $\{w \in \{a, b\}^\omega \mid |w|_a = \infty\}$.

to state 2 but can choose to remain in state 1. This is done using a nondeterministic choice which is depicted in Fig. 9.3 with an auxiliary $\vee$-node.

The argument for why we have $L(\mathcal{B}) = L$ proceeds along the same lines as for $\mathcal{A}$ in Ex. 9.3: any accepting run will have one branch of the form 0^ω, some branches of the form 0^+1^ω on any word $w \notin L$, respectively all other branches of the form $0^+1^+2^\omega$ on words $w \in L$. Hence, all branches have infinitely many accepting states iff the underlying word belongs to L.

There is one minor difference to the analysis on branches in runs of $\mathcal{A}$, though: in a branch of the form $0^i 1^j 2^\omega$, j is not determined anymore by the distance from the i-th position to *the next* position carrying an a. Instead, it is the distance between the i-th position and *some* future position carrying an a. In other words, the purpose of state 1 in both $\mathcal{A}$ and $\mathcal{B}$ is to check for the future occurrence of a letter a which then leads to a transition into state 2. Whilst $\mathcal{A}$ does this as soon as it is possible, $\mathcal{B}$ can choose to do so with any future a. Note that $\mathcal{B}$ also has non-accepting runs on words in L that arise from never taking the transition from 1 to 2 even though it would be possible.

A run of $\mathcal{B}$ on $(ba)^\omega$ is shown in Fig. 9.4. It is not memoryless because different branches that visit state 1 on the same level use different symbols a to transition into state 2.

Memoryless runs are the key to algorithmic properties of ABA since they can be represented as DAGs of fixed width, namely the number of different states of the underlying ABA. So we aim, again, for the result that memoryless runs suffice in the sense that whenever a word is accepted by an ABA then this is witnessed by the existence of a memoryless run. This cannot be proved, though, as it was done for AFA on finite words. Runs are infinite trees now, and these cannot be constructed by induction on their height. Alternatively, the result for AFA can be shown by turning a non-memoryless run into a memoryless one by successively replacing subtrees. It is also not possible to simply argue for the existence of a memory-less run that is obtained by successively replacing subtrees that violate memorylessness, because the final result is only obtained in the limit of this process and not after some final replacement. In this case, we additionally need a measure for the progress made towards obtaining a memoryless run when doing these successive replacements which allows us to argue that the limit of this process has the desired property.

Definition 9.5 Let ρ be a run of an ABA $\mathcal{A} = (Q, \Sigma, q_I, \delta, F)$ on a word $w \in \Sigma^\omega$. The *rank* of a node v, written rk_v, is the maximal k in a sequence $v_0, \ldots, v_k$ such that

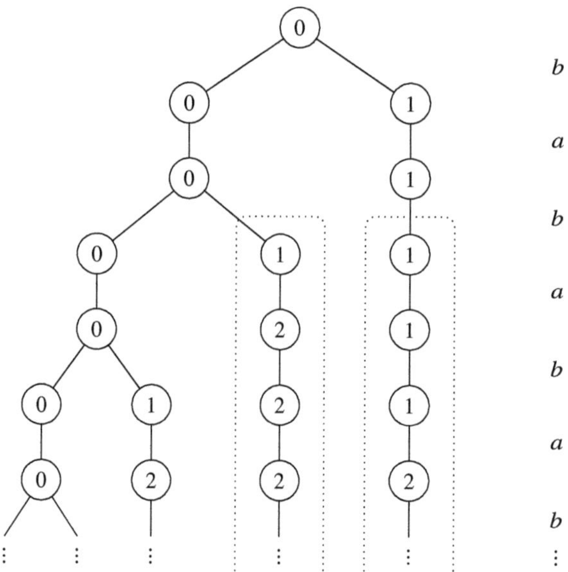

Fig. 9.4 Non-memoryless run of the ABA from Ex. 9.4 on the word $(ba)^\omega$.

- $v = v_0$,
- for all $i \in [k]$ we have: v_{i+1} is a successor of v_i in ρ,
- $\rho(v_k) \in F$ and $\rho(v_i) \notin F$ for all $i < k$.

In particular we have $rk_v = 0$ if $\rho(v) \in F$, and $rk_v = \infty$ if there is a path v through ρ starting in v that never visits an accepting state.

A *level* of the run ρ is a maximal set of nodes that are all located at equal distance from the root node. The rank of a level V is the maximal rank of all its nodes: $rk_V := \max\{rk_v \mid v \in V\}$.

Lemma 9.6 *Let* $\mathcal{A} = (Q, \Sigma, q_I, \delta, F)$ *be an ABA and* ρ *be a run of* $\mathcal{A}$ *on some* $w \in \Sigma^\omega$. *Then* ρ *is accepting iff every level in* ρ *has finite rank.*

Proof We will show that indeed the following four statements are equivalent, from which the lemma's claim follows immediately, since it prescribes the equivalence of two of these.

a) Every node in ρ has finite rank.
b) Every level in ρ has finite rank.
c) Infinitely many levels have finite rank.
d) The run ρ is accepting.

"(a) $\Rightarrow$ (b)" This is a consequence of the fact that ρ is a finitely-branching tree. Hence, if V is a level then $|V| < \infty$ and therefore $\max\{rk_v \mid v \in V\} < \infty$ if $rk_v < \infty$ for all $v \in V$.

"(b) $\Rightarrow$ (c)" Trivial.

"(c) $\Rightarrow$ (d)" By contradiction. Suppose that ρ was not accepting. I.e. it contains some path $v_0, v_1, \ldots$ that visits accepting states only finitely often. Let $m := \max\{i \mid \rho(v_i) \in F\}$. By assumption, m exists. Moreover, we have $rk_{v_i} = \infty$ for all $i > m$ as each such v_i is clearly the source of a path that does not visit accepting states anymore.

Now let $V_0, V_1, \ldots$ be the levels of ρ in descending order. Note that $v_i \in V_i$ for all $i \geq 0$. Since the rank of a level can never be smaller than the rank of any of its elements, we have $rk_{V_i} = \infty$ for all $i > m$ as well. This shows that there can be at most finitely many levels with finite rank.

"(d) $\Rightarrow$ (a)" By contradiction. Suppose there was some node v such that $rk_v = \infty$. Then there would be a path $v_0, v_1, \ldots$ starting in v that does not visit accepting states. Since the distance of v to the root is finite, there can be at most finitely many accepting states on the unique path starting in the root of ρ, traversing to v and then continuing along $v_1, v_2, \ldots$ Hence, ρ would contain a path that does not visit accepting states infinitely often and, therefore, ρ would not be accepting. $\qquad\square$

We say that a run ρ of $\mathcal{A}$ on w with levels $V_0, V_1, \ldots$ is *memoryless* on level i if there are no two nodes $v, v' \in V_i$ such that $\rho(v) = \rho(v')$ but the two subtrees t under v and t' under v' differ. Clearly, ρ is memoryless if it is memoryless on all levels $i \geq 0$.

Lemma 9.7 *Let $n \geq 1$, $\mathcal{A} = (Q, \Sigma, q_I, \delta, F)$ be an ABA, $w \in \Sigma^\omega$ and ρ be an accepting run of $\mathcal{A}$ on w that is memoryless on levels $0, \ldots, n - 1$. Then there is a run $\widehat{\rho}$ of $\mathcal{A}$ on w that is memoryless on levels $0, \ldots, n$, and the rank of the i-th level in $\widehat{\rho}$ is bounded by the rank of the i-th level in ρ.*

Proof Let $w = a_0 a_1 \ldots$, and $V_0, V_1, \ldots$ be the levels of ρ in descending order. If V_n does not contain two nodes that violate the property of being memoryless on level n, then simply take $\widehat{\rho} := \rho$. Otherwise let $v, v' \in V_n$ such that $\rho(v) = \rho(v')$ but the subtree t' rooted at v' differs from the subtree t rooted at v. W.l.o.g. we assume $rk_v \leq rk_{v'}$.

Let ρ' result from ρ by replacing the subtree t' rooted at v' with the subtree t. We claim that ρ' is also an accepting run of $\mathcal{A}$ on w. Since $\rho(v') = \rho(v)$, the fact that the labels of successor nodes form a model of the transition function at the respective position, is not violated: let v'' be the parent node of v', residing on level V_{n-1}, and let $M \subseteq V_n$ be the set of its successor nodes. By assumption we have $\{\rho(u) \mid u \in M\} \models \delta(\rho(v''), a_{n-1})$. Hence, we also have

$$\{\rho(u) \mid u \in (M \setminus \{v'\}) \cup \{v\}\} \models \delta(\rho(v''), a_{i-1}) \, .$$

Thus, the replacement of t' by (a copy of) t preserves the property of being a run of $\mathcal{A}$ on w. It should be clear that this operation cannot increase the rank of any level because the levels in ρ' are subsets of the respective levels in ρ.

Since each level of a run is finite, in particular $|V_n| < \infty$, this process can be iterated with potentially other pairs of nodes on level i until one obtains a run $\widehat{\rho}$ that is memoryless on level n as well. Since levels $V_0, \ldots, V_{n-1}$ are left untouched, $\widehat{\rho}$ has the properties demanded in the lemma's statement. $\square$

This allows us now to prove that it suffices to consider memoryless runs only for determining whether a given ABA accepts a given word.

Theorem 9.8 *Let $\mathcal{A} = (Q, \Sigma, q_I, \delta, F)$ be an ABA and $w \in \Sigma^\omega$. We have $w \in L(\mathcal{A})$ iff there is a memoryless accepting run of $\mathcal{A}$ on w.*

Proof "$\Leftarrow$" Trivial. "$\Rightarrow$" Assume that ρ is an accepting run of $\mathcal{A}$ on w. According to Lemma 9.6, all its ranks are finite. We now construct a sequence $\rho_0, \rho_1, \ldots$ of runs of $\mathcal{A}$ on w as follows. Let $\rho_0 := \rho$, and let $\rho_i := \widehat{\rho_{i-1}}$ for $i > 0$ according to Lemma 9.7. Then the following holds for any $n \geq 0$:

a) ρ_n is memoryless on levels $0, \ldots, n$. This is trivially true for ρ_0 since level 0 in a run cannot contain two different nodes, and it follows for $n > 0$ by induction using Lemma 9.7.

b) ρ_n is accepting. Again, this can be shown by induction. It is true for $n = 0$ by assumption. Suppose it is true for some $n \geq 0$. According to Lemma 9.6, the ranks of all levels in ρ_n are finite. According to Lemma 9.7, the ranks of levels in ρ_{n+1} are bounded by the ranks of the respective levels in ρ_n, so they must be finite as well. Using Lemma 9.6 again, we get that ρ_{n+1} is accepting as well.

c) Let $m > n$. Then ρ_m and ρ_n agree on levels $0, \ldots, m$. In other words, the construction of this sequence successively fixes the levels one-by-one.

Because of property (b), this sequence has a limit ρ^* which is defined level-wise as follows: its i-th level is the i-th level of all ρ_n for $n \geq i$. Note that this is well-defined. An immediate consequence of this is that ρ^* would be memoryless, provided that it is a run, because each of its levels has undergone the construction from Lemma 9.7 that eliminates violations of memorylessness on that level. But, likewise, ρ^* is easily seen to be a run of $\mathcal{A}$ on w. For this it suffices to consider an arbitrary node v on some arbitrary level n. Since this node and its successors also exists in all ρ_i for $i > n$, the transition relation must be satisfied at node v in ρ^*.

It remains to be seen that ρ^* is also accepting. According to Lemma 9.6 it suffices, again, to show that all its levels have finite ranks. Note that this is the case for each ρ_n, $n \geq 0$. Let $V_0, V_1, \ldots$ be the levels of ρ^*, and let $n \geq 0$. We make use of part (c) of the observations above, namely the fact that the n-th level V_n of ρ^* is also the n-th level of all ρ_i for $i \geq n$. Note that their ranks are all finite, even though they may not be the same for all such i. However, since the ranks of levels do not increase in the sequence $\rho_0, \rho_1, \ldots$, there is some k such that $rk_{V_n} = k$ in all but finitely many ρ_i. Hence, this rank only depends on the ranks of nodes on the next k levels. In other words, levels $V_n, \ldots, V_{n+k}$ of ρ^* agree with the respective levels in all ρ_i for $i \geq n + k$. Since the rank of V_n in these is finite, so must be the rank of V_n in ρ^*. $\square$

As mentioned in Chp. 3 already, memoryless runs can be represented as DAGs instead of trees, by simply sharing common subtrees on the same level. Fig. 9.5 shows a DAG representation of a (memoryless) run of the ABA $\mathcal{B}$ from Ex. 9.4. A general bound on the width of such DAGs – the maximal size of a level – in terms of

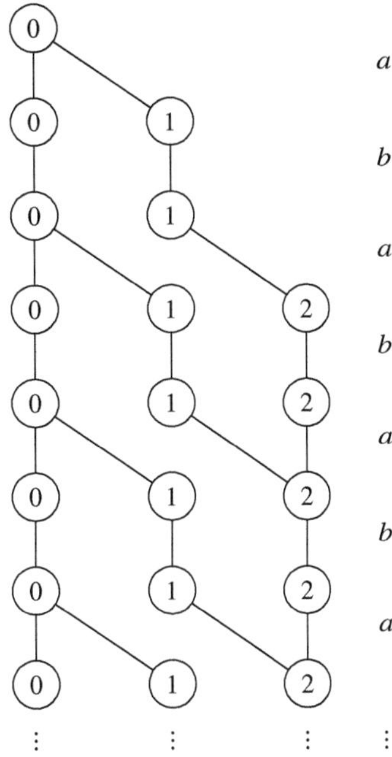

Fig. 9.5 DAG representation of a memoryless run of the ABA from Ex. 9.4 on the word $(ab)^\omega$.

the number of states of the underlying ABA is obtained immediately. We therefore also identify a level as a set of nodes in a memoryless run with the set of their labels.

9.2 A Game-Theoretic Semantics

As in the case of alternating automata on finite words, cf. Chp. 3, it is possible to explain acceptance of a word by an ABA in terms of winning strategies for one of two players in a game of perfect information. The role of the two players is the same, given an ABA $\mathcal{A}$ and a word $w \in \Sigma^\omega$: player 0's aim is to show that $w \in L(\mathcal{A})$, and player 1 wants to show that $w \notin L(\mathcal{A})$. The game progresses through the word, letter by letter, and through $\mathcal{A}$'s state space. It should be clear that this cannot be cast into the framework of reachability games anymore since, in general, acceptance of a word is not determined by a finite prefix of the word only. Hence, we need to extend the game-theoretic framework. We first introduce *Büchi games* as abstract two-player games of *infinite* duration and then make use of them to explain acceptance of a word by an ABA in terms of winning strategies in such games.

9.2.1 Büchi Games

Much of the technical development for the theory of reachability games, as introduced in Sect. 3.4, like the notions of players, arenas, plays, strategies, etc. can be re-used here as well.

Definition 9.9 A *Büchi game* is a $\mathcal{G} = (V, V_0, V_1, v_I, E, F)$ s.t. (V, E) is a directed graph with left-total and finitely-branching edge relation, $V = V_0 \uplus V_1$ is the partition of the node set into nodes owned by either of the two players, $v_I \in V$ is a designated initial node in the game, and $F \subseteq V$ is a designated set of accepting nodes.

The notions of plays, strategies, positional strategies and attractors are defined in the same way as they are for reachability games. The only difference lies in the interpretation of the winning condition, also given as a set F of nodes: a play $\rho = v_0, v_1, \ldots$ is *winning* for player 0, if $Inf(\rho) \cap F \neq \varnothing$, i.e. if it contains infinitely many accepting nodes. Otherwise it is winning for player 1.

Remember that, given a game $\mathcal{G} = (V, V_0, V_1, v_I, E, F)$, the attractor $Attr_p(T)$ of a set $T \subseteq V$ is the set of all nodes from which player p can force a play to eventually reach T. Recall that the construction of an attractor region, as given in Def. 3.23, assumes the graph underlying the game to be finitely-branching. This is the reason for the same requirement in Def. 9.9 above. It is equally possible to consider Büchi games of infinite branching degree, but then some of the technical developments, in particular the definition of attractors, would have to be extended.

It is not a surprise that attractors played a major role for the question of determining the winner in a reachability game. They seem less useful in Büchi games. However, note that, while player 0 attempts to enforce the set F to be reached in a reachability game, she needs to enforce *repeated* visits to F in a Büchi game. This leads to the following definition.

Definition 9.10 Let $\mathcal{G} = (V, V_0, V_1, v_I, E, F)$ be a Büchi game and $T \subseteq V$. We use the abbreviations $\Diamond T := \{v \in V \mid vE \cap T \neq \varnothing\}$ and $\Box T := \{v \in V \mid vE \subseteq T\}$.

The *repeated attractor* of $T \subseteq V$ for player $p \in \{0, 1\}$ is $rAttr_p(T) := \bigcap_{k \in \mathbb{N}} rAttr_p^k(T)$ where $rAttr_p^0(T) := V$ and

$$rAttr_p^{k+1}(T) := Attr_p\big(T \cap \big((V_p \cap \Diamond rAttr_p^k(T)) \cup (V_{1-p} \cap \Box rAttr_p^k(T))\big)\big)$$

for $k \geq 0$.

Thus, $rAttr_p^k(T)$ consists of all nodes from which player p can enforce at least k repeated visits to set T and, thus, $rAttr_p(T)$ is the set of all nodes from which player p can enforce infinitely many visits to T.

We will use games to show that alternating Büchi automata can easily be complemented into alternating co-Büchi automata by a conceptually simple dualisation construction. Its correctness proof is not that simple, though. It is the reason for introducing Büchi games in the first place, and we need the fundamental result of determinacy again.

Theorem 9.11 *Let $\mathcal{G}$ be a Büchi game, $p \in \{0, 1\}$.*

a) Exactly one of the players has a winning strategy for $\mathcal{G}$.

b) Player p has a winning strategy for $\mathcal{G}$ iff player p has a positional winning strategy for $\mathcal{G}$.

Proof Let $\mathcal{G} = (V, V_0, V_1, v_I, E, F)$ be a Büchi game. We will show the more general statement that for every $v \in V$, one of the players has a winning strategy for the game (V, V_0, V_1, v, E, F). Then surely one of the players must have a winning strategy for the game started in v_I. This then shows part (a) of the theorem, and part (b) follows by inspection of the construction which is easily seen to yield positional strategies.

We claim that

- player 0 has a positional winning strategy from all nodes in $rAttr_0(F)$, and
- player 1 has a positional winning strategy from all nodes in $V \smallsetminus rAttr_0(F)$.

For the former, suppose that $v \in rAttr_0(F) = \bigcap_{k \in \mathbb{N}} rAttr_0^k(F)$. Then, in particular, $v \in Attr_0(F)$. Hence, player 0 can enforce any play starting in v to reach F. Moreover, by the definition of $rAttr_0^k(F)$, she can then enforce such plays to progress to a node from which she can do so again. Hence, this combination of attractor strategies guarantees her to repeatedly visit nodes in F, and it is positional. The crucial insight here is given by the following argument. Suppose that this did not guarantee her to visit accepting nodes infinitely often. Then there would be some play conforming to this strategy that contains only finitely, say k many accepting nodes. This then contradicts the assumption that $v \in rAttr_0^{k+1}(F)$ which demands every play conforming to this strategy to visit accepting nodes at least $k + 1$ many times.

Now for the second claim, take a node $v \in V \smallsetminus rAttr_0(F)$. Player 1 has an even simpler strategy, namely an avoidance strategy. Note that $Attr_0(rAttr_0(F)) \subseteq rAttr_0(F)$, and consider two cases: if $v \in V_1$ then there must be some $w \in vE$ such that $w \notin Attr_0(rAttr_0(F))$, for otherwise if $vE \subseteq Attr_0(rAttr_0(F))$ then we would have $v \in Attr_0(rAttr_0(F))$ by the definition of an attractor and, hence, $v \in rAttr_0(F)$. In other words, when it is player 1's turn to move in a node outside of $rAttr_0(F)$, he can always move to some node that is also outside of $rAttr_0(F)$.

In the second case we have $v \in V_0$. By a similar argument, we must have $vE \subseteq V \smallsetminus Attr_0(rAttr_0(F))$ for otherwise, if there was some $w \in vE \cap Attr_0(rAttr_0(F))$ we would have $v \in Attr_0(rAttr_0(F)) \subseteq rAttr_0(F)$. In other words, player 0 cannot enforce a play to leave $V \smallsetminus rAttr_0(F)$.

This clearly defines a positional strategy σ_1 for player 1: for every $v \in V_1 \cap (V \smallsetminus rAttr_0(F))$ pick an arbitrary $w \in vE \cap (V \smallsetminus rAttr_0(F))$. Whenever a play visits v, move to w, i.e. $\sigma_1(v) := w$.

It remains to be seen that this is indeed a winning strategy, i.e. that every play conforming to this strategy is winning for player 1 or, equivalently, only visits accepting states finitely often. Suppose that this was not the case, i.e. there was a play $\rho = v_0, v_1, \ldots$ conforming to σ_1 such that there are $i_0 < i_1 < \ldots$ with $v_{i_j} \in F$ for all $j \geq 0$. This is not enough to obtain a contradiction right away because we need to contradict the assumption that $v_0 \in V \smallsetminus rAttr_0(F)$, i.e. we need to show that $v_0 \in rAttr_0(F)$. But there may be other choices in $\mathcal{G}$ from the nodes in ρ that lead to different plays and that need to be considered in an argument about attractors. We therefore assume that player 1's strategy σ_1 is best in the sense that choices other than those of the form $v \mapsto \sigma_1(v)$ would lead to earlier visits of accepting states in subsequent plays. Then we have $v_0 \in Attr_0(\{v_{i_j}\})$ for every $j \geq 0$. Since $v_{i_j} \in F$ for all $j \geq 0$, we get $v_0 \in rAttr_0(F)$, contradicting the assumption. $\qquad\square$

Definition 9.12 A *co-Büchi game* is a $\mathcal{G} = (V, V_0, V_1, v_I, E, F)$ defined like a Büchi game with the only difference that player 0 wins a play iff it eventually traverses through accepting states only.

Given a Büchi, resp. co-Büchi game $\mathcal{G} = (V, V_0, V_1, v_I, E, F)$, the *dual game* is the co-Büchi, resp. Büchi game $\overline{\mathcal{G}} := (V, V_1, V_0, v_I, E, V \setminus F)$.

Hence, a game is dualised by swapping the players' choices and dualising the winning condition. Note that a strategy σ for player p in $\mathcal{G}$ becomes a strategy for player $1 - p$ in $\overline{\mathcal{G}}$ because of the swapping of the roles. Moreover, it is player 1's goal, for example, to enforce plays that eventually only traverse through $V \setminus F$ for the winning condition F in a Büchi game. This is then exactly the winning condition in the dual co-Büchi game (for player 0). The following theorem is therefore easy to prove.

Theorem 9.13 *Let $\mathcal{G}$ be a Büchi or co-Büchi game. Player 0 wins $\mathcal{G}$ (with a positional strategy) iff player 1 wins $\overline{\mathcal{G}}$ (with a positional strategy).*

A consequence of determinacy in Thm. 9.11 and this duality principle is the following.

Corollary 9.14 *Let $\mathcal{G}$ be a Büchi or co-Büchi game, $p \in \{0, 1\}$. Player p has a (positional) winning strategy for $\mathcal{G}$ iff p does not have a winning strategy for $\overline{\mathcal{G}}$.*

9.2.2 Acceptance as a Game

As said above, the main purpose of the introduction of Büchi games is to provide a game-theoretic characterisation of acceptance of a word by an ABA, and then to use the determinacy result – which is most insightful in this context of such abstract games – in subsequent developments regarding ABA and their use for ω-regular languages, in particular an alternative proof of complementation closure.

As in the case of finite words, we define the acceptance game as a product of a given word with a given alternating automaton. However, we choose a slightly different format for the nodes and edges in the game, simply because it makes the link between dualisation of games (above) and of automata (below) easier to form. In these games, players closely follow the Boolean formulas of the ABA's transition function. In contrast to this, the acceptance games for AFA and finite words were more semantical in nature with their alternating moves between player 0 choosing models of such formulas, and player 1 choosing states in these models. There is no conceptual difference between these two versions, and the reason for defining the

ABA acceptance games differently to the AFA acceptance games is just to present both ways. We leave it as an exercise to define acceptance games for ABA in which the players choose alternatingly.

Definition 9.15 Let $\mathcal{A} = (Q, \Sigma, q_I, \delta, F)$ be an ABA and $w = a_0 a_1 \ldots \in \Sigma^\omega$. Let $\Phi := Q \cup \{ f \mid \exists q \in Q, a \in \Sigma \text{ s.t. } f \text{ is a subformula of } \delta(q, a) \}$.

The *acceptance game* for $\mathcal{A}$ and w is the Büchi game $\mathcal{G}_{\mathcal{A},w} = (V, V_0, V_1, v_I, E, F')$ where $V := \Phi \times \mathbb{N}$ and V_0 consists of all nodes of the form (q, i) for $q \in Q$ and those of the form $(f \vee g, i)$ whereas V_1 consists of all other nodes, i.e. those of the form $(f \wedge g, i)$. The edge relation in this game is given as

$$\begin{aligned}
E \;:=\; & \{((f_0 \vee f_1, i), (f_j, i)) \mid j \in \{0, 1\}, i \geq 0\} \\
\cup\; & \{((f_0 \wedge f_1, i), (f_j, i)) \mid j \in \{0, 1\}, i \geq 0\} \\
\cup\; & \{((q, i), (\delta(q, a_i), i + 1)) \mid q \in Q, i \geq 0\} .
\end{aligned}$$

The initial node is $(q_I, 0)$ and the winning condition is $F' := F \times \mathbb{N}$.

The acceptance game $\mathcal{G}_{\mathcal{A},w}$ can therefore be seen as both players moving two tokens, one on the underlying ABA, the other on the word. Whenever the automaton token is on a state q, we read off the letter a that the word token is on, place the token at the root of the syntax tree of the positive Boolean formula $\delta(q, a)$, and move the word token to the next letter. Note that this move is deterministic. It has been assigned to player 0 for no particular reason. Since there is no choice involved, one could equally assign such moves to player 1. The cleanest solution would in fact be to introduce deterministic nodes not belonging to either of the players. At least this would fit best with dualisation. On the other hand, this would cause extra work in arguing that these are still two-player games etc.

The other moves are pretty much self-explanatory. If the automaton token is on a disjunction, then player 0, who wants to show that the underlying word is accepted, needs to provide proof for that by proposing an appropriate disjunct. Note that, instead of proposing a model of a formula, it suffices to choose which disjunct will be satisfied by such a model. Likewise, if a conjunction is reached, player 1 picks the conjunct that he believes would not be satisfied subsequently.

The main result of this section then is the observation that the game-theoretic semantics is equivalent to the semantics based on run trees.

Theorem 9.16 *Let $\mathcal{A}$ be an ABA and $w \in \Sigma^\omega$. Player 0 wins $\mathcal{G}_{\mathcal{A},w}$ iff $w \in L(\mathcal{A})$.*

Proof Let $\mathcal{A} = (Q, \Sigma, q_I, \delta, F)$ and $w = a_0 a_1 \ldots \in \Sigma^\omega$.

"$\Leftarrow$" Suppose that $w \in L(\mathcal{A})$, i.e. there is an accepting run ρ of $\mathcal{A}$ on w. In particular, its root is labelled with q_I.

We (recursively) call a node (f, i) of $\mathcal{G}_{\mathcal{A},w}$ *true*, if one of three cases holds:

- $f = q$ for some $q \in Q$, and there is a node v on level i (starting with the root at level 0) in ρ labelled with q;
- $f = g_1 \vee g_2$ and (g_j, i) is true for some $j \in \{1, 2\}$;
- $f = g_1 \wedge g_2$ and (g_j, i) is true for both $j \in \{1, 2\}$.

This allows us to define a simple strategy for player 0 in $\mathcal{G}_{\mathcal{A},w}$: she plays to preserve truth. It remains to be seen that this is possible and that it is a winning strategy.

For the former, suppose the play hits a node of the form (q,i) and then continues deterministically with $\delta(q,a_i)$. By truth of (q,i) there is a node v on level i in ρ such that $\rho(v) = q$. By construction of run trees, the set M of successors of v on level $i+1$ satisfies $M \vDash \delta(q,a_i)$. A simple induction on the structure of positive Boolean formulas shows that $(\delta(q,a_i),i+1)$ is then true as well.

The fact that player 0 can preserve truth in a move from a node of the form $(f \vee g, i)$, resp. player 1 has to preserve truth in a move from a node of the form $(f \wedge g, i)$ is in fact part of this induction.

Hence, this is a viable strategy for player 0, i.e. she can maintain the invariant of moving to true nodes only. The fact that this is a winning strategy is even easier to see: it should be clear that any play conforming to this strategy is also a path through ρ. Hence, it contains infinitely many accepting states from F by assumption, and the play therefore satisfies the Büchi winning condition.

"$\Rightarrow$" Likewise, from a winning strategy σ for player 0 in the game $\mathcal{G}_{\mathcal{A},w}$ we can iteratively construct an accepting run of $\mathcal{A}$ on w. First of all, because of Thm. 9.11 we can assume σ to be positional.

We start with the root labelled with q_I at level 0. Whenever a path in this partial run tree ends in a node v with label q_i on level i, we extend the construction of the tree at this node as follows. Note that node (q_i,i) has a unique successor $(\delta(q_i,a_i),i+1)$ in $\mathcal{G}_{\mathcal{A},w}$. Moreover, $\delta(q_i,a_i)$ is a finite formula, and the game rules follow the structure of this formula. Strategy σ resolves disjunctions in it. We collect the set M of states q' that eventually occur in the form of a node $(q',i+1)$ by following all plays conforming to σ. Again, a straightforward induction on the structure of Boolean formulas shows that $M \vDash \delta(q_i,a_i)$. For every node $q' \in M$ we expand the run tree construction with a node on level $i+1$ labelled with q'.

This guarantees that the structure obtained in the limit of this process is a complete run tree. The fact that it is also accepting follows again from the observation that every path in this run tree corresponds to a play in $\mathcal{G}_{\mathcal{A},w}$ conforming to σ. Thus, it also sees accepting states infinitely often. $\square$

It should be clear that the entire construction could also be carried out for alternating co-Büchi automata (AcoBA), defined syntactically like ABA, but accepting a word only if there is a run such that eventually all paths of the run traverse through accepting states only. Consequently, the acceptance game of an AcoBA and a word becomes a co-Büchi game, defined accordingly.

9.3 Expressiveness

We can use Thm. 9.8 to tackle the converse of Thm. 9.2, i.e. the question after an upper bound on the expressive power of ABA. As mentioned earlier, ABA do not exceed the expressivity of ω-regular languages. It is possible to construct an NBA from an ABA that recognises the same language.

9.3.1 Alternation Elimination

One may expect the translation of an alternating automaton into a nondeterministic one to be similarly complex in terms of the involved combinatorics as the construction of a deterministic automaton from a nondeterministic one. This is not the case, though, at all. The step from an ABA to an NBA can be realised with a relatively simple extension of the well-known powerset construction.

Intuitively, the NBA guesses levels of a memoryless run of the underlying ABA. This is essentially a powerset construction. The next level in a memoryless run consists of the union of models of the transition function applied to the nodes of the previous level and the corresponding letter in the input word. Since models of Boolean formulas are not necessarily unique, there can be several possibilities for the node labels in the next level of such a run, and nondeterminism is used to guess one that will eventually lead to an accepting run.

Clearly, this is not sufficient to check for the existence of a memoryless *accepting* run. The NBA also needs to ensure that every path in this run will see accepting states infinitely often. This is surprisingly easy to do: with each set of states forming the labels of a level in a memoryless run of the underlying ABA, it also remembers a subset thereof, namely those state that occur on paths which still need to visit an accepting state. At the beginning, the subset is full, i.e. from all states on the current level we still need to see accepting states. In other words: we still need to prove that all of them have finite rank. Whenever any of these states, that are successively transformed by the powerset construction into successors and successors of successors etc., is an accepting state, it is eliminated from this subset. This leads to the following effect. If a node has finite rank then eventually all its descendants disappear from the subset. If it has infinite rank, i.e. there is a path from it that never visits accepting states, then this subset never gets empty. So the subset must become empty infinitely often when the underlying ABA run is accepting. This provides the Büchi acceptance condition for the resulting automaton. The construction presented in the following theorem is known as the *Miyano-Hayashi construction*, named after its inventors.

Theorem 9.17 *For every ABA $\mathcal{A}$ of size n there is an NBA $\mathcal{B}$ of size at most 3^n such that $L(\mathcal{B}) = L(\mathcal{A})$.*

Proof Let $\mathcal{A} = (Q, \Sigma, q_I, \delta, F)$. W.l.o.g. we assume that $q_I \notin F$. We construct $\mathcal{B} := (3^Q, \Sigma, q_I', \Delta, F')$ as follows. First of all, note that $3^Q \simeq \{(S, T) \mid Q \supseteq S \supseteq T\}$, and we can identify states of $\mathcal{B}$ as pairs (S, T) of sets of states of $\mathcal{A}$ such that the second is a subset of the first. In accordance with the intuitive description above, let $q_I' := (\{q_I\}, \{q_I\})$.

Its transition relation is given as follows. Let $(S, T) \in 3^Q$ and $a \in \Sigma$ be given. We have $(S', T') \in \Delta((S, T), a)$ iff the following holds.

a) S' is a minimal (w.r.t. '$\subseteq$') model of $\bigwedge_{q \in S} \delta(q, a)$. In particular, for every $q \in S$ there is some $S_q' \subseteq S'$ such that S_q' is a minimal model of $\delta(q, a)$.
b) $T' := (\bigcup \{S_q' \mid q \in T\}) \setminus F$ if $T \neq \varnothing$, and $T' := S' \setminus F$ otherwise.

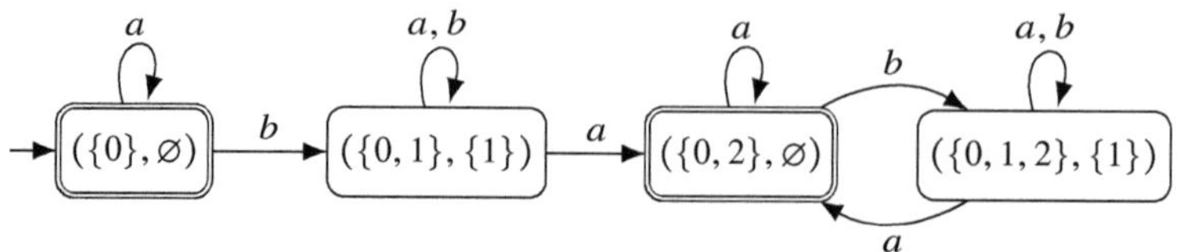

Fig. 9.6 NBA for $\{w \in \{a,b\}^\omega \mid |w|_a = \infty\}$ resulting from the ABA in Fig. 9.3.

At last, let $F' := 2^Q \times \{\varnothing\}$.

The claim on the size of $\mathcal{B}$ should be clear. It may take an extra state to satisfy the assumption of $q_I \notin F$. However, this does not need to be carried out explicitly. If $q_I \in F$ then simply let $q_I' := (\{q_I\}, \varnothing)$.

Correctness of this construction remains to be seen, i.e. that $L(\mathcal{B}) = L(\mathcal{A})$. For this, it is useful to note that, in a run $(S_0, T_0), (S_1, T_1), \ldots$ of $\mathcal{B}$ on any word, each T_{i+1} is uniquely determined by S_{i+1} and T_i. In particular, in order to construct such a run, it suffices to construct the sequence $S_0, S_1, \ldots$ and T_0.

"$\supseteq$" Let $w = a_0 a_1 \ldots \in L(\mathcal{A})$. According to Thm. 9.8 there is a memoryless run ρ of $\mathcal{A}$ on w. As observed above, ρ can be represented as a DAG with each level $S_0, S_1, S_2, \ldots$ forming a subset of Q. Clearly we have $S_0 = \{q_I\}$. Moreover, for all $i \in \mathbb{N}$ we have $S_{i+1} \vDash \bigwedge_{q \in S_i} \delta(q, a_i)$.

Let $T_0 := \{q_I\}$. According to the remark above, this uniquely defines a run $\rho' := (S_0, T_0), (S_1, T_1), \ldots$ of $\mathcal{B}$ on w. It remains to be seen that ρ' is accepting, i.e. that $T_i = \varnothing$ for infinitely many i. We first observe that, for all $i \geq 0$ with $T_i \neq \varnothing$ we have $rk_{T_{i+1}} < rk_{T_i}$ because T_i cannot contain accepting states. Moreover, we have $rk_{T_{i+1}} > rk_{T_i}$ only if $T_i = \varnothing$. According to Lemma 9.6, the ranks of all S_i are finite, and then so are the ranks of all T_i, respectively the maxima of the ranks of all the nodes in each of the T_i. But then there must be infinitely many i such that $T_i = \varnothing$ which means that ρ' visits accepting states from F' infinitely often and is therefore accepting. Thus, $w \in L(\mathcal{B})$.

"$\subseteq$" Suppose that $\rho = (S_0, T_0), (S_1, T_1), \ldots$ is an accepting run of $\mathcal{B}$ on $w = a_0 a_1 \ldots \in \Sigma^\omega$. It is easy to construct a memoryless run ρ' of $\mathcal{A}$ on w by using $S_0, S_1, \ldots$ as its levels and connecting each node on level i to the corresponding nodes on level $i + 1$ that form a model of the transition function at that node and the corresponding input letter.

Again, it remains to be seen that ρ' is accepting, i.e. that every branch through this memoryless run visits accepting states infinitely often. We do this by contradiction. Suppose there was a branch $v_0, v_1, \ldots$ in ρ' such that $\rho'(v_i) \notin F$ for all but finitely many i. Hence, there is a maximal n such that $\rho'(v) \notin F$ for all $i > n$. On the other hand, since ρ is supposed to be accepting, there are infinitely many i such that $T_i = \varnothing$. Take the least such i with $i > n$. Since $v_i \in S_i$ and $v_{i+1} \in S_{v_i} \setminus F$ we have $v_{i+1} \in T_{i+1}$. This argument can now be iterated ad infinitum: since v_{i+1} is a successor of v_i, it is part of the corresponding S_{v_i}, so if $v_i \in T_i$ then $v_{i+1} \in T_{i+1}$. But this contradicts the assumption that eventually $T_j = \varnothing$ for some $j > i$ again. $\square$

Example 9.18 Take the ABA from Fig. 9.3 that recognises $\{w \in \{a, b\}^\omega \mid |w|_a = \infty\}$. Applying the construction of Thm. 9.17 to it results in the NBA shown in Fig. 9.6. It is clearly not of optimal size. The rightmost two states form the typical structure of an NBA for this language, especially when the a-loop in the non-accepting state on the right is removed. This transition does not add anything to the recognised language since it is always more beneficial to take the a-transition into the accepting state to the left.

The initial state and its right neighbour can also clearly be removed, since they are only useful for recognising the special word a^ω (which is also recognised by the third state) and any prefix containing at least one b, which would also be taken care of by the third or fourth state from the left.

9.3.2 Universal and Deterministic Automata

It is worth noting that the cause for nondeterminism in the NBA resulting from an ABA is the possibility of Boolean formulas to have several different models, even minimal ones. This is only the case when these formulas contain disjunctions. We make this formal, and in the same step also consider alternating automata with the co-Büchi acceptance condition.

Definition 9.19 An *alternating co-Büchi automaton* (AcoBA) is defined syntactically like an ABA, and runs on ω-words are also trees defined in the same way, but they are accepting when each branch eventually traverses through accepting states only.

Let $A = (Q, \Sigma, q_I, \delta, F)$ be an ABA, resp. AcoBA such that $\delta(q, a)$ is a disjunction of elements of Q. We regard this as a nondeterministic automaton (NBA / NcoBA). If $\delta(q, a)$ consists of a pure conjunction of states in Q, then A is said to be a *universal automaton* (UBA / UcoBA).

A closer inspection of the construction in Thm. 9.17 yields the following, based on the observation that minimal models of purely conjunctive formulas are unique. The proof is left as an easy execise.

Lemma 9.20 *Let* $f \in \mathbb{B}^+(Q)$ *be of the form* $\bigwedge_{q \in M} q$ *for some* $M \subseteq Q$. *Then* $M \vDash Q$ *and for every* $N \subseteq Q$ *with* $N \vDash Q$ *we have* $M \subseteq N$.

This means that ABA which happen to be universal get turned into deterministic Büchi automata.

Corollary 9.21 *For every UBA* A *of size n there is a DBA* B *of size at most* 3^n *such that* $L(B) = L(A)$.

Next we want to show that alternating Büchi automata are easily complemented into alternating co-Büchi automata by a simple dualisation construction.

Definition 9.22 Let Q be a finite set and $f \in \mathbb{B}^+(Q)$. The *dual formula* to f is $\overline{f}$, defined inductively by

$$\overline{q} := q \ , \quad \overline{f_1 \wedge f_2} := \overline{f_1} \vee \overline{f_2} \ , \quad \overline{f_1 \vee f_2} := \overline{f_1} \wedge \overline{f_2} \ .$$

Let $\mathcal{A} = (Q, \Sigma, q_I, \delta, F)$ be an ABA, resp. AcoBA. The *dual automaton* to $\mathcal{A}$ is the AcoBA, resp. ABA $\overline{\mathcal{A}} := (Q, \Sigma, q_I, \overline{\delta}, Q \setminus F)$ where $\overline{\delta}(q, a) := \overline{\delta(q, a)}$ for any $q \in Q$ and $a \in \Sigma$.

Now we can make use of the fact that the acceptance games for ABA were defined such that moves closely follow the structure of the Boolean formulas. The duality between Büchi and co-Büchi automata lifts to the duality between Büchi and co-Büchi acceptance games. A formal proof of the following statement is omitted as it is fairly easy to see by unravelling the definitions of dual games and dual automata.

Lemma 9.23 *Let $\mathcal{A}$ be an ABA, resp. AcoBA. Then $\overline{\mathcal{G}_{\overline{\mathcal{A}}, w}} = \mathcal{G}_{\mathcal{A}, w}$.*

Strictly speaking, the two games are not equal but winner-equivalent. There is a slight subtlety arising from the fact that the acceptance game contains deterministic moves which we arbitrarily assigned to player 0, and in the dualisation construction for games, they become moves assigned to player 1. To obtain equality between $\overline{\mathcal{G}_{\overline{\mathcal{A}}, w}}$ and $\mathcal{G}_{\mathcal{A}, w}$ one would have to reassign these moves back to player 0. Since these moves are deterministic, and the owner of these nodes is irrelevant to any interesting question about such games, we simply keep the lemma's statement as it is.

Lemma 9.23 can then be used to prove correctness of the complementation construction on automata.

Theorem 9.24 *For every ABA / NBA / NcoBA $\mathcal{A}$ of size n over alphabet Σ there is an AcoBA / UcoBA / UBA $\overline{\mathcal{A}}$ of size at most n such that $L(\overline{\mathcal{A}}) = \Sigma^\omega \setminus L(\mathcal{A})$, and vice-versa.*

Proof The construction of $\overline{\mathcal{A}}$ from an ABA, resp. AcoBA $\mathcal{A}$ as the dual automaton has been given above. It is not hard to see that it yields a UcoBA from an NBA etc. Also, the claim on the size is immediately verified. It remains to be seen that $w \in L(\overline{\mathcal{A}})$ iff $w \notin L(\mathcal{A})$ for an arbitrary $w \in \Sigma^\omega$. This is a consequence of previous results as follows.

$$w \in L(\overline{\mathcal{A}}) \quad \overset{\text{Thm. 9.16}}{\Longleftrightarrow} \quad \text{player 0 wins } \mathcal{G}_{\overline{\mathcal{A}}, w} \quad \overset{\text{Thm. 9.13}}{\Longleftrightarrow} \quad \text{player 1 wins } \overline{\mathcal{G}_{\overline{\mathcal{A}}, w}}$$

$$\overset{\text{Lem. 9.23}}{\Longleftrightarrow} \quad \text{player 1 wins } \mathcal{G}_{\mathcal{A}, w}$$

$$\overset{\text{Thm. 9.11}}{\Longleftrightarrow} \quad \text{player 0 does not win } \mathcal{G}_{\mathcal{A}, w} \quad \overset{\text{Thm. 9.16}}{\Longleftrightarrow} \quad w \notin L(\mathcal{A})$$

For the cases of $\mathcal{A}$ not being a general ABA or AcoBA, one only needs to check that that corresponding dualisations specialise accordingly. $\square$

One can observe that the Miyano-Hayashi construction, originally used to transform an ABA into an NBA, can be used to transform an NcoBA into a DcoBA. This is not too surprising. Determinisation in this case means checking that amongst

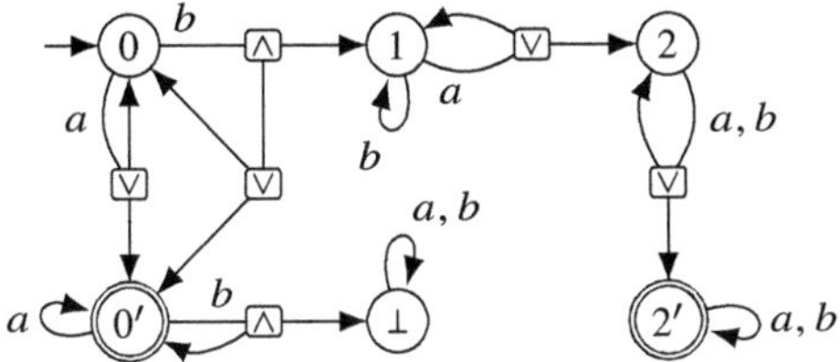

Fig. 9.7 Result of an attempt to turn an AcoBA into an ABA by extending the corresponding translation from NcoBA to NBA.

all runs of the NcoBA there is an accepting one, i.e. one that eventually traverses accepting states only. This is exactly what is done in the alternation-elimination procedure for ABA with the only difference that the mechanism involving a second set of microstates is used to check for the *non*-existence of a path eventually containing *non*-accepting states only. The following theorem even shows that determinisation of co-Büchi automata is a by-product of the developments so far.

Theorem 9.25 *For every NcoBA $\mathcal{A}$ of size n there is a DcoBA $\mathcal{B}$ of size at most 3^{n+1} such that $L(\mathcal{B}) = L(\mathcal{A})$.*

Proof Take an NcoBA of size n. According to Thm. 9.24, it can be complemented into a UBA of size at most $n + 1$. According to Cor. 9.21 this can be determinised directly into a DBA of size at most 3^{n+1}. But this can be complemented again into a DcoBA of the same size recognising the language of the original NcoBA, according to Thm. 6.32. □

9.4 Complementation via Alternating Automata

We revisit the problem of constructing, given an NBA for some language L, an NBA for its complement $\overline{L}$. Alternation may promise to be helpful for this, given that alternating automata offer an easy complementation mechanism via dualisation. Unfortunately, unlike the case of automata on finite words, such constructions are only very simple when the acceptance condition is allowed to be dualised as well. This is why Thm. 9.24 turns an ABA into an AcoBA and vice-versa. If there was a way to mimic, say, a co-Büchi condition by a Büchi condition in an alternating automaton, then this could open up the way for an alternative complementation construction for Büchi automata. We first remark that the simple construction of Thm. 6.34 that turns an NcoBA into an NBA by guessing the moment after which no more non-accepting states are being seen, cannot be used for alternating automata.

Example 9.26 Take the ABA $\mathcal{A}$ from Ex. 9.4 that is shown in Fig. 9.3 and simply regard it as an AcoBA. The language it recognises also happens to be $(b^*a)^\omega$ as well, the same as its language regarded as an ABA.

If we were to attempt to transform it into an ABA using the same trick as for nondeterministic automata, we would add a copy q' for every accepting state q, and give each original state the possibility to transition into those new copies. It is not immediately clear what this means in the context of an alternating automaton. The most sensible interpretation seems to be that every state p in the Boolean formula $\delta(q, a)$ for any q, a is replaced by the disjunction between p and the new copy p', if p was accepting. Otherwise it simply remains to be p.

The transitions for the new copy states q' are inherited from their origins q. However, only transitions into new states should be possible. This means that any p in $\delta(q', a)$ for a new copy q' should be replaced by p' if p was accepting, or by *false* otherwise. We can mimic this Boolean value by one additional state $\bot$ that accepts nothing. Executing this construction on $\mathcal{B}$ would result in the ABA shown in Fig. 9.7.

It does not accept $(b^*a)^\omega$. Specifically, consider the word $(ab)^\omega$ that should be accepted. In state 0 and upon reading a it can choose to loop back to state 0 or to go over into $0'$. The latter is problematic because afterwards, it can only successfully read a^ω as any b would take it into state $\bot$. Thus, on $(ab)^\omega$ it can never move into $0'$. But it cannot always loop back to 0 either because this would clearly create a path in a run that visits state 0 only and is therefore not accepting.

Instead, a more elaborate construction is needed. One of the key pieces here is the fact that runs of alternating co-Büchi automata can also be assumed to be memory-less. The proof is left as an exercise.

Lemma 9.27 *Let $\mathcal{A}$ be an AcoBA and $w \in L(\mathcal{A})$. Then there is a memoryless run of $\mathcal{A}$ on w.*

In order to transform an AcoBA into an ABA we now equip memoryless runs with additional information so that the co-Büchi acceptance condition in the original run can be formulated as a Büchi acceptance condition in the extended run. An ABA can then guess and verify that additional information. It is given here in terms of a ranking of nodes in a run of an AcoBA, and this is not the same as the ranking used for runs of ABA in Def. 9.5.

Definition 9.28 Let $\mathcal{A} = (Q, \Sigma, q_I, \delta, F)$ be an AcoBA of size n, $w \in \Sigma^\omega$ and ρ be a memoryless run of $\mathcal{A}$ on w. Let V be the set of nodes underlying ρ.

A *ranking* of ρ is a function $\ell : V \rightarrow \{1, \ldots, 2n\}$, satisfying the following for all $v, v' \in V$, $q \in Q$.

(I) If v' is a successor of v then $\ell(v') \leq \ell(v)$.
(II) If $\rho(v) = q$ and $\ell(v)$ is odd then $q \in F$.
(III) Every (necessarily infinite) path in ρ contains infinitely many nodes v such that $\ell(v)$ is odd.

Rankings are witnesses of acceptance.

Theorem 9.29 *If there is a ranking for a memoryless run ρ of an AcoBA then ρ is accepting.*

Proof Let ρ be a memoryless run and ℓ be a ranking on it. Take an infinite branch $v_0, v_1, \ldots$ of ρ. Condition (I) in the definition of a ranking states that $\ell(v_0) \geq \ell(v_1) \geq \ldots$ Since ranking values are finite, there is some $n \geq 0$ and some k such that $\ell(v_i) = k$ for all $i \geq n$. According to condition (III), k must be odd because it is the only value that occurs infinitely often on this branch. Because of condition (II), we have that $\rho(v_i)$ is an accepting state for all $i \geq n$. Hence, this branch, and therefore any branch, satisfies the co-Büchi condition. $\qquad\square$

The converse holds as well but requires a bit more work. Fix an AcoBA $\mathcal{A} = (Q, \Sigma, q_I, \delta, F)$ of size n and an accepting run ρ of it on some word $w \in \Sigma^\omega$. Let V be the set of all nodes in ρ.

For two nodes $v, v' \in V$ we write $v' \to^* v'$ if v' is a *descendant* of v, i.e. v' is located in the subtree of ρ rooted at v. Note that $v \to^* v$ in particular for any v. We write $v \to v'$ if v' is a *successor* of v.

We inductively construct sets of nodes $S_0 \subseteq S_1 \subseteq S_2 \subseteq \ldots$ in a run ρ as follows. Let $S_0 := \varnothing$ and, for all $i \geq 0$:

$$S_{2i+1} := \{ v \mid \text{for all } v' \text{ s.t. } v \to^* v' : v' \in S_{2i} \text{ or } \rho(v') \in F \}$$

$$S_{2i+2} := \{ v \mid \text{for all but finitely many } v' \text{ s.t. } v \to^* v' : v' \in S_{2i} \text{ or } \rho(v') \in F \}$$

The following properties about these sets are easy to verify.

Lemma 9.30 *For all $i \geq 0$ and nodes v, v' of an AcoBA run with associated sets $S_0, S_1, \ldots$ we have*

a) $S_{2i} \subseteq S_{2i+1} \subseteq S_{2i+2}$.
b) If $v \to^* v'$ and $v \in S_i$ then $v' \in S_i$.

Lemma 9.31 *Let V be the set of all nodes of an accepting run ρ of some AcoBA, and $S_0, S_1, \ldots$ be as constructed above. Let $i > 0$ such that $|V \setminus S_{2i}| = \infty$. Then $S_{2i+2} \supsetneq S_{2i}$.*

Proof We have $S_{2i+2} \supseteq S_{2i}$ by Lemma 9.30 (a). Hence, all that remains to be seen is that $S_{2i+2} \setminus S_{2i} \neq \varnothing$.

Suppose this was not the case, i.e. $S_{2i+2} = S_{2i}$. Then every node in $V \setminus S_{2i}$ would have infinitely many descendants that are not labelled with accepting states and do not belong to $V \setminus S_{2i}$ themselves. This allows us to construct an infinite path violating the co-Büchi condition. We begin with an arbitrary node $v_0 \in V \setminus S_{2i}$. It must have some descendant $v_1 \in V \setminus S_{2i}$ that is not labelled with an accepting state. This can be continued to form a sequence $v_0, v_1, \ldots$ with $v_0 \to^* v_1 \to^* \ldots$, i.e. an infinite path on which infinitely many non-accepting states occur, contradicting the assumption that ρ is accepting. $\qquad\square$

Lemma 9.32 *Let $S_0, S_1, \ldots$ be as constructed above for some memory-less run ρ of an AcoBA with n states. Let $0 \leq i \leq n$. There is an m_i such that for every $m \geq m_i$, the m-th level of ρ contains at most $n - i$ nodes not belonging to S_{2i}.*

Proof We show this by induction on i. We assume that the run is given as a DAG. Then the claim is trivially true for $i = 0$ because the maximal width of a memory-less run in a minimal DAG representation is n. We have $S_0 = \varnothing$, so every node does not belong to S_0 but there are only n nodes, hence, at most $n - 0 = n$ many nodes do not belong to S_0 for every level.

So suppose the statement is true for some $i < n$. We show that it is also true for $i + 1$. We distinguish two cases. Let V denote the set of all nodes in the run ρ.

Case 1, $|V \setminus S_{2i}| < \infty$. Then we immediately get $S_{2i+2} = V$ for the following reason. If there are only finitely many nodes not belonging to S_{2i} then the root node belongs to S_{2i+2}. According to Lemma 9.30 (b), every node belongs to S_{2i+2}. Hence, every level contains 0 nodes not belonging to S_{2i+2}, and therefore at most $n - (i + 1)$ nodes. Thus, $m_{i+1} := 0$ proves the claim in this case.

Case 2, $|V \setminus S_{2i}| = \infty$. According to Lemma 9.31 (a) we have $S_{2i+2} \supsetneq S_{2i}$. Take some $v_0 \in S_{2i+2} \setminus S_{2i}$. We argue that there is a path through ρ, starting in v_0 such that all its nodes belong to $S_{2i+2} \setminus S_{2i}$. For this it suffices to show that every node $v' \in S_{2i+2} \setminus S_{2i}$ must have some successor v'' that also belongs to $S_{2i+2} \setminus S_{2i}$. Note that $v'' \in S_{2i+2}$ holds even for all successors v'' of a node $v' \in S_{2i+2}$, according to Lemma 9.30 (b). So suppose that all successors of v' belonged to S_{2i}. Then, again with Lemma 9.30 (b), all descendants belonged to S_{2i} as well, and so all but finitely many descendants of v' would belong to S_{2i} and so would v' as well.

Thus, there are nodes $v_0, v_1, \dots$ that form a path $v_0 \to v_1 \to \dots$ with $v_j \in S_{2i+2} \setminus S_{2i}$ for all $j \geq 0$. Then let $m_{i+1} := \max\{\ell, m_i\}$ where ℓ is the level of node v_0. By the induction hypothesis, all levels below m_i contain at most $n - i$ nodes not belonging to S_{2i}. Moreover, there is a path starting on level m_{i+1} or above that contains nodes in $S_{2i+2} \setminus S_{2i}$. Hence, every level $m \geq m_{i+1}$ contains at most $n - i - 1 = n - (i + 1)$ many nodes not belonging to $S_{2i+2} = S_{2(i+1)}$. $\qquad\qquad\square$

An immediate consequence of this is a bound on the length of the chain $S_0 \subseteq S_1 \subseteq \dots \subseteq S_{2n+2}$. From Lemma 9.32 for $i = n$ we get some m_n such that all levels $m \geq m_n$ contain at most $n - n = 0$ nodes not belonging to S_{2n}. Hence, the entire DAG contains only finitely many nodes not belonging to S_{2n}. Therefore, every node must belongs to S_{2n+2}.

With a little bit of further insight, we can get a slightly tighter bound.

Lemma 9.33 *Let $S_0, S_1, \dots$ be as constructed above for some memoryless run ρ of an AcoBA $\mathcal{A}$ on some word w, and let V be the set of nodes in ρ. Then $S_{2n} = V$.*

Proof With the reasoning above we already now that $S_0 \subseteq \dots \subseteq S_{2n} \subseteq S_{2n+2} = V$. Also, if $S_{2i} = S_{2i+2}$ for some i then $S_{2i} = S_{2j}$ for all $j \geq i$. So suppose that $S_{2n} \neq V$, i.e. $S_{2n+2} \setminus S_{2n} \neq \varnothing$. Then we must have

$$\varnothing = S_0 \subsetneq S_2 \subsetneq \dots \subsetneq S_{2n-2} \subsetneq S_{2n} \subsetneq S_{2n+2} = V$$

which is only possible if, for all $i = 1, \dots, n$, there is some m_i such that all levels below m contain *exactly* $n - i$ nodes not belonging to S_{2i}. Now take $i = n - 1$. All levels below m_{i-1} contain exactly one node not belonging to S_{2n-2}. These necessarily form a path starting on level m_{i-1}. Since the underlying run is accepting, this path

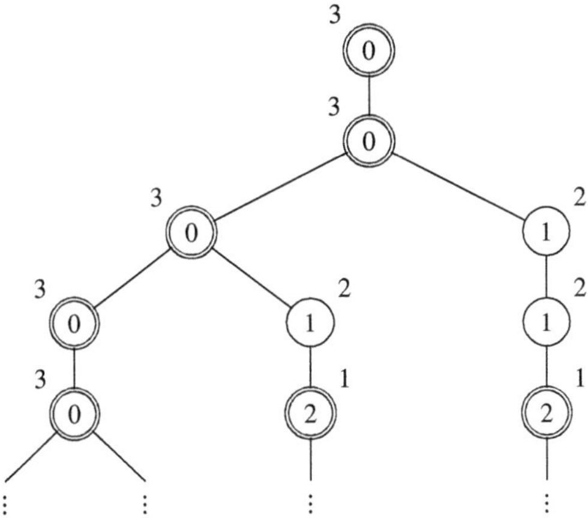

Fig. 9.8 Run of an AcoBA with a ranking.

must satisfy the co-Büchi condition, i.e. it must eventually traverse through accepting states only. But then it can contain only finitely many nodes not belonging to S_{2n-2} or being labelled with an accepting state. Hence, every node belongs to $S_{2n-2+2} = S_{2n}$ indeed. $\square$

We are now in a position to prove the converse of Thm. 9.29.

Theorem 9.34 *Let ρ be a memoryless run of an AcoBA. If ρ is accepting then there is a ranking for ρ.*

Proof We construct the ranking ℓ as follows. Let V be the set of nodes of ρ. For every $v \in V$ let $\ell(v) := \min\{i \mid v \in S_{2i}\}$. It remains to be seen that this indeed defines a ranking. We check the three properties stated in Def. 9.28.

(I) Suppose $v \to v'$. According to Lemma 9.30 (b) we have $v' \in S_j$ whenever $v \in S_j$ for every $j \geq 0$. Hence, $\ell(v') \leq \ell(v)$.

(II) Suppose $\ell(v)$ is odd for some v, i.e. $\ell(v) = 2i+1$ for some i. Then all descendants of v are labelled with accepting states or belong to S_{2i}. But then $\rho(v)$ must be an accepting state for otherwise we would have $\ell(v) \leq 2i$.

(III) Suppose that $v_0, v_1, v_2, \ldots$ is an infinite path through ρ. We need to show that the sequence $\ell(v_0), \ell(v_1), \ldots$ contains infinitely many odd numbers. So suppose that $\ell(v_j)$ was even for some $j \geq 0$, i.e. $\ell(v_j) = 2i + 2$ for some i. Then all but finitely many descendants of v_j are labelled with accepting states or belong to S_{2i}. Thus, there must be some $k \geq j$ such that all descendants of v_k have this property. But then $\ell(v_k) \leq 2i + 1$. Hence, each even number in the sequence $\ell(v_0), \ell(v_1), \ldots$ must be followed by one that is strictly smaller. So this sequence must contain infinitely many odd numbers. $\square$

Example 9.35 Reconsider the ABA $\mathcal{A}$ from Ex. 9.3, recognising the language $(b^*a)^\omega$. We now regard it as an AcoBA. First we note that it accepts the same language, and this is simply because every path in a run eventually cycles through one of the three states $0, 1, 2$, of which 0 and 2 are accepting. Thus, such a path contains infinitely many accepting states iff it contains at most finitely many non-accepting states.

Fig. 9.8 shows how the run of $\mathcal{A}$ that is also shown in Fig. 9.2 can be given a ranking with the numbers $3, 2, 1$. Rankings that only use the numbers 1 and 2, or even just the number 1 do not exist for this run. The reason for this is the existence of nodes that have infinitely many descendants that are not labelled with accepting states. Nevertheless, every path contains finitely many non-accepting states only, and so the run is accepting.

We can now use rankings to construct, given an AcoBA, an equivalent ABA.

Theorem 9.36 *For every AcoBA $\mathcal{A}$ of size n there is an ABA $\mathcal{B}$ of size at most $2n^2 + 1$ such that $L(\mathcal{B}) = L(\mathcal{A})$.*

Proof Let $\mathcal{A} = (Q, \Sigma, q_I, \delta, F)$ be an AcoBA. We construct the ABA $\mathcal{B} := (Q', \Sigma, q'_I, \delta', F')$ with $Q' := \{\bot\} \cup Q \times \{1, \ldots, 2n\}$, $q'_I := (q_I, 2n)$, $F' := \{(q, i) \mid i$ is odd $\}$ and

$$\delta(\bot, a) := \bot$$

$$\delta((q, i), a) := \begin{cases} \bot & , \text{ if } q \notin F \text{ and } i \text{ is odd} \\ \delta(q, a)|_i & , \text{ otherwise} \end{cases}$$

where $(\varphi \vee \psi)|_i = \varphi|_i \vee \psi|_i$, $(\varphi \wedge \psi)|_i = \varphi|_i \wedge \psi|_i$ and $q|_i = \bigvee_{j \leq i}(q, j)$.

Intuitively, $\mathcal{B}$ guesses a ranking in the form of an additional number for every node in a memoryless run of $\mathcal{A}$ on some w. The transition relation ensures properties of a ranking, namely that the numbers cannot increase along a path in a run, and that odd numbers are only assigned to nodes with accepting states.

The bound on the size of $\mathcal{B}$ is obvious. Correctness of the construction follows from Thm. 9.29, 9.34 and Lemma 9.33. The two former show that a ranking exists iff the underlying run is accepting, and the latter shows that the individual numbers in a ranking can be restricted to $\{1, \ldots, 2n\}$. It is then easy to read off a run of $\mathcal{A}$ and a ranking from a run of $\mathcal{B}$ and, conversely, construct a run of $\mathcal{B}$ from a run of $\mathcal{A}$ and a corresponding ranking. $\qquad\square$

While Thm. 9.36 is interesting in itself because it shows how alternation interacts with the Büchi and co-Büchi acceptance conditions, its most important application is in complementation for Büchi automata.

Corollary 9.37 *For every NBA $\mathcal{A}$ of size n there is an NBA $\overline{\mathcal{A}}$ of size at most $3^{2n^2 + 4n + 3}$ such that $L(\overline{\mathcal{A}}) = \Sigma^\omega \setminus L(\mathcal{A})$.*

Proof Take an NBA with n states. This can be viewed as an ABA of size at most $n + 1$. One extra state may be needed in order to make the transition function total, as it is required for ABA. According to Thm. 9.24 this can easily be complemented into an AcoBA of size $n + 1$. Using the construction of Thm. 9.36 we can turn this into an equivalent ABA of size at most $2(n + 1)^2 + 1 = 2n^2 + 4n + 3$. At last, we can turn this into an NBA of the prescribed size using Thm. 9.17. $\qquad\square$

The complementation construction underlying Cor. 9.37 with an upper bound of $2^{\mathcal{O}(n^2)}$ on the involved blowup is asymptotically worse than the $2^{\mathcal{O}(n \log n)}$ that can be achieved with determinisation constructions. However, it is conceptually and combinatorially simpler, and it can be implemented symbolically for instance.

9.5 Weak Automata

Ex. 9.26 and 9.35 considered ABA that can equally be seen as AcoBA without changing the accepted language. This is due to a structural property called *weakness* that we examine closer in this section. An interesting observation that we will study in more detail later on, is that the ABA resulting from the construction in Thm. 9.36 always have this property.

9.5.1 Weak Büchi and co-Büchi Automata

We begin by formalising weakness.

Definition 9.38 An ABA, resp. AcoBA $\mathcal{A} = (Q, \Sigma, q_I, \delta, F)$ is called *weak*, abbreviated then as a WABA, resp. WAcoBA, if its state set can be partitioned into $Q = Q_1 \cup \ldots \cup Q_n$ for some $n \geq 1$ such that

- for all $i = 1, \ldots, n$: $Q_i \subseteq F$ or $Q_i \cap F = \varnothing$,
- there is a partial order $\geq$ on the set $\{Q_1, \ldots, Q_n\}$ such that for any $q, q' \in Q$, $a \in \Sigma$ and $i, j \in \{1, \ldots, n\}$ with $q \in Q_i$ and $q' \in Q_j$ the following holds: if q' occurs in $\delta(q, a)$ then $Q_i \geq Q_j$.

There is another characterisation of weakness that is slightly easier to use. The proof of the following lemma is left as an exercise.

Lemma 9.39 *An ABA, resp. AcoBA is weak iff there is a function $\Phi : Q \to \mathbb{N}$ such that for all $q, q' \in Q$:*

- *if $\Phi(q) = \Phi(q')$ then $q \in F$ iff $q' \in F$,*
- *if q' occurs in $\delta(q, a)$ for some $a \in \Sigma$ then $\Phi(q') \leq \Phi(q)$.*

One can regard the function Φ as a symbolic representation of the partition that is demanded in the definition of weakness.

With this slightly alternative characterisation at hand we remark that any ABA $\mathcal{B}$ that results from an arbitrary AcoBA $\mathcal{A}$ via the construction in Thm. 9.36 is indeed weak. It is not hard to verify that the function Φ, defined by $\Phi(q, i) = i$ and $\Phi(\bot) = 0$, satisfies the requirements in Lemma 9.39. Also note that the ABA from Ex. 9.3 and 9.4 are weak: take $\Phi(q) = 2 - q$ for their states $q \in \{0, 1, 2\}$ for example.

Next we observe that weakness is a strong requirement that makes the Büchi and co-Büchi conditions collapse to a single acceptance condition.

Lemma 9.40 *Let ρ be a run of a WABA or WAcoBA and $\pi = q_0, q_1, \ldots$ be an infinite path in ρ. Then there are infinitely many accepting states in π iff there are finitely many non-accepting states in π only.*

Proof Let Φ witness the weakness of the underlying automaton. Since π is a path in a run, each q_{i+1} obviously occurs in $\delta(q_i, a)$ for some a. Hence, we must have $\Phi(q_0) \geq \Phi(q_1) \geq \ldots$. Since the range of Φ is finite, there must be some $m \geq 0$ such that $\Phi(q_i) = \Phi(q_m)$ for all $i \geq m$. Thus, either all q_i for $i \geq m$ are accepting, or all of them are not accepting. In either case, π satisfies both the Büchi and the co-Büchi condition, or it does not satisfy either of them. $\square$

It is because of this observation that we drop the explicit consideration of co-Büchi automata in the following and simply speak about WABA only, knowing that every WAcoBA is in fact just a WABA.

An interesting consequence of this collapse to a single automaton model is obtained for complementation. Remember that alternating automata are easy to complement for as long as one accepts the dualisation of the acceptance condition. However, as we have just seen: in the context of weak automata, the dual of a Büchi condition is again a Büchi condition, and so we get the following result of complementation as an immediate consequence of Thm. 9.24 and Lemma 9.40.

Corollary 9.41 *For every WABA $\mathcal{A}$ of size n over alphabet Σ there is a WABA $\overline{\mathcal{A}}$ of size at most n such that $L(\overline{\mathcal{A}}) = \Sigma^\omega \setminus L(\mathcal{A})$.*

A follow-up consequence of this is the perhaps surprising result that weak alternating Büchi automata are no weaker than arbitrary alternating Büchi automata in terms of expressiveness.

Theorem 9.42 *For every ABA $\mathcal{A}$ of size n there is a WABA $\mathcal{B}$ of size at most $2n^2 + 1$ such that $L(\mathcal{B}) = L(\mathcal{A})$.*

Proof Start with an ABA $\mathcal{A}$ of size n and dualise it into an AcoBA of size n that recognises $\Sigma^\omega \setminus L(\mathcal{A})$ according to Thm. 9.24. Then apply the construction from Thm. 9.36 to obtain a WABA of size at most $2n^2 + 1$ for this complemented language. Then apply Cor. 9.41 to complement the language again, obtaining a WABA for $L(\mathcal{A})$ of this size. $\square$

One may therefore question the choice of the term *weakness* which may suggest that the corresponding class of automata should perhaps recognise less than all ω-regular languages. The point to note here is that syntactic weakness as a structural property of the transition functions in finite automata is recovered by the stronger branching mode in alternating automata. One can apply the definition of weakness to purely nondeterministic automata, resulting in models like WNBA. It turns out that these are in fact weaker than NBA and thus do not recognise all ω-regular languages.

Theorem 9.43 *There is no WNBA that recognises* $\{w \in \{a,b\}^\omega \mid |w|_a = \infty\}$.

Proof By contradiction. Suppose there was a WNBA $\mathcal{A} = (Q, \{a,b\}, q_I, \delta, F)$ with its weakness witnessed by some function Φ. Clearly, $|\{\Phi(q) \mid q \in Q\}| \leq |Q|$, i.e. there can be at most $|Q|$ many Φ-values. Let $n := |Q|$, $w := (ab^n)^\omega \in L$ and let $\rho = q_0, q_1, \ldots$ be an accepting run of $\mathcal{A}$ on w. Note that $\Phi(q_0) \geq \Phi(q_1) \geq \ldots$ by assumption. Hence, there must be some $m \geq 0$ such that $\Phi(q_i) = \Phi(q_m)$ for all $i \geq m$. Most of all, since states with equal Φ-values need to have the same acceptance type, i.e. both being accepting or both being non-accepting, and ρ contains infinitely many accepting states, we must have $q_i \in F$ for all $i \geq m$. Now, since $n = |Q|$, there must be some i, j with $i \leq m < j \leq i+n$ such that $q_j = q_i$ and the part $q_i, \ldots, q_j$ of ρ only contains b-transitions. Note that ρ continuously contains parts with n consecutive b-transitions, and each such part contains $n+1$ states. Since $q_i, \ldots, q_j$ are all accepting and the last state in this sequence equals the first, we can construct an accepting run of the form $q_0, q_1, \ldots, (q_i, \ldots, q_{j-1})^\omega$ on a word of the form $(ab^n)^* ab^\omega$ which should not be accepted. $\qquad\square$

9.5.2 Weak Parity Automata

We extend the concept of weakness to automata accepting with a parity condition. A natural way to interpret the informal requirement that two states, which are given the same value by a function Φ witnessing weakness, should have the same acceptance type, is for those states to have the same priority. Then weakness boils down to the requirement that transitions only ever lead to states that do not have a higher priority than the one just visited.

Definition 9.44 An *alternating parity automaton* (APA) is a $\mathcal{A} = (Q, \Sigma, q_I, \delta, \Omega)$ as usual, in particular with $\delta : Q \times \Sigma \to \mathbb{B}^+(Q)$, and $\Omega : Q \to \mathbb{N}$.

Runs of APA are trees just like they are for ABA. Such a run ρ is *accepting* if the parity condition Ω holds on every path π through ρ, i.e. $\max\{\Omega(q) \mid q \in \mathit{Inf}(\pi)\}$ is even. The notions of language and size of an APA are defined as usual, respectively derived from this.

Such an APA is *weak* or a WAPA, if there is a function $\Phi : Q \to \mathbb{N}$ such that for all $q, q' \in Q$:

- if $\Phi(q) = \Phi(q')$ then $\Omega(q) = \Omega(q')$,
- if q' occurs in $\delta(q, a)$ for some $a \in \Sigma$ then $\Phi(q') \leq \Phi(q)$.

There is, again, a slightly different characterisation of weakness that may make reasoning about WAPA a bit easier. It rephrases parity acceptance in the context of a weak structure of the underlying automaton in terms of simple reachability of high priorities, not repeated reachability.

Lemma 9.45 *Let* $\mathcal{A} = (Q, \Sigma, q_I, \delta, \Omega)$ *be a WAPA. There is a function* $\Omega' : Q \to \mathbb{N}$ *such that a run* ρ *of* $\mathcal{A}$ *on any* $w \in \Sigma^\omega$ *is accepting iff* $\max\{\Omega'(q_i) \mid i \geq 0\}$ *is even for every path* $q_0, q_1, \ldots$ *in* ρ.

Proof Let $\mathcal{A}$ be given as above with function Φ witnessing its weakness. W.l.o.g. we can assume that $\Phi(q)$ is even iff $\Omega(q)$ is even, for any $q \in Q$. This can easily be achieved by successively increasing Φ-values, if necessary, simultaneously for states of Ω-priorities 0 or more, then 1 or more, etc.

Now let m be an even upper bound to $\{\Phi(q) \mid q \in Q\}$, and define $\Omega' : Q \to \mathbb{N}$ via $\Omega'(q) = m - \Phi(q)$. Clearly, we have $\Omega'(q_0) \leq \Omega'(q_1) \leq \ldots$ for any path $\pi = q_0, q_1, \ldots$ of any run ρ because $\Phi(q_0) \geq \Phi(q_1) \geq \ldots$ Hence, if ρ is accepting, and the greatest Ω-priority p seen infinitely often on any path π in it is even then weakness demands that $\Omega(q_i) = p$ for all but finitely many i. By the definition of weakness, $\Phi(q_i)$ is also even for those q_i, and by the assumption on Φ and Ω' made above, the sequence of Ω'-values of π is (not necessarily strictly) monotonically increasing and reaches p, i.e. $\max\{\Omega'(q_i) \mid i \geq 0\}$ is even for such a path π. □

It is because of this lemma that we consider the acceptance condition in WAPA as a reachability condition. In a sense, one can just use the auxiliary function Ω' as the acceptance condition. So we can consider WAPA to be of the form $(Q, \Sigma, q_I, \delta, \Omega)$ just like an arbitrary APA, but a run is accepting when the highest priority on every path is even. Note that this is a semantic rather than syntactic condition and in fact not exactly a restriction but a redefinition of how acceptance is defined.

One may be inclined to think that acceptance by simple reachability is too weak to capture all ω-regular languages. On the other hand, we have seen examples of such languages that rely on repeated reachability like $(b^*a)^\omega$ and can be recognised by a WABA. Now, as just pointed out, weakness in WABA is defined structurally whereas for WAPA it is defined semantically. On the other hand, there are clear connections: every path of a run of an alternating automaton must eventually get trapped in a strongly connected component (SCC) of the transition graph, and weakness implies that no two states in an SCC contribute differently to acceptance. So intuitively, acceptance in a WABA is also a reachability question, namely the question of reaching (and not leaving anymore) an SCC with accepting states. The WABA of Ex. 9.3 can directly be turned into a WAPA for the same language by giving it the weak parity acceptance condition $\Omega(q_i) := i$.

We show that this correspondence does not only hold intuitively for chosen examples, but that WABA and WAPA can be translated into one another by means of relatively simple constructions. The proof of the following theorem follows the same lines as the construction in the proof of Lemma 9.45 above. It is left as an exercise.

Theorem 9.46 *For every WABA $\mathcal{A}$ of size n there is a WAPA $\mathcal{B}$ of size at most n such that $L(\mathcal{B}) = L(\mathcal{A})$.*

The converse is slightly more involved as the estimation in the blowup in size suggests.

Theorem 9.47 *For every WAPA $\mathcal{A}$ of size n there is a WABA $\mathcal{C}$ of size at most n^2 such that $L(\mathcal{C}) = L(\mathcal{A})$.*

Proof Let $\mathcal{A} = (Q, \Sigma, q_I, \delta, \Omega)$ be a WAPA with $|Q| = n$. Clearly, $|\{\Omega(q) \mid q \in Q\}| \leq n$. Since acceptance is not determined by the actual values in Ω but rather by their relation to one another w.r.t. '$\leq$', and by their parity, we can always eliminate gaps in the range of Ω or uniformly reduce all values by an even number so that we have $\Omega : Q \to \{0,\ldots,n-1\}$ or $\Omega : Q \to \{1,\ldots,n\}$. Then let $M := \{\Omega(q) \mid q \in Q\}$ be the set of occurring priorities.

In an intermediate step we construct another WAPA $\mathcal{B} := (Q \times M, \Sigma, (q_I, \Omega(q_I)), \delta', \Omega')$ via $\delta'((q,i),a) = \delta(q,a)|_i$ where

$$q|_i = (q, \max\{i, \Omega(q)\}) \ , \quad (f \vee g)|_i = f|_i \vee g|_i \ , \quad (f \wedge g)|_i = f|_i \wedge g|_i$$

for all $q \in Q$, $i \in M$. Moreover, $\Omega'(q,i) := i$ for all $(q,i) \in Q \times M$.

Thus, $\mathcal{B}$ runs a simulation of $\mathcal{A}$ and records, in the second components of its states, the maximum of all the priorities seen so far. It should be clear with the considerations above on the possibility to compress priorities that the size of $\mathcal{B}$ is bounded by n^2. We claim that it is equivalent to $\mathcal{A}$, i.e. that $L(\mathcal{B}) = L(\mathcal{A})$.

We only consider the "$\subseteq$"-part. The "$\supseteq$"-part is analogous. Suppose there is an accepting run ρ of $\mathcal{B}$ on a word $w \in \Sigma^*$. By projection onto the first components of each state pair, we obtain a run ρ' of $\mathcal{A}$ on w. To see that it is also an accepting one, take an arbitrary path $\pi' = q_0, q_1, \ldots$ in ρ' that results from the projection of a path $\pi = (q_0, i_0), (q_1, i_1), \ldots$ in ρ. It should be clear that we have $i_0 \leq i_1 \leq \ldots$ and that the maximal priority m occurring in this sequence is even. Since $i_0 = \Omega(q_I)$ and $i_{j+1} = \max\{i_j, \Omega(q_j)\}$ for any $j \geq 0$, there must indeed be some $j \geq 0$ such that $\Omega(q_j) = m$ and $\Omega(q_k) \leq m$ for all $k \neq j$. Thus, the maximal priority occurring in π' is even, and so ρ is also accepting.

The last step that is required to prove the theorem's statement is to turn $\mathcal{B}$ into an equal-sized WABA $\mathcal{C} := (Q \times M, \Sigma, (q_I, \Omega(q_I)), \delta', F)$ where $F = \{(q,i) \mid i$ is even$\}$. Weakness is witnessed by the function Φ with $\Phi(q,i) := m - i$ where m is the maximal Ω-priority occurring in $\mathcal{A}$. It does indeed satisfy the requirements for weakness: its values are never increasing along transitions because priorities are never decreasing. Clearly, two states with the same Φ-value either both belong to F or both belong to $(Q \times M) \setminus F$. $\qquad\square$

At last, we remark that an analogous semantical weakening of the acceptance condition into a simple reachability condition fails for weak alternating Büchi automata. I.e. if weakness in alternating Büchi automata was defined via the reachability of an accepting state, rather than the reachability of an accepting SCC and the ability to remain within, then the resulting class of languages recognised by such automata would be strictly included in the class of ω-regular languages.

A concrete example of a language that cannot be recognised in this way is $L = a^\omega \cup a^* b^\omega$. It needs to have an accepting run ρ on $w = a^\omega$. This run cannot have finite paths of unbounded length that do not contain accepting states. By Kőnig's Lemma (Thm. 7.7), it would also contain an infinite path with no accepting states contradicting the assumption that ρ is accepting. Thus, there must be some level k in ρ such that every path contains an accepting state on a level that is at most k. It should be clear that any word which shares the same prefix with w of length n will also be accepted because a run can be constructed by extending ρ after n levels accordingly. In particular, $a^n b a^\omega$ would be accepted but does not belong to L.

Bibliographic Notes

See also the bibliographic notes on alternating finite automata on finite words in Chp. 3, including some notes on alternation as a general computational concept.

The study of alternation in the context of finite automata on infinite objects was started by Muller and Schupp [MS87] in the wider context of automata operating on infinite trees. Part III of this book studies automata and logics over such structures. It should be clear, though, that infinite words are simply special trees of branching degree 1. Hence, a theory of alternating automata on infinite trees immediately specialises to one of alternating automata on infinite words.

More to the point, though, alternating automata on infinite words with their runs being trees, bear connections to nondeterministic automata on infinite trees, and these yield the key to decision procedure for logics an trees. Kupferman and Vardi studied this connection in detail [KV98].

The powerset-like translation of an ABA into an NBA is also known as the *breakpoint construction* or, named after its inventors, the *Miyano-Hayashi construction* [MH84]. It was originally formulated for exactly such purposes, namely for alternating automata. The fact that the same construction can be used to determinise nondeterministic co-Büchi automata appears to be folklore.

For a long time, it was not known whether the bound of 3^n in the blowup incurring in the Miyano-Hayashi construction was optimal. A lower bound of $\Omega(2^n)$ is of course easily inherited from corresponding results about automata on finite words. Boker, Kupferman and Rosenberg eventually managed to show that 3^n is indeed optimal [BKR10]. They also studied the problem of alternation removal further, in particular with the aim of identifying subclasses of alternating automata for which alternation could be removed more easily.

Weakness in alternating automata was introduced and studied by Muller, Saoudi and Schupp [MSS88]. The translation from ABA to WABA via AcoBA presented here, showing that weak alternating automata are expressively complete with respect to ω-regular languages, is due to Kupferman and Vardi [KV01]. Likewise, the result showing that memoryless runs suffice for ABA is also due to them.

A lot more work on alternating automata can be found in the literature in the context of program verification. See the bibliographic notes of Chp. 10 for pointers to such work.

A topic that is not covered in this chapter, and in fact not in this book at all, is that of minimising alternating automata. Because of their use in program verification, especially due to the ability to directly translate logics into alternating automata – studied in some detail in Chp. 10 – much attention has been paid to this problem in the literature, cf. work by Wilke and others [FW02, FW05, EWS05] and Mayr and Clemente [CM10, MC13].

Kőnig's Lemma, that is mentioned in the last section, is a classical result in combinatorics which first appeared in a paper by Kőnig [Kőn27], see also the bibliographic notes for Chp. 7.

Exercises

Exercise 99 Prove Thm. 9.2. *Hint:* Consider the proof of Thm. 3.10.

Exercise 100 Take the ABA $\mathcal{B}$ from Ex. 9.4 and the word $w = (ba)^\omega$.

a) Construct an accepting run ρ of $\mathcal{B}$ with levels $V_0, V_1, \ldots$ such that there are $i_0 < i_1 < \ldots$ so that, for $j \geq 0$, level V_{i_j} contains at least j many nodes of the same label that are at the roots of mutually different subtrees.
b) Construct the memoryless run ρ^* that is obtained from ρ of part (a) using the construction of Thm. 9.8.

Exercise 101 Define acceptance games for ABA in which the players make their moves alternately by player 0 choosing models of Boolean formulas, and player 1 subsequently picking a state in the model to continue with.

Exercise 102 Show that ABA are exponentially more succinct than NBA: construct a family $(L_n)_{n \geq 0}$ of languages over some alphabet Σ such that there is a function $f : \mathbb{N} \to \mathbb{N}$ and

- each L_n is recognised by some ABA of size $\mathcal{O}(f(n))$, and
- the smallest NBA recognising L_n requires size $2^{\Omega(f(n))}$.

Hint: Extend the proof of a similar result for AFA/NFA to the case of infinite words.

Exercise 103 Prove Lemma 9.20.

Exercise 104 Is every ω-regular language recognisable by a universal Büchi automaton? Prove or refute. In the latter case, give an example of a language that divides the two classes.

Exercise 105 Prove Lemma 9.27. *Hint:* This is simpler than the corresponding construction for alternating Büchi automata, cf. Thm. 9.8. It does not necessarily require a limit construction but can almost be done inductively.

Exercise 106 Prove Lemma 9.30.

Exercise 107 Prove Lemma 9.39.

Exercise 108 Prove Thm. 9.46.

Chapter 10
Linear-Time Temporal Logic

In this chapter we study another logic interpreted over infinite words. It differs from MSO fundamentally in that there are no quantifiers for sets of positions and consequently no variables either. Instead it obtains reasonable expressiveness through the use of *temporal operators* which is also where the name *temporal logic* derives from.

In *linear-time temporal logics*, an (infinite) word is intuitively seen as a sequence of temporally ordered events, represented by letters of the underlying finite alphabet. A formula is interpreted in a single position of such a word. Intuitively this can be seen as the present moment. The suffix after that position forms the temporal future, and the prefix before that position forms the past. Here we consider a future-only temporal logic, i.e. its temporal operators can only be used to make assertions about something happening in the future or the present moment. Despite this fundamentally different structure, the simple temporal logic LTL considered here is easily seen to be embeddable into MSO, even into FO.

The intuition of a temporally ordered sequence of events is reminiscent of how automata can be seen to read a word stepwise. We study direct translations of temporal formulas into equivalent Büchi automata that are more efficient than those obtained through the embedding of LTL into FO and then MSO.

The main use and purpose of temporal logics like LTL is found in program specification and verification where a program is abstractly seen as a collection of possible executions or runs that can be regarded as infinite words over some finite alphabet. One of the most fundamental problems there is the so-called *model checking problem*: given a finite abstract description of a program P and a formula φ of LTL specifying desired program behaviour, decide whether all executions of P satisfy φ. We will see how Büchi automata can be used to solve this problem algorithmically.

© The Author(s), under exclusive
license to Springer-Verlag GmbH, DE, part of Springer Nature 2025
M. Hofmann and M. Lange, *Automata Theory and Logic*,
https://doi.org/10.1007/978-3-662-72154-4_10

10.1 Syntax and Semantics

10.1.1 Alphabets of Atomic Propositions

We recall the translation of MSO formulas into NFA in Chapter 2. A normalised MSO formula $\varphi(X_1, \ldots, X_n)$ over alphabet Σ with no first-order and n free second-order variables is being translated into an NFA $\mathcal{A}_\varphi$ over the alphabet $\Sigma \times \{0, 1\}^n$. Hence, it operates on words over Σ with n additional tracks filled by symbols 0 and 1. Likewise, every position is equipped with a binary vector of length n, encoding the information of which positions belong to the interpretation of which second-order variable.

The considerations on finite automata in the previous chapters assumed nothing of the underlying alphabet other than it being a finite set. This clearly covers the case of alphabets of the form $\Sigma \times \{0, 1\}^n$ as well, and this is one of the reasons for why the translation of MSO into finite automata, NFA or NBA, could be done inductively. Likewise, we should be able to make use of the developed automata theory for alphabets of the form $\{0, 1\}^n$ as well. Rather than seeing its elements as vectors of the form $(b_1, \ldots, b_n)$ encoding the interpretation of some second-order variables $X_1, \ldots, X_n$ of a fixed order, one could equally use $2^{\{X_1, \ldots, X_n\}}$ as the underlying alphabet, especially when it does not get changed in constructions (as it is the case for modularly translating MSO formulas into NFA or NBA).

Moreover, for every finite alphabet Σ there is clearly some number n such that $|\Sigma| \le 2^n$, so that the elements of Σ can be encoded as subsets of $\{1, \ldots, n\}$. Thus, it should be possible to carry out the entire development of a theory of finite automata over alphabets of that form as well. This is what we do here for LTL, simply because it conforms to the way that LTL is traditionally presented and also used in program verification. To allow for even more flexibility, intuition and meaningfulness in writing program specifications, we start with a finite set $\mathcal{P} = \{p, q, \ldots\}$ of so-called *atomic propositions* from which we implicitly derive an alphabet $2^{\mathcal{P}}$. Thus, infinite words in this chapter are infinite sequences of sets of atomic propositions, for instance $\{p\}, \{p, q\}, \{p, q\}, \varnothing, \{p\}, \ldots$. Note that these propositions are nothing but second-order variables. The only difference is the fact that there is no quantification over these variables in LTL, and this is why we use lowercase letters $p, q, \ldots$ that perhaps suggest a more static interpretation than the one normally associated with quantifiable variables.

Example 10.1 Let $\mathcal{P} = \{g, y, r\}$ modelling a *green*, a *yellow* and a *red* light. Then

$$\{w \in (2^{\mathcal{P}})^\omega \mid w(0) = \{r\} \text{ and } \forall i \in \mathbb{N} : w(i) \in \{\{g\}, \{y\}, \{r\}, \{y, r\}\},$$
$$w(i) = \{g\} \Rightarrow w(i + 1) \in \{\{g\}, \{y\}\},$$
$$w(i) = \{y\} \Rightarrow w(i + 1) \in \{\{y\}, \{r\}\},$$
$$w(i) = \{r\} \Rightarrow w(i + 1) \in \{\{r\}, \{y, r\}\},$$
$$w(i) = \{y, r\} \Rightarrow w(i + 1) = \{g\},$$
$$\exists j > i \text{ s.t. } w(j) \ne w(i)\}$$

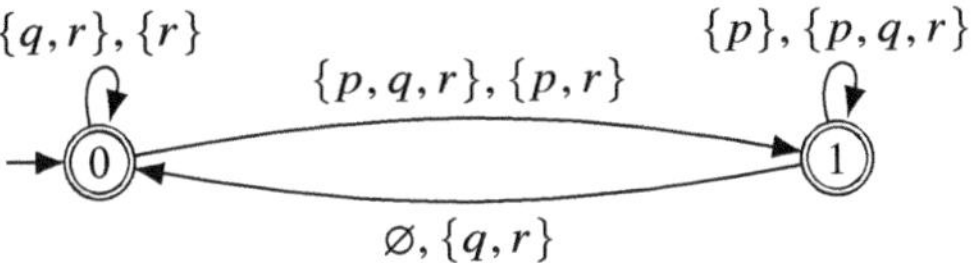

Fig. 10.1 NBA for the language defined in Ex. 10.2.

is the set of executions of a standard traffic light system in which the yellow-red-phase only lasts for one time unit, the three other phases last for an arbitrary non-zero and finite amount of time units and the traffic light shows red at the beginning.

The fact that the derived alphabet is of exponential size in the number of underlying propositions can be an inconvenience for constructing automata with transition relations of type $Q \times 2^{\mathcal{P}} \times Q$ for some state set Q.

Example 10.2 Let $\mathcal{P} = \{p, q, r\}$ and consider the language of all words $a_0 a_1 \ldots \in$ $(2^{\mathcal{P}})^{\omega}$ such that for all $i \in \mathbb{N}$ we have $r \in a_{i+1}$ iff $p \in a_i$ implies $q \in a_{i+1}$. I.e. at every moment $i \geq 1$, proposition r signals whether q at this moment has correctly followed an occurrence of p in the previous moment.

Fig. 10.1 shows an NBA for this language. It should be clear that it only needs two states in order to remember whether p occurred in the previous moment or not. The alphabet size is 8 leading to several transitions that share source and target state.

We introduce a form of representation of automata, respectively their transition relations, that is more suitable for such alphabets of sets of atomic propositions. All it needs is to see that a propositional formula α over $\mathcal{P}$ represents a set of sets of atomic propositions, namely the set of all its models, and this corresponds to a set of alphabet letters. Hence, we can use propositional formulas to represent multiple transitions in such an automaton.

Definition 10.3 Let $\mathcal{P}$ be a set of atomic proposition. A *Boolean* or *propositional formula* over $\mathcal{P}$ is one that is built from elements of $\mathcal{P}$ using Boolean connectives $\neg, \vee, \wedge, \rightarrow, \leftrightarrow, \ldots$ The satisfaction relation between an alphabet symbol $a \in 2^{\mathcal{P}}$ and such a formula f, $a \models f$, is defined in the usual way, i.e.

$$
\begin{array}{lll}
a \models q & \text{iff} & q \in a \\
a \models \neg f & \text{iff} & a \not\models f \\
a \models f \vee g & \text{iff} & a \models f \text{ or } a \models g \\
a \models f \wedge g & \text{iff} & a \models f \text{ and } a \models g \\
a \models f \rightarrow g & \text{iff} & a \models f \text{ implies } a \models g \\
a \models f \leftrightarrow g & \text{iff} & a \models f \text{ iff } a \models g
\end{array}
$$

etc. We write $\mathbb{B}(\mathcal{P})$ for the set of Boolean formulas over $\mathcal{P}$.

A *symbolic NBA* is an $\mathcal{A} = (Q, \Sigma, q_I, \delta, F)$ just like an NBA but with δ being a finite subset of $Q \times \mathbb{B}(\mathcal{P}) \times Q$. A run of $\mathcal{A}$ on a word $a_0 a_1 \ldots \in (2^{\mathcal{P}})^{\omega}$ is a sequence

$q_0, q_1, \ldots$ of states such that $q_0 = q_I$ and for every $i \in \mathbb{N}$ there is some $f_i \in \mathbb{B}(\mathcal{P})$ such that $(q_i, f_i, q_{i+1}) \in \delta$ and $a_i \vDash f_i$.

All other concepts like size, accepting run, recognised language, etc. are as they are for ordinary NBA.

Note that being symbolic is a property that only affects the transition relation of a finite automaton. It is not tied to NBA in particularly. We can therefore assume that any kind of automaton can be represented symbolically, regardless of their (state-based) acceptance condition.

Example 10.4 Reconsider the language defined in Ex. 10.2 with the NBA show in Fig. 10.1. A symbolic NBA for the same language is the following.

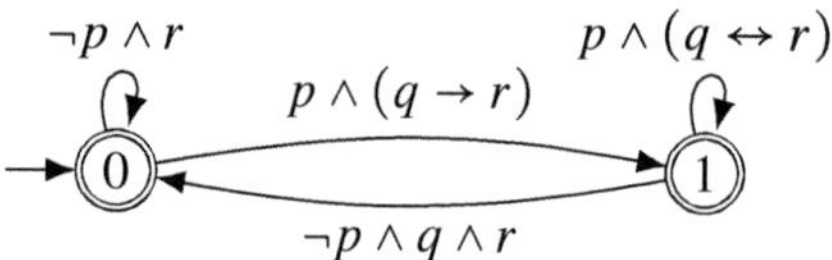

The use of propositional formulas enables a symbolic representation of the labels on transitions with equal sources and targets. In this small example, 8 transitions collapse into 4. We leave it as an exercise to show that symbolic NBA can have exponentially fewer transitions than those based on explicit representations.

10.1.2 Formulas Built from Temporal Operators

We start by defining the syntax of the *linear-time temporal logic* LTL.

Definition 10.5 Let $\mathcal{P}$ be a set of propositions. Formulas of LTL over $\mathcal{P}$ are given by the grammar

$$\varphi \ ::= \ p \mid \varphi \vee \varphi \mid \neg\varphi \mid \mathsf{X}\varphi \mid \varphi \mathsf{U} \varphi$$

where $p \in \mathcal{P}$.

Besides the usual abbreviations of further Boolean operators, including $\mathsf{tt} :=$ $q \vee \neg q$ for some $q \in \mathcal{P}$ and $\mathsf{ff} := \neg\mathsf{tt}$, we also use the following.

$$\varphi \mathsf{R} \psi := \neg(\neg\varphi \mathsf{U} \neg\psi) \ , \quad \mathsf{F}\varphi := \mathsf{tt} \mathsf{U} \varphi \ , \quad \mathsf{G}\varphi := \neg\mathsf{F}\neg\varphi$$

We introduce the following convention about the precedence of operators: unary ones bind stronger than binary ones, the temporal ones bind stronger than Boolean ones, and the precedence between U and R needs to be made explicit with parentheses.

The set $Sub(\varphi)$ of *subformulas* of φ is inductively defined as follows.

$$
\begin{aligned}
Sub(q) \ &:= \ \{q\} & Sub(\varphi \vee \psi) \ &:= \ \{\varphi \vee \psi\} \cup Sub(\varphi) \cup Sub(\psi) \\
Sub(\neg\varphi) \ &:= \ \{\neg\varphi\} \cup Sub(\varphi) & Sub(\varphi \mathsf{U} \psi) \ &:= \ \{\varphi \mathsf{U} \psi\} \cup Sub(\varphi) \cup Sub(\psi) \\
Sub(\mathsf{X}\varphi) \ &:= \ \{\mathsf{X}\varphi\} \cup Sub(\varphi)
\end{aligned}
$$

The *size* of φ is $|\varphi| := |Sub(\varphi)|$.

Note that the definition of the size of an LTL formula is a reasonable one. It measures the space needed for a succinct representation that shares common subformulas.

Example 10.6 Let $\varphi_0 := q$ for some atomic proposition q and $\varphi_{n+1} := X(\varphi_n \wedge \neg X\varphi_n)$. Then $|\varphi_n| = 1 + 4n$, i.e. the size of formulas in the sequence $(\varphi_n)_{n\geq 0}$ grows linearly. However, when writing them out fully, their string representations grow exponentially because of the double occurrence of φ_n in φ_{n+1}, see for instance φ_3 which is

$$X\Big(\overbrace{X\big(\underbrace{X(q \wedge \neg Xq)}_{\varphi_1} \wedge \neg X\, X(q \wedge \neg Xq)}^{\varphi_2} \big) \Big) \wedge \neg X\, X\Big(\overbrace{X(q \wedge \neg Xq)}^{\varphi_2} \wedge \neg X\, X(q \wedge \neg Xq) \big) \Big) \,.$$

The *temporal operators* U, X, R, F, G have particular meanings that are being explained formally below. They are read as *"until"*, *"next"*, *"release"*, *"finally"* and *"generally"*, and these names already suggest what kind of temporal connectives they represent in order to form statements about temporal connections between occurrences of events in an infinite word.

Just as with MSO, which is in fact a family of logics, namely MSO *over an underlying alphabet* Σ, LTL is to be understood as LTL *over a given set of atomic propositions*. Nevertheless, and as we did with MSO, we will simply speak of LTL and assume that the underlying set of atomic propositions P can be inferred from the context. It is also not the case that the model-theoretic properties of LTL heavily depend on P.

Formulas of LTL are interpreted over infinite words with an implicit moment of reference.

Definition 10.7 Let P be given and $\Sigma := 2^P$. The semantics of LTL is inductively defined as follows. Let $w = a_0 a_1 \ldots \in \Sigma^\omega$ and $i \in \mathbb{N}$.

$$
\begin{array}{lll}
w, i \vDash p & \text{iff} & p \in a_i \\
w, i \vDash \varphi \vee \psi & \text{iff} & w, i \vDash \varphi \text{ or } w, i \vDash \psi \\
w, i \vDash \neg\varphi & \text{iff} & w, i \nvDash \varphi \\
w, i \vDash X\varphi & \text{iff} & w, i + 1 \vDash \varphi \\
w, i \vDash \varphi \, U \, \psi & \text{iff} & \text{there is } k \geq i, \text{ s.t. } w, k \vDash \psi \\
& & \text{and for all } j : i \leq j < k \text{ implies } w, j \vDash \varphi
\end{array}
$$

Two LTL formulas φ and ψ are *equivalent*, written $\varphi \equiv \psi$, if for all $w \in \Sigma^\omega$ and all $i \in \mathbb{N}$ we have $w, i \vDash \varphi$ iff $w, i \vDash \psi$.

The *language* of an LTL formula φ is $L(\varphi) := \{w \in \Sigma^\omega \mid w, 0 \vDash \varphi\}$, thus consisting of all words whose initial moment satisfies φ. We also write $w \vDash \varphi$ as an abbreviation for $w, 0 \vDash \varphi$.

The semantics immediately explains why the operator X is read as *"next"* or *"at the next moment"*: an LTL formula φ holds in particular moments or positions of an infinite word, and the formula $X\varphi$ holds at all those position that precede one at which φ holds.

The formal semantics also suggests why the temporal operator U is read as "*until*": let φ and ψ be LTL formulas and consider the composed formula $\varphi\,U\,\psi$. It is true at a given position i iff there is some moment k (later or the same as i) at which ψ holds, and all moments from i and up to k need to satisfy φ. Thus, $\varphi\,U\,\psi$ is true at those moments from which on φ holds until ψ holds eventually, as it is the case in the following picture for instance. We depict an infinite word $w = a_0a_1\ldots$ as an infinite sequence of temporally ordered events, and write LTL formulas as labels of a moment at which they are supposed to hold.

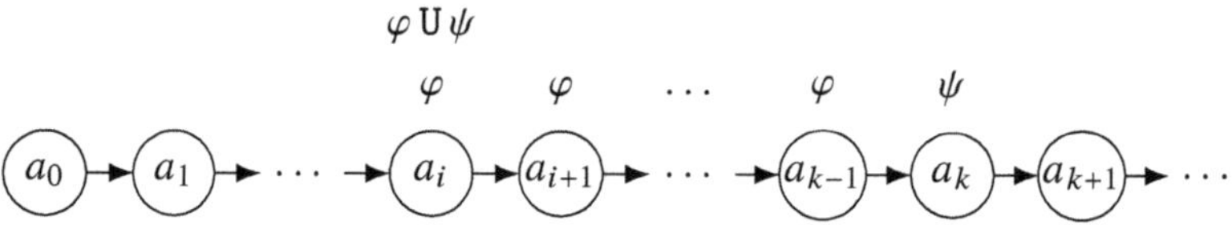

Note that $k = i$ is possible, and that the moment k at which ψ holds, must indeed exist. I.e. the fact that φ holds for all $j \geq i$ is not sufficient to conclude that $\varphi\,U\,\psi$ holds at moment i.

Remember that $F\psi$ is just an abbreviation for $tt\,U\,\psi$, i.e. a *finally*-formula is just a special case of an *until*-formula. Since the left argument tt trivially holds in any position of any word, all that $F\psi$ demands of a moment i is therefore that there is some moment $k \geq i$ at which its argument ψ holds, in other words that ψ holds *finally* or *eventually*, shown as follows.

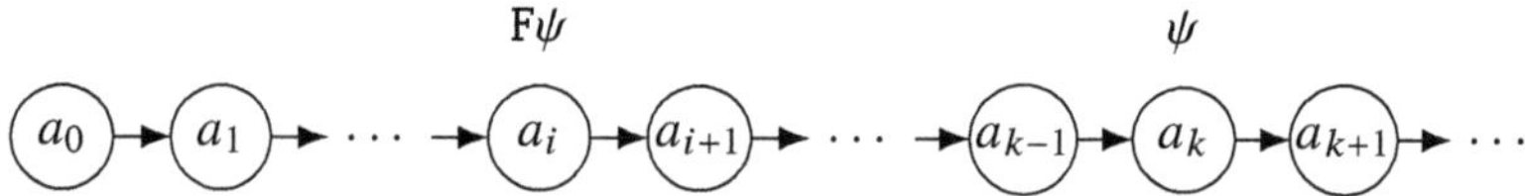

Again, we can have $k = i$. Thus, $\psi \to F\psi$ is a tautology in LTL for example, and so is $\psi \to \varphi\,U\,\psi$.

The operator G is dual to F in the sense of the abbreviation $G\psi = \neg F\neg\psi$. Thus, $G\psi$ holds if it is not the case that some point in the future or present moment does not satisfy ψ, in other words if ψ is satisfied henceforth or *generally* from the current point in time.

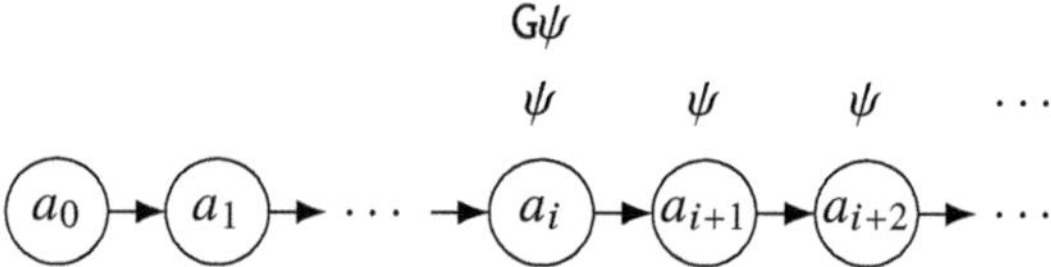

In the same sense R is dual to U. Remember that $\varphi\,R\,\psi = \neg(\neg\varphi\,U\,\neg\psi)$. It is a bit more difficult to depict, though, since there are two ways that a formula of the form $\neg\varphi\,U\,\neg\psi$ can be unfulfilled. First, it could be that $\neg\psi$ never holds, i.e. all moments into the future satisfy ψ. Second, it could be the case that $\neg\psi$ holds at some point in the future but it is not the case that $\neg\varphi$ holds continuously up to the first such moment. Hence, we get the following two situations depicting typical cases in which $\varphi \, \mathsf{R} \, \psi$ holds. In the first one, ψ holds generally.

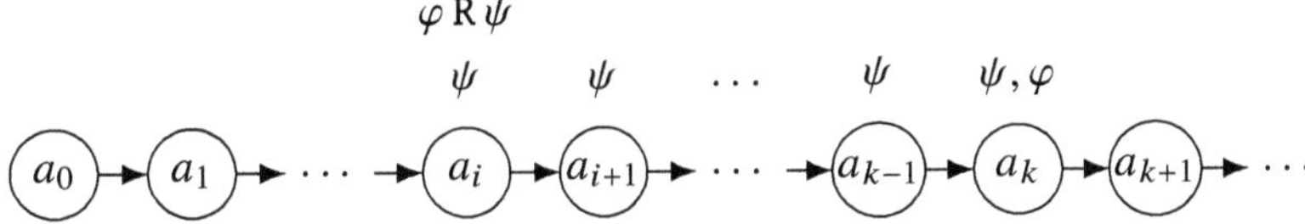

In the second situation, φ has *released* the necessity of ψ to hold continuously.

Example 10.8 It is possible to express "*q holds infinitely often*" in LTL as $\mathsf{GF}q$. It literally says that at every point into the future there is a point somewhere into the future where q holds. In other words, "*infinitely often*" is achieved by combining the operators G and F to "*always eventually*".

Strictly speaking, $\mathsf{GF}q$ says that q holds infinitely often after the moment of interpretation. Since there are only finitely many moments before any such moment, we get that $w, i \models \mathsf{GF}q$ iff $w, 0 \models \mathsf{GF}q$ for any $w \in \Sigma^\omega$ and $i \in \mathbb{N}$. This is also expressed by the equivalence $\mathsf{FGF}\varphi \equiv \mathsf{GF}\varphi$.

The language of all words in which infinitely many positions contain q if infinitely many positions contain p can be defined in LTL by $\mathsf{GF}p \to \mathsf{GF}p$.

Example 10.9 We ask whether there is an LTL formula describing the language L that contains the single word $(ab)^\omega$ only for some alphabet $\Sigma = \{a, b\}$. In general, we of course assume that $\Sigma = 2^{\mathcal{P}}$ for some set $\mathcal{P}$ of atomic propositions. In this case, it could just be $\mathcal{P} = \{q\}$, and L could equally be described as $(\{q\} \, \varnothing)^\omega$ or, more symbolically, as $(q \, \neg q)^\omega$ for example.

In general, given an alphabet $\Sigma = 2^{\mathcal{P}}$, each letter $a \in \Sigma$ induces a *characteristic formula*

$$\chi_a \; := \; \left(\bigwedge_{p \in a} p \right) \wedge \left(\bigwedge_{p \notin a} \neg p \right) .$$

Then the LTL formula

$$\chi_a \wedge \mathsf{G}\big((\chi_a \to \mathsf{X}\chi_b) \wedge (\chi_b \to \mathsf{X}\chi_a) \big)$$

defines the language $\{(ab)^\omega\}$.

Note that L of the previous example can be regarded as the property of seeing letter a at position i iff i is even. We remark without proof that the language of words of the form $(a(a + b))^\omega$, i.e. the property of seeing letter a at every even position, is not LTL-definable. The reason is that LTL-definable languages are also FO-definable, and we recall that the language of finite words of even length is MSO-but not FO-definable. The same principles that restrict the expressiveness of FO on finite words also do so on infinite words. In particular, genuine counting properties like *"something holds at every k-th position"* for $k > 1$ are not FO-expressible.

The fact that FO is an upper bound on the expressiveness of LTL is a direct consequence of the fact that the semantics of LTL is essentially given in FO.

Theorem 10.10 *Every LTL-definable language is FO-definable.*

Proof Given an LTL formula φ, we inductively construct an FO formula $tr_x(\varphi)$ with a single free first-order variable x such that for all words $w \in \Sigma^\omega$, all $i \in \mathbb{N}$ and all first-order variables x we have

$$w, i \vDash \varphi \quad \text{iff} \quad w, [x \mapsto i] \vDash tr_x(\varphi) \, .$$

The construction of $tr_x(\varphi)$ for an arbitrary variable x is straightforward. The only technicality arises from the fact that in FO, we use atomic letters, while LTL uses atomic propositions. Hence, we define

$$
\begin{aligned}
tr_x(q) &:= \bigvee \{ a(x) \mid a \in \Sigma, q \in a \} \\
tr_x(\varphi \vee \psi) &:= tr_x(\varphi) \vee tr_x(\psi) \\
tr_x(\neg\varphi) &:= \neg tr_x(\varphi) \\
tr_x(\mathsf{X}\varphi) &:= tr_x(\varphi)[succ(x)/x] \\
tr_x(\varphi\,\mathsf{U}\,\psi) &:= \exists y.y \geq x \wedge tr_y(\psi) \wedge \forall z.x \leq z < y \rightarrow tr_z(\varphi)
\end{aligned}
$$

where y, z in the last clause are fresh variables different from x.

The theorem's claim is then established using the FO formula $tr_x(\varphi)[0/x]$ for an LTL formula φ, i.e. first translating it for an arbitrary position represented by some variable x, and in the end fixing that position to be the first in an underlying word.$\square$

10.1.3 Temporal Equivalences

When handling LTL formulas algorithmically it will be convenient to assume them to be normalised, in particular with respect to occurrences of the negation operator. For this we promote some of the operators that were introduced as abbreviations only, to first-class citizens.

Definition 10.11 An LTL formula over $\mathcal{P}$ is in *negation normal form* (NNF) if it is built from literals of the form q, $\neg q$ for some $q \in \mathcal{P}$ and constants tt, ff using the connectives $\vee, \wedge, \mathsf{X}, \mathsf{U}$ and R.

This has an effect on the definition of the set of subformulas of a given LTL formula φ.

Example 10.12 Let $\varphi := \mathsf{G}(p \rightarrow \mathsf{F}q)$. When taking this as a formula in the pure syntax given in Def. 10.5, it is to be seen as an abbreviation for

$$\neg\big(\neg(q \vee \neg q)\, \mathsf{U} \,\neg(\neg p \vee (q \vee \neg q)\, \mathsf{U}\, q)\big)$$

where we re-use q in order to define $\mathsf{tt} := q \vee \neg q$. This formula then has 11 different subformulas. When taking it as a formula in the syntax of negation normal forms, it should be considered as an abbreviation for

$$\mathsf{ff}\,\mathsf{R}\,(\neg p \vee \mathsf{tt}\,\mathsf{U}\,q)$$

which has 8 subformulas.

It should be clear that, while the actual size of a formula may vary depending on whether it is measured against negation normal form or the original syntax, there can be at most a linear difference between the two measures. Hence, we will be liberal about this difference and simply continue to speak about the size of a formula.

Before we remark that every LTL formula can easily be normalised into NNF, we list some useful LTL equivalences about temporal operators. All can be proved by inspection of the semantics and some then follow easily from others. Carrying out the proofs in detail is left as an exercise.

Lemma 10.13 *For all φ, ψ the following hold.*

$$
\begin{array}{rclcrcl}
\neg\mathsf{X}\varphi &\equiv& \mathsf{X}\neg\varphi & \qquad & \mathsf{X}(\varphi\,\mathsf{U}\,\psi) &\equiv& \mathsf{X}\varphi\,\mathsf{U}\,\mathsf{X}\psi \\
\neg(\varphi\,\mathsf{U}\,\psi) &\equiv& \neg\varphi\,\mathsf{R}\,\neg\psi & & \mathsf{X}(\varphi\,\mathsf{R}\,\psi) &\equiv& \mathsf{X}\varphi\,\mathsf{R}\,\mathsf{X}\psi \\
\neg(\varphi\,\mathsf{R}\,\psi) &\equiv& \neg\varphi\,\mathsf{U}\,\neg\psi & & \mathsf{X}\mathsf{F}\varphi &\equiv& \mathsf{F}\mathsf{X}\varphi \\
\neg(\varphi\,\mathsf{U}\,\psi) &\equiv& \mathsf{G}\neg\psi \vee \neg\psi\,\mathsf{U}\,(\neg\varphi \wedge \neg\psi) & & \mathsf{X}\mathsf{G}\varphi &\equiv& \mathsf{G}\mathsf{X}\varphi \\
\mathsf{X}\mathsf{tt} &\equiv& \mathsf{tt} & & \mathsf{X}\mathsf{ff} &\equiv& \mathsf{ff}
\end{array}
$$

The relation '$\equiv$' on LTL formulas is not only an equivalence relation but in fact also a congruence with respect to all logical operators in LTL in the sense of the following lemma. It can easily be shown by induction on the structure of χ, and this is left as an exercise again. By $\chi[\psi/\varphi]$ we denote the formula that arises from χ by uniformly replacing every occurrence of φ as a subformula of χ by ψ.

Lemma 10.14 *For all LTL formulas φ, ψ, χ with $\varphi \equiv \psi$ we have $\chi \equiv \chi[\psi/\varphi]$.*

Being a congruence is not a particularly remarkable fact. It is used in many reasoning steps, though, namely whenever an equivalence between formulas is proved by replacing subformulas of it with equivalent ones, and this is a reasoning step that is naturally assumed to be sound.

Corollary 10.15 *For every LTL formula φ there is an LTL formula φ' in NNF such that $\varphi' \equiv \varphi$ and $|\varphi'| \leq 2 \cdot |\varphi|$.*

Proof Using the deMorgan laws $\neg(\varphi \vee \psi) \equiv \neg\varphi \wedge \neg\psi$ and $\neg(\varphi \wedge \psi) \equiv \neg\varphi \vee \neg\psi$, double negation elimination $\neg\neg\varphi \equiv \varphi$, commutativity between negation and the temporal *next* and the duality between U and R as stated in Lemma 10.13, we can push negation successively inwards until it occurs at most in front of atomic propositions, at the expense of possibly turning U-operators into R-operators.

The size estimation follows from the observation that multiple occurrences of negated subformulas can be put into the same NNF, and that pushing negation inwards preserves the structure of the syntax tree but may, in the worst case, add an extra layer of formulas above the tree's leaves. $\qquad\square$

10.1.4 Unfoldings of Temporal Operators

In the following we will consider translations of LTL formulas into Büchi automata. They rely on a characterisation of the temporal operators U and R known as their *unfoldings* – a formula equivalent to $\varphi\,\mathsf{U}\,\psi$ for instance that contains $\varphi\,\mathsf{U}\,\psi$ underneath a X-operator.

Lemma 10.16 *For all $\varphi,\psi \in LTL$ we have:*

a) $\varphi\,\mathsf{U}\,\psi \equiv \psi \vee (\varphi \wedge \mathsf{X}(\varphi\,\mathsf{U}\,\psi))$,
b) $\varphi\,\mathsf{R}\,\psi \equiv \psi \wedge (\varphi \vee \mathsf{X}(\varphi\,\mathsf{R}\,\psi))$.

Proof (a) We only show the "$\Rightarrow$"-part. The "$\Leftarrow$"-part is entirely analogous.

Suppose that $w,i \vDash \varphi\,\mathsf{U}\,\psi$. Then there is $k \geq i$ with $w,k \vDash \psi$ and $w,j \vDash \varphi$ for all j with $i \leq j < k$. We distinguish between two cases.

a) Case 1, $k = i$. Then we clearly have $w,i \vDash \psi$.
b) Case 2, $k > i$. Then we have $w,i \vDash \varphi$. Consider position $i + 1$ in w. Note that $k \geq i + 1$, $w,k \vDash \psi$ and $w,h \vDash \varphi$ for all j with mit $i \leq j < k$, so in particular for all j with $i + 1 \leq j < k$. Hence, we have $w,i + 1 \vDash \varphi\,\mathsf{U}\,\psi$ and therefore $w,i \vDash \mathsf{X}(\varphi\,\mathsf{U}\,\psi)$. Altogether we get that $w,i \vDash \varphi \wedge \mathsf{X}(\varphi\,\mathsf{U}\,\psi)$.

Since one of both cases must be true for any such i, we get $w,i \vDash \psi \vee (\varphi \wedge \mathsf{X}(\varphi\,\mathsf{U}\,\psi))$.

(b) This then follows from (a) using standard reasoning about negation in propositional logic (deMorgan laws, double negation elimination/introduction) and some equivalences from Lemma 10.13. We have

$$
\begin{aligned}
\varphi\,\mathsf{R}\,\psi \;&\equiv\; \neg\neg(\varphi\,\mathsf{R}\,\psi) \;\equiv\; \neg(\neg\varphi\,\mathsf{U}\,\neg\psi) \;\equiv\; \neg\big(\neg\psi \vee (\neg\varphi \wedge \mathsf{X}(\neg\varphi\,\mathsf{U}\,\neg\psi))\big) \\
&\equiv\; \neg\neg\psi \wedge \neg(\neg\varphi \wedge \mathsf{X}(\neg\varphi\,\mathsf{U}\,\neg\psi)) \;\equiv\; \neg\neg\psi \wedge (\neg\neg\varphi \vee \neg\mathsf{X}(\neg\varphi\,\mathsf{U}\,\neg\psi)) \\
&\equiv\; \neg\neg\psi \wedge (\neg\neg\varphi \vee \mathsf{X}\neg(\neg\varphi\,\mathsf{U}\,\neg\psi)) \;\equiv\; \psi \wedge (\varphi \vee \mathsf{X}(\varphi\,\mathsf{R}\,\psi))
\end{aligned}
$$

which proves the claim. $\qquad\square$

Lemma 10.16 suggests a method for checking whether a given word with some position i satisfies a given LTL formula $\varphi\,\mathsf{U}\,\psi$: first, check whether position i satisfies ψ. If this is the case then return *yes*. Otherwise check whether it satisfies φ. If this is not the case then return *no*. Otherwise move to position $i + 1$ and repeat this procedure.

It should be clear that, if this procedure ever produces an answer *yes* or *no*, then this is truly an answer to the question whether the original position i satisfies $\varphi \, U \, \psi$. But what if this is deferred indefinitely? Then no position $k \geq i$ satisfies ψ but all of them satisfy φ. The latter is less relevant than the former for the observation that then position i cannot satisfy $\varphi \, U \, \psi$ because this demands the existence of some position $k \geq i$ satisfying ψ. Hence, this intuitive procedure, based on the unfolding of U-formulas according to Lemma 10.16 which prescribes conditions on what needs to hold *locally*, also comes with a *global* condition: in order for $\varphi \, U \, \psi$ to hold, this recursion needs to stop eventually and produce the answer *yes* because some position has been found at which ψ holds.

While this reasoning is quite high-level and leaves open questions after the representation of an infinite word and how to check whether the subformulas φ, ψ hold at a given position, it shows that proper decision procedures for LTL which handle U-formulas by unfolding need to take such limit conditions into account.

A natural question that arises concerns the R-operator. Likewise, one may imagine that in order to check whether a position i in a given word satisfies $\varphi \, R \, \psi$, one first checks whether it satisfies ψ and returns *no* if it does not. Otherwise one checks whether it satisfies φ and returns *yes* if it does, or continues this procedure with the next position $i + 1$. Again, any answer obtained in finite time correctly says whether $\varphi \, R \, \psi$ is satisfied at position i, and the interesting question then is: what is the correct answer in case that this procedure goes on forever? One may be tempted to also say that the answer should be *no*, perhaps because it feels unnatural to derive a positive answer from such non-well-founded reasoning. However, when looking closer, we see that the answer should be *yes*. If this process never derives an answer in finite time, then any position $k \geq i$ has passed the test for satisfying ψ. So position i satisfies $G\psi$ and therefore $\varphi \, R \, \psi$, regardless of the fact that no such position satisfies φ (because this would have caused the check to terminate at some point).

Another way of seeing that infinite deferral in checking $\varphi \, R \, \psi$ is a reason for it to hold, is the duality between R and U. Remember that $\varphi \, R \, \psi \equiv \neg(\neg\varphi \, U \, \neg\psi)$. The outer negation on the right-hand side can be interpreted as inverting the answers *yes*/*no* in a check for $\neg\varphi \, U \, \neg\psi$. Hence, if the answer is not derived in finite time but deferred to the limit, it is *no* by the argumentation based on the semantics of U-formulas above, and consequently it is inverted into a *yes* for the question whether the corresponding R-formula holds.

The following two sections present translations of LTL formulas into Büchi automata – nondeterministic and alternating ones. Both make use of the unfoldings of U- and R-formulas. The global conditions – an U-formula may only be unfolded finitely often while a R-formula can be unfolded infinitely often – are ensured by the acceptance conditions.

10.2 Nondeterministic Büchi Automata for LTL

We have of course already provided a way to translate LTL formulas into equivalent Büchi automata: LTL can easily be translated into FO according to Thm. 10.10; every FO formula is obviously also an MSO formula; and MSO formulas can be translated into equivalent NBA via Lemma 5.35. The problem with this approach is that, while the first two steps incur no blowup at all, the last one from MSO to NBA incurs a non-elementary blowup in general. The reason for this is the necessity of an exponential blowup for every negation, and negation cannot be eliminated from MSO formulas since there is no way to directly handle universal quantification on the automata side.

Now, the quantification in LTL is only first-order and very restricted. For instance, a formula of the form $\varphi \, \mathsf{U} \, \psi$ translates into a quantification pattern of the form $\exists \ldots \forall \ldots$, and a formula of the form $\varphi \, \mathsf{R} \, \psi$ translates into one of the form $\forall \ldots \exists \ldots$ Thus, it is reasonable to assume that not one of them is more difficult than the other in a possible translation into NBA, and using Cor. 10.15, we can avoid successive complementation steps altogether. This is indeed the case, but there is another small technicality to handle, and we do so by introducing yet another automaton model for languages of infinite words.

10.2.1 Generalised Büchi Automata

Remember the construction showing that the class of ω-regular languages is closed under intersections, cf. Thm. 5.17. The technical challenge was to come up with a single Büchi acceptance condition that realises acceptance by two Büchi acceptance conditions simultaneously. This could have been no problem at all if automata were equipped with multiple Büchi acceptance conditions so that an accepting run needs to satisfy all of them. This is exactly what happens in generalised Büchi automata, and it is not a surprise that the construction showing that they do not exceed the expressive power of NBA makes use of the same trick as is used in the proof of Thm. 5.17 to show closure under intersections.

Definition 10.17 A *generalised (nondeterministic) Büchi automaton* (GNBA) is an $\mathcal{A} = (Q, \Sigma, I, \delta, \mathcal{F})$ with Q, Σ, δ as for an NBA, but with a set of initial states $I \subseteq Q$ and a set $\mathcal{F} = \{F_1, \ldots, F_k\} \subseteq 2^Q$ of acceptance sets.

The *size* of the GNBA $\mathcal{A}$ is, as usual, $|Q|$, and its *index* is k.

A run ρ of a GNBA on a word $w = a_0 a_1 \ldots \in \Sigma^\omega$ is defined as for an NBA but it is allowed to start in an arbitrary $q_0 \in I$. It is *accepting* if $Inf(\rho) \cap F_i \neq \varnothing$ for all $i = 1, \ldots, k$.

Thus, the way that GNBA are presented here includes two generalisations: having potentially multiple initial states and having potentially multiple acceptance sets. We remark that the generalisation to multiple initial states is only done for convenience, and that it is always possible to transform such GNBA into ones that only have

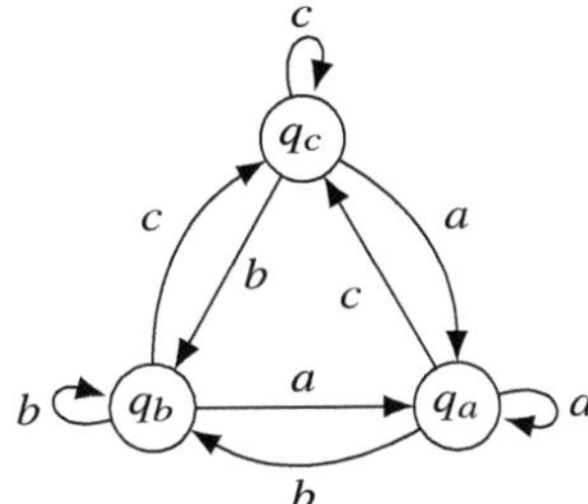

Fig. 10.2 Transition function of the GNBA for the language of words containing infinitely many symbols a and infinitely many symbols b.

a single initial state by introducing this as a new one which inherits its outgoing transitions from all original initial states. The reason for calling GNBA generalised is really the extension to potentially multiple acceptance sets, i.e. the fact that a run needs to hit not just one but possibly many different sets infinitely often.

Example 10.18 GNBA can be quite convenient, particularly to represent languages that come as intersections of Büchi-recognisable languages. Let $L := \{w \in \{a,b,c\}^\omega \mid |w|_a = \infty$ and $|w|_b = \infty\}$. It is recognised by the GNBA shown in Fig. 10.2. It simply remembers in its state space the last letter that was read. Any non-empty set of states can be used as initial states since all three recognise the same language anyway, regardless of any accepting condition. With the generalised Büchi condition $\{\{q_a\}, \{q_b\}\}$ we ensure that both symbols a and b need to be seen infinitely often in a word for it to be accepted.

It should be clear that GNBA can recognise every NBA-definable language; an NBA with acceptance set F can be seen as a GNBA with a single acceptance set $\{F\}$. Given the statements above about the connection between GNBA and the intersection closure of the class of ω-regular languages, it is not surprising that the converse holds as well. Naturally, the construction is reminiscent of the one proving intersection closure of the class of NBA-recognisable languages (cf. Thm. 5.17). So the translation from GNBA to NBA comes with a mild blowup.

Theorem 10.19 *For every GNBA $\mathcal{A}$ of size n and index k there is an NBA $\mathcal{B}$ of size at most $n \cdot k + 1$ such that $L(\mathcal{B}) = L(\mathcal{A})$.*

Proof Let $\mathcal{A} = (Q, \Sigma, I, \delta, \mathcal{F})$ with $\mathcal{F} = \{F_0, \ldots, F_{k-1}\}$ be a GNBA. Take a new state q_I and define the NBA $\mathcal{B}$ as

$$(Q \times [k] \cup \{q_I\}, \Sigma, q_I, \Delta, F_0 \times \{0\})$$

where

$$\big((q,i), a, (p,j)\big) \in \Delta \quad \text{iff} \quad (q,a,p) \in \delta \text{ and } j = \begin{cases} i+1 \bmod k & \text{, if } q \in F_i, \\ i & \text{, otherwise,} \end{cases}$$

$$\big(q_I, a, (p, 0)\big) \in \Delta \quad \text{iff} \quad \text{there is } q \in I \text{ with } (q, a, p) \in \delta$$

for all $q, p \in Q, i, j \in [k], a \in \Sigma$.

So intuitively, $\mathcal{A}$'s state space is enriched with a counter that points to the index of the next acceptance set from which a state needs to be seen. This is based on the principle that in a run which sees states from all F_i infinitely often, there will be a first occurrence of a state from F_0, eventually followed by an occurrence of a state from F_1, etc. Once a state from F_{k-1} has been seen in this order, we repeat the entire procedure from the beginning. Formally, we have $L(\mathcal{B}) = L(\mathcal{A})$ because of the following reasoning.

"$\subseteq$" Let $\rho = q_I, (q_1, i_1), (q_2, i_2), \ldots$ be an accepting run of $\mathcal{B}$ on a word $w = a_0 a_1 \ldots \in \Sigma^\omega$. Then there must be some $q_0 \in I$ such that $(q_0, a_0, q_1) \in \delta$. The sequence $\rho' = q_0, q_1, q_2, \ldots$ then forms a run of $\mathcal{A}$ on w.

Since ρ is accepting, there must be infinitely many j such that $(q_j, i_j) \in F_0 \times \{0\}$, i.e. $i_j = 0$ and $q_j \in F_0$. According to the definition of Δ, we have $i_{j+1} = 1$ for every such j. Since the second components of the states only ever change from h to $h + 1 \bmod k$ when the first component is a member of F_h, we get that between two occurrences of states from $F_0 \times \{0\}$ we must have seen states from $F_h \times \{h\}$ for all $h \in [k]$. Hence, ρ' is an accepting run of $\mathcal{A}$ on w.

"$\supseteq$" Let $\rho = q_0, q_1, \ldots$ be an accepting run of $\mathcal{A}$ on a word $w = a_0 a_1 \ldots \in \Sigma^\omega$. Hence, for every $h \in [k]$ and every $j \in \mathbb{N}$ there is $i \geq j$ with $q_i \in F_h$. We call this the *progression property* for the moment.

Now extend ρ to a run $\rho' := q_I, (q_1, i_1), (q_2, i_2), \ldots$ of $\mathcal{B}$ as follows: let $i_1 := 0$, and whenever i_j is determined, then let i_{j+1} be the unique value in $[k]$ such that $((q_j, i_j), a_j, (q_{j+1}, i_{j+1})) \in \Delta$. By inspection of the construction of Δ we see that it exists uniquely.

Because of the progression property, the sequence $i_1, i_2, \ldots$ is not eventually stable, but it forms a word from $(0^+ 1^+ \ldots (k-1)^+)^\omega$. Hence, it contains infinitely many symbols 0. Moreover, since it also contains infinitely many transitions from a 0 to a 1, ρ' must contain infinitely many states from $F_0 \times \{0\}$ and is therefore an accepting run on w. □

10.2.2 From LTL to Generalised Büchi Automata

In the following we assume that a given LTL formula has been normalised into NNF already. We give a direct translation from an LTL formula into an equivalent GNBA which can then be composed with the construction in the proof of Thm. 10.19 to obtain an NBA equivalent to the LTL formula. The translation from LTL into GNBA is not modular, i.e. it does not proceed by induction on the structure of the formula, as is the case for MSO for instance. Instead it is monolithic, and for this we need a concept that extends the definition of subformulas slightly.

Definition 10.20 Let θ be an LTL formula in NNF. The *Fischer-Ladner closure* of θ is the smallest set $FL(\theta)$ that contains θ and satisfies the following for all φ, ψ.

- If $\varphi \vee \psi \in FL(\theta)$ or $\varphi \wedge \psi \in FL(\theta)$ then $\{\varphi, \psi\} \subseteq FL(\theta)$,
- if $X\varphi \in FL(\theta)$ then $\varphi \in FL(\theta)$,
- if $\varphi \,U\, \psi \in FL(\theta)$ then $\{\varphi, \psi, X(\varphi \,U\, \psi)\} \subseteq FL(\theta)$,
- if $\varphi \,R\, \psi \in FL(\theta)$ then $\{\varphi, \psi, X(\varphi \,R\, \psi)\} \subseteq FL(\theta)$.

The following estimation on the size of the Fischer-Ladner closure of a formula follows directly from the observation that the Fischer-Ladner closure adds to the set of subformulas of a formula in NNF, at most one more formula for each temporal U- or R-formula.

Lemma 10.21 *Let φ be an LTL formula in NNF. Then $|FL(\varphi)| \leq 2 \cdot |\varphi|$.*

The Fischer-Ladner closure of φ can be seen as the set of formulas that are of interest when trying to establish whether φ holds at a particular position of a given word, making use of the unfoldings of temporal formulas. Based on this we introduce another concept, namely that of a Hintikka set. Such sets can be seen as being closed under logical consequence. For instance, suppose we say that $\varphi \wedge \psi$ is true at some position i of a word w. Then this will also be true for φ and for ψ. Likewise, if $\varphi \vee \psi$ is true, then so must be one of the two disjuncts, etc.

Definition 10.22 Let θ be an LTL formula in NNF over $\mathcal{P}$. A set $M \subseteq FL(\theta)$ is called a *Hintikka set* if it satisfies the following for all φ, ψ.

- If $\varphi \vee \psi \in M$ then $\varphi \in M$ or $\psi \in M$,
- if $\varphi \wedge \psi \in M$ then $\varphi \in M$ and $\psi \in M$,
- if $\varphi \,U\, \psi \in M$ then $\psi \in M$ or $\{\varphi, X(\varphi \,U\, \psi)\} \subseteq M$,
- if $\varphi \,R\, \psi \in M$ then $\{\psi, \varphi\} \subseteq M$ or $\{\psi, X(\varphi \,R\, \psi)\} \subseteq M$.

Such a Hintikka set M is called *propositionally consistent* if $\mathrm{ff} \notin M$ and there is no $p \in \mathcal{P}$ such that $\{p, \neg p\} \subseteq M$.

We write $\mathcal{H}(\theta)$ for the set of all propositionally consistent Hintikka sets for θ, $\mathcal{P}^+(M)$ for the set of all positive literals in M, i.e. $\mathcal{P}^+(M) := M \cap \mathcal{P}$, and $\mathcal{P}^-(M)$ for the set of all negative literals in M, i.e. $\mathcal{P}^-(M) := M \cap \{\neg p \mid p \in \mathcal{P}\}$.

Note that propositional consistency is not the same as consistency in the standard logical sense or even satisfiability. For instance, $\{Xq, X\neg q\}$ is clearly unsatisfiable but it is propositionally consistent in the sense that it has a propositional model that simply assigns *true* or *false* to each proposition which is either an atomic one or a formula that begins with a X-operator.

Since propositional consistency is the only concept of consistency we consider here, we simply drop the qualification "propositional" and speak of consistent sets.

Fix an LTL formula θ for the remainder of this section. The goal is to construct a GNBA $\mathcal{A}_\theta$ such that $L(\mathcal{A}_\theta) = L(\theta)$ and $|\mathcal{A}_\theta|$ is elementary in $|\theta|$.

As states we use consistent Hintikka sets. Such states intuitively contain all the subformulas of θ or, more precisely, all the elements of its Fischer-Ladner closure that need to be satisfied at the current position i of a word that is to be accepted from this state. Note that such sets need to be Hintikka sets: if a conjunction is supposed to be satisfied by such a position, then both conjuncts need to be as well, etc. Moreover, it needs to be consistent since no position can satisfy ff or q and $\neg q$ at the same time. However, propositional consistency suffices. It is perfectly fine to assume that some position i satisfies $\mathrm{X}q$ and $\mathrm{X}\neg q$. The transition relation will ensure that such hidden inconsistencies will eventually – here already after one step – become propositional inconsistencies.

We can use nondeterminism to guess the set of formulas that need to hold in the next position. Temporal operators are handled by their unfoldings where U-formulas need special treatment through the acceptance condition in order to ensure that every unfolding terminates eventually.

Let $\varphi_1 \mathbin{U} \psi_1, \ldots, \varphi_k \mathbin{U} \psi_k$ be an enumeration of all U-formulas in $FL(\theta)$. We construct the GNBA $\mathcal{A}_\theta$ as $(\mathcal{H}(\varphi), \Sigma, I, \delta, \mathcal{F})$ where $I := \{M \in \mathcal{H}(\theta) \mid \theta \in M\}$ consists of all such states that contain θ.

The transition relation is given as follows. We have

$$(M, a, M') \in \delta \quad \text{iff} \quad \text{for all } \mathrm{X}\psi \in M : \psi \in M'$$

for any $M, M' \in \mathcal{H}(M), a \in 2^{\mathcal{P}}$ such that $\mathcal{P}^+(M) \subseteq a$ and $\{q \mid \neg q \in \mathcal{P}^-(M)\} \cap a = \varnothing$.

At last, there are k acceptance sets, one for each U-formula in the Fischer-Ladner closure of θ. We have $\mathcal{F} := \{F_1, \ldots, F_k\}$ where

$$F_i := \{M \mid \varphi_i \mathbin{U} \psi_i \notin M \text{ or } \psi_i \in M\}$$

for all $i = 1, \ldots, k$. Hence, the acceptance set associated with the i-th U-formula consists of all states that contain its right argument whenever they contain the formula itself. In other words, a good state in the sense of ensuring termination of the unfolding process for the i-th U-formula $\varphi_i \mathbin{U} \psi_i$ is one that does not contain $\varphi_i \mathbin{U} \psi_i$ in which case there is no termination needed to be guaranteed, or it contains ψ_i which is exactly what needs to happen for the unfolding not be deferred to later moments anymore.

There is no need to treat R-formulas in the acceptance condition. Their satisfaction is guaranteed entirely locally through unfolding which can either stop or go on ad infinitum.

Example 10.23 Let $\theta = \mathrm{G}(p \to \mathrm{XF}q)$. Strictly speaking we would have to transform θ into NNF, including the rewriting of G and F as R and U. It should be clear, though, that the general construction could equally be formulated for formulas including subformulas of such kind. We leave it as an exercise to extend the general construction correspondingly. Here we carry it out for a θ that is only normalised into $\mathrm{G}(\neg p \vee \mathrm{XF}q)$.

The Fischer-Ladner closure of θ is

$$\{\mathrm{G}(\neg p \vee \mathrm{XF}q), \mathrm{XG}(\neg p \vee \mathrm{XF}q), \neg p \vee \mathrm{XF}q, \neg p, \mathrm{XF}q, \mathrm{F}q, q\}$$

containing six elements.

There are way less than $2^6 = 64$ subsets thereof which are consistent Hintikka sets. Moreover, it suffices to construct the GNBA $\mathcal{A}_\theta$ on-the-fly, i.e. starting will all potential initial states and then only constructing the part that is reachable from these.

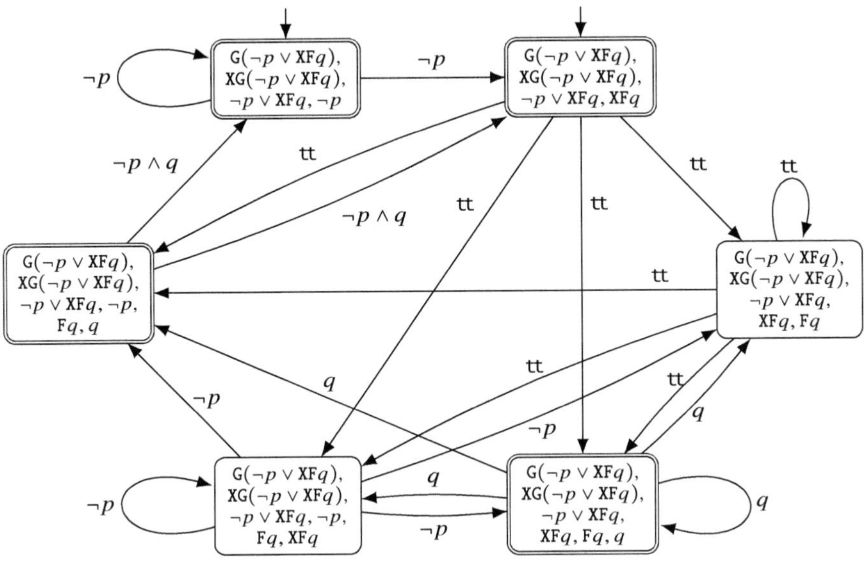

Fig. 10.3 GNBA with a single acceptance set, obtained for the LTL formula $G(p \rightarrow XFq)$.

Moreover, it is sufficient to construct these Hintikka sets in a minimal way, i.e. to only include what needs to be included according to Def. 10.22 and the construction of the transition relation.

Note that any consistent Hintikka set containing $\theta = G(\neg p \vee XFq)$ also needs to contain $X\theta$ and $\neg p \vee XFq$. Hence, there are two initial states for $\mathcal{A}_\theta$, namely

$$M_0 \ := \ \{G(\neg p \vee XFq), XG(\neg p \vee XFq), \neg p \vee XFq, \neg p\} \text{ and}$$
$$M_1 \ := \ \{G(\neg p \vee XFq), XG(\neg p \vee XFq), \neg p \vee XFq, XFq\}$$

We proceed to construct the GNBA as a symbolic automaton. For this it suffices to note that, given a state M, in order to find out its successors, we do not need to iterate through all $a \in 2^{\mathcal{P}}$ and all possible consistent Hintikka sets M' to check whether $(M, a, M') \in \delta$. Instead, we can extract a symbolic representation f of all such a from M itself: simply take $f := \bigwedge(\mathcal{P}^+(M) \cup \mathcal{P}^-(M))$, i.e. conjoin all literals occurring in M conjunctively.

Likewise, the set of possible successors of M is obtained by collecting all formulas χ such that $X\chi \in M$ and then extending this to a consistent Hintikka sets, for which there may be several possibilities in general.

For instance, take state M_0 as defined above. Its outgoing transitions can symbolically be labelled with $\neg p$, and each successor must contain θ. Hence, M_0 and M_1 are the two successors of M_0.

Now consider M_1. It contains no literals. Hence, each outgoing transition is labelled with $\bigwedge \varnothing$, i.e. tt. Its successors need to contain both θ and Fq, and this leads

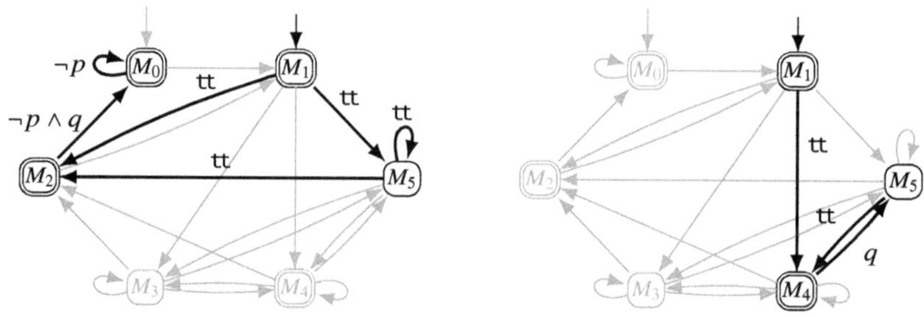

Fig. 10.4 Shape of accepting runs for two families of words described in Ex. 10.23.

to four more consistent Hintikka sets.

$$M_2 := \{G(\neg p \vee XFq), XG(\neg p \vee XFq), \neg p \vee XFq, \neg p, Fq, q\}$$
$$M_3 := \{G(\neg p \vee XFq), XG(\neg p \vee XFq), \neg p \vee XFq, \neg p, Fq, XFq\}$$
$$M_4 := \{G(\neg p \vee XFq), XG(\neg p \vee XFq), \neg p \vee XFq, XFq, Fq, q\}$$
$$M_5 := \{G(\neg p \vee XFq), XG(\neg p \vee XFq), \neg p \vee XFq, XFq, Fq\}$$

From these, we do not obtain any new states in this manner. The automaton's entire transition relation is shown in Fig. 10.3 in a simplified way. Note that every reachable consistent Hintikka set must contain $\theta, X\theta$ and $\neg p \vee XFq$, so their content is in fact entirely determined by the answers to the following questions.

- Is $\neg p$ included or XFq (or both)?
- If Fq is included, is q also included or XFq (or both)?

Due to the excessive use of nondeterminism and the use of symbolic transition labels it is not easy to see that $\mathcal{A}_\theta$ accepts exactly those words in which every position containing p is followed by a position containing q. One of the obstacles is the fact that p only occurs negatively in the transition labels. So take a word which only has finitely many positions containing p, and some position containing q after the last position containing p. It is accepted by a run of the form that is shown on the left of Fig. 10.4. As a second example, take a word that contains p everywhere, and q at every even position. It is accepted by the run shown on the right of that figure.

We need to show that this construction does not only work in this example.

Theorem 10.24 *For every LTL formula θ in NNF with k U-subformulas there is a GNBA $\mathcal{A}_\theta$ of size at most $2^{2 \cdot |\theta|}$ and index k such that $L(\mathcal{A}_\theta) = L(\theta)$.*

Proof The construction of $\mathcal{A}_\theta$ is shown above. The estimation on its index is trivially seen to be true. The statement on its size is obtained using Lemma 10.21 stating that $|FL(\theta)| \leq 2 \cdot |\theta|$ and the fact that a consistent Hintikka set is a subset of $FL(\theta)$.

It remains to be seen that $L(\mathcal{A}_\theta) = L(\theta)$. Let $\varphi_1 U \psi_1, \ldots, \varphi_k U \psi_k$ be an enumeration of all U-formulas in $FL(\theta)$ in no particular order.

"⊇" Suppose that $w = a_0 a_1 \ldots \in L(\theta)$, i.e. $w, 0 \vDash \theta$. For every $i \in \mathbb{N}$ we define the set $M_i := \{\psi \in FL(\theta) \mid w, i \vDash \psi\}$. Then we have $\theta \in M_0$ by assumption and for every $i \in \mathbb{N}$ the following hold.

(I) $M_i \in \mathcal{H}(\theta)$, i.e. each M_i is a consistent Hintikka set.
(II) If $\mathsf{X}\psi \in M_i$ then $\psi \in M_{i+1}$.
(III) $\mathcal{P}^+(M_i) \subseteq a_i$ and $\{q \mid \neg q \in \mathcal{P}^-(M_i)\} \cap a_i = \varnothing$.
(IV) For every $j \in \{1, \ldots, k\}$ with $\varphi_j \mathsf{U} \psi_j \in M_i$ there is some $i' \geq i$ such that $\psi_j \in M_{i'}$. This is a consequence of the fact that every U-formula that holds somewhere must be satisfied at a later moment, more specifically its right argument must hold eventually.

Because of (I) we have that $M_0, M_1, \ldots$ is a sequence of states in $\mathcal{A}_\theta$. $\mathcal{A}_\varphi$. Because of the observation that $\theta \in M_0$ this sequence begins in an initial state. Because of (II) and (III) this sequence forms a valid run on w. Because of (IV) it is accepting. Hence, $w \in L(\mathcal{A}_\theta)$.

"⊆" Suppose that $w = a_0 a_1 \ldots \in L(\mathcal{A}_\theta)$, i.e. there is an accepting run $\rho = M_0, M_1, \ldots$ of $\mathcal{A}_\theta$ on w. We will show by induction on the structure of LTL formulas that for all $\varphi \in FL(\theta)$ with $\varphi \in M_i$ we have $w, i \vDash \varphi$. It should be clear that then we have $w, 0 \vDash \theta$, i.e. $w \in L(\theta)$, in particular because M_0 must contain θ.

Case $\varphi = q$ for some $q \in \mathcal{P}$. Suppose that $q \in M_i$. Note that then $q \in \mathcal{P}^+(M_i)$ in particular. Since ρ is accepting, it is infinite, and so it must take a transition from M_i to M_{i+1} under the alphabet symbol a_i. By construction of the transition relation we have $\mathcal{P}^+(M_i) \subseteq a_i$, i.e. in particular $q \in a_i$ and therefore $w, i \vDash q$.

Case $\varphi = \neg q$ for some $q \in \mathcal{P}$. By the same reasoning as in the previous case we get that $w, i \nvDash q$, resp. $w, i \vDash \neg q$ because $\neg q \in \mathcal{P}^-(M_i)$ and, thus, $q \notin a_i$.

Case $\varphi = \psi_1 \vee \psi_2$ or $\varphi = \psi_1 \wedge \psi_2$. Here, $w, i \vDash \varphi$ follows immediately from the inductive hypothesis for either or both of ψ_1, ψ_2 and the fact that M_i is a Hintikka set, i.e. it needs to contain both conjuncts of a conjunction, and one disjunct of a disjunction.

Case $\varphi = \mathsf{X}\psi$. Suppose that $\varphi \in M_i$. By the construction of the transition relation we have $\psi \in M_{i+1}$. By the hypothesis, we get $w, i + 1 \vDash \psi$, and so $w, i \vDash \varphi$.

Case $\varphi = \psi_1 \mathsf{U} \psi_2$. Note that there is some $\ell \in \{1, \ldots, k\}$ such that φ is the ℓ-th U-formula in the enumeration fixed above. Suppose now that $\varphi \in M_i$. By the definition of a Hintikka set and the transition relation, we have $\psi_2 \in M_i$ or $\psi_1 \in M_1$ and $\varphi \in M_{i+1}$. The second option can be unrolled further: we have $\psi_2 \in M_{i+1}$ or $\psi_1 \in M_{i+1}$ and $\varphi \in M_{i+2}$, etc. Since ρ is accepting, the sequence $M_i, M_{i+1}, M_{i+2}, \ldots$ must eventually hit the acceptance set F_ℓ, i.e. they cannot all contain ψ_1 and φ. Instead, some state in this sequence, say M_j for some $j \geq i$, must contain ψ_2. Let j be chosen minimal. Then $\psi_1 \in M_h$ for $i \leq h < j$. We can now apply the hypothesis for ψ_1 and M_h for such h, as well as to ψ_2 and M_j, and get that $w, j \vDash \psi_2$ and $w, h \vDash \psi_1$ for all h with $i \leq h < j$. Hence, $w, i \vDash \varphi$.

Case $\varphi = \psi_1 \mathsf{R} \psi_2$. Similar to the previous case we get that $\{\psi_1, \psi_2\} \subseteq M_i$ or $\psi_2 \in M_i$ and $\varphi \in M_{i+1}$. Again, this can be unrolled but this time there is no argument ensuring termination of this unrolling. Hence, either $\psi_2 \in M_h$ for all $h \geq i$, or there is some $j \geq i$ such that $\psi_1 \in M_j$, and $\psi_2 \in M_h$ for all h with $i \leq h \leq j$. Applying the hypothesis again to all ψ_1 and ψ_2 and the corresponding Hintikka sets, we get that $w, i \vDash \psi_1 \mathrel{R} \psi_2$ in both these cases. $\square$

Putting Cor. 10.15, Thm. 10.24 and 10.19 together, we obtain the goal of a translation from LTL into NBA of elementary complexity.

Corollary 10.25 *For every LTL formula φ there is an NBA $\mathcal{A}_\varphi$ of size $2^{\mathcal{O}(|\varphi|)}$ such that $L(\mathcal{A}_\varphi) = L(\varphi)$.*

10.3 From LTL to Very Weak Alternating Automata

While alternation generally allows languages to be represented with exponentially smaller automata then nondeterministic ones, and they are arguable closer to logical formulas with Boolean conjunctions and disjunctions, they do not provide a more efficient way to translate MSO into automata. The problem there is that existential quantification over second-order variables is handled by alphabet projection which is only sound for nondeterministic automata.

It is reasonable to ask whether this is still an obstacle for a much weaker logic like LTL, especially since LTL does not feature quantification over variables, let alone second-order ones. The answer is no, i.e. alternating automata provide a framework for a direct translation from LTL formulas that results in smaller automata than the NBA obtained in the previous section that are generally of exponential size.

As it turns out, the automata obtained from LTL formulas have a very special form. They are not only weak in the sense of Sect. 9.5 but in fact syntactically even more specialised which we call being *very weak*.

For a positive Boolean formula $f \in \mathbb{B}^+(Q)$ and some $q \in Q$ we simply write $q \in f$ to state that q occurs syntactically in f.

Definition 10.26 Let $\mathcal{A} = (Q, \Sigma, q_0, \delta, F)$ be an ABA. It is called *very weak* (VWABA) if there is a partial order '$\leq$' on Q such that for all $a \in \Sigma$ and all $q, q' \in Q$ with $q' \in \delta(q, a)$ we have $q' \leq q$.

Very weak alternating automata are also known as being *counter-free*. The reason is that a loop of length k through the transition table can be seen as the automaton's ability to "count modulo k." Now the presence of a total order with the requirement that transitions do not ascend in this order, precludes the existence of loops of length greater than 1.

This is only a very crude intuitive explanation for what being counterfree means. It does not mean that a language which intuitively requires counting modulo some k greater than 1 cannot be VWABA-definable.

Example 10.27 The language $(ab)^\omega \cup (ba)^\omega$ is recognised by the ABA shown in Fig. 10.5. It is easily seen to be very weak by employing any of the three partial orders that satisfy $0 > 1 > 3$ and $0 > 2 > 3$. Then transitions in this ABA only ever lead to states that are smaller or equal in this order.

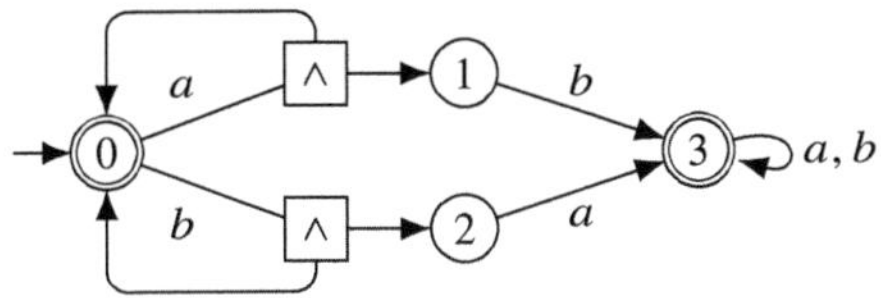

Fig. 10.5 Very weak ABA recognising $(ab)^\omega \cup (ba)^\omega$.

It should be clear that every VWABA is also a WABA, i.e. being very weak is a restriction of the concept of being weak. Remember that a weak alternating automaton is one whose state space can be partitioned such that each part either consists of accepting states or of non-accepting states only, and there is a partial order on the parts such transitions never lead to parts that are greater in this order. A very weak automaton is then a weak automaton in which every part of the partition is a singleton set only.

Unlike WABA, VWABA are less expressive than general ABA, i.e. their expressiveness is genuinely below that of ω-regular languages. Ex. 10.27 is slightly misleading by suggesting that when recognising a word of the form $(ab)^\omega$, one would do counting modulo 2. A language that cannot be recognised by VWABA is, for example $\{a_0a_1 \ldots \in \{a,b\}^\omega \mid \forall i \in \mathbb{N} : a_{2i} = a\}$. This does indeed require proper counting modulo 2 in order to know whether a letter is required to be a or nor, whereas no counting is needed to recognise $(ab)^\omega \cup (ba)^\omega$: one simply needs to verify alternation between each two adjacent input symbols.

A formal proof of this upper bound on the expressiveness of VWABA would require a bit more machinery, for instance the introduction of Ehrenfeucht-Fraïssé games on infinite words, as well as showing that they capture exactly the expressiveness of FO and LTL. While this is true, we will only show equi-expressiveness between LTL and VWABA here. We begin with the translation of formulas into automata. It essentially shows that an LTL formula can directly be regarded as a VWABA.

Theorem 10.28 *For every LTL formula φ there is a VWABA $\mathcal{A}_\varphi$ of size $\mathcal{O}(|\varphi|)$ such that $L(\mathcal{A}_\varphi) = L(\varphi)$.*

Proof According to Cor. 10.15 we can assume φ to be given in NNF. This incurs a linear blowup only. We define the ABA $\mathcal{A}_\varphi$ as

$$(Sub(\varphi) \cup \{\mathrm{tt}, \mathrm{ff}\}, \Sigma, \varphi, \delta, F)$$

where Σ is the alphabet underlying φ. The state space consists of all subformulas of φ with possibly additional formulas tt and ff that are needed in order to ensure that the transition function can always assign a successor state. It is defined inductively on the structure of φ for all $a \in \Sigma$ as follows.

$$\delta(\mathrm{tt}, a) \ := \ \mathrm{tt}$$
$$\delta(\mathrm{ff}, a) \ := \ \mathrm{ff}$$

$$
\delta(p,a) \;:=\; \begin{cases} \text{tt} & \text{, if } p \in a \\ \text{ff} & \text{, otherwise} \end{cases}
$$

$$
\delta(\neg p,a) \;:=\; \begin{cases} \text{ff} & \text{, if } p \in a \\ \text{tt} & \text{, otherwise} \end{cases}
$$

$$
\begin{aligned}
\delta(\psi_1 \vee \psi_2, a) &:= \delta(\psi_1,a) \vee \delta(\psi_2,a) \\
\delta(\psi_1 \wedge \psi_2, a) &:= \delta(\psi_1,a) \wedge \delta(\psi_2,a) \\
\delta(\mathsf{X}\psi, a) &:= \psi \\
\delta(\psi_1 \,\mathsf{U}\, \psi_2, a) &:= \delta(\psi_2,a) \vee (\delta(\psi_1,a) \wedge \psi_1 \,\mathsf{U}\, \psi_2) \\
\delta(\psi_1 \,\mathsf{R}\, \psi_2, a) &:= \delta(\psi_2,a) \wedge (\delta(\psi_1,a) \vee \psi_1 \,\mathsf{R}\, \psi_2)
\end{aligned}
$$

Note that this is well-defined in the sense that $\delta(\psi,a)$ can unambiguously be written down as soon as $\delta(\psi',a)$ is known for the maximal genuine subformulas ψ' of ψ. Also note that in state $\psi_1 \vee \psi_2$ for example, $\mathcal{A}_\varphi$ employs existential branching, but it does not branch into ψ_1 or ψ_2, instead it branches into the options provided as the successors of ψ_1 and ψ_2. The reason simply is that an automaton progresses to the next position in a word in every step, whereas disjunction in the logic intuitively remains in the current state.

Intuitively, $\mathcal{A}_\varphi$ checks, when being in state ψ, whether ψ is satisfied in the current position of the underlying word. Hence, it is not surprising that φ itself is the initial state.

At last, let $F := \{\text{tt}\} \cup \{\psi_1 \,\mathsf{R}\, \psi_2 \mid \psi_1 \,\mathsf{R}\, \psi_2 \in Sub(\varphi)\}$. Thus, the states in which $\mathcal{A}_\varphi$ is allowed to reside forever are given by the R-subformulas, besides the special state tt. The reason for this becomes clearer when considering the fact that the transitions from states which are not U- or R-subformulas always lead to genuinely smaller formulas (apart from the two Boolean constants tt and ff). Hence, the only states that can be seen infinitely often on a path of a run are such subformulas or tt or ff.

Three properties of $\mathcal{A}_\varphi$ need to be verified. (i) The statement about it being of size linear in $|\varphi|$ should be clear. (ii) $\mathcal{A}_\varphi$ is indeed a VWABA. To witness this, take the relation '$\leq$' on its state space defined by

$$
\psi' \leq \psi \quad \text{iff} \quad \psi' \in \{\text{tt}, \text{ff}\} \cup Sub(\psi)
$$

which is easily seen to be a partial order. Moreover, transitions never lead to states that are greater in this order.

(iii) At last, it remains to be seen that $\mathcal{A}_\varphi$ is correct, i.e. that $L(\mathcal{A}_\varphi) = L(\varphi)$.

"$\subseteq$" We show that for every accepting run ρ of $\mathcal{A}_\varphi$ on a word $w = a_0 a_1 \ldots \in \Sigma^\omega$ whose root is labelled with $\psi \in Sub(\varphi) \cup \{\text{tt}\}$ we have $w \in L(\psi)$. This can be done by induction on the structure of ψ. The case of $\psi = \text{tt}$ is trivial.

Suppose that $\psi = q$ for some $q \in \mathcal{P}$. According to the definition of $\mathcal{A}_\varphi$'s transition function, the root node v_0 has a single successor v_1 (labelled tt). This is only possible if $q \in a_0$. Hence, $w \models q$. The case of $\psi = \neg q$ is done analogously.

Suppose that $\psi = \psi_1 \vee \psi_2$. By hypothesis, if there is an accepting run on w with root label ψ_i then $w \vDash \psi_i$ for $i \in \{1, 2\}$. Remember that $\delta(\psi_1 \vee \psi_2, a_0) = \delta(\psi_1, a_0) \vee \delta(\psi_2, a_0)$, and that any model M of a Boolean formula $f \vee g$ is also a model of f or of g. Hence, an accepting run of w with root label $\psi_1 \vee \psi_2$ can be turned into an accepting run on w with root label ψ_i for some $i \in \{1, 2\}$. By the hypothesis, we have $w \vDash \psi_i$, and therefore $w \vDash \psi_1 \vee \psi_2$, i.e. $w \in L(\psi)$.

The case of $\psi = \psi_1 \wedge \psi_2$ is similar. An accepting run with root label $\psi_1 \wedge \psi_2$ can be turned into accepting runs with root labels ψ_1 and ψ_2 by simply changing the root label accordingly. This is possible because any model M of a positive Boolean formula $f \wedge g$ is also one of f and of g. The induction hypothesis then yields $w \vDash \psi_i$ for both $i \in \{1, 2\}$ and, thus, $w \in L(\psi)$.

Suppose that $\psi = X\psi'$. Note that the root of an accepting run with root label ψ has a single successor labelled ψ', and the subtree rooted there is an accepting run on $v = a_1 a_2 \ldots$ By the hypothesis we have $v \vDash \psi'$ and therefore $w \vDash X\psi'$, i.e. $w \in L(\psi)$.

This leaves only the cases of the two temporal operators U and R open. These are certainly the most interesting ones.

Suppose that $\psi = \psi_1 U \psi_2$. Remember that $\delta(\psi, a_0) = \delta(\psi_2, a_0) \vee (\delta(\psi_1, a_0) \wedge \psi)$. Hence, there are two possibilities for the shape of an accepting run on w with root label ψ.

- The successors of the root node form a model of $\delta(\psi_2, a_0)$. In this case, we can change the root label to ψ_2 and the result is still an accepting run. By the hypothesis we get $w \vDash \psi_2$ and therefore $w \vDash \psi_1 U \psi_2$, i.e. $w \in L(\psi)$.
- The successors of the root node form a model of $\delta(\psi_1, a_0) \wedge \psi$. Since ψ_1 is a genuine subformula of ψ, the latter cannot occur in $\delta(\psi_1, a_0)$. Hence, the successors of the root node can be split as follows: one is labelled ψ, and the others form a model of $\delta(\psi_1, a_0)$. Now, ψ is clearly not smaller than ψ itself so we cannot apply the induction hypothesis to it. However, we can observe that ψ, being an U-formula, is not an accepting state. Moreover, the reasoning about the shape of the run at the top labelled ψ can be applied to the node labelled ψ on level 1 as well. This way, we obtain a path through ρ of nodes all labelled ψ. Since ψ is non-accepting, this cannot be an infinite path. Hence, it must eventually end with some node on some level k, labelled ψ such that its successors form a model of $\delta(\psi_2, a_k)$. We can apply the induction hypothesis here to obtain $a_k \ldots \vDash \psi_2$. We can also apply it to all previous nodes on this path and similar reasoning to the case of conjunctions above to obtain $a_j a_{j+1} \ldots \vDash \psi_1$ for all $j \in [k]$. But then $w \vDash \psi_1 U \psi_2$, i.e. $w \in L(\psi)$.

At last, suppose that $\psi = \psi_1 R \psi_2$. This is done similarly to the previous case. The only difference is the observation that here state ψ is accepting. So the run ρ contains a path that is either infinite and contains nodes labelled ψ only. In this case we can decompose the transition function for R-formulas and see that $a_j a_{j+1} \ldots \vDash \psi_2$ for all $j \geq 0$. Or this path is finite in which case it ends on some level k, and with similar reasoning as above we also obtain $a_k a_{k+1} \ldots \vDash \psi_1$. In either case we get $w \vDash \psi_1 R \psi_2$, i.e. $w \in L(\psi)$.

"$\supseteq$" Suppose that $w = a_0 a_1 \ldots \in L(\varphi)$, i.e. $w \vDash \varphi$. We can construct, by induction on the structure of φ, an accepting run ρ_φ of $\mathcal{A}_\varphi$.

If $\varphi = \mathrm{tt}$ then simply let ρ_φ consist of a single path with all nodes labelled tt. The case of $\varphi = \mathrm{ff}$ is impossible because $w \nvDash \mathrm{ff}$. The cases of $\varphi = \psi_1 \vee \psi_2$ and $\varphi = \psi_1 \wedge \psi_2$ are handled as above using the observation that models of disjuncts are also models of disjunctions, etc. Thus, an accepting run ρ_{ψ_i} with root label ψ_i can be turned into an accepting run $\rho_{\psi_1 \vee \psi_2}$ simply by relabelling the root node.

If $\varphi = \mathrm{X}\psi$ than simply add a new node above the root of ρ_ψ on w and label it $\mathrm{X}\psi$ to obtain an accepting run witnessing that $aw \vDash \mathrm{X}\psi$ for any $a \in \Sigma$.

If $\varphi = \psi_1 \, \mathrm{U} \, \psi_2$, then take k such that $a_k \ldots \vDash \psi_2$ and $a_j \ldots \vDash \psi_1$ for all $j < k$. We can now create a sequence of accepting runs $\rho_k, \ldots, \rho_0$ as follows. Let ρ_k be an accepting run witnessing $a_k \ldots \vDash \psi_2$ which exists according to the hypothesis for ψ_2. Change its root label to φ. Note that this is sound because if $a_k \ldots \vDash \psi_2$ then $a_k \ldots \vDash \varphi$.

Now suppose that ρ_j has been constructed already. To obtain ρ_{j-1}, take a new root node with label φ and two kinds of successors: one successor that is the root of ρ_j, the others obtained as the successors of the root node in an accepting run witnessing $a_{j-1} \ldots \vDash \psi_1$. By the construction of the transition function, in particular the fact that $M \cup \{\varphi\}$ is a model of $\delta(\varphi, a_{j-1})$ if M is a model of $\delta(\psi_1, a_{j-1})$, the obtained tree ρ_{j-1} is a run on $a_{j-1} a_j \ldots$ It is accepting because every infinite path is also an infinite path in one of the subtrees that are being glued together in this construction. Thus, we can take ρ_φ as ρ_0 obtained in this way.

As last, if $\varphi = \psi_1 \, \mathrm{R} \, \psi_2$, then ρ_φ is constructed in a similar way. Note that, if $w \vDash \varphi$ then $w \vDash \psi_2 \, \mathrm{U} \, (\psi_1 \wedge \psi_2)$ or $w \vDash \mathrm{G}\psi_2$. In the first case, ρ_φ can be constructed as in the general case for U-formulas. In the second case, to take an infinite path of nodes all labelled φ, and each of them receives, as additional successors, the successors of the root node of ρ_{ψ_2} which exists by hypothesis. Again, the result is an accepting run ρ_φ with root labelled φ because its infinite paths are either those that have a suffix in one of the accepting runs that are obtained by induction, or it is the single extra infinite path which is labelled φ all along and, φ being a R-formula, consists of accepting states only. $\qquad\square$

The converse of Thm. 10.28 is in fact true as well: VWABA capture exactly the expressive power of LTL. The following lemma formulates a key observation used in the proof of that result.

Lemma 10.29 *Let $\varphi, \psi \in LTL$ over $\mathcal{P}$, and $L \subseteq \Sigma^\omega$ where $\Sigma = 2^{\mathcal{P}}$.*

a) If L is the least language such that $L = L(\psi) \cup (L(\varphi) \cap \Sigma L)$ then $L = L(\varphi \mathrm{U} \psi)$.
b) If L is the greatest language such that $L = L(\psi) \cap (L(\varphi) \cup \Sigma L)$ then $L = L(\varphi \mathrm{R} \psi)$.

Proof Here, least and greatest is said in reference to the partial order '$\subseteq$' on languages. In both cases, it is easy to see, because of the equivalences

$$\varphi \, \mathrm{U} \, \psi \;\equiv\; \psi \vee (\varphi \wedge \mathrm{X}(\varphi \, \mathrm{U} \, \psi))$$
$$\varphi \, \mathrm{R} \, \psi \;\equiv\; \psi \wedge (\varphi \vee \mathrm{X}(\varphi \, \mathrm{R} \, \psi))$$

that $L(\varphi\,U\,\psi)$, resp. $L(\varphi\,R\,\psi)$ is a solution to the corresponding equation. It remains to be seen that it is the least solution in case of the U-formula and the greatest in the other case.

(a) Suppose L is such that $L = L(\psi) \cup (L(\varphi) \cap \Sigma L)$. We need to show that $L(\varphi\,U\,\psi) \subseteq L$. Take some $w \in L(\varphi\,U\,\psi)$, i.e. there is a $k \in \mathbb{N}$ s.t. $w, k \vDash \psi$ and $w, j \vDash \varphi$ for all $j < k$. For $i \in \mathbb{N}$ let w_i denote the i-th suffix of w with $w_0 = w$. Then we have

$$w_k \;\in\; L(\psi) \;\subseteq\; L(\psi) \cup (L(\varphi) \cap \Sigma L) \;=\; L\,.$$

Moreover, for every $i > 0$ with $w_i \in L$ we have

$$w_{i-1} \;\in\; L(\varphi) \cap \Sigma L \;\subseteq\; L(\psi) \cup (L(\varphi) \cap \Sigma L) \;=\; L\,.$$

Thus, we have $w_0 = w \in L$ which was to be shown.

(b) Suppose here that $L = L(\psi) \cap (L(\varphi) \cup \Sigma L)$. The claim is that $L(\varphi\,R\,\psi)$ is the greatest solution to the corresponding equation, so we need to show that $L \subseteq L(\varphi\,R\,\psi)$. Take some $w \in L$. Again, let w_i denote its i-th suffix for $i \in \mathbb{N}$. We have

$$w_0 \;=\; w \;\in\; L \;=\; L(\psi) \cap (L(\varphi) \cup \Sigma L)$$

and therefore $w, 0 \vDash \psi$ and, additionally, $w, 0 \vDash \varphi$ or $w_1 \in L$. Applying the same reasoning to w_1 yields $w, 1 \vDash \psi$, and $w, 1 \vDash \varphi$ or $w, 2 \in L$. Thus, either there is some k such that $w, i \vDash \psi$ for all $i \leq k$ and $w, k \vDash \varphi$. Or there is no such k and we have $w, i \vDash \psi$ for all $i \in \mathbb{N}$. In both cases we have $w, 0 \vDash \varphi\,R\,\psi$, i.e. $w \in L(\varphi\,R\,\psi)$ which was to be shown. $\qquad\square$

The distinction between least and greatest solutions is necessary. For example, Lemma 10.29 states that $L(p\,U\,q)$ is the least L such that $L = L(q) \cup (L(p) \cap \Sigma L)$. This equation has another solution, namely $L(p\,U\,q \vee Gp)$. It is not hard to verify that

$$L(p\,U\,q \vee Gp) \;=\; L(q) \cup (L(p) \cap \Sigma L(p\,U\,q \vee Gp))\,.$$

Moreover, we clearly have $L(p\,U\,q \vee Gp) \supseteq L(\varphi\,U\,\psi)$, so this second solution is indeed greater-or-equal.

Finding a non-greatest solution to the corresponding equation for R-formulas is left as an exercise.

We use this lemma to show that the language of a VWABA is LTL-definable. In the following theorem, we assume the alphabet size, resp. number of atomic propositions to be fixed. Otherwise the size estimation becomes more complicated.

Theorem 10.30 *For every VWABA $\mathcal{A}$ there is an LTL formula $\varphi_{\mathcal{A}}$ of size $2^{\mathcal{O}(|\mathcal{A}|)}$ such that $L(\varphi_{\mathcal{A}}) = L(\mathcal{A})$.*

Proof Let $\mathcal{A} = (Q, \Sigma, q_I, \delta, F)$ be a VWABA with $Q = \{q_0, \ldots, q_{n-1}\}$. W.l.o.g. we assume that the partial order '$\leq$' witnessing that $\mathcal{A}$ is indeed a VWABA, satisfies $q_i > q_j$ for all $0 \leq i < j < n$. This means in particular that all states must be reachable from the initial state which is of course a reasonable assumption, and that $q_I = q_0$.

For $i \in [n]$ let $L_i := L(Q, \Sigma, q_i, \delta, F)$ consist of all words that are accepted by $\mathcal{A}$ when started in state q_i. We construct, for each $i = n - 1, \ldots, 0$, an LTL formula φ_i such that $L(\varphi_i) = L_i$. When constructing φ_i we can assume φ_j to be constructed already for any $j > i$. It should be clear that $\varphi_{\mathcal{A}} := \varphi_0$ is then a formula correctly describing the language of $\mathcal{A}$.

In each step, we obtain φ_i as a solution to a recursive description of L_i. The construction distinguishes two cases.

Case 1, $q_i \notin F$. The language L_i of all words accepted by $\mathcal{A}$ when started in state q_i is the least solution of the equation

$$L_i = \bigcup_{a \in \Sigma} tr_a(\delta(q_i, a)) \tag{10.1}$$

where $tr_a(\psi_1 \vee \psi_2) := tr_a(\psi_1) \cup tr_a(\psi_2)$, $tr_a(\psi_1 \wedge \psi_2) := tr_a(\psi_1) \cap tr_a(\psi_2)$ and $tr_a(q_j) := \{a\}\Sigma^\omega \cap \Sigma L_j$.

Note that $\delta(q_i, a)$ cannot contain any state q_j with $j < i$, and for all $j > i$, L_j is already described by an LTL formula φ_j. The right-hand side of (10.1) is a positive Boolean combination of terms of the form $\{a\}\Sigma^\omega$ for some $a \in \Sigma$, and terms ΣL_j for some $j \geq i$. The entire expression can be rewritten into disjunctive normal form, i.e. a union of intersections, and divided into those intersections that contain ΣL_i and those that do not. Hence, we have

$$L_i = \underbrace{\left(\bigcup_{j=1}^{n_1} \bigcap_{h=1}^{m_{1,j}} \alpha_{j,h} \right)}_{\alpha} \cup \underbrace{\left(\left(\bigcup_{j=1}^{n_2} \bigcap_{h=1}^{m_{2,j}} \beta_{j,h} \right) \cap \Sigma L_i \right)}_{\beta} \tag{10.2}$$

where all $\alpha_{j,h}$ and $\beta_{j,h}$ are terms of the form $\{a\}\Sigma^\omega$ for some $a \in \Sigma$ or ΣL_j for some $j > i$. The part on the right of the top-level union additionally uses the distributivity law for $\cup$ and $\cap$ to extract the common factor ΣL_i from all the conjunctions that contain it.

Next we observe that the two languages α and β are definable in LTL by formulas φ_α and φ_β respectively, simply as Boolean combinations of formulas of the form χ_a for language terms $\{a\}\Sigma^\omega$, and $X\varphi_j$ for language terms ΣL_j.

The last step is then given by the observation that L_i is, as the least solution to the equation $L_i = \alpha \cup (\beta \cap \Sigma X)$, expressible in LTL as $\varphi_i := \varphi_\beta \, U \, \varphi_\alpha$ according to Lemma 10.29.

Case 2, $q_i \in F$. This is done in the same way, but here we derive an equation in conjunctive normal form as $L_i = \alpha \cap (\beta \cup \Sigma L_i)$ with the terms α and β not containing ΣL_i itself. Also, we are now interested in the greatest solution to this equation because an accepting run can contain a path that cycles through q_i.

According to Lemma 10.29, L_i is then described by $\varphi_i := \varphi_\beta \, R \, \varphi_\alpha$ where φ_α and φ_β are, as in the previous case, LTL formulas for the languages expressed by α and β respectively.

While correctness of $\varphi_{\mathcal{A}}$ follows immediately from this construction, we need to verify the claim on its size. The construction only creates linearly many formulas of the form φ_i, namely one for each state of $\mathcal{A}$, and each step relies on the transformation of a Boolean formula into disjunctive or conjunctive normal form. The blowup involved in this is at most exponential: a formula in disjunctive or conjunctive normal form over $|\Sigma| + |Q|$ elementary formulas can be seen as a set of sets of these n formulas. Hence, there are at most 2^{2^n} of them but each is of size $\mathcal{O}(2^n)$ at most. Note that these exponential blowups do not get iterated: in the construction for φ_i, all φ_j with $j > i$ can be seen as fixed and elementary for the conversion into disjunctive and conjunctive normal forms. $\qquad\square$

Example 10.31 Take the VWABA $\mathcal{A}$ from Fig. 10.5 over $\Sigma = \{a, b\}$. The partial order witnessing its very weakness is already compatible with the state names. I.e. in order to derive an LTL formula for $L(\mathcal{A})$, we can proceed by successively constructing $\varphi_3, \varphi_2, \varphi_1, \varphi_0$ in this order.

We have $L(\varphi_3) = \Sigma^\omega$, i.e. we can simply take $\varphi_3 := \mathrm{tt}$. We could also carry out the construction and compute the largest solution to the equation

$$X = \{a\}X \cup \{b\}X = \{a,b\}X = \Sigma^\omega \cap (\varnothing \cup \Sigma X)$$

as $\mathrm{ff}\,\mathsf{R}\,\mathrm{tt}$. Note that $L(\mathrm{ff}) = \varnothing$ and $L(\mathrm{tt}) = \Sigma^\omega$. Since $\mathrm{ff}\,\mathsf{R}\,\mathrm{tt} \equiv \mathsf{G}\,\mathrm{tt} \equiv \mathrm{tt}$, we obtain the same φ_3 in this case.

Next we compute φ_2. The corresponding equation is

$$X = \{a\}L(\varphi_3) = \{a\}L(\varphi_3) \cup (\varnothing \cap \Sigma X)$$

with corresponding solution $\mathrm{ff}\,\mathsf{U}\,(\chi_a \wedge \mathsf{X}\varphi_3) \equiv \chi_a \wedge \mathsf{X}\mathrm{tt} \equiv \chi_a =: \varphi_2$.

We equally obtain φ_1 as χ_b. Since there is no recursion in the equations in these two cases we obtain unique solutions, i.e. least and greatest solutions coincide. Strictly speaking, we were looking for the least solution because states 1 and 2 are non-accepting. The fact that we could equally have chosen the greatest solutions since they are the same, is reflected by the fact that the language of $\mathcal{A}$ remains unchanged when these two states or one of them is made accepting.

At last, the equation for obtaining φ_0 is

$$\begin{aligned}
X &= \{a\}(L(\varphi_1) \cap X) \cup \{b\}(L(\varphi_2) \cap X) \\
&= (\{a\}L(\varphi_1) \cap \{a\}X) \cup (\{b\}L(\varphi_2) \cap \{b\}X) \\
&= (\{a\}L(\varphi_1) \cap \Sigma X) \cup (\{b\}L(\varphi_2) \cap \Sigma X) \\
&= (\{a\}L(\varphi_1) \cup \{b\}L(\varphi_2)) \cap \Sigma X = (\{a\}L(\varphi_1) \cup \{b\}L(\varphi_2)) \cap (\varnothing \cup \Sigma X)
\end{aligned}$$

whose greatest solution is described by

$$\mathrm{ff}\,\mathsf{R}\,((\chi_a \wedge \mathsf{X}\varphi_1) \vee (\chi_b \wedge \mathsf{X}\varphi_2)) \equiv \mathsf{G}((\chi_a \wedge \mathsf{X}\chi_b) \vee (\chi_b \wedge \mathsf{X}\chi_a)) =: \varphi_0$$

which is indeed an LTL formula describing $(ab)^\omega \cup (ba)^\omega$.

We remark that, when dealing with alphabets of the form $\Sigma = 2^{\mathcal{P}}$, it is useful to work with a slightly different format for the transition function as it leads to smaller Boolean expressions in general. Note that

$$Q \times 2^{\mathcal{P}} \to \mathcal{B}^{+}(Q) \;\simeq\; Q \to (2^{\mathcal{P}} \to \mathcal{B}^{+}(Q))$$

for a state set Q in general. Moreover, the type $2^{\mathcal{P}} \to \mathcal{B}^{+}(Q)$ can be internalised when allowing positive Boolean formulas over states and literals of propositions, i.e. possibly negated propositions. Reconsider the VWABA for the language $(ab)^{\omega} \cup (ba)^{\omega}$ from Fig. 10.5. Suppose that the underlying alphabet $\{a, b\}$ has arisen from a singleton set of propositions $\mathcal{P} = \{p\}$, and $a = \{p\}$, $b = \varnothing$. Then the transition function of that VWABA can be written as a function of type $Q \to \mathbb{B}^{+}(Q \cup \mathcal{P} \cup \mathcal{P}^{-})$ where $\mathcal{P}^{-} := \{\neg q \mid q \in \mathcal{P}\}$ as follows.

q	$\delta(q)$
0	$0 \wedge ((p \wedge 1) \vee (\neg p \wedge 2))$
1	$\neg p \wedge 3$
2	$p \wedge 3$
3	3

10.4 An Application: Formal Verification

An important application of LTL is its use as a formal specification language for properties of dynamic systems with discrete state spaces. Such systems arise from hardware or software, and "dynamic" here simply indicates that such systems evolve in time by experiencing state changes. This happens for instance for hardware circuits that compute, in a sequence of cycles, values in registers depending on changing input signals. It also occurs with software: executing a program is typically done in a sequence of atomic steps that change the underlying memory which gives rise to a natural notion of state of a program.

Both hardware and software are often modelled to be nondeterministic. For instance, the states that a circuit goes through will depend on the values of the (unknown) input signals. The same happens for software whose concrete behaviour is determined by user input. There are other reasons for modelling such systems nondeterministically. For example programs with components working in parallel may be executed in a number of interleaving ways.

We focus our attention on non-terminating programs like components of an operating systems, sensors continuously delivering data, etc. This is not a restrictive view but rather a more general one since terminating programs can always be seen as non-terminating ones that eventually reside in a specific state of termination. On the other hand, there is no similarly simple way to model non-terminating behaviour using terminating programs.

We introduce a simple, intuitive model of such dynamic systems, called *labelled transition systems*. It is very reminiscent of finite automata, and this is in fact what allows formal specifications of program behaviour to be formally verified. In this setup, an LTS specifies program behaviour in terms of all the possible sequences of states changes it can do in its execution. A formal specification given as an LTL formula determines desired or undesired program behaviour. Checking the overall

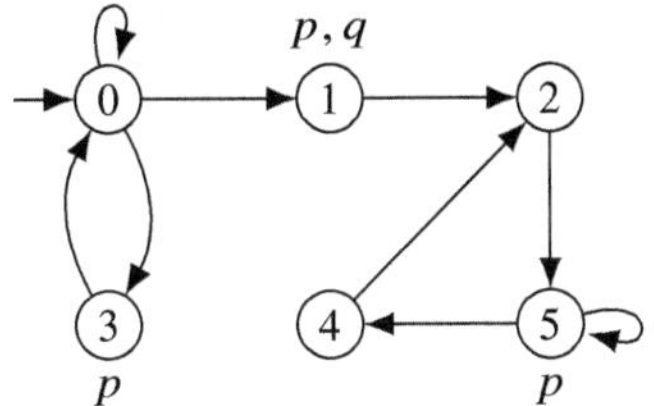

Fig. 10.6 Example of a transition system modelling a program with six states.

behaviour against it then decides whether the program is correct with respect to this specification or contains an error. Such a check is done using an automaton, specifically an NBA, that is equivalent to the given LTL formula.

10.4.1 Labelled Transition Systems and Traces

Definition 10.32 Let $\mathcal{P}$ be a finite set of propositions. A *labelled transition system* (LTS) over $\mathcal{P}$ is a $\mathcal{T} = (S, \longrightarrow, I, \lambda)$ where $(S, \longrightarrow)$ is a finite, directed graph with node set S and edge relation "$\longrightarrow$" that is assumed to be left-total, i.e. for every $s \in S$ there is some $t \in S$ such that $s \longrightarrow t$. Furthermore, $I \subseteq S$ is a set of designated *initial states*, and $\lambda : S \to 2^{\mathcal{P}}$ labels states with sets of propositions.

The size of the LTS $\mathcal{T}$ is measured in terms of the number of its states: $|\mathcal{T}| := |S|$, even though the number of transitions can be quadratic in that.

An LTS naturally represents the behaviour of a state-based program in time. Each maximal path through the underlying graph is a possible execution of the modelled system. Initial states can be used to restrict the executions' starts. This is very natural for programs that are run starting at particular lines of code and with assumed initial values for their variables.

Example 10.33 An example of an LTS is shown in Fig. 10.6. It represents an abstract program that can assume six different states, and the valid state changes are given by the edge relation in this graph. The model of this program is nondeterministic, there is no unique successor state in states 0 and 5.

The states' labels represent atomic propositions that hold true in the respective states. In a concrete example, this could represent some truth value like *"the green light is on"* etc.

One may wonder where to see the program in a more traditional form in this LTS. This is a somehow meaningless quest: the LTS *is* the program. It is given a very simple semantics: the finite graph represents possibly infinitely many infinite paths starting in its initial states. This is nothing more than a language of ω-words over the alphabet induced by the powerset of the underlying set of propositions.

However, not all examples need to be as abstracted away from programs in a more traditional form.

Example 10.34 Consider a system of three components running in parallel, one of which is a producer that adds items to a queue Q for as long as it has not reached its maximal capacity. The other two are consumers that remove items when Q is non-empty. Their behaviour is given in pseudocode as follows.

<table>
<tr><td>

1: **procedure** PRODUCER
2:     **while** *true* **do**
3:         **if** $\neg Q$*.full* **then**
4:             Q*.addItem*

</td><td>

1: **procedure** CONSUMER
2:     **while** *true* **do**
3:         **if** $\neg Q$*.empty* **then**
4:             Q*.removeItem*

</td></tr>
</table>

Fig. 10.7 shows an LTS modelling the system in wich each step of the entire system consists of a single step of one of its components. Here we assume that the capacity of the shared queue Q is 2. The states of the entire system can be described as a quadruple (c_1, p, c_2, q) where $p, c_i \in \{3, 4\}$ point to the line in the code that is to be executed next in the producer and the two consumers, and $q \in \{0, 1, 2\}$ represents the number of items currently held by Q. We ignore the outer while loops and start the system in state $(3, 3, 3, 0)$. Note that each component has transitions from line 3 to either 3 and 4, and from line 4 back to line 3 again. For brevity, we write 3330 instead of $(3, 3, 3, 0)$ etc.

The acute reader may have noticed that, besides the described states, the system can also enter an error state in two different ways. This is modelled by the addition of states *undr* and *over* representing failures because of queue under-, resp. overflows.

While it may not be imminent to see from the pure source code how a queue underflow can occur for instance, Fig. 10.7 reveals what the problem is. Simply take any path from the initial state 3330 to the failure state *undr*, for example

$$3330 \rightarrow 3430 \rightarrow 3331 \rightarrow 4331 \rightarrow 4341 \rightarrow 4330 \rightarrow undr \ .$$

Note that a transition from $c_1 3 c_2 q$ to $c_1 4 c_2 q$ means that the producer has checked that the queue is not full and gets ready to insert another item. A transition from $3p c_2 q$ to $4p c_2 q$ means that the first consumer has checked that the queue is not empty and is getting ready to remove the next item. The same holds for the second consumer and a change from state $c_1 p 3 q$ to $c_1 p 4 q$. Hence, the path above corresponds to the following program execution, starting with the empty queue:

a) Producer checks for non-fullness and inserts. Queue now holds one item.
b) Consumer 1 checks for non-emptiness and gets ready to remove but does not remove yet. Queue still holds one item.
c) Consumer 2 checks for non-emptiness and removes the item. Queue now is empty.
d) Consumer 1 executes the action to remove one item which fails.

As mentioned above, there is an implicit formal semantics to LTS as models of programs via the set of executions.

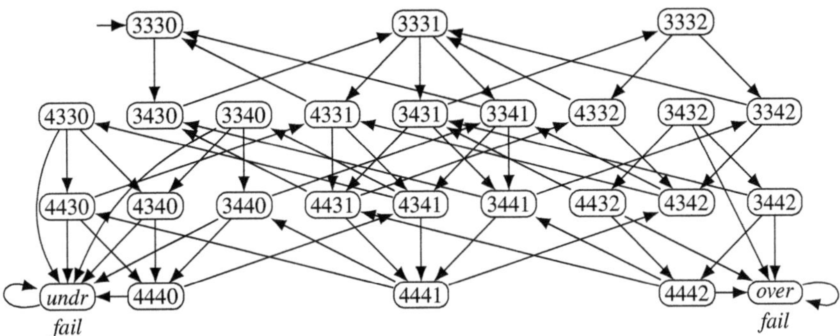

Fig. 10.7 Labelled transition system modelling the global behaviour of a producer and two consumers interacting via a queue of bounded capacity.

Definition 10.35 Let $\mathcal{T} = (S, \longrightarrow, I, \lambda)$ be an LTS over $\mathcal{P}$. A *path* (in $\mathcal{T}$) is an infinite sequence $\pi = s_0, s_1, \ldots \in S^\omega$ such that $s_0 \in I$ and $s_i \longrightarrow s_{i+1}$ for all $i \in \mathbb{N}$.

The path $\pi = s_0, s_1, \ldots$ induces the *trace* $\lambda(s_0), \lambda(s_1), \ldots$ in $\mathcal{T}$. We write $L(\mathcal{T})$ for the set of all traces induced by some path in $\mathcal{T}$.

Note that $L(\mathcal{T})$ is a language of ω-words over $2^{\mathcal{P}}$. It is not hard to see that it is ω-regular, at least for the LTS as they are defined here, namely based on finite state spaces. We remark that LTS can of course also be defined to be of possibly infinite size, and then their languages exceed ω-regularity in general. This also raises questions about finite representability etc. which are beyond the scope of this short introduction to LTS and their use in program specification and verification.

We recall the concept of weakness of an automaton which we studied predominantly with regards to alternating automata. The concept can equally be used for nondeterministic automata, though. Remember that an automaton is weak if its state set can be partitioned such that each part consists entirely of accepting or of non-accepting states only, and each cycle of transitions remains within a single part.

Theorem 10.36 *Let $\mathcal{T}$ be a (finite) LTS. There is a WNBA $\mathcal{A}_{\mathcal{T}}$ of size $|\mathcal{T}| + 1$ such that $L(\mathcal{A}_{\mathcal{T}}) = L(\mathcal{T})$.*

Proof Let $\mathcal{T} = (S, \longrightarrow, I, F)$ be an LTS over $\mathcal{P}$. Take a new state s_I such that $s_I \notin S$. We construct the NBA $\mathcal{A}_{\mathcal{T}}$ as $(S \cup \{s_I\}, \Sigma, s_I, \delta, S \cup \{s_I\})$ where $\Sigma = 2^{\mathcal{P}}$ as usual and, for all $s, t \in S$ and $a \in \Sigma$:

$$(s, a, t) \in \delta \quad \text{iff} \quad s \longrightarrow t \text{ and } a = \lambda(t) .$$

Additionally, we have $(s_I, \lambda(t), t) \in \delta$ for every $t \in I$.

The claim on the size of $\mathcal{A}_{\mathcal{T}}$ is easily seen to be true. It is equally easy to see that $\mathcal{A}_{\mathcal{T}}$ is indeed weak since all its states are final.

At last, we have $L(\mathcal{A}_{\mathcal{T}}) = L(\mathcal{T})$ because of the following consideration. First note that every run in $\mathcal{A}_{\mathcal{T}}$ is an accepting one since there are no non-accepting states. Then a path $\pi = s_0, s_1, \ldots$ with corresponding trace $w = \lambda(s_0), \lambda(s_1), \ldots$ induces a necessarily accepting run $\rho = s_I, \lambda(s_0), s_0, \lambda(s_1), s_1, \ldots$ through $\mathcal{A}_{\mathcal{T}}$ on w. Conversely, the projection of an accepting run to the underlying word is a trace in $\mathcal{T}$. $\qquad\square$

10.4.2 Model Checking

The *model checking problem* for LTL is: given a finite LTS $\mathcal{T}$ and an LTL formula φ, do all traces of $\mathcal{T}$ satisfy the specification φ, i.e. is $L(\mathcal{T}) \subseteq L(\varphi)$? This formalises the following task: given a model $\mathcal{T}$ of a dynamic state-based system and a specification φ of correct runtime behaviour, do all possible executions of the system adhere to this specification? Note the implicit universal quantification over all traces. So in this setting which is also called the linear-time framework vs. the so-called branching-time framework, a program is identified with the set of its possible runs, and correctness means that all possible runs are correct w.r.t. a specification about their behaviour in time which is modelled as an infinite sequence of moments. Likewise, a program is correct w.r.t. φ if it does not have a run that does not satisfy φ.

The model checking problem for LTL can be solved algorithmically using the translation from LTL into NBA (Cor. 10.25), together with the view of an LTS as an NBA of at most exponential size accepting all its traces (Thm. 10.36). Hence, model checking for LTL reduces (via an exponential-time reduction) to the inclusion problem for NBA which itself requires exponential time to solve, leading to a decision procedure that is doubly exponential in the size of the formula. This is not optimal, though.

First, we have

$$L(\mathcal{T}) \subseteq L(\varphi) \quad \text{iff} \quad L(\mathcal{T}) \cap \overline{L(\varphi)} = \varnothing \quad \text{iff} \quad L(\mathcal{T}) \cap L(\neg\varphi) = \varnothing$$

i.e. by making use of the fact that LTL is closed under negation we can reduce the model checking problem to the problem of emptiness of the intersection of two ω-regular languages. Since negating an LTL formula incurs at most a linear blowup by adding a negation symbol on top and turning the result into NNF, required for further procedures, while complementing an NBA incurs an exponential blowup, we have saved one exponential and reduced the complexity of model checking to singly exponential time.

Second, while ω-regular languages are closed under intersections (Thm. 5.17), the construction with an extra counter in the product NBA is unnecessarily complex for the purposes here. According to Cor. 10.25, $L(\neg\varphi)$ can be expressed by an NBA $\mathcal{A}_{\neg\varphi}$, and according to Thm. 10.36, $L(\mathcal{T})$ can be expressed by a WNBA $\mathcal{A}_{\mathcal{T}}$, so we have

$$L(\mathcal{T}) \cap L(\neg\varphi) = \varnothing \quad \text{iff} \quad L(\mathcal{A}_{\mathcal{T}}) \cap L(\mathcal{A}_{\neg\varphi}) = \varnothing \,.$$

Hence, model checking LTL reduces to the emptiness problem for the intersection of an NBA- and a WNBA-definable language. We observe that such an intersection can be recognised by a simpler NBA than the one that is obtained via the general construction for the intersection of two NBA-definable languages.

Theorem 10.37 *Let A be an NBA and B be a WNBA. There is an NBA C of size at most $|A| \cdot |B|$ such that $L(C) = L(A) \cap L(B)$.*

Proof Let $A = (Q, \Sigma, q_I, \delta, F)$ and $B = (Q', \Sigma, q'_I, \delta', F')$. We construct C via a straightforward product construction as $(Q \times Q', \Sigma, (q_I, q'_I), \Delta, F \times F')$ with

$$\big((q, q'), a, (p, p')\big) \in \Delta \quad \text{iff} \quad (q, a, p) \in \delta \text{ and } (q', a, p') \in \delta' .$$

The claim on the size of C is obvious. It remains to be seen that $L(C) = L(A) \cap L(B)$. The key insight here is, not surprisingly, that a run ρ in C defines a run ρ_1 in A and a run ρ_2 in B on the same word by projection onto the first, resp. second component in the visited states. Likewise, two such runs ρ_1 in A and ρ_2 in B on the same word w can be fused into a run ρ on w in C.

"$\supseteq$" So suppose that ρ_1 and ρ_2 are accepting, i.e. $Inf(\rho_1) \cap F \neq \emptyset$ and $Inf(\rho_2) \cap F' \neq \emptyset$. Since B is a WNBA, ρ_2 eventually traverses through accepting states from F' only. Now consider the fused run ρ. It eventually traverses through states from $Q \times F'$ only, and it contains infinitely many states from $F \times Q'$. Hence, $Inf(\rho) \cap F \times F' \neq \emptyset$ and it is therefore accepting as well.

"$\supseteq$" This is even simpler and does not use that fact that B is a WNBA. Suppose that $Inf(\rho) \cap F \times F' \neq \emptyset$. Then clearly $Inf(\rho_1) \cap F \neq \emptyset$ and $Inf(\rho_2) \cap F' \neq \emptyset$ since ρ_1 and ρ_2 are obtained as projections of ρ. So these are both accepting and the underlying word therefore belongs to the languages of both A and B. $\qquad \square$

This yields all the ingredients needed to solve the model checking problem for LTL.

Theorem 10.38 *The model checking problem for LTL formulas φ over finite LTS T can be solved in time $|T| \cdot 2^{O(|\varphi|)}$ and polynomial space.*

Proof Let T and φ be given. Deciding whether $L(T) \subseteq L(\varphi)$ is done by constructing

- the WNBA A_T of size $O(|T|)$ in time $|T|^{O(1)}$ using Thm. 10.36,
- the NBA $A_{\neg\varphi}$ of size $2^{O(|\varphi|)}$ in time $2^{O(|\varphi|)}$ using Cor. 10.25,
- an NBA for $L(A_T) \cap L(A_{\neg\varphi})$ of size $|T| \cdot 2^{O(|\varphi|)}$

and checking its language for emptiness in time that is polynomial in its size.

The claim on the lower space consumption of this procedure uses the observation that the product automaton can be built on-the-fly and that emptiness of an NBA can be checking in nondeterministic logarithmic space in the size of the automaton which is exponential in the size of the input $|T| + |\varphi|$. This leads to a nondeterministic, polynomial-space procedure, and a result known as Savitch's Theorem states that it can then also be done in deterministic polynomial space. $\qquad \square$

Bibliographic Notes

Temporal logics have arisen from work in philosophy, especially the development of *tense logic* by Prior [Pri57] for the formalisation of temporal statements. LTL in its current form was then introduced to computer science by Pnueli [Pnu77] for the purposes discussed here, namely the specification of program behaviour and, in a slightly weaker form, also by Kröger [Krö77, Krö87].

The automata-theoretic approach to LTL, in particular via nondeterministic Büchi automata, was then developed primarily by Vardi and Wolper [VW94, Var96]. The direct and relatively straightforward correspondence between LTL and very weak alternating Büchi automata has been observed by Löding and Thomas [LT00]. The use of automata corresponding to LTL formulas in program verification also led to many attempts to improve such constructions in practice, e.g. [GPVW95, GO01].

There is more to the theory of LTL-definable languages than what is contained in this chapter, and is only hinted at with Thm. 10.10 stating that LTL-definable languages are FO-definable. The converse holds as well, but it is conceptually and combinatorially a lot more complex and also does not necessarily involve finite automata. The result is usually known as *Kamp's Theorem* [Kam68] but it was proved for a version of LTL that also includes past-time operators, i.e. symmetric versions of U and R that regard previous rather than succeeding positions in a word. A step that completes the result that every FO-definable language is also LTL-definable is then given by *Gabbay's Separation Theorem* [Gab89] which states that every LTL formula with future- and past-time operators is equivalent over ω-words to one with future-time operators only. The combinatorial intricacies involved in the proof of Kamp's Theorem have called for attempts to provide simpler translations from FO into LTL, cf. [GPSS80, HR07, Rab14].

As with languages of finite words, first-order logic defines a robust subclass of the class of ω-regular languages. The concept of star-freeness can be extended to infinite words as well so that it corresponds exactly to FO-, resp. LTL-definability. This has mainly been explored by Thomas [Tho79]. Wilke has characterised this class in terms of a structural property of NBA known as counter-freeness [Wil99a], and this corresponds closely to an algebraic characterisation of this class via aperiodic monoids. The equi-expressiveness of these and first-order logic is a classic result by Schützenberger [Sch65]. Diekert and Gastin [DG08] present a rather full picture of the different models that all define this class, including temporal logic LTL.

The standard translation from LTL into first-order logic can be made to use only three variables. Combined with a translation back from first-order logic into LTL, cf. Gabbay et al. [GPSS80], one obtains that every star-free, resp. FO-definable property of ω-words is already definable in FO using three variables only. Etessami at al. showed that the two-variable fragment of FO corresponds exactly to the fragment of LTL using only the unary temporal operators *Next*, *Finally* and *Generally*.

LTL has traditionally been used for specifying infinite runs of systems, i.e. in the world of ω-words. It is not hard to define an interpretation over finite words only, essentially introducing two versions of the next-time operator. The resulting logic, often called LTL_f [GV13], is said to have interesting applications in areas of artificial intelligence like planning, and has therefore gained a lot of separate interest in recent years.

For many purposes in program specification, LTL is considered to be too weak, but MSO is considered to be too impractical as it requires to much expertise to be used correctly. This calls for extensions of LTL with increased expressiveness but similarly pragmatic interface in terms of temporal operators. Several attempts have been made at creating such specification languages. The temporal operator U can be enhanced with regular expressions refining it to only allow particular future moments at which it gets fulfilled. This idea is taken from Dynamic Logic [HKT00] and leads to an extension of LTL that can express all ω-regular properties [HT99]. The Linear-Time μ-Calculus [BB89, Var88] employs fixpoint quantifiers to explicitly express least and greatest recursively defined sets of positions in a word, just as U and R do in a very restricted form. This also makes it reach ω-regular expressiveness but it suffers from similar disdain as a language usable in practice for program verification. The *Property Specification Language* (PSL) [EF06] has emerged from an attempt to standardise temporal logic used in program verification making use of regular expressions similar to Dynamic Logic mentioned earlier. A commonality between the three extensions is not only ω-regular expressiveness, it is also the case that the automata-theoretic approach to LTL, either via nondeterministic or alternating automata can typically be extended to richer formalisms like these, cf. [Var08], in case of Dynamic Linear-Time Temporal Logic [HT99] and PSL [BFH05] more easily than for the Linear-Time μ-Calculus [Kai97].

At last, LTL is a de facto standard for temporal logics and is therefore routinely discussed in overview work on temporal logic in general (which spans a lot more than just LTL) [Eme90, HR07] as well as textbooks on (temporal) logic and/or automata [HR04, DGL16, EB23] or on program verification techniques [BK08, CGK$^+$18].

Savitch's Theorem, used in the proof of Thm. 10.38 to estimate the complexity of LTL's model checking problem, is a result in computational complexity stating that nondeterministic Turing machines can be simulated by deterministic ones at a quadratic blowup in space [Sav70]. Hence, any nondeterministic space-complexity class equals its deterministic counterpart if the resource bound is closed under squaring. In particular, NPSPACE equals PSPACE.

Exercises

Exercise 109 Construct LTL formulas that define the following languages over the alphabet $\Sigma = 2^{\{p,q\}}$ where $a = \varnothing$, $b = \{p\}$, $c = \{q\}$ and $d = \{p,q\}$.

a) $a^*b^*c^*\Sigma^\omega$
b) $(a^+b^+c^+d^+)^\omega$
c) $\{w \in \Sigma^\omega \mid |w|_a = \infty \Rightarrow |w|_b = \infty\}$
d) $(\Sigma^*a\Sigma^*b\Sigma^*c)^\omega$
e) $\{w \in \Sigma^\omega \mid$ between each two symbols d in w there is at least one $c\}$

Exercise 110 Let φ be an LTL formula over a finite set $\mathcal{P}$ of propositions. The formula φ' results from φ by replacing every occurrence of a proposition p in it by the characteristic formula $\chi_{\{p\}}$. Prove or refute the following statements.

a) If φ is satisfiable then so is φ'.
b) If φ is unsatisfiable then so is φ'.

Exercise 111 For $n \geq 1$ let $\mathcal{P}_n := \{q_1, \ldots, q_n\}$ and $L_n := \{a_0 a_1 \ldots \mid \forall i = 1, \ldots, n : \exists j \in \mathbb{N} \text{ with } q_i \in a_j\}$.

a) Construct LTL formulas φ_n of size $\mathcal{O}(n)$ such that $L(\varphi_n) = L_n$.
b) Construct NBA $\mathcal{A}_n$ such that $L(\mathcal{A}_n) = L_n$.
c) Show that every NBA $\mathcal{B}_n$ for L_n needs to have at least 2^n many states.
   Hint: Construct 2^n many different words $w_1, \ldots, w_{2^n}$ that all belong to L_n so that $\mathcal{B}_n$ needs to reach pairwise different states after some fixed number of steps when reading these w_i in an accepting run. This can be achieved such that otherwise, two of these runs could be combined to an accepting run on a word from $\overline{L_n}$.

Exercise 112 Show that, for any LTL formulas φ, ψ we have $\varphi \equiv \psi$ iff $L(\varphi) = L(\psi)$. *Hint:* This may seem obvious, and it is certainly the case that the "only if"-direction follows immediately from the definitions. But the "if"-direction needs an additional argument.

Exercise 113 Prove Lemma 10.13.

Exercise 114 Which of the following LTL formulas are tautologies, i.e. are satisfied by any ω-word of the underlying alphabet? Explain why. For those bi-implications that are not tautologies, explain which of the two implicational directions fails.

a) $\mathsf{G}\varphi \wedge \mathsf{G}\psi \leftrightarrow \mathsf{G}(\varphi \wedge \psi)$
b) $\mathsf{F}\mathsf{G}\varphi \leftrightarrow \mathsf{G}\mathsf{F}\varphi$
c) $\mathsf{F}\varphi \vee \mathsf{F}\psi \leftrightarrow \mathsf{F}(\varphi \vee \psi)$
d) $\mathsf{G}\mathsf{F}\mathsf{G}\varphi \leftrightarrow \mathsf{F}\mathsf{G}\mathsf{F}\varphi$
e) $\mathsf{G}\varphi \vee \mathsf{G}\psi \leftrightarrow \mathsf{G}(\varphi \vee \psi)$

f) $\mathsf{G}\mathsf{F}\mathsf{G}\varphi \leftrightarrow \mathsf{F}\mathsf{F}\mathsf{G}\varphi$
g) $\mathsf{F}\varphi \wedge \mathsf{F}\psi \leftrightarrow \mathsf{F}(\varphi \wedge \psi)$
h) $\mathsf{X}(\psi\mathsf{U}(\varphi \wedge \psi)) \vee \mathsf{G}\mathsf{X}\psi \leftrightarrow (\mathsf{X}\varphi)\mathsf{R}(\mathsf{X}\psi)$
i) $(\mathsf{G}\varphi \to \mathsf{F}\psi) \leftrightarrow \varphi\mathsf{U}(\psi \vee \neg\varphi)$
j) $(\varphi\mathsf{U}\psi)\mathsf{U}\chi \leftrightarrow \chi \vee ((\varphi\vee\psi)\mathsf{U}(\psi \wedge \mathsf{X}\chi))$

Exercise 115 Prove the following statement in analogy to Lemma 10.16, without using the definition of G as a special case of an R or via U and negations: for all φ we have $\mathsf{G}\varphi \equiv \varphi \wedge \mathsf{X}\mathsf{G}\varphi$.

Exercise 116 Find LTL formulas φ, ψ and a language L over alphabet Σ such that $L = L(\psi) \cap (L(\varphi) \cup \Sigma L)$ but $L \neq L(\varphi\mathsf{R}\psi)$. Verify that indeed $L \subsetneq L(\varphi\mathsf{R}\psi)$ holds.

Exercise 117 Construct LTL formulas formalising the following statements as well as NBA recognising the language of ω-words that satisfy these statements.

a) Proposition p holds at the next moment at which q holds.
b) Proposition p holds for as long as q holds.
c) Whenever q holds somewhere then p must have held somewhere before that.

d) Proposition q is true at finitely many moments only.

Exercise 118 Construct an accepting run of the GNBA that is obtained by the construction of Thm. 10.24 for the LTL formula $G(p \, U \, \neg p)$ on the word $bba(ab)^\omega$ where $a = \{p\}$, $b = \varnothing$.

Exercise 1 Construct the GNBA for the LTL formula $\varphi = G((FXq) \, U \, \neg q)$ according to the description in the proof of Thm. 10.24.

Hint: To simplify this, it is possible to restrict attention to minimal Hintikka sets, i.e. those that contain the formulas that must be contained and then are closed under the rules for Hintikka sets but do not contain any further additional formulas.

Exercise 119 Let $\mathcal{P} = \{p, q\}$. Construct VWABA for the languages defined by the following LTL formulas.

a) $Gp \wedge Fq$
b) $G(p \, U \, q)$

Exercise 120 Design a direct translation from VWABA into equivalent GNBA. *Hint:* Use the principles presented in the translations from VWABA to LTL and from LTL to GNBA.

Exercise 121 Find a path from state 3330 to state *over* in the LTS of Fig. 10.7 and explain what behaviour causes the queue overflow in terms of interleaving steps of the three components in the underlying programs.

Explain, similarly, why state 3432 is unreachable from the initial state while the somehow "dual" state 4340 is reachable.

**Part III
Trees**

Chapter 11
Automata on Finite Trees

Words are used to model computational phenomena like linear sequences of events or signals, runs of a deterministic program, etc. A natural generalisation of a word is a tree. Not only do trees play a significant role in computer science as data structures, for instance in binary search trees, they also naturally generalise the model of a sequence of events with a designated starting point and a unique successor at each moment, to a model of runs of nondeterministic programs for instance: instead of a unique next moment there may be several possible next moments. Reasoning about the entirety of the behaviour of such a program – instead of all its single runs only – then requires it to be viewed as a tree.

The three chapters of this part present an automata theory over trees, again with a particular focus on its applicability to logics. So, as with the cases of finite and infinite words, we develop some machinery that allows us to translate reasoning problems over trees into computational problems. It turns out that the very generic formalism of Monadic Second-Order Logic, which also has a natural interpretation over trees, retains decidability of its main decision problems like satisfiability and validity. Again, a rich theory of automata operating on trees, including fundamental results like effective complementability, is the key ingredient. This then opens up the possibility to automatically reason about the behaviour of certain nondeterministic programs, namely those with finite state-spaces for instance.

The step from words to trees or, equivalently, the extension of such sequences of events to having multiple successors, yet again comes with a price in terms of the involved combinatorics, as it was the case with the transition from finite to infinite words. We therefore consider the case of finite trees first. It can be seen as a warm-up for the more intricate case of infinite trees, to be dealt with in the next chapter, but it is also useful in its own right because of the ubiquitous use of finite trees as data structures in computer science besides the search trees mentioned above. Other examples include parse trees for context-free languages, abstract data types and XML documents. We will discuss selected applications of an automata theory over finite trees at the end of this chapter.

M. Hofmann and M. Lange, *Automata Theory and Logic*,
https://doi.org/10.1007/978-3-662-72154-4_11

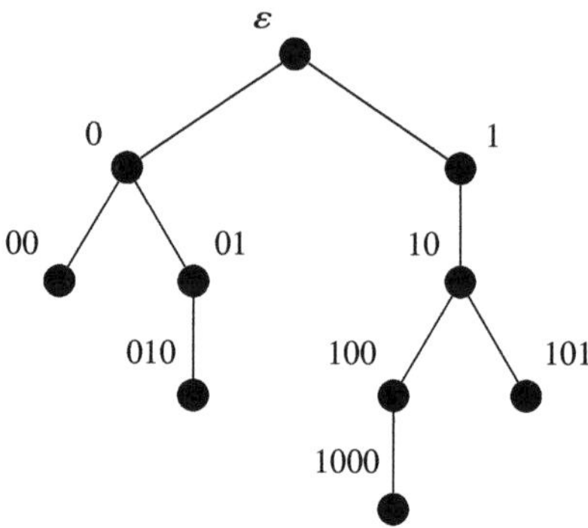

Fig. 11.1 A finite, ordered tree.

11.1 Finite Trees

11.1.1 Trees and Tree Languages

While it is intuitively clear what a tree is, a formal definition is certainly needed
in order to explain further concepts like an automaton's run on a tree, etc. Such
a definition has been given already, though, namely as Def. 7.3 in the context of
using finite trees to refine the powerset construction for the determinisation of Büchi
automata. Again, we consider *ordered trees* here which means that there is a total
order on the children of each *node*, i.e. amongst these there is a leftmost and every
other has a designated left sibling.

We recall that a *finite tree* is then a finite set $T \subseteq \mathbb{N}^*$ which satisfies *parent closure*
and *left-sibling closure*, i.e. the following two properties.

- Whenever $vi \in T$ for some $v \in \mathbb{N}^*$ and $i \in \mathbb{N}$ then $v \in T$.
- Whenever $vi \in T$ for some $v \in \mathbb{N}^*$ and $i \geq 1$ then $v(i-1) \in T$.

Recall that the first condition (parent closure) ensures that each node in the tree has a
parent node, apart from the root. The second condition (left-sibling closure) ensures
that for every node in the tree that is a child but not the leftmost child of another
node, its left sibling is also an element of the tree. It also means that the children of
node v are numbered $v0, v1, v2, \ldots$ from left to right.

The name of each node encodes its position in the tree by listing the directions
one has to take starting at the root node ε. For instance, node 3 19 0 2 is located at
the position that one reaches when starting at the root, then moving on to its fourth
child (i.e. the one with number 3), then to the twentieth child of that node, then to
the first of that one and then to the third.

Example 11.1 Fig. 11.1 shows the graphical and perhaps more familiar representation of the tree $\{\varepsilon, 0, 00, 01, 010, 1, 10, 100, 1000, 101\}$.

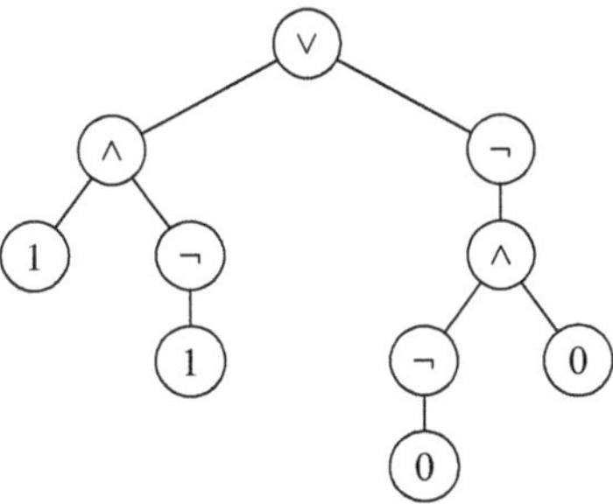

Fig. 11.2 A Boolean expression as a tree over the ranked alphabet of Boolean constants and operators.

The trees we consider as objects generalising words are not only ordered but also *ranked*. This means that the underlying alphabet Σ, still considered to be a finite set of symbols, comes with a ranking function $rk_\Sigma : \Sigma \to \mathbb{N}$ that assigns a *rank* or *arity* to each alphabet symbol. Σ is then called a *ranked alphabet* in this case. We will not consider unranked trees, hence whenever we speak of an alphabet Σ we will mean a ranked alphabet, and we will write rk_Σ for the corresponding ranking function. We will also write Σ_d for the set $\{a \in \Sigma \mid rk_\Sigma(a) = d\}$ of symbols of rank d. Hence, $\Sigma = \Sigma_0 \cup \Sigma_1 \cup \ldots \cup \Sigma_m$ for some maximal rank $m \in \mathbb{N}$.

Definition 11.2 Let Σ be a ranked alphabet and T be a finite tree in the above sense. A Σ-*tree* with domain T is a mapping $t : T \to \Sigma$ such that for all $v \in T$ and all $a \in \Sigma$ with $t(v) = a$ we have: $rk_\Sigma(a) = |\{i \in \mathbb{N} \mid vi \in T\}|$. Let $\mathcal{T}_\Sigma^*$ denote the set of all finite Σ-trees with arbitrary domain.

We will simply speak of a tree t instead of a Σ-tree over domain T since the domain can usually be inferred and the underlying alphabet is usually given by the context. Note that $\mathcal{T}_\Sigma^*$ adopts the role of Σ^* from the world of finite words in the world of finite trees. The notation for the set of all trees is different because it is slightly more tedious (but not impossible) to define the set of all ranked ordered trees as the result of an iterative process just like the notion Σ^* suggests.

An immediate consequence of Def. 11.2 is the fact that two nodes in a ranked tree that carry the same alphabet symbol also must have the same number of children. Moreover, ranked trees are finitely-branching, i.e. each node has at most finitely many children. The number is even bounded, not only because nodes are finite, but also because alphabets are finite, so some symbol must have maximal rank.

Recall that a language was, so far, just a (possibly infinite) set of words. Likewise we will refer to a set of trees $L \subseteq \mathcal{T}_\Sigma^*$ as a *tree language* or simply as a *language* since trees are our main objects of interest from now on. Languages of words will only play very specific roles in this, and then we will use the terms *word language* and *tree language* to distinguish between these two kinds when in danger of confusion.

Example 11.3 Let $\Sigma = \{0, 1, \neg, \wedge, \vee\}$ with

$$rk_\Sigma(0) \;=\; rk_\Sigma(1) \;:=\; 0 \;\;,\;\; rk_\Sigma(\neg) \;:=\; 1 \;\;,\;\; rk_\Sigma(\wedge) \;=\; rk_\Sigma(\vee) \;:=\; 2\,.$$

A ranked, ordered tree over this alphabet naturally represents a Boolean expression over the constants 0 and 1 and the operators of negation, conjunction and disjunction. For example, the expression $(1 \wedge \neg 1) \vee \neg(\neg 0 \wedge 0)$ represents the Σ-tree shown in Fig. 11.2 whose domain is exactly the finite ordered tree shown in Fig. 11.1.

An example of a tree language is therefore the language of all (representations) of Boolean expressions in this sense. This is a trivial example though, as it simply is $\mathcal{T}_\Sigma^*$ for this ranked alphabet Σ. Note that not only can every Boolean expression over these operators be represented as a Σ-tree as done above; but every Σ-tree also represents such a Boolean expression.

A non-trivial language of Σ-trees for this Σ is the set of all Boolean expressions that evaluate to 1 under the usual evaluation rules for the Boolean operators. The tree shown in Fig. 11.2 belongs to this language, but the tree obtained from it by replacing the symbol 0 with the symbol 1 at node 101 does not belong to it.

The connection between terms and trees brought out in the previous example is not coincidental. Not only do terms naturally have tree representations, but each tree can also be represented as a term. The infix notation used in the example above is more readable for terms that contain familiar binary operators like Boolean or arithmetical ones. Prefix notation is more natural for abstract alphabets. For example, the tree

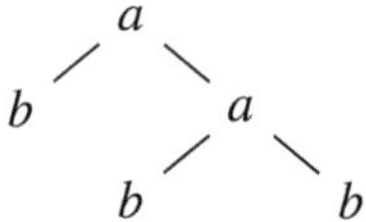

over the ranked alphabet $\Sigma = \Sigma_0 \cup \Sigma_2$ with $\Sigma_0 = \{b\}$, $\Sigma_2 = \{a\}$, would be written as the term $a(b, a(b, b))$ using prefix notation.

It is worth pointing out explicitly that the ranking of an alphabet implicitly partitions its symbols into those that can occur at leaves, namely those whose rank is zero, and those that can occur at genuine inner nodes, namely those whose rank is strictly greater than zero.

11.1.2 Two Different Directions

We will consider two kinds of finite automata operating on finite, ranked and ordered trees. Both are generalisations of the model of an NFA operating on finite words. The distinction of the two models is owed to the special structure of trees. Note that an NFA is intuitively seen as reading a word from left to right. Regular languages are closed under reversals, though, so one could also consider them as operating from right to left. In fact, a run of an NFA on a finite word $a_0 a_1 \ldots a_{n-1}$ of length n is just a labelling of each symbol with matching pairs of states: the one that the automaton is in before reading the letter and the one that it is in afterwards. The latter of course needs to coincide with the one that it is in before reading the letter to the right. So forming a run of an NFA on a word of length n can be seen as filling the positions between each two letters and before the first and after the last with states in a way that respects the transition table as follows.

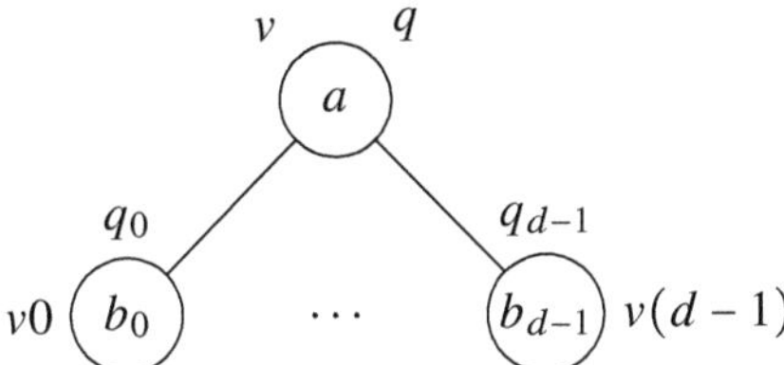

If we tried to lift this construction to trees we would be placing the automaton's states between the tree's nodes, in particular in places between the tree's levels. This is not impossible but a more natural approach would perhaps be to label the tree's nodes with states in a run, for instance like this:

Here we see a node with name v and its children with names $v0, \ldots, v(d-1)$. The parent node is labelled with the symbol a, and its children carry symbols $b_0, \ldots, b_{d-1}$. The nodes are additionally labelled with states, namely q at the parent node and $q_0, \ldots, q_{d-1}$ at the children as part of a potential run.

To see the potential for two types of automata in this picture, re-consider the picture for runs of NFA on finite words, in particular one such triple like (q_1, a_1, q_2). The intuitive understanding of the NFA reading the word from left to right is reflected in the mathematical dependency that the state q_2 in this case is determined from the combination of q_1 and a_1. However, one could equally define NFA to be reading words from right to left, meaning that the combination of q_2 on the right and the letter a_1 determines which states are allowed to be written down on the left like q_1. Either way ultimately results in the same class of languages accepted by such automata, namely the regular ones. Closure under reversal, respectively the way that it is proved, shows that there is no conceptual difference between the two modes reading from left to right or right to left.

However, for trees there is a conceptual difference. First note that because of the way that we drew trees as growing downwards, the directions from-left-to-right and from-right-to-left now correspond to top-down and bottom-up. This is just a representational difference, though, not a conceptual one. However, in top-down mode, the automaton is supposed to be in state q before it reads the node label a, and then it moves to the combination of states $(q_0, \ldots, q_{d-1})$. In bottom-up mode, it determines the state q from the combination of the tuple $(q_0, \ldots, q_{d-1})$ and the symbol a. This makes a conceptual difference because a tuple like $(q_0, \ldots, q_{d-1})$ can encode more information than a single state. So in top-down mode, the automaton would have to determine the next states from the information that is given by the letter being read and a single state, in bottom-up mode it has more information available to determine the next state.

We will make these intuitive explanations formal in the following. In particular, top-down and bottom-up tree automata are distinguished by the type of their transition tables. Before we get to these definitions we need to point out a perhaps strange effect of the choice that runs should be labellings of the tree's nodes with states. Then a run has exactly as many levels as the underlying tree which would correspond to a situation in the world of words where runs are exactly as long as the underlying words. It is not hard to see that an automaton model with initial and final states would then only accept languages that are either invariant in the first or the last letter, i.e. languages of the form ΣL, resp. $L\Sigma$ for some regular language L. This can be fixed by not starting in a fixed initial state but in a state that depends on the first letter of the word. Likewise one could replace accepting states by an accepting mode that takes the currently read letter into consideration. This then needs to be done for tree automata as well, and it turns out that such initial or final assignments can simply be incorporated into the transition table. This is why top-down automata for example will have initial states but no final ones as their usual function is provided by the transition table. Likewise, bottom-up automata will have final states but no initial ones.

11.2 Direction Bottom-Up

11.2.1 Bottom-Up Tree Automata

Definition 11.4 A (nondeterministic) *bottom-up tree automaton* (NbuTA) is an $\mathcal{A} = (Q, \Sigma, \delta, F)$ where

- Q is a finite set of states,
- Σ is a ranked alphabet with corresponding ranking function rk_Σ and some maximal rank $m := \max\{rk_\Sigma(a) \mid a \in \Sigma\}$,
- the transition table is a collection $\delta = \delta_0 \cup \ldots \cup \delta_m$ of separate transition tables for each possible rank d with $\delta_d \subseteq Q^d \times \Sigma_d \times Q$ for all $d = 0, \ldots, m$,
- $F \subseteq Q$ is a set of designated accepting states.

As usual, the *size* of the NbuTA $\mathcal{A}$ is $|Q|$.

The partitioning of the transition table into transition relations for each rank is only done in order to precisely give the type of these relations, but these are dependent: the length of the tuple of states that the automaton is in – more precisely: that label the children of a node – depends on the rank of the alphabet letter that is being read next.

As usual, we sometimes regard a relation of type $Q^d \times \Sigma_d \times Q$ as a function of type $Q^d \times \Sigma_d \to 2^Q$ and write $q \in \delta((q_0, \ldots, q_{d-1}), a)$ instead of $((q_0, \ldots, q_{d-1}), a, q) \in \delta$. This is also needed to meaningfully define a deterministic variant of an NbuTA.

Definition 11.5 A *deterministic bottom-up tree automaton* (DbuTA) is an $\mathcal{A} = (Q, \Sigma, \delta, F)$ like an NbuTA except that δ is a collection of functions $\delta_d : Q^d \times \Sigma_d \to Q$ for each possible rank $d = 0, \ldots, \max\{rk_\Sigma(a) \mid a \in \Sigma\}$.

We extend the flexibility introduced above in regarding the transition table of an NbuTA as relations or as functions, whatever is more convenient, to the point where we regard a function of type $Q^d \times \Sigma_d \to Q$ as a special function of type $Q^d \times \Sigma_d \to 2^Q$ that returns, on every input, a singleton state. Then every DbuTA can immediately be regarded as an NbuTA, and their difference intuitively is that, once children of a node in a tree are labelled with states, these and the node's alphabet symbol label determine either several possibilities or a unique possibility to extend the state labelling to the node itself.

These considerations have already appealed to an intuitive notion of a run of an NbuTA on a finite, ranked and ordered Σ-tree as a labelling of the tree's nodes with states. It is time to formalise this properly.

Definition 11.6 Let $\mathcal{A} = (Q, \Sigma, \delta, F)$ be an NbuTA, and $t \in \mathcal{T}_\Sigma^*$. A *run* of $\mathcal{A}$ on t is a mapping $\rho : dom(t) \to Q$ satisfying

$$\rho(v) \in \delta_d((\rho(v0), \ldots, \rho(v(d-1))), t(v))$$

for all $v \in dom(t)$ where $d = rk_\Sigma(t(v))$.

Such a run ρ is called *accepting* if $\rho(\varepsilon) \in F$. The (tree) language accepted by $\mathcal{A}$ is, as usual, $L(\mathcal{A}) := \{t \in \mathcal{T}_\Sigma^* \mid$ there is an accepting run of $\mathcal{A}$ on $t\}$.

So a run of $\mathcal{A}$ on t is indeed just a labelling of t's nodes with states of $\mathcal{A}$ that respects the transition relations in the sense that each tuple $((q_0, \ldots, q_{d-1}), a, q)$ of children's label $(q_0, \ldots, q_{d-1})$ and parent's symbol a and state label q must be a legal combination according to the finitely many combinations prescribed by the transition relations.

A perhaps more interesting question regards the seemingly disappeared initial states. An NbuTA does not have initial states, so one may perhaps think that runs cannot be formed in a bottom-up style because there is no beginning for this process. Or perhaps the labelling could be started in an arbitrary state. Neither interpretation is correct, and the correct one is seen by carefully analysing the definitions of an NbuTA and its runs. Note that the transition function δ is composed of one for each rank, in particular there is a transition function $\delta_0 : Q^0 \times \Sigma_0 \to 2^Q$ for alphabet symbols of rank 0. As stated further above, these are exactly the symbols that can occur in leaf positions of a Σ-tree. Moreover, $Q^0 = \{()\} =: \mathbf{1}$, and a function of type $\mathbf{1} \times \Sigma_0 \to 2^Q$ can easily be seen as a function of type $\Sigma_0 \to 2^Q$. Note that an argument to a function whose values are drawn from a singleton domain does not allow any variation in the function's values, hence it can be ignored. We will also do this and consider the special case of the transition function for rank 0 to be some $\delta_0 : \Sigma_0 \to 2^Q$. And this is in fact where the initial states are hiding. Remember that a run on a tree with k levels also has k levels, and this is why we cannot have fixed initial and final states but one type has to depend on the symbols read at the beginning or end. So NbuTA do not have initial *states* but an *initial assignment* δ_0

that (nondeterministically) selects states as labels of leaf nodes depending on the alphabet symbols at these leaves.

Accordingly, a DbuTA should assign a unique state to a leaf node, but this can also depend on the symbol at the leaf.

We also simplify the notation for the transition functions of rank 1 and write $q \in \delta(p, a)$ instead of $q \in \delta((p), a)$ for example. I.e. we identify tuples of length 1 with their content or, likewise, consider δ_1 to be of type $Q \times \Sigma_1 \to 2^Q$ instead of $Q^1 \times \Sigma_1 \to 2^Q$.

Example 11.7 Reconsider the example of the tree language of all Boolean expressions that evaluate to 1, modelled as trees over the ranked alphabet Σ defined in Ex. 11.3. It is recognisable by a DbuTA, namely $\mathcal{A} := (\{0, 1\}, \Sigma, \delta, \{1\})$ with the three transition functions for ranks 0, 1 and 2 given as follows.

<table>
<tr><td>

δ_0	
a	$\delta_0(a)$
0	0
1	1

δ_1		
q	a	$\delta_1(q, a)$
0	$\neg$	1
1	$\neg$	0

</td><td>

δ_2		
(q_0, q_1)	a	$\delta_2((q_0, q_1), a)$
$(0, 0)$	$\wedge$	0
$(0, 1)$	$\wedge$	0
$(1, 0)$	$\wedge$	0
$(1, 1)$	$\wedge$	1
$(0, 0)$	$\vee$	0
$(0, 1)$	$\vee$	1
$(1, 0)$	$\vee$	1
$(1, 1)$	$\vee$	1

</td></tr>
</table>

Note that in the expression $\delta_0(0) = 0$, each of the three occurrences of the symbol 0 has a different meaning. The 0 in the index refers to the rank, i.e. the table for δ_0 lists the initial assignments that depend on the symbol at a leaf node. These symbols can be 0 or 1, and the 0 in the argument position of $\delta_0(0)$ refers of course to the alphabet symbol 0 of rank 0. Finally, the 0 on the right-hand side refers to the state that $\mathcal{A}$ enters in a leaf node labelled with the alphabet symbol 0.

The choice of states as 0 and 1, equal to the alphabet symbols or rank 0, is not made to be deliberately confusing. The DbuTA formalises the usual bottom-up evaluation of a Boolean expression over constants 0 and 1. This assigns a Boolean value of 0 or 1 to each subexpression. The value of subexpressions 0 and 1 is 0, respectively 1, and the value of a composed subexpression depends on the value of its maximal subexpressions and the rules for evaluating the Boolean operator at the top of the subexpression. This is exactly what is formalised in terms of a run of this DbuTA: each node in an underlying Σ-tree represents a subexpression, and the state assigned to a node in a run of $\mathcal{A}$ is exactly the value of that subexpression. Hence, it is fair to say that $\mathcal{A}$ formalises the usual bottom-up evaluation of Boolean expressions. It should also be clear that state 1 is the only accepting state: a Boolean expression evaluates to 1 iff the state reached at its root is 1.

A run of $\mathcal{A}$ on the tree representing the Boolean expression $(1 \wedge \neg 1) \vee \neg(\neg 0 \wedge 0)$ as shown in Fig. 11.2 is shown in Fig. 11.3. The states 0 and 1 are shown as labels near the tree's nodes. It is easy to confirm that they equal the value of the

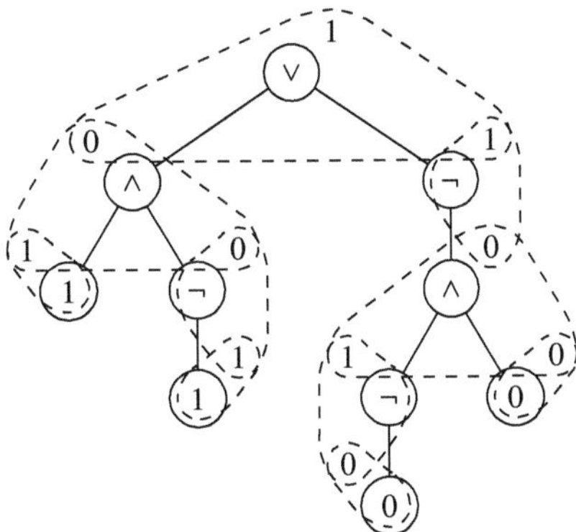

Fig. 11.3 Run of the DbuTA $\mathcal{A}$ from Ex. 11.7 on the tree from Fig. 11.2.

corresponding subexpression represented by the subtree rooted at each such node. The areas enclosed with a dashed line represent the transitions; they can all be found in the tables above. At last, the run is accepting since the root is labelled with the accepting state 1.

11.2.2 Determinisation

As with automata on words, an interesting question arising with the general models of nondeterministic and the special model of deterministic bottom-up tree automata is: does the deterministic variant have the same expressive power as the nondeterministic one? In other words: can NbuTA be transformed into DbuTA? The answer is positive: one can technically adjust the well-known powerset construction for NFA in order to obtain such a translation.

Theorem 11.8 *For every NbuTA $\mathcal{A}$ of size n there is a DbuTA $\mathcal{B}$ of size at most 2^n such that $L(\mathcal{B}) = L(\mathcal{A})$.*

Proof Let $\mathcal{A} = (Q, \Sigma, \delta, F)$. We construct the DbuTA $\mathcal{B} := (2^Q, \Sigma, \Delta, F')$ with $F' := \{S \subseteq Q \mid S \cap F = \varnothing\}$ and transition function Δ given rankwise via

$$\Delta_d((S_0, \ldots, S_{d-1}), a) := \{q \mid \exists q_0 \in S_0 \ldots \exists q_{d-1} \in S_{d-1} \text{ s.t.}$$
$$q \in \delta((q_0, \ldots, q_{d-1}), a)\} \, .$$

The claim on the size of $\mathcal{B}$ is obvious. It remains to be seen that $L(\mathcal{B}) = L(\mathcal{A})$.

"$\supseteq$" Suppose that $t \in L(\mathcal{A})$, i.e. there is an accepting run ρ of $\mathcal{A}$ on t. Since $\mathcal{B}$ is a DbuTA, it has a unique run ρ' on t, and all that remains to be done is to check that it is accepting. This is the case because the following invariant holds for all nodes v of t: $\rho(v) \in \rho'(v)$. This is easily seen to be the case for leaves v since ρ' labels these with the set of all states that could possibly occur at this node in a run of $\mathcal{A}$, in particular the run ρ, and therefore it includes $\rho(v)$.

For inner nodes this invariant is maintained because of the construction of Δ: take some node v with children $v0, \ldots, v(d-1)$. By the hypothesis we have $\rho(vi) \in \rho'(vi)$ for all $i = 0, \ldots, d-1$. Since ρ is a run of $\mathcal{A}$ it must respect the transition relation δ, so we have $\rho(v) \in \delta((\rho(v0), \ldots, \rho(v(d-1))), a)$ and therefore $\rho(v) \in \Delta((S_0, \ldots, S_{d-1}), a)$ for any sets $S_0, \ldots, S_{d-1}$ containing $\rho(v0), \ldots, \rho(v(d-1))$ componentwise.

Iterating this invariant eventually yields $\rho(\varepsilon) \in \rho'(\varepsilon)$. Since ρ is accepting we have $\rho(\varepsilon) \in F$, i.e. $\rho(\varepsilon) \in F \cap \rho'(\varepsilon)$ which shows that $\rho'(\varepsilon)$ is an accepting state of $\mathcal{B}$ and so ρ' is accepting, too.

"$\subseteq$" Let ρ' be an accepting run of $\mathcal{B}$ on some tree t. We claim that we can extract an accepting run ρ of $\mathcal{A}$ on t from it. We do this in a top-down manner.

At first, consider the root ε of t. We have $\rho'(\varepsilon) \cap F \neq \varnothing$, so $\rho'(\varepsilon)$ must contain some state, say, $q_\varepsilon \in F$. If there are several ones, pick an arbitrary one and let $\rho(\varepsilon) := q_\varepsilon$. Now remember that ρ' is a run of $\mathcal{B}$ that must adhere to the transition function Δ, i.e. we have $q_\varepsilon \in \Delta((\rho'(0), \ldots, \rho'(d-1)), t(\varepsilon))$ where d is the rank of the symbol $t(\varepsilon)$. Hence, there must be states $q_0, \ldots, q_{d-1}$ of $\mathcal{A}$ such that $q_i \in \rho'(i)$ for all $i = 0, \ldots, d-1$ and $q_\varepsilon \in \delta((q_0, \ldots, q_{d-1}), t(\varepsilon))$. The states $q_0, \ldots, q_{d-1}$ therefore witness the inclusion of q_ε in $\rho'(\varepsilon)$, and they all belong to $\rho'(i)$ for the corresponding children $0, \ldots, d-1$ of t's root. So this yields states at the level below the root that can be used to extend ρ: let $\rho(i) := q_i$ for $i = 0, \ldots, d-1$.

It should be clear that this one-step construction of selecting nodes in the labels of the run ρ' that are connected via δ is not restricted to the root and can be continued at every other node down to the leaves, picking a state q_v from $\rho'(v)$ for any node v. At the leaves we then selected nodes that the initial assignment in ρ could nondeterministically choose, hence, ρ is indeed a run of $\mathcal{A}$ on t. It is accepting because $\rho(\varepsilon)$ was chosen to belong to F. $\qquad\square$

11.2.3 Closure Properties

An immediate consequence of determinisability is closure of the class of NbuTA-recognisable languages under complements. As with automata on finite words, the deterministic variant yields a simple complementation procedure.

Theorem 11.9 *For every DbuTA $\mathcal{A}$ of size n over some ranked alphabet Σ there is a DbuTA $\overline{\mathcal{A}}$ of size n such that $L(\overline{\mathcal{A}}) = T_\Sigma^* \setminus L(\mathcal{A})$.*

Proof Let $\mathcal{A} = (Q, \Sigma, \delta, F)$. Simply define $\overline{\mathcal{A}}$ as $(Q, \Sigma, \delta, Q \setminus F)$. Determinism of $\mathcal{A}$ clearly carries over to $\overline{\mathcal{A}}$, so on any tree they both have a unique run ρ only (which is necessarily the same run). Since $\rho(\varepsilon) \notin F$ iff $\rho(\varepsilon) \in Q \setminus F$ we have that ρ is accepting for $\overline{\mathcal{A}}$ iff it is not accepting for $\mathcal{A}$ and vice-versa. $\qquad\square$

Putting the previous two theorems together yields closure of the class of NbuTA-recognisable languages under complements.

Corollary 11.10 *For every NbuTA $\mathcal{A}$ of size n over some ranked alphabet Σ there is an NbuTA $\overline{\mathcal{A}}$ of size at most 2^n such that $L(\overline{\mathcal{A}}) = \mathcal{T}_\Sigma^* \setminus L(\mathcal{A})$.*

It is not too hard to see that this class is also closed under unions since nondeterminism is available. Closure under intersections is then an immediate consequence of this using the deMorgan laws. A more efficient construction is obtained by lifting the product construction used for NFA to NbuTA. Details are left as an exercise.

Theorem 11.11 *For every NbuTA $\mathcal{A}_1, \mathcal{A}_2$ of sizes n_1 and n_2 respectively there is an NbuTA $\mathcal{B}$ of size at most . . .*

a) $n_1 + n_2$ such that $L(\mathcal{B}) = L(\mathcal{A}_1) \cup L(\mathcal{A}_2)$,
b) $n_1 \cdot n_2$ such that $L(\mathcal{B}) = L(\mathcal{A}_1) \cap L(\mathcal{A}_2)$.

Recall the definition of the class of regular languages of finite words as the closure of finite languages under unions, concatenations and Kleene iterations. This raises the question after the closure of the class of NbuTA-recognisable languages (as a candidate for a tree analogue to the class of regular word languages) under concatenations and iterations. We remark that such closure results also hold, but we do not investigate this in detail here. The reason simply is that the concatenation of two tree languages – based on the concatenation of two trees – is a bit more cumbersome to define as there is not a unique way to extend a tree t_1 "at its end" by another tree t_2, especially not in the ranked setting. One way to do this is to invent a special symbol, say $\bigcirc$, of rank 0, and tree concatenation of t_1 with t_2 is then performed by replacing one of t_1's leaves that carries the "hole" symbol $\bigcirc$ with t_2. This process can also naturally be iterated.

It is not hard to imagine that two NbuTA $\mathcal{A}_1$ and $\mathcal{A}_2$ can be combined so that the result accepts a tree iff it is the concatenation of some tree from $L(\mathcal{A}_1)$ with one from $L(\mathcal{A}_2)$. This requires a bit more bookkeeping than the concatenation construction on words since the tree resulting from the concatenation of t_1 and t_2 then has some leaves from t_1 and others from t_2, etc. It may also be more convenient to perform this construction for top-down tree automata, to be studied next, which of course immediately raises the question after their effective equi-expressiveness.

Before we study this next automaton model, we briefly mention another important closure result, namely that for homomorphisms. Again, the richer structure of trees compared to words requires a few more technicalities. Recall that a (word) homomorphism $\hat{h}$ was the natural extension of a morphism $h : \Sigma \to \Delta^*$ for some alphabets Σ, Δ, to a mapping of type $\Sigma^* \to \Delta^*$. This cannot be directly lifted to ranked trees.

Definition 11.12 Let Σ, Δ be ranked alphabets. A *rank-preserving morphism* is a mapping $h : \Sigma \to \Delta$ such that $rk_\Delta(h(a)) = rk_\Sigma(a)$ for all $a \in \Sigma$.

It naturally induces a *(rank-preserving) tree homomorphism* $\hat{h} : \mathcal{T}_\Sigma^* \to \mathcal{T}_\Delta^*$ via $\hat{h}(t)(v) = h(v)$ for any $t \in \mathcal{T}_\Sigma^*$ and any $v \in dom(t)$.

Note that $dom(\hat{h}(t)) = dom(t)$ for any t and any rank-preserving tree homomorphism h, i.e. tree homomorphisms are defined in a way that they do not alter the structure of a tree. This is not the most general definition that is possible, but it suffices for our purposes.

Not too surprising, the image of an NbuTA-recognisable languages under a rank-preserving tree homomorphism is also NbuTA-recognisable. The proof is left as an exercise.

Lemma 11.13 *Let Σ, Δ be tree alphabets and $h : \Sigma \to \Delta$ be rank-preserving. For every NbuTA $\mathcal{A}$ of size n there is an NbuTA $\mathcal{B}$ of size at most n such that $L(\mathcal{B}) = \hat{h}(L(\mathcal{A}))$.*

We may refer to this result also sloppily by saying that NbuTA-recognisable languages are closed under rank-preserving tree homomorphisms. This is either not meaningful or too weak, strictly speaking, since there is not just one class of NbuTA-recognisable languages, but one such class for every ranked alphabet.

11.3 Direction Top-Down

We develop a second automaton model that, intuitively, traverses trees starting from the root down to their leaves. As discussed at length above, though, this is really just an intuition rather than a mathematical fact. We will see that top-down and bottom-up automata are essentially the same, at least in their nondeterministic variant.

11.3.1 Top-Down Tree Automata

Definition 11.14 Let Σ be a ranked alphabet as above and $m := \max\{rk_\Sigma(a) \mid a \in \Sigma\}$. A *nondeterministic top-down tree automata* (NtdTA) is an $\mathcal{A} = (Q, \Sigma, q_I, \delta)$ such that

- Q is a finite set of states,
- $q_I \in Q$ is a designated initial state,
- the transition table is a collection $\delta = \delta_0 \cup \delta_1 \cup \ldots \cup \delta_m$ of transition relations, one for each rank, such that $\delta_d \subseteq Q \times \Sigma_d \times Q^d$ for each $d = 0, \ldots, m$.

As usual, we may use such a δ_d as a function of type $Q \times \Sigma_d \to 2^{Q^d}$ and write $(q_1, \ldots, q_d) \in \delta(q, a)$ for instance.

A *deterministic top-down tree automaton* (DtdTA) is such an NtdTA where $|\delta(q, a)| \leq 1$ for every $q \in Q$, $a \in \Sigma$.

As with bottom-up automata, alphabet symbols of rank 0 and 1 introduce a little bit of notational clutter which we can avoid. We identify Q^1 and Q again and write $q' \in \delta(q, a)$ instead of $(q') \in \delta(q, a)$ when $a \in \Sigma_1$.

For the case of rank 0 note that $2^{Q^0} = \{\varnothing, \{()\}\}$. Hence, a relation of type $Q \times \Sigma_0 \times Q^0$, resp. a function of type $Q \times \Sigma_0 \to 2^{Q^0}$ can be seen as returning, for any state q and any alphabet symbol of rank 0, one of two answers: either $\varnothing$ or $\{()\}$. These can be interpreted as *false* and *true*, and this interpretation is not far fetched: the set $\delta(q, a)$ contains the possibilities to label the children of some tree node v that carries the symbol a, with tuples of states. Hence, for a leaf node v carrying an a, $\delta(q, a) = \varnothing$ means that there is no possibility to continue the labelling past v in a run; and $\delta(q, a) = \{()\}$ means there is exactly one possibility to label v's zero children, namely with the empty tuple of states. This defines, in a natural way, an acceptance condition: we write $\bot$, resp. $\top$ instead of $\varnothing$, resp. $\{()\}$, and then $\delta(q, a) = \bot$ means unsuccessful finishing of a branch in a run, and $\delta(q, a) = \top$ means successful finishing. In this way, NtdTA, that do not have explicit accepting or final states, do indeed have a final assignment in terms of δ_0, just like NbuTA have an initial assignment.

Definition 11.15 A *run* of an NtdTA $\mathcal{A} = (Q, \Sigma, q_I, \delta)$ on a Σ-tree t is a $\rho : dom(t) \rightarrow Q$ that satisfies the following.

- $\rho(\varepsilon) = q_I$,
- $(\rho(v0), \ldots, \rho(v(d-1))) \in \delta_d(\rho(v), t(v))$ for all ranks $d \geq 1$, all $a \in \Sigma_d$ and all $v \in dom(t)$ such that $t(v) = a$.

Such a run ρ is *accepting* if $\delta(\rho(v), t(v)) = \top$ for all leaf nodes $v \in dom(t)$.

The language of the NtdTA $\mathcal{A}$ is, as usual, $L(\mathcal{A}) := \{t \mid$ there is an accepting run of $\mathcal{A}$ on $t\}$.

We remark that there is a slightly shorter way to define an accepting run: simply demand the statement in the second bullet not just for all $d \geq 1$ but for all $d \geq 0$. The case of $d = 0$ is exactly what is stated in the additional requirement above for a run to be accepting. Hence, if the requirements on a run were formulated for all $d \geq 0$, then all runs would be accepting. This would not render non-accepting runs suddenly as accepting. It just means that non-accepting runs would not be classified as runs at all anymore, and the class of NtdTA-recognisable languages remains exactly the same.

Example 11.16 Let $\Sigma = \{a, b, c\}$ with $rk_\Sigma(a) = rk_\Sigma(b) = 2$, and $rk_\Sigma(c) = 0$. The language of all Σ-trees that contain at least one occurrence of the letter b is NtdTA-recognisable, for instance by the automaton $\mathcal{A} := (\{q^-, q^+\}, \Sigma, q^-, \delta)$ with the following transitions.

$$\begin{aligned}
\delta(q^-, a) &= \{(q^-, q^+), (q^+, q^-)\} & \delta(q^+, a) &= \{(q^+, q^+)\} \\
\delta(q^-, b) &= \{(q^+, q^+)\} & \delta(q^+, b) &= \{(q^+, q^+)\} \\
\delta(q^-, c) &= \bot & \delta(q^+, c) &= \top
\end{aligned}$$

$\mathcal{A}$ uses its state q^- to signal, at any node v, that the subtree under v is still required to contain some b. Clearly this is what is needed for the root node; hence, q^- is the starting state. The state q^+ is used to signal that no requirement holds anymore. This is why $\mathcal{A}$ moves from state q^- to q^+ at both children when seeing a b for instance. At last, the entire tree contains some b if no more requirement to see a b is signalled at any leaf node.

Nondeterminism is used in the transition out of state q^- with the symbol a. So $\mathcal{A}$ effectively guesses the position at which to find a symbol b in the underlying tree.

δ_0

q	a	$\delta_0(q, a)$
0	0	$\top$
1	0	$\bot$
0	1	$\bot$
1	1	$\top$

δ_1

q	a	$\delta_1(q, a)$
0	$\neg$	1
1	$\neg$	0

δ_2

q	a	$\delta_2(q, a)$
0	$\wedge$	$\{(0, 0), (0, 1), (1, 0)\}$
1	$\wedge$	$\{(1, 1)\}$
0	$\vee$	$\{(0, 0)\}$
1	$\vee$	$\{(0, 1), (1, 0), (1, 1)\}$

Fig. 11.4 Transition table of an NtdTA recognising Boolean expressions that evaluate to 1.

We consider a second example which can be used to compare top-down with bottom-up tree automata.

Example 11.17 Recall the language of all Boolean expressions that evaluates to 1, modelled as trees over the ranked alphabet $\Sigma = \Sigma_0 \cup \Sigma_1 \cup \Sigma_2$ with $\Sigma_0 = \{0, 1\}$, $\Sigma_1 = \{\neg\}$ and $\Sigma_2 = \{\wedge, \vee\}$.

A NtdTA recognising this language is $(\{0, 1\}, \Sigma, 1, \delta)$ with transition table δ shown in Fig. 11.4. Intuitively, it guesses the value at each subexpression that this evaluates to, using its two states $0, 1$. Surely, it has to start with state 1 at the root as the entire expression is supposed to evaluate to 1. When encountering a negation symbol, the state is flipped. At a conjunction, for instance, in state 1 there is only one possibility that this could be the value of that subexpression, namely when both its subexpressions evaluate to 1 as well. This is why there is only one transition to $(1, 1)$. There are three possibilities, though, for the value to become 0, namely when one or both its subexpressions evaluate to 0. The NtdTA uses nondeterminism to guess which of these is the case and continues to confirm its guess.

The behaviour at leaf nodes is then clear: the value of a subexpression at a leaf node is its label, so the NtdTA simply confirms that the state reached at that leaf node equals its label.

There are obvious differences between the top-down automaton in this example and the bottom-up automaton in Ex. 11.7, most notably the fact that the bottom-up automaton is deterministic while it is unclear how to avoid nondeterminism in the top-down variant for this language. On the other hand, there are also notable commonalities, in particular the transition table of the NtdTA in Fig. 11.4 seems to be obtainable from the DbuTA's in Ex. 11.7 simply by mirroring the tuples in the transition relation.

11.3.2 Expressiveness

Not only does the introduction of this second automaton model, but also this example in particular, raise two questions: is the deterministic variant of top-down automata also as expressive as the nondeterministic one, as it is the case for bottom-up automata? And how does the expressive power of top-down automata relate to the bottom-up ones? The answer to the first question is negative in fact, so DtdTA are in fact weaker than NtdTA in expressiveness. And the answer to the second question is: in their nondeterministic variant, top-down and bottom-up automata are equi-expressive.

We will prove the equi-expressiveness result first. The size estimations in the following two lemmas already suggest that the translations between these two models are simple.

Lemma 11.18 *For every NtdTA $\mathcal{A}$ of size n there is an NbuTA $\mathcal{B}$ of size n such that $L(\mathcal{B}) = L(\mathcal{A})$.*

Proof Let $\mathcal{A} = (Q, \Sigma, q_I, \delta)$ be an NtdTA. We construct the NbuTA $\mathcal{B}$ as $(Q, \Sigma, \delta', \{q_I\})$ where

$$q \in \delta'((q_1, \ldots, q_d), a) \quad \text{iff} \quad (q_1, \ldots, q_d) \in \delta(q, a)$$

for any $q \in \Sigma_d$ and any rank d.

The size estimation on $\mathcal{B}$ is obvious, and the fact that it accepts the same language as $\mathcal{A}$ is a direct consequence of the fact that a run ρ of $\mathcal{A}$ on some tree t is a run of $\mathcal{B}$ on t and vice-versa. Moreover, it is accepting for $\mathcal{A}$ iff it is accepting for $\mathcal{B}$ since $\rho(\varepsilon) = q_I$ in both cases, and we have $\delta(\rho(v), t(v)) = \top$ iff $\rho(v) \in \delta(t(v))$ for every leaf node v. Hence, ρ is in the initial state for $\mathcal{A}$ on ε, resp. in the only accepting state for $\mathcal{B}$; the assignment of states to leaf nodes is a final assignment for $\mathcal{A}$ and an initial assignment for $\mathcal{B}$. $\square$

The proof already suggests that the converse direction is equally simple: an NbuTA can equally be regarded as an NtdTA. There is only a tiny technical difference, though: while in the direction above the NtdTA's initial state becomes the single accepting state of the NbuTA, an NbuTA may in general have several accepting states but the corresponding NtdTA is required to have a single initial state. We can employ the usual trick of adding a new state that nondeterministically mimics the top-down behaviour of any of NbuTA's accepting states. This is standard procedure, so a formal proof for this direction is omitted.

Lemma 11.19 *For every NbuTA $\mathcal{A}$ of size n there is an NtdTA $\mathcal{B}$ of size at most $n + 1$ such that $L(\mathcal{B}) = L(\mathcal{A})$.*

Putting these two lemmas together we obtain equi-expressiveness of the two tree automaton models.

Theorem 11.20 *A tree language is NtdTA-recognisable iff it is NbuTA-recognisable.*

Equi-expressiveness only holds because of the availability of nondeterminism which allows an NtdTA in a state q at some node v to guess the tuple of states $(q_1, \ldots, q_d)$ at v's children that an NbuTA came from when it entered q and vice-versa. Note that we do not only have equi-expressiveness but basically equality of the models. It makes use of the fact that

$$Q \times \Sigma_d \times Q^d \;\simeq\; Q^d \times \Sigma_d \times Q$$

for any $d \geq 0$. Coming back to the proposition that a word automaton does not really read a word from left to right and a tree automaton does not really read a tree from top to bottom or from bottom to top but only provides – in the form of its transition table – local rules for labelling a tree with states, it is not surprising that a NtdTA can directly be seen as an NbuTA and vice-versa. The transition table of either model provides rules that declare certain combinations of a state at a node, an alphabet symbol at that node, and states at the node's children to be valid in a run.

The equivalence between NtdTA and NbuTA is a strong argument for considering this model to be a rightful extension of the NFA model to trees. We will therefore allow ourselves to speak of a (nondeterministic) *tree automaton* (NTA) and use the bottom-up or top-down mode, whatever is more convenient in that situation. We also call a tree language *regular* when it is recognised by some NTA.

With NtdTA, NbuTA and DbuTA sharing the same exressiveness, it may be tempting to assume that DtdTA also recognise the same class of languages. This is not the case, though, and the counterexample shows that nondeterminism is sometimes needed in top-down mode when a decision needs to be made about which of several subtrees should possess certain properties.

Theorem 11.21 *There are regular tree languages that cannot be recognised by a DtdTA.*

Proof Let $\Sigma = \{a, b, c\}$ with $rk_\Sigma(a) = 2$ and $rk_\Sigma(b) = rk_\Sigma(c) = 0$. Consider the simple tree language $L := \{t_1, t_2\}$ with $t_1 := a(b, c)$ and $t_2 := a(c, b)$. It is not hard to see that it can be recognised by an NTA, for instance $(\{q_a, q_b, q_c\}, \Sigma, q_a, \delta)$ with

$$\delta(q_a, a) = \{(q_b, q_c), (q_c, q_b)\}, \quad \delta(q_b, b) = \top, \quad \delta(q_c, c) = \top$$

and $\delta(q, x) = \varnothing$, resp. $\delta(q, x) = \bot$ in all other cases.

Now suppse that $\mathcal{A} = (Q, \Sigma, q_I, \delta)$ is a DtdBA such that $L(\mathcal{A}) = L$. Since $t_1 \in L(\mathcal{A})$ there is an accepting run ρ_1 of $\mathcal{A}$ on t_1. So there are states $q_1 := \rho_1(0)$ and $q_2 := \rho_1(1)$ with $(q_1, q_2) \in \delta(q_I, a)$. Since $\mathcal{A}$ is deterministic, we even have $\delta(q_I, a) = \{(q_1, q_2)\}$. Moreover, we have $\delta(q_1, b) = \top$ and $\delta(q_2, c) = \top$, for otherwise ρ_1 would not be an accepting run.

Now consider $\mathcal{A}$'s behaviour on t_2. Note that $t_2(\varepsilon) = a = t_1(\varepsilon)$, so any run ρ_2 of $\mathcal{A}$ on t_2 must satisfy $\rho_2(\varepsilon) = q_I$, $\rho_2(0) = q_1$ and $\rho_2(1) = q_2$, for otherwise $\mathcal{A}$ would not be deterministic. Moreover, since ρ_2 is also accepting, we must have $\delta(q_1, c) = \top = \delta(q_2, b)$.

Now consider the tree $t_3 := a(b, b)$. Clearly, $t_3 \notin L$. We can construct a run ρ_3 of $\mathcal{A}$ on t_3: we naturally have $\rho_3(\varepsilon) = q_I$. Since $t_3(\varepsilon) = a$ we can apply the transition from q_I via a to (q_1, q_2) and get $\rho_3(0) = q_1$, $\rho_3(1) = q_2$. Now note that $t_3(0) = b$ and $\rho_3(0) = q_1$ and, as worked out above, $\delta(q_1, b) = \top$. Likewise, $t_3(1) = b$, $\rho_3(1) = q_2$ and $\delta(q_2, b) = \top$. Thus, ρ_3 is an accepting run of $\mathcal{A}$ on t_3, contradicting the assumption that $L(\mathcal{A}) = L$. $\qquad\qquad\square$

11.3.3 Decision Problems

As with automata on words, automata on trees will serve as the computational backbone for deciding logics interpreted over trees. This of course requires the corresponding problems on the automata side, most of all the non-emptiness problem, to be decidable. It is not hard to see that this is the case for NTA.

One possibility to determine whether $L(\mathcal{A}) \neq \varnothing$ for some given NTA $\mathcal{A} = (Q, \Sigma, \delta, F)$, here regarded as an NbuTA, is to compute the set of productive states in a saturation process. Then every state $q \in Q$ such that $\delta(q, a) = \top$ for some $a \in \Sigma_0$ is *productive* in the sense that there is a run on some tree whose root label is q. The tree simply consists of a single node labelled with that symbol a, which is both leaf and root. Moreover, suppose that $P \subseteq Q$ is a set of states that are already confirmed to be productive in this sense, and $q \in Q \setminus P$. If there is some $a \in \Sigma_d$, $d > 0$, such that $q \in \delta((q_1, \ldots, q_d), a)$ for some $q_1, \ldots, q_d \in P$, then q can also be marked as productive. A tree that has a run of $\mathcal{A}$ ending in q at its root can be constructed by putting corresponding trees for $q_1, \ldots, q_d$ under a new root labelled a.

It should be clear that the set of productive symbols can be computed in a terminating process, even in time that is polynomial in the size of $\mathcal{A}$. This requires the alphabet to be fixed, though. Moreover, it is not hard to show that this is a sound and complete characterisation of non-emptiness in the sense that $L(\mathcal{A}) \neq \varnothing$ iff some $q \in F$ is marked as productive during this process. This then establishes decidability of the non-emptiness problem for NbuTA, and therefore also for NtdBA as they can be transformed into one another easily. We give a different proof, though, making use of the reachability games introduced in Chp. 3. This serves as a link and preparation for the material in the following chapter which studies automata on infinite trees, and it should be clear that such inductive reasoning about productive states cannot be applied there anymore because infinite trees are not inductive data structures.

Theorem 11.22 *The non-emptiness problem for NTA is decidable in polynomial time.*

Proof We show that non-emptiness of an NtdBA (and therefore also an NbuTA) can be characterised as a reachability game. Let $\mathcal{A} = (Q, \Sigma, q_I, \delta)$ be an NtdTA with $\Sigma = \Sigma_0 \cup \ldots \cup \Sigma_m$, i.e. m is the maximal rank of a symbol in Σ. $\mathcal{A}$ induces the reachability game $\mathcal{G}_{\mathcal{A}} = (V, V_0, V_1, v_I, E, F)$ with the following components.

- The node set is $V := (Q \times \{0\}) \cup (\bigcup_{i=0}^{m} Q^i \times \{1\})$, i.e. nodes are either pairs $(q, 0)$ with some automaton state q, or are pairs $((q_1, \ldots, q_d), 1)$ for some d-tuple of automaton states. In fact, it suffices to restrict ourselves to those tuples that occur in the image of some transition of $\mathcal{A}$, as all other tuples will not be reachable in $\mathcal{G}_{\mathcal{A}}$ from the initial node anyway.
- The partition into nodes belonging to player 0 and those belonging to player 1 is encoded into the nodes themselves: we have $V_0 := Q \times \{0\}$ and V_1 then consists of the remaining nodes. Hence, player 0 makes a choice when given an automaton state, player 1 makes a choice when given a tuple of states that could be used to label the children of a node.

- The initial node is $(q_I, 0)$, i.e. player 0 begins.
- The game's edges are given as follows.

$$E := \bigcup_{d=1}^{m} \left(\bigcup_{a\in\Sigma} \{((q,0),((q_1,\ldots,q_d),1)) \mid (q_1,\ldots,q_d) \in \delta(q,a)\} \right.$$
$$\left. \cup \; \{(((q_1,\ldots,q_d),1),(q_i,0)) \mid i \in \{1,\ldots,d\}\} \right)$$

Thus, whenever it is player 0's turn in a state q, she chooses a transition from q to some tuple $(q_1,\ldots,q_d)$ via some d-ary symbol. Player 1 then responds by picking one of the states in this tuple. These games are therefore strictly turn-based.

- The winning condition for player 0 in the form of a set of game nodes to be reached is $F := \{(q,0) \mid \exists a \in \Sigma_0 \text{ s.t. } \delta(q,a) = \top\}$. I.e. it consists of all states that can label a leaf in an accepting run of $\mathcal{A}$ on some tree.

It should be clear that the size of $\mathcal{G}_\mathcal{A}$ is polynomial in the size of $\mathcal{A}$. The degree of the polynomial may depend on the maximal rank in Σ, hence for the theorem's statement to be true we need to require Σ to be fixed. By Thm. 3.26, reachability games can be solved in polynomial time. This immediately establishes a polynomial bound on the time complexity of the non-emptiness problem for NTA.

It remains to be seen that $\mathcal{G}_\mathcal{A}$ correctly characterises non-emptiness for $\mathcal{A}$, i.e. that player 0 has a winning strategy for $\mathcal{G}_\mathcal{A}$ iff $L(\mathcal{A}) \neq \varnothing$.

"$\Leftarrow$" Suppose $t \in L(\mathcal{A})$ and ρ is an accepting run of $\mathcal{A}$ on t. We define a strategy σ_0 for player 0 as follows. Note that, in general, such a strategy is a function of type $V^*V_0 \to V$. Since these games are strictly turn-based, it suffices to define σ_0 for histories of even length. Moreover, the second component in each game node, that only signals whose turn it is, is irrelevant for this, and so we can represent the history of a game as a sequence $H = q_0, \mathbf{q_0}, q_1, \mathbf{q_1}, \ldots, q_{n-1}, \mathbf{q}_{n-1}, q_n$ such that q_i is an element of the tuple $\mathbf{q}_{i-1}$ for all $i = 1,\ldots,n-1$. Note that H defines a unique node $v(H)$ in t via $v(q_0) := \varepsilon$, and $v(H, \mathbf{q}_{n-1}, q_n) := v(H)d$ where q_n occurs in position d in $\mathbf{q}_{n-1}$ (starting with 0).

This can be seen as player 0 tracing a path through t in order to guide her choices. Then let $\sigma_0(H) := (\mathbf{q}, 1)$ such that the children of $v(H)$ are labelled with $\mathbf{q}$ in ρ. In other words, player 0 does not just trace the play as a branch through t. She also performs her choices according to the state labelling in ρ. Meanwhile, player 1 responds by picking one particular state and therefore implicitly selects a child node. Note that several children could be labelled with the same state but player 1 can only choose the state, not the exact direction. This state then determines the extension of the branch that player 0 follows by one more level. If the selected state q occurs multiple times then she simply extends the branch in any of the matching directions.

It is easy to see that this is indeed a winning strategy for player 0 because eventually the constructed branch in t will have to hit a leaf node v, and by the assumption that ρ is an accepting run, we have $\rho(v) \in F$, i.e. the play has reached a final node.

"$\Rightarrow$" Suppose that player 0 has a winning strategy for $\mathcal{G}_\mathcal{A}$. According to Thm. 3.25 she has a *positional* strategy σ_0. This can be used to iteratively construct a tree t with an accepting run ρ. Let $\rho(\varepsilon) := q_I$. The root label $t(\varepsilon)$ of t is obtained from

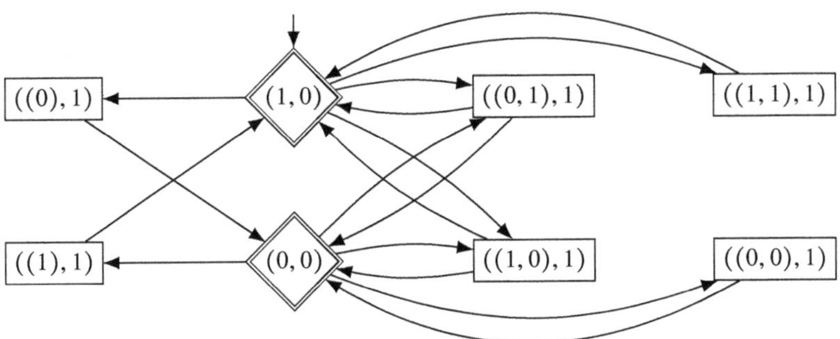

Fig. 11.5 Non-emptiness as a reachability game, here for the NTA from Ex. 11.7.

$\sigma_0(q_I, 0)$. Since σ_0 is a winning strategy, there must be some $a \in \Sigma_d$ for some d such that $\sigma_0(q_I, 0) = (\mathbf{q}, 1)$ and $\mathbf{q} \in \delta(q_I, a)$. Then set $t(\varepsilon) := a$. If $d = 0$ then we are finished, otherwise continue the process with the d children $0, \ldots, d - 1$ and the states in $\mathbf{q}$.

Since σ_0 is a winning strategy, every play must eventually reach F which ensures that the construction on every branch eventually terminates with some state q and symbol $a \in \Sigma_0$ such that $\delta(q, a) = \top$. This means that ρ is in fact accepting. $\qquad\square$

Example 11.23 The reachability game $\mathcal{G}_A$ for the NTA A of Ex. 11.7, recognising the set of all Boolean expressions that evaluate to true, is shown in Fig. 11.5.

It is trivially seen to be won by player 0 because the starting node $(1, 0)$, corresponding to state 1 and marking player 0's turn next, is the reachability target. The reason for this is the existence of a very small tree representing a Boolean expression that evaluates to 1, namely the constant 1 itself. The corresponding run marks it with state 1, and this is why this node is part of the winning condition.

The moves player 0 can make from her two states to the left correspond to the choice of the symbol $\neg$. It changes the state accordingly; player 1 has not real choice here. The moves to the four states on the right correspond to choices of transitions under the symbols $\wedge$ and $\vee$.

Every Boolean expression that evaluates to 1 induces a winning strategy for player 0 in this game. Take for instance the expression $\neg 1 \vee (1 \wedge \neg 0)$. The strategy that is induced by it is best shown as a tree itself, namely the one in Fig. 11.6. It shows, when read from top to bottom, a move for player 0 in response to all possible player-1 moves occurring in such a play. The branching on the right to two nodes of the form $(1, 0)$ can be interpreted as two different ways that player 1 can choose to continue with state 1 after being given the transition into $(1, 1)$.

Interestingly, while every tree in $L(A)$ induces a strategy in $\mathcal{G}_A$ for player 0, not every strategy corresponds uniquely to a tree. For example, the Boolean expression $\neg 1 \vee (1 \vee \neg 0)$ gives rise to the same strategy. The reason is the fact that the strategy

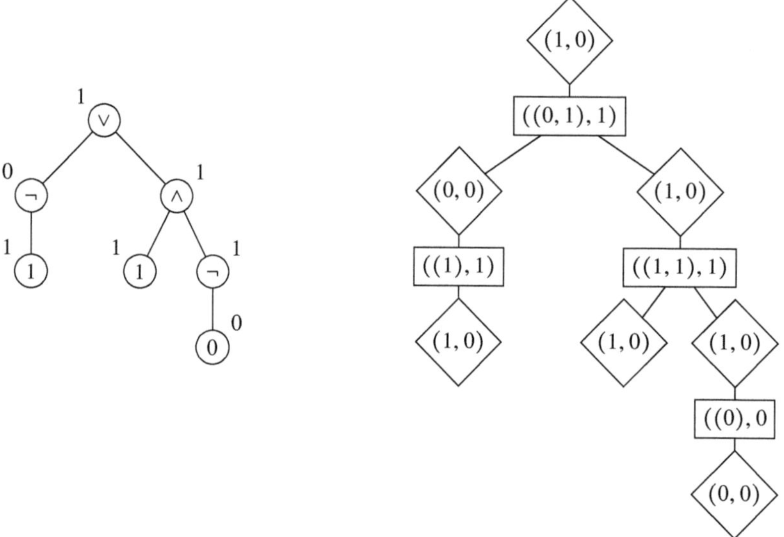

Fig. 11.6 Every tree in the language of an NTA $\mathcal{A}$ induces a winning strategy for player 0 in the non-emptiness game $\mathcal{G}_{\mathcal{A}}$, here for the NTA from Ex. 11.7 and the tree shown on the left with a corresponding accepting run.

only depends on the structure of the tree and the accepting run on it, but not directly on the tree's alphabet symbols.

Decidability of non-emptiness, together with effective closure properties, in particular closure under complements (Cor. 11.10) and intersections (Thm. 11.11) yields decidability of the other standard decision problems as well. Since complementation incurs an exponential blowup, we obtain decidability in exponential time for these other problems.

Corollary 11.24 *The universality, subsumption and equivalence problems for NTA are decidable in exponential time.*

11.4 Monadic Second-Order Logic on Finite Trees

An important application of decidability of non-emptiness for tree automata is, again, decidability of the satisfiability problem for logics that can effectively be translated into NTA. A natural candidate for such a logic is Monadic Second-Order Logic interpreted over trees. At close inspection, one sees that a formal definition of such a logic in analogy to MSO over (finite) words requires a few technical adjustments.

As usual, first-order variables should be interpreted as positions in a tree, and second-order variables as sets of positions. While a formula like $x < y$ has a very natural interpretation on words with their total order on positions, one could allow formulas like these in the syntax and interpret the symbol '$<$' as the (generator of the) partial order given by the positions in the tree with the root being the minimal element. This would be oblivious to the order on children, though. For example, the trees $a(b, c)$ and $a(c, b)$ would be indistinguishable.

In order to remedy this, we can recall that in the presence of second-order quantification, '$<$' on words was expressible using the successor function. This gives rise to an extension of the word logic MSO[*succ*] to a tree logic: we introduce several successor functions $succ_i$ that map each node to its i-th child (if it exists). One just has to be aware of potential conflicts with the alphabet ranks. For instance, the formula

$$\exists x \exists y \exists z. \overbrace{(\neg \exists x'.succ_0(x',x))}^{\psi_1} \wedge \overbrace{a(x) \wedge b(y) \wedge c(z)}^{\psi_2} \wedge$$
$$\underbrace{succ_0(x,y) \wedge succ_1(x,z)}_{\psi_3} \wedge \underbrace{\neg \exists v.succ_0(y,v) \vee succ_0(z,v)}_{\psi_4}$$

is then satisfied by exactly the tree $a(b, c)$. It demands the existence of three nodes x, y, z such that

a) x has no predecessor, i.e. no parent, so it must be the root node (ψ_1),
b) x, y and z are labelled with a, b and c accordingly (ψ_2),
c) y is the first child of x and z is the second (ψ_3),
d) neither y nor z have a first successor, so no successor at all, i.e. they are leaves (ψ_4).

On the other hand, the formula

$$\varphi(x) \ := \ \exists x_0 \exists x_1 \exists x_2.a(x) \wedge \bigwedge_{i=0}^{2} succ_i(x,x_i)$$

is satisfied by a node v in a tree when it is labelled with a and has at least three successors. This is of course not possible over a ranked alphabet which gives the letter a the rank 2.

There are several possibilities to overcome this small technical issue. A restrictive option is to define this variant of MSO only for particular alphabets, for instance to demand that every rank is either 0 or 2. But even then one would have to be able to see whether a formula demands some node to have two or zero children, and this essentially boils down to deciding satisfiability again. So we refrain from trying to solve the problem syntactically and simply accept that there are formulas like $\varphi(x)$ above that are unsatisfiable because of a mismatch in demands on the ranks of certain nodes.

Definition 11.25 Let Σ be a ranked alphabet and $m := \max\{rk_\Sigma(a) \mid a \in \Sigma\}$. Again, we fix two countable and disjoint sets $\mathcal{V}_1 = \{x, y, \ldots\}$ of *first-order variables* and $\mathcal{V}_2 = \{X, Y, \ldots\}$ of *second-order variables*. Formulas of *Monadic Second-Order Logic* (MSO) are given by the following grammar.

$$\varphi \; ::= \; succ_i(x,y) \mid X(x) \mid a(x) \mid \varphi_1 \vee \varphi_2 \mid \neg\varphi \mid \exists x\, \varphi \mid \exists X\, \varphi$$

where $a \in \Sigma$, $x, y \in \mathcal{V}_1$, $X \in \mathcal{V}_2$ and $0 \le i < m$.

All the syntactical concepts like formula size, set of subformulas, free and bound variables, first-order formulas, etc. carry over from MSO over words to this logic straightforwardly.

We will also use the acronym MSO for Monadic Second-Order Logic over trees since it will always be clear from the context whether we consider the variant interpreted over words or the one interpreted over trees. We will of course also use other logical symbols like $\wedge$, $\rightarrow$ etc. which can be introduced via the standard abbreviations.

The interpretation of an MSO formula over a Σ-tree is also straightforwardly extended from words.

Definition 11.26 Let Σ be a ranked alphabet, $t \in \mathcal{T}_\Sigma^*$, and $I : (\mathcal{V}_1 \rightarrow dom(t)) + (\mathcal{V}_2 \rightarrow 2^{dom(t)})$ be an *assignment* of the first-order variables by nodes in t and the second-order variables by sets of such nodes, resp. positions.

We say that the *interpretation* of t and I *satisfies* the MSO formula φ, if $t, I \vDash \varphi$ holds according to the following rules.

$$
\begin{array}{lll}
t, I \vDash succ_i(x, y) & \text{iff} & I(y) = vi \text{ whenever } I(x) = v \\
t, I \vDash X(x) & \text{iff} & I(x) \in I(X) \\
t, I \vDash a(x) & \text{iff} & t(I(x)) = a \\
t, I \vDash \varphi \vee \psi & \text{iff} & t, I \vDash \varphi \text{ or } t, I \vDash \psi \\
t, I \vDash \neg\varphi & \text{iff} & t, I \nvDash \varphi \\
t, I \vDash \exists x\, \varphi & \text{iff} & \text{there is } v \in dom(t) \text{ such that } w, I[x \mapsto v] \vDash \varphi \\
t, I \vDash \exists X\, \varphi & \text{iff} & \text{there is } M \subseteq dom(t) \text{ such that } w, I[X \mapsto M] \vDash \varphi
\end{array}
$$

Semantical notions like equivalence between two formulas etc., are defined as they are for formulas interpreted over words. Again, the interpretation of a formula φ without free variables in a tree is independent of any variable assignment, in which case we also simply write $t \vDash \varphi$ instead of $t, I \vDash \varphi$ for some arbitrary I. Then such a sentence defines a tree language in the usual way via $L(\varphi) := \{t \in \mathcal{T}_\Sigma^* \mid t \vDash \varphi\}$.

The root of a tree is obviously definable using a first-order formula, and so are all children of a node. We make use of this and introduce the following abbreviations for arbitrary formulas $\psi(x)$, first-order variables y and directions i.

$$
\begin{array}{rcl}
\psi(\varepsilon) & := & \exists x.(\neg\exists y.succ_0(y,x)) \wedge \psi(x) \\
\psi(succ_i(y)) & := & \exists x.succ_i(y,x) \wedge \psi(x)
\end{array}
$$

Example 11.27 Reconsider the example representing Boolean expressions as trees over the ranked alphabet $\{0, 1, \neg, \wedge, \vee\}$. The aim is to exemplify the use of MSO by defining the set of all such Boolean expressions that evaluate to 1 in MSO. In order to avoid an awkward look of the formula arising from the use of $\neg, \wedge, \vee$ both as alphabet symbols and as logical symbols in the formula, we use $a_\neg$, $a_\wedge$ and $a_\vee$ to denote the alphabet symbols of ranks 1 and 2.

Then the language of all such expressions that evaluate to 1 is defined by the following sentence.

$$\exists T \exists F. \big(\forall v. T(v) \leftrightarrow \neg F(v)\big) \wedge T(\varepsilon) \wedge$$

$$\forall v. \bigg(T(v) \rightarrow \Big(\neg 0(v) \wedge \big(a_\neg(v) \rightarrow F(succ_0(v))\big)\Big) \wedge$$

$$\big(a_\wedge(v) \rightarrow T(succ_0(v)) \wedge T(succ_1(v))\big) \wedge$$

$$\big(a_\vee(v) \rightarrow T(succ_0(v)) \vee T(succ_1(v))\big)\Big) \wedge$$

$$\bigg(F(v) \rightarrow \Big(\neg 1(v) \wedge \big(a_\neg(v) \rightarrow T(succ_0(v))\big)\Big) \wedge$$

$$\big(a_\wedge(v) \rightarrow F(succ_0(v)) \vee F(succ_1(v))\big) \wedge$$

$$\big(a_\vee(v) \rightarrow F(succ_0(v)) \wedge F(succ_1(v))\big)\Big)\bigg)$$

It states that the nodes of a given Σ-tree can be labelled with predicates T, F so that they form a partition on the nodes, the root belongs to T and the classification follows the usual evaluation rules for Boolean operators so that a node v belongs to the interpretation of T iff the subexpression at this node evaluates to 1, and likewise for F and 0.

We can use the same automata-theoretic approach to MSO over finite trees as used for MSO of finite or infinite words: an MSO formula over finite trees can be normalised to only contain second-order variables, and then we can inductively translate it into an NTA over an extended alphabet that is used to encode a valuation of the free second-order variables in the formula. Details are left as an exercise.

Theorem 11.28 *For every MSO sentence φ over some ranked alphabet Σ there is an NTA $\mathcal{A}_\varphi$ such that $L(\mathcal{A}_\varphi) = L(\varphi)$.*

The fact that $\mathcal{A}_\varphi$ is effectively constructible from φ and non-emptiness for NTA was established to be decidable in Thm. 11.22 then immediately yields decidability for MSO again.

Corollary 11.29 *The satisfiability problem for MSO over finite trees is decidable.*

Since MSO features negation, problems like validity of a formula or equivalence between two formulas can immediately be reduced to the satisfiability problem.

Corollary 11.30 *The validity and equivalence problem for MSO over finite trees is decidable.*

It should be clear that the lower bounds established for MSO over words immediately carry over to the world of trees since every word over an alphabet Σ can be encoded as tree over an alphabet $\Sigma' := \Sigma \cup \{\#\}$ with all letters from Σ seen as unary symbols and one extra symbol # of rank 0 to mark the end of a word with an extra leaf node. Since L is regular iff $L\#$ is regular, this does not change the fact that lower bounds on the satisfiability of MSO over words immediately carry over to MSO over trees. In particular, satisfiability is not decidable in elementary time.

One could argue that satisfiability for MSO over ranked alphabets other than those in which one letter has rank 0 and all others have rank 1, is not covered by this argument. So perhaps MSO over ranked alphabets with all letters having rank either 2 or 0 could be easier to decide. It is not difficult, though, to refute this by encoding words as trees in a different way, for instance by degenerate trees in which every node has two successors, of which at least one is a leaf.

Not surprisingly, MSO over finite trees is also strong enough to express the existence of a run of an NTA on a given tree. Spelling this out is also left as an exercise.

Theorem 11.31 *For every NTA $\mathcal{A}$ there is an MSO formula $\varphi_\mathcal{A}$ of size polynomial in $|\mathcal{A}|$ such that $L(\varphi_\mathcal{A}) = L(\mathcal{A})$.*

Hence, MSO over finite trees, NbuTA, NtdTA and DbuTA all have the same expressive power, and that of DtdBA is weaker.

11.5 Applications

We study two applications of automata over finite trees. The first one considers the question of equality of two terms of a simply typed λ-calculus under certain congruences. The second one shows that tree automata can be used in database querying, namely for semi-structured data, i.e. XML documents. We assume some basic familiarity with the concepts of XML and the λ-calculus.

11.5.1 Higher-Order Matching

The simply typed λ-calculus can be seen as an abstract programming language with types and no recursion. Types τ are defined inductively via

$$\tau \quad ::= \quad \mathsf{o} \mid \tau_1, \ldots, \tau_n \to \tau$$

where o is some base type. The type constructor $\to$ is used to build types of functions with arguments. For instance, the type

$$\mathsf{o}, (\mathsf{o}, \mathsf{o} \to \mathsf{o}) \to (\mathsf{o} \to \mathsf{o})$$

describes functions that take two arguments and return a function. The first argument is a value of the base type, and the second argument is a binary function on the basetype. The return value is a unary function on the base type. An example of a function of this type is the specialisation function $sp : (x, f) \mapsto f_x$ where $f_x(y) = f(x, y)$.

The order of a type describes the nesting depth of functions in arguments. It is defined via

$$ord(\mathsf{o}) := 0 \ , \quad ord(\tau_1, \ldots, \tau_n \to \tau) := \max\left(\{ord(\tau)\} \cup \{1 + ord(\tau_i) \mid i = 1, \ldots, n\}\right)$$

We assume a set S of constants and function symbols, each associated with a type, and a set X of variable names. The set of *terms* of S is then given by the following grammar.

$$t, t_i \ ::= \ f \mid x \mid \lambda x_1, \ldots, x_n.t \mid t(t_1, \ldots, t_n)$$

where $f \in S, x \in X$.

This grammar also allows non-well-typed terms. We restrict attention to well-typed terms. A stringent definition requires the introduction of a simple typing system. Here we introduce this on a less formal level since the concept is quite intuitive: every function symbol f has a type τ by assumption which we write as $f : \tau$. Variables x need to be given types as well. If $x_1 : \tau_1, \ldots, x_n : \tau_n$ and $t : \tau$, then the term $\lambda x_1, \ldots, x_n.t$ has type $\tau_1, \ldots, \tau_n \to \tau$. At last, if $t_1 : \tau_1, \ldots, t_n : \tau_n$ and $t : \tau_1, \ldots, \tau_n \to \tau$, then $t(t_1, \ldots, t_n) : \tau$.

A well-typed term then has a unique type τ, which gives terms an order as well via $ord(t) := n$ if $t : \tau$ and $ord(\tau) = n$.

Now suppose that the set of functions and constants is finite and only contains objects with types of the form $\mathsf{o}^n \to \mathsf{o}$ where $\tau^n \to \tau'$ is an abbreviation for

$$\underbrace{\tau, \ldots, \tau}_{n \text{ times}} \to \tau'$$

and $\tau^0 \to \tau'$ is just τ'.

Such a finite set S induces a ranked tree alphabet Σ where $rk_\Sigma(f) = n$ if $f : \mathsf{o}^n \to \mathsf{o}$. In particular, constant symbols have rank 0 and may occur at leaf nodes in trees representing terms of such types.

We are interested in solving third-order matching equations. These are equations of the form

$$x(s_1, s_2, \ldots, s_n) \ \approx \ t$$

for terms s_i of type $\tau_i = \mathsf{o}^{n_i} \to \mathsf{o}$ for some n_i that contain no free variables, and t is a variable-free term of type o. The variable x therefore must have type $\tau_1, \ldots, \tau_n \to \mathsf{o}$.

Solving such an equation means computing a term t' that makes the equation above true when substituted in for the variable x. This would be a rather trivial problem if '$\approx$' denoted syntactical equality. It is used to denote so-called $\beta\eta$-equality which is the congruence that is obtained by allowing (sub)terms to be rewritten according to the rules

$$(\beta) \qquad (\lambda x_1, \ldots, x_n.t)(t_1, \ldots, t_n) \ \approx \ t[t_1/x_1, \ldots, t_n/x_n]$$

$$(\eta) \qquad \lambda x_1, \ldots, x_n.t(x_1, \ldots, x_n) \ \approx \ t \quad \text{if } x_1, \ldots, x_n \text{ do not occur in } t$$

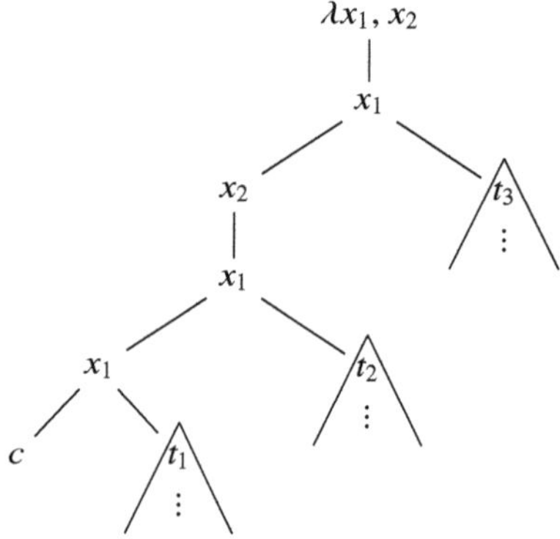

Fig. 11.7 A λ-term as a tree over a ranked alphabet.

where $t[t_1/x_1,\ldots,t_n/x_n]$ denotes the term that results from t by simultaneously replacing each free occurrence of the variable x_i with the term t_i.

Example 11.32 Let $S = \{c, f\}$ with $c : \mathsf{o}$ and $f : \mathsf{o}, \mathsf{o} \to \mathsf{o}$. Consider the equation

$$x\big((\lambda y_1, y_2.y_1), (\lambda y_3.f(y_3, y_3))\big) \;\approx\; f(c,c) . \tag{11.1}$$

A possible solution is $x = \lambda x_1, x_2.x_2(c)$ since

$$(\lambda x_1, x_2.x_2(c))\big((\lambda y_1, y_2.y_1), (\lambda y_3.f(y_3, y_3))\big) \;\approx\; (\lambda y_3.f(y_3, y_3))(c)$$
$$\approx\; f(c,c)$$

by two applications of the β-rule.

Another possible solution is $x = \lambda x_1, x_2.x_1(f(c,c), c)$ since, equally,

$$(\lambda x_1, x_2.x_1(f(c,c), c))\big((\lambda y_1, y_2.y_1), (\lambda y_3.f(y_3, y_3))\big)$$
$$\approx\; (\lambda y_1, y_2.y_1)(f(c,c), c) \;\approx\; f(c,c) .$$

Also, any term of the form $\lambda x_1, x_2.x_1(x_2(x_1(x_1(c, t_1), t_2)), t_3)$ for arbitrary t_1, t_2, t_3 is a solution of that equation.

Not only can so-called ground terms like $f(c,c)$ with no λ-abstractions be represented as trees over an alphabet that is naturally ranked by the types of the involved symbols. Even terms with λ-abstractions can be seen as trees simply by additionally regarding the operator of the λ-abstraction as a unary symbol. The tree representation of $\lambda x_1, x_2.x_1(x_2(x_1(x_1(c, t_1), t_2)), t_3)$ for example is shown in Fig. 11.7.

Example 11.33 We continue the previous example. The goal is now to construct a DbuTA $\mathcal{A}$ that recognises exactly the solutions to equation (11.1) above. In addition to the symbols c of rank 0, x_2 and $\lambda x_1, x_2$ of rank 1, and x_1 and f of rank 2 we

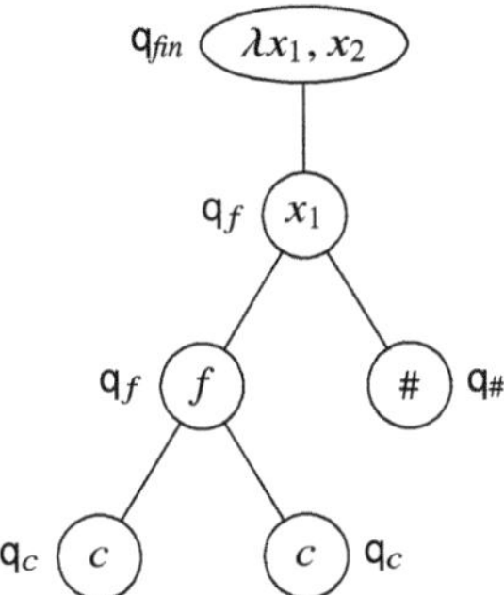

Fig. 11.8 Accepting run of the DbuTA from Ex. 11.33 for the term $\lambda x_1, x_2.x_1(f(a,a),\#)$.

use another symbol # that should be read as a placeholder for an arbitrary term. Naturally, its rank is 0, i.e. it is used as a leaf in a tree representation of a term.

The DbuTA will have four states $q_c, q_f, q_\#, q_{fin}$. The first two correspond to subterms of the right-hand side of (11.1). Recall that the goal is not to recognise terms syntactically but to recognise terms which equal some given term modulo $\beta\eta$-congruence. This is why state q_f for instance may occur in a run at some node whose subtree is not $f(c,c)$.

The state $q_\#$ is used to recognise arbitrary subterms represented by the symbol #, and the state q_{fin} is used to signal the successful completion of a run, i.e. it is the only final state.

The transitions table δ is given as follows.

<table>
<tr><td colspan="2">δ_0</td><td></td><td colspan="3">δ_1</td><td></td><td colspan="3">δ_2</td></tr>
<tr><td>a</td><td>$\delta_0(a)$</td><td></td><td>q</td><td>a</td><td>$\delta_1(q,a)$</td><td></td><td>(q_1,q_2)</td><td>a</td><td>$\delta_2((q_1,q_2),a)$</td></tr>
<tr><td>c</td><td>q_c</td><td></td><td>q_f</td><td>x_2</td><td>q_f</td><td></td><td>(q_c,q_c)</td><td>f</td><td>q_f</td></tr>
<tr><td>$\#$</td><td>$q_\#$</td><td></td><td>q_f</td><td>$\lambda x_1,x_2$</td><td>q_{fin}</td><td></td><td>$(q_c,q_\#)$</td><td>x_1</td><td>q_c</td></tr>
<tr><td></td><td></td><td></td><td></td><td></td><td></td><td></td><td>$(q_f,q_\#)$</td><td>x_1</td><td>q_f</td></tr>
</table>

Consider, for instance, the term $\lambda x_1, x_2.x_1(f(c,c),\#)$. An accepting run on its tree representation can be constructed easily and is shown in Fig. 11.8. One can equally show that $\lambda x_1, x_2.x_1(x_2(x_1(x_1(c,\#),\#)),\#)$ is being accepted. On the other hand, $\lambda x_1, x_2.x_2(x_1(f(c,c),\#))$ is not being accepted since $\mathcal{A}$ gets stuck on it.

$\mathcal{A}$'s functionality can be explained as follows. A term t with two variables x_1 and x_2 should possess a run of $\mathcal{A}$ with label q_c, resp. q_f at the root node iff $t[x_1 := \lambda y_1, y_2.y_1, x_2 := \lambda y_3.f(y_3,y_3)]$ reduces to c, resp. $f(c,c)$ under $\beta\eta$-rewritings. Moreover, the run on t should assign $q_\#$ to the root node iff $t[x_1 := s_1, x_2 := s_2]$ reduces to #. This can be shown by induction on the height of t, assuming $\beta\eta$-normal form of t.

This example can be generalised to solve arbitrary matching equations of the same form as Eq. 11.1.

Theorem 11.34 *For every third-order matching equation $\mathcal{E}$ one can construct a DbuTA of polynomial size that recognises exactly the solutions to $\mathcal{E}$.*

Proof Let $\mathcal{E}$ be of the form $x(s_1, s_2, \ldots, s_n) \approx t$ for a variable-free term t of type o and closed terms $s_1, \ldots, s_n$ of types $o^{n_i} \to o$. We construct the desired DbuTA as $\mathcal{A}_{\mathcal{E}} := (Q, \Sigma, \delta, F)$ where Σ and the rankings of its symbols are naturally given through the function symbols, variables and λ-abstraction operations occurring in $s_1, \ldots, s_n, t$ with an additional symbol # as a placeholder for arbitrary subterms.

The state set is $Q := \{q_u \mid u \text{ is a subterm of } t\} \cup \{q_\#, q_{fin}\}$. There is only one final state: $F := \{q_{fin}\}$.

The transition rules are given as follows. We have

$$\delta_1(q_t, \lambda x_1, \ldots, x_n) \;=\; q_{fin}$$

to mark the successful parsing of a tree. As in the previous example, state $q_\#$ is used to mark subterms that are irrelevant for the solution, using the following transition rule.

$$\delta(\#) \;=\; q_\#$$

For every subterm $v = f(u_1, \ldots, u_m)$ of the right-hand side t of $\mathcal{E}$ with $v \neq \# \neq u_i$ for all $i = 1, \ldots, m$, we add the transition

$$\delta((q_{u_1}, \ldots, q_{u_m}), f) \;=\; q_v \,.$$

If $s_i(u_1, \ldots, u_n) \approx v$ under $\beta\eta$-equivalence such that $v \neq \#$ (while $u_i = \#$ is allowed), we also add the rule

$$\delta((q_{u_1}, \ldots, q_{u_n}), x_i) \;=\; q_v \,.$$

The size estimation on $\mathcal{A}_{\mathcal{E}}$ is obvious. For correctness one shows by induction on the height of a tree t that $\mathcal{A}_{\mathcal{E}}$ has a run on t with the root label q_u iff $t(s_1, \ldots, s_n) \approx u$ from which the claim immediately follows that $\mathcal{A}_{\mathcal{E}}$ recognises exactly the tree representations of solutions to $\mathcal{E}$. Details are left as an exercise. $\square$

11.5.2 Tree Automata for XML Data Processing

Tree automata play an important role for semi-structured data, i.e. data recorded in XML documents. Tree automata can be used for type checking of XML documents, also known as XML schema checking, and transformation scripts. XML document, traditionally represented as a string with nested opening and closing *tags*, is in fact tree-shaped which each section from opening to closing tags forming a subtree. The principle can be seen in Fig. 11.9. The tag names then become tree alphabet symbols.

The example in Fig. 11.9 shows a potential technical mismatch: in an XML document there is no guarantee that sections with equal tags always have the same number of included subsections, so that the tag can have a well-defined rank as a tree alphabet symbol. We will not go into the details of how to fix this. For the relatively

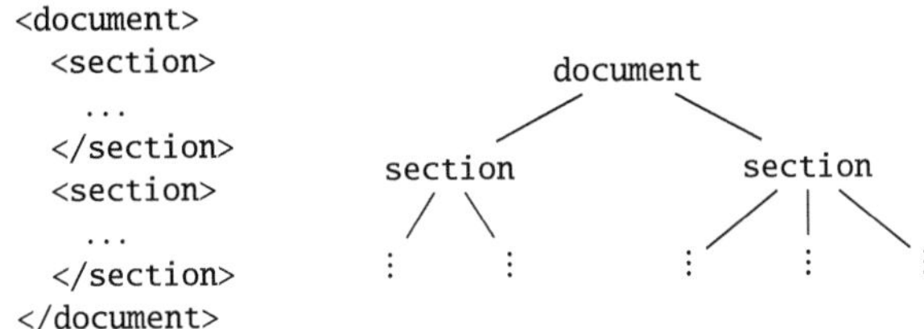

Fig. 11.9 XML document in traditional representation and when regarded as a tree.

shallow treatment of XML as an application domain for automata on finite trees it suffices to assume that XML documents have been modified to have this property, either by using different symbols for tags of different ranks, or by reshaping the tree into a binary one, etc.

For transformation scripts that are written in a functional style, a combination of type checking (in a programming language) and tree automata can be used to obtain an approximative XML type checking in the following sense. Suppose schemas, i.e. descriptions of XML-documents of a particular structure, *In* and *Out* are given, as well as a program P that is supposed to transform XML documents of the form described by *In* into documents of a form described by *Out*. If type checking of P confirms that this program has the type *In* → *Out* then it is guaranteed that documents of type *In* are always transformed into documents of type *Out*. However, it is only approximative in the sense that there may be programs which do this but are not found to have type *In* → *Out*. The advantage of this approach is simplicity and efficiency of the type checking method whilst using a general-purpose programming language.

Alternatively it is possible to obtain an exact type checking analysis based on *transducers*, i.e. automata with output. Transducers are not discussed here any further.

As a concrete example we consider the transformation language XDuce, a functional programming language for manipulating XML documents. XML data can be used both as input or output of a function in XDuce. It possesses standard data types like `Float`, `String`, etc. For XML data there are user-defined types that basically correspond to XML schemas.

An XDuce type definition defines potentially several types by mutual recursion. Each type definition names an XML tag and the content of the section enclosed in the corresponding opening and closing tags in terms of the types of its subsections. It uses intuitive regular expression notation to describe valid lists of subsections that can occur within a section.

Example 11.35 The following is an XDuce type definition.

```
type Addrbook = addrbook[Person*]
type Person = person[(Name,Tel?,Email*)]
type Name = name[String]
type Tel = tel[String]
```

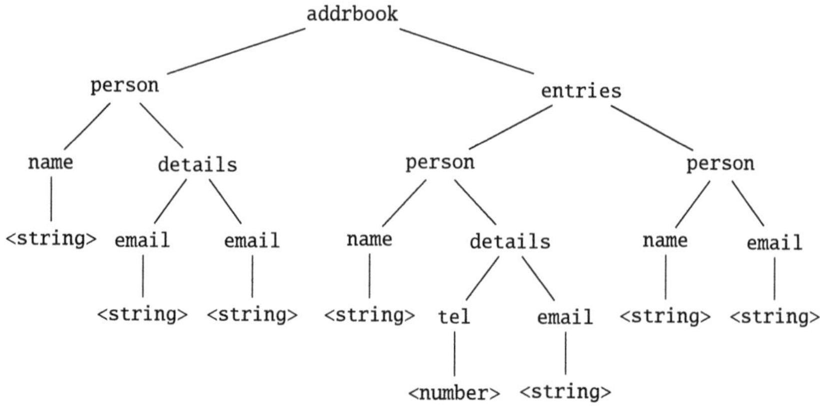

Fig. 11.10 Encoding of an XML document as a tree using additional alphabet symbols to guarantee unique ranks.

```
type Email = email[String]
```

It hierarchically defines five types of XML documents. By convention, the first type listed is the type of an entire document, and the others are used as types of subdocuments corresponding to subtrees in a tree representation. The type `Person` for example defines subtrees that start with the symbol `person` and have at least one child node of type `Name` with one optional next child of type `Tel` and then arbitrarily many further children of type `Email`.

An example XML document of type `Addrbook` is the following.

```
<addrbook>
  <person>
    <name>Haruo Hosoya</name>
    <email>hahosoya@xduce.jp</email>
    <email>haruo@xduce.jp</email>
  </person>
  <person>
    <name>Jerome Vouillon</name>
    <tel>123-456-789</tel>
    <email>vouillon@xduce.fr</email>
  </person>
  <person>
    <name>Benjamin Pierce</name>
    <email>pierce@xduce.edu</email>
  </person>
</addrbook>
```

A possible representation as a ranked tree is shown in Fig. 11.10. It abstracts away from the actual values of the name, address, telephone number and email sections. These values are represented by the symbols <string> and number of rank 0.

The representation uses additional symbols of rank 2 in order to produce a ranked tree. For instance, `entries` is used to model a list of more than two `person` nodes, and `details` is used similarly to cope with cases in which, in addition to a name, there is more than one email address or one phone number in that person's record.

It is not hard to construct a tree automaton recognising the language of all trees that represent XML documents of type `Addrbook`, once an encoding of such documents as ranked trees is fixed. XDuce encodes XML documents internally using ranked trees.

Bibliographic Notes

The study of finite automata on finite trees goes back to work by Doner [Don70] and by Thatcher and Wright [TW68] who generalised the notion of finite automata operating on words, seen as finite monadic algebras, to finite algebras with operations of higher arity. This way, an automaton can be seen as classifying terms, and words are just special terms in which all function symbols have arity 1. They observed that the theory of finite automata on words can essentially be lifted to a theory of automata on trees and therefore a theory of regular tree languages with all essential results being preserved, like determinisability, decidability, closure properties, etc. The main driving force was – following the work of Büchi, Elgot and Trakhtenbrot [BE58, Tra61] – the establishing of decidability results for logics like MSO on finite trees or WS2S, the Weak Monadic Logic of Two Successors.

A notable difference shows up in computational complexity. The membership problem for word languages can be solved in nondeterministic logarithmic space, whereas it is hard for polynomial time for tree automata. Such results are often folklore and cannot necessarily be traced back to a particular piece of work in the literature. The universality problem for automata on words is complete for the class PSPACE [MS73] whereas for words it is complete for EXPTIME [Sei90] and therefore presumably harder.

There is an online book project started in 2007 by Comon et al. [CDG$^+$07] which is dedicated to the study of tree automata and their applications. It naturally contains many more references and of course also a far deeper study of this topic than this chapter here can provide.

Matching problems, as presented in the first application in this chapter, occur in many applications, for instance in compilation of pattern matching expression as they are traditionally used in functional programming languages like ML and Haskell, but also increasingly introduced into object-oriented languages like Scala or C#. To clarify terminology: a *matching* equation is one in which the variables for which a solution is to be found, only occur on one side. If variables occur on both sides, then the problem is known as *unification*.

For a general introduction into the topic of unification see the handbook article by Baader and Snyder [BS01a]. An introduction into higher-order unification and matching problems in particular is given by Dowek in the same handbook [Dow01]. The description of higher-order objects needs a formalism like the λ-calculus, invented by Church through a series of papers ending in the introduction of the typed

λ-calculus [Chu40]. The literature contains a lot of material dedicated to this subject and useful as an introduction, for instance the textbooks by Barendregt [Bar85] and Hankin [Han04].

The algorithm presented here for third-order matching is due to Comon and Jurski [CJ97] and can be extended up to order five. Decidability of the matching problem for arbitrary orders had been open for a long time until Stirling finally showed that it is indeed decidable [Sti09]. This is only true for equality modulo $\beta\eta$-reductions. The problem becomes undecidable when only β-reductions are considered [Loa03].

The XML querying and processing language XDuce was developed by Pierce und Hosoya [HP03]. Hosoya has also written a comprehensive book on the foundations of XML querying and processing using tree automata [Hos10]. There is also an overview article by Schwentick on this topic [Sch07b]. Both provide not only further references but also a much deeper introduction and study of this connection. This includes, first of all, the lifting of the technical concept of tree automata to unranked trees which are more suitable to model XML documents than ranked trees, as the examples above suggest. This has led to the study of different kinds of tree automata operating on unranked trees, i.e. trees in which nodes can have arbitrarily many children regardless of the node's label. Such include stepwise tree automata [CNT04] and tree-walking automata [AU71], introduced originally for parsing of context-free languages long before XML was invented. These then became a popular domain of application for tree automata.

Such a theory of querying languages for unranked trees would be incomplete without the study of suitable logics to express their properties. An overview of such logics based on First-Order and Monadic Second-Order Logic is given by Libkin [Lib06].

Transducers, as briefly mentioned in Sect. 11.5.2 but not studied in any kind of detail here, are finite automata with output. They therefore realise functions, for instance from trees to trees. For a general introduction to transducers see the textbook by Berstel [Ber79] for instance. For a closer look at tree transducers see the corresponding chapter in the book by Comon et al. [CDG$^+$07]. For a specific look at tree transducers for XML processing see the book by Hosoya [Hos10] for instance.

Exercises

Exercise 122 Find a ranked alphabet that can be used to model Boolean expressions over the constants $0, 1$ and over variables $x_0, x_1, \ldots$ with the typical Boolean operators. *Hint:* Since it may be cumbersome to differentiate between subscript and ordinary symbols, it may be helpful to work with a representation of these variables that does not rely on subscript symbols, for instance $x(0), x(1), x(2), \ldots$ using decimal representations of numbers. This causes a little problem, though, as the index 0 clashes with the constant 0. Could this be alleviated by allowing alphabets to be finite multisets, so that one symbol can have several ranks? Perhaps it is easier to use different symbols for the Boolean constants then.

Exercise 123 Let $\Sigma = \{a, b, c, d\}$ with $rk_\Sigma(a) = rk_\Sigma(b) = 2$ and $rk_\Sigma(c) = rk_\Sigma(d) = 0$. Determine, for each of the following languages, whether they can be recognised by a nondeterministic or even a deterministic top-down tree automaton. In the positive case, construct such an automaton, in the negative case give an argument for why the language is not regular.

a) $L_1 := \{t \in \mathcal{T}_\Sigma^* \mid$ the path $\varepsilon, 0, 01, 010, 0101, 01010, \ldots$ in t contains an even number of occurrences of the symbol $a\}$,

b) $L_2 := \{t \in \mathcal{T}_\Sigma^* \mid t$ is not balanced $\}$,

c) $L_3 := \{t \in \mathcal{T}_\Sigma^* \mid$ there are two leaves u, v in t such that $t(u) = c$, $t(v) = d$ and u is further to the left of $v\}$,

d) $L_4 := \{t \in \mathcal{T}_\Sigma^* \mid t$ contains exactly 239 leaves that are labelled with $c\}$.

Exercise 124 Let $\Sigma := \{0, 1, \neg, \wedge, \vee, x, y, z\}$ be the extension of the ranked alphabet from Ex. 11.3 used to model Boolean expressions over the constants 0 and 1, by symbols x, y, z of rank 0. This way we can represent Boolean expressions that contain the variables x, y and z, like $(\neg x \vee (1 \wedge z)) \wedge \neg(y \wedge \neg z)$.
Construct NbuTA over Σ for the following languages.

a) The set of all expressions in *negation normal form*, i.e. expressions that are built from the literals $0, 1, x, y, z, \neg x, \neg y, \neg z$ using only the operators $\wedge$ and $\vee$.

b) The set of all *monotonic* expressions where an expression is said to be monotonic if the number of negation symbols on every path of its syntax tree that ends in a variable is even.

c) The set of expressions in *disjunctive normal form*, i.e. expressions of the form $\bigvee_{i=1}^{n} \bigwedge_{j=1}^{m_i} \ell_{i,j}$ for some $n, m_1, \ldots, m_n \geq 0$ such that each $\ell_{i,j}$ is a literal in the sense of part (a).

d) The set of all expressions that evaluate to 1 under *any* valuation of the variables x, y, z.

e) The set of all expressions that contain at most $n_\neg$ occurrences of negation symbols, at most $n_\wedge$ subexpressions that are conjunctions and at most $n_\vee$ subexpressions that are disjunctions, for some arbitrary but fixed $n_\neg, n_\wedge, n_\vee \in \mathbb{N}$.

f) Similar to the previous language but now the numbers of occurrences of the symbols $\neg$, $\wedge$, $\vee$ should each be some given $n_\neg, n_\wedge, n_\vee$ modulo some given $m_\neg, m_\wedge, m_\vee \geq 1$.

Exercise 125 Show that the set of all parse trees of a context-free language is a regular tree language. *Hint:* You may assume that the grammar has been normalised such that all rules are of the form $A \to BC$ or $D \to a$ for some nonterminal symbols A, B, C, D and a some terminal symbol a (ε-free Chomsky normal form), and that additionally, whenever there is a rule of the form $A \to BC$ then there is no rule of the form $A \to a$ for the same nonterminal A.

Exercise 126 Prove Thm. 11.11.

Exercise 127 Prove Lemma 11.13.

Exercise 128 Let $\mathcal{A} = (Q, \Sigma, \delta, F)$ be an NbuTA. Define a sequence of sets of states $P_i \subseteq Q$ for $i = 0, \ldots$ as follows. We have $P_0 := \emptyset$ and

$$P_i \;\; := \;\; \bigcup_{d \geq 0} \bigcup_{a \in \Sigma_d} \bigcup \{\delta_d((q_1, \ldots, q_n), a) \mid q_1, \ldots, q_d \in P_{i-1}\}$$

for each $i \geq 1$. Finally, let $P^* := \bigcup_{i \geq 0} P_i$.

a) Show that $P_i \subseteq P_{i+1}$ for all $i \geq 0$. *Hint:* Use induction on i.
b) Show that there is an n such that $P^* = P_n$.
c) Show that the following holds for any $q \in Q$ and any $i \in \mathbb{N}$: we have $q \in P_i$ iff there is a tree t of height at most i such that $t \in L(\mathcal{A}_q)$ where $\mathcal{A}_q := (Q, \Sigma, \delta, \{q\})$.
d) Conclude that the non-emptiness problem for NTA is decidable in polynomial time.
e) Derive a small model theorem for NTA, i.e. give a function $f : \mathbb{N} \to \mathbb{N}$ that grows as gently as possible such that for every NTA $\mathcal{A}$ of size n either $L(\mathcal{A}) = \emptyset$ or there is a tree $t \in L(\mathcal{A})$ of size at most $f(n)$.

Exercise 129 Write an FO formula that defines the set of all Boolean expressions in conjunctive normal form over a fixed set of variables $V := \{x_1, \ldots, x_k\}$, i.e. expressions of the form $\bigwedge_{i=1}^{n} \bigvee_{j_i=1}^{m_i} \ell_{i,j_i}$ where each ℓ_{i,j_i} is either x_h or $\neg x_h$ for some $h \in \{1, \ldots, k\}$. The ranked alphabet is given as $\Sigma_0 = V$, $\Sigma_1 = \{\neg\}$ and $\Sigma_2 = \{\wedge, \vee\}$.

Exercise 130 Prove Thm. 11.28 and 11.31 along the lines of the proofs of Thm. 2.10 and 2.16.

Exercise 131 Show that MSO over an alphabet $\Sigma = \Sigma_0 \cup \Sigma_2$ is not elementarily decidable. *Hint:* Show how to transform a formula φ of MSO over words into an equi-satisfiable MSO tree formula φ' over this alphabet such that φ' only has models in which every non-leaf node has at least one child that is a leaf node. Such degenerate trees are essentially one path from the root to a node with two leaf children, and this path can easily encode a word.

Exercise 132 Show that $\lambda x_1, x_2.x_1(x_2(x_1(x_1(a, t_1), t_2)), t_3)$, for any terms t_1, t_2, t_3, is a solution for the equation

$$x\big((\lambda y_1, y_2.y_1), (\lambda y_3.f(y_3, y_3))\big) \;\; \approx \;\; f(a, a)$$

where $a : 0$, $f : 0, 0 \to 0$.

Exercise 133 a) Construct an accepting run of the DbuTA from Ex. 11.33 on the term $\lambda x_1, x_2.x_1(x_2(x_1(x_1(a, \#), \#)), \#)$.
b) Show that $\lambda x_1, x_2.x_2(x_1(f(a, a), \#))$ is not being accepted by this DbuTA.

Exercise 134 Complete the details that are left out in the proof of Thm. 11.34.

Exercise 135 Construct an NTA that recognises exactly the tree representations like the one given in Fig. 11.10 of those XML documents that have the type `Addrbook` as defined in Ex. 11.35. *Hint:* Rewrite the XDuce type definition of `addrbook` first using the additional symbols from Fig. 11.10 like `details` etc., so that each type refers to a binary symbol.

Chapter 12
Parity Games

The automata-logic correspondence, starting with automata on finite words, whose fundamentals are presented in Chp. 2, has been extended in two directions: Chp. 5 considers infinite words, and Chp. 11 considers finite trees. In all three cases, Monadic Second-Order Logic has been shown to be equi-expressive to a natural model of finite automata over the respective word or tree structures.

A natural question to ask concerns the unification of both extensions: is there also a similar automata-logic correspondence over *infinite* trees? The answer is yes and will be studied in detail in Chp. 13. However, remember that both extensions – to infinite words and to finite trees – separately introduced some additional combinatorial difficulty, so a theory of finite automata over infinite trees can be expected not only to inherit both but perhaps even introduce further technical obstacles.

These combinatorial difficulties usually arise from the combination of two necessities: something that objects against easy complementation constructions like nondeterminism or the branching structure in trees, and complementation closure as a must in order to handle logical negation in a translation from formulas to automata. The central combinatorial result used to obtain complementation closure for finite automata over infinite trees is positional determinacy of parity games.

Parity games can be seen as extensions of Büchi games as studied in Chp. 9, and determinacy again describes the phenomenon of there always being one player who has a winning strategy for a given game. Positional determinacy means that these winning strategies can even be assumed to be positional, resp. memoryless.

This chapter introduces parity games, proves positional determinacy and presents an algorithmic solution to the main problem of solving, i.e. to determine the winner in a given game.

12.1 Games, Plays and Strategies

Parity games are two-player games of infinite duration in which player 0's winning plays satisfy a given parity condition. Just like reachability games, parity games are played on directed graphs whose node set is partitioned into nodes belonging to players 0 and 1, respectively. The main difference to reachability games is the fact that, in a reachability game, player 0 wins a play after a finite amount of time. Player 1's wins are determined after infinitely many steps only, namely when the target set has *not* been reached. But determinacy of reachability games allows us to compute the winning region for one player only in order to automatically obtain the winning region for the other player as well. And the winning region for the player who wins plays after finitely many steps can easily be characterised and computed using attractors.

The winner of a play in a parity game is not determined after finitely many steps, and this is true for both players. The nodes in a parity game are equipped with priorities (from a finite set of natural numbers), and player 0 wins a play if the highest priority seen infinitely often is even. Likewise, player 1 wins all other plays, and by demanding that plays are always of infinite duration, these are exactly the plays in which the highest priority seen infinitely often is odd. Hence, there is no way to determine the winner of a play by looking at a finite prefix only.

Most of the concepts associated with the formal study of two-player games on directed graphs can simply be copied verbatim from reachability games to parity games.

Definition 12.1 A *parity game* is a $\mathcal{G} = (V, V_0, V_1, v_I, E, \Omega)$ where V is a set of nodes partitioned into nodes V_0 owned by player 0 and nodes V_1 owned by player 1, $v_I \in V$ is a designated starting node, and $E \subseteq V \times V$ is a left-total and finitely branching relation determining possible moves in the game. The winning condition for plays is given as a parity condition $\Omega : V \to \mathbb{N}$ which is required to have a finite range, i.e. $|\{\Omega(v) \mid v \in v\}| < \infty$.

A *play* is an infinite sequence $\pi = v_0, v_1, \ldots$ such that $v_0 = v_I$ and $(v_i, v_{i+1}) \in E$ for all $j \geq 0$. Such a play π is winning for player 0 if $\limsup_{i \to \infty} \Omega(v_i) \equiv 0 \bmod 2$, i.e. the maximal priority occurring infinitely often in π is even. Player 1 wins the play if this is odd.

A *strategy* for player i is a function $\sigma_i : V^* V_i \to V$ that respects the edge relation, i.e. $(\pi u, \pi u \sigma_i(\pi u)) \in E$ for all finite plays $\pi \in V^*$ and all nodes $u \in V_i$. It is a *winning strategy* if player i is the winner for any play $\pi = v_0, v_1, \ldots$ that conforms to this strategy in the sense that for all $j \geq 0$ such that $v_j \in V_i$ we have $v_{j+1} = \sigma_i(v_0 \ldots v_j)$.

The strategy σ_i is *positional* if $\sigma_i(\pi u) = \sigma_i(\pi' u)$ for all $\pi, \pi' \in V^*$ and all $u \in V_i$, i.e. the choices that it describes are only dependent on the current position in a play, not its history. A positional strategy is usually given as a function $\sigma_i : V_i \to V$.

We will often be concerned with finite parity games only, especially when considering the problem of algorithmically solving a game, i.e. determining the existence of winning strategies for either of the players. Finite parity games are clearly finitely branching. For infinite parity games, the requirement of being finitely branching is included just because it simplifies some technical constructions slightly, in particular that of an attractor region and strategy which will also play a significant role here. Nevertheless, all results on parity games developed here also hold for infinite games with infinite branching degree.

On the other hand, the requirement of there being only finitely many priorities in a game is a genuine restriction. Equivalently, it requires some node in the game to have maximal priority. This is needed for the winner of a play to be determined, and subsequently for positional determinacy to hold, as the following example shows. We also restrict our attention to infinite parity games of at most countable size. This will avoid the need to reason using the axiom of choice in some parts.

Example 12.2 Consider the infinite game

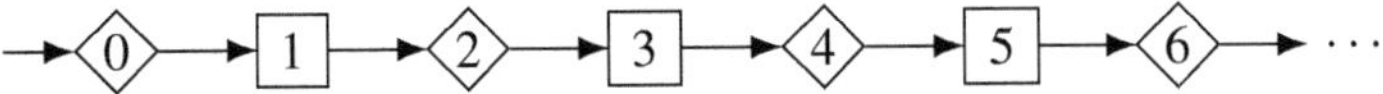

with nodes' priorities shown inside the nodes. As usual, we depict nodes owned by player 0 with diamond shapes (possibly stretched horizontally) and nodes owned by player 1 as squares (or rectangles).

We refrain from calling this game a parity game because it violates the property of having a maximal priority. Clearly, there is only one play in this game, and it would not be won by any of the player because $\limsup_{i \to \infty} i$ does not exist and is therefore neither even nor odd.

Moreover, no player can have a winning strategy. While both players clearly have exactly one strategy, it is not winning since there are no winning plays for either player. One could argue that both players have a *non-losing strategy* which is a concept that becomes relevant in games which allow draws between the players. Here we stick to games in which every play has a unique winner, though.

12.2 Basic Properties

12.2.1 Games with no Particular Initial Node

Sometimes it is convenient to take on a more global view onto a parity game by not fixing a particular starting node and consider parity games of the form $\mathcal{G} = (V, V_0, V_1, E, \Omega)$ with V, V_0, V_1, E and Ω as above. In this case, a play may start in any node, not just a designated starting node, and a winning strategy is then one for a player and a particular node $v \in V$, guaranteeing her or him to win any play that starts in v. This leads to the notion of a *winning region* for player p, usually denoted W_p, of all nodes v such that player p has a winning strategy for the game starting in node v. We will also say that player p *wins node v* if $v \in W_p$.

Determinacy of a parity game $\mathcal{G}$ with node set V is then simply the property of $W_0 \cup W_1 = V$. Note that $W_0 \cap W_1 = \varnothing$ is trivially always the case since no node can be won by both players at the same time. Hence, determinacy can be seen as the ability to partition the node set of a game into two parts, each of them won by one of the players. *Positional determinacy* refers to the property that additionally, each node in the winning region W_p is won by player p with a positional strategy.

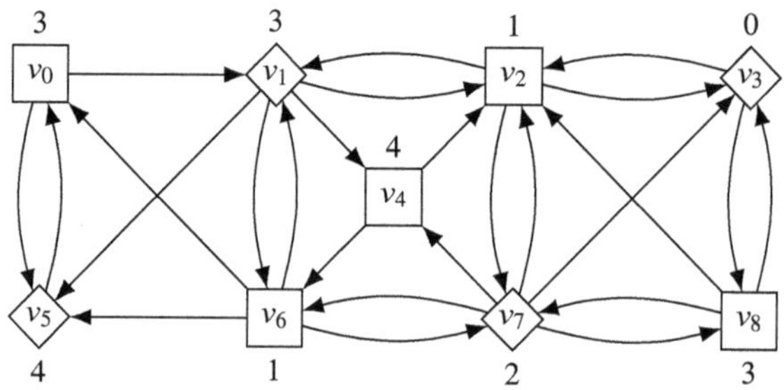

Fig. 12.1 A parity game with nine nodes and priorities $0, \ldots, 4$.

Example 12.3 Fig. 12.1 shows a finite parity game with node set $V = \{v_0, \ldots, v_8\}$. The priorities are given as labels to the nodes. They are drawn from the range $\{0, \ldots, 4\}$ in this case.

One can easily check that positional determinacy is given for this particular game. The winning regions are $W_0 = \{v_0, v_1, v_5, v_6, v_7\}$ and $W_1 = \{v_2, v_3, v_4, v_8\}$. A positional winning strategy for player 0 to win node v_0 for example is given as

$$\sigma_0 : \{v_1 \mapsto v_5, v_5 \mapsto v_0\}$$

with arbitrary values on the other nodes v_3 and v_7 owned by player 0. It is also a strategy to win nodes v_1 and v_5. Note that all plays conforming to this strategy and starting in node v_0 are of the form $(v_0(v_5 + v_1v_5))^\omega$. Hence, the greatest priority occurring infinitely often in them is always 4.

A positional strategy for player 0 to win from node v_7 is

$$\sigma_0' : \{v_1 \mapsto v_5, v_5 \mapsto v_0, v_7 \mapsto v_6\}$$

with the value on v_3 being arbitrary. It induces two kinds of plays that conform to it: those that eventually loop within $\{v_0, v_1, v_5\}$ as above and are won by player 0 because of priority 4, and those of the form $(v_7v_6)^\omega$ that are won by her because of priority 2. Likewise, σ_0' also wins node v_6 for player 0.

In this particular example it is easy to see that there is also a positional winning strategy with which player 0 uniformly wins her entire winning region. Strategy σ_0' extends σ_0 in a way that was said to be allowed for σ_0. So σ_0' is not only winning for nodes v_6 and v_7 but also for nodes v_0, v_1 and v_5. In fact, it would be more precise to say that σ_0' can be extended to a positional winning strategy for all nodes in W_0 by giving it an arbitrary value on v_3.

12.2.2 Uniform Winning Strategies

The previous example raises the question after the possibility to generalise the observation on uniformity: given a winning region W_p for player p, i.e. winning strategies σ_v for player p to win node $v \in W_i$, is there also one strategy σ that wins all nodes in W_p? And is it positional provided that all σ_v are positional? The answer is yes to both questions. We will concentrate on the case of positional strategies only. The case for general strategies is analogous and only requires a notational extension in the reasoning below.

The crucial observation for the ability to conjoin strategies into uniform ones is formalised in the next lemma. Its proof is left as an exercise. To be able to state it succinctly, we introduce the following notation for nodes v, u of a parity game $\mathcal{G} = (V, V_0, V_1, E, \Omega)$ and a positional strategy σ for some player p. We write $v \overset{\sigma}{\rightsquigarrow} u$ if u occurs in some play starting in v that conforms to σ. It can formally be defined inductively via

- $v \overset{\sigma}{\rightsquigarrow} v$ for any v, σ.
- $v \overset{\sigma}{\rightsquigarrow} u$ if $u \neq v$ and there is a $u' \in V$ such that $v \overset{\sigma}{\rightsquigarrow} u'$ and

  - $u' \in V_p$ and $u = \sigma(u')$, or
  - $u' \in V_{1-p}$.

Lemma 12.4 *Let $p \in \{0, 1\}$, $\mathcal{G}$ be a parity game with node set V, $v \in V$ and σ be a positional strategy that guarantees player p to win v. Then σ also wins any node v' for player p such that $v \overset{\sigma}{\rightsquigarrow} v'$.*

With this we can prove the aforementioned existence of uniform strategies that win all nodes of a winning region. The trick here is the following. Suppose we have a set W of nodes that are won by player p in a game $\mathcal{G}$ and positional winning strategies σ_v for any node $v \in W$. Since the node set of the underlying game $\mathcal{G}$ is assumed to be countable, we can enumerate W as $v_0, v_1, \ldots$ Note that W does not necessarily need to be infinite; the case of a finite W is simply subsumed in the following reasoning. We write σ_i instead of σ_{v_i}.

Consider σ_0. It guarantees player p to win node v_0, but also all nodes v' such that $v_0 \overset{\sigma_0}{\rightsquigarrow} v'$, according to Lemma 12.4. Let $W_0 := \{v' \mid v_0 \overset{\sigma_0}{\rightsquigarrow} v'\}$. If $W_0 \supseteq W$ then we have obviously already found the required strategy. Otherwise there is a smallest j such that $v_j \in W \setminus W_0$, i.e. we do not have $v_0 \overset{\sigma_0}{\rightsquigarrow} v_j$. More generally, there is a smallest j such that σ_0 does not guarantee winning v_j.

Intuitively, we may try to construct a strategy that guarantees winning $W_0 \cup \{v_j\}$ as follows: when visiting a node in W_0, play according to σ_0; otherwise, in node v_j, play according to σ_j. This is not a complete description of a strategy in general, though, because it may be the case that a play starting in v_j leads to some node $u \in V_p \setminus (W_0 \cup \{v_j\})$, and this strategy does not prescribe a choice in u. This seems to be easily fixed by considering the set $W_j := \{v' \mid v_j \overset{\sigma_j}{\rightsquigarrow} v'\}$ instead of just $\{v_j\}$. This causes another problem, though: we may have $W_0 \cap W_j \neq \varnothing$, i.e. some node

u may be reachable from both v_0 and v_j with the corresponding strategies, and $\sigma_0(u) \neq \sigma_j(u)$ may be possible. So we may have to determine explicitly how player p should choose in u.

This can be done, though, with another simple observation, namely that no finite prefix of a play is determines the winner of a play. In other words, a player can play according to some arbitrary strategy for any finite amount of time and then start using a winning strategy, and this will still be a winning strategy provided that the strategy that is used to form a prefix of a play does not leave the player's winning region. This principle can even be iterated: let $\sigma_0', \ldots, \sigma_{n-1}'$ be strategies for player p, not necessarily winning. Construct a new strategy σ' that asks player p to play according to σ_0' for a while, then according to σ_1' for a while, etc. until σ_{n-1}' is used. Now suppose this reaches some node u from which player p has a winning strategy σ_n', and there she continues using σ_n'. Then this overall strategy is a winning strategy for each node in which she could start to use strategy σ_0' and so on in this way.

This allows us to construct a strategy with which player p uniformly wins $W_0 \cup W_j$: on nodes for which both prescribe a choice, follow strategy σ_0. Equally, one could follow strategy σ_j and dismiss the choices prescribed by σ_0 instead. However, when merging infinitely many strategies into a single one, order matters because we need to ensure that the resulting strategy only ever requires player p to swap the underlying strategy finitely many times or, equally, to eventually stick to one of these strategies.

Lemma 12.5 *Let $\mathcal{G}$ be a parity game with node set V, $p \in \{0,1\}$ be a player and $W \subseteq V$ a set of positions such that there are positional winning strategies σ_v for player p to win any node $v \in W$. Then there is also a positional strategy σ that is winning any node $v \in W$ for player p.*

Proof Let $\mathcal{G} = (V, V_0, V_1, E, \Omega)$, $p \in \{0,1\}$ and $W \subseteq V$ be given, as well as positional winning strategies σ_v for player p to win any node $v \in W$. Let W be enumerated as $v_0, v_1, \ldots$ and define $W_i := \{v' \mid v_i \overset{\sigma_i}{\rightsquigarrow} v'\}$, as well as $W' := \bigcup_{i=0}^{\infty} W_i$. We have $W' \supseteq W$, so it suffices to define a positional strategy σ that uniformly wins all nodes in W' for player p. We define it via $\sigma(v) := \sigma_m(v)$ where $m := \min\{i \mid v \in W_i\}$. Clearly, this is a positional strategy for all nodes in W'. It remains to be seen that it is winning for player p for any such node.

Let $\pi = u_0, u_1, u_2, \ldots$ be a play that conforms to strategy σ. By definition of the sets W_i, we have for all $i, j \geq 0$: if $u_j \in W_i$ then $u_{j+1} \in W_i$. Hence, the sequence $m_0, m_1, \ldots$ with $m_j := \min\{i \mid u_j \in W_i\}$ is monotonically decreasing. Since $m_0 \in \mathbb{N}$, the set $\{m_0, m_1, \ldots\}$ is finite which means that there is an $n \geq 0$ such that $m_j = m_n$ for all $j \geq n$. In other words, the play $u_n, u_{n+1}, \ldots$ conforms to strategy σ_n and is therefore winning for player p, i.e. $\limsup_{i \to \infty} \Omega(u_{n+i}) \equiv p \bmod 2$. Since the limes superior of a sequence is invariant under adding prefixes we have that $\limsup_{i \to \infty} \Omega(u_i) \equiv p \bmod 2$ as well which shows that π is indeed winning for player p, and σ is therefore a winning strategy for player p. $\qquad \square$

Example 12.6 Consider the infinite parity game shown in Fig. 12.2. It is easy to see that the positional strategy σ_i defined via

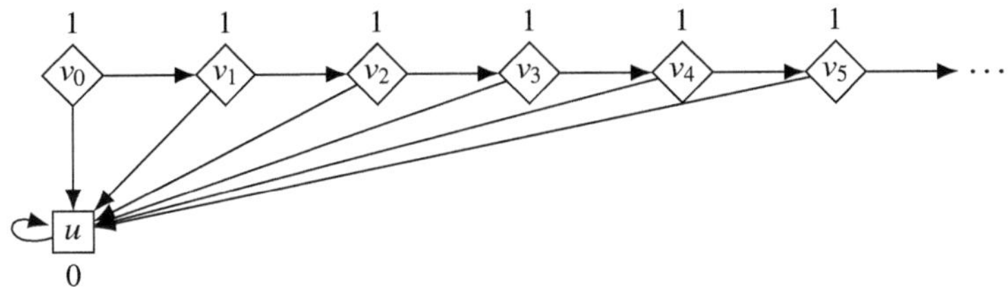

Fig. 12.2 An infinite parity game showing that winning strategies need to be merged in a well-founded way to obtain a uniform winning strategy.

$$\sigma_i(v_j) \ := \ \begin{cases} u & , \text{ if } j = i \\ v_{j+1} & , \text{ otherwise} \end{cases}$$

is winning all nodes v_j for player p such that $j \leq i$, by successively moving right towards v_i and then down to u where the play ultimately loops and priority 0 makes player 0 the winner.

So the winning region for player 0 is the entire node set. A uniform strategy for player 0 to win all nodes is obtained by means of the construction in Lemma 12.5 for instance by taking the natural order $v_0, v_1, \ldots$ as an enumeration for the relevant part of the node set. The strategy obtained from this order is σ defined by $\sigma(v_j) = u$ for any $j \in \mathbb{N}$, i.e. it makes player 0 move directly down to node u.

The need for a well-founded order on the winning strategies is shown by considering a non-well-founded way to merge them, i.e. to make player change strategies infinitely often. Let σ' be defined by $\sigma'(v_j) := \sigma_{j+1}(v_j)$. Hence, when playing according to σ' and starting in v_0, player 0 first moves to v_1 since σ_1 requires her to do so. There she swaps over to strategy σ_2 which takes her to v_2, and so on. This is clearly not a winning strategy for her because it results in the play $v_0, v_1, v_2, \ldots$ that is won by player 1.

12.2.3 Priority Compression

We state the rather obvious observation that priorities in a parity game can uniformly be shifted by an even amount without changing the winning regions and associated strategies. The same principle has also been observed to apply to NPA, yielding a language-preserving transformation there, cf. Lemma 6.9. The construction is even sound if priorities are not shifted uniformly but in a way that preserves their parities and their order. The proof is left as an exercise.

Lemma 12.7 *Let* $\mathcal{G} = (V, V_0, V_1, E, \Omega)$ *be a parity game and* $\Omega' : V \to \mathbb{N}$ *such that*

- $\Omega(v) \leq \Omega(u)$ *iff* $\Omega'(v) \leq \Omega'(u)$ *for all* $v, u \in V$,
- $\Omega(v) \equiv \Omega'(v) \bmod 2$ *for all* $v \in V$.

Let $\mathcal{G}' := (V, V_0, V_1, E, \Omega')$. Then any winning strategy σ for player p in $\mathcal{G}$ is also a winning strategy for player p and the same nodes in $\mathcal{G}'$ and vice-versa.

Consequently, such transformations on the priorities do not change the winning regions in a parity game.

12.3 Winning Parity Games

Again, positional determinacy of parity games means that any node of any parity game is won by exactly one of the players. While it is easy to see that every node is won by *at most* one of the players 0 and 1 – assuming both have a winning strategy, there is a unique play that conforms to both these strategies and the highest priority occurring infinitely often in this play would therefore have to be both even and odd at the same time – the tricky part is to show that every node is won by *at least* one of the players. Why should player $1-p$ have a winning strategy for the game starting in some node v, simply because player p does not?

12.3.1 Subgames

In order to prove the result formally we need the construction of a subgame.

Definition 12.8 Let $\mathcal{G} = (V, V_0, V_1, E, \Omega)$ be a parity game and $U \subseteq V$. We abbreviate $V \smallsetminus U$ as $\overline{U}$. The *subgame* of $\mathcal{G}$ resulting from the removal of U is $\mathcal{G} \smallsetminus U := (V \smallsetminus U, V_0 \cap \overline{U}, V_1 \cap \overline{U}, E \cap (\overline{U} \times \overline{U}), \Omega|_{\overline{U}})$ with $\Omega|_{\overline{U}}(v) = \Omega(v)$ for all $v \in \overline{U}$.

Note that $\mathcal{G} \smallsetminus U$ is in general not a parity game, and calling it a subgame is at least questionable. The removal of nodes from U can leave nodes in $\mathcal{G} \smallsetminus U$ that do not have successors. Take for instance the parity game $\mathcal{G}$ in Fig. 12.2. Then $\mathcal{G} \smallsetminus \{u\}$ is a parity game and so is $\mathcal{G} \smallsetminus \{v_i \mid i \text{ is odd }\}$. However, $\mathcal{G} \smallsetminus \{v_1, u\}$ is not a parity game anymore since it leaves node v_0 with no successor.

The reason why we still speak of a *subgame* $\mathcal{G} \smallsetminus U$ is that we will only use this construction for particular sets U which satisfy a condition that is sufficient for $\mathcal{G} \smallsetminus U$ to be a parity game. For this we recall the definition of an *attractor* (cf. Sect. 3.4.2) – i.e. the set of all nodes from which a player can enforce a visit to a particular region in the underlying graph. More specifically, the attractor of a set of nodes U for player p is

$$Attr_p(U) := \bigcup_{i \in \mathbb{N}} Attr_p^i(U)$$

where $Attr_p^0(U) := U$ and

$$Attr_p^{i+1}(U) := Attr_p^i(U) \cup \{v \in V_p \mid vE \cap Attr_p^i(U) \neq \varnothing\}$$
$$\cup \{v \in V_{1-p} \mid vE \subseteq Attr_p^i(U)\}.$$

An *attractor strategy* for player p is a positional strategy to win the reachability game with such a target U: on a node $v \in Attr_p^i(U)$ for $i > 0$ move to a successor u such that $u \in Attr_p^j(U)$ for some $j < i$.

Lemma 12.9 *Let $\mathcal{G} = (V, V_0, V_1, E, \Omega)$ be a parity game, $U \subseteq V$, and $p \in \{0, 1\}$. Then $\mathcal{G} \setminus Attr_p(U)$ is a parity game.*

Proof All that remains to be seen is that the edge relation in $\mathcal{G} \setminus Attr_p(U)$ is left-total. So take a node $v \in V \setminus Attr_p(U)$ and assume, for the sake of contradiction, that $vE \subseteq Attr_p(U)$. But then $v \in Attr_p(U)$ by the definition of an attractor as well, so $v \notin V \setminus Attr_p(U)$. $\qquad\qquad\square$

Henceforth, when we speak of a subgame $\mathcal{G} \setminus U$ for some node set U we assume that it is indeed a parity game, for instance because U is attractor-closed. We need two technical observations regarding subgames and attractor-closures.

Lemma 12.10 *Let $\mathcal{G}$ be a parity game with node set V, $p \in \{0, 1\}$, $U \subseteq V$ such that $Attr_p(U) \subseteq U$ and $\mathcal{G} \setminus U$ the subgame induced by U. Suppose σ is a strategy for player $\overline{p} := 1 - p$ with which she wins some node v in $\mathcal{G} \setminus U$. Then she also wins v with σ in $\mathcal{G}$.*

Proof This is a simple consequence of the fact that any play in $\mathcal{G}$ that conforms to σ and starts in node v is a play within $\mathcal{G} \setminus U$. Note that, by following σ, player $\overline{p}$ will never make a move out of $V \setminus U$ for otherwise σ would not be a strategy for her in $\mathcal{G} \setminus U$. On the other hand, since $Attr_p(U) \subseteq U$ by assumption, and therefore $Attr_p(U) = U$ in fact, player p cannot make a move in $\mathcal{G}$ from some node in $v \in V_p \setminus U$ to some some in U for otherwise we would have $v \in Attr_p(U) \subseteq U$ contradicting the assumption that $v \notin U$. $\qquad\qquad\square$

Lemma 12.11 *Let $\mathcal{G}$ be a parity game, $p \in \{0, 1\}$ and W_p be the set of all nodes for which player p has a (positional) winning strategy. Then $Attr_p(W_p) \subseteq W_p$.*

Proof Suppose there was some node $v \in Attr_p(W_p) \setminus W_p$. It is possible to construct a winning strategy for player p and node v as follows: play according to the attractor strategy for as long as a play visits nodes in $Attr_p(W_p) \setminus W_p$; once it reaches W_p, continue playing according to the winning strategy that exists by assumption. If the latter is positional then so is this combined strategy. Also, since following the attractor strategy guarantees a visit to W_p eventually, the winning of any play conforming to this combined strategy is solely determined by the greatest priority occurring infinitely often after a visit to W_p, i.e. the play is winning for player p. $\square$

12.3.2 Positional Determinacy

With the considerations above we can finally prove positional determinacy.

Theorem 12.12 *Let $\mathcal{G}$ be a parity game with node set V and W_0, W_1 be the set of nodes that are won by either of the players respectively. Then we have $W_0 \cup W_1 = V$. Moreover, for both $p \in \{0, 1\}$ there is a positional winning strategy σ_p with which player p wins all the nodes in W_p.*

Proof Let $\mathcal{G} = (V, V_0, V_1, E, \Omega)$ and $k := \max\{\Omega(v) \mid v \in V\}$. Remember that k is assumed to exist. We prove the claim by induction on k. The base case is given by $k = 0$, i.e. all nodes have priority 0. It should be clear that in this case $W_0 = V$ and $W_1 = \varnothing$, and therefore $W_0 \cup W_1 = V$. Moreover, any positional strategy for player 0 is a winning strategy since any play only ever sees priority 0. At last, it should be clear that positional strategies always exist since the graphs underlying parity games are assumed to be left-total, i.e. every node has a successor, and every function assigning arbitrary successors to nodes is a positional strategy.

Now let $k > 0$. W.l.o.g. we assume k to be even. The case of an odd k is entirely symmetric with only the roles of players 0 and 1 swapped. Let W_0 be the set of nodes which are won by player 0 with some positional strategy. According to Lemma 12.5, player 0 also has a positional strategy σ_0 with which she uniformly wins all nodes in W_0.

It remains to be seen that player 1 has a positional strategy with which he wins all nodes in $V \setminus W_0$. Using Lemma 12.5 it suffices to show that he has positional winning strategies for any node $v \in V \setminus W_0$.

According to Lemma 12.9 and 12.11 we have $Attr_0(W_0) \subseteq W_0$ and that $\mathcal{G}' := \mathcal{G} \setminus W_0$ is indeed a parity game. Its node set is obviously $V \setminus W_0$. We now distinguish two cases depending on whether or not the highest priority k from $\mathcal{G}$ occurs in $\mathcal{G}'$.

(I) Suppose first that k does not occur in $V \setminus W_0$. Then the induction hypothesis yields a partition of the node set of the game $\mathcal{G} \setminus W_0$ into winning regions W_0' and W_1' together with positional winning strategies σ_0', σ_1' such that player p wins every node in W_p' with strategy σ_p'. According to Lemma 12.10, player 1 wins all the nodes in W_1' with his strategy σ_1' in $\mathcal{G}$ as well. We now claim that $W_0' = \varnothing$ which then yields $W_1' = V \setminus W_0$ showing that player 1 has a positional winning strategy for all the nodes which are not won by player 0 with a positional strategy.

So suppose there was some $v \in W_0'$, i.e. player 0 wins v with strategy σ_0' in $\mathcal{G} \setminus W_0$. Then consider the following combined strategy for player 0 and the game $\mathcal{G}$ starting in v: on nodes in $V \setminus W_0$ play according to strategy σ_0', and on nodes in W_0 play according to strategy σ_0. This is indeed a winning strategy for her because there are only two kinds of plays that conform to this strategy: those that stay entirely within $V \setminus W_0$, and those that eventually move into W_0 and remain there forever because player 1 cannot leave W_0, and player 0 does not leave W_0 by following a winning strategy. So the greatest priority occurring infinitely often in any of these plays must be even as well, and this combined strategy is a winning strategy for player 0 in $\mathcal{G}$, showing that indeed $v \in W_0$ in the first place and therefore $v \notin V \setminus W_0$.

(II) In the second case we have that priority k occurs somewhere in $V \setminus W_0$. Let $K := \{v \in V \setminus W_0 \mid \Omega(v) = k\}$. We consider $A := Attr_0(K)$, i.e. the set of all positions in $\mathcal{G}'$ from which player 0 can enforce a visit to K. According to Lemma 12.9, $\mathcal{G}'' := \mathcal{G}' \setminus A = (\mathcal{G} \setminus W_0) \setminus A$ is a parity game. Clearly, the highest priority occurring in it is strictly less than k, so the induction hypothesis yields a partitioning of

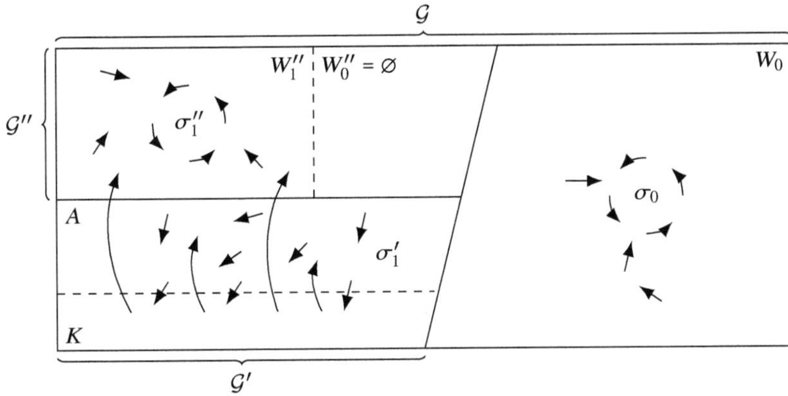

Fig. 12.3 The situation in part (II) of the proof of Thm. 12.12.

$V \smallsetminus (W_0 \cup A)$ into winning regions W_0'' and W_1'', together with positional strategies σ_0'', σ_1'' for the two players to win the nodes in W_0'' and W_1'' respectively.

The situation is shown in Fig. 12.3. The right side consists of W_0 – the set of nodes for which player 0 has a positional winning strategy. The left side is then the subgame $\mathcal{G}' = \mathcal{G} \smallsetminus W_0$, and the upper part of this is its subgame $\mathcal{G}'' = \mathcal{G}' \smallsetminus A$. It is partitioned into W_0'' and W_1''. We need to argue for each of the regions $W_0'', W_1'', A \smallsetminus K$ and K that either player 1 has a positional winning strategy in $\mathcal{G}$ for the nodes in these regions or the regions are in fact empty (because player 0 has a positional winning strategy for any node assumed to be in it, in which case it is in fact already included in W_0).

The easiest part is W_1''. Note that it is the winning region of player 1, i.e. player 0's opponent, in a subgame induced by the attractor for player 0. Hence, according to Lemma 12.10, player 1 wins all nodes in W_1'' not only in $\mathcal{G}''$ but also in $\mathcal{G}$.

Next consider $A \smallsetminus K$. By the definition of an attractor, all edges from nodes in $V_1 \cap (A \smallsetminus K)$ do not lead to nodes outside of $A \smallsetminus K$. In the supergame $\mathcal{G}$, there could be additional edges into W_0, though. Such edges are not beneficial to player 1 because player 0 wins any play taking such an edge with her strategy σ_0. Since player 1 not only cannot escape region A but also cannot prevent a play from ultimately reaching K, it suffices to consider region K, and the same findings apply to region $A \smallsetminus K$ as well.

First we observe that there can be no node $v \in K$ such that $v \in Attr_0^j(\{v\})$ for some $j > 0$. In other words, there is no node in K that player 0 can repeatedly enforce to visit. If this was the case, then this node would belong to W_0 because any play within A that visits some node in K infinitely often is winning for player 0. This gives a positional strategy for player 1 on A: let $v_1, v_2, \ldots$ be an enumeration of the nodes in K such that for all i, j with $1 \le i < j$: if $v_i \notin Attr_0(\{v_j\})$. Then on any node $v \in A \cap V_1$, player 1 moves to the successor $u \in vE$ that belongs to $Attr_0(\{v_j\})$ for the least j if it exists. Note that it may not exist because edges from nodes in K do not necessarily have to lead into A. However, they cannot lead into W_0 because then such nodes would belong to W_0. Hence, they must lead into W_0'' or W_1''.

This defines a positional strategy σ_1' for player 1 on $A = (A \smallsetminus K) \cup K$ which leaves the region W_0'' to be considered: in a node $v \in V_1$, move to the successor that belongs to $Attr_0(\{v_j\})$ for the smallest j if it exists. Otherwise move into $\mathcal{G}''$. Note that σ_1' is not necessarily a winning strategy; it is only winning if it eventually leads into W_1'' and not W_0''. We complete the two cases by arguing that $W_0'' = \varnothing$. We cannot use Lemma 12.10 to reason here because $\mathcal{G}''$ is obtained as a subgame of $\mathcal{G}$ induced by removing regions W_0 and A that are attractor-closed for player 0, not necessarily for her opponent.

So suppose that $W_0'' \neq \varnothing$, i.e. there is some node in $V \smallsetminus (W_0 \cup A)$ that is won by player 0 with a winning strategy σ_0'' in $\mathcal{G}''$. Consider the effect of using σ_0'' in $\mathcal{G}$. Upon visiting a node in V_0, player 0 makes her choices according to σ_0'' and stays within W_0''. However, when visiting a node $v \in V_1$, player 1 could now make use of edges that are additionally available to him by leading out of W_0''. They cannot lead into W_1'', though, for otherwise v would belong to W_1'' already. Likewise, they cannot lead into A because – using the argument above – the play would ultimately end up in W_1'', so v would also belong to W_1'' then. At last, player 1 would not make use of additional edges that lead into W_0 since player 0 wins there. So any play starting in a node $v \in W_0''$ and conforming to σ_0'' that is winning for player 0 in $\mathcal{G}$ will either eventually lead into W_0 or stay within W_0'' forever. But then v is won by player 0 in $\mathcal{G}$ and therefore we already have $v \in W_0$ which contradicts the assumption that $W_0'' \neq \varnothing$.

Thus, we get that $V \smallsetminus W_0 = W_1$ where W_1 is the set of nodes that are won by player 1 in $\mathcal{G}$, and a positional strategy for player 1 is obtained as the combination of the two positional strategies σ_1' and σ_1'' with every play conforming to σ_1 eventually conforming to σ_1'' and therefore being winning for player 1. $\qquad\square$

The proof of Thm. 12.12 shows that (positional) winning strategies in parity games can be obtained by consecutively merging attractor strategies. We remark that the proof in its form above needs to be slightly extended for infinite games in which nodes may have infinitely many successors. For games played on finitely-branching graphs, the definition of an attractor via an iteration over all natural numbers suffices. For infinitely-branching graphs, it needs to be extended to an iteration indexed by ordinal numbers.

Example 12.13 Reconsider the parity game shown in Fig. 12.1. It is easy to check that player 1 has a positional strategy to win the nodes in $W_1 = \{v_2, v_3, v_4, v_8\}$. To show that his opponent, i.e. player 0, has a positional winning strategy for the remaining nodes $\{v_0, v_1, v_5, v_6, v_7\}$, we first determine the highest priority in this region which needs to be good for her. Otherwise we would have had to start with the other player's winning region.

Here the highest priority is 4, and the set of nodes with the priority is $\{v_5\}$. Its attractor for player 0 is $\{v_5, v_0, v_1\}$. The subgame obtained by removing this attractor only contains nodes $\{v_6, v_7\}$. The induction hypothesis divides this node set into winning regions for players 0 and 1. In fact, both nodes are won by player 0 because there are only two plays in this subgame: $(v_5v_6)^\omega$ and $(v_6v_5)^\omega$. Both are clearly won by player 0.

By composing this with the attractor strategy for player 0 to reach $\{v_5\}$ we obtain the following positional winning strategy for her on $\{v_0, v_1, v_5, v_6, v_7\}$.

- The attractor strategy demands her to move from v_1 to v_5.
- The induction hypothesis yields the move from v_7 to v_6.
- The move back from a node with highest priority into its own attractor is realised by going from v_5 to v_0.

12.4 Solving Parity Games

The proof of Thm. 12.12 is not constructive, not even for finite parity games, since it assumes the winning region for one player to be given already. Thus, it does not immediately yield an algorithm for *solving parity games*, i.e. for the following problem.

> **given:** a finite parity game $\mathcal{G}$
> **compute:** the sets W_0, W_1 of winning regions together with winning
> strategies for each of the players

We restrict our attention to finite parity games in order to safely keep the problem computable. We will not strictly distinguish this problem from the associated decision problem which asks, given a parity game $\mathcal{G}$ and a node v, whether v belongs to W_0 or W_1. Likewise one could turn the computation of a winning strategy into a decision problem by asking, given a finite path $v_1, \ldots, v_n$ through $\mathcal{G}$ and some $u \in v_n E$, whether a winning strategy for player p exists to win node v_1 that maps $v_1, \ldots, v_n$ to u.

12.4.1 Theoretical Complexity

With Thm. 12.12 we can of course restrict our attention to positional strategies only. This yields the first result on the complexity of solving parity games.

Theorem 12.14 *The problem of solving a parity game belongs to NP $\cap$ co-NP.*

Proof Inclusion in NP is shown using the usual guess-and-verify technique: given $\mathcal{G} = (V, V_0, V_1, E, \Omega)$, guess positional strategies σ_0, σ_1 for both of the players. Note that these are objects of the form $V \to V$, i.e. we only need to guess one successor node for each node in the game. This can obviously be done in time $\mathcal{O}(|E|)$.

In order to verify that each σ_p is a winning strategy for player p we construct the subgame

$$\mathcal{G}_p \; := \; \mathcal{G} \setminus \left(V \setminus \left(\bigcup \{ vE \mid v \in V_{1-p} \} \cup \{ \sigma_p(v) \mid v \in V_p \} \right) \right) .$$

It is obtained by removing all successors of a p-node that player p does not ever move to when conforming to strategy σ_p. The graph underlying $\mathcal{G}_p$ then contains exactly those plays that conform to σ_p. Thus, in order to verify that σ_p is a winning strategy, it suffices to check that the highest priority on every simple loop in $\mathcal{G}_p$ is good for player p. This can be done as follows for example. Say we need to verify that there is no simple cycle on which the highest priority is odd, i.e. we consider $\mathcal{G}_0$. We iterate through all odd priorities r occurring in $\mathcal{G}_0$, remove all nodes with priorities greater than r and compute an SCC decomposition of the remaining graph. If it contains a non-trivial SCC, i.e. one with at least one edge, and a node of priority r, then such a cycle is found. The entire verification can therefore be done in time $\mathcal{O}(k \cdot |E|)$ where k is the index of $\mathcal{G}$, i.e. the number of different priorities used in it.

Inclusion in co-NP is then a simple consequence of the symmetric nature of positional determinacy for parity games: in order to decide that v does *not* belong to W_p it suffices to decide that it belongs to W_{1-p} which can be done in the same way as above. $\qquad\square$

12.4.2 A Recursive Algorithm

A deterministic algorithm can be based on the principles used in the proof of positional determinacy. Of course, an algorithm cannot simply assume that the winning region W_0 (and winning strategy σ_0) for player 0 is already given and then only construct a winning strategy on W_1. However, the principle of induction over the number of priorities can be used equally to compute the division into W_0 and W_1. It works as follows.

Let $\mathcal{G} = (V, V_0, V_1, E, \Omega)$ be a finite parity game and K be the set of nodes whose priority is maximal. W.l.o.g. we assume this priority to be even; otherwise the players need to be swapped in the following reasoning.

First we compute the attractor $A_0 := Attr_0(K)$, i.e. the set of positions from which player 0 can enforce a single visit of a node with highest (and even) priority. According to Lemma 12.9, $\mathcal{G} \setminus A_0$ is a parity game. Clearly the number of priorities in $\mathcal{G} \setminus A_0$ is strictly smaller than that in $\mathcal{G}$ since $K \subseteq A_0$.

So we can recursively solve the subgame $\mathcal{G} \setminus A_0$ and obtain winning regions W_0', W_1' with associated positional winning strategies σ_0', σ_1'. According to Lemma 12.10, σ_1' is not only a winning strategy for player 1 in the subgame $\mathcal{G} \setminus A_0$ but also in the supergame $\mathcal{G}$. Thus, W_1' is at least part of the winning region W_1 for player 1 in $\mathcal{G}$.

If $W_1' = \varnothing$ then player 0's winning region in $\mathcal{G}$ is the entire node set because every play in $\mathcal{G}$ must either eventually be trapped in $\mathcal{G} \setminus A_0$ (and therefore won by player 0), or visit K infinitely often which also makes her the winner because nodes in K have highest and even priority.

However, if $W_1' \neq \varnothing$ then the winning region for player 1 in $\mathcal{G}$ could encompass more than just W_1'. For instance, there may be nodes in player 0's attractor A_0 for K from which on player 0 is of course able to enforce one visit to K, but perhaps not repeatedly, i.e. in the long run player 1 may be able to enforce a visit to W_1'.

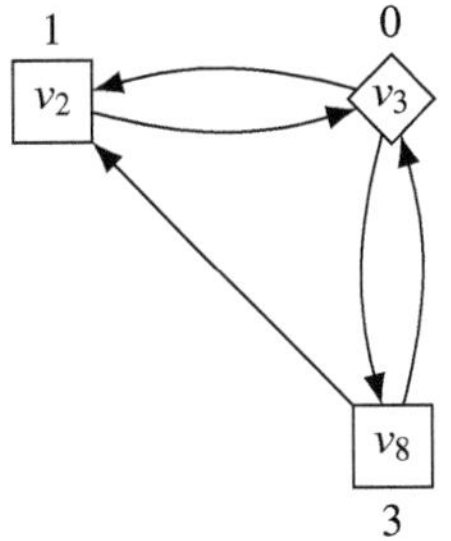
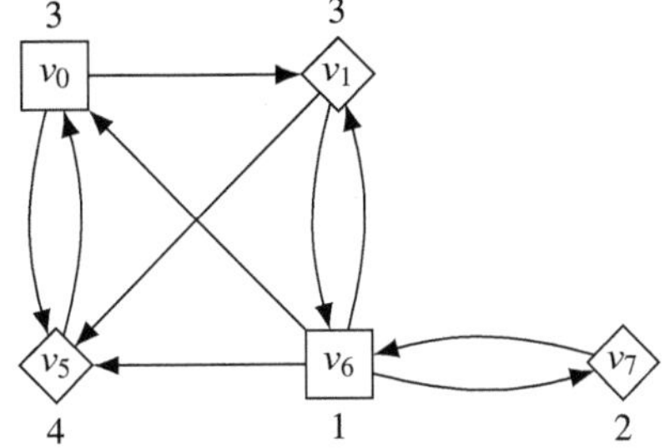

Fig. 12.4 Subgames to be considered when solving the parity game in Fig. 12.1.

We therefore then compute $A_1 := Attr_1(W_1')$. It should be clear that player 1 does not only win $\mathcal{G}$ on W_1' but in fact on A_1 which includes W_1'. The subgame $\mathcal{G} \setminus A_1$ may contain nodes that are won by either player 0 or player 1 in $\mathcal{G}$: for instance, player 0 may win a node by repeatedly enforcing a visit to K from there. On the other hand, player 1 may win a node because he can enforce a play that visits K only finitely often but a lower odd priority infinitely often that then determines the winner. Such a node is not necessarily included in W_1' because of some potential preliminary visits to K.

Now remember that the division of $\mathcal{G} \setminus A_1$ into nodes won by each of the players is only necessary when $W_1' \neq \varnothing$ and therefore $A_1 \neq \varnothing$. Hence, $\mathcal{G} \setminus A_1$ is strictly smaller than $\mathcal{G}$.

This gives us an algorithm for solving finite parity games which handles the solving of subgames by recursion. It is well-founded because the game passed to the recursive calls is strictly smaller than the original one. In the first case, even the number of priorities is strictly smaller. So all that remains is to explain how to solve the base cases which are games with only a single priority or only a single node. Clearly, games with a single node can only have one priority, so the former case suffices in fact as a base case.

Solving games with a single priority is of course trivial since that priority's parity determines the winner for all nodes in the game, and any strategy is a winning strategy. In particular, positional winning strategies always exist.

Example 12.15 Reconsider the game $\mathcal{G}$ shown in Fig. 12.1. The set of nodes with highest priority is $\{v_4, v_5\}$, and their priority is 4. Hence, we need to calculate its 0-attractor $A_0 := Attr_0(\{v_4, v_5\}) = \{v_0, v_1, v_4, v_5, v_6, v_7\}$. The subgame $\mathcal{G} \setminus A_0$ is shown in Fig. 12.4 on the left. It contains three nodes with priorities $0, 1, 3$. At this point we can employ Lemma 12.7 and squeeze the number of priorities by changing node v_8's priority from 3 to 1. Since this preserves all parities and the order amongst all nodes' priorities, winning regions and strategies are also preserved in this step.

Normally, we would continue recursively but it is not hard to see what the solution to the subgame with these three nodes needs to be. So we partition them directly into winning regions for players 0 and 1. Player 1 can win all three nodes with any of

---

Algorithm 2 A recursive algorithm for solving finite parity games.

```
 1: procedure SolveGame(𝒢 = (V, V₀, V₁, E, Ω))
 2:     k ← max{Ω(v) | v ∈ V}
 3:     if k is even then p ← 0 else p ← 1
 4:     K ← {v ∈ V | Ω(v) = k}
 5:     if K = V then                                  ▷ only one priority left in the game
 6:         Wₚ ← V; W₁₋ₚ ← ∅
 7:         let σₚ be an arbitrary positional strategy on V, σ₁₋ₚ be undefined everywhere
 8:     else
 9:         Aₚ ← Attrₚ(K)
10:         (W₀′, W₁′, σ₀′, σ₁′) ← SolveGame(𝒢 \ Aₚ)
11:         if W₁′₋ₚ = ∅ then
12:             Wₚ ← V; W₁₋ₚ ← ∅
13:             let σₚ extend σₚ′(v) by an attractor strategy on Aₚ and arbitrary choices on K
14:             let σ₁₋ₚ be undefined everywhere
15:         else
16:             A₁₋ₚ ← Attr₁₋ₚ(W₁′₋ₚ)
17:             (W₀″, W₁″, σ₀″, σ₁″) ← SolveGame(𝒢 \ A₁₋ₚ)
18:             Wₚ ← Wₚ″; W₁₋ₚ ← W₁″₋ₚ ∪ A₁₋ₚ
19:             σₚ ← σₚ″
20:             let σ₁₋ₚ extend σ₁′₋ₚ ∪ σ₁″₋ₚ by an attractor strategy on A₁₋ₚ
21:     return (W₀, W₁, σ₀, σ₁)
```

---

his two positional strategies, for example $\sigma_1' = \{v_2 \mapsto v_3, v_8 \mapsto v_2\}$. Thus, we have $W_1' = \{v_2, v_3, v_8\}$ and $W_0' = \varnothing$.

We now need to consider player 1's attractor for W_1' in $\mathcal{G}$ which is $A_1 := Attr_1(W_1') = \{v_2, v_3, v_4, v_8\}$ as well as the subgame $\mathcal{G} \setminus A_1$. It is shown in Fig. 12.4 on the right.

We would now have to solve this recursively by considering the set of nodes with highest priority, which is $\{v_5\}$, and its 0-attractor $\{v_0, v_1, v_5, v_6, v_7\}$ since the priority of node $\{v_5\}$ is even again. The removal of this region results in the empty game. In other words, player 0 has a positional winning strategy on all nodes of this subgame simply by playing the attractor strategy and extending this with an arbitrary choice for a move in the target v_5 of this attractor strategy, for instance $\sigma_0'' = \{v_1 \mapsto v_5, v_5 \mapsto v_0, v_7 \mapsto v_6\}$. This can be arbitrary here (within the subgame) since the attractor comprises the entire subgame, so after reaching node v_5 and then moving to an arbitrary successor, player 0 can repeatedly enforce a visit to node v_5. On the other hand, node v_5 only has a single successor, so there are no options other than to move to node v_0 anyway.

This solves the entire game $\mathcal{G}$: player 1's winning region is $W_1 = \{v_2, v_3, v_4, v_8\}$, resulting as the union of A_1 – the 1-attractor of the winning region of the subgame in the first recursive call – with his winning region from the second recursive call which is empty. His positional winning strategy is therefore just $\sigma_1 := \sigma_1'$.

Player 0's winning region is $W_0 = \{v_0, v_1, v_5, v_6, v_7\}$, resulting from the second recursive call. Her positional winning strategy is $\sigma_0 := \sigma_0''$.

The recursive algorithm described above is given in pseudocode in Alg. 2. Given a finite parity game $\mathcal{G}$ with node set W, it computes a quadruple $(W_0, W_1, \sigma_0, \sigma_1)$ such that W_0, W_1 is a partition of V into the winning regions for players 0 and 1, and each σ_p is a positional winning strategy for player p defined on the domain W_p for $p \in \{0, 1\}$.

The two recursive calls are the reason for an exponential running time. It is the game's size that decreases genuinely in both calls, despite of the algorithm's focus on the number of priorities. It is therefore fair to estimate its runtime as being exponential in the number of nodes. On the other hand, the number of priorities decreases in one of these recursive calls, and while this number can clearly never exceed the number of nodes, it is often much smaller. A more accurate estimation of the algorithm's runtime is therefore achieved by considering these two parameters separately.

Theorem 12.16 *Alg. 2 solves parity games with n nodes, k priorities and e edges in time* $\mathcal{O}(e \cdot n^k)$.

Proof Termination of the algorithm has been argued above by pointing out that the size of the games in the recursive calls is always genuinely smaller than that of the original game. For correctness we refer to the algorithm's description above which essentially argues why nodes in the returned sets W_0, W_1 are won by the respective players with the returned strategies σ_0, σ_1. We focus on the estimation of an upper bound on its runtime.

We argue that there is a constant c such that Alg. 2's runtime can be bounded by $c \cdot e \cdot n^k$. To see this we describe the runtime $T(n, k, e)$ via the recurrence

$$
\begin{aligned}
T(1, k, e) &= \mathcal{O}(e) \\
T(n, 1, e) &= \mathcal{O}(e) \\
T(n, k, e) &= T(n-1, k-1, e) + T(n-1, k, e) + \mathcal{O}(e) \qquad \text{for } n, k \geq 2 .
\end{aligned}
$$

The first two terms on the right-hand side of the last clause describe the time needed in the recursive calls; the summand $\mathcal{O}(e)$ comes from the need to compute attractors which can be done using breadth-first search on the inverse of the underlying graph and is therefore possible in time $\mathcal{O}(e)$. Any other steps like the evaluation of the conditions in if-statements or the composition of strategies and winning regions is subsumed by this. This also holds for the bases cases in the two first clauses. More precisely, we can assume that the algorithm takes at most $c \cdot e$ steps for some constant c in each call, not counting steps taken in recursive subcalls.

We show that $T(n, k, e) \leq c \cdot e \cdot n^k$ from which the theorem's claim on the worst-case runtime follows immediately. It is obviously true for $n = 1$ or $k = 1$. So assume that $n, k \geq 2$. We first observe that then we get

$$(n-1)^{k-1} + (n-1)^k + 1 \ \leq \ 2 \cdot (n-1)^k + 1 \ \leq \ n^k . \tag{12.1}$$

Then consider the third clause in the recurrence for $T(n, k, e)$ above. We verify the runtime estimation as follows.

$$\begin{aligned}
T(n,k,e) \;&=\; T(n-1,k-1,e) + T(n-1,k,e) + c\cdot e \\
&\le\; c\cdot e\cdot(n-1)^{k-1} + c\cdot e\cdot(n-1)^{k} + c\cdot e \\
&=\; c\cdot e\cdot\big((n-1)^{k-1} + (n-1)^{k} + 1\big) \;\le\; c\cdot e\cdot n^{k}
\end{aligned}$$

using (12.1). $\square$

Bibliographic Notes

Two-player games with a parity condition as a winning condition were first studied by Mostowski [Mos91]. They remain probably the most well-researched concept amongst those that appear in this book. The reason seems to be that on one hand, they come with a very natural definition and an elegant game theory, in particular the fact that they are positionally determined [EJ91]. On the other hand, this is, to this day, unmatched on the complexity-theoretical side.

Their membership in NP $\cap$ co-NP already makes them a rare object of study since not many natural problems are known to belong to this class without also belonging to P. It also makes solving parity games very unlikely to be NP-complete since this would clearly yield NP $=$ co-NP. Instead, membership in NP $\cap$ co-NP is often seen as an indication that a problem should really belong to P but a polynomial deterministic algorithm simply has not been found yet. This belief may even be supported by the fact that solving parity games even belongs to UP $\cap$ coUP [Jur98], i.e. it has algorithms for solving from the point of both players with unique nondeterministic choices that lead to success.

The fact that no deterministic polynomial-time algorithm has been found yet for solving parity games is not due to lack of trying. The algorithm presented here is due to Zielonka [Zie98], based on an algorithm by McNaughton for solving Muller games [McN93]. The following years saw a multitude of – conceptually often very different – algorithms proposed for solving parity games, all with worst-case running times that are asymptotically at least exponential in the number of priorities. It is usually possible to reduce the dependency on the index k to $\frac{k}{2}$, an effect that had also been observed in fixpoint evaluation algorithms [Sei96, BCJ^{+}97].

One of the first parity game solving algorithms with such running time is Jurdzinski's Small Progress Measures algorithm [Jur00]. It also provides the guiding idea for a reduction to the satisfiability problem for propositional logic [HKLN12], opening up the possibility to leverage the power of SAT solvers for parity game solving.

The observation of a close connection between parity games and the model checking problem for the modal μ-calculus [EJS01, Sti95], an important specification language for program verification, has opened up the possibility to use model checking technology for solving parity games (and vice-versa), for instance Stevens and Stirling's model checking games [SS98], Cleaveland's tableaux [Cle90] or fixpoint iteration [BFL14, vDR19].

The first major break-through in the search for a polynomial-time algorithm was made by Jurdzinski et al. with the Dominion Decomposition algorithm of genuine subexponential running time, depending exponentially on $\sqrt{n}$ only for games of size n [JPZ08]. Randomised algorithms with similar expected subexponential running times had already been found before by Vorobyov et al. [PV01, BSV03]

Another interesting speed-up in asymptotic running time was achieved by Schewe's Big-Step algorithm [Sch17] which replaces the base cases in Zielonka's recursive algorithm and carefully balances the recursion tree to achieve a running time that is exponential in a puzzling $\frac{k}{3}$ instead of the much more natural $\frac{k}{2}$.

For a long time, strategy improvement – more of a class of algorithms than a single algorithm – had been believed to be a polynomial algorithm, simply lacking a runtime analysis that is careful enough to reveal this. This was based on the fact that its instances like Jurdzinski and Vöge's for example [VJ00] were only ever observed to perform linearly many steps (with each of them taking low polynomial time) on any benchmark. In much celebrated work, Friedmann was finally able to handcraft games revealing an exponential lower bound on its worst-case runtime [Fri09]. Lower bounds in terms of specific families of games that are hard to solve had been known for certain other algorithms before, e.g. [Jur00]. Friedmann and others subsequently crushed hopes that some other variant of strategy improvement [Fea10, FHZ11, Fri11d, Fri13, AF17, DFH23] as well as the Stevens-Stirling [Fri10] or the Zielonka algorithm [Fri11c] would have polynomial running time, cf. [Fri11b].

Strategy improvement is typically formulated as a global algorithm determining the winner for all nodes in a game. There are, however, also on-the-fly versions that determine the winner for a designated initial node only [FL12b] which is often more useful in practical applications.

One may argue that this only leads to a never ending game, taking turns in improving an algorithm and providing a lower bound for that improvement. Some effort has also gone into the design of families of games that are hard for several (strategy improvement) algorithms [Fri11a] or are even universally hard for conceptually different algorithms [BDM20].

Meanwhile, more progress has been made on upper bounds. Another much celebrated result was the first deterministic algorithm that runs in quasi-polynomial time, i.e. depending exponentially only on $\log n$ for games of size n (with a non-constant base), by Calude et al. [CJK$^+$17]. The main idea used there to lower the complexity is the use of so-called *universal trees* as very succinct representations for relevant data like set of nodes. These have subsequently been used to improve existing algorithms [JL17, Par19, LPSW22, JMT22] and invent new ones [Leh18, CDHS18, FJdK$^+$19, Par20, ANP21, PW23] that also achieve quasi-polynomial running time.

One may hope that a polynomial runtime is just one step ahead, but this hope is not justified as shown by Czerwinski et al. who give lower bounds of quasi-polynomial time for solving parity games based on techniques as they are used in the listed algorithms [CDF$^+$19].

A different direction of research into solving parity games is motivated by their use (without really any viable alternatives) in decision procedures for logics, in particular over infinite trees, and in program verification in general. Some effort has gone into creating tools that solve parity games efficiently in practice like PGSOLVER [FL09] and OINK [vD18], often based on the use of heuristics rather than algorithms with best asymptotic worst-case behaviour, e.g. [SMPS21].

There are close connections between parity games and other two-player games of perfect information, in particular pay-off games and stochastic games [HK66, ZP96]. This relationship was used for example in the development of strategy improvement as an approach to solving parity games. The algorithm by Jurdziński and Vöge is based on a strategy improvement algorithm for mean pay-off games by Puri [Pur95] which in turn is based on an algorithm for stochastic games by Hoffman and Karp [HK66]. The latter is reminiscent of the simplex algorithm for solving linear programs [Dan60], which is another example of an algorithmic problem that has escaped a polynomial solution for a long time [Kha80] and for which algorithms are still being studied.

The second parity game shown in Fig. 12.5 and referred to in Exc. 140 is due to Buhrke et al. [BLV96].

Exercises

Exercise 136 Let $\mathcal{G}$ be a two-player game of perfect information and infinite duration (i.e. all plays are infinite) played on a directed graph with node set V such that its set of plays is partitioned into two sets of plays, namely those won by player 0 and those won by player 1. Let W_0 and W_1 be the sets of nodes from which player 0, resp. player 1 has a winning strategy. Show that $W_0 \cap W_1 = \varnothing$.

Exercise 137 Determine winning strategies for player 1 for each of the nodes v_2, v_4 and v_8 in the parity game shown in Fig. 12.1.

Exercise 138 Prove Lemma 12.4.

Exercise 139 Prove Lemma 12.7.

Exercise 140 Solve the two parity games shown in Fig. 12.5 using the Zielonka algorithm (Alg. 2). The nodes have not been given explicit names; instead it is the nodes' priorities that are shown inside the nodes. As usual, player-0 nodes are drawn as diamonds, player-1 nodes as boxes.

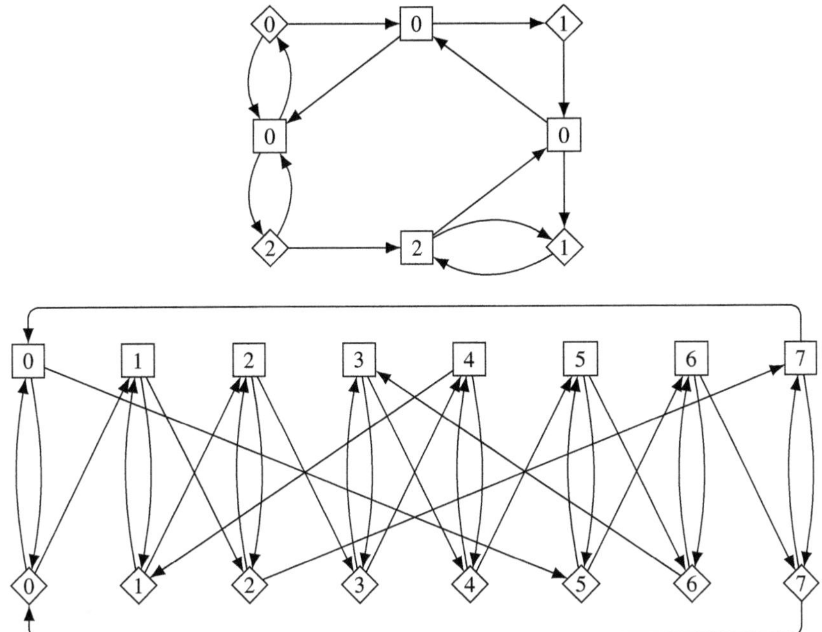

Fig. 12.5 Games to solve using Alg. 2.

Chapter 13
Automata on Infinite Trees

A natural question that arises with the study of finite automata operating on finite words and the two extensions to infinite words and finite trees, concerns their combination. Consequently, in this chapter we will study finite automata operating on infinite trees. Any tree whose underlying node set is infinite can of course be called infinite, but we consider only finitely-branching trees in which every node has finitely many successors only. Hence, there are only finitely many nodes on each level, and such infinite trees are indeed infinitely deep. We continue to demand that trees are ordered and ranked, i.e. there is always an implicit total order on the children of any node, and the node's label determines the number of its children.

It should be clear that a conceptually much different extension to the models introduced in the previous chapter would be needed in order to study automata operating on infinitely-branching trees. Hence, finitely-branching but otherwise infinite trees should allow us to combine the extensions seen in Chp. 11 concerning the transition relations in tree automata, and in Chp. 5 and 6 regarding acceptance conditions, leading rather straightforwardly to an automaton model operating on infinite trees.

For simplicity, we also demand not only that some path in such infinite trees is infinite but that in fact all paths are infinite. In other words, such infinite trees have no leaves. For applications that may require leaf nodes in infinite trees it is always possible to extend finite paths ad infinitum by introducing a new symbol of arbitrary non-zero arity that marks an ending of a path in the application's sense, yet the technical demand of all paths being infinite is fulfilled.

It should be clear that only top-down tree automata can meaningfully be extended to operate on infinite trees since there are no leaves that bottom-up automata could start in. On the other hand, the distinction between nondeterministic bottom-up and top-down tree automata is an artificial one only made for intuitive purposes. Again, a tree automaton operating on infinite trees is nothing more than a finite set of rules that describes locally legal possibilities to label the tree's nodes with certain combinations of states, taking a node's label from the underlying alphabet into account, together with a global condition known as the acceptance condition. This way, one could equally argue that a tree automaton is neither top-down nor bottom-up, or both at the same time.

The distinction was important when studying deterministic variants, showing that top-down determinism is weaker than bottom-up determinism. Now, on infinite trees one can rightfully argue that bottom-up determinism is a meaningless concept because, if there are no leaves to deterministically start a run on, then it is useless to be able to continue the construction of such a run deterministically afterwards. So we have that deterministic automata on infinite words are weaker (than their nondeterministic variants), at least for the Büchi acceptance condition, and that deterministic top-down tree automata are weaker. It should be clear that top-down deterministic Büchi tree automata do not have the full expressive power of their nondeterministic variants since the counterexamples and proofs for infinite words and finite trees can trivially be extended to infinite trees.

This is not the only way to lose expressiveness, though. It turns out that there is even a gap between the Büchi acceptance condition and others with regards to expressiveness. This is why we define tree automata operating on infinite trees with one of the richer conditions and study the expressiveness of the Büchi condition as a fragment thereof. We will mostly stick to the parity acceptance condition since the use of Rabin, Streett or Muller conditions does not yield greater expressiveness, but algorithmic approaches offered by parity automata turn out to be a bit nicer than those for the other models.

An immediate question that arises with any of these conditions that are properties of infinite, linear sequences is how to apply them to runs of tree automata that are trees. A natural way is to demand the acceptance condition to be fulfilled on *all* paths of a run. This raises some fundamental questions. For instance, complementability is unclear, even for deterministic automata, since the negation of all paths in a run satisfying a parity condition is an existential property, and it is not immediate to see that this should be expressible as an acceptance condition with universal path quantification again. In fact, complementation of tree automata requires some deeper combinatorial insights.

13.1 Parity Tree Automata

13.1.1 Infinite Trees and Tree Languages

Infinite trees over a ranked alphabet Σ with ranking function rk_Σ are defined like finite trees, just as infinite sets $t \subseteq \mathbb{N}^*$ satisfying parent- and left-sibling closure, as well as ranks: if $t(v) = a$ for some $v \in \mathbb{N}^*$ and $a \in \Sigma$, then $v(d-1) \in t$ but $vd \notin t$ for $d = rk_\Sigma(a)$. As before, we write Σ_d for the set of symbols from Σ of rank d. We also let $\mathcal{T}_\Sigma^\omega$ denote the set of all infinite trees over Σ.

A simple way to ensure infiniteness of t is to demand that all symbols $a \in \Sigma$ have positive rank: $rk_\Sigma(a) > 0$ for all $a \in \Sigma$. A *path* in such infinite trees is then an infinite sequence $\varepsilon, d_1, d_1 d_2, d_1 d_2 d_3, \ldots$ of nodes in this tree, sometimes also more conveniently denoted as the ω-word $d_1 d_2 d_3 \ldots$

We define parity tree automata by combining the definitions of a tree automaton for the transition table and a parity (word) automaton for the acceptance condition.

Definition 13.1 A *nondeterministic parity tree automaton* (NPTA) is an $\mathcal{A} = (Q, \Sigma, q_I, \delta, \Omega)$ where Q is a finite set of states, Σ is a ranked alphabet with implicit ranking function rk_Σ and no symbols of rank 0, and $q_I \in Q$ is a designated initial state. The transition relation δ is a collection $\delta = \delta_1 \cup \delta_2 \cup \ldots \cup \delta_m$ where $m := \max\{rk_\Sigma(a) \mid a \in \Sigma\}$, and

$$\delta_d \;\subseteq\; Q \times \Sigma_d \times Q^d$$

for all $d = 1, \ldots, m$.

The *size* of an NPTA is, as usual, measured as the number of its states. Its *index* is, as with NPA, $|\Omega(Q)|$ where $\Omega(Q) := \{\Omega(q) \mid q \in Q\}$.

As before, we make use of the fact that a relation of type $Q \times \Sigma_d \times Q^d$ can be seen as a function of type $Q \times \Sigma_d \to 2^{Q^d}$ and write $(q_1, \ldots, q_d) \in \delta(q, a)$ for instance instead of $(q, a, (q_1, \ldots, q_d)) \in \delta$.

NPTA operate on infinite trees. The notions of runs, accepting runs and tree languages are obtained by straightforwardly combining the concepts for tree automata and parity word automata.

Definition 13.2 A *run* of an NPTA $\mathcal{A} = (Q, \Sigma, q_I, \delta, \Omega)$ on an infinite Σ-tree t is a function $\rho : dom(t) \to Q$ such that $\rho(\varepsilon) = q_I$ and for all $v \in dom(t)$, all $d \geq 1$ and all $a \in \Sigma$ we have

$$(\rho(v0), \ldots, \rho(v(d-1))) \in \delta_d(\rho(v), a)$$

whenever $rk_\Sigma(a) = d$ and $t(v) = a$.

Such a run is *accepting* if for all paths $\pi = v_0, v_1, v_2, \ldots$ in t we have that $\max\{\Omega(\rho(v)) \mid v \in Inf(\pi)\}$ is even where $Inf(\pi)$ denotes the set of all nodes that occur infinitely often in the sequence π.

As usual, $L(\mathcal{A})$ is said to be the *(tree) language* of the NPTA $\mathcal{A}$, and it simply consists of all trees on which $\mathcal{A}$ has some accepting run.

We do not introduce an algebraic definition of languages of infinite trees as it was done for finite and infinite words, leading to the notion of (ω-)regular word languages. We simply call a language of infinite trees *regular* if it is NPTA-recognisable.

Example 13.3 Let $\Sigma = \{a, b, c\}$ with $rk_\Sigma(a) = rk_\Sigma(b) = rk_\Sigma(c) = 2$. The set L_1 of all (necessarily full binary) trees over Σ in which every path that contains infinitely many symbols b also contains infinitely many symbols c is NPTA-recognisable. It is recognised by the NPTA $\mathcal{A}_1 = (\{q_a, q_b, q_c\}, \Sigma, q_a, \delta, \Omega)$ where $\delta(q, x) = \{(q_x, q_x)\}$ for all $x \in \Sigma$. The acceptance condition is given as $\Omega(q_a) = 0$, $\Omega(q_b) = 1$ and $\Omega(q_c) = 2$.

A run of $\mathcal{A}_1$ on a tree t essentially shifts a node label x to both children as a label with state q_x. The parity condition is the one also seen for detecting word properties of the form of an implication between two conditions on the infinite occurrences of letters, cf. Ex. 6.8. Seeing a symbol b is potentially bad or has to be remedied by seeing a symbol c. This is why seeing a b triggers the visit of a state with on odd priority, namely 1. Seeing a c remedies this in the sense that the priority 2, which occurs then, is greater and even. At last, seeing an a is harmless in the sense of the tree property, so it triggers the lowest even priority 0.

The NPTA $\mathcal{A}_1$ is essentially obtained from the standard NPA for the language L of all ω-words over $\{a, b, c\}$ that have infinitely many symbols c unless they have finitely many symbols b only. The tree language L_1 in this example is of course obtained by a straightforward extension of the word language L with universal quantification over paths. Likewise, the NPTA $\mathcal{A}_1$ is obtained by a straightforward extension of the standard DPA for L, simply by turning a successor state in a transition into a tuple of matching arity of duplicates of that successor state. It is worth noting that this construction only works in general for deterministic word automata. We will examine the connection between tree languages of the form "all paths ... " and word languages in more detail in the context of complementation later on.

Example 13.4 Let Σ be as in the previous example and L_2 be the set of all trees on which some path contains infinitely many symbols b but only finitely many symbols c. It is also NPTA-recognisable, namely by the NPTA $\mathcal{A}_2 = (\{q_0, q_a, q_b, q_c\}, \Sigma, q_a, \delta, \Omega)$ with

$$\Omega(q_0) = 0 \ , \ \ \Omega(q_a) = 1 \ , \ \ \Omega(q_b) = 2 \ , \ \ \Omega(q_c) = 3$$

and the transitions

$$\delta(q_y, x) \ := \ \{(q_x, q_0), (q_0, q_x)\} \ \ , \ \ \ \delta(q_0, x) \ := \ \{(q_0, q_0)\}$$

for any $x, y \in \Sigma$.

$\mathcal{A}_2$ uses nondeterminism to guess a path through an underlying tree and verifies using the states q_a, q_b, q_c and their priorities $1, 2, 3$, that this path indeed contains infinitely many symbols b but only finitely many symbols c.

The NPTA $\mathcal{A}_3 = (\{q_0, q_a, q_b\}, \Sigma, q_a, \delta, \Omega)$ with Ω and δ defined as above, but only for q_0, q_a, q_b then recognises the set of all trees over $\{a, b\}$ only in which some path contains infinitely many symbols b. Its index is three since it uses priorities $0, 1, 2$. It is possible to reduce its index to two, namely priorities 1 and 2, though. State q_0 can be given priority 2 because any path of a run that visits state q_0 then stays in state q_0 forever. Hence, once this state occurs on a path with the original priority 0, no priority 1 can occur below this, and one can safely lift all these priorities to 2 without making more branches of the run satisfy the parity condition, and so the language is preserved.

The NPTA $\mathcal{A}_1$ in Ex. 13.3 does not use nondeterminism; it is deterministic in the usual sense.

Definition 13.5 An NPTA $\mathcal{A} = (Q, \Sigma, q_I, \delta, \Omega)$ is said to be *deterministic* (DPTA), if $|\delta(q, a)| \leq 1$ for all $q \in Q$ and all $a \in \Sigma$.

It is not hard to see that DPTA are weaker in expressiveness than NPTA. The example that separates the expressive power of DtdTA from NTA in Thm. 11.21 can easily be extended to one on infinite trees. Spelling out the details is left as an exercise.

Theorem 13.6 *a) There are NPTA-recognisable tree languages that are not DPTA-recognisable.*
 b) The class of DPTA-recognisable languages is not closed under complementation.

Part (b) of this theorem is hinted at by the two examples above. Note that L_2 is in fact the complement of the language L_1. The fact that $\mathcal{A}_2$ is not a DPTA is of course no proof for the claim that L_2 is not DPTA-recognisable. But it is possible to carry out the proof of part (a) with L_2 as an example. Likewise, the principles used in the proof of Thm. 11.21 can also be applied to show that L_2 is not DPTA-recognisable.

Thm. 13.6 highlights an important difference in the automata theory of infinite trees compared to that on infinite words: while the parity condition is strong enough to enable determinisation of word automata, a simple dualisation construction does not work for tree deterministic parity automata anymore. It is also pointless to try to determinise tree automata into those with a Muller condition, because a tree automaton with a Muller condition could easily be transformed into a parity tree automaton using the LAR construction of Thm. 6.28, and this preserves determinism.

13.1.2 Büchi Tree Automata

It is fair to ask why we introduced tree automata with a parity acceptance condition straight away rather than to start with Büchi automata which may perhaps seem to be reasonable given the exposition in Chp. 5 and Chp. 6 for ω-words. The answer is that, unlike the case for words, Büchi tree automata are strictly weaker in expressiveness than parity tree automata. They also do not enjoy closure under complements. Thus, they are not a good model for a theory of regular languages of infinite trees. Instead we call a language of infinite trees regular iff it is NPTA-recognisable.

A *nondeterministic Büchi tree automaton* (NBTA) is defined straightforwardly, just like an NPTA but with a set of accepting states, and a run on a tree is accepting when every branch visits accepting states infinitely often. Alternatively, an NPTA of index 2 with a smaller odd and a greater even priority, for example 1 and 2, can be called an NBTA.

We aim to show that there are regular languages of infinite trees that cannot be recognised by NBTA. An example of such a language L_0 can be constructed over the ranked alphabet $\Sigma = \{a, b\}$ with $rk_\Sigma(a) = rk_\Sigma(b) = 2$. L_0 consists of all Σ-trees such that every path contains finitely many symbols b only.

It is not hard to see that L_0 is regular. An NPTA, even a DPTA recognising it can easily be constructed. Details are left as an exercise.

Lemma 13.7 *The language L_0 is regular.*

We use a pumping argument to show the expressive weakness of NBTA. As usual, the first key step is to construct a sequence of pumpable candidates, here in the form of (necessarily binary) Σ-trees t_n, defined for $n \geq 0$ by

$$t_n(v) \;:=\; \begin{cases} b & , \text{ if } v \in (0^*1)^{\leq n} \text{ and } v \neq \varepsilon \,, \\ a & , \text{ otherwise.} \end{cases}$$

For example, t_0 is the tree that is labelled with symbols a only; t_1 is the tree in which only nodes of the form 0^*1 are labelled b, i.e. only the right children of a node on the leftmost path from the root. Slightly abusing term representation we get that

$$t_n \;=\; a(t_n, b(t_{n-1}, t_{n-1}))$$

for all $n > 0$.

A crucial observation is the following. It may be tempting to try to prove it by induction on n, but this is not possible since t_n contains itself as a genuine subtree.

Lemma 13.8 *For all $n \geq 0$ we have $t_n \in L_0$.*

Proof Fix $n \geq 0$ and suppose that $t_n \notin L_0$, i.e. t_n contains an infinite path π with infinitely many symbols b. Such a path can be represented as an ω-word $d_0 d_1 d_2 \ldots \in \{0, 1\}^\omega$.

We distinguish two cases. First suppose that π is of the form $(0 + 1)^* 0^\omega$. Then it has only finitely many occurrences of 1, i.e. it forks to the right only finitely many times. But a letter b is only found at a node that is the right child of its parent. Hence, this path cannot contain infinitely many symbols b.

Suppose therefore that π is of the form $(0^*1)^\omega$, i.e. it forks to the right infinitely often. Now we make use of the fact that not every right child of a node is labelled with b. Instead this is only the case if the unique path from the root to that child encounters at most n forks to the right. But this is obviously only true for the first n nodes that are right children of their parents on π. Hence, such a path π cannot contain infinitely many symbols b either. $\square$

We also need an unravelling construction on trees. We define it for binary trees only since this suffices for our purposes here. The construction can easily be applied to trees with nodes of arbitrary branching degrees, but it is more tedious to define formally when there are nodes of differing branching degrees.

For two words $u, v \in \{0, 1\}^*$ we write $u \leq v$ if u is a prefix of v. When taken as nodes in a tree, $u \leq v$ means that u occurs on the unique finite path from t's root to v.

Let t be an infinite binary tree, $u \in \{0, 1\}^*$ and $v \in \{0, 1\}^+$. The *unravelling* of t w.r.t. u and uv is the tree $t[u \leftarrow v]$ that is intuitively obtained by removing the subtree under node uv and instead pasting an infinite repetition of the subtree under u in there. Fig. 13.1 depicts this construction schematically. Formally, we have

$$t[u \leftarrow v](w) \;:=\; \begin{cases} t(uz) & , \text{ if } w \text{ is of the form } uv^+z \text{ for some } z \text{ s.t. } v \not\leq z \\ t(w) & , \text{ otherwise} \end{cases}$$

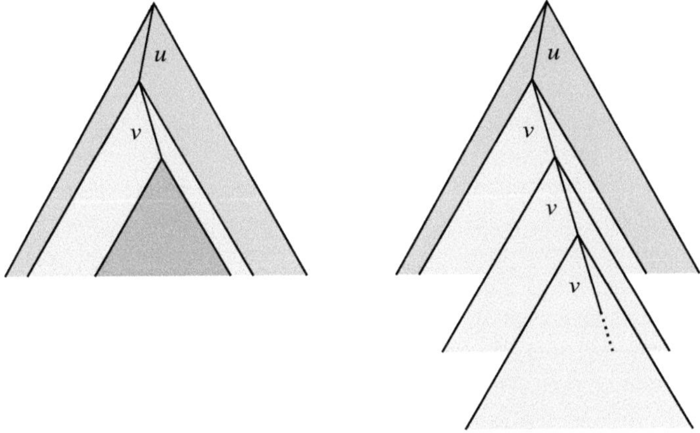

Fig. 13.1 The unravelling (right) of a tree (left) with respect to nodes u and uv.

for any $w \in \{0,1\}^*$.

Lemma 13.9 *Let t be a binary Σ-tree, $u \in \{0,1\}^*$, $v \in \{0,1\}^+$ and $a \in \Sigma$ such that $t(uw) = a$ for some $w \prec v$. Then $t[u \leftarrow v]$ contains a path on which a occurs infinitely often.*

Theorem 13.10 *There are regular languages of infinite trees that are not NBTA-recognisable.*

Proof Take the language L_0 of binary $\{a, b\}$-trees on which every path contains finitely many symbols b only, as constructed above. According to Lemma 13.7 it is regular. It remains to be seen that it is not NBTA-recognisable.

Suppose, for the sake of contradiction, that $L_0 = L(\mathcal{A})$ for some NBTA $\mathcal{A} = (Q, \Sigma, q_I, \delta, F)$ with $F \subseteq Q$. Let $n := |F|$ and consider t_n. According to Lemma 13.8, we have $t_n \in L_0$, so there must be an accepting run ρ of $\mathcal{A}$ on t_n. In particular, every path of the run tree ρ contains infinitely many nodes from F.

Next we construct a sequence of paths π_i, numbers m_i and states f_i for $i = 0, \ldots, n$ as follows. Start with $\pi_0 := 0^\omega$. Since ρ contains infinitely many accepting states on π_0 there must be some m_0 such that $f_0 := \rho(0^{m_0}) \in F$. Next consider the path $\pi_1 := 0^{m_0} 1 0^\omega$. Again, it must contain infinitely many accepting states. Hence, there is some $m_1 \in \mathbb{N}$ and $f_1 \in F$ such that $\rho(0^{m_0} 1 0^{m_1}) = f_1$. In general, when $m_0, \ldots, m_i$ have been found, let $\pi_{i+1} := 0^{m_0} 1 0^{m_1} 1 \ldots 1 0^{m_i} 1 0^\omega$. Then use the fact that ρ must assign accepting states to infinitely many states on this path, in particular to some state that occurs on the suffix of the form 0^ω. This defines m_{i+1} and f_{i+1}.

Now remember that $n = |F|$, hence there must be some i, j with $0 \le i < j \le n$ such that $f_i = f_j$. Let $u := 0^{m_0} 1 \ldots 1 0^{m_i}$ and $v := 1 0^{m_{i+1}} 1 \ldots 1 0^{m_j}$. Note that the symbol b occurs somewhere on the path from u to uv in t_n, namely at node $u1$ because $i < n$. According to Lemma 13.9, $t^* := t_n[u \leftarrow v]$ contains a path with infinitely many symbols b, so we have $t^* \notin L_0$.

On the other hand, one can construct an accepting run ρ^* of $\mathcal{A}$ on t^*. It is obtained by lifting the unravelling construction from t_n to t^* to ρ. This is locally sound, i.e. ρ^* is only composed of transitions that are valid according to δ because they all occur in ρ and $\rho(u) = \rho(uv)$.

Now there are two types of paths in ρ^* or, equally, in t^*: almost every path eventually proceeds like a path in ρ, namely as soon as it deviates from uv^ω. The suffix after the deviation point is the suffix of some path in ρ, hence it contains infinitely many accepting states. But the only remaining path uv^ω also contains infinitely many accepting states because u and v were constructed in a way that guarantees that some accepting state is seen between u and uv.

Hence, this unravelling or pumping has created a tree t^* that is also accepted by $\mathcal{A}$ but does not belong to L_0. Thus, we have $L(\mathcal{A}) \neq L_0$ contradicting the assumption. $\square$

The second weakness of NBTA mentioned above is then just a consequence of this.

Corollary 13.11 *The class of NBTA-recognisable language is not closed under complements.*

Proof This follows immediately from the previous result by observing that the complement $\overline{L}$ of the language L used in the proof of Thm. 13.10 above, is in fact NBTA-recognisable. Note that $\overline{L}$ consists of all trees that have a path with infinitely many symbols b. An NBTA for this language is given at the end of Ex. 13.4. $\square$

13.1.3 Closure Properties

The main goal is, as before, to show that the class of languages of infinite trees that are recognised by NPTA, is closed under complements. This bears the combined difficulties of several similar tasks: we have seen in Chp. 5 that complementation on infinite words involves some combinatorial difficulties; clearly these are implicitly present for infinite trees as well. Complementation closure was given for finite trees, but it needed deterministic bottom-up tree automata. On the other hand, only deterministic top-down automata can meaningfully be constructed for infinite trees. Deterministic top-down automata were not helpful in achieving complementation closure for finite trees; so clearly they will not be helpful here either. In addition, we have just seen that we cannot work restrict attention to the simple Büchi condition, so working with parity tree automata may induce further complications.

In the end, complementation closure for NPTA-recognisable languages, i.e. regular languages of infinite trees, does hold indeed. The construction will need some other closure properties which we discuss here. The first one – closure under unions – is imminent due to the presence of nondeterminism in the automaton model.

Lemma 13.12 *For every NPTA $\mathcal{A}_1, \mathcal{A}_2$ of sizes n_1, n_2 and indices k_1, k_2 there is an NPTA $\mathcal{B}$ of size at most $n_1 + n_2 + 1$ and index at most $\max\{k_1, k_2\}$ such that $L(\mathcal{B}) = L(\mathcal{A}_1) \cup L(\mathcal{A}_2)$.*

Closure under intersections is also given, but it requires a little bit more thought. It either follows from complementation closure using the deMorgan laws, or one can attempt to directly construct an NPTA via a product construction that simulates two given NPTA on a tree. This is problematic, though, because the resulting acceptance condition is naturally a conjunction of two parity conditions, and it is not that easy to express it as a parity condition again. One possibility is to regard it as a Muller condition and translate it back into a parity condition using the LAR construction. This leads to the following estimation. Details are left as an exercise.

Lemma 13.13 *For every NPTA $\mathcal{A}_1, \mathcal{A}_2$ of sizes n_1, n_2 and indices k_1, k_2 there is an NPTA $\mathcal{B}$ of size $\mathcal{O}((n_1 \cdot n_2) \cdot (k_1 \cdot k_2)!)$ and index $\mathcal{O}(k_1 \cdot k_2)$ such that $L(\mathcal{B}) = L(\mathcal{A}_1) \cap L(\mathcal{A}_2)$.*

The next construction is that of a homomorphism. Recall that the class of regular languages of finite words is closed under homomorphisms based on arbitrary morphisms $h : \Sigma \to \Delta^*$ for two alphabets Σ and Δ. It would of course be more precise to say that homomorphisms preserve regularity, given that there is not just one class of regular languages on which homomorphisms act as a mapping, but they transform languages over one alphabet into languages over another.

Lifting this to the world of infinite words already required a restriction to be imposed, namely closure under non-deleting homomorphisms, i.e. those that are based on a morphism of type $\Sigma \to \Delta^+$ for two alphabets Σ, Δ. This guarantees that the image of an infinite word is an infinite word again. Lifting it to tree languages required a further restriction, namely that of being rank-preserving (cf. Def. 11.12). It is not hard to see that without this construction the homomorphic image of a tree is either not well-defined, or a naïve attempt at making it well-defined, for instance by copying subtrees in order to satisfy rank conditions, will break regularity of homomorphic images.

So as with finite trees, we will consider homomorphisms on infinite trees only when they are based on rank-preserving morphisms $h : \Sigma \to \Delta$, i.e. when $rk_\Delta(h(a)) = rk_\Sigma(a)$ for every $a \in \Sigma$. This then induces a homomorphism $\hat{h} : \mathcal{T}_\Sigma^\omega \to \mathcal{T}_\Delta^\omega$ naturally via $\hat{h}(t)(v) = h(t(v))$ for every $v \in dom(t)$. Moreover, this is lifted to tree languages via $\hat{h}(L) := \{\hat{h}(t) \mid t \in L\}$.

We then have that homomorphisms based on rank-preserving morphisms preserve regularity of languages of infinite trees. The proof is left as an exercise.

Lemma 13.14 *For every NPTA $\mathcal{A}$ of size at most n over some ranked alphabet Σ and every rank-preserving morphism $h : \Sigma \to \Delta$ there is an NPTA $\mathcal{B}$ of size at most n such that $L(\mathcal{B}) = \hat{h}(L(\mathcal{A}))$.*

We will apply Lemma 13.14 mainly for rank-preserving *projections* which are special morphisms operating on alphabets of the form Σ^k for some $k \geq 1$ by deleting certain elements of these tuples. While this is not a concept particularly linked to trees – see for instance the use of projections in the construction of NFA from MSO formulas over finite words (Thm. 2.16) – the next construction is trivial for word languages and only interesting for genuine tree languages.

Definition 13.15 Let Σ be a ranked alphabet, $m := \max\{rk_\Sigma(a) \mid a \in \Sigma\}$ and $D :=$ $\{0, \ldots, m-1\}$. A tree $t \in \mathcal{T}_\Sigma^\omega$ determines a set $Tr(t)$ of *guided traces* as words over $\Sigma \times D$ as follows. We have

$$(a_0, d_0), (a_1, d_1), (a_2, d_2), \ldots \in Tr(t) \quad \text{iff} \quad a_i = t(d_0 \ldots d_{i-1}) \text{ for all } i \geq 0 \, .$$

Now let $L \subseteq (\Sigma \times D)^\omega$ be a language of infinite Σ-words. The language $L^\triangle$ is the language of infinite trees whose guided traces all belong to L, i.e. $t \in L^\triangle$ iff $Tr(t) \subseteq L$.

It is helpful to intuitively consider the construction of $L^\triangle$ as follows: given a language of words $L \subseteq (\Sigma \times D)^\omega$. Each of them can be seen as a trace, i.e. the concatenated labels of a path, in a tree. The second components determine the path in the tree that this trace comes from.

Example 13.16 Let $\Sigma = \{a, b\}$ with $rk_\Sigma(a) = rk_\Sigma(b) = 2$. Consider the language

$$L \;:=\; (a, 0)^\omega + (a, 0)^*(a, 1)\big((b, 0) + (b, 1)\big)^\omega$$

of guided traces. Then $L^\triangle$ contains exactly one tree, namely the binary tree whose root is labelled a, and in which

- the left child of an a-node is an a-node again,
- the right child of an a-node is a b-node and
- both children of a b-node are b-nodes.

Consider, on the other hand, the guided-trace languages L_n for $n \geq 0$ defined by

$$L_n \;:=\; \{(x_0, d_0), (x_1, d_1), \ldots \in (\{a, b\} \times \{0, 1\})^\omega \mid |\{i \mid x_i = b\}| \leq n\} \, .$$

Then $L_n^\triangle$ consists of exactly those Σ-trees such that every path contains at most n occurrences of the symbol b.

Clearly, it is possible to have $L^\triangle = \varnothing$ even though $L \neq \varnothing$, simply when L does not contain enough guided traces. For instance, let $L = (a, 0)^*(a, 1)\big((b, 0) + (b, 1)\big)^\omega$. Then $L^\triangle = \varnothing$ because L does not contain a trace for the path 0^ω, even though the labels of that path could be considered to be entirely determined by the information given for other paths.

Lemma 13.17 *For every DPA $\mathcal{A}$ of size n and index k recognising a language of guided traces, there is a DPTA $\mathcal{B}$ of size n and index k such that $L(\mathcal{B}) = L(\mathcal{A})^\triangle$.*

Proof Let a ranked alphabet Σ be given with its associated set of directions D, and $\mathcal{A} = (Q, \Sigma \times D, q_I, \delta, \Omega)$ be a DPA over $\Sigma \times D$ with $n = |Q|$ and $k = |\{\Omega(q) \mid q \in Q\}|$. We construct the DPTA $\mathcal{B} := (Q, \Sigma, q_I, \delta', \Omega)$ under demand via

$$\delta'(q, a) \;:=\; \big(\delta\big(q, (a, 0)\big), \delta\big(q, (a, 1)\big), \ldots, \delta\big(q, (a, d-1)\big)\big)$$

for every $q \in Q$, $a \in \Sigma$ and $d = rk_\Sigma(a)$. Note that $\mathcal{B}$ is in fact deterministic.

The claim on the size of $\mathcal{B}$ is clear. It remains to be seen that $L(\mathcal{B}) = L(\mathcal{A})^{\triangle}$. For the direction "$\subseteq$" it suffices to check that an accepting run of $\mathcal{B}$ on some tree t can be decomposed into all paths occurring in this run, and each of them belongs to $L(\mathcal{A})$, making use of the fact that the parity condition of an NPTA applies to *all* paths in an accepting run. Hence, the set of all guided traces of t is included in $L(\mathcal{A})$ and so $t \in L(\mathcal{A})^{\triangle}$.

The direction "$\supseteq$" is seen in the same way. However, here we need the requirement of $\mathcal{A}$ being deterministic. Then we have that each two guided traces τ_1, τ_2 that are accepted by $\mathcal{A}$, have accepting runs that share a common prefix which is at least as long as the longest common prefix of τ_1 and τ_2. This is why it is possible to assemble an accepting run of $\mathcal{B}$ on t from accepting runs of $\mathcal{A}$ on all guided traces from t. $\square$

It is not possible to carry out the construction using a nondeterministic Büchi or parity automaton for the language of guided traces, even when allowing the resulting tree automaton to be nondeterministic.

Example 13.18 Take the ranked alphabet $\Sigma = \{a, b\}$ with both symbols having rank 2, and consider $L = (\Sigma \times D)^*(\{a\} \times D)^{\omega}$ where $D = \{0, 1\}$. The language $L^{\triangle}$ consists of all trees such that every path only contains finitely many symbols b.

Take the most obvious NBA for L, for example the following.

$$\xymatrix{ & \Sigma \times D & & \{a\} \times D \\ \to q_0 \ar[rr]^{\{a\} \times D} & & q_1 }$$

An attempt to construct an NPTA for $L^{\triangle}$ along the lines of the proof of Lemma 13.17 above yields the NBTA $(\{q_0, q_1\}, \Sigma, q_0, \delta, \{q_1\})$ with

$$\begin{aligned} \delta(q_0, a) \;=\; \delta(q_0, b) &\;=\; \{(q_0, q_0), (q_0, q_1), (q_1, q_0), (q_1, q_1)\}, \\ \delta(q_1, a) &\;=\; \{(q_1, q_1)\}, \\ \delta(q_1, b) &\;=\; \varnothing. \end{aligned}$$

This tree automaton does not accept the tree t given by

$$t(v) \;=\; \begin{cases} b & , \text{ if } v \in 0^*1, \\ a & , \text{ otherwise} \end{cases}$$

even though it belongs to $L^{\triangle}$. The reason for this is the fact that an accepting run would have to eventually contain the accepting state q_1 on the path 0^{ω}, but then no node label b could be processed in the subtree under this node. On the other hand, every node on the path 0^{ω} has one child labelled b.

13.2 Complementation Closure

Positional determinacy of parity games is the combinatorial result which allows us to prove closure of the class of languages recognised by NPTA under complements. Remember that complementation of automata comes with several obstacles in general: for a start, we do not face the same problems of those introduced by a Büchi condition since the parity condition lends itself to an easy dualisation. However, NPTA are nondeterministic, so simply dualising the acceptance condition does not work. Additionally, NPTA are tree automata, so even if they were deterministic a simple dualisation procedure would not be sufficient because the acceptance condition with its universal quantification over paths in a tree would be dualised into an existential quantification over paths.

Despite these obstacles, complementation closure for NPTA holds indeed. In order to use positional determinacy of parity games we need to link them to the acceptance of trees by NPTA.

13.2.1 Acceptance as a Parity Game

We define, given an NPTA $\mathcal{A}$ and a tree t over the same ranked alphabet Σ, a parity game that is won by player 0 iff $t \in L(\mathcal{A})$. Intuitively, the game is played by moving two tokens around, one residing on a state in $\mathcal{A}$ and the other on a node in t. Initially, they are placed in $\mathcal{A}$'s initial state and on t's root node.

The game proceeds in rounds. In each round with the tokens on a state q and a node v, first player 0 selects a tuple from the transition table. More specifically, let $a = t(v)$ be the symbol at the tree's marked node and $d := rk_{\Sigma}(a)$. Then player 0 chooses a tuple $(q_0, \ldots, q_{d-1}) \in \delta(q, a)$. Player 1 then responds by choosing a number $i \in [d]$, after which the token in the NPTA is moved to q_i and the tree token is moved to node vi.

Because of their roles, specifically where they perform their choices in this turn-based game, the players are often also referred to as *Automaton* (player 0) and *Pathfinder* (player 1). Here we stick to the names 0 and 1 to remain consistent with the game terminology used so far.

We give a more formal definition of this acceptance game for NPTA.

Definition 13.19 Let Σ be a ranked alphabet, $m := \max\{rk_{\Sigma}(a) \mid a \in \Sigma\}$, $\mathcal{A} = (Q, \Sigma, q_I, \delta, \Omega)$ be an NPTA over Σ and $t \in \mathcal{T}_{\Sigma}^{\omega}$. The *acceptance game* for $\mathcal{A}$ and t is the parity game $\mathcal{G}_{\mathcal{A},t} := (V, V_0, V_1, v_I, E, \Omega')$ defined as follows.

- There are two kinds of positions in this game. The distinction coincides with the partition of positions belonging to either of the players. As usual, V is the disjoint union of V_0 and V_1 which are defined as follows.

  - The first kind consists of pairs of automaton states and tree nodes. These belong to player 0: $V_0 := Q \times dom(t)$.

– Player-1 positions are pairs of automaton state tuples from the transition table and tree nodes:

$$V_1 \ := \ \left(\bigcup_{q \in Q} \bigcup_{d=1}^{m} \bigcup_{a \in \Sigma_d} \delta_d(q,a) \right) \times dom(t)$$

Note that some confusion may arise with alphabet symbols of rank 1 unless we carefully distinguish a single state from the singleton tuple containing that state. In other words, the player-0 position (q, v) should be distinguished from the player-1 position $((q), v)$.

- The initial position in the game is $v_I := (q_I, \varepsilon)$.
- The game is strictly turn-based, i.e. we have $E \subseteq V_0 \times V_1 \cup V_1 \times V_0$. Specifically, we have

$$\begin{aligned} E \ := \ & \{((q,v),((q_0,\ldots,q_{d-1}),v)) \mid (q_0,\ldots,q_{d-1}) \in \delta_d(q,t(v))\} \\ & \cup \ \{((q_0,\ldots,q_{d-1}),v),(q_i,vi)) \mid i \in \{0,\ldots,d-1\}\} \ . \end{aligned}$$

- The winning condition in this game is given by inheritance of the priorities from the automaton's acceptance condition:

$$\Omega'(q,v) := \Omega(q) \qquad \text{and} \qquad \Omega'((q_0,\ldots,q_{d-1}),v) := 0$$

for all $d \leq m$.

Theorem 13.20 *Let A be an NPTA over some ranked alphabet Σ and $t \in T_\Sigma^\omega$. Player 0 wins the acceptance game $\mathcal{G}_{A,t}$ iff $t \in L(A)$.*

Proof Let $A = (Q, \Sigma, q_I, \delta, \Omega)$ and $t \in T_\Sigma^\omega$ be given.

"$\Leftarrow$" Suppose there is an accepting run ρ of A on t. It can immediately be regarded as a representation of a positional winning strategy σ_0 for player 0 in $\mathcal{G}_{A,t}$. Note that $\rho(\varepsilon) = q_I$. Hence, the initial position (q_I, ε) of $\mathcal{G}_{A,t}$ is a pair (q, v) such that $q = \rho(v)$. By ensuring that this is an invariant under the players' choices, it suffices to define σ_0 on pairs (q, v) that satisfy this property.

So suppose some (q, v) is given such that $\rho(v) = q$. Let $a := t(v)$ and $d := rk_\Sigma(a)$. By definition, v has d many ordered children $v0, \ldots, v(d-1)$, and ρ labels them with states $q_0, \ldots, q_{d-1}$ respectively, such that $(q_0, \ldots, q_{d-1}) \in \delta_d(q, a)$. This determines player 0's choice: $\sigma_0(q, v) := ((q_0, \ldots, q_{d-1}), v)$. Note that, no matter which $i \in [d]$ player 1 chooses subsequently, the resulting position in the game is (q_i, vi), and the invariant still holds because $\rho(vi) = q_i$ for all such i.

Finally, it remains to be seen that σ_0 is indeed a winning strategy. Take any play

$$\pi \ = \ \underbrace{(q_0, v_0)}_{v_0'}, \underbrace{((\ldots), v_0)}_{v_1'}, \underbrace{(q_1, v_1)}_{v_2'}, \underbrace{((\ldots), v_1)}_{v_3'}, \underbrace{(q_2, v_2)}_{v_4'}, \underbrace{((\ldots), v_2)}_{v_5'}, \ldots$$

conforming to σ_0. Then

$$\limsup_{i \to \infty} \Omega'(v_i') \ = \ \limsup_{i \to \infty} \Omega'(v_{2i}') \ = \ \limsup_{i \to \infty} \Omega(q_i) \ .$$

The former equality holds because the positions $v_1', v_3', \dots$ with odd indices all have priority 0, so they do not contribute to the limes superior in this sequence. The second equation simply uses the definition of Ω'. Now note that for such a play π, the sequence $v_0, v_1, \dots$ forms a path through t, and so $q_0, q_1, \dots$ is a sequence of state labels in ρ along a path in t. By the assumption that ρ is an accepting run, $\limsup_{i \to \infty} \Omega(q_i)$ is even, and then so is the maximal priority occurring infinitely often in π which makes it winning for player 0. Hence, σ_0 is indeed a winning strategy.

"$\Rightarrow$" Suppose that player 0 has a winning strategy σ_0 for the acceptance game $\mathcal{G}_{A,t}$. We use this to construct an accepting run ρ of $\mathcal{A}$ on t. All we need to do for this is to define a state label $\rho(v)$ for every $v \in dom(t)$ such that the greatest priority of the sequence of states along any path through t is even. It is not strictly necessary but simplifies the construction when we assume that σ_0 is indeed positional. This is a valid assumption according to Thm. 12.12.

We start with the root label $\rho(\varepsilon) := q_I$. Now suppose that for some node $v \in dom(t)$, $\rho(v)$ is already defined. We use this to define $\rho(vi)$ for all successors vi of v. Simply consult $\sigma_0(\rho(v), v)$. Note that for $v = \varepsilon$, σ_0 must provide a choice. Similar to the other direction in the proof above we will maintain this invariant, so we can assume that σ_0 does indeed provide a choice in the player-0 position $(\rho(v), v)$. We have $\sigma_0(\rho(v), v) = (q_0, \dots, q_{d-1})$ for some d and $q_0, \dots, q_{d-1}$. Then let $\rho(vi) := q_i$ for $i \in [d]$.

The limit of this process provides a complete labelling ρ of t's nodes with automaton states. This forms a run of $\mathcal{A}$ on t, and the run starts in $\mathcal{A}$'s initial state. It therefore just remains to be seen that it is accepting. Very much as in the other direction of the proof above, every path in ρ corresponds to a play conforming to σ_0. Since such plays are winning for player 0, and this can only be determined by the priorities on the player-0 nodes (since the others all have priority 0), the greatest priority seen infinitely often along any path in ρ is also even, and ρ is therefore accepting. $\qquad\square$

Without the assumption in the second half of this proof that σ_0 is positional, the construction of ρ-labels of successor nodes in t would simply have to consult what σ_0 prescribes not just in a position (q, v) but after playing through a history $(q_0, v_0), \dots, (q_n, v_n)$ (with appropriate player-1 nodes in between) where $v_0, \dots, v_n$ form a finite path from the root in t.

An immediate consequence of determinacy of parity games (Thm. 12.12) and Thm. 13.20 is the following.

Corollary 13.21 *Let $\mathcal{A}$ be an NPTA over some ranked alphabet Σ and $t \in \mathcal{T}_\Sigma^\omega$. Player 1 has a positional winning strategy for the acceptance game $\mathcal{G}_{A,t}$ iff $t \notin L(\mathcal{A})$.*

13.2.2 The Complementation Construction

We will make use of Cor. 13.21 to construct, given an NPTA $\mathcal{A}$, an NPTA $\overline{\mathcal{A}}$ that accepts the complement of $\mathcal{A}$'s language. The underlying idea is the following.

1. A (positional) winning strategy for player 1 in the acceptance game for $\mathcal{A}$ and some tree t, witnessing the fact that $t \notin L(\mathcal{A})$, can be regarded as a labelling of t's nodes over an extended, yet finite alphabet.
2. The language of guided traces of such annotated trees is ω-regular, hence recognisable by a deterministic parity word automaton. This can be turned into a deterministic parity tree automaton recognising the language of trees annotated in this way.
3. A simple projection construction yields the language of trees on which player 1 has a winning strategy for the corresponding acceptance game, i.e. $\overline{L(\mathcal{A})}$.

For the remainder of this section, we fix an NPTA $\mathcal{A} = (Q, \Sigma, q_I, \delta, \Omega)$ and carry out the complementation construction with respect to $\mathcal{A}$. Likewise, this fixes the underlying alphabet Σ. Let $m := \max\{rk_\Sigma(a) \mid a \in \Sigma\}$ and $D := [m]$.

In order to grasp the intuition behind the construction of the complement NPTA $\overline{\mathcal{A}}$, it is helpful to imagine an arbitrary tree $t \in \mathcal{T}_\Sigma^\omega$ to be given, in particular one that satisfies $t \notin L(\mathcal{A})$, and then to consider the requirements on $\overline{\mathcal{A}}$ in terms of the acceptance game $\mathcal{G}_{\mathcal{A},t}$.

According to Cor. 13.21, player 1 has a positional winning strategy σ_1 for $\mathcal{G}_{\mathcal{A},t}$. It tells player 1 which direction to move to in any situation when it is his turn, i.e. in a position of the form $((q_0, \ldots, q_{d-1}), v)$ for some tuple $(q_0, \ldots, q_{d-1}) \in Q^{\leq m}$ occurring in the image of the transition function δ, and some node $v \in dom(t)$. So σ_1 can be seen as a function of type $dom(t) \times Q^{\leq m} \to D$. This can be reformulated using the following observation – also known as *(Un-)Currying* – where $\simeq$ is used to denote the existence of an isomorphism between function spaces.

Lemma 13.22 *For all sets A, B, C we have $A \times B \to C \simeq A \to (B \to C)$.*

Now let $S := Q^{\leq m} \to D$. Using Lemma 13.22, σ_1 can be seen as having type $dom(t) \to S$. Note that S is finite and independent of t. In fact, it only depends on $\mathcal{A}$'s state space and the underlying alphabet Σ.

This opens up the possibility to construct an NPTA that, given an arbitrary $t \in \mathcal{T}_\Sigma^\omega$, checks whether $t \notin L(\mathcal{A})$ by guessing an element from S at every node in t, and verifying that the consecutive guesses comprise a winning strategy for player 1.

In order to do so, we construct a new ranked alphabet $\Sigma \times S$ where $rk_{\Sigma \times S}(a, S) := rk_\Sigma(a)$ for all $a \in \Sigma$ and $S \in S$. We will use the projection functions $proj_1, proj_2$ defined by

$$proj_1(a, S) := a \qquad \text{and} \qquad proj_2(a, S) := \sigma$$

and the former's extension as a rank-preserving homomorphism $\overline{proj_1} : \mathcal{T}_{\Sigma \times S}^\omega \to \mathcal{T}_\Sigma^\omega$ on trees as well as its natural extension to tree languages. This allows us to characterise non-membership of a tree t in the language of the NPTA $\mathcal{A}$ by the existence of a labelling on that tree that represents such a winning strategy for player

1. Equivalently, it is characterised by the existence of a pre-image with this property under the homomorphism $\widetilde{proj_1}$. The next observation follows immediately from Cor. 13.21 and Lemma 13.22.

Lemma 13.23 *Let $t \in \mathcal{T}_\Sigma^\omega$. We have $t \notin L(\mathcal{A})$ iff there is a tree $t' \in \mathcal{T}_{\Sigma \times \mathcal{S}}^\omega$ such that*

(I) $\widetilde{proj_1}(t') = t$ and
(II) the function $\sigma_1 : Q^{\leq m} \times dom(t) \to D$, defined by

$$\sigma_1(\mathbf{q}, v) \ := \ proj_2(t'(v))(\mathbf{q})$$

is a positional winning strategy for player 1 in the acceptance game $\mathcal{G}_{\mathcal{A},t}$.

Now let L' be the set of all trees $t' \in \mathcal{T}_{\Sigma \times \mathcal{S}}^\omega$ that satisfy condition (II) in Lemma 13.23, i.e. the set of all trees extending a tree t over Σ by node labels that conjunctively represent a positional winning strategy for player 1 in the acceptance game for $\mathcal{A}$ and t. This gives us a simple characterisation of the complement of $\mathcal{A}$'s language.

Lemma 13.24 *We have $\mathcal{T}_\Sigma^\omega \setminus L(\mathcal{A}) = \widetilde{proj_1}(L')$.*

This follows immediately from Lemma 13.23. The more important point to make here, though, is that this lemma reduces the construction of an NPTA for $\mathcal{T}_\Sigma^\omega$ to an NPTA for L'. According to Lemma 13.14, NPTA-recognisability is preserved by rank-preserving homomorphisms. Hence, if L' is NPTA-recognisable then so is $\mathcal{T}_\Sigma^\omega \setminus L(\mathcal{A})$.

So we need to study the possibility to construct an NPTA over $\Sigma \times \mathcal{S}$ that checks condition (II) from Lemma 13.23. In order to do so, we need to analyse what makes a labelling of nodes in a tree t with elements of $\mathcal{S} = Q^{\leq m} \to D$ a winning strategy for player 1. Note that an element $S \in \mathcal{S}$ can essentially be seen as a table telling player 1 how to react to a previous move by player 0 in the acceptance game $\mathcal{G}_{\mathcal{A},t}$, when the automaton token was on a state q and the tree token is on a node v, and player 0 has chosen some $(q_0, \ldots, q_{d-1}) \in \delta(q, v)$. More specifically, S can be seen as telling player 1 which direction to choose in each case that player 0 chooses some state tuple $\mathbf{q}$. We therefore also call such an $S \in \mathcal{S}$ a *local strategy profile*.

When actually playing the game, player 1 would therefore make the choice prescribed by this strategy, i.e. choose to continue the play in the direction $S(\mathbf{q})$. This has a particular consequence regarding the view onto t with local strategy profiles S as additional node labels. Take some node $v \in dom(t)$ for some tree $t \in \mathcal{T}_\Sigma^\omega$, and a local strategy profile S. Suppose that player 0 has chosen some state tuple $\mathbf{q}$. Then $S(\mathbf{q})$ determines a direction in which player 1 – the *Pathfinder* – wants the play to pursue. Say $rk_\Sigma(t(v)) = d$ for some $d \in \mathbb{N}$, so we can assume $0 \leq S(\mathbf{q}) < d$. Node v has d children $v0, \ldots, v(d-1)$, with local strategy profiles $S_0, \ldots, S_{d-1}$ associated with them, for instance as explicit labels. Only one of them is interesting for player 1, namely S_i for $i = S(\mathbf{q})$. By choosing direction i – more precisely by following the choice i that is prescribed by his strategy – the i-th state q_i in $\mathbf{q}$ is selected, and in the next round player 0 continues with a choice of another tuple $\mathbf{q}' \in \delta(q_i, t(vi))$.

In the end, we need to construct an NPTA over $\Sigma \times \mathcal{S}$ for the language L'. In order to do so we take a path-based view onto trees in $\mathcal{T}_{\Sigma \times \mathcal{S}}^{\omega}$. Remember that we can construct tree languages from languages of guided traces, i.e. infinite words over an alphabet that extends the (unranked version of the) tree alphabet with directions. Hence, a natural candidate for describing trees in L' via guided traces is $\Sigma \times \mathcal{S} \times D$. Consider the condition laid out in the following lemma that determines whether a guided trace over this alphabet is part of a tree in L'. It follows immediately from Lemma 13.23 as it only reformulates that statement from a point of view onto guided traces.

Lemma 13.25 *Let* $t' \in \mathcal{T}_{\Sigma \times \mathcal{S}}^{\omega} \setminus L(\mathcal{A})$. *A* $\rho = (a_0, S_0, d_0), (a_1, S_1, d_1), \ldots \in (\Sigma \times \mathcal{S} \times D)^{\omega}$ *is a guided trace of* t' *iff for all sequences* $q_0, q_1, \ldots \in Q^{\omega}$ *and* $\mathbf{q}_0, \mathbf{q}_1, \ldots \in (Q^{\leq m})^{\omega}$ *the following holds. If*

(i) $q_0 = q_I$ *and*
(ii) for all $i \geq 1$ *we have* $q_i = p_d$ *where* $d = S_{i-1}(\mathbf{q}_{i-1})$ *and* $\mathbf{q}_{i-1} = (p_0, \ldots, p_r) \in$
  $\delta(q_{i-1}, a_{i-1})$ *for some* $r < m$,

then

(iii) $\limsup_{i \to \infty} \Omega(q_i)$ *is odd.*

At this point, the proof of complementability of an NPTA-recognisable language is essentially finished because conditions (i)–(iii) in Lemma 13.25 are easily seen to be MSO-definable. Thus, the set of guided traces of trees in L' is ω-regular, and we can build a DPA recognising it which can be used to build a parity tree automaton for L', even a deterministic one. Using homomorphism closure we also obtain an NPTA for $\overline{A}$.

This approach has one disadvantage, though. Writing down condition (ii) from Lemma 13.25 in MSO results in a formula of exponential size as it has to address all $S \in \mathcal{S}$ for instance, and $|\mathcal{S}| = |D|^{|Q^{\leq m}|} \in 2^{n^{\mathcal{O}(1)}}$ since $|D|$ and m only depend on the original alphabet Σ. Determinisation introduces another exponential, resulting in a doubly exponential complementation procedure for NPTA only. A better complexity bound is obtained by constructing automata checking the conditions in Lemma 13.25 directly. For this, we extend the underlying alphabet even further to

$$\Delta := \Sigma \times \mathcal{S} \times D \times Q \times Q^{\leq m}$$

so that a word in Δ^{ω} represents a guided trace of a tree in $\mathcal{T}_{\Sigma \times \mathcal{S}}^{\omega}$, together with two infinite sequences, one of states, and the other of state tuples from $\mathcal{A}$'s transition table. To see why this is advantageous, we reformulate Lemma 13.25 as follows, only using standard transformations between universal and existential quantification, as well as between implications and conjunctions involving negations.

Lemma 13.26 *Let* $t' \in \mathcal{T}_{\Sigma \times \mathcal{S}}^{\omega} \setminus L(\mathcal{A})$. *A* $\rho = (a_0, S_0, d_0), (a_1, S_1, d_1), \ldots \in (\Sigma \times \mathcal{S} \times D)^{\omega}$ *is a guided trace of* t' *iff it is not the case that there are sequences* $q_0, q_1, \ldots \in Q^{\omega}$ *and* $\mathbf{q}_0, \mathbf{q}_1, \ldots \in (Q^{\leq m})^{\omega}$ *such that*

(i) $q_0 = q_I$ *and*

(ii) for all $i \geq 1$ we have $q_i = p_d$ where $d = S_{i-1}(\mathbf{q}_{i-1})$ and $\mathbf{q_{i-1}} = (p_0, \ldots, p_r) \in$
$\delta(q_{i-1}, a_{i-1})$ for some $r < m$, and
(iii) $\limsup_{i \to \infty} \Omega(q_i)$ is even.

Next we consider the possibility to recognise such words in Δ^ω by NPA.

Lemma 13.27 *Let $w = (a_0, S_0, d_0, q_0, \mathbf{q}_0), (a_1, S_1, d_1, \mathbf{q}_1), \ldots \in \Delta^\omega$. There is a*

*a) DPA of size $k + 1$ and index k that accepts w iff $q_0 = q_I$ and $\limsup_{i \to \infty} \Omega(q_i)$
is even,*
*b) DcoBA of size n that accepts w iff for all $i \geq 1$ we have $q_i = p_d$ where $d =$
$S_{i-1}(\mathbf{q}_{i-1})$ and $\mathbf{q_{i-1}} = (p_0, \ldots, p_r) \in \delta(q_{i-1}, a_{i-1})$ for some $r < m$.*

Proof (a) The DPA contains one state p of priority p itself, for each priority occurring in $\mathcal{A}$. It deterministically moves to state $\Omega(q)$ upon reading any symbol $(a, S, d, q, \mathbf{q}) \in \Delta$. One additional state is needed to check that the first alphabet symbol contains the initial state q_I in its fourth component.

(b) The DcoBA contains one state per $q \in Q$ to remember the last state in the state sequence. It naturally starts with q_I. Upon reading the alphabet symbol $(a, S, d, q', \mathbf{q})$ in state q it proceeds deterministically to state q' if $\mathbf{q} \in \delta(q, a)$ and q' is the d-th component of $S(\mathbf{q})$. Otherwise, it just stops. All states are accepting, i.e. it only rejects a word by stopping. $\qquad\square$

This allows us to formulate complementation closure for NPTA-recognisable languages with an optimal singly exponential blowup only.

Theorem 13.28 *Let $\mathcal{A}$ by an NPTA of size n and index k. There is an NPTA $\overline{\mathcal{A}}$ of size at most $2^{\mathcal{O}(nk^2 \log nk)}$ and index $\mathcal{O}(nk^2)$ such that $L(\overline{\mathcal{A}}) = \mathcal{T}_\Sigma^\omega \setminus L(\mathcal{A})$.*

Proof Let $\mathcal{A} = (Q, \Sigma, q_I, \delta, \Omega)$ be an NPTA. The construction of an NPTA for the complement language is outlined above in consecutive steps. With Lemma 13.27 we can construct a DPA of size $k + 1$ and index k, as well as a DcoBA of size n such that the intersection of their languages is exactly the set of all words $w \in \Delta^\omega$ that represent a guided trace from L', extended with sequences of states and state tuples representing possible choices by player 0 in an acceptance game on $\mathcal{A}$, such that w satisfies conditions (i)–(iii) of Lemma 13.26.

According to Lemma 6.37, this intersection can be recognised by an NPA of size $\mathcal{O}(k \cdot n)$ and index $k + 1$ and therefore by an NBA $\mathcal{B}$ of size $\mathcal{O}(k^2 \cdot n)$. Using the standard projection construction onto the alphabet $\Sigma \times \mathcal{S} \times D$, we obtain an NBA of the same size that accepts a guided trace of a tree in L' iff there are accompanying sequences of states and state tuples that extend it to a word accepted by $\mathcal{B}$. Using Cor. 7.26 we obtain an equivalent DPA of size $2^{\mathcal{O}(k^2 \cdot n \cdot \log(k^2 \cdot n))} = 2^{\mathcal{O}(nk^2 \log nk)}$ and index $\mathcal{O}(nk^2)$.

Complementation of DPA is possible without an additional blowup, cf. Thm. 6.11. Hence we get a DPA of the same size and index that accepts exactly the guided traces of trees in the language L', according to Lemma 13.26. With Lemma 13.17, there is a DPTA of the same size and index that recognises $L(\mathcal{B})^\triangle$, i.e. L'. Note that it is a tree language over $\Sigma \times \mathcal{S}$ where $\mathcal{S} = Q^{\leq m} \to D$, and Lemma 13.24 establishes that its homomorphic projection onto Σ is exactly $L(\mathcal{A})$. An NPTA for it can be obtained using Lemma 13.14 which also does not incur any further blowup in size or index.$\square$

We carry out the complementation construction for a small example that is not entirely trivial. Even this induces intermediate steps of significant complexity to be done manually. We therefore simplify steps wherever possible.

Example 13.29 Let $\Sigma = \{a, b\}$ with $rk_\Sigma(a) = rk_\Sigma(b) = 2$. Consider the language

$$L = \{t \in \mathcal{T}_\Sigma^\omega \mid \text{there is a path in } t \text{ that contains only symbols } a\}\,.$$

It is recognised by the NPTA $\mathcal{A} = (Q, \Sigma, q_1, \delta, \Omega)$ where $Q = \{q_a, q_*\}$, $\Omega(q_a) = 0 = \Omega(q_*)$ and

$$\begin{aligned}
\delta(q_a, a) &:= \{(q_a, q_*), (q_*, q_a)\}\,, \\
\delta(q_a, b) &:= \varnothing\,, \\
\delta(q_*, x) &:= \{(q_*, q_*)\} \quad \text{for all } x \in \Sigma\,.
\end{aligned}$$

The goal is to construct an NPTA recognising $\mathcal{T}_\Sigma^\omega \setminus L$, i.e. those trees in which every path contains at least one b. It is of course an easy exercise to construct an NPTA for this language directly, even an NBTA. However, we will show that a methodological construction along the lines of the proof of Thm. 13.28 will also arrive at a tree automaton for the complement of L. This is made easier in parts by the fact that $\mathcal{A}$'s acceptance condition is very simple with a single priority only.

First note that there are three state pairs in the image of δ. Let $\Pi := \{(q_a, q_*), (q_*, q_a), (q_*, q_*)\}$. Hence, the set of local strategy profiles $\mathcal{S}$ could be seen as the finite function space $\Pi \to \{0, 1\}$ resulting in 8 local strategy profiles instead of 16 of type $Q^2 \to \{0, 1\}$. However, not every state pair from Π occurs in $\delta(q, x)$ for any $q \in Q$ and $x \in \Sigma$. So we can restrict our attention to the relevant pairs, i.e. those choices in an acceptance game on $\mathcal{A}$ that are feasible in the sense that they give a response for player 1 to any state pair that player 0 can choose but no response to state pairs that player 0 cannot choose. This gives us a reduced set $\mathcal{S} := \{S_*^0, S_*^1, S_a^{00}, S_a^{01}, S_a^{10}, S_a^{11}\}$ of 6 local strategy profiles.

The naming convention is the following: the subscript index denotes the state from which player 0 chooses a transition. There is only one choice in state q_* and two choices in state q_a. This gives two possibilities for player 1 to react in the former case – either go left or right – and four possibilities to react in the latter case, encoded by directions $d_1 d_2$ in the superscript meaning that the strategy tells player 1 to go into direction d_1 in response to the first state pair and direction d_2 in response to the second. Spelled out as partial functions they are as follows.

S_*^0	S_*^1	S_a^{00}	S_a^{01}	S_a^{10}	S_a^{11}
$(q_*, q_*)\mid 0$	$(q_*, q_*)\mid 1$	$(q_a, q_*)\mid 0$	$(q_a, q_*)\mid 0$	$(q_a, q_*)\mid 1$	$(q_a, q_*)\mid 1$
		$(q_*, q_a)\mid 0$	$(q_*, q_a)\mid 1$	$(q_*, q_a)\mid 0$	$(q_*, q_a)\mid 1$

Next we need to construct an NPA over the alphabet

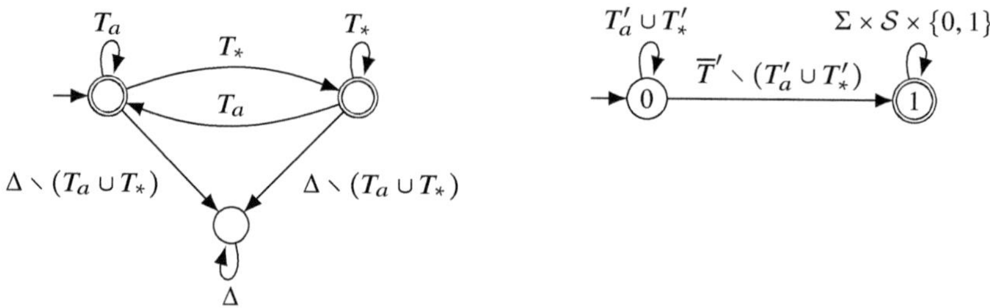

Fig. 13.2 Word automata used in the complementation construction in Ex. 13.29, with the right one obtained from the left one by projection, determinisation and complementation.

$$\Delta \; := \; \Sigma \times \mathcal{S} \times \{0,1\} \times Q \times \Pi$$

that recognises words satisfying the conditions (I)–(III) of Lemma 13.26. According to Lemma 13.27 this can be done modularly by constructing a DPA that checks conditions (I) and (III) and then intersecting it with a DcoBA that checks condition (II).

The DPA for condition (III) in this case is trivial: it only has a single state with priority 0 and a transition looping on this state with any symbol from Δ. The reason is that it only checks that the states in the third components of all symbols in a word over Δ satisfy the parity condition, but the priorities of all states are 0 anyway and so condition (III) boils down to the universal language.

Hence, it suffices to construct an automaton checking conditions (I) and (II). The DcoBA $\mathcal{B}$ shown on the left in Fig. 13.2 does this. Note that $|\Delta| = 144$, so spelling out all transition labels is already infeasible in this small example. The important ones are those tuples $(x, S, d, q, (q_0, q_1))$ for which we have $(q_1, q_2) \in \delta(q', x)$ for some q' and $q = q_{S(q_0,q_1)}$. This is satisfied by the following 20 tuples.

$$
\begin{array}{ll}
T_a \left\{
\begin{array}{ll}
(a, S_a^{00}, 0, q_a, (q_a, q_*)), & (a, S_a^{10}, 0, q_*, (q_a, q_*)), \\
(a, S_a^{00}, 1, q_a, (q_a, q_*)), & (a, S_a^{10}, 1, q_*, (q_a, q_*)), \\
(a, S_a^{00}, 0, q_*, (q_a, q_*)), & (a, S_a^{10}, 0, q_*, (q_a, q_*)), \\
(a, S_a^{00}, 1, q_*, (q_a, q_*)), & (a, S_a^{10}, 1, q_*, (q_a, q_*)), \\
(a, S_a^{01}, 0, q_a, (q_a, q_*)), & (a, S_a^{11}, 0, q_*, (q_a, q_*)), \\
(a, S_a^{01}, 1, q_a, (q_a, q_*)), & (a, S_a^{11}, 1, q_*, (q_a, q_*)), \\
(a, S_a^{01}, 0, q_a, (q_a, q_*)), & (a, S_a^{11}, 0, q_a, (q_a, q_*)), \\
(a, S_a^{01}, 1, q_a, (q_a, q_*)), & (a, S_a^{11}, 1, q_a, (q_a, q_*)),
\end{array}
\right. \\
T_* \left\{
\begin{array}{ll}
(b, S_*^{0}, 0, q_*, (q_*, q_*)), & (b, S_*^{1}, 0, q_*, (q_*, q_*)), \\
(b, S_*^{0}, 1, q_*, (q_*, q_*)), & (b, S_*^{1}, 1, q_*, (q_*, q_*))
\end{array}
\right.
\end{array}
$$

Next we need to project its language onto $\Sigma \times \mathcal{S} \times \{0,1\}$ and then construct a DPA for it. The projection introduces nondeterminism in general. Let $T'_a := \{(x, S, d) \mid$

$\exists q, q_0, q_1$ s.t. $(x, S, d, q, (q_0, q_1)) \in T_a\}$ and likewise for T'_*. This is unproblematic because $T'_a \cap T'_* = \varnothing$. Hence, this particular projection preserves the determinism between the two accepting states in $\mathcal{B}$. However, projecting the labels from $\Delta \smallsetminus (T_a \cup T_*)$ yields triples that are also included in T'_a or T'_*. To be precise, let $\overline{T}' := \{(x, S, d) \mid \exists q, q_0, q_1$ s.t. $(x, S, d, q, (q_0, q_1)) \notin T_a \cup T_*\}$. Then we have

$$
\begin{aligned}
T'_a &:= \{a\} \times \{S_a^{00}, S_a^{01}, S_a^{10}, S_a^{11}\} \times \{0, 1\} \\
T'_* &:= \{b\} \times \{S_*^0, S_*^1\} \times \{0, 1\} \\
\overline{T}' &:= \{a\} \times \{S_*^0, S_*^1\} \times \{0, 1\} \cup \{b\} \times \{S_a^{00}, S_a^{01}, S_a^{10}, S_a^{11}\} \times \{0, 1\} \cup T'_a \cup T'_*
\end{aligned}
$$

so the overlap between the projected transitions in $\mathcal{B}$ is very pristine: any transition from an accepting state to an accepting state can also be taken to the non-accepting state. A small deterministic automaton for the complement of $\mathcal{B}$'s language after projection is then obtained by observation of two facts: (I) the two accepting states recognise the same language and can be merged; (II) moving to the non-accepting state is never helpful since it is a trap. Hence, determinism can be achieved simply by deleting those transitions into the non-accepting state whose label can also lead to an accepting one. Since the automaton (after projection and removal of useless transitions) is deterministic and weak, it can easily be complemented by swapping the status of accepting and non-accepting states. The resulting DPA $\overline{\mathcal{B}}$ is shown in Fig. 13.2 on the right. Note that it is in fact already a DcoBA.

Next we interpret its language as a set of guided traces in trees over $\Sigma \times \mathcal{S}$ and construct a DPTA recognising $L(\overline{\mathcal{B}})^\triangle$ according to Lemma 13.17. Its complete transition table has $2 \cdot 2 \cdot 6 = 24$ entries – one for each combination of a state in $\overline{\mathcal{B}}$ and an alphabet symbol from $\Sigma \times \mathcal{S}$ – but many transitions lead to the same target, so it can be presented succinctly as

$$
\delta'(0, (a, S)) = (0, 0) \ , \quad \delta'(0, (b, S)) = (1, 1) \ , \quad \delta'(1, (b, S)) = (1, 1)
$$

for any $S \in \mathcal{S}$ in all cases. The acceptance condition is inherited from $\overline{\mathcal{B}}$, here just a co-Büchi condition with 1 as the only accepting state.

At last, we obtain the desired complemented NPTA $\overline{\mathcal{A}}$ by a final projection onto the alphabet Σ which is particularly easy in this case, leading to the tree automaton $\overline{\mathcal{A}} := (\{0, 1\}, \Sigma, 0, \delta'', \Omega')$ where

$$
\delta''(0, a) = (0, 0) \ , \quad \delta'(0, b) = (1, 1) \ , \quad \delta'(1, b) = (1, 1)
$$

and $\Omega'(0) = 1$, $\Omega'(1) = 0$. It should be clear that $L(\overline{\mathcal{A}}) = T_\Sigma^\omega \smallsetminus L(\mathcal{A})$.

13.3 Decision Problems

In order to use NPTA for logical decision problems we need to study decidability and complexity of the corresponding decision problems on the automata side, in particular the (non-)emptiness problem.

13.3.1 Non-Emptiness via Parity Games

Non-emptiness turns out to be decidable, using essentially the same techniques as those employed for automata on infinite words. First, for non-emptiness the exact labelling of a tree in the automaton's language with alphabet symbols is irrelevant. Second, finiteness of the automaton's state space and the nature of the parity acceptance condition guarantee the existence of finitely representable trees in each non-empty language of an NPTA.

Independence on the exact alphabet symbols is shown using a transformation into an NPTA whose transitions do not depend on the symbol read in one step. This essentially amounts to the use of homomorphism closure for a morphism that maps all symbols of the underlying alphabet to a single one. While this is very easily done for word automata, it requires a little bit more technical care for tree automata because such a homomorphism would generally not be rank-preserving.

Definition 13.30 Let $A = (Q, \Sigma, q_I, \delta, \Omega)$ be an NPTA and $m := \max\{rk_\Sigma(a) \mid a \in \Sigma\}$. Let $\Sigma^- := \{a\}$ for some alphabet symbol $a \in \Sigma$ such that $rk_\Sigma(a) = m$. By finiteness of Σ, such an a exists.

Define an NPTA A^- as $(Q, \Sigma^-, q_I, \delta^-, \Omega)$ where

$$\delta^-(q, a) = \{(\underbrace{q_0, \ldots, q_{d-1}, \ldots, q_{d-1}}_{m}) \mid \exists b \in \Sigma, rk_\Sigma(b) = d \text{ and } (q_0, \ldots, q_{d-1}) \in \delta(q, b)\}$$

for all $q \in Q$.

Intuitively, A^- recognises a tree t iff it is possible to relabel and reduce it to a tree recognised by A by removing subtrees in order to adjust the ranks for the original symbols in Σ. The exact construction is given in the proof of the following lemma, making the statement of A^-'s language formal.

Lemma 13.31 *Let A be an NPTA over some alphabet Σ and A^- be the NPTA obtained from it according to Def. 13.30. We have $L(A) \neq \emptyset$ iff $L(A^-) \neq \emptyset$.*

Proof Let $A = (Q, \Sigma, q_I, \delta, \Omega)$, $\Sigma^- = \{a\}$ be the singleton alphabet underlying A^-, and m the maximal rank of a symbol in Σ.

"$\Rightarrow$" Suppose $t \in L(A)$ for some $t \in \mathcal{T}_\Sigma^\omega$. Let t' be the complete m-branching tree with $t'(v) = a$ for all $v \in [m]^*$. We claim that $t' \in L(A^-)$. This is seen most easily by realising that t' can be obtained from t by

- changing the label at every node to a, and
- successively, in a top-down way starting with the root level, adding copies of the right-most subtree under each node for as long as it has less than m children.

Note that this corresponds exactly to the construction on the transition function in Def. 13.30. Thus, an accepting run ρ on t can be turned into an accepting run ρ' on t' via

$$\rho'(v') := \begin{cases} \rho(v') & , \text{if } v' \in dom(t), \\ \rho(v) & , \text{otherwise where } v' \text{ resulted as a copy of } v \in dom(t) \end{cases}$$

for any $v' \in [m]^*$. The crucial insight here is that any path $q_0, q_1, \ldots$ through the run ρ' is also a path through the run ρ. Since that is an accepting one, the greatest priority seen infinitely often on all such paths is even, and so ρ' is also accepting.

"$\Leftarrow$" Suppose that $t' \in L(\mathcal{A}^-)$. Since the underlying alphabet Σ^- is a singleton, t' is even unique, namely it is the m-branching tree with all nodes labelled a, as the previous part of the proof noted. Let ρ' be an accepting run of $\mathcal{A}^-$ on t'. We can turn this successively – again in a level-by-level way starting at the root – into a tree $t \in \mathcal{T}_\Sigma^\omega$ with an accepting run ρ of $\mathcal{A}$ on it.

Take a node $v \in dom(t')$ on the currently considered level of t', i.e. the root node at the very beginning of this process. Let $\rho'(v) = q$ for some $q \in Q$. So there is some $(q_0, \ldots, q_{m-1}) \in \delta'(q, a)$ such that $\rho'(vi) = q_i$ for $i \in [m]$. By the construction of $\mathcal{A}^-$, there is some $b \in \Sigma$ such that $(q_0, \ldots, q_{d-1}) \in \delta(q, b)$ where $d = rk_\Sigma(b)$, and $q_j = q_{d-1}$ for all $j = d, \ldots, m-1$. Then remove all nodes vj for $j > d$ from t', change the label at v to b, and continue the process with all (finitely many) remaining nodes on the same level as v, resp. the next level when level $|v|$ is completed.

This turns t' consecutively into the desired tree t. The run ρ on it is simply given as the restriction of ρ' to $dom(t)$. Hence, every path in ρ is also a path in ρ', and so ρ is accepting. $\qquad\square$

Lemma 13.31 does not only remove the distinction between different alphabet symbols in a non-emptiness check, it reduces non-emptiness to the membership problem for a fixed tree t_a, namely the full m-branching tree with uniform node labels where m depends only on the original alphabet. This is a simple consequence of the fact that the language of such an NPTA $\mathcal{A}^-$ is either $\varnothing$ or $\{t_a\}$, since no other trees over the underlying alphabet Σ^- exist.

This immediately opens up the route for a decision procedure for non-emptiness: according to Thm. 13.20, membership of a given tree in the language of an NPTA can be expressed in terms of a parity game. This, together with Lemma 13.31 therefore yields the following characterisation of NPTA non-emptiness.

Corollary 13.32 *Let $\mathcal{A}$ be an NPTA over some alphabet Σ, m the maximal rank in Σ, $\mathcal{A}^-$ the reduct of $\mathcal{A}$ according to Def. 13.30 and t_a the full m-branching tree over the alphabet of $\mathcal{A}^-$. Then $L(\mathcal{A}) \neq \varnothing$ iff player 0 wins the acceptance game $\mathcal{G}_{\mathcal{A}^-, t_a}$.*

While finite parity games can be solved algorithmically, Thm. 13.20 only yields infinite parity games in general. The reason, though, lies solely in the underlying tree, and here the fixed tree t_a obviously has a very small finite representation. This is enough to bound the size of the acceptance game $\mathcal{G}_{\mathcal{A}^-,t_a}$ as a finite one and obtain decidability of the non-emptiness problem for NPTA.

Theorem 13.33 *The non-emptiness problem for NPTA with n states, e edges and k priorities can be solved in time $\mathcal{O}(e^{k+2})$ for any fixed underlying alphabet, provided that $n \le e$.*

Proof Let $\mathcal{A} = (Q,\Sigma,q_I,\delta,\Omega)$ be given, and $m := \max\{rk_\Sigma(a) \mid a \in \Sigma\}$, $n = |Q|$, $k = |\{\Omega(q) \mid q \in Q\}|$, and $e = |\delta| \cdot m$. According to Cor. 13.32 it suffices to analyse the size of $\mathcal{G}_{\mathcal{A}^-,t_a}$ where $\mathcal{A}^- = (Q,\{a\},q_I,\delta',\Omega)$ is the singleton-alphabet NPTA resulting from $\mathcal{A}$ according to Def. 13.30. In particular, $\mathcal{A}^-$ agrees with $\mathcal{A}$ in terms of number of states, transitions and their index.

The crucial insight now is the existence of a finite parity game $\mathcal{G}'$ that is equivalent to the infinite acceptance game $\mathcal{G}_{\mathcal{A}^-,t_a}$ because of a one-to-one correspondence between the plays in the two games, and a matching between their nodes that respects the ownership and the priorities. We define $\mathcal{G}'$ as $(V,V_0,V_1,v_I,E,\Omega')$ where

- $V_0 := Q$, $V_1 := \{\mathbf{q} \mid \exists q \in Q \text{ s.t. } \mathbf{q} \in \delta'(q,a)\}$, $V := V_0 \cup V_1$ as usual, and $v_I = q_I$,
- $E = \{(q,\mathbf{q}) \mid q \in Q, \mathbf{q} \in \delta'(q,a)\} \cup \{((q_1,\ldots,q_m),q_i) \mid i \in \{1,\ldots,m\}\}$,
- $\Omega'(q) = \Omega(q)$ for $q \in V_0$ and $\Omega'(\mathbf{q}) = 0$ for $\mathbf{q} \in V_1$.

A winning strategy for player 0 in $\mathcal{G}'$ then immediately carries over to a winning strategy for player 0 in $\mathcal{G}_{\mathcal{A}^-,t_a}$, even a positional one, such that node q is won by player 0 in $\mathcal{G}'$ iff node (q,v) is won by player 0 in $\mathcal{G}_{\mathcal{A}^-,t_a}$ for arbitrary $v \in [m]^*$. In particular, player 0 either wins the initial nodes of both games or none of them.

A winning strategy for player 0 in $\mathcal{G}_{\mathcal{A}^-,t_a}$ does not immediately carry over to a winning strategy for player 0 in $\mathcal{G}'$, not even when it is positional. The reason is that a positional strategy in $\mathcal{G}_{\mathcal{A}^-,t_a}$ may technically predict different choices in nodes of the form (q,v) and (q,v') for $v,v' \in dom(t_a)$ with $v \ne v'$, but $\mathcal{G}'$ treats v and v' as the same because the subtrees under both of them are isomorphic. In other words: t_a has a finite representation using a single tree node only, and $\mathcal{G}'$ is constructed as the product of the NPTA $\mathcal{A}^-$, not with the infinite tree t_a itself but with its single-node representation.

However, determinacy of parity games (Thm. 12.12) comes in handy here: instead of transforming a winning strategy for player 0 in $\mathcal{G}_{\mathcal{A}^-,t_a}$ into one for her in $\mathcal{G}'$ it suffices to argue that the existence of a winning strategy for player 1 in $\mathcal{G}'$ implies the existence of one for him in $\mathcal{G}_{\mathcal{A}^-,t_a}$. This is done in exactly the same way as for player 0.

Thus, in order to check $\mathcal{A}$ for non-emptiness it suffices to solve the parity game $\mathcal{G}$ with $(n+e)$ nodes, k priorities and at most $n \cdot m \cdot e$ edges, which can be done – cf. Thm. 12.16 – in time $\mathcal{O}(nme(n+e)^k) = \mathcal{O}(e^{k+2})$ since m is constant and we can assume w.l.o.g. that $n \le e$. $\square$

13.3.2 Complexity, Expressiveness and Consequences

Recall that non-emptiness for automata on finite words is a simple reachability problem that can be solved in non-deterministic logarithmic space, and this is still true when considering infinite words and their automaton models like Büchi and parity automata. For trees, the situation is slightly different. Non-emptiness for languages of finite trees can be checked in polynomial time, but the step to infinite trees probably incurs higher complexity: so far, it is only known to be polynomially solvable for NPTA with a bounded number of priorities, for instance for Büchi tree automata. This immediately raises the question after a fixed bound k on the number of priorities such that NPTA of index k accept all regular languages of infinite trees. This is not the case, as the following theorem states. A proof would require a few more technical developments and is not presented here.

Theorem 13.34 *Let Σ be an arbitrary alphabet such that $|\Sigma| \geq 2$. For every $k \geq 1$ there is some $k' \geq k$ and an $L \subseteq \mathcal{T}_\Sigma^\omega$ that is recognisable by an NPTA of index k' but not recognisable by any NPTA of index k.*

One may think that it is the inherent refusal of parity games to admit a polynomial-time algorithm because of which one should attempt to find a direct solution for the non-emptiness problem for NPTA instead. This does not make things easier, though. A polynomial-time algorithm for NPTA emptiness would imply a polynomial-time algorithm for solving parity games. The proof is left as an exercise.

An immediate consequence of the combination of decidability of non-emptiness (Thm. 13.33) and the effective closure under complements (Thm. 13.28) is the decidability of the other standard decision problems associated with types of automata.

Corollary 13.35 *The universality, subsumption and equivalence problems for NPTA are solvable in exponential time.*

13.3.3 Finitely Representable Trees

Often one is not only interested in the answer to the question of non-emptiness of the language of a given tree automaton, but additionally needs to have a witness in terms of some tree in the language in case that it is non-empty. This is the natural extension of the decision problem to a computation problem, and such witnesses play an important role in applications in program verification for instance, where such a tree may encode the part of the set of runs of a program that violates some correctness specification.

Trees are infinite objects in this setting, and one cannot expect an arbitrary infinite tree to be constructible in finite time. So it is not immediately clear that the decidable decision problem of non-emptiness gives rise to a computable computation problem. It hinges on the fact that every non-empty language that is recognised by an NPTA

contains a tree that can be finitely represented. This also merits the use of the term
"regular" for languages recognised by NPTA.

Note that this is comparable to the corresponding problem for automata on infinite
words. By Büchi's Theorem, every non-empty ω-regular language over an alphabet
Σ contains a word of the form uv^ω for some $u \in \Sigma^*, v \in \Sigma^+$. The only difference is
the lack (so far) of a language like ω-regular expressions which provides a formal
notion of finite representability for infinite trees.

Definition 13.36 Let Σ be a ranked alphabet. A tree $t \in \mathcal{T}_\Sigma^\omega$ is called *finitely representable* if it contains only finitely many mutually non-isomorphic subtrees. The
size of t is the number of such subtrees.

A natural representation of a tree is a system of equations

$$t_1 \;=\; a_1\big(t_{i_{1,1}},\ldots,t_{i_{1,\sigma(a_1)}}\big)$$

$$\vdots$$

$$t_n \;=\; a_n\big(t_{i_{n,1}},\ldots,t_{i_{n,\sigma(a_n)}}\big)$$

over variables $t_1,\ldots,t_n$ for trees in $\mathcal{T}_\Sigma^\omega$, and each right-hand side being a term of the
form $a(t_1,\ldots,t_d)$ with $d = rk_\Sigma(a)$. It represents a tree whose root node is labelled a
and whose d children are, successively, the trees represented by the right-hand sides
of the equations for $t_1,\ldots,t_d$.

In fact, every infinite tree is represented by an infinite system of such equations
with one equation for each node in the tree. Here we restrict our attention to finite
systems of equations which can be seen as several nodes in the tree sharing the same
description, i.e. the subtrees rooted at these nodes being isomorphic. Thus, finite
systems of n equations represent exactly the finitely representable trees of size n.

Example 13.37 The tree t_a used in the proof of Thm. 13.33 – the full tree of
branching degree m for some m with all nodes labelled a for some symbol a –
is finitely representable and of size 1. It contains exactly one isomorphism class
of subtrees, namely t_a itself, since the subtrees at the children of its root are all
isomorphic to t_a. It is therefore represented by the equation system $t_a = a(t_a,\ldots,t_a)$.

Let $n \geq 0$. The tree t_n over $\Sigma = \{a,b\}$ with $rk_\Sigma(a) = rk_\Sigma(b) = 2$ defined by

$$t(v) \;=\; \begin{cases} b & \text{, if } v \in L((0^*1)^n), \\ a & \text{, otherwise} \end{cases}$$

is finitely representable. Note that it contains a b at every node that is reached on a
path which takes a turn to the right at most n times.

Every tree t_n is finitely representable and of size $2n+1$. There is an infinite system
of equations representing them all uniformly, namely

$$
\begin{aligned}
&\ \vdots &&&&\ \vdots \\
t_n^{\text{lft}} &= a(t_n^{\text{lft}}, t_n^{\text{rgt}}) && t_n^{\text{rgt}} &= b(t_{n-1}^{\text{lft}}, t_{n-1}^{\text{rgt}}) \\
&\ \vdots &&&&\ \vdots \\
t_1^{\text{lft}} &= a(t_0, t_0) && t_1^{\text{rgt}} &= b(t_0, t_0) \\
t_0 &= a(t_0, t_0)
\end{aligned}
$$

for every $n \geq 2$. Note that each tree with index n only depends on the $2n + 1$ trees with indices at most n. Hence, each $t_n := t_n^{\text{lft}}$ is indeed represented by a finite system of equations.

A detailed analysis of the proof of Thm. 13.33 yields the desired result about finitely representable witnesses for non-emptiness of NPTA-recognisable languages.

Theorem 13.38 *Let A be an NPTA of size n. We have $L(A) \neq \varnothing$ iff there is a finitely representable tree t of size at most n such that $t \in L(A)$.*

Proof The direction "$\Leftarrow$" is obvious. For the direction "$\Rightarrow$" let $A = (Q, \Sigma, q_I, \delta, \Omega)$ and assume that $L(A) \neq \varnothing$. So player 0 has a positional winning strategy σ_0 for the game $\mathcal{G}(A^-, t_a)$ where A^- results from A with the construction of Def. 13.30 changing its alphabet to a singleton $\Sigma' = \{a\}$.

This strategy has type $Q \times dom(t_a) \to Q^m$ where $m = rk_{\Sigma'}(a)$. Since $|dom(t_a)| = 1$ we can in fact assume that the type of σ_0 is $Q \to Q^m$.

We now use σ_0 to create a finitely representable tree, represented by the variable t_{q_I} in the system that contains one equation

$$
t_q = b(t_{q_{i_1}}, \ldots, t_{q_{i_d}})
$$

for each $q \in Q$ where $\sigma_0(q) = (q_{i_1}, \ldots, q_{i_d}, \ldots, q_{i_d}) \in Q^m$ with $(q_{i_1}, \ldots, q_{i_d}) \in \delta(q, b)$ for $b \in \Sigma$ and $rk_\Sigma(b) = d$. Note that this incorporates a partial reversal of the simplification construction that turns A into A^-: we consider the positional strategy σ_0 in the acceptance game for A^- (and t_a) because t_a gives us a negligible set of tree nodes, and A is defined over a different alphabet than t_a, but we ultimately need a representation of a tree in $L(A)$, not $L(A^-)$.

This system of equations is well-defined. By assumption, $\sigma_0(q_I)$ is defined, for otherwise player 0 would not win the node (q_I, t_a) and therefore not the game itself. Here we write (q_I, t_a) instead of (q_I, ε) for the root node ε of t_a. The reason will be clear in a moment.

Since player 1 controls the directions in the acceptance game, σ_0 must be defined for every player-0 position that can be reached next, namely every position of the form (q_i, t_a) for all $i = 1, \ldots, d$, where $\sigma_0(q_I, t_a) = (q_1, \ldots, q_d)$. Here, we identify a subtree with its root node and write t_a for the root of any subtree that is isomorphic to the tree t_a. This also proves the point that σ_0 can be assumed to only depend on Q, and not on $dom(t_a)$.

So consider the tree t_{q_I} represented by this system of equations. Clearly, it has size at most n. It remains to be seen that $t_{q_I} \in L(A)$. It is not hard to see that there is a run of A on t_{q_I}. It labels the root of each node represented by t_q with the state q. It is even accepting because σ_0 is a winning strategy, and every sequence of states that forms a path in this run on t_{q_I} is a subsequence of a play in $\mathcal{G}(\mathcal{A}^-, t_a)$ conforming to σ_0, namely the subsequence of player-0 nodes. They are interleaved with player-1 nodes, but these all have priority 0, so the greatest priority occurring infinitely often on the subsequence of player-0 nodes is the greatest priority occurring infinitely often in the play, and this must be even by assumption. $\qquad\square$

Bibliographic Notes

Automata recognising languages of infinite trees are studies in detail in the book on tree automata by Comon et al. [CDG$^+$07], unpublished but available online. Automata on infinite trees also do feature in other textbooks on automata in a more general setting, for instance [KN10, PP04], as well as Thomas' articles in the Handbook of Theoretical Computer Science [Tho90] and the Handbook of Languages, Automata and Logic [Tho97]. The topic also plays a role in a broader framework in parts in Thomas' Festschrift [FGW08], and in a collection edited by Grädel, Thomas and Wilke [GTW02].

A chapter by Löding of the Handbook of Automata Theory is also devoted to the theory of infinite trees [Löd21]. This chapter also contains a detailed exposition of the complementation closure result for tree automata. It introduces and uses alternating tree automata which are easier to complement, and a simulation construction for them by nondeterministic ones. This does not make an essential but rather a notational difference only to the construction presented here because acceptance of a tree by an alternating automaton can equally be seen as a game, and simulation of an alternating automaton by a nondeterministic one is essentially the construction of an automaton recognising a winning strategy for one of the players.

Alternating automata on infinite trees have first been studied by Muller and Schupp [MS87, MS95], in particular with regards to their use for proving closure under complements for regular languages of infinite trees, as well as by Saoudi [SMS90, Sao91].

Vardi, Wolper et al. studied automata operating on infinite trees, mainly for the purpose of obtaining complexity-theoretically optimal decision procedures for branching-time temporal logics [VW86, CVW86, KVW00].

Complementation closure for regular languages of infinite trees is a much celebrated result known as *Rabin's Theorem* [Rab69]. It answered a natural question arising with Büchi's decidability proof for Second-Order Logic of One Successor (S1S), namely concerning the decidability of Second-Order Logic with monadic predicates over structures that provide more than one successor function, so-called SnS. While the high-level structure of this result as it is presented here, cf. Thm. 13.28, is in line with Rabin's original construction, it has to be said that much of the elegance is owed to positional determinacy of parity games which was not available to Rabin at the time. The path via parity automata and games, as it is presented here, is due to Gurevich and Harrington [GH82].

Since Büchi tree automata are expressively too weak [Rab70], Rabin first had to introduce a stronger acceptance condition, nowadays known as the Rabin condition. This introduces a bit more technical difficulty compared to the use of parity tree automata because, due to their lack of symmetry, Rabin games do not enjoy positional determinacy. They are determined, but only player 0 has positional strategies in general, cf. [KK91]. Player 1 can only be assumed to have finite-memory strategies which is sufficient, though, for the construction of tree automata for complement languages in the end.

The relative weakness of Büchi tree automata, in particular their lack of complementation closure, called for further studies into their expressiveness, in particular possible correspondences to logics over trees [Kai95, Sku02].

Büchi tree automata are clearly parity tree automata, using only the priorities 1 and 2. So a natural question asks whether there is any fixed set of priorities that suffices to recognise all regular languages of infinite trees. The answer is negative and has first been given in terms of the need for unbounded nestings of fixpoints in the modal μ-calculus, cf. [Koz83], the so-called strictness of the alternation hierarchy [Bra98a, Len96, Bra98b]. This result also holds for ranked trees [Bra99, Arn99]. Since formulas of the modal μ-calculus are essentially alternating parity tree automata (APTA), this hierarchy immediately implies a strict hierarchy of expressiveness for APTA w.r.t. their indices. It is even the case that increasing the index by 1 strictly increases their expressive power. The proof relies on complementation closure which can easily be done for APTA without an increase in index. For nondeterministic automata, this involves an increase though, in general. Hence, the stratification w.r.t. their indices also yields a strict hierarchy of expressiveness for NPTA, but higher expressiveness is not necessarily already achieved by increasing the index by 1 but may require more than one additional priority.

The existence of finitely representable infinite trees witnessing non-emptiness of the language of a tree automaton not necessarily with a parity condition but with others like Rabin or Muller, was shown by Hossley and Rackoff [HR72] who gave a decision procedure for non-emptiness by a reduction to the non-emptiness problem for automata on finite trees.

Exercises

Exercise 141 Construct NPTA for the following languages over $\Sigma = \{a, b, c\}$ where $rk_\Sigma(x) = 2$ for all $x \in \Sigma$.

a) $L_1 = \{t \in \mathcal{T}_\Sigma^\omega \mid t = a(b(t,t), b(t,t))\}$,
b) $L_2 = \{t \in \mathcal{T}_\Sigma^\omega \mid t(\varepsilon) = a$ and $\forall v :$ if $t(v) = a$ then $t(v110) = a = t(v001)\}$,
c) $L_3 = \{t \in \mathcal{T}_\Sigma^\omega \mid$ for all paths w of t we have that $|w|_a = \infty$ implies $|w|_b = \infty\}$,
d) $L_5 = \{t \in \mathcal{T}_\Sigma^\omega \mid t$ has a path with infinitely many symbols a, and it has a path with infinitely many symbols $b\}$.

In each case, explain whether the language is also recognisable by a DPTA, an NBTA or even a DBTA.

Exercise 142 Prove Thm. 13.6.

Exercise 143 Prove Lemma 13.7.

Exercise 144 Prove Lemma 13.12 and 13.13.

Exercise 145 Prove Lemma 13.14.

Exercise 146 Let $L \subseteq \mathcal{T}_\Sigma^\omega$ for some ranked alphabet Σ with associated set of directions D. Define $Tr(L) := \bigcup \{ Tr(t) \mid t \in L \} \subseteq (\Sigma \times D)^\omega$ to be the set of all guided traces of trees from L.

a) Show that $Tr(L)$ is ω-regular if L is a regular tree language.
b) Consider the following attempt at a determinisation procedure for NPTA. Given an NPTA $\mathcal{A}$, use part (a) to compute an NBA for $Tr(L(\mathcal{A}))$. Then use Lemma 13.17 to compute a DPTA for $Tr(L(\mathcal{A}))^\triangle$. Why does this not yield a DPTA for $L(\mathcal{A})$?

Exercise 147 Prove Lemma 13.22.

Exercise 148 Consider the NPTA $\mathcal{A} = (Q, \Sigma, 0, \delta, \Omega)$ where $\Sigma = \{a, b\}$ with $rk_\Sigma(a) = rk_\Sigma(b) = 2$ and $Q = \{0, 1, \bullet\}$, $\Omega(0) = \Omega(1) = 1$, $\Omega(\bullet) = 0$ and the following transitions.

$$\begin{aligned}
\delta(0, a) &= \{(0, 1), (1, 0)\} & \delta(0, b) &= \{(0, 0), (1, 1), (\bullet, \bullet)\} \\
\delta(1, a) &= \{(0, 0), (1, 1)\} & \delta(1, b) &= \{(0, 1), (1, 0)\} \\
\delta(\bullet, a) &= \varnothing & \delta(\bullet, b) &= \{(\bullet, \bullet)\}
\end{aligned}$$

a) Determine $L(\mathcal{A})$.
b) Consider the tree $t \in \mathcal{T}_\Sigma^\omega$, finitely represented by the following system of equations.

$$\begin{aligned}
t &= b(a(b(a(t_b, a(t_b, t_b)), a(t_b, t_b)), a(t_b, t_b)), t_b) \\
t_b &= b(t_b, t_b)
\end{aligned}$$

We have $t \notin L(\mathcal{A})$. Construct a tree $t' \in \mathcal{T}_{\Sigma \times S}^\omega$ for $S := Q^2 \to \{0, 1\}$ such that $\overline{proj_1}(t') = t$ and $\overline{proj_2}(t')$ defines a positional winning strategy for player 1 in the game $\mathcal{G}_{\mathcal{A}, t}$.

Exercise 149 Consider the NPTA $\mathcal{A} = (\{0, 1\}, \Sigma, 0, \delta, \Omega)$ with $\Sigma = \{a, b\}$, $rk_\Sigma(a) = rk_\Sigma(b) = 2$, $\Omega(0) = 1$, $\Omega(1) = 2$ and

$$\delta(0, a) = \{(0, 0)\} \ , \quad \delta(0, b) = \{(1, 1)\} \ , \quad \delta(1, x) = \{(1, 1)\}$$

for $x \in \Sigma$.

a) Determine $L(\mathcal{A})$.

b) Let ρ be a guided trace of a tree in $T_\Sigma^\omega \setminus L(\mathcal{A})$. Explain why ρ must be of the form $(x_0, S_0, d_0), (x_1, S_1, d_1), \ldots$ with $x_i \in \Sigma$, $S_i \in \{0,1\}^2 \to \{0,1\}$, $d_i \in \{0,1\}$ for all $i \geq 0$ such that

$$(\forall n.x_n = a) \ \vee$$

$$\Big(\exists m.(x_m = b) \ \wedge \ (\forall n < m.x_n = a) \ \wedge$$

$$\exists n.\big(n \leq m \wedge S_n(0,0) \neq d_n\big) \vee \big(n > m \wedge S_n(1,1) \neq d_n\big)\Big)$$

is satisfied.

c) Construct an NPTA $\overline{\mathcal{A}}$ that recognises $T_{\overline{\mathcal{A}}}^\omega \setminus L(\mathcal{A})$.

Exercise 150 Let $\mathcal{G}$ be a parity game with n nodes, e many edges and of index k.

a) Construct an NPTA $\mathcal{A}_\mathcal{G}$ such that $L(\mathcal{A}) \neq \varnothing$ iff $\mathcal{G}$ is won by player 0.

b) Argue that a polynomial-time algorithm for NPTA non-emptiness would entail a polynomial-time algorithm for solving parity games, by checking that $\mathcal{A}_\mathcal{G}$ is small enough to transfer polynomial-time bounds between the algorithms.

Chapter 14
Logics on Infinite Trees

As with automata on infinite words and finite trees, automata as studied in the previous chapter provide a relatively simple computational model for specifying properties of infinite trees. Such trees can be seen as abstractions of runs of reactive programs for instance, for which the exact next step is not predetermined (as in infinite words) but may depend on some external input.

While automata open up the path to decidability for the main decision problems in the background, they can be cumbersome as specification formalisms in the foreground. For example, programs are typically only considered to be correct when they satisfy several specifications, i.e. correctness is often expressed as a conjunction. While the class of NPTA is closed under intersections, and an NPTA for the intersection of finitely many NPTA-definable languages can be constructed effectively, it is barely possible to find the automata for the single parts in the structure of the resulting automaton for the intersection. This can make debugging difficult.

Suppose that $\bigcap_{i=1}^{n} L(\mathcal{A}_i)$ for some NPTA $\mathcal{A}_1, \ldots, \mathcal{A}_n$ describes the branching runs of a program that are seen to be correct, and a decision procedure determines this language to be empty. It is then difficult to attribute this directly to one or several involved NPTA.

One step to alleviate this – at least on the side of a user interface – is the use of logical specification languages because specifications for tree languages can be built more modularly using formulas rather than automata directly. The price to pay is of course the fact that formulas are tougher to handle algorithmically, and this is where automatic translations into automata come into play again. So using formulas instead of automata directly does not solve all problems, but they can provide a sometimes more usable interface for specifying such languages.

A natural logic to consider is of course Monadic Second-Order Logic over infinite trees. We adopt the few small syntactic modifications implemented in Sect. 11.4 in order to obtain an MSO logic whose formulas can speak about (finite) trees, compared to MSO over words. The extension to infinite trees is then purely semantical and straightforward. We are of course mainly interested in the satisfiability problem for this logic, and it is, again, complementation closure for a corresponding automaton model – here: NPTA – that provides the key to its decidability.

One might rightfully argue that MSO is perhaps not the most suitable specification language for applications in the specification and verification of reactive programs and systems, as it requires some deeper familiarity with formal logic. Moreover, its expressive power can sometimes be seen as too high for particular purposes. This is the reason why more application-targeted specification formalisms like the linear-time temporal logic LTL discussed in Chp. 10 have been invented and studied.

Temporal logic can also be interpreted over trees. It only requires an adjustment in the notion of time, as already hinted at above. In (discrete) *linear-time* temporal logics the future is considered to be determined in the sense that for every moment there is a unique future moment. A temporal model then naturally is a word: a linear sequence of moments, each of which comes with some particular properties, here abstracted away into a single alphabet symbol.

One may equally consider the future not to be predetermined in the sense that for every moment, there are several possible future moments, and the exact moment that is taken in some run is chosen by some uncontrollable principle like the external environment of a computer system, user input, randomness etc. The time model underlying this view is known as *branching time*. Note that our task is not to determine the answer to the perhaps philosophical question of whether linear or branching time is the right interpretation of the world. In computer science, both have their right to exist, and it is the requirements imposed by an application that determine which is the correct one to use.

After briefly studying MSO on infinite trees, following the standard recipe of the automata-logic connection for obtaining decidability, we turn our attention to two temporal logics interpreted over infinite trees: the so-called *full branching-time temporal logic* CTL* can be seen as a natural extension of the linear-time temporal logic LTL from Chp. 10 to tree models. The *modal μ-calculus* $\mathcal{L}_\mu$ extends a very small fragment of First-Order Logic (interpreted in tree structures) by so called *fixpoint quantifiers*. They can be seen as restricted versions of the generally more powerful second-order quantifiers. Decidability of satisfiability for both logics is everything but obvious. However, it immediately follows from translations into MSO.

14.1 Monadic Second-Order Logic

14.1.1 Syntax and Semantics

The syntax of MSO, interpreted over infinite trees over some ranked alphabet Σ, is exactly the same as the one for MSO over finite Σ-trees, see Def. 11.25. For convenience, we repeat it here.

$$\varphi \ ::= \ succ_i(x, y) \mid X(x) \mid a(x) \mid \varphi_1 \vee \varphi_2 \mid \neg\varphi \mid \exists x\, \varphi \mid \exists X\, \varphi$$

As usual, x, y are first-order variables, X is a second-order variable from some underlying countable set of variables $\mathcal{V} = \mathcal{V}_1 \cup \mathcal{V}_2$, $a \in \Sigma$ and $i \in \mathbb{N}$. The formula

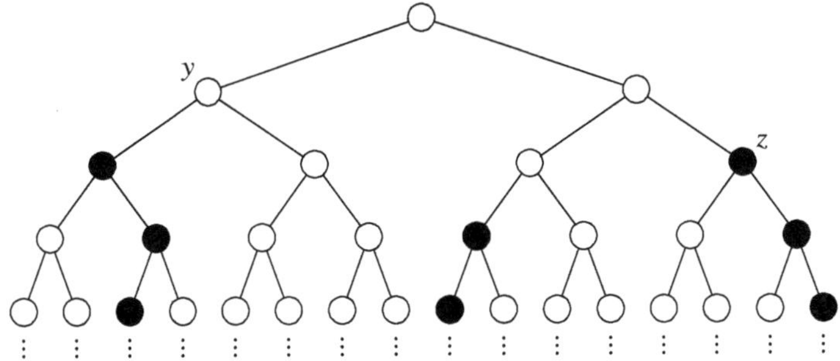

Fig. 14.1 Binary tree with variable assignment for first-order variables y, z and some second-order variable.

$succ_i(x, y)$ is used to state that the node in a tree that is referred to with y is the i-th successor of the node referred to by x, starting from $i = 0$.

Other logical operators like conjunctions, universal quantification etc. are introduced as abbreviations in the usual way. All the other syntactical concepts like formula size, the first-order fragment, etc. apply here as well of course.

The interpretation of a formula in a tree $t \in \mathcal{T}_\Sigma^\omega$, together with a variable assignment $I : (\mathcal{V}_1 \to dom(t)) + (\mathcal{V}_2 \to 2^{dom(t)})$ is defined as usual, cf. Def. 11.26. Naturally, second-order quantification now ranges over finite and infinite sets of nodes in a tree.

The usual semantical concepts like equivalence, satisfiability and language $L(\varphi)$ of a sentence φ are defined in the usual way.

Equality is not explicitly introduced in the syntax of MSO. As with (monadic) second-order logics in general, equality is definable via $x = y := \forall X.X(x) \leftrightarrow X(y)$.

14.1.2 Capturing Paths

Remember that over words, equality is equally definable using pure Boolean operators via $x = y := \neg(x < y) \wedge \neg(y < x)$. This does of course require the relation '$<$' to be available, and MSO above has been introduced without it. It will be convenient to have, though. Before we show how to obtain it as an abbreviation, we need to remark that '$<$' on words is interpreted by the total order of all the positions in the word. A natural way to interpret such a symbol in a tree is the partial order obtained via $u < v$ iff there is a $w \in \mathbb{N}^+$ such that $v = uw$, i.e. if v is located somewhere "underneath" u in the underlying tree.

Example 14.1 We aim to construct an MSO formula $\varphi_<(y, z)$ that is true in a tree t under some variable assignment I iff $I(x) < I(y)$ via the partial-order interpretation of '$<$' described above.

It is tempting to say that z is located underneath y if it is possible to start a path from y that eventually hits z, i.e. if there is a set X of nodes that contains y, also contains some successor of every node in it, and also contains y. This bears several problems, though.

First of all, this informal construction recipe is clearly symmetric in y and z. Hence, a formalisation in MSO – which is clearly possible – could not define $\varphi_<$ as desired because it would not distinguish the case of z located underneath y from the case in which y is located underneath z. In fact, it would not even distinguish these from the case in which both are equal. This could easily be fixed though. Instead of demanding that X contains y, we demand that X contains some successor of y. However, there is a much more profound problem with this attempt.

Consider the situation depicted in Fig. 14.1. It shows a binary tree and an assignment I of two first-order variables y, z such that $I(y) = 0$ and $I(z) = 11$, as well as of a second-order variable X. Its interpretation is shown in black circles, i.e. we have $I(X) = \{00, 11, 001, 100, 111, \ldots\}$.

Clearly, $0 \not< 11$. Hence, $\varphi_<$ should not be satisfied under this assignment I. However, $I(X)$ contains some successor of $I(y)$, contains $I(z)$ and is closed under successors. At least it is easy to imagine that the interpretation of X extends further down the tree so that every black circle node has one successor that is also a black circle node.

Fig. 14.1 shows why the characterisation of '<' via the three properties above is insufficient: it does not require that y and z are ultimately *connected* via X. In fact, the monotonic use of X in this description means that it can be interpreted as a set of paths rather than a single path, and it suffices for some path in this set to contain a successor of y and another to contain z.

It may then be tempting to turn the construction around and demand that there is a set which contains z, is closed under *predecessors* and contains some successor of y. However, logically this is exactly the same. Note that $succ_i(x, x')$ does not only state that x' is the i-th successor or x but equally that x is the (unique) predecessor of x'.

In the end, it is helpful, though, to think in terms of an ascending path from z to y, but we need to exclude the possibility of a second-order variable to be interpretable by multiple paths or path-like sets. We first define

$$\varphi_{\leq}(y, z) \;\; := \;\; \forall X.\big(X(z) \wedge preds(X) \wedge nomerge(X)\big) \to X(y)$$

where

$$succ(x', x) \;\; := \;\; \bigvee_{i=0}^{d-1} succ_i(x', x)$$

$$preds(X) \;\; := \;\; \forall x. X(x) \to \big(\forall x'.succ(x', x) \to X(x)\big)$$

$$nomerge(X) \;\; := \;\; \forall x. \bigwedge_{i=0}^{d-2} \bigwedge_{j=i+1}^{d-1} \forall x' \forall x''.succ_i(x, x') \wedge succ_j(x, x'') \to$$

$$\neg\big(X(x') \wedge X(x'')\big)$$

and d is the maximal rank of symbols in the underlying alphabet. It states that every set X which contains z and is closed under predecessors, and additionally never contains two different successors of some node, also contains y. The only sets that satisfy the first two conditions are paths from the root to z and perhaps beyond. Now, that fact that every such set must contain y means that it must be located on the unique path from the root to z. Hence, we have $t, I \vDash \varphi_\le(y, z)$ iff $I(y) \le I(z)$ in the partial order induced by reachability in t.

Then we can simply define $\varphi_<(y, z) := \varphi_\le(y, z) \wedge \neg(y = z)$. For this, it is of course necessary to define equality via second-order quantification as done above, not via '$<$' itself.

We allow ourselves to simply write $y < z$ and $y \le z$ instead of $\varphi_<(y, z)$ and $\varphi_\le(y, z)$ just as we do with $y = z$ for instance.

In the following section on temporal logic we will need MSO's ability to quantify over paths, i.e. to express that some second-order variable evaluates to a path starting in a particular node.

Lemma 14.2 *Let Σ be given. There is an MSO formula $Path(X, z)$ such that for every $t \in T_\Sigma^\omega$ and every variable assignment I in t we have $t, I \vDash Path(X, z)$ iff $I(X)$ forms a single path through t starting in $I(z)$.*

Proof It suffices to observe that a path in a tree starting in some node v is a set X of nodes that contains v, contains some successor for every node in it, and additionally has two properties: It does not contain any ancestor of z, and each two nodes in X are comparable w.r.t. '$\le$'. Thus, we can construct the formula under demand as

$$Path(X, z) := X(z) \wedge \big(\forall y.X(y) \to \exists x.succ(y, x) \wedge X(x)\big) \wedge$$
$$\big(\forall y.y < z \to \neg X(y)\big) \wedge \big(\forall x \forall y.X(x) \wedge X(y) \to x \le y \vee y \le x\big)$$

where $succ(y, x)$ is defined as in Ex. 14.1. $\qquad\square$

One may wonder why Σ needs to be given. Note that subformulas like $y \le x$ depend on some maximal rank of symbols in the underlying alphabet.

14.1.3 Decidability

The main decision problems for MSO over infinite trees are decidable, as they are for MSO over finite and infinite words, and over finite trees. The backbone of a decision procedure is, again, the effective ability to translate formulas into equivalent automata, in this case NPTA. For this to work inductively, the same tricks can be applied as before.

First, we adopt a special syntax of MSO that only contains second-order variables and a special predicate $Sing(X)$ which is true under some variable assignment I iff

$|I(X)| = 1$. This allows us to express first-order quantification as relativised second-order quantification. Similar adjustments have to be made to replace the formula construct $succ_i(x, y)$ by some $Succ_i(X, Y)$ operating on second-order variables.

Once first-order variables are eliminated, an interpretation (t, I) with t being a tree over a ranked alphabet Σ and $I : \{X_1, \ldots, X_n\} \to 2^{dom(t)}$, can be regarded as a tree over the alphabet $\Sigma \times \{0, 1\}^n$ in the natural way with the j-th component of the additional vector of binary values at a node v determining whether or not $v \in I(X_j)$. Thus, if $t \in \mathcal{T}_\Sigma^\omega$ then $t_I \in \mathcal{T}_{\Sigma \times \{0,1\}^n}^\omega$ where t_I is the natural representation of t and I in this sense. For this to be well-defined, we need to set ranks as $rk_{\Sigma \times \{0,1\}^n}(a, b_1, \ldots, b_n) = rk_\Sigma(a)$. As a consequence, any projection of type $\Sigma \times \{0, 1\}^n \to \Sigma \times \{0, 1\}^m$ for any $0 \le m < n$ that erases the same $n - m$ symbols from each n-tuple of binary values, induces a rank-preserving homomorphism.

Then again, it is possible to construct NPTA for atomic MSO formulas in this specialised syntax, and effective closure under unions (Lemma 13.12), rank-preserving homomorphisms (Lemma 13.14) and complements (Thm. 13.28) can be used to build automata inductively for larger formulas possibly containing free variables. Spelling out the details of this construction is left as an exercise.

Theorem 14.3 *For every MSO sentence φ over a ranked alphabet Σ there is an NPTA $\mathcal{A}_\varphi$ such that $L(\mathcal{A}_\varphi) = L(\varphi)$.*

Thus, satisfiability of MSO over infinite trees also reduces to non-emptiness for NPTA which is decidable according to Thm. 13.33.

Corollary 14.4 *Satisfiability for MSO over infinite trees is decidable.*

Note that Thm. 14.3 only states the existence of equivalent NPTA for MSO sentences. However, the considerations above clearly show that such NPTA are also effectively computable. Cor. 14.4 states decidability of satisfiability for arbitrary formulas, even though Thm. 14.3 is only formulated for sentences. One can either extend the statement in Thm. 14.3 accordingly as it needs to be done for an inductive proof, but then one has to inject the notion of representation of a variable valuation by a node label extension into the notion of equivalence. Alternatively, one can easily see that satisfiability of an arbitrary formula $\varphi(X_1, \ldots, X_n, x_1, \ldots, x_n)$ reduces to satisfiability of a sentence, namely in this case the one for

$$\exists X_1 \ldots \exists X_n \exists x_1 \ldots \exists x_n \, \varphi(X_1, \ldots, X_n, x_1, \ldots, x_n) \, .$$

Likewise, decidability of satisfiability carries over to the other main logical decision problems, and this can either be shown by making the step from, say, equivalence to emptiness on the automata side, constructing an NPTA whose language is empty iff two given ones define the same language. Or it can be seen on the logical side with $\varphi \equiv \psi$ iff $\neg(\varphi \leftrightarrow \psi)$ is unsatisfiable.

Corollary 14.5 *Validity and equivalence for MSO over infinite trees are decidable.*

14.2 Full Branching-Time Logic

The so-called full branching time temporal logic CTL* extends the linear-time temporal logic LTL by quantifiers for paths so that its formulas can naturally be interpreted in nodes of a tree.

14.2.1 Syntax and Semantics

We recall the syntax of LTL which is built from atomic propositions using Boolean operators and the temporal operators X (*Next*) and U (*Until*) with several derived operators like F (*Finally*), G (*Generally*) and R (*Release*).

Formulas were said to be interpreted in ω-words over the alphabet $2^{\mathcal{P}}$, but actually they are interpreted in a position in a word, namely the first, as the standard translation into FO shows. Since every ω-word clearly has a unique first position, it is fair to say that LTL formulas are interpreted in words.

CTL* extends LTL by two additional operators E ("*there is a path*") and A ("*for all paths*"). This makes formulas interpretable in nodes of a tree, at least some formulas. Take, for instance, the LTL formula $\varphi = Xp$ that does not make use of the new operators, stating "*p holds in the next moment.*" It is meaningless to ask whether node 010 for instance, in a binary $2^{\mathcal{P}}$-labelled tree, satisfies φ because node 010 does not have a single successor which could be probed for satisfying p. Instead, it has two: 0100 and 0101.

On the other hand, the CTL* formula $\varphi' := A\varphi$ could be satisfied by this node. It states that p holds on *all* paths (starting in the node under consideration). This is clearly possible for a tree t, namely when $p \in t(0100)$ and $p \in t(0101)$.

In order to avoid pitfalls with uninterpretable formulas, the syntax of CTL* contains two types of formulas, namely *state formulas* and *path formulas*. They are built by mutual recursion. A state formula is interpretable in a node of a tree, so it is what we are interested in after all. A path formula is interpretable on a path in a tree. Path formulas are essentially just LTL formulas over propositions and state formulas, and path quantifiers turn path into state formulas.

Before we can define the syntax formally, we need to briefly address the issue of the underlying alphabet. As with LTL, CTL* is mainly used for the specification of runs of programs, and for modelling purposes it is more handy to assume an underlying set of propositions $\mathcal{P}$ of which multiple ones or none can hold in a state. This is not in line with the model of Σ-trees for a ranked alphabet Σ where every node is labelled with exactly one alphabet symbol. A simple way to overcome this is, as done for LTL, to associate, with a finite set of propositions $\mathcal{P}$, the alphabet $\Sigma = 2^{\mathcal{P}}$. This was not a problem in the case of LTL, leading to ω-words over an alphabet which is of exponential size in the number of underlying propositions but of course still finite. In the case of trees, we need a ranked alphabet, though, and explicitly fixing the rank of each symbol $a \subseteq \mathcal{P}$ defeats the purpose of working with propositions instead of the associated and generally much larger set of alphabet symbols. For simplicity, we assume a fixed rank $d > 1$ such that $rk_{2^{\mathcal{P}}}(a) = d$ for all $a \subseteq \mathcal{P}$. This will allow us to appeal to results for MSO and NPTA, interpreted in trees over a ranked alphabet.

The case of $d = 1$ does not have to be excluded, but 1-ary trees are of course just ω-words, and one can easily check – with the semantics given below – that the state formulas $\mathsf{E}\psi$ and $\mathsf{A}\psi$ are satisfied by a node in a 1-ary tree, i.e. an ω-word, iff the unique path starting in this node satisfies the path formula ψ. Hence, in case of $d = 1$, the extension by path quantifiers adds no extra expressive power, and CTL^* is just the same as LTL. This is why we generally assume $d \geq 1$ but implicitly understand that only the cases $d > 1$ are really interesting.

Definition 14.6 Let $\mathcal{P}$ be a set of atomic propositions. State (φ) and path (ψ) formulas of the full branching-time temporal logic CTL^* are given by the grammar

$$\varphi \ := \ p \mid \varphi \vee \varphi \mid \neg\varphi \mid \mathsf{E}\psi$$
$$\psi \ := \ \varphi \mid \psi \vee \psi \mid \neg\psi \mid \mathsf{X}\psi \mid \psi \,\mathsf{U}\, \psi$$

where $p \in \mathcal{P}$.

Other Boolean connectives are introduced as abbreviations in the usual way. The same holds for other temporal operators that make up path formulas, as they were introduced within LTL. At last, we abbreviate $\neg\mathsf{E}\neg\varphi$ as $\mathsf{A}\varphi$.

The size $|\varphi|$ of a CTL^* formula φ is the number of distinct subformulas it has. These can be state or path formulas. When we speak of a *CTL^* formula* we usually mean a CTL^* state formula.

As said above, CTL^* state formulas are interpreted in nodes of a tree. Def. 14.6 allows formulas to be built over an infinite set of atomic propositions. Clearly, if $|\mathcal{P}| = \infty$ then $|2^{\mathcal{P}}| = \infty$, and it seems that we cannot use $2^{\mathcal{P}}$ as an alphabet for labelling the nodes in trees, at least not in the context of recognising trees using finite automata. However, every CTL^* formula can clearly only contain finitely many atomic propositions, and this also holds for a finite set of CTL^* formulas. When studying infinite families of CTL^* formulas, we assume them to be built over the same finite set of atomic propositions, even though the set of all CTL^* formulas may not satisfy this property.

Definition 14.7 Let $d \geq 1$, $\mathcal{P}$ be a finite set of propositions, $\Sigma := 2^{\mathcal{P}}$ with $rk_\Sigma(a) := d$ for all $a \subseteq \mathcal{P}$, and $t \in \mathcal{T}_\Sigma^\omega$. We write $\Pi_t(v)$ for the set of paths through t that start in node v, i.e. $\pi \in \Pi_t(v)$ iff $\pi = v, vi_1, vi_1i_2, \ldots$ for some $i_1, i_2, \ldots$ with $0 \leq i_j < d$ for all $j \in \mathbb{N}$.

The interpretation of a CTL^* state formula φ in a node $v \in dom(t)$ and of a CTL^* path formula ψ on a path π through t is explained by simultaneous induction on the structure of φ and ψ.

$$
\begin{aligned}
t, v &\vDash p && \text{iff} && p \in t(v) \\
t, v &\vDash \varphi_1 \vee \varphi_2 && \text{iff} && t, v \vDash \varphi_1 \text{ or } t, v \vDash \varphi_2 \\
t, v &\vDash \neg\varphi && \text{iff} && t, v \nvDash \varphi
\end{aligned}
$$

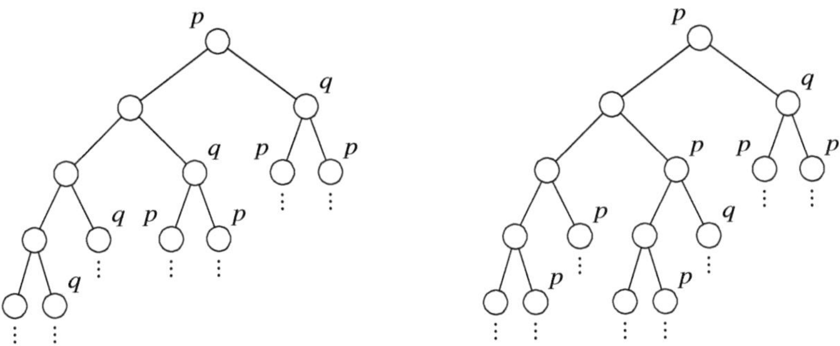

Fig. 14.2 Two finitely representable trees used to separate CTL* formulas in Ex. 14.8.

$$t, v \models \mathsf{E}\psi \qquad \text{iff} \quad \text{there is } \pi \in \Pi_t(v) \text{ s.t. } t, \pi \models \psi$$

$$t, \pi \models \varphi \qquad \text{iff} \quad t, v_0 \models \varphi$$

$$t, \pi \models \psi_1 \vee \psi_2 \quad \text{iff} \quad t, \pi \models \psi_1 \text{ or } t, \pi \models \psi_2$$

$$t, \pi \models \neg\psi \qquad \text{iff} \quad t, \pi \not\models \psi$$

$$t, \pi \models \mathsf{X}\psi \qquad \text{iff} \quad t, \pi^1 \models \psi$$

$$t, \pi \models \psi_1 \mathsf{U} \psi_2 \quad \text{iff} \quad \text{there is } k \geq 0 \text{ with } t, \pi^k \models \psi_2 \text{ and for all } m < k : t, \pi^m \models \psi_1$$

where $\pi(0) = v_0$ and $\pi^k = v_k, v_{k+1}, \ldots$ for any $k \geq 0$ if $\pi = v_0, v_1, \ldots$

We say that a tree t is a *model* of a state formula φ, written $t \models \varphi$ for short, if $t, \varepsilon \models \varphi$. The *language* $L(\varphi) \subseteq \mathcal{T}_\Sigma^\omega$ consists of all models of φ. Two state formulas φ, φ' are equivalent, written $\varphi \equiv \varphi'$ as usual, if $L(\varphi) = L(\varphi')$. A formula φ is *valid*, written $\models \varphi$, if $L(\varphi) = \mathcal{T}_\Sigma^\omega$.

Note that there is a slight ambiguity in the definition of the language of a CTL* formula. Since there is no obligation to use up all propositions in a formula, a CTL* formula over $\mathcal{P}$ is also a CTL* formula over $\mathcal{P}'$ whenever $\mathcal{P} \subseteq \mathcal{P}'$. We assume that the underlying set of propositions is always fixed. If it is not given explicitly, then it is safe to assume it to be smallest in the sense that it only contains those propositions that occur in a given formula, resp. set of formulas.

Example 14.8 Let $\mathcal{P} = \{p, q\}$. A tree node that satisfies a proposition p may also be called a p-node, and likewise for q. Remember that a proposition holds at some node in a tree when it is included in the label of that node which is a set of propositions.

The formula $\varphi_1 := \mathsf{E}(\mathsf{GF}p \wedge \mathsf{FG}\neg q)$ states that on some path in a given tree, there are infinitely many p-nodes but only finitely many q-nodes.

Consider the following two finitely representable binary trees t_1, t_1' over $2^\mathcal{P}$ where $a_p = \{p\}$, $a_q = \{q\}$ and $b = \varnothing$.

$$t_1 = a_p(t_2, t_3) \qquad\qquad t_1' = a_p(t_2', t_3')$$
$$t_2 = b(t_2, t_3) \qquad\qquad t_2' = b(t_2', t_1')$$

$$t_3 \;=\; a_q(t_1, t_1) \qquad\qquad\qquad t_3' \;=\; a_q(t_1', t_1')$$

They are unfolded to a few levels in Fig. 14.2 with t_1 on the left and t_1' on the right.

We have $t_1 \not\models \varphi_1$ because between two p-nodes in t_1, there is a q-node. Hence, every path that contains infinitely many p-nodes must also contain infinitely many q-nodes, and so no path can contain infinitely many p-nodes but only finitely many q-nodes.

On the other hand, $t_1' \models \varphi_1$ because it clearly contains paths with repeating parts without any q-nodes but containing p-nodes. Hence, there is such a path under question, for example the path $(01)^\omega$.

Now consider the CTL* formula $\varphi_2 := \mathrm{AGF}p \wedge \mathrm{EFG}\neg q$. It states that all paths contain p-nodes infinitely often and some path contains only finitely many q-nodes. This is not the same as φ_1. A witness for the distinction between these two formulas is t_1' because $t_1' \not\models \varphi_2$. This is easily seen because not every path in t_1' contains infinitely many p-nodes, for example 0^ω, so the first conjunct of φ_2 is already violated by t_1'.

Likewise, we have $t_1 \not\models \varphi_2$ for the same reason. A slightly more complicated argument uses the observation that φ_1 is weaker than φ_2 in the sense that the implication $\varphi_2 \to \varphi_1$ is valid. This is not difficult to see: let t be a given tree over $2^{\mathcal{P}}$, and suppose that $t \models \varphi_2$. Then all its paths contain infinitely many p-nodes and some path π contains finitely many q-nodes only. So there is a path, namely π, that contains infinitely many p-nodes and finitely many q-nodes only. Hence, $t \models \varphi_1$ which proves that $\models \varphi_2 \to \varphi_1$. By pure Boolean reasoning we also have $\models \neg\varphi_1 \to \neg\varphi_2$. In other words, if a tree does not satisfy φ_1 it also cannot satisfy φ_2. Since t_1 does not satisfy φ_1 as established above, we also have $t_1 \not\models \varphi_2$.

At last, consider $\varphi_3 := \mathrm{EF}(p \wedge \mathrm{EG}\neg q)$. It simply states that a given tree has a p-node from which a path can be started that does not contain any q-node. This is clearly the case for both t_1 and t_1', witnessed by the root node in both cases. So $t_1 \models \varphi_3$ and $t_1' \models \varphi_3$.

The latter is also a consequence of the fact that $\models \varphi_1 \to \varphi_3$, i.e. φ_3 is weaker than φ_1, together with the fact established above that $t_1' \models \varphi_1$.

To see that the implication $\varphi_1 \to \varphi_3$ is indeed valid, consider an arbitrary tree t over $2^{\mathcal{P}}$ that satisfies φ_1, i.e. it contains a path $\pi = v_0, v_1, \dots$ with infinitely many p-nodes and finally many q-nodes only. There must be a last q-node on this path in the sense that there is a $k \in \mathbb{N}$ such that $v_k, v_{k+1}, \dots$ all are not q-nodes. Of course it is possible that there is not a single q-node on the path, but the important point to note here is that it is always possible to find some suffix $\pi^k = v_k, v_{k+1}, \dots$ of π that does not contain q-nodes at all. Now v_k is clearly reachable from t's root, and it is the first node on a path, namely π^k, with no q-nodes. Hence, $t \models \varphi_3$.

We have that φ_1 and φ_3 are not equivalent either. The two properties are separated by t_1 as we have $t_1 \models \varphi_3$, witnessed by the root node and the path 0^ω, but $t_1 \not\models \varphi_1$ as established above. So we have $\not\models \varphi_3 \to \varphi_1$.

We develop a second example which shows how CTL* is useful as a specification language for reactive systems.

Example 14.9 Consider a system made up of n consumer processes $C_0, \ldots, C_{n-1}$. They may signal *requests* (for some resource), using atomic propositions r_i for $i \in [n]$. A scheduler, also part of the system, is used to keep track of requests and grant requests on a particular basis. Granting a request for process C_i is signalled by an atomic proposition g_i for $i \in [n]$. The CTL* formula

$$\varphi_0 \ := \ \bigwedge_{i=0}^{n-1} \mathsf{AGF} r_i$$

states that every process issues requests over and over again.

The scheduler maintains a FIFO buffer in which it stores requests. Thus, reaching an r_i-state can be seen as adding process C_i's request to the buffer unless the buffer already contains a request from this process in which case the new request is simply discarded. The CTL* formula

$$\varphi_1 \ := \ \bigwedge_{\substack{i=0 \\ }}^{n-1} \bigwedge_{\substack{j=0 \\ j \neq i}}^{n-1} \mathsf{A}\neg\left(r_i \wedge \mathsf{X}\left(\neg g_i \ \mathsf{U} \left(r_j \wedge \neg g_i \wedge \mathsf{X}(\neg g_i \ \mathsf{U} \ g_j) \right) \right) \right)$$

states that the requests are granted in the same order in which they are issued (without the discarded ones).

A desirable property is so-called starvation freedom – the fact that every request is eventually granted. This is expressed by the following formula.

$$\varphi_2 \ := \ \mathsf{AG} \bigwedge_{i=0}^{n-1} (r_i \to \mathsf{AF} g_i)$$

The conjunction $\varphi_0 \wedge \varphi_1 \wedge \varphi_2$ of these three properties is then satisfiable iff this specification of a scheduling system is viable.

The aim of the next section is to establish decidability of the main logical decision problems for CTL*, in particular the satisfiability problem. For this, it is useful to observe that CTL* formulas are essentially nestings of LTL formulas, preceded by path quantifiers.

Lemma 14.10 *Let φ be a CTL* state formula over $\mathcal{P}$. There are some $n \in \mathbb{N}$, propositions $f_1, \ldots, f_{n-1}$ all not belonging to $\mathcal{P}$, LTL formulas $\psi_1, \ldots, \psi_n$ and CTL* state formulas $\varphi_1, \ldots, \varphi_n$ such that*

- *ψ_i is an LTL formula over $\mathcal{P} \cup \{f_1, \ldots, f_{i-1}\}$ for all $i = 1, \ldots, n$,*
- *$\varphi_i = \mathsf{E}\psi_i[\psi_{i-1}/f_{i-1}, \ldots, \psi_1/f_1]$ for all $i = 1, \ldots, n$,*
- *φ is a Boolean combination of $\varphi_1, \ldots, \varphi_n$.*

Proof Let φ be given. Take n to be the number of existential path quantifiers in φ, i.e. the number of distinct subformula of the form $\mathsf{E}\psi$. According to Def. 14.6, φ is a Boolean combination of such formulas, and each such ψ is a path formula, i.e. an LTL formula over the original propositions or smaller state formulas. A straightforward decomposition and introduction of new propositions to abbreviate such smaller state formulas yields the desired ψ_i and φ_i. $\qquad\qquad\square$

14.2.2 Decidability

With the tools worked out so far, in particular decidability of satisfiability for MSO over Σ-trees for a given Σ via the construction and analysis of NPTA, it is not difficult to see that the satisfiability problem for CTL^* is also decidable. This can be shown by embedding CTL^* effectively into MSO. And it is not a surprise that this is possible: according to Lemma 14.10, CTL^* formulas are just nestings of path quantified LTL formulas. LTL can easily be translated into FO, and MSO is expressive enough to quantify over sets and state that they must form a path. All that needs to be done is to relativise the FO formulas obtained from the LTL subformulas to the corresponding paths.

Theorem 14.11 *Let $\varphi \in CTL^*$ over some finite $\mathcal{P}$. There is an MSO formula Φ over the alphabet $2^{\mathcal{P}}$ such that $L(\Phi) = L(\varphi)$ and $|\Phi| = \mathcal{O}(|\varphi|)$.*

Proof First we define a function $tr'_{X,z}$ that translates an LTL formula into an MSO formula over infinite trees with two free variables: a second-order variable X and a first-order variable z. The resulting MSO formula cannot be equivalent to the LTL formula in a strict sense since they are interpreted over different kinds of structures. Instead, the following holds. Let t be a tree over some alphabet $2^{\mathcal{P}}$ for some suitable $\mathcal{P}$, and d be the uniform rank for all symbols in $2^{\mathcal{P}}$. For a path $\pi = v_0, v_1, \ldots$ and an LTL formula ψ we have

$$\pi, i \models \psi \quad \text{iff} \quad t, [X \mapsto P, z \mapsto v_i] \models tr'_{X,z}(\psi)$$

where $P := \{v_0, v_1, \ldots\}$. Note that the satisfaction relation on the right-hand side is the one for MSO over infinite trees, on the left it is the one for LTL where the path π is naturally interpreted as an ω-word over $2^{\mathcal{P}}$.

In other words, if the second-order variable X denotes a path, and z denotes a node on this path, then $tr'_{X,z}(\psi)$ should express that the remaining part of this path starting in z satisfies ψ. Before we can formulate the details of this translation, we need an auxiliary predicate. We write $z \leq_X y$ to say that the node addressed by y is further down the tree on the path X than the node z. This strict order induced by the path X is expressible in MSO as follows. Node y is further down the X-path than z if every set that contains the (necessarily unique) successor of z that belongs to X, and is closed under successors that belong to X, must also contain y. This is formalised in MSO straightforwardly as follows.

$$z <_X y \; := \; \forall Z.\Big(\bigwedge_{i=0}^{d-1} \forall z'.succ_i(z,z') \wedge X(z') \to Z(z') \Big) \wedge$$

$$\Big(\forall z' \forall z''.Z(z') \wedge X(z'') \wedge \bigvee_{i=0}^{d-1} succ_i(z',z'') \to Z(z'') \Big) \to Z(y)$$

Likewise, we can define the non-strict version of this order predicate by $z \leq_X y :=$ $z = y \vee z <_X y$.

With this, we can formulate the semantics of LTL in MSO, relativised to a path X straightforwardly as follows.

$$tr'_{X,z}(q) := \bigvee_{\substack{a \subseteq \mathcal{P} \\ q \in a}} a(x) \quad \text{if } q \in \mathcal{P}$$

$$tr'_{X,z}(\psi_1 \vee \psi_2) := tr'_{X,z}(\psi_1) \vee tr'_{X,z}(\psi_2)$$

$$tr'_{X,z}(\neg\psi) := \neg tr'_{X,z}(\psi)$$

$$tr'_{X,z}(\mathsf{X}\psi) := \exists y. \bigvee_{i=0}^{d-1} succ_i(z,y) \wedge X(y) \wedge tr'_{X,y}(\psi)$$

$$tr'_{X,z}(\psi_1 \,\mathsf{U}\, \psi_2) := \exists y.z \leq_X y \wedge X(y) \wedge tr'_{X,y}(\psi_2) \,\wedge$$
$$\forall x.z \leq_X x \wedge x <_X y \rightarrow tr'_{X,x}(\psi_1)$$

We have $|tr'_{X,z}(\psi)| = \mathcal{O}(|\psi|)$, at least if $\mathcal{P}$ is assumed to be fixed. Moreover, the branching degree d is fixed as well.

Building on this, we can devise a translation tr_z from CTL* formulas into MSO formulas over infinite trees that are equivalent in the following sense. The resulting formula $tr_z(\varphi)$ contains a free first-order variable z. For every tree t over $2^{\mathcal{P}}$ we have $t \in L(\varphi)$ iff $t, [z \mapsto \varepsilon] \models tr_z(\varphi)$. This is of course not strong enough to be used inductively because the evaluation of temporal operators shifts the point of reference further down in a tree, so we need a more general correctness statement that takes arbitrary nodes into account for it to be suitable as an inductive invariant. Indeed, we have that $t[v] \models \varphi$ iff $t, [z \mapsto v] \models tr_z(\varphi)$ for any tree t and node $v \in dom(t)$ where $t[v]$ is used to denote the subtree rooted at node v. Then we have

$$tr_z(q) := \bigvee_{\substack{a \subseteq \mathcal{P} \\ q \in a}} a(x)$$

$$tr_z(\varphi_1 \vee \varphi_2) := tr_z(\varphi_1) \vee tr_z(\varphi_2)$$

$$tr_z(\neg\varphi) := \neg tr_z(\varphi)$$

$$tr_z(\mathsf{E}\psi) := \exists X.Path(X,z) \wedge tr'_{X,z}(\psi)$$

where $Path(X,z)$ states that X is a path starting in node x. Lemma 14.2 shows that this is expressible in MSO.

So the functions $tr'_{X,z}$ allow us to translate a genuine LTL formula, and the functions tr_z then allow us to translate a CTL* state formula whose path subformulas are pure LTL formulas. At last, we make use of the decomposition property for CTL* formulas laid out in Lemma 14.10 by extending the translation functions $tr'_{X,z}$, defined for LTL formulas over $\mathcal{P}$, to LTL formulas over the original propositions in $\mathcal{P}$ and new auxiliary propositions f that are being replaced by CTL* state formulas via

$$tr'_{X,z}(f)[\varphi/f] := tr_z(\varphi)$$

to obtain a translation for arbitrary CTL* formulas into MSO over infinite trees. Correctness follows immediately from the observation that the requirements on how the two translation functions yield equivalent formulas in a particular sense, are in fact induction invariants. The claim on the size of the resulting MSO formula is also easily verified, provided that – as said above – the set of underlying propositions and the branching degree of the underlying trees are considered to be fixed.

In a final step, we need to fix the interpretation of the free variable z in $tr_z(\varphi)$ for a CTL* formula φ, to the root of an underlying tree. So the MSO sentence Φ, demanded by the theorem's statement, can be obtained as

$$\Phi \ := \ \exists z.(\neg\exists y \bigvee_{i=0}^{d-1} succ_i(y,z)) \wedge tr_z(\varphi)$$

which does not exceed the size bounds either and clearly fixes the interpretation of z to the root node. $\qquad\square$

An immediate consequence of this effective translation from CTL* into equivalent MSO sentences and Cor. 14.4 and 14.5 is decidability of the satisfiability problem as well as other associated decision problems for CTL*.

Corollary 14.12 *The satisfiability, validity and equivalence problems for CTL* over d-ary trees are decidable.*

The decision procedure obtained in this way is not optimal from a complexity-theoretic point of view. Remember that satisfiability for MSO over finite words cannot be solved in elementary time, and this of course carries over to infinite words, finite and infinite trees since finite words can easily be encoded in them or are special cases anyway. The height of the tower of exponentials in the worst-case time complexity is due to the alternations between existential and universal (second-order) quantifications in an MSO formula or, equivalently, existential quantification and negation. The translation from CTL* into MSO constructed in the proof of Thm. 14.11 does not create formulas of bounded quantifier alternation depth. Hence, it is not just due to the lack of a better worst-case runtime analysis because of which we only get a non-elementary decision procedure for CTL* this way.

By a direct translation into tree automata, or – very much related – a direct formulation of the satisfiability problem as a parity game solving problem, one can obtain a better complexity bound.

Proposition 14.13 *The satisfiability, validity and equivalence problems for CTL* are decidable in doubly exponential time.*

This is optimal; these problems are indeed complete for 2ExpTime.

14.2.3 Expressiveness

Note that Prop. 14.13 does not only improve on Cor. 14.12 in terms of a significantly better complexity bound. It is also more general in that it makes a statement about satisfiability over the class of trees of arbitrary (even infinite) branching degree whereas the automata-theoretic method leading to Cor. 14.12 requires the underlying alphabet to be ranked first and thus only decides these problems for a class of trees with fixed, and in particular bounded branching degrees.

So one question that arises immediately with this is: is there a bound on the branching degree necessary to satisfy a satisfiable CTL^* formula? If this was not the case, then Cor. 14.12 would only yield a semi-decision procedure for general CTL^* satisfiability without further involvement. However, such a bound does indeed exist. We state it here without a proof either since it requires a much deeper study of the theory of temporal logics.

Proposition 14.14 *Let φ be a CTL^* formula with at most n distinct subformulas of the form $E\psi$. If φ is satisfiable then it is satisfied by a tree of branching-degree at most $n + 1$.*

Together with this result, Cor. 14.12 then also yields decidability over the class of all trees.

Another question that arises with Thm. 14.11 is of course the one after the converse direction: is every MSO-definable property of infinite trees already CTL^*-definable? The answer is no. CTL^*-definable properties are *bisimulation-invariant* which, intuitively and on infinite trees not necessarily of the same branching-degree, can be explained as follows. Let t be a tree and t' result from it by successively

- re-ordering the children under some node, including the subtrees under them, and
- duplicating subtrees or removing duplicates of subtrees.

Then t and t' cannot be distinguished by any CTL^* formula. On the other hand, MSO is able to count numbers of children to some degree, and is also generally aware of the order in which the children of some node are given. Hence, MSO is not bisimulation-invariant.

Example 14.15 Let $\Sigma = \{a, b, c\}$ with $rk_\Sigma(a) = 3$, $rk_\Sigma(b) = rk_\Sigma(c) = 1$. Consider the two trees t and t' defined by

$$t = a(t_b, t_b, t_c) \,, \quad t' = a(t_b, t_c, t_c) \,, \quad t_b = b(t_b) \,, \quad t_c = c(t_c) \,.$$

Then t and t' are distinguished by the MSO formula

$$\exists r.\left(\neg \exists y \bigvee_{i=0}^{2} succ_i(y,r)\right) \wedge \exists x.succ_1(r,x) \wedge b(x)$$

which is in fact already an FO formula. On the other hand, one can show by induction on the structure of CTL^* formulas that $t \models \varphi$ iff $t' \models \varphi$ for all φ.

14.3 The Modal μ-Calculus

We consider a second prominent logic for program specification purposes that can be interpreted over infinite trees. The modal μ-calculus extends modal logic with fixpoint quantifiers. Modal logic can be seen as what remains of FO when it is restricted to the specification of bisimulation-invariant properties, see the brief discussion on the expressive power of CTL* above. There is, of course, a much simpler approach via a very intuitive syntax, and bisimulation-invariance is then a result following from the semantics rather than an imposition.

14.3.1 Modal Logic

Models of formulas continue to be trees, and for pragmatic purposes we continue to define logical formulas on the basis of atomic propositions from some set $\mathcal{P}$ from which we derive a tree alphabet $2^{\mathcal{P}}$, at least when $|\mathcal{P}|$ is finite. For simplicity we assume that all alphabet symbols have some fixed rank $d \geq 1$. Again, the case of $d = 1$ boils down to words and is only included as it is not harmful.

Definition 14.16 Let $\mathcal{P}$ be a set of atomic propositions. Formulas of *modal logic* (ML) over $\mathcal{P}$ are given by the grammar

$$\varphi \quad ::= \quad q \mid \varphi \vee \varphi \mid \neg \varphi \mid \Diamond \varphi$$

where $q \in \mathcal{P}$.

Besides the usual Boolean operators we introduce one more abbreviation: $\Box \varphi :=$ $\neg \Diamond \neg \varphi$.

The size of an ML formula is given as the number of distinct subformulas in it.

The operators $\Diamond$ and $\Box$ are read as *"there is a successor"*, resp. *"for all successors."* They can be seen as versions of the operators $succ_i(x, y)$ in FO/MSO, restricted in two ways:

- The order amongst the children of a node is irrelevant. There is no i-th successor anymore, at least not for the logic. There is only *some* successor. Of course some successor will reside at a particular position amongst the children of a node, but the logic has no means to distinguish their indices anymore.
- As with temporal logics like CTL*, formulas are interpreted in a node of a tree. This takes over the role of the variable x in $succ_i(x, y)$, and then y is not needed either because the interpretation of a formula of the form $\Diamond \varphi$ in an implicitly given node x entails the interpretation of φ in a successor node y which is now the implicitly given nameless node. This is why ML does not contain any (first-order) variables, but this is of course not new as the same mechanism is used in CTL*.

ML can also be obtained as the fragment of CTL* that forbids the use of the operator U, at least with some simple syntactical equivalence-preserving transformations. Then $\diamond$ and $\square$ are nothing more than **EX** and **AX** in CTL*.

Formulas of ML are interpreted in a node of a tree, very much in the same way as it is done for CTL*.

Definition 14.17 Let $\mathcal{P}$ be a finite set of propositions and $\Sigma := 2^{\mathcal{P}}$ with $rk_\Sigma(a) = d$ for all $a \subseteq \mathcal{P}$ and some $d \geq 1$. The satisfaction relation between a tree $t \in \mathcal{T}_\Sigma^\omega$ and a node $v \in dom(t)$ on one side and an ML formula φ on the other is explained inductively as follows.

$$
\begin{aligned}
t, v &\models q & \text{iff} \quad & q \in t(v) \\
t, v &\models \varphi \vee \psi & \text{iff} \quad & t, v \models \varphi \text{ or } t, v \models \psi \\
t, v &\models \neg \varphi & \text{iff} \quad & t, v \not\models \varphi \\
t, v &\models \diamond \varphi & \text{iff} \quad & \text{there is } i < d \text{ s.t. } t, vi \models \varphi
\end{aligned}
$$

A tree t satisfies an ML formula φ, written $t \models \varphi$, if $t, \varepsilon \models \varphi$. The language of an ML formula φ is, as usual, $L(\varphi) := \{t \mid t \models \varphi\}$. Other semantical concepts like equivalence between formulas etc. are defined in the usual way.

It is not hard to see that ML can be embedded straightforwardly into FO over trees, simply because the semantics of an ML formula is pretty much given as an FO formula over trees, and the root of a tree can be addressed in FO. We omit a formal proof as it would only repeat those two observations.

Theorem 14.18 *For every $\varphi \in ML$ over $\mathcal{P}$ there is a $\varphi' \in FO$ over $2^{\mathcal{P}}$ such that $L(\varphi') = L(\varphi)$ and $|\varphi'| = \mathcal{O}(|\varphi|)$.*

It should not be surprising to hear that ML is not as expressive as FO, exactly for the lack of ability to distinguish bisimilar trees, i.e. those that only differ from each other through the order and multiplicities of subtrees at every node. Ex. 14.15, giving two trees that are distinguishable in FO but not in CTL*, covers ML as well. This is also not a surprise as ML can equally easily be embedded into CTL*.

Theorem 14.19 *For every $\varphi \in ML$ over $\mathcal{P}$ there is a $\varphi' \in CTL^*$ over $\mathcal{P}$ such that $L(\varphi') = L(\varphi)$ and $|\varphi'| = \mathcal{O}(|\varphi|)$.*

The proof details are left as an exercise. Again, a natural question asks about the converse direction. CTL* is strictly more expressive than ML, though. The key observation for a proof of the following theorem is: any given $\varphi \in ML$ contains a finite number of modal operators only. In fact, it has a finite *modal depth $md(\varphi)$* which is the maximal number of modal operators occurring on any path in the syntax tree of φ.

Theorem 14.20 *Suppose that $|\mathcal{P}| \geq 1$. There are tree languages over $2^{\mathcal{P}}$ that are definable in CTL* which are not definable in ML.*

Proof Let $\mathcal{P} = \{p, \ldots\}$. Consider the language L of trees containing a p-node somewhere. We have $L = L(\mathrm{EF}p)$, so this language is CTL^*-definable. A straightforward induction on the structure of ML formulas φ shows: let t, t' be two d-ary trees such that $t(v) = t'(v)$ for all $v \in [d]^*$ with $|v| \le md(\varphi) + 1$. Then $t \vDash \varphi$ iff $t' \vDash \varphi$.

Now suppose there was an ML formula φ such that $L(\varphi) = L$. Then it must have some modal depth $k := md(\varphi)$. Consider the two trees t_k, t'_k with

$$t_k(v) \;\; := \;\; \begin{cases} \varnothing & , \text{ if } |v| \le k \\ \{p\} & , \text{ otherwise} \end{cases}$$

and $t'_k(v) = \varnothing$ for all $v \in [d]^*$. Clearly, we have $t \in L$ and $t' \notin L$. On the other hand, the previous induction shows that $t_k \in L(\varphi)$ iff $t'_k \in L(\varphi)$. Thus, $L(\varphi) \ne L$ contradicting the assumption. $\qquad\qquad\square$

14.3.2 Fixpoint Quantifiers

The previous theorem shows that it is debatable whether ML should be considered as a logic for infinite trees since every formula can only assess the first k levels of a tree for some fixed k. One may argue that ML is therefore rather a logic for finite trees, especially since the interpretation of the modal operators goes well with trees that appear to be too shallow: a formula $\Diamond\varphi$, interpreted in a node with no children, would simply evaluate to false, and consequently $\Box\varphi$ would evaluate to true in this case regardless of φ.

However, modal logic is not our primary goal here; that is its extension by fixpoint quantifiers, resulting in the logic known as the modal μ-calculus. It is capable of expressing such properties like the one used in the proof of Thm. 14.20, i.e. fixpoint quantifiers must provide a mechanism for accessing nodes at arbitrary depth in a tree. And then infinite trees are of course a suitable model for the interpretation of such formulas.

In other words, we are searching for a method to extend ML in a generic way so that properties like $\mathrm{EF}p$ become definable. By generic we mean the addition of a small and certainly finite set of operators in order to not just express $\mathrm{EF}p$ but all sorts of other properties that may be useful for program specification purposes. The next fair question is: why not simply take CTL^* which is an extension of ML, cf. Thm. 14.19? One could say that CTL^* results from ML by the addition of an *infinite* set of operators, namely $\mathrm{E}\psi$ for any path formula ψ. Of course some regularity in the syntax is given since path formulas themselves are only built from finitely many operators. However, in the strict sense, it is correct to say that CTL^* achieves higher expressive power through infinitely many operators on the level of formulas that are interpreted in a node of a tree.

The modal μ-calculus, to be introduced in the following, does in fact provide such an extension using only a single operator (and its dual version). It looks like we also have to introduce second-order variables, which could be argued to be an extension by infinitely many operators, but they are in fact already there. They are just not that visible. Take an ML formula φ over some propositions $\mathcal{P} = \{p_1, \ldots, p_n\}$. A model is a tree whose nodes are labelled with subsets of $\mathcal{P}$ or, equivalently, with vectors from $\{0, 1\}^n$ representing subsets of such ordered sets.

This can also be seen as a tree over a singleton alphabet $\{\bullet\}$ whose nodes are *additionally* labelled with such subsets. We also simply write $\mathbf{1}$ for such an alphabet with an anonymous symbol in it. And this change of perspective is of course something that has occurred several times before, in particular when translating MSO formulas with free second-order variables into automata over an extended alphabet, cf. Sect. 2.2.2 for example. So an interpretation $t \in \mathcal{T}_{2^{\mathcal{P}}}^{\omega}$ for an ML formula over $\mathcal{P}$ is nothing more than an interpretation consisting of a tree $t_0 \in \mathcal{T}_1^{\omega}$, namely the tree that is obtained from t by removing all labels, together with an assignment $I : \mathcal{P} \to 2^{dom(t_0)}$. Hence, propositions are nothing more than second-order variables. It is merely a matter of taste that distinguishes them, namely whether they should by interpreted by the labels *in* the tree, or by additional labels *on* the tree. This is no structural difference, though, just one of notation.

Moreover, there is no need to restrict ourselves to the two extremes, i.e. to either regard them all as atomic propositions or all as second-order variables. It is perfectly possible to regard some as propositions and others as variables. In the end, they all have to be interpreted by a set of nodes in a tree for a formula to evaluate to true or false. This is why we extend the syntax of ML by second-order variables from some set $\mathcal{V}_2 = \{X, Y, \ldots\}$ that are treated syntactically just like propositions, i.e. $\Diamond(p \wedge \Box X)$ is an ML formula for example. Note that these variables are in fact *monadic* second-order variables, even though they look like they are 0-ary. But this is only the appearance resulting from the fact that in modal logic, there is always a single anonymous point of reference.

The distinction between propositions p and second-order variables X is only made so that it is clear what interpretation an underlying tree needs to provide, namely values for the propositions p. The interpretation for variables X is supposed to be obtained during the evaluation process, namely through (fixpoint) quantifiers.

We extend the semantics accordingly. A formula φ with second-order variables $X_1, \ldots, X_n$ is interpreted in a tree $t \in \mathcal{T}_{2^{\mathcal{P}}}^{\omega}$ with the aid of an assignment $I : \{X_1, \ldots, X_n\} \to 2^{dom(t)}$ in the usual way:

$$t, I, v \vDash X \quad \text{iff} \quad v \in I(X)$$

Def. 14.17 can easily be rewritten accordingly by passing I recursively through the clauses for subformulas.

The next necessary shift in perspective reveals such formulas with free variables to represent functions on the powerset of the domain of a tree.

Definition 14.21 Let φ be an ML formula over $\mathcal{P}$ and $\mathcal{V}_2$, $X \in \mathcal{V}_2$, $t \in \mathcal{T}_{2^{\mathcal{P}}}^{\omega}$ and $I : \mathcal{V}_2 \to 2^{dom(t)}$. This induces a mapping $[\![\varphi]\!]_I^t : 2^{dom(t)} \to 2^{dom(t)}$ via

$$[\![\varphi]\!]_I^t(U) := \{v \in dom(t) \mid t, I[X \mapsto U], v \vDash \varphi\}$$

where $I[X \mapsto U]$ is the update of I at position X with U, i.e.

$$I[X \mapsto U](Y) \; := \; \begin{cases} U & , \text{ if } Y = X \, , \\ I(Y) & , \text{ otherwise} \end{cases}$$

for all $Y \in \mathcal{V}_2$.

Thus, $[\![\varphi]\!]_I^t$ returns, given a set U, the set of all nodes v in t that satisfy φ, provided that the variable X is interpreted as U. We also write the result of this function, when applied to U, as $[\![\varphi]\!]_{I[X \mapsto U]}^t$.

Such a function is *monotonic* on t if for all $U, U' \subseteq dom(t)$, we have

$$U \subseteq U' \quad \text{implies} \quad [\![\varphi]\!]_{I[X \mapsto U]}^t \subseteq [\![\varphi]\!]_{I[X \mapsto U']}^t \, .$$

ML formulas define monotonic mappings in this respect, at least when the use of the negation symbol is restricted. We say that φ is *positive* in X if all occurrences of X are under an even number of negation symbols in the syntax tree of φ. The proof of the following lemma is by a straightforward induction on the structure of ML formulas. Details are left as an exercise.

Lemma 14.22 *Let φ be an ML formula over $\mathcal{P}$ and $\mathcal{V}_2$, $X \in \mathcal{V}_2$, $t \in \mathcal{T}_{2^\mathcal{P}}^\omega$ and $I : \mathcal{V}_2 \to 2^{dom(t)}$. If φ is positive in X then $U \mapsto [\![\varphi]\!]_{I[X \mapsto U]}^t$ is monotonic.*

In order to let an ML formula φ with a second-order variable X – or rather its associated mapping $U \mapsto [\![\varphi]\!]_{I[X \mapsto U]}^t$ – define properties of nodes in a tree t, such mappings need to give us particular values in terms of some designated set of nodes in a tree. A natural way to obtain a set of nodes from such a mapping is given by *fixpoints*: consider the mapping $U \mapsto [\![\varphi]\!]_{I[X \mapsto U]}^t$ as an equation

$$U \; = \; [\![\varphi]\!]_{I[X \mapsto U]}^t \tag{14.1}$$

for given φ, t, I and X, i.e. as the definition of a set $U \subseteq dom(t)$ that equals $[\![\varphi]\!]_{I[X \mapsto U]}^t$. This immediately raises further questions: do such sets exists? If they are not guaranteed to exist at least for a syntactically definable class of formulas then this mechanism is not good as an extension of ML because it would lead to formulas with undefined truth values. Moreover, even if such values always exist, are they unique? If they can be guaranteed to exist in any case and be unique then this does indeed provide a mechanism for extending ML with certain expressive power as the following example shows. If they exist but are not necessarily unique, then we may have to refine the selection of such values, i.e. let the semantics of these new operators choose certain solutions to equation (14.1).

Example 14.23 Let $\mathcal{P} = \{p\}$ and $\varphi(X, Y) = (p \wedge \Diamond X) \vee \Diamond Y$. Let t be an arbitrary tree over $\Sigma = 2^\mathcal{P}$. For simplicity, we assume its branching degree to be 2. The argument for other values is exactly the same, though.

There are two second-order variables in φ, giving us the two equations

$$U \; = \; [\![(p \wedge \Diamond X) \vee \Diamond Y]\!]_{I[X \mapsto U]}^t \tag{14.2}$$

$$U = [\![(p \wedge \Diamond X) \vee \Diamond Y]\!]^t_{I[Y \mapsto U]} \tag{14.3}$$

for any given mapping $I : \{X, Y\} \to 2^{dom(t)}$. In the first case, it is of course sufficient for I to provide a value for Y but not necessarily for X, and vice-versa in the second case.

We consider the second equation first. We claim that the set

$$Y_{\min} := \{v \in dom(t) \mid \exists wi \in \{0,1\}^+ \text{ s.t. } p \in t(vw) \text{ and } vwi \in I(X)\}$$

consisting of all ancestors of a node that is labelled p and which has a successor belonging to X is in fact a solution to equation (14.3). For this we need to show that $Y_{\min} = [\![(p \wedge \Diamond X) \vee \Diamond Y]\!]^t_{I[Y \mapsto Y_{\min}]}$. For the direction from left to right take a node v and a suffix $wi \in \{0,1\}^+$ witnessing that $v \in Y_0$. We then have $v \in [\![(p \wedge \Diamond X) \vee \Diamond Y]\!]^t_{I[Y \mapsto Y_{\min}]}$ by induction on the length of w. The opposite direction is shown in the same way.

The set $Y_{\min}$ is not the only solution to equation (14.3), though. The set $Y_{\max} := dom(t)$ is also a solution. There are many more; any solution is obtained as the union of $Y_{\min}$ with an arbitrary set of full paths starting in the root of the underlying tree.

So the names $Y_{\min}$ and $Y_{\max}$ are not chosen coincidentally. These are in fact the least and greatest solutions in $2^{dom(t)}$ with sets of nodes partially ordered by the subsumption relation '$\subseteq$', i.e. they are the *least* and *greatest fixpoints* of this equation, depending on I of course. Out of all fixpoints, $Y_{\min}$ stands out as a perhaps particularly interesting one, as it defines exactly the set of nodes which can reach a p-node that has a successor in X. This set is not ML-definable. The property $Y_{\max}$ is of course just the universal property that is already ML-definable by the formula tt.

Now say that equation (14.3) defines the set $Y_{\min}$, still depending on a value for X of course. Consider equation (14.2). The way that X is used in φ is not too dissimilar to the way that Y is used. Hence, the reasoning for finding fixpoints of (14.2) is similar. The smallest fixpoint $X_{\min}$ consists of nodes from which there is a finite path through p-nodes (including the starting node) to an immediate predecessor of a node in Y. The greatest fixpoint is obtained by adding all nodes that lie on a path through p-nodes only.

The solutions to (14.3) depend on a value for X which is supposedly fixed as a solution to (14.2) which depends on a value of Y that, in turn, is getting fixed through equation (14.3). So in order to let formula φ denote a well-defined value, we need not only choose which kind of fixpoint is supposed to be defined for each variable. We also need to impose an order between these two equations. One way of doing so is to take the greatest fixpoint of (14.2) and give this equation priority over (14.3) which is supposed to give a least fixpoint. The largest set $X_{\max}$ that equals $[\![(p \wedge \Diamond X) \vee \Diamond Y]\!]^t_{[X \mapsto X_{\max}, Y \mapsto Y_{\min}]}$ where $Y_{\min}$ is the least set that equals $[\![(p \wedge \Diamond X) \vee \Diamond Y]\!]^t_{I[Y \mapsto Y_{\min}]}$ for any given value of X, is the set of all nodes from which there is a path that visits p-nodes infinitely often.

In order to comprehend the final conclusion in this example, some more fixpoint theory may be needed. The theory of fixpoint approximations is particularly helpful. It states that least fixpoints can be obtained as limits of an iterative process starting from the least set $\varnothing$, and greatest fixpoints can dually be obtained by iterating from above, starting with $dom(t)$. So in order to determine this set defined by a greatest solution for X and a least solution for Y depending on X, one can fix $I(X) = dom(t)$ and determine the least solution $Y^1_{\min}$ of (14.3) under this I. It consists of all nodes that are ancestors of a p-node. Then let $I(X) := Y^1_{\min}$ and determine the least solution of (14.3) again. This yields the set $Y^2_{\min}$ of all nodes from which there is a path visiting at least two p-nodes. The i-th iteration defines the set of all nodes from which there is a path visiting at least i p-nodes. Note that this forms a descending chain of sets of nodes, i.e. every iteration potentially removes nodes. The theory of fixpoint approximations states that the greatest fixpoint of the underlying equation is the limit of this chain, i.e. the set of all nodes that do not get removed in any iteration which is exactly the set of all nodes from which there is a path containing an infinite number of p-nodes.

The example provides some questions to be answered when designing the syntax of an extension of ML by operators for fixpoints of modal equations: we need to state the kinds of fixpoints that are to be selected in each case, and when using multiple second-order variables, the order in which they depend on each other needs to be fixed. Neither is particularly problematic: we introduce two operators μ and ν that syntactically act as quantifiers for second-order variables and provide the distinction between least and greatest fixpoints. The second point is naturally addressed by the subformula order, as it is the case with quantification in MSO for instance: inner quantifiers depend on the values for variables quantified further outside in a formula. The formula $\nu X.\mu Y.(p \wedge \Diamond X) \vee \Diamond Y$ then states "there is a path on which p occurs infinitely often."

14.3.3 Syntax and Semantics

We are using the terms "the least" and "the greatest fixpoint" as if they were always unique. This is in fact the case but it requires a little bit more insight, needed to provide a well-defined semantics for the extension of ML by such quantifiers. We introduce the syntax first as it makes it easier to reason about semantical issues like uniqueness afterwards.

Definition 14.24 Let $\mathcal{P}$ be a set of atomic propositions and $\mathcal{V}_2$ be a set of second-order variables. Formulas of the *modal μ-calculus* $\mathcal{L}_\mu$ are given by

$$\varphi \ ::= \ q \mid X \mid \varphi \vee \varphi \mid \neg\varphi \mid \Diamond\varphi \mid \mu X.\varphi$$

where $q \in \mathcal{P}$ and $X \in \mathcal{V}_2$. Additionally, every formula φ must satisfy the *positivity requirement*: take any subformula $\mu X.\psi$ of φ. Then every occurrence of the variable X must be under an even number of negation symbols inside of ψ.

Apart from the usual other Boolean connectives and the modal operator $\Box$ we introduce the abbreviation $\nu X.\varphi := \neg\mu X.\neg\varphi[\neg X/X]$ where $\varphi[\neg X/X]$ is the formula that results from φ by replacing every free occurrence of X by $\neg X$. Here, μX acts as a binder for the variable X, i.e. occurrences of X under this operator are not free.

It is not strictly necessary but good practice to require that every variable gets bound at most once in a formula.

Example 14.25 Consider

$$\varphi_1 \ := \ \neg\mu X.\neg\mu Y.\neg(\neg p \vee \neg\Diamond\neg X) \vee \Diamond Y \ .$$

It is well-formed in that it satisfies the positivity requirement. However, $\varphi_2 := \neg\mu X.\neg\mu X.\neg(\neg p \vee \neg\Diamond\neg X) \vee \Diamond X$ does not, even though it results from φ_1 by a simple renaming of Y to X. This introduces a new variable capturing, though, and now there are three negation symbols in the syntax tree between the occurrence of X in the left disjunct and the binding operator which is the inner μX. In φ_1, the corresponding binding operator is the outer one, and there are four negation symbols on the corresponding part in the syntax tree, i.e. an even number.

One has to be a bit careful with the introduced abbreviations. First, by using the equivalences $\varphi \wedge \psi \equiv \neg(\neg\varphi \vee \neg\psi)$, $\Box\varphi \equiv \neg\Diamond\neg\varphi$ and $\nu X.\varphi \equiv \neg\mu X.\neg\varphi[\neg X/X]$ to rewrite formulas, one only introduces or removes an even number of negation symbols on every syntax path between a variable and its binder. Hence, it does not matter whether the positivity requirement is demanded within the original syntax or in the extended syntax with abbreviations. Take, for instance, $\varphi_1' := \nu X.\mu Y.(p \wedge \Diamond X) \vee \Diamond Y$ which results from φ_1 by strict introduction of the abbreviations ν and $\wedge$ wherever possible. It clearly satisfies the positivity requirement because it does not contain any negation symbols at all. When rewriting φ_2 in the same way we obtain $\varphi_2' := \nu X.\mu X.(p \wedge \Diamond\neg X) \vee \Diamond X$ which does not satisfy the positivity requirement because it contains one negation symbol on a path between a variable and its binder.

Likewise, one must not discount hidden negations in abbreviations like '$\rightarrow$'.

The reason for the positivity requirement is monotonicity of the semantic function associated with a formula containing a free variable. In order to formulate this precisely, we need to give semantics to formulas of $\mathcal{L}_\mu$, and in order to appeal to the rather vague statement of $\mu X.\varphi$ denoting "the least set of nodes that solves the equation $X = \varphi(X)$" (which would somehow rely on the introduction of the mentioned function) we present a fundamental result in fixpoint theory known as the *Knaster-Tarski Theorem* (Prop. 14.27 below). It allows us to specify least and greatest solutions of such equations concisely.

Recall that a *lattice* is a partial order $(M, \leq)$ in which infima $x \sqcap y$ and suprema $x \sqcup y$ exist for all $x, y \in M$. By associativity, distributivity and idempotence of $\sqcap$ and $\sqcup$, infima $\bigsqcap N$ and suprema $\bigsqcap N$ exist for all *finite* $N \subseteq M$. The lattice $(M, \leq)$ is *complete* if infima and suprema also exist for arbitrary subsets, in particular infinite ones. It is a standard exercise to show that powersets form complete lattices.

Lemma 14.26 *Let M be an arbitrary set. Then $(2^M, \subseteq)$ is a complete lattice with infima and suprema given by $\cap$ and $\cup$, resp. $\bigcap$ and $\bigcup$.*

An example of an incomplete lattice is the set of all *finite* subsets of an infinite set. Let $2_{\text{fin}}^{\mathbb{N}} := \{N \subseteq \mathbb{N} \mid |N| < \infty\}$. Then $(2_{\text{fin}}^{\mathbb{N}}, \subseteq)$ is a lattice but it is not complete.

The following proposition is known as the *Knaster-Tarski Theorem*.

Proposition 14.27 *Let $(M, \leq)$ be a complete lattice, $f : M \to M$ be monotonic, i.e. $f(x) \leq f(y)$ whenever $x \leq y$ for arbitrary $x, y \in M$.*

a) f has a unique least fixpoint μf and a unique greatest fixpoint νf.
b) We have $\mu f = \bigsqcap\{x \in M \mid f(x) \leq x\}$ and $\nu f = \bigsqcup\{x \in M \mid x \leq f(x)\}$.

We can now use Lemma 14.26 and Prop. 14.27 in order to give formulas of $\mathcal{L}_\mu$ a well-defined meaning when interpreted in nodes of a tree $t \in \mathcal{T}_\Sigma^\omega$ for a ranked alphabet Σ of the form $2^{\mathcal{P}}$. The set giving rise to a powerset lattice according to Lemma 14.26 is just $dom(t)$.

Definition 14.28 Let $\mathcal{P}$ be given and $\Sigma := 2^{\mathcal{P}}$ be ranked with $d = rk_\Sigma(a)$ for all $a \subseteq \mathcal{P}$. Let $t \in \mathcal{T}_\Sigma^\omega$. The denotation $[\![\varphi]\!]_I^t$ of an $\mathcal{L}_\mu$ formula φ over $\mathcal{P}$ and some $\mathcal{V}_2$ in t under a variable assignment $I : \mathcal{V}_2 \to 2^{dom(t)}$ is defined inductively as follows.

$$
\begin{aligned}
[\![q]\!]_I^t &:= \{v \in dom(t) \mid q \in t(v)\} \\
[\![X]\!]_I^t &:= I(X) \\
[\![\varphi \vee \psi]\!]_I^t &:= [\![\varphi]\!]_I^t \cup [\![\psi]\!]_I^t \\
[\![\neg\varphi]\!]_I^t &:= dom(t) \setminus [\![\varphi]\!]_I^t \\
[\![\Diamond\varphi]\!]_I^t &:= \{v \in dom(t) \mid \exists i < d \text{ s.t. } vi \in [\![\varphi]\!]_I^t\} \\
[\![\mu X.\varphi]\!]_I^t &:= \bigcap\{V \subseteq dom(t) \mid [\![\varphi]\!]_{I[X \mapsto V]}^t \subseteq V\}
\end{aligned}
$$

Here, $I[X \mapsto V]$ denotes the variable interpretation that maps X to V and Y to $I(Y)$ for any $Y \neq X$.

We also write $t, v, I \vDash \varphi$ if $v \in [\![\varphi]\!]_I^t$. Since $[\![\varphi]\!]_I^t$ only depends on the I-values of the free variables in φ, we also simply write $t, v \vDash \varphi$ instead of $t, v, [\,] \vDash \varphi$ for closed formulas φ.

While the path to a semantics for $\mathcal{L}_\mu$ via the Knaster-Tarski Theorem avoids problems with ill-defined formulas, it does not provide a way to easily grasp the meaning of such formulas. An easier grasp of intuition is obtained when defining the semantics via parity games, as it is done with the acceptance games for tree automata. The two ways are equivalent, i.e. formulas denote the same sets of nodes under both semantics. The game-theoretic semantics, however, comes with an increased difficulty to argue that satisfiability is decidable which is almost trivial for the denotational semantics, see below. This is why we stick to the denotational semantics and aid the intuition for reading formulas by stating that least fixpoints should be read as necessarily terminating recursion, and greatest fixpoints as potentially infinite recursion. This is also reflected in another general theorem from the theory of fixpoints, known as *Kleene's Fixpoint Theorem*.

A *chain* in a partial order $(M, \leq)$ is a sequence $x_0 < x_1 < x_2 < \ldots$ of elements from M. Its length is measured using ordinal numbers in general. The *height* of a lattice is the supremum of the length of any chain in it. The Kleene Fixpoint Theorem then entails that the least fixpoint of a monotone function $f : M \to M$ on a complete lattice of height at most ω can be obtained as the limit of the sequence $\bot, f(\bot), f(f(\bot)), \ldots$ where $\bot$ is the least element of M.

Proposition 14.29 *Let $(M, \leq)$ be a complete lattice of height at most ω, $f : M \to M$ monotonic. Then $\bigsqcup_{i \geq 0} f^i(\bot)$ is the least fixpoint of f where $f^0(\bot) := \bot$ and $f^{i+1}(\bot) := f(f^i(\bot))$.*

The scenario that we are in does not strictly meet these criteria: for a tree $t \in \mathcal{T}_\Sigma^\omega$, the height of the complete lattice $(2^{dom(t)}, \subseteq)$ is generally more than ω. However, one can show that, for any $\mathcal{L}_\mu$ formula $\varphi(X)$ with a free variable X and every *finitely branching* tree t, the limit of the chain $V_0 \subseteq V_1 \subseteq V_2 \subseteq \ldots$ of length at most ω, where $V_0 := \varnothing$ and $V_{i+1} := [\![\varphi]\!]^t_{I[X \mapsto V_i]}$, is the least fixpoint of the mapping $V \mapsto [\![\varphi]\!]^t_{I[X \mapsto V]}$. The i-th element of this chain is also known as the i-th *approximant* of the fixpoint at the limit.

This iterative approach can be used to understand the meaning of formulas.

Example 14.30 Let $\mathcal{P} = \{q, \ldots\}$. The language of all trees that contain a q-node is definable in $\mathcal{L}_\mu$ via $\mu X.q \vee \Diamond X$. To see that this is indeed the case, consider an arbitrary tree t over $2^\mathcal{P}$ and the approximants $V_0, V_1, \ldots$ for this fixpoint formula. We have $V_0 = \varnothing$ by definition and then $V_1 := [\![q \vee \Diamond X]\!]^t_{[X \mapsto \varnothing]} = [\![q \vee \Diamond ff]\!]^t_{[]}$. Since $\Diamond ff \equiv ff$ and $q \vee ff \equiv q$ we get that V_1 consists of exactly the set of q-nodes in $dom(t)$.

Then consider $V_2 := [\![q \vee \Diamond X]\!]^t_{[X \mapsto V_1]}$. Since V_1 is clearly defined by the formula q, we also have $V_2 = [\![q \vee \Diamond q]\!]^t_{[]}$, so V_2 consists of all nodes that satisfy q or have an immediate successor that satisfies q. We write $[]$ for the empty variable assignment which is clearly sufficient to interpret formulas with no free variables. Note also that $V_2 = V_1 \cup [\![\Diamond q]\!]^t_{[]}$ which is not a surprise since the approximants are bound to form an ascending chain.

This can be iterated to reveal that V_i consists of all nodes which satisfy q or have a successor which satisfies q or itself has a successor, and so on. Likewise, V_i extends V_{i+1} by those nodes which reside $i - 1$ levels above a q-node. In other words, V_i consists of those nodes from which a q-node can be reached in at most $i - 1$ steps.

The limit of the chain $V_0 \subseteq V_1 \subseteq V_2 \subseteq \ldots$ is $V^* := \bigcup_{i \geq 0} V_i$, consisting of all nodes in t from which a q-node is reachable. According to the Kleene Fixpoint Theorem, it coincides with $[\![\mu X.q \vee \Diamond X]\!]^t_{[]}$. Hence, when interpreted in the root of t, $\mu X.q \vee \Diamond X$ states that some node in t must be a q-node.

Now consider $\nu X.q \vee \Diamond X$. Greatest fixpoints can equally be approximated, starting from the lattice's top element and forming a descending chain. So here we start with $V_0 := dom(t)$. Then $V_1 := [\![q \vee \Diamond X]\!]^t_{[X \mapsto dom(t)]} = [\![q \vee \Diamond tt]\!]^t_{[]}$. So V_1 consists of all nodes that satisfy q or have a successor. Since every node in an infinite tree – at least according to the tree model considered here – has a successor, we have $\Diamond tt \equiv tt$ over the class of ranked trees with non-zero ranks, and $q \vee tt \equiv tt$ anyway, so $V_1 = dom(t) = V_0$, and the greatest fixpoint is reached with the 0-th approximant already. In other words, $\nu X.q \vee \Diamond X \equiv tt$.

A non-trivial property is expressed by $\nu X.q \wedge \Diamond X$. We start with $V_0 = dom(t)$. Then $V_1 = [\![q \wedge \Diamond X]\!]^t_{[X \mapsto V_0]} = [\![q]\!]^t_{[]}$, i.e. V_1 consists of all q-nodes as well, as in the case of the approximation for $\mu X.q \vee \Diamond X$. However, the next approximant already differs. We have $V_2 = [\![q \wedge \Diamond X]\!]^t_{[X \mapsto V_1]} = [\![q \wedge \Diamond q]\!]^t_{[]}$ consisting of all q-nodes that have a q-successor. Iterating this reveals that V_i consists of all nodes from which there is a path of $i + 1$ successive q-nodes. The limit here is the infimum over all approximants, i.e. $V^* := \bigcap_{i \geq 0} V_i$, and it should be clear that exactly the nodes from which there is an infinite path of q-nodes, belong to all V_i, i.e. to the greatest fixpoint. Hence, $\nu X.q \wedge \Diamond X$ states "there is an infinite path of q-nodes."

The formulas considered in the previous example are simple in the sense that they only contain a single fixpoint operator. The principles can equally be applied to form approximants for fixpoint subformulas in a formula containing potentially several fixpoint operators. This requires a bit more bookkeeping, though, which does not necessarily help the acquisition of the correct intuition about what properties are expressed by which formulas. Especially when fixpoint alternation comes into play – the nesting of fixpoints of different kinds – this gets trickier, not only from a pragmatic point of view but also algorithmically.

Take for instance a formula $\varphi(X,Y)$ with two free variables. Then $\nu X.\mu Y.\varphi(X,Y)$ and $\mu X.\nu Y.\varphi(X,Y)$ do not express the same property in general, see also Ex. 14.23. Take $\nu X.\mu Y.\varphi(X,Y)$. The way to build approximants for the fixpoints is then to start with the initial value for the variable X of the *outer* fixpoint, carry out a whole iteration for the inner fixpoint with Y, starting from its initial value $\varnothing$. The limit then determines the first approximant for the outer X. With this new value for X, one has to carry out a whole fixpoint iteration for the inner one again.

Example 14.31 Reconsider the formula $\varphi := \nu X.\mu Y.(q \wedge \Diamond X) \vee \Diamond Y$ from Ex. 14.23, proclaiming the existence of a path with infinitely many q-nodes.

The first inner iteration for Y with a fixed interpretation of X as tt yields the set of all nodes which can reach a q-node. Note that $(q \wedge \Diamond \mathsf{tt}) \vee \Diamond Y \equiv q \vee \Diamond Y$ over models in which every node has a successor. In the second iteration, we recompute the inner least fixpoint with a value of X fixed to that set. This yields the set of all nodes from which a q-node is reachable that has a successor belonging to the set constructed in the previous iteration. I.e. we get the set of all nodes from which there is a path containing two q-nodes. The limit of this construction then yields the set of all nodes from which there is a path containing infinitely many q-nodes.

A result known as the *Bekić Lemma* gives a shortcut through such a nested iteration when the fixpoints are of the same kind. This does not carry over to alternations between least and greatest fixpoints for which these iterations need to be nested.

One can also regard this iterative process as running through the formula recursively. A greatest fixpoint variable can be seen infinitely often, but the recursion through a least fixpoint variable needs to terminate at some point. However, when checking whether a given node in a given tree satisfies a formula like $\nu X.\mu Y.(q \wedge \Diamond X) \vee \Diamond Y$ by tracing which parts are satisfied and forming a path stepwise, one ultimately recurses through X and Y infinitely often in general. It is then the outermost fixpoint variable that determines whether the formula is satisfied or not. The reason simply is that the recursion of the outermost one corresponds to one fixpoint iteration, whereas the infinitely many occurrences of the inner one, interrupted infinitely often by the outer one, correspond to infinitely many terminating fixpoint iterations for the inner one.

This intuition is reminiscent of a parity condition. In fact, it is possible to define acceptance games, also known as *model checking games*, for determining whether a given tree satisfies a given $\mathcal{L}_\mu$ formula. These games are special parity games.

14.3.4 Decidability

Decidability of the satisfiability problem for $\mathcal{L}_\mu$ is less obvious without some deeper insights provided by the theory of fixpoints, in particular the Knaster-Tarski Theorem. It enables the formulation of the semantics of $\mathcal{L}_\mu$ formulas like $\mu X.\varphi$ as second-order properties. Note that a formulation along the lines of "node v belongs to the least fixpoint of the function derived from φ" is not a (monadic) second-order property because it quantifies over functions.

Theorem 14.32 *Let $\mathcal{P}$ be given and $\Sigma := 2^{\mathcal{P}}$. For every $\mathcal{L}_\mu$ formula φ over $\mathcal{P}$ there is an MSO formula Φ over Σ such that $L(\Phi) = L(\varphi)$ and $|\Phi| = \mathcal{O}|\varphi|$.*

Proof As in the case of the temporal logic CTL*, whose formulas are also interpreted in given nodes in a tree, we first translate every $\mathcal{L}_\mu$ formula φ into an MSO formula $tr_x(\varphi)$ with a free variable x such that $t, v, I \models \varphi$ iff $t, I[x \mapsto v] \models tr_x(\varphi)$ for any $t \in \mathcal{T}_\Sigma^\omega$, and $v \in dom(t)$ and any assignment $I : \mathcal{V}_2 \to 2^{dom(t)}$. Hence, the MSO formula $tr_x(\varphi)$ uses the same second-order variables as φ. It uses additional first-order variables of which exactly one is free.

$$
\begin{aligned}
tr_x(q) &:= \bigvee_{\substack{a \subseteq \mathcal{P} \\ q \in a}} a(x) \\[1em]
tr_x(X) &:= X(x) \\
tr_x(\varphi \vee \psi) &:= tr_x(\varphi) \vee tr_x(\psi) \\
tr_x(\neg\varphi) &:= \neg tr_x(\varphi) \\
tr_x(\Diamond\varphi) &:= \exists y. \bigvee_{i=0}^{d-1} succ_i(x, y) \wedge tr_y(\varphi) \\
tr_x(\mu X.\varphi) &:= \forall X.\big(\forall y. tr_y(\varphi) \to X(y)\big) \to X(x)
\end{aligned}
$$

The fact that $tr_x(\varphi)$ is correct according to the requirement outlined above, is immediate since the translation tr_x only formulates the semantics of an $\mathcal{L}_\mu$ formula in MSO. The last clause makes use of Prop. 14.27. Moreover, for a fixed set $\mathcal{P}$, the translation also clearly incurs a linear blowup only. $\qquad\square$

Consequently, decidability for MSO over trees carries over to $\mathcal{L}_\mu$.

Corollary 14.33 *The satisfiability, validity and equivalence problems for $\mathcal{L}_\mu$ are decidable.*

As with CTL*, the embedding into MSO does not yield an optimal decision procedure. Formulas of $\mathcal{L}_\mu$ with nested least and greatest fixpoints clearly lead to MSO formulas with unbounded nestings between universal quantifiers and negation or, equivalently, universal and existential quantifiers, leading to a non-elementary upper bound only. However, satisfiability (and the other problems) for $\mathcal{L}_\mu$ can in fact be decided in singly exponential time. This requires some deeper insights, though, for instance on the automata side via alternating tree automata.

Proposition 14.34 *The satisfiability, validity and equivalence problems for $\mathcal{L}_\mu$ are decidable in exponential time.*

Again, this is optimal; these problems are complete for ExpTime.

Bibliographic Notes

For reference to work on MSO over trees, also known as SnS – the *Second-Order Logic of n Successor Relations* – see the bibliographic notes of the previous chapter since work on MSO is tightly linked to tree automata. In particular, Rabin's celebrated decidability proof for this logic [Rab69] is one of the cornerstones of the automata-logic connection.

The full branching-time temporal logic CTL* was proposed by Emerson and Halpern [EH86] as a means to unify two kinds of temporal logics with incomparable expressiveness and different complexities: the linear-time temporal logic LTL with PSpace-complete model checking and satisfiability checking problems [SC85, LP00] on one hand, capable of expressing fairness properties for example; and Clarke and Emerson's branching-time temporal logic CTL on the other hand with polynomial-time model checking [EC82, CES86] but an ExpTime-complete satisfiability problem and without the ability to express fairness [EH85].

The fact that satisfiability for CTL* is decidable was readily seen. It is an easy exercise to show that CTL* has the tree model property and that it can be embedded into the decidable logic MSO over trees. However, this only gives a non-elementary decision procedure. An optimal, doubly exponential one was found by Emerson and Sistla [EJ00] using a direct translation into tree automata. Prop. 14.14 was proved by them to establish correctness of such a translation.

The search for an elementary decision procedure for CTL* did not arrive at an optimal one straight away. At that time, only McNaughton's doubly exponential determinisation procedure for Büchi automata was available [McN66]. Emerson und Sistla showed that the particular automata needed in a decision procedure for CTL* could be determinised at a singly exponential blowup only, leading to a triply exponential decision procedure for CTL* [ES84b]. An improved emptiness test for tree automata [EJ00] then results in a doubly exponential procedure only.

It is possible to replace the perhaps sometimes too rigid framework of tree automata in a decision procedure for a logic like CTL* by more flexible tableaux [FLL10], or to formulate the satisfiability problem directly in terms of two-player games [FLL13]. Both approaches still rely on determinisation for ω-word automata, though, and do not differ in essence from a direct approach via tree automata.

Doubly exponential time had been established as a lower bound by Vardi and Stockmeyer earlier already [VS85], showing that the integration of the entire linear-time temporal logic LTL into CTL does genuinely increase the latter's complexity. This is perhaps not too surprising, but the lower bound already holds for the fragment known as CTL$^+$ [JL03] which disallows immediate nestings of temporal operators. This is in fact surprising because the expressive power of CTL$^+$ does not exceed that of CTL [EH85], unlike the case of CTL*. So the increase in complexity from the branching-time temporal logic CTL to the full branching-time temporal logic CTL* is not owed to an increase in expressiveness but an exponential increase in succinctness, i.e. the need for exponentially sized formulas expressing certain properties in CTL that can be expressed in CTL$^+$ using formulas of (low) polynomial size. The literature contains at least three different proofs for the succinctness gap between CTL$^+$ and CTL [Wil99b, Lan08, AI03].

Temporal logics, including CTL*, are also extensively covered, regarding questions of computational complexity, expressive power and their model theory, in a handbook article by Emerson [Eme90], and in textbooks on model checking [CGK$^+$18, BK08] or solely on temporal logics themselves with branching-time temporal logics either featured extensively [DGL16] or just briefly [KM08].

The modal μ-calculus in the form presented here was proposed by Kozen [Koz83] under the name *propositional μ-calculus*, building on earlier proposals by Park [Par70] and de Bakker and de Roever [dBdR72]. The different terminology is simply used, then, to distinguish it from logics over non-finite data like arithmetic for example, whereas the name "modal μ-calculus" emphasises the extension of modal logic in it.

The Knaster-Tarski Theorem (Prop. 14.27) was first proved by Knaster [Kna28] for the special case of powerset lattices only, and then later by Tarski [Tar55] for general complete lattices. A proof can be found in Winskel's textbook on programming language semantics for example [Win93].

Kleene proved his Fixpoint Theorem in a more general form than stated here for complete lattices and monotone functions (Prop. 14.29), namely for complete partial orders and Scott-continuous functions. The exact origin in the literature amongst Kleene's work is hard to trace. A precise formulation and proof can be found in a textbook on domain theory for example [SLG94].

A formulation and proof of the Bekić Lemma can be found in a collection of Bekić's work [Bek84].

The parity games that characterise the model checking, resp. acceptance problem for $\mathcal{L}_\mu$ were formulated by Stirling [Sti95].

Decidability of the satisfiability problem for the modal μ-calculus over trees was easily seen, precisely for the simple translation into MSO due to the Knaster-Tarski characterisation of fixpoints. As with CTL*, this is not optimal as it yields

a non-elementary decision procedure only. Again, an optimal upper bound had
been found after some intermediate progress [SE89, KP83], by Emerson and Jutla
[EJ00] with an automata-theoretic decision procedure that runs in singly exponential
time. It is based on alternating tree automata [MS87] which have not been covered
here explicitly. The concept of alternation can straightforwardly be lifted to tree
automata, though. Formulas of the modal μ-calculus can also straightforwardly be
translated into alternating tree automata. The core of a decision procedure then lies
in a translation into nondeterministic tree automata [MS95] for which non-emptiness
can be decided, cf. Thm. 13.33. The key is to limit the blowup in the translation to an
at most exponential one [EJ00] which then results in a singly exponential procedure
overall. This is optimal. The satisfiability problem for Propositional Dynamic Logic
[FL79, HKT00], which can easily be embedded linearly into $\mathcal{L}_\mu$, was shown to be
hard for the class EXPTIME by Fischer and Ladner [FL79].

The translation from μ-calculus formulas into alternating tree automata is not
reversible. This is simply due to the fact that tree automata can see the order and
multiplicity of successor nodes. A restriction of tree automata that is oblivious to
this and then corresponds exactly to $\mathcal{L}_\mu$ in expressive power is given by so-called
symmetric tree automata [Wil01]. The technical term for the equivalence relation
behind this is *bisimilarity*, a formal concept of program equivalence studied by
Milner [Mil80]. A celebrated result on the expressive power of $\mathcal{L}_\mu$ states that every
MSO property which is bisimulation-invariant can be expressed in $\mathcal{L}_\mu$, shown by
Janin and Walukiewicz [JW96]. This lifts a result known as the *van Benthem-Rosen-
Theorem* [vB76, Ros97] for the first-order world, stating ML captures exactly the
bisimulation-invariant properties definable in FO, see also some overview articles
on this topic [vB84, GO07].

For a further view onto the connection between the modal μ-calculus and tree
automata see also the corresponding chapter [Zap02] in the collection [GTW02].

The concept of fixpoint alternation has been studied at great depth. The most
accepted way to measure the entanglement between fixpoints is the one proposed
by Niwiński [Niw97], but there is also the weaker one by Emerson and Lei [EL86].
Bradfield has shown that the alternation hierarchy is strict [Bra98a], i.e. more fixpoint
alternation properly gives higher expressive power. This also holds over trees [Arn99,
Bra99]. See also the bibliographic notes for Chp. 13 which contains a few more
references and explanations.

The modal μ-calculus is also studied in detail in two handbook articles by Bradfield and Stirling [BS01b, BS07], a survey by Lenzi [Len05], a textbook on the logic
itself by Arnold and Niwiński [AN01], and chapters in textbooks on temporal logics
[DGL16], reactive systems [GM14] or model checking [CGK$^+$18].

A question that may arise with the introduction of two logics, CTL* and $\mathcal{L}_\mu$,
that can both be embedded into MSO over infinite trees, is concerned with their
expressive power relative to one another. An immediate consequence of the fact that
CTL*-definable properties are bisimulation-invariant and the Janin-Walukiewicz
result mentioned above, is the fact that CTL* can be embedded into $\mathcal{L}_\mu$. A direct
and effective translation has been given by Dam for instance [Dam94].

Exercises

Exercise 151 Write down an MSO formula $\varphi(X)$ over an arbitrary ranked alphabet Σ and with a free second-order variable X such that $t, I \models \varphi$ iff $|\mathcal{I}(X)|$ is finite and even, for an arbitrary Σ-tree t.

Exercise 152 Write down MSO formulas with suitable free variables that formalise the following properties.

a) Node y is right of node x, i.e. it has an ancestor that is a sibling to the right of x.
b) Every path contains finitely many symbols a only.

Exercise 153 Prove Thm. 14.3.

Exercise 154 Determine for each pair of the following four CTL* formulas over propositions $p_1, \ldots, p_n$ whether or not they are equivalent. In case they are not, construct a tree that separates them in the sense that it is a model of one but not the other, and determine whether one of them implies the other, i.e. whether an implication either way is valid.

$$\bigwedge_{i=1}^{n} \mathsf{AGF} p_i \;, \qquad \mathsf{A} \bigwedge_{i=1}^{n} \mathsf{GF} p_i \;, \qquad \mathsf{AG} \bigwedge_{i=1}^{n} \mathsf{F} p_i \;, \qquad \mathsf{AGF} \bigwedge_{i=1}^{n} p_i$$

Exercise 155 Consider the two trees t, t' from Ex. 14.15. Show that $t \models \varphi$ iff $t' \models \varphi$ for all CTL* state formulas φ. *Hint:* This can be done by induction on the structure of formulas but the statement needs to be generalised. Find a relation $R \subseteq dom(t) \times dom(t')$ such that whenever $(v, v') \in R$ then $t[v] \models \varphi$ iff $t'[v'] \models \varphi$ for an arbitrary state formula φ where $t[v]$ denotes the subtree of t rooted at v etc. Generalise this suitably for path formulas as well.

Exercise 156 Let t be a tree over some Σ, $v \in dom(t)$, $d := rk_\Sigma(t(v)) > 1$ and $\sigma : [d] \to [d]$ be a permutation such that the subtrees $t[vi]$ and $t[v\sigma(i)]$ are not isomorphic for at least some $i \in [d]$.

Let t' result from t by applying the permutation σ to the children of node v, i.e. $dom(t') = dom(t)$ but

$$t'(u) \;=\; \begin{cases} t(u\sigma(i)w) & \text{, if } u = viw \text{ for some } i \in [d], w \in \mathbb{N}^* \\ t(u) & \text{, otherwise} \end{cases}$$

for all $u \in dom(t')$.

Construct an MSO sentence φ such that $t \models \varphi$ and $t' \not\models \varphi$ or vice-versa. Can φ be formalised in FO already?

Hint: First show that for every pair of non-isomorphic trees there is a formula $\psi(x)$ that distinguishes the two when x is mapped to their respective root nodes.

Exercise 157 Is the formula $\varphi_0 \wedge \varphi_1 \wedge \varphi_2$ given in Ex. 14.9 satisfiable? If so, construct a model for it.

Exercise 158 Prove or refute the following statements for CTL*, resp. $\mathcal{L}_\mu$ formulas φ and $d \in \mathbb{N}$.

a) If φ is satisfiable in the class of trees of branching degree d then it is also satisfiable in the class of trees of branching-degree $d + 1$.
b) If φ is satisfiable in the class of trees of branching degree $d + 1$ then it is also satisfiable in the class of trees of branching-degree d.

Exercise 159 Prove Thm. 14.19.

Exercise 160 Prove Lemma 14.22.

Exercise 161   a) Prove Lemma 14.26.
b) Show that $(2^{\mathbb{N}}_{\text{fin}}, \subseteq)$ is incomplete as a lattice.

Exercise 162 Show that $\nu X . \varphi$ does indeed define the greatest fixpoint of the mapping induced by $\varphi(X)$, i.e. show that

$$[\![\nu X . \varphi]\!]^t_I \;=\; \bigcup \{V \subseteq dom(t) \mid V \subseteq [\![\varphi]\!]^t_I\}$$

for any tree t and any variable assignment I.

Exercise 163 What properties of nodes are being expressed by the following $\mathcal{L}_\mu$ formulas?

a) $\mu X . X$
b) $\nu X . X$
c) $\mu X . \Diamond X$
d) $\mu X . q \vee \Box X$

Index

References

[AB00]   A. Ayari and D. Basin. Bounded model construction for monadic second-order logics. In *Proc. 12th Conf. on Computer Aided Verification, CAV'00*, volume 1855 of *Lect. Notes in Comp. Sci.*, pages 99–112. Springer, 2000.

[ACC⁺10]   P. A. Abdulla, Y.-F. Chen, L. Clemente, L. Holík, C.-D. Hong, R. Mayr, and T. Vojnar. Simulation subsumption in Ramsey-based Büchi automata universality and inclusion testing. In *Proc. 22nd Conf. on Computer Aided Verification, CAV'10*, volume 6174 of *Lect. Notes in Comp. Sci.*, pages 132–147. Springer, 2010.

[ACC⁺11]   P. A. Abdulla, Y.-F. Chen, L. Clemente, L. Holík, C.-D. Hong, R. Mayr, and T. Vojnar. Advanced Ramsey-based Büchi automata inclusion testing. In *Proc. 22nd Conf. on Concurrency Theory, CONCUR'11*, volume 6901 of *Lect. Notes in Comp. Sci.*, pages 187–202. Springer, 2011.

[AF17]   D. Avis and O. Friedmann. An exponential lower bound for Cunningham's rule. *Math. Progr.*, 161(1-2):271–305, 2017.

[AHU83]   A. V. Aho, J. E. Hopcroft, and J. D. Ullman. *Data Structures and Algorithms*. Comp. Sci. and Inform. Proc. Addison-Wesley, 1st edition, 1983.

[AI01]   M. Adler and N. Immerman. An $n!$ lower bound on formula size. In *Proc. 16th Symp. on Logic in Computer Science, LICS'01*, pages 197–208. IEEE, 2001.

[AI03]   M. Adler and N. Immerman. An $n!$ lower bound on formula size. *ACM Trans. Comput. Logic*, 4(3):296–314, 2003. Cf. [AI01].

[AN01]   A. Arnold and D. Niwiński. *Rudiments of μ-calculus*, volume 146 of *Studies in Logic and the Foundations of Mathematics*. North-Holland, 2001.

[ANP21]   A. Arnold, D. Niwinski, and P. Parys. A quasi-polynomial black-box algorithm for fixed point evaluation. In *Proc. 29th Conf. on Computer Science Logic, CSL'21*, volume 183 of *LIPIcs*, pages 9:1–9:23. Schloss Dagstuhl - Leibniz-Zentrum für Informatik, 2021.

[Ard60]   D. N. Arden. Delayed logic and finite state machines. In *Theory of Computing Machine Design*, pages 1–35. U. of Michigan Press, Ann Arbor, 1960.

[Arn99]   A. Arnold. The modal μ-calculus alternation hierarchy is strict on binary trees. *RAIRO Theor. Inform. Appl.*, 33:329–339, 1999.

[AU71]   A.V. Aho and J.D. Ullman. Translations on a context free grammar. *Inform. Control*, 19(5):439–475, 1971.

[Bar85]   H. P. Barendregt. *The λ-calculus - its syntax and semantics*, volume 103 of *Studies in logic and the foundations of mathematics*. North-Holland, 1985.

[BB89]   B. Banieqbal and H. Barringer. Temporal logic with fixed points. In *Proc. Coll. on Temporal Logic in Specification*, volume 398 of *Lect. Notes in Comp. Sci.*, pages 62–73. Springer, 1989.

[BCJ$^+$97] A. Browne, E. M. Clarke, S. Jha, D. E. Long, and W. Marrero. An improved algorithm for the evaluation of fixpoint expressions. *Theor. Comp. Sci.*, 178(1–2):237–255, 1997. Cf. [LBC$^+$94].

[BDM20] M. Benerecetti, D. Dell'Erba, and F. Mogavero. Robust worst cases for parity games algorithms. *Inform. Comp.*, 272:104501, 2020.

[BE58] J. Büchi and C. C. Elgot. Decision problems of weak second order arithmetics and finite automata, Part I. *Notices Amer. Math. Soc.*, 5:834, 1958.

[Bek84] H. Bekić. *Programming Languages and Their Definition, Selected Papers*, volume 177 of *LNCS*. Springer, 1984.

[Ber79] J. Berstel. *Transductions and context-free languages*. Teubner, Stuttgart, 1979.

[Ber80] L. Berman. The complexity of logical theories. *Theor. Comp. Sci.*, 11(1):71–77, 1980.

[BFH05] D. Bustan, D. Fisman, and J. Havlicek. Automata constructions for PSL. Technical Report MCS05-04, The Weizmann Inst. of Science, 2005.

[BFL14] F. Bruse, M. Falk, and M. Lange. The fixpoint-iteration algorithm for parity games. In *Proc. 5th Symp. on Games, Automata, Logics and Formal Verification, GandALF'14*, volume 161 of *EPTCS*, pages 116–130, 2014.

[BG00] A. Blumensath and E. Grädel. Automatic structures. In *Proc. 15th Symp. on Logic in Computer Science, LICS'00*, pages 51–62. IEEE, 2000.

[BK08] C. Baier and J.-P. Katoen. *Principles of Model Checking*. MIT Press, 2008.

[BKR10] U. Boker, O. Kupferman, and A. Rosenberg. Alternation removal in Büchi automata. In *Proc. 37th Coll. on Automata, Languages and Programming, ICALP'10*, volume 6199 of *Lect. Notes in Comp. Sci.*, pages 76–87. Springer, 2010.

[BLO12] S. Breuers, C. Löding, and J. Olschewski. Improved Ramsey-based Büchi complementation. In *Proc. 15th Conf. on Foundations of Software Science and Computational Structures, FOSSACS'12*, volume 7213 of *Lect. Notes in Comp. Sci.*, pages 150–164. Springer, 2012.

[BLV96] N. Buhrke, H. Lescow, and J. Vöge. Strategy construction in infinite games with Streett and Rabin chain winning conditions. In *Proc. 2nd Workshop on Tools and Algorithms for Construction and Analysis of Systems, TACAS'96*, volume 1055 of *Lect. Notes in Comp. Sci.*, pages 207–224. Springer, 1996.

[Bok18] U. Boker. Why these automata types? In *Proc. 22nd Conf. on Logic for Programming, A.I. and Reasoning, LPAR'18*, volume 57 of *EPiC Series in Comp.*, pages 143–163. EasyChair, 2018.

[Bra96] J. C. Bradfield. The modal μ-calculus alternation hierarchy is strict. In *Proc. 7th Conf. on Concurrency Theory, CONCUR'96*, volume 1119 of *Lect. Notes in Comp. Sci.*, pages 233–246. Springer, 1996.

[Bra98a] J. C. Bradfield. The modal μ-calculus alternation hierarchy is strict. *Theor. Comput. Sci.*, 195(2):133–153, 1998. Cf. [Bra96].

[Bra98b] J. C. Bradfield. Simplifying the modal μ-calculus alternation hierarchy. In *Proc. 15th Symp. on Theoretical Aspects of Computer Science, STACS'98*, volume 1373 of *Lect. Notes in Comp. Sci.*, pages 39–49. Springer, 1998.

[Bra99] J. C. Bradfield. Fixpoint alternation: Arithmetic, transition systems, and the binary tree. *RAIRO Theor. Inform. Appl.*, 33(4/5):341–356, 1999.

[BS01a] F. Baader and W. Snyder. Unification theory. In *Handbook of Automated Reasoning*, pages 445–532. Elsevier and MIT Press, 2001.

[BS01b] J. Bradfield and C. Stirling. Modal logics and μ-calculi: an introduction. In J. Bergstra, A. Ponse, and S. Smolka, editors, *Handbook of Process Algebra*, pages 293–330. Elsevier, 2001.

[BS07] J. Bradfield and C. Stirling. Modal μ-calculi. In P. Blackburn, J. van Benthem, and F. Wolter, editors, *Handbook of Modal Logic: Studies in Logic and Practical Reasoning Volume 3*, pages 721–756. Elsevier, 2007.

[BSV03] H. Björklund, S. Sandberg, and S. G. Vorobyov. A discrete subexponential algorithm for parity games. In *Proc. 20th Symp. on Theoretical Aspects of Computer Science, STACS'03*, volume 2607 of *Lect. Notes in Comp. Sci.*, pages 663–674. Springer, 2003.

[Büc60]   J. Büchi. Weak second order logic and finite automata. *Z. Math. Logik, Grundlag. Math.*, 5:66–62, 1960.

[Büc62]   J. R. Büchi. On a decision method in restricted second order arithmetic. In *Proc. Congress on Logic, Method, and Philosophy of Science*, pages 1–12, Stanford, CA, USA, 1962. Stanford Univ. Press.

[Büc73]   J. R. Büchi. The monadic second order theory of ω_1. In G. H. Müller and D. Siefkes, editors, *Decidable Theories II: The Monadic Second Order Theory of All Countable Ordinals*, pages 1–127. Springer, 1973.

[BVW94]   O. Bernholtz, M. Y. Vardi, and P. Wolper. An automata-theoretic approach to branching-time model checking. In *Proc. 6th Conf. on Computer Aided Verification, CAV'94*, volume 818 of *Lect. Notes in Comp. Sci.*, pages 142–155. Springer, 1994.

[CDF$^+$19]   W. Czerwinski, L. Daviaud, N. Fijalkow, M. Jurdzinski, R. Lazic, and P. Parys. Universal trees grow inside separating automata: Quasi-polynomial lower bounds for parity games. In *Proc. 30th Symp. on Discrete Algorithms, SODA'19*, pages 2333–2349. SIAM, 2019.

[CDG$^+$07]   H. Comon, M. Dauchet, R. Gilleron, C. Löding, F. Jacquemard, D. Lugiez, S. Tison, and M. Tommasi. Tree automata techniques and applications. Available on: https://inria.hal.science/hal-03367725, 2007. release October, 12th 2007.

[CDHS18]   K. Chatterjee, W. Dvorák, M. Henzinger, and A. Svozil. Quasipolynomial set-based symbolic algorithms for parity games. In *Proc. 22nd Conf. on Logic for Programming, Artificial Intelligence and Reasoning, LPAR-22*, volume 57 of *EPiC Series in Computing*, pages 233–253. EasyChair, 2018.

[CE81]   E. M. Clarke and E. A. Emerson. Design and synthesis of synchronization skeletons using branching-time temporal logic. In *Proc. Workshop on Logics of Programs*, volume 131 of *LNCS*, pages 52–71. Springer, 1981.

[CES83]   E. M. Clarke, E. A. Emerson, and A. P. Sistla. Automatic verification of finite state concurrent systems using temporal logic specifications. In *Proc. 10th Symp. on Principles of Programming Languages, POPL'83*, pages 117–126. ACM, 1983.

[CES86]   E. M. Clarke, E. A. Emerson, and A. P. Sistla. Automatic verification of finite-state concurrent systems using temporal logic specifications. *ACM Trans. Program. Lang. Sys.*, 8(2):244–263, 1986. Cf. [CES83].

[CGK$^+$18]   E. M. Clarke, O. Grumberg, D. Kroening, D. A. Peled, and H. Veith. *Model checking*. MIT Press, 2nd edition, 2018.

[Cho74]   Y. Choueka. Theories of automata on omega-tapes: A simplified approach. *J. Comp. Sys. Sci.*, 8(2):117–141, 1974.

[Chu40]   A. Church. A formulation of the simple theory of types. *J. Symb. Log.*, 5(2):56–68, 1940.

[CJ97]   H. Comon and Y. Jurski. Higher-order matching and tree automata. In *Proc. 11th Conf. on Computer Science Logic, CSL'97*, volume 1414 of *Lect. Notes in Comp. Sci.*, pages 157–176. Springer, 1997.

[CJK$^+$17]   C. S. Calude, S. Jain, B. Khoussainov, W. Li, and F. Stephan. Deciding parity games in quasipolynomial time. In *Proc. 49th Symp. on Theory of Computing, STOC'17*, pages 252–263. ACM, 2017.

[CKS81]   A. K. Chandra, D. C. Kozen, and L. J. Stockmeyer. Alternation. *J. Assoc. Comp. Mach.*, 28(1):114–133, 1981. Cf. [Koz76, CS76].

[Cle90]   R. Cleaveland. Tableau-based model checking in the propositional μ-calculus. *Acta Inform.*, 27(8):725–748, 1990.

[CLRS22]   T. H. Cormen, C. E. Leiserson, R. L. Rivest, and C. Stein. *Introduction to algorithms*. MIT Press, 4th edition, 2022.

[CM10]   L. Clemente and R. Mayr. Multipebble simulations for alternating automata (extended abstract). In *Proc. 21th Conf. on Concurrency Theory, CONCUR'10*, volume 6269 of *Lect. Notes in Comp. Sci.*, pages 297–312. Springer, 2010.

[CNT04]   J. Carme, J. Niehren, and M. Tommasi. Querying unranked trees with stepwise tree automata. In *Proc. 15th Conf. on Rewriting Techniques and Applications, RTA'04*, volume 3091 of *Lect. Notes in Comp. Sci.*, pages 105–118. Springer, 2004.

[CS76]   A. K. Chandra and L. J. Stockmeyer. Alternation. In *Proc. 17th Symp. on Foundations of Computer Science, FOCS'76*, pages 98–108. IEEE, 1976.

[CVW86]   C. Courcoubetis, M. Y. Vardi, and P. Wolper. Reasoning about fair concurrent programs. In *Proc. 18th Symp. on Theory of Computing, STOC'86*, pages 283–294. ACM, 1986.

[CZ09]   T. Colcombet and K. Zdanowski. A tight lower bound for determinization of transition labeled Büchi automata. In *Proc. 36th Coll. on Automata, Languages and Programming, ICALP'09*, volume 5556 of *Lect. Notes in Comp. Sci.*, pages 151–162. Springer, 2009.

[Dam92]   M. Dam. CTL* and ECTL* as fragments of the modal μ-calculus. In *Proc. 17th Coll. on Trees in Algebra and Programming, CAAP'92*, volume 581 of *Lect. Notes in Comp. Sci.*, pages 145–164. Springer, 1992.

[Dam94]   M. Dam. CTL* and ECTL* as fragments of the modal μ-calculus. *Theor. Comp. Sci.*, 126(1):77–96, 1994. Cf. [Dam92].

[Dan60]   G. B. Dantzig. Inductive proof of the simplex method. *IBM J. Res. Dev.*, 4(5):505–506, 1960.

[dBdR72]   J. W. de Bakker and W. P. de Roever. A calculus for recursive program schemes. In M. Nivat, editor, *Proc. IRIA Symp. on Automata, Formal Languages and Programming*. North-Holland, 1972.

[DFH23]   Y. Disser, O. Friedmann, and A. V. Hopp. An exponential lower bound for Zadeh's pivot rule. *Math. Progr.*, 199(1):865–936, 2023. Cf. [Fri11d].

[DG08]   V. Diekert and P. Gastin. First-order definable languages. In J. Flum, E. Grädel, and T. Wilke, editors, *Logic and Automata: History and Perspectives*, Texts in Logic and Games, pages 261–306. Amsterdam Univ. Press, 2008.

[DGL16]   S. Demri, V. Goranko, and M. Lange. *Temporal Logics in Computer Science*. Cambridge Tracts in Theoretical Computer Science. Cambridge Univ. Press, 2016.

[DGPR21]   K. Doveri, P. Ganty, F. Parolini, and F. Ranzato. Inclusion testing of Büchi automata based on well-quasiorders. In *Proc. 32nd Conf. on Concurrency Theory, CONCUR'21*, volume 203 of *LIPIcs*, pages 3:1–3:22. Schloss Dagstuhl - Leibniz-Zentrum für Informatik, 2021.

[DGW24]   K. Doveri, P. Ganty, and C. Weil-Kennedy. A uniform framework for language inclusion problems. In *Taming the Infinities of Concurrency - Essays Dedicated to Javier Esparza on the Occasion of his 60th Birthday*, volume 14660 of *Lect. Notes in Comp. Sci.*, pages 155–171. Springer, 2024.

[DHL06]   C. Dax, M. Hofmann, and M. Lange. A proof system for the linear time μ-calculus. In *Proc. 26th Conf. on Foundations of Software Technology and Theoretical Computer Science, FSTTCS'06*, volume 4337 of *Lect. Notes in Comp. Sci.*, pages 274–285. Springer, 2006.

[Don70]   J. Doner. Tree acceptors and some of their applications. *J. Comp. Sys. Sci.*, 4(5):406–451, 1970.

[Dow01]   G. Dowek. Higher-order unification and matching. In *Handbook of Automated Reasoning*, pages 1009–1062. Elsevier and MIT Press, 2001.

[DR09]   L. Doyen and J.-F. Raskin. Antichains for the automata-based approach to model-checking. *Log. Meth. Comp. Sci.*, 5(1), 2009.

[DR10]   L. Doyen and J.-F. Raskin. Antichain algorithms for finite automata. In *Proc. 16th Conf. on Tools and Algorithms for the Construction and Analysis of Systems, TACAS'10*, volume 6015 of *Lect. Notes in Comp. Sci.*, pages 2–22. Springer, 2010.

[EB23]   J. Esparza and M. Blondin. *Automata Theory – An Algorithmic Approach*. MIT Press, 2023.

[EC82]   E. A. Emerson and E. M. Clarke. Using branching time temporal logic to synthesize synchronization skeletons. *Sci. Comp. Progr.*, 2(3):241–266, 1982. Cf. [CE81].

[EF06] C. Eisner and D. Fisman. *A Practical Introduction to PSL*. Series on Integrated Circuits and Systems. Springer, 2006.

[EH82] E. A. Emerson and J. Y. Halpern. Decision procedures and expressiveness in the temporal logic of branching time. In *Proc. 14th Symp. on Theory of Computing, STOC'82*, pages 169–180. ACM, 1982.

[EH83] E. A. Emerson and J. Y. Halpern. "Sometimes" and "Not never" revisited: On branching versus linear time. In *Proc. 10th Symp. on Principles of Programming Languages, POPL'83*, pages 127–140. ACM, 1983.

[EH85] E. A. Emerson and J. Y. Halpern. Decision procedures and expressiveness in the temporal logic of branching time. *J. Comp. Sys. Sci.*, 30:1–24, 1985. Cf. [EH82].

[EH86] E. A. Emerson and J. Y. Halpern. "Sometimes" and "Not never" revisited: On branching versus linear time temporal logic. *J. Assoc. Comp. Mach.*, 33(1):151–178, 1986. Cf. [EH83].

[Ehr61] A. Ehrenfeucht. An application of games to the completeness problem for formalized theories. *Fund. Math.*, 49:129–141, 1961.

[Eil74] S. Eilenberg. *Automata, languages, and machines. A.* Pure and Applied Math. Academic Press, 1974.

[EJ88] E. A. Emerson and C. S. Jutla. The complexity of tree automata and logics of programs (extended abstract). In *Proc. 29th Symp. on Foundations of Computer Science, FOCS'88*, pages 328–337. IEEE, 1988.

[EJ91] E. A. Emerson and C. S. Jutla. Tree automata, μ-calculus and determinacy. In *Proc. 32nd Symp. on Foundations of Computer Science*, pages 368–377, San Juan, Puerto Rico, 1991. IEEE.

[EJ00] E. A. Emerson and C. S. Jutla. The complexity of tree automata and logics of programs. *SIAM J. Comp.*, 29(1):132–158, 2000. Cf. [EJ88].

[EJS93] E. A. Emerson, C. S. Jutla, and A. P. Sistla. On model-checking for fragments of μ-calculus. In *Proc. 5th Conf. on Computer Aided Verification, CAV'93*, volume 697 of *Lect. Notes in Comp. Sci.*, pages 385–396. Springer, 1993.

[EJS01] E. A. Emerson, C. S. Jutla, and A. P. Sistla. On model checking for the μ-calculus and its fragments. *Theor. Comp. Sci.*, 258(1–3):491–522, 2001. Cf. [EJS93].

[EL86] E. A. Emerson and C. L. Lei. Efficient model checking in fragments of the propositional μ–calculus. In *Symposion on Logic in Computer Science*, pages 267–278, Washington, D.C., USA, 1986. IEEE.

[Elg61] C. C. Elgot. Decision problems of finite automata design and related arithmetics. *Trans. Amer. Math. Soc.*, 98:21–52, 1961.

[Eme90] E. A. Emerson. Temporal and modal logic. In J. van Leeuwen, editor, *Handbook of Theor. Comp. Sci.*, volume B: Formal Models and Semantics, chapter 16, pages 996–1072. Elsevier and MIT Press, 1990.

[ES83] E. A. Emerson and A. P. Sistla. Deciding branching time logic: A triple exponential decision procedure for CTL*. In *Proc. Workshop on Logics of Programs*, volume 164 of *LNCS*, pages 176–192. Springer, 1983.

[ES84a] E. A. Emerson and A. P. Sistla. Deciding branching time logic. In *Proc. 16th Symp. on Theory of Computing, STOC'84*, pages 14–24. ACM, 1984.

[ES84b] E. A. Emerson and A. P. Sistla. Deciding full branching time logic. *Inform. Control*, 61(3):175–201, 1984. Cf. [ES83, ES84a].

[EWS05] K. Etessami, T. Wilke, and R. A. Schuller. Fair simulation relations, parity games, and state space reduction for Büchi automata. *SIAM J. Comp.*, 34(5), 2005.

[Far02] B. Farwer. ω-Automata. In E. Grädel, W. Thomas, and Th. Wilke, editors, *Automata, Logics, and Infinite Games*, volume 2500 of *Lect. Notes in Comp. Sci.*, pages 3–21. Springer, 2002.

[Fea10] J. Fearnley. Exponential lower bounds for policy iteration. In *Proc. 37th Coll. on Automata, Languages and Programming, ICALP'10*, volume 6199 of *Lect. Notes in Comp. Sci.*, pages 551–562. Springer, 2010.

[FGW08]   J. Flum, E. Grädel, and T. Wilke, editors. *Logic and Automata: History and Perspectives [in Honor of Wolfgang Thomas]*, volume 2 of *Texts in Logic and Games*. Amsterdam Univ. Press, 2008.

[FHJ⁺17]   T. Fiedor, L. Holík, P. Jank, O. Lengál, and T. Vojnar. Lazy automata techniques for WS1S. In *Proc. 23rd Conf. on Tools and Algorithms for the Construction and Analysis of Systems, TACAS'17*, volume 10205 of *Lect. Notes in Comp. Sci.*, page 407–425. Springer, 2017.

[FHZ11]   O. Friedmann, T. D. Hansen, and U. Zwick. Subexponential lower bounds for randomized pivoting rules for the simplex algorithm. In *Proc. 43rd Symp. on Theory of Computing, STOC'11*, pages 283–292. ACM, 2011.

[FJdK⁺19]   J. Fearnley, S. Jain, B. de Keijzer, S. Schewe, F. Stephan, and D. Wojtczak. An ordered approach to solving parity games in quasi-polynomial time and quasi-linear space. *J. Softw. Tools Technol. Transf.*, 21(3):325–349, 2019. Cf. [FJS⁺17].

[FJS⁺17]   J. Fearnley, S. Jain, S. Schewe, F. Stephan, and D. Wojtczak. An ordered approach to solving parity games in quasi polynomial time and quasi linear space. In *Proc. 24th Symp. on Model Checking of Software, SPIN'17*, pages 112–121. ACM, 2017.

[FJY90]   A. Fellah, H. Jürgensen, and S. Yu. Constructions for alternating finite automata. *Int. J. Comput. Math.*, 35(1-4):117–132, 1990.

[FKL13]   O. Friedmann, F. Klaedtke, and M. Lange. Ramsey goes visibly pushdown. In *Proc. 40th Coll. on Automata, Languages, and Programming, ICALP'13*, volume 7966 of *Lect. Notes in Comp. Sci.*, pages 224–237. Springer, 2013.

[FKL15]   O. Friedmann, F. Klaedtke, and M. Lange. Ramsey-based inclusion checking for visibly pushdown automata. *ACM Trans. Comput. Log.*, 16(4):34, 2015. Cf. [FKL13].

[FKV04]   E. Friedgut, O. Kupferman, and M. Y. Vardi. Büchi complementation made tighter. In *Proc. 2nd Conf. on Automated Technology for Verification and Analysis, ATVA'04*, volume 3299 of *Lect. Notes in Comp. Sci.*, pages 64–78. Springer, 2004.

[FKV06]   E. Friedgut, O. Kupferman, and M. Y. Vardi. Büchi complementation made tighter. *J. Found. Comp. Sci.*, 17(4):851–868, 2006. Cf. [FKV04].

[FL77]   M. J. Fischer and R. E. Ladner. Propositional modal logic of programs (extended abstract). In *Proc. 9th Symp. on Theory of Computing, STOC'77*, pages 286–294. ACM, 1977.

[FL79]   M. J. Fischer and R. E. Ladner. Propositional dynamic logic of regular programs. *J. Comp. Sys. Sci.*, 18(2):194–211, 1979. Cf. [FL77].

[FL09]   O. Friedmann and M. Lange. Solving parity games in practice. In *Proc. 7th Symp. on Automated Technology for Verification and Analysis, ATVA'09*, volume 5799 of *Lect. Notes in Comp. Sci.*, pages 182–196, 2009.

[FL10]   O. Friedmann and M. Lange. Local strategy improvement for parity game solving. In *Proc. 1st Symp. on Games, Automata, Logic, and Formal Verification, GandALF'10*, volume 25 of *Elect. Proc. in Theor. Comp. Sci.*, pages 118–131, 2010.

[FL12a]   O. Friedmann and M. Lange. Ramsey-based analysis of parity automata. In *Proc. 18th Conf. on Tools and Algorithms for the Construction and Analysis of Systems, TACAS'12*, volume 7214 of *Lect. Notes in Comp. Sci.*, pages 64–78. Springer, 2012.

[FL12b]   O. Friedmann and M. Lange. Two local strategy improvement schemes for parity game solving. *J. Found. of Comp. Sci.*, 23(3):669–685, 2012. Cf. [FL10].

[FLL10]   O. Friedmann, M. Latte, and M. Lange. A decision procedure for CTL* based on tableaux and automata. In *Proc. 5th Joint Conf. on Automated Reasoning, IJCAR'10*, volume 6173 of *Lect. Notes in Comp. Sci.*, pages 331–345. Springer, 2010.

[FLL13]   O. Friedmann, M. Latte, and M. Lange. Satisfiability games for branching-time logics. *Log. Meth. Comp. Sci.*, 9(4), 2013. Cf. [FLL10].

[FR74]   M. J. Fischer and M. O. Rabin. Super-exponential complexity of Presburger arithmetic. In R. M. Karp, editor, *Complexity of computation*, volume 7 of *SIAM-AMS Proceedings*, page 27–41. AMS, 1974. Cf. [FR98].

[FR79]   J. Ferrante and C. W. Rackoff. *The computational complexity of logical theories*, volume 718 of *Lect. Notes in Math.* Springer, 1979.

[FR98]   M. J. Fischer and M. O. Rabin. Super-exponential complexity of Presburger arithmetic. In *Quantifier Elimination and Cylindrical Algebraic Decomposition*, Texts and Monographs in Symb. Comp., pages 122–135. Springer, 1998.

[Fra54]   R. Fraïssé. Sur quelques classifications des systèmes de relations. *Publ. Sci. Univ. Alger. Sér. A*, 1:35–182, 1954.

[Fri09]   O. Friedmann. An exponential lower bound for the parity game strategy improvement algorithm as we know it. In *Proc. 24th Symp. on Logic in Computer Science, LICS'09*, pages 145–156. IEEE, 2009.

[Fri10]   O. Friedmann. The Stevens-Stirling-algorithm for solving parity games locally requires exponential time. *J. Found. Comp. Sci.*, 21(3):277–287, 2010.

[Fri11a]   O. Friedmann. An exponential lower bound for the latest deterministic strategy iteration algorithms. *Log. Meth. Comput. Sci.*, 7(3), 2011.

[Fri11b]   O. Friedmann. *Exponential Lower Bounds for Solving Infinitary Payoff Games and Linear Programs*. PhD thesis, LMU Munich, 2011.

[Fri11c]   O. Friedmann. Recursive algorithm for parity games requires exponential time. *RAIRO Theor. Inform. Appl.*, 45(4):449–457, 2011.

[Fri11d]   O. Friedmann. A subexponential lower bound for Zadeh's pivoting rule for solving linear programs and games. In *Proc. 15th Conf. on Integer Programming and Combinatoral Optimization, IPCO'11*, volume 6655 of *Lect. Notes in Comp. Sci.*, pages 192–206. Springer, 2011.

[Fri13]   O. Friedmann. A superpolynomial lower bound for strategy iteration based on snare memorization. *Discr. Appl. Math.*, 161(10-11):1317–1337, 2013.

[FV10]   S. Fogarty and M. Y. Vardi. Efficient Büchi universality checking. In *Proc. 16th Conf. on Tools and Algorithms for the Construction and Analysis of Systems, TACAS'10*, volume 6015 of *Lect. Notes in Comp. Sci.*, pages 205–220, 2010.

[FV12]   S. Fogarty and M. Y. Vardi. Büchi complementation and size-change termination. *Log. Meth. Comp. Sci.*, 8(1), 2012.

[FW02]   C. Fritz and T. Wilke. State space reductions for alternating Büchi automata. In *Proc. 22nd Conf. on Foundations of Software Technology and Theoretical Computer Science, FSTTCS'02*, volume 2556 of *Lect. Notes in Comp. Sci.*, pages 157–168, 2002.

[FW05]   C. Fritz and T. Wilke. Simulation relations for alternating Büchi automata. *Theor. Comp. Sci.*, 338(1-3):275–314, 2005.

[Gab89]   D. Gabbay. The declarative past and imperative future: Executable temporal logic for interactive systems. In *Proc. Conf. on Temporal Logic in Specification*, volume 398 of *Lect. Notes in Comp. Sci.*, pages 409–448. Springer, 1989.

[GH82]   Y. Gurevich and L. Harrington. Trees, automata, and games. In *Proc. 14th Symp. on Theory of Computing, STOC'82*, pages 60–65. ACM, 1982.

[GKL+07]   E. Grädel, P. G. Kolaitis, L. Libkin, M. Marx, J. Spencer, M. Y. Vardi, Y. Venema, and S. Weinstein. *Finite model theory and its applications*. Springer, 2007.

[GM14]   J. F. Groote and M. R. Mousavi. *Modeling and Analysis of Communicating Systems*. MIT Press, 2014.

[GO01]   P. Gastin and D. Oddoux. Fast LTL to Büchi automata translation. In *Proc. 13th Conf. on Computer Aided Verification, CAV'01*, volume 2102 of *Lect. Notes in Comp. Sci.*, pages 53–65. Springer, 2001.

[GO07]   V. Goranko and M. Otto. Model theory of modal logic. In P. Blackburn, J. F. A. K. van Benthem, and F. Wolter, editors, *Handbook of Modal Logic*, volume 3 of *Studies in Log. and Pract. Reason.*, pages 249–329. North-Holland, 2007.

[Göd31]   K. Gödel. Über formal unentscheidbare Sätze der Principia Mathematica und verwandter Systeme I. *Monatshefte für Mathematik und Physik*, 38(1):173–198, 1931.

[GPSS80]   D. Gabbay, A. Pnueli, S. Shelah, and J. Stavi. The temporal analysis of fairness. In *Proc. 7th Symp. on Principles of Programming Languages, POPL'80*, pages 163–173. ACM, 1980.

[GPVW95]   R. Gerth, D. Peled, M. Vardi, and P. Wolper. Simple on-the-fly automatic verification of linear temporal logic. In *Proc. Symp. on Protocol Specification Testing and Verification, PSTV'95*, pages 3–18. Chapman & Hall, 1995.

[GS53]   D. Gale and F. M. Stewart. *Infinite Games with Perfect Information*, pages 245–266. Princeton Univ. Press, 1953.

[GTW02]   E. Grädel, W. Thomas, and T. Wilke, editors. *Automata, Logics, and Infinite Games: A Guide to Current Research*, volume 2500 of *Lect. Notes in Comp. Sci.* Springer, 2002.

[GV13]   G. De Giacomo and M. Y. Vardi. Linear temporal logic and linear dynamic logic on finite traces. In *Proc. 23rd Joint Conf. on A.I., IJCAI'13*, pages 854–860. IJCAI/AAAI, 2013.

[Haa18]   C. Haase. A survival guide to Presburger arithmetic. *ACM SIGLOG News*, 5(3):67–82, 2018.

[Han04]   C. Hankin. *An introduction to λ-calculi for computer scientists*, volume 2 of *Texts in Computing*. King's College Publ., 2004.

[Har78]   M. A. Harrison. *Introduction to Formal Language Theory*. Addison-Wesley, 1978.

[HK66]   A. Hoffman and R. M. Karp. On nonterminating stochastic games. *Management Sci.*, 12:359–370, 1966.

[HKLN12] K. Heljanko, M. Keinänen, M. Lange, and I. Niemelä. Solving parity games by a reduction to SAT. *J. Comp. Sys. Sci.*, 78:430–440, 2012. Cf. [Lan05].

[HKT00]   D. Harel, D. Kozen, and J. Tiuryn. *Dynamic Logic*. MIT Press, 2000.

[HMU01]   J. E. Hopcroft, R. Motwani, and J. D. Ullman. *Introduction to Automata Theory, Languages, and Computation*. Addison-Wesley, 3 edition, 2001.

[Hos10]   H. Hosoya. *Foundations of XML Processing: The Tree-Automata Approach*. Cambridge Univ. Press, 2010.

[HP03]   H. Hosoya and B. C. Pierce. XDuce: A statically typed XML processing language. *ACM Trans. Internet Techn.*, 3(2):117–148, 2003.

[HR72]   R. Hossley and C. Rackoff. The emptiness problem for automata on infinite trees. In *Proc. 13th Symp. on Switching and Automata Theory, SWAT'72*, pages 121–124. IEEE, 1972.

[HR04]   M. Huth and M. D. Ryan. *Logic in computer science - modelling and reasoning about systems*. Cambridge Univ. Press, 2 edition, 2004.

[HR07]   I. Hodkinson and M. Reynolds. Temporal logic. In P. Blackburn, J. Van Benthem, and F. Wolter, editors, *Handbook of Modal Logic*, volume 3 of *Studies in Logic and Practical Reasoning*, pages 655–720. Elsevier, 2007.

[Hro84]   J. Hromkovič. On the power of alternation in finite automata. In *Proc. 11th Symp. on Mathematical Foundations of Computer Science, MFCS'84*, volume 176 of *Lect. Notes in Comp. Sci.*, pages 322–329. Springer, 1984.

[Hro85]   J. Hromkovič. On the power of alternation in automata theory. *J. Comp. Sys. Sci.*, 31(1):28–39, 1985. Cf. [Hro84].

[HT99]   J. G. Henriksen and P. S. Thiagarajan. Dynamic linear time temporal logic. *Annals Pure Appl. Logic*, 96(1–3):187–207, 1999.

[HU80]   J. Hopcroft and J. Ullman. *Introduction to Automata Theory, Languages, and Computation*. Addison-Wesley, N. Reading, MA, 1980.

[IJW92]   O. H. Ibarra, T. Jiang, and H. Wang. A characterization of exponential-time languages by alternating context-free grammars. *Theor. Comp. Sci.*, 99(2):301–315, 1992.

[Imm99]   N. Immerman. *Descriptive Complexity*. Springer, New York, 1999.

[JL03]   J. Johannsen and M. Lange. CTL$^+$ is complete for double exponential time. In *Proc. 30th Coll. on Automata, Logics and Programming, ICALP'03*, volume 2719 of *LNCS*, pages 767 – 775. Springer, 2003.

[JL17]   M. Jurdzinski and R. Lazic. Succinct progress measures for solving parity games. In *Proc. 32nd Symp. on Logic in Computer Science, LICS'17*, pages 1–9. IEEE, 2017.

[JMT22]   M. Jurdzinski, R. Morvan, and K. S. Thejaswini. Universal algorithms for parity games and nested fixpoints. In *Principles of Systems Design - Essays Dedicated to Thomas A. Henzinger on the Occasion of His 60th Birthday*, volume 13660 of *Lect. Notes in Comp. Sci.*, pages 252–271. Springer, 2022.

[JPZ06]   M. Jurdziński, M. Paterson, and U. Zwick. A deterministic subexponential algorithm for solving parity games. In *Proc. 17th Symp. on Discrete Algorithms, SODA'06*, pages 114–123. ACM/SIAM, 2006.

[JPZ08]   M. Jurdzinski, M. Paterson, and U. Zwick. A deterministic subexponential algorithm for solving parity games. *SIAM J. Comput.*, 38(4):1519–1532, 2008. Cf. [JPZ06].

[Jur98]   M. Jurdziński. Deciding the winner in parity games is in UP∩co-UP. *Inf. Process. Lett.*, 68(3):119–124, 1998.

[Jur00]   M. Jurdziński. Small progress measures for solving parity games. In *Proc. 17th Symp. on Theoretical Aspects of Computer Science, STACS'00*, volume 1770 of *Lect. Notes in Comp. Sci.*, pages 290–301. Springer, 2000.

[JW96]   D. Janin and I. Walukiewicz. On the expressive completeness of the propositional μ-calculus with respect to monadic second order logic. In *Proc. 7th Conf. on Concurrency Theory, CONCUR'96*, volume 1119 of *LNCS*, pages 263–277. Springer, 1996.

[Kai95]   R. Kaivola. On modal μ-calculus and Büchi tree automata. *Inform. Proc. Lett.*, 54(1):17–22, 1995.

[Kai97]   R. Kaivola. *Using Automata to Characterise Fixed Point Temporal Logics*. PhD thesis, LFCS, Div. of Inform., The Univ. of Edinburgh, 1997. Tech. Rep. ECS-LFCS-97-356.

[Kam68]   H. W. Kamp. *On tense logic and the theory of order*. PhD thesis, Univ. of California, 1968.

[Kha80]   L.G. Khachiyan. Polynomial algorithms in linear programming. *USSR Comp. Math. and Math. Physics*, 20(1):53–72, 1980.

[Kin81]   K. N. King. Alternating multihead finite automata (extended abstract). In *Proc. 8th Coll. on Automata, Languages and Programming, ICALP'81*, volume 115 of *Lect. Notes in Comp. Sci.*, pages 506–520. Springer, 1981.

[Kin88]   K. N. King. Alternating multihead finite automata. *Theor. Comp. Sci.*, 61:149–174, 1988. Cf. [Kin81].

[KK91]   N. Klarlund and D. Kozen. Rabin measures and their applications to fairness and automata theory. In *Proc. 6th Symp. on Logic in Computer Science, LICS'91*, pages 256–265. IEEE, 1991.

[Kla91]   N. Klarlund. Progress measures for complementation of ω-automata with applications to temporal logic. In *Proc. 32nd Symp. on Foundations of Computer Science, FOCS'91*, pages 358–367. IEEE, 1991.

[Kla99]   N. Klarlund. A theory of restrictions for logics and automata. In *Proc. 11th Conf. on Computer Aided Verification, CAV'99*, volume 1633 of *Lect. Notes in Comp. Sci.*, pages 406–417. Springer, 1999.

[Kla04]   F. Klaedtke. On the automata size for Presburger arithmetic. In *Proc. 19th Symp. on Logic in Computer Science, LICS'04*, pages 110–119. IEEE, 2004.

[Kla08]   F. Klaedtke. Bounds on the automata size for Presburger Arithmetic. *ACM Trans. Comput. Logic*, 9(2), 2008. Cf. [Kla04].

[Kle43]   S. C. Kleene. Recursive predicates and quantifiers. *Trans. Amer. Math. Soc.*, 53(1):41–73, 1943.

[Kle56]   S. C. Kleene. Representation of events in nerve nets and finite automata. In C. E. Shannon and J. McCarthy, editors, *Automata Studies*, pages 3–42. Princeton Univ. Press, Princeton, N.J., 1956.

[KM08]   F. Kröger and S. Merz. *Temporal Logic and State Systems*. Texts in Theor. Comp. Sci. An EATCS Series. Springer, 2008.

[KN10]   B. Khoussainov and A. Nerode. *Automata theory and its applications*. Springer, 2010.

[Kna28]   B. Knaster. Un théorèm sur les fonctions d'ensembles. *Annals Soc. Pol. Math*, 6:133–134, 1928.

[Kol07]   P. G. Kolaitis. On the expressive power of logics on finite models. In *Finite Model Theory and Its Applications*, pages 27–123. Springer, 2007.

[Kőn27]   D. Kőnig. Über eine Schlussweise aus dem Endlichen ins Unendliche. *Acta litterarum ac scientiarum Regiae universitatis Hungaricae Francisco-Josephinae. Sectio: Acta scientiarum mathematicarum*, 3:121–130, 1927.

[Koz76]   D. Kozen. On parallelism in Turing machines. In *Proc. 17th Symp. on Foundations of Computer Science, FOCS'76*, pages 89–97. IEEE, 1976.

[Koz82]   D. Kozen. Results on the propositional μ-calculus. In *Proc. 9th Coll. on Automata, Languages and Programming, ICALP'82*, volume 140 of *LNCS*, pages 348–359. Springer, 1982.

[Koz83]   D. Kozen. Results on the propositional μ-calculus. *Theor. Comp. Sci.*, 27:333–354, 1983. Cf. [Koz82].

[KP83]   D. Kozen and R. Parikh. A decision procedure for the propositional μ-calculus. In *Proc. Workshop on Logics of Programs*, volume 164 of *Lect. Notes in Comp. Sci.*, pages 313–325. Springer, 1983.

[Krö77]   F. Kröger. LAR: A logic of algorithmic reasoning. *Acta Inform.*, 8:243–266, 1977.

[Krö87]   F. Kröger. *Temporal Logic of Programs*. Springer, 1987.

[Kup18]   O. Kupferman. Automata theory and model checking. In *Handbook of Model Checking*, pages 107–151. Springer, 2018.

[KV97]   O. Kupferman and M. Y. Vardi. Weak alternating automata are not that weak. In *Proc. 5th Israel Symp. on Theory of Computing and Systems, ISTCS'97*, pages 147–158. IEEE, 1997.

[KV98]   O. Kupferman and M. Y. Vardi. Weak alternating automata and tree automata emptiness. In *Proc. 30th Symp. on Theory of Computing, STOC'98*, pages 224–233. ACM, 1998.

[KV01]   O. Kupferman and M. Y. Vardi. Weak alternating automata are not that weak. *ACM Trans. Comput. Logic*, 2(3):408–429, 2001. Cf. [KV97].

[KVW00]   O. Kupferman, M. Y. Vardi, and P. Wolper. An automata-theoretic approach to branching-time model checking. *J. Assoc. Comp. Mach.*, 47(2):312–360, 2000. Cf. [BVW94].

[Lad77]   R. E. Ladner. Application of model theoretic games to discrete linear orders and finite automata. *Inform. Control*, 33(4):281–303, 1977.

[Lan05]   M. Lange. Solving parity games by a reduction to SAT. In *Proc. Workshop on Games in Design and Verification, GDV'05*, 2005.

[Lan08]   M. Lange. A purely model-theoretic proof of the exponential succinctness gap between CTL^+ and CTL. *Inform. Proc. Lett.*, 108:308–312, 2008.

[LBC$^+$94] D. E. Long, A. Browne, E. M. Clarke, S. Jha, and W. R. Marrero. An improved algorithm for the evaluation of fixpoint expressions. In *Proc. 6th Conf. on Computer Aided Verification, CAV'94*, volume 818 of *Lect. Notes in Comp. Sci.*, pages 338–350. Springer, 1994.

[Leh18]   K. Lehtinen. A modal μ perspective on solving parity games in quasi-polynomial time. In *Proc. 33rd Symp. on Logic in Computer Science, LICS'18*, pages 639–648. ACM, 2018.

[Len96]   G. Lenzi. A hierarchy theorem for the μ-calculus. In *Proc. 23rd Coll. on Automata, Languages and Programming, ICALP'96*, volume 1099 of *Lect. Notes in Comp. Sci.*, pages 87–97. Springer, 1996.

[Len05]   G. Lenzi. The modal μ-calculus: a survey. *Task Quarterly*, 9(3):293–316, 2005.

[Lib06]   L. Libkin. Logics for unranked trees: An overview. *Log. Meth. Comput. Sci.*, 2(3), 2006.

[LJBA01]   C. S. Lee, Neil D. Jones, and A. M. Ben-Amram. The size-change principle for program termination. In *Proc. 28th Symp. on Principles of Programming Languages, POPL'01*, pages 81–92. ACM, 2001.

[LLS78]   R. E. Ladner, R. J. Lipton, and L. J. Stockmeyer. Alternating pushdown automata (preliminary report). In *Proc. 19th Symp. on Foundations of Computer Science, FOCS'78*, pages 92–106. IEEE, 1978.

[LLS84]   R. E. Ladner, R. J. Lipton, and L. J. Stockmeyer. Alternating pushdown and stack automata. *SIAM J. Comp.*, 13(1):135–155, 1984. Cf. [LLS78].

[Loa03]   R. Loader. Higher order beta matching is undecidable. *Logic J. IGPL*, 11(1):51–68, 2003.

[Löd99]   C. Löding. Optimal bounds for transformations of omega-automata. In *Proc. 19th Conf. on Foundations of Software Technology and Theoretical Computer Science, FSTTCS'99*, volume 1738 of *Lect. Notes in Comp. Sci.*, pages 97–109. Springer, 1999.

[Löd21]   C. Löding. Automata on infinite trees. In J.-E. Pin, editor, *Handbook of Automata Theory*, pages 265–302. Europ. Math. Society Publ. House, 2021.

[LP00]   O. Lichtenstein and A. Pnueli. Propositional temporal logics: Decidability and completeness. *Logic J. IGPL*, 8(1):55–85, 2000.

[LPSW22]   K. Lehtinen, P. Parys, S. Schewe, and D. Wojtczak. A recursive approach to solving parity games in quasipolynomial time. *Log. Meth. Comp. Sci.*, 18(1), 2022.

[LSL84]   R. E. Ladner, L. J. Stockmeyer, and R. J. Lipton. Alternation bounded auxiliary pushdown automata. *Inform. Control*, 62(2/3):93–108, 1984.

[LT00]   C. Löding and W. Thomas. Alternating automata and logics over infinite words. In *Proc. 1st Conf. on Theoretical Computer Science, TCS'00*, volume 1872 of *Lect. Notes in Comp. Sci.*, pages 521–535. Springer, 2000.

[Mar75]   D. A. Martin. Borel determinacy. *Ann. Math.*, 102:363–371, 1975.

[MC13]   R. Mayr and L. Clemente. Advanced automata minimization. In *Proc. 40th Symp. on Principles of Programming Languages, POPL'13*, pages 63–74. ACM, 2013.

[McN66]   R. McNaughton. Testing and generating infinite sequences by a finite automaton. *Inform. Control*, 9(5):521–530, 1966.

[McN93]   R. McNaughton. Infinite games played on finite graphs. *Annals Pure Appl. Logic*, 65(2):149–184, 1993.

[MH84]   S. Miyano and T. Hayashi. Alternating finite automata on omega-words. *Theor. Comp. Sci.*, 32(3):321–330, 1984.

[Mic88]   M. Michel. Complementation is more difficult with automata on infinite words. Technical Report 15, Centre national d'études des télécommunications, Paris, 1988.

[Mil80]   R. Milner. *A Calculus of Communicating Systems*, volume 94 of *Lect. Notes in Comp. Sci.* Springer, 1980.

[Mos91]   A. W. Mostowski. Games with forbidden positions. Technical report, Univ. of Gdańsk, 1991.

[MP71]   R. McNaughton and S. Papert. *Counter-Free Automata*. MIT Press, Cambridge, Mass., 1971.

[MS72]   A. R. Meyer and L. J. Stockmeyer. The equivalence problem for regular expressions with squaring requires exponential space. In *Proc. 13th Symp. on Switching and Automata Theory*, pages 125–129. IEEE, 1972.

[MS73]   A. R. Meyer and L. J. Stockmeyer. Word problems requiring exponential time. In *Proc. 5th Symp. on Theory of Computing, STOC'73*, pages 1–9, New York, 1973. ACM.

[MS84]   D. Muller and P. Schupp. Alternating automata on infinite objects: determinacy and Rabin's theorem. In *Proc. Ecole de Printemps d'Informatique Théoretique on Automata on Infinite Words*, volume 192 of *Lect. Notes in Comp. Sci.*, pages 100–107. Springer, 1984.

[MS87]   D. E. Muller and P. E. Schupp. Alternating automata on infinite trees. *Theor. Comp. Sci.*, 54(2-3):267–276, 1987. Cf. [MS84].

[MS95]   D. E. Muller and P. E. Schupp. Simulating alternating tree automata by nondeterministic automata: New results and new proofs of the theorems of Rabin, McNaughton and Safra. *Theor. Comp. Sci.*, 141(1–2):69–107, 1995.

[MSS88]   D. E. Muller, A. Saoudi, and P. E. Schupp. Weak alternating automata give a simple explanation of why most temporal and dynamic logics are decidable in exponential time. In *Proc. 3rd Symp. on Logic in Computer Science, LICS'88*, pages 422–427. IEEE, 1988.

[Mul63]   D. E. Muller. Infinite sequences and finite machines. In *Proc. 4th Symp. on Switching Circuit Theory and Logical Design*, pages 3–16. IEEE, 1963.

[Ner58]   A. Nerode. Linear automaton transformations. *Proc. Amer. Math. Soc.*, 9(4):541–544, 1958.

[Niw97]   D. Niwiński. Fixed point characterization of infinite behavior of finite-state systems. *Theor. Comp. Sci.*, 189(1–2):1–69, 1997.

[Opp78]   D. C. Oppen. A $2^{2^{2^{pn}}}$ upper bound on the complexity of Presburger arithmetic. *J. Comp. Sys. Sci.*, 16:323–332, 1978.

[Par70]   D. Park. Fixpoint induction and proof of program semantics. In *Machine Intelligence*, volume 5, pages 59–78. Edinburgh Univ. Press, 1970.

[Par19]   P. Parys. Parity games: Zielonka's algorithm in quasi-polynomial time. In *Proc. 44th Symp. on Mathematical Foundations of Computer Science, MFCS'19*, volume 138 of *LIPIcs*, pages 10:1–10:13. Schloss Dagstuhl - Leibniz-Zentrum für Informatik, 2019.

[Par20]   P. Parys. Parity games: Another view on Lehtinen's algorithm. In *Proc. 28th Conf. on Computer Science Logic, CSL'20*, volume 152 of *LIPIcs*, pages 32:1–32:15. Schloss Dagstuhl - Leibniz-Zentrum für Informatik, 2020.

[Pit06]   N. Piterman. From nondeterministic Büchi and Streett automata to deterministic parity automata. In *Proc. 21st Symp. on Logic in Computer Science, LICS'06*, pages 255–264. IEEE Computer Society, 2006.

[Pnu77]   A. Pnueli. The temporal logic of programs. In *Proc. 18th Symp. on Foundations of Computer Science, FOCS'77*, pages 46–57, Providence, RI, USA, 1977. IEEE.

[PP86]   D. Perrin and J.-E. Pin. First-order logic and star-free sets. *J. Comp. Sys. Sci.*, 32(3):393–406, 1986.

[PP04]   D. Perrin and J.-E. Pin. *Infinite words – automata, semigroups, logic and games*, volume 141 of *Pure and applied mathematics series*. Elsevier, 2004.

[Pre27]   M. Presburger. Über die Vollständigkeit eines gewissen Systems der Arithmetik ganzer Zahlen, in welchen die Addition als einzige Operation hervortritt. In *Comptes Rendus du Premier Congrès des Mathématiciens des Pays Slaves*, pages 92–101, 395, Warsaw, 1927.

[Pri57]   A. N. Prior. *Time and modality*. Oxford Univ. Press, Oxford, UK, 1957.

[Pur95]   A. Puri. *Theory of hybrid systems and discrete event systems*. PhD thesis, Univ. of California, Berkeley, 1995.

[PV01]   V. Petersson and S. Vorobyov. A randomized subexponential algorithm for parity games. *Nordic J. Computing*, 8(3):324–345, 2001.

[PW23]   P. Parys and A. Wiacek. Improved complexity analysis of quasi-polynomial algorithms solving parity games. In *Proc. 19th Conf. on Computability in Europe, CiE'23*, volume 13967 of *Lect. Notes in Comp. Sci.*, pages 275–286. Springer, 2023.

[Rab69]   M. O. Rabin. Decidability of second-order theories and automata on infinite trees. *Trans. Amer. Math. Soc.*, 141(5):1–35, Jul. 1969.

[Rab70]   M. O. Rabin. Weakly definable relations and special automata. In *Proc. Coll. on Mathematical Logic and Foundations of Set Theory*, volume 59 of *Studies in Logic and the Found. of Math.*, pages 1–23. Elsevier, 1970.

[Rab72]   M. O. Rabin. *Automata on Infinite Objects and Church's Problem*. AMS, 1972.

[Rab14]   A. Rabinovich. A proof of Kamp's theorem. *Log. Meth. Comp. Sci.*, 10(1), 2014.

[Ram30]   F. P. Ramsey. On a problem in formal logic. *Proc. London Math. Soc. (3)*, 30:264–286, 1930.

[Ros97]   E. Rosen. Modal logic over finite structures. *J. Log. Lang. Inf.*, 6(4):427–439, 1997.

[RS59]   M. O. Rabin and D. Scott. Finite automata and their decision problems. *IBM J. Research and Dev.*, 3:114–125, 1959.

[Saf88]   S. Safra. On the complexity of ω-automata. In *Proc. 29th Symp. on Foundations of Computer Science, FOCS'88*, pages 319–327. IEEE, 1988.

[Saf89]   S. Safra. *Complexity of automata on infinite objects*. PhD thesis, Weizmann Inst. of Sci., Rehovot, Israel, 1989.

[Saf92]   S. Safra. Exponential determinization for ω-automata with strong-fairness acceptance condition (extended abstract). In *Proc. 24th Symp. on the Theory of Computing, STOC'92*, pages 275–282. ACM, 1992.

[Sao91]   A. Saoudi. Generalized automata on infinite trees and Muller-McNaughton's theorem. *Theor. Comp. Sci.*, 84(2):165–177, 1991.

[Sav69]   W. J. Savitch. Deterministic simulation of nondeterministic Turing Machines. In *Proc. 1st Symp. on Theory of Computing, STOC'69*, pages 247–248. ACM, 1969.

[Sav70]   W. J. Savitch. Relationships between nondeterministic and deterministic tape complexities. *J. Comp. Sys. Sci.*, 4:177–192, 1970. Cf. [Sav69].

[SC82]   A. P. Sistla and E. M. Clarke. The complexity of propositional linear temporal logics. In *Proc. 14th Symp. on Theory of Computing, STOC'82*, pages 159–168. ACM, 1982.

[SC85]   A. P. Sistla and E. M. Clarke. The complexity of propositional linear temporal logics. *J. Assoc. Comp. Mach.*, 32(3):733–749, 1985. Cf. [SC82].

[Sch65]   M. P. Schützenberger. On finite monoids having only trivial subgroups. *Inform. Control*, 8(2):190–194, 1965.

[Sch72]   M. P. Schützenberger. A propos du relation rationelles fonctionnelles. In *Proc. Coll. on Automata, Languages and Programming, ICALP'72*, pages 103–114. North-Holland, 1972.

[Sch02]   S. Schwoon. Determinization and complementation of Streett automata. In E. Grädel, W. Thomas, and T. Wilke, editors, *Automata Logics, and Infinite Games: A Guide to Current Research*, volume 2500 of *Lect. Notes in Comp. Sci.*, pages 79–91. Springer, 2002.

[Sch07a] S. Schewe. Solving parity games in big steps. In *Proc. 27th Conf. on Foundations of Software Technology and Theoretical Computer Science, FSTTCS'07*, volume 4855 of *Lect. Notes in Comp. Sci.*, pages 449–460. Springer, 2007.

[Sch07b] T. Schwentick. Automata for XML - a survey. *J. Comp. Sys. Sci.*, 73(3):289–315, 2007.

[Sch09a] S. Schewe. Büchi complementation made tight. In *Proc. 26th Symp. on Theoretical Aspects of Computer Science, STACS'09*, volume 3 of *LIPIcs*, pages 661–672. Schloss Dagstuhl – Leibniz-Zentrum für Informatik, 2009.

[Sch09b] S. Schewe. Tighter bounds for the determinisation of Büchi automata. In *Proc. 12th Conf. on Foundations of Software Science and Computation Structures, FOSSACS'09*, volume 5504 of *Lect. Notes in Comp. Sci.*, pages 167–181. Springer, 2009.

[Sch17]   S. Schewe. Solving parity games in big steps. *J. Comp. Sys. Sci.*, 84:243–262, 2017. Cf. [Sch07a].

[SE84]   R. S. Streett and E. A. Emerson. The propositional μ-calculus is elementary. In *Proc. 11th Coll. on Automata, Languages, and Programming, ICALP'84*, volume 172 of *Lect. Notes in Comp. Sci.*, pages 465–472. Springer, 1984.

[SE89]   R. S. Streett and E. A. Emerson. An automata theoretic decision procedure for the propositional μ-calculus. *Inform. Comp.*, 81(3):249–264, 1989. Cf. [SE84].

[Sei89]   H. Seidl. Deciding equivalence of finite tree automata. In *Proc. 6th Symp. on Theoretical Aspects of Computer Science, STACS'89*, volume 349 of *Lect. Notes in Comp. Sci.*, pages 480–492. Springer, 1989.

[Sei90]   H. Seidl. Deciding equivalence of finite tree automata. *SIAM J. Comp.*, 19(3):424–437, 1990. Cf. [Sei89].

[Sei96]   H. Seidl. Fast and simple nested fixpoints. *Inform. Proc. Lett.*, 59(6):303–308, 1996.

[Sha81]   M. Sharir. A strong-connectivity algorithm and its applications in data flow analysis. *Comp. Math. Appl.*, 7(1):67–72, 1981.

[Sip13]   M. Sipser. *Introduction to the Theory of Computation*. Course Technology, 3rd edition, 2013.

[Sku02]   J. Skurczynski. A characterization of Büchi tree automata. *Inform. Process. Lett.*, 81(1):29–33, 2002.

[SLG94]   V. Stoltenberg-Hansen, I. Lindström, and E. R. Griffor. *Mathematical theory of domains*, volume 22 of *Cambridge Tracts in Theor. Comp. Sci.* Cambridge Univ. Press, 1994.

[SMPS21] A. Di Stasio, A. Murano, V. Prignano, and L. Sorrentino. Improving parity games in practice. *Ann. Math. Artif. Intell.*, 89(5-6):551–574, 2021.

[SMS90]   A. Saoudi, D. E. Muller, and P. E. Schupp. Recognizable infinite tree sets and their complexity. In *Proc. 10th Conf. on Foundations of Software Technology and Theor. Comp. Sci., FSTTCS'90*, volume 472 of *Lect. Notes in Comp. Sci.*, pages 91–103. Springer, 1990.

[SS98]   P. Stevens and C. Stirling. Practical model-checking using games. In *Proc. 4th Conf. on Tools and Algorithms for the Construction and Analysis of Systems, TACAS'98*, volume 1384 of *Lect. Notes in Comp. Sci.*, pages 85–101. Springer, 1998.

[Sti95]   C. Stirling. Local model checking games. In *Proc. 6th Conf. on Concurrency Theory, CONCUR'95*, volume 962 of *Lect. Notes in Comp. Sci.*, pages 1–11. Springer, 1995.

[Sti06]   C. Stirling. A game-theoretic approach to deciding higher-order matching. In *Proc. 33rd Coll. on Automata, Languages and Programming, ICALP'06*, volume 4052 of *Lect. Notes in Comp. Sci.*, pages 348–359. Springer, 2006.

[Sti09]   C. Stirling. Decidability of higher-order matching. *Log. Meth. Comp. Sci.*, 5(3), 2009. Cf. [Sti06].

[Sto74]   L. J. Stockmeyer. *The complexity of decision problems in automata theory and logic.* PhD thesis, MIT, 1974.

[Str82]   R. S. Streett. Propositional dynamic logic of looping and converse is elementarily decidable. *Inform. Control*, 54(1/2):121–141, 1982.

[Str94]   H. Straubing. *Finite Automata, Formal Logic, and Circuit Complexity.* Birkhäuser, 1994.

[SV12]   S. Schewe and T. Varghese. Tight bounds for the determinisation and complementation of generalised Büchi automata. In *Proc. 10th Symp. on Automated Technology for Verification and Analysis, ATVA'12*, volume 7561 of *Lect. Notes in Comp. Sci.*, pages 42–56. Springer, 2012.

[SVW83]   A. P. Sistla, M. Y. Vardi, and P. Wolper. Reasoning about infinite computation paths. In *Proc. 24th Symp. on Foundations of Computer Science, FOCS'83*, pages 185–194. IEEE, 1983.

[SW11]   R. Sedgewick and K. Wayne. *Algorithms.* Addison-Wesley, 4th edition, 2011.

[SY00]   K. Salomaa and S. Yu. Alternating finite automata and star-free languages. *Theor. Comput. Sci.*, 234(1-2):167–176, 2000.

[Tar55]   A. Tarski. A lattice-theoretical fixpoint theorem and its application. *Pac. J. Math.*, 5:285–309, 1955.

[Tar72]   R. E. Tarjan. Depth-first search and linear graph algorithms. *SIAM J. Comp.*, 1:146–160, 1972.

[TB73]   B. A. Trakhtenbrot and J. M. Barzdin. *Finite automata.* Fundamental studies in computer science. North-Holland, 1973.

[Tho79]   W. Thomas. Star-free regular sets of ω-sequences. *Inform. Control*, 42(2):148–156, 1979.

[Tho81]   W. Thomas. A combinatorial approach to the theory of ω-automata. *Inform. Control*, 48:261–283, 1981.

[Tho90]   W. Thomas. Automata on infinite objects. In J. van Leeuwen, editor, *Handbook of Theor. Comp. Sci. Volume B: Formal Models and Semantics*, pages 133–191. Elsevier and MIT Press, 1990.

[Tho97]   W. Thomas. Languages, automata, and logic. In G. Rozenberg and A. Salomaa, editors, *Handbook of Formal Languages, Vol. 3: Beyond Words*, pages 389–455. Springer, 1997.

[Tra61]   B. A. Trakhtenbrot. Finite automata and logic of monadic predicates (in Russian). *Doklady Akademii Nauk SSSR*, 140:326–329, 1961.

[TW68]   J. W. Thatcher and J. B. Wright. Generalized finite automata theory with an application to a decision problem of second-order logic. *Math. Sys. Theory*, 2(1):57–81, 1968.

[TWD20]   C. Tian, W. Wang, and Z. Duan. Making Streett determinization tight. In *Proc. 35th Symp. on Logic in Computer Science, LICS'20*, pages 859–872. ACM, 2020.

[Var88]   M. Y. Vardi. A temporal fixpoint calculus. In *Proc. Conf. on Principles of Programming Languages, POPL'88*, pages 250–259. ACM, 1988.

[Var96]   M. Y. Vardi. *An Automata-Theoretic Approach to Linear Temporal Logic*, volume 1043 of *Lect. Notes in Comp. Sci.*, pages 238–266. Springer, 1996.

[Var08]   M. Y. Vardi. From Church and Prior to PSL. In *25 Years of Model Checking – History, Achievements, Perspectives*, volume 5000 of *Lect. Notes in Comp. Sci.*, pages 150–171. Springer, 2008.

[vB76]   J. van Benthem. *Modal Correspondence Theory.* PhD thesis, Univ. of Amsterdam, 1976.

[vB84]   J. van Benthem. Correspondence theory. In D. Gabbay and F. Guenthner, editors, *Handbook of Philosophical Logic, Volume II: Extensions of Classical Logic*, pages 167–247. D. Reidel, 1984.

[vD18]   T. van Dijk. Oink: An implementation and evaluation of modern parity game solvers. In *Proc. 24th Conf. on Tools and Algorithms for the Construction and Analysis of Systems, TACAS'18*, volume 10805 of *Lect. Notes in Comp. Sci.*, pages 291–308. Springer, 2018.

[vDR19]   T. van Dijk and B. Rubbens. Simple fixpoint iteration to solve parity games. In *Proc. 10th Symp. on Games, Automata, Logics, and Formal Verification, GandALF'19*, volume 305 of *EPTCS*, pages 123–139, 2019.

[VJ00]   J. Vöge and M. Jurdziński. A discrete strategy improvement algorithm for solving parity games. In *Proc. 12th Conf. on Computer Aided Verification, CAV'00*, volume 1855 of *Lect. Notes in Comp. Sci.*, pages 202–215. Springer, 2000.

[VS85]   M. Y. Vardi and L. Stockmeyer. Improved upper and lower bounds for modal logics of programs. In *Proc. 17th Symp. on Theory of Computing, STOC'85*, pages 240–251, Baltimore, USA, 1985. ACM.

[VW84]   M. Y. Vardi and P. Wolper. Automata-theoretic techniques for modal logics of programs (extended abstract). In *Proc. 16th Symp. on Theory of Computing, STOC'84*, pages 446–456. ACM, 1984.

[VW86]   M. Y. Vardi and P. Wolper. Automata-theoretic techniques for modal logic of programs. *J. Comp. Sys. Sci.*, 32:183–221, 1986. Cf. [VW84].

[VW94]   M. Y. Vardi and P. Wolper. Reasoning about infinite computations. *Inform. Comp.*, 115(1):1–37, 1994. Cf. [SVW83].

[WDHR06] M. De Wulf, L. Doyen, T. A. Henzinger, and J.-F. Raskin. Antichains: A new algorithm for checking universality of finite automata. In *Proc. 18th Conf. on Computer Aided Verification, CAV'06*, volume 4144 of *Lect. Notes in Comp. Sci.*, pages 17–30. Springer, 2006.

[WDMR08] M. De Wulf, L. Doyen, N. Maquet, and J.-F. Raskin. Antichains: Alternative algorithms for LTL satisfiability and model-checking. In *Proc. 14th Conf. on Tools and Algorithms for the Construction and Analysis of Systems, TACAS'08*, volume 4963 of *Lect. Notes in Comp. Sci.*, pages 63–77. Springer, 2008.

[Wil99a] T. Wilke. Classifying discrete temporal properties. In *Proc. 16th Symp. on Theoretical Aspects of Computer Science, STACS'99*, volume 1563 of *Lect. Notes in Comp. Sci.*, pages 32–46. Springer, 1999.

[Wil99b] T. Wilke. CTL$^+$ is exponentially more succinct than CTL. In *Proc. 19th Conf. on Foundations of Software Technology and Theoretical Computer Science, FSTTCS'99*, volume 1738 of *LNCS*, pages 110–121. Springer, 1999.

[Wil01]   T. Wilke. Alternating tree automata, parity games, and modal μ-calculus. *Bull. Belgian Math. Soc.*, 8(2):359–391, 2001.

[Win93]   G. Winskel. *The Formal Semantics of Programming Languages: An Introduction*. MIT Press, 1993.

[Zap02]   J. Zappe. Modal μ-calculus and alternating tree automata. In E. Grädel, W. Thomas, and T. Wilke, editors, *Automata Logics, and Infinite Games: A Guide to Current Research*, volume 2500 of *Lect. Notes in Comp. Sci.*, pages 171–184. Springer, 2002.

[Zie98]   W. Zielonka. Infinite games on finitely coloured graphs with applications to automata on infinite trees. *Theor. Comp. Sci.*, 200(1–2):135–183, 1998.

[ZP95]   U. Zwick and M. Paterson. The complexity of mean payoff games. In *Proc. 1st Conf. on Computing and Combinatorics, COCOON'95*, volume 959 of *Lect. Notes in Comp. Sci.*, pages 1–10. Springer, 1995.

[ZP96]   U. Zwick and M. Paterson. The complexity of mean payoff games on graphs. *Theor. Comp. Sci.*, 158(1–2):343–359, 1996. Cf. [ZP95].